Teaching Physical Education Today

THOMPSON
EDUCATIONAL

Teaching Physical Education Today

Canadian Perspectives

Edited by
Daniel B. Robinson
& Lynn Randall

Information on how to obtain copies of this book is available at:
Website: www.thompsonbooks.com
E-mail: publisher@thompsonbooks.com
Telephone: (416) 766–2763
Fax: (416) 766–0398

Library and Archives Canada Cataloguing in Publication

   Teaching physical education today : Canadian perspectives / Daniel B. Robinson and Lynn Randall, editors.

Includes bibliographical references and index.
ISBN 978-1-55077-231-9 (pbk.)

      1. Physical education and training--Study and teaching--Canada.
I. Robinson, Daniel B., 1974-, editor of compilation II. Randall, Lynn, 1965-, editor of compilation

GV365.5.C3T43 2013   372.86'0440971   C2013-902419-0

Production Editor: Katy Bartlett
Cover Design: Gary Blakeley, Blakeley Words+Pictures
Proofreader: Gillian Buckley

Every reasonable effort has been made to acquire permission for copyrighted materials used in this book and to acknowledge such permissions accurately. Any errors called to the publisher's attention will be corrected in future printings.

We acknowledge the support of the Government of Canada through the Canada Book Fund for our publishing activities.

Printed in Canada.

1 2 3 4 5   18 17 16 15 14 13

Table of Contents

Preface

Physical education pedagogues from across the nation have contributed to *Teaching Physical Education Today: Canadian Perspectives*. Through Physical and Health Education Canada's Council of University Professors and Researchers (CUPR), a network of the nation's most notable physical education experts were invited to contribute to this text. More specifically, twenty-four professors from sixteen Canadian universities in the nine provinces with physical education teacher education (PETE) programs have contributed as chapter authors. These twenty-four professors and an additional sixteen from another five Canadian universities contributed as reviewers. In all then, *Teaching Physical Education Today* has been shaped by the perspectives of over forty university professors from over twenty universities across Canada.

Notwithstanding the collective expertise that was brought to bear in writing *Teaching Physical Education Today*, as much as possible the editors tried to ensure that each chapter retained the author's individual perspective, point of view, and style. That is, the authors were allowed, and indeed encouraged, to exercise a considerable autonomy as they wrote their chapters. Readers should therefore keep in mind that each chapter presents essentially that author's perspective on the topic, and should be prepared to judge the content of each chapter in the context of other works on the subject as well as their own practical experiences.

Acknowledgements

We would like to thank all of the chapter authors for their involvement in writing *Teaching Physical Education Today: Canadian Perspectives*. We are similarly grateful to all of the reviewers who helped shape the content of various chapters within the text. Thank you, also, to Drs. Tim Fletcher, Barb Olmsted, and David Chorney for their contributions as editorial team consultants. We also wish to thank Katy Bartlett and Keith Thompson from Thompson Educational Publishing for supporting our initial vision and the realized end product.

Most of all, thank you to our students, who give both our peers and ourselves a reason to contribute to this text. It is to our students that *Teaching Physical Education Today: Canadian Perspectives* is dedicated.

Reviewers

Karen Sirna	Douglas College
Colin Higgs	Memorial Univeristy of Newfoundland
Dwayne Sheehan	Mount Royal University
Tom Ryan	Nipissing University
Lynn Lavalleé	Ryerson University
Amanda Stanec	St. Francis Xavier University
Joy Butler	University of British Columbia
Daniel Balderson	University of Lethbridge
Joannie Halas	University of Manitoba
Lee Shaefer	University of Regina
Louise Humbert	University of Saskatchewan
Sandy Gibbons	University of Victoria
Tim Hopper	University of Victoria
Aniko Varpalotai	University of Western Ontario

Foreword

The book *Teaching Physical Education Today: Canadian Perspectives*, comes at a critical time for emerging health and physical educators. As a profession, we have evolved from a discipline first funded by the militia, where drill sergeants barked out commands to prepare young boys for military service (see Chapter 1), to a profession that is now concerned with the holistic and healthy development of all students. The book is an essential read for those entering the physical education (PE) profession as it provides a vital foundation for delivering quality PE programs.

As you read this book you will be inspired by Canada's leading scholars in PE as they share their expertise and experiences across a number of important topics. For example, how do you develop a vision for teaching PE based on what is important to teach (see Chapter 2)? How can games become a vehicle to foster the development of personal and social responsibility (see Chapter 3)? How do we ensure that ALL students have equal and equitable access to quality PE (see Chapters 7, 8, and 9)? How can we use technology in effective and efficient ways (Chapter 15)? And why is the development of health literacy and physical literacy critical to ensuring that the next generation of students will be more active and healthier than the current generation (see Chapters 13 and 14)? This book will also provide you with effective teaching tools such as planning for instruction (Chapter 4), delivering effective lessons (Chapter 5), providing a safe environment (Chapter 10), and assessing with student learning in mind (Chapter 6). You will also be challenged to think critically and reflect upon the information provided, and will have an opportunity to enrich your understanding through numerous case study examples.

We have reached a critical period in the development of healthy Canadian students (or more accurately, we are lacking in this development). If current trends continue, the students of the twenty-first century are at risk of experiencing a shorter life expectancy than their parents due to their unhealthy choices and physical inactivity (Ludwig, 2007). Only nine percent of boys and four percent of girls in Canada meet the national guidelines for daily physical activity (Active Healthy Kids Canada, 2011). Fourteen percent of Canadians aged four to seventeen "... experience clinically important mental disorders" (Waddell, McEwan, Shepherd, Offord, & Hua, 2005, p. 226). Given that every student in Canada is required to take PE throughout primary school and part of secondary school, physical education has been identified as one of the most important places to have a positive impact on the health of Canadian children.

However, how we teach is often just as important, if not more important, than what we teach. Simply rolling out a ball and letting your students play will not lead to good long-term health and physical activity behaviours. Purposeful planning that uses that ball, for example, in a way that is reflective of effective pedagogy as outlined by the various authors in this book can result in positive outcomes such as enhanced skill development, interpersonal skills, critical thinking, cultural awareness, and fitness improvements. For physical education to have the type of impact that is required in today's society, and that people are expecting from it, will require a change in praxis for many. And it starts with you. I know that after reading this book and learning from and reflecting upon the advice from experts across Canada that you will be inspired to help both current and future students to lead the kind of healthy and active lives that result from a quality physical education program.

James Mandigo
Brock University

Editors

Daniel B. Robinson, PhD, is an Assistant Professor in the Faculty of Education at St. Francis Xavier University. He teaches undergraduate courses in elementary and secondary physical education curriculum and instruction. He also teaches graduate courses in current research in curriculum and instruction in physical education, administration of inclusive schools, curriculum theory, and school and teaching effectiveness. Dr. Robinson's research focuses on culturally responsive physical education, gender and physical education, and Teaching Games for Understanding (TGfU).

Lynn Randall, PhD, is an Associate Professor in the Faculty of Education at the University of New Brunswick. She teaches undergraduate courses in elementary and secondary physical education curriculum and instruction. She also teaches graduate courses in current issues in curriculum and instruction. Dr. Randall's research focuses on physical education and pre-service physical education teacher education.

Contributing Authors

Joe Barrett, EdD, is an Assistant Professor in the Faculty of Education at Brock University. He teaches undergraduate courses in heath and physical education, health policy, and coaching studies. He also teaches graduate courses in physical education pedagogy and curriculum. Dr. Barrett's research focuses on health policy, health and physical education, and daily physical activity.

Stephen Berg, PhD, is an Assistant Professor in the Faculty of Education at the University of British Columbia. He teaches undergraduate courses in physical education, health and career education, and early years education. Dr. Berg's research focuses on physical education, health education, and children's physical activity.

Antony Card, EdD, is an Associate Professor and Associate Vice-President (Research) for the Grenfell Campus of Memorial University of Newfoundland. He has taught undergraduate courses in growth and development and physical education pedagogy. He also teaches online graduate courses in physical education leadership and comprehensive school health. Dr. Card's research focuses on physical education, youth health, and health promoting schools.

Catherine Casey, PhD, is an Associate Professor in the Faculty of Education at the University of Manitoba. She teaches physical education/health education curriculum and instruction courses at the elementary and secondary level. She also teaches graduate courses in current research in physical education/health education pedagogy and curriculum theory. Dr. Casey's research focuses on physical education/health education, policy effectiveness, teacher preparedness, and physical education/health education pedagogy through experiential learning.

David Chorney, PhD, is an Associate Professor in the Faculty of Education at the University of Alberta. He teaches undergraduate courses in physical education pedagogy and curriculum and instruction. He also teaches graduate courses in conceptualizing the field of physical education. Dr. Chorney's research focuses on physical education teacher education, pedagogy in physical education, and technology integration in physical education.

Tim Fletcher, PhD, is an Assistant Professor in the School of Human Kinetics and Recreation at Memorial University of Newfoundland. He teaches undergraduate courses in elementary physical education and sociology of sport. He also teaches graduate courses in physical education and culture and qualitative inquiry. Dr. Fletcher's research focuses on pre-service teacher education and teacher identity.

Nick Forsberg, PhD, is a Professor in the Faculty of Education at the University of Regina. He teaches undergraduate courses in pedagogy of physical education and pedagogical practices of outdoor education. He also teaches graduate courses in exploring well-being through health, outdoor, and physical education (HOPE), interdisciplinary studies in outdoor education, and philosophy, foundations, and frameworks of physical education. Dr. Forsberg's research focuses on physical education student teacher (e)merging identity formation, Teaching for Personal and Social Responsibility (TPSR), and solo and solitude in the wilderness.

Nancy R. Francis, EdD, is a Professor in the Faculty of Applied Health Sciences at Brock University. She teaches undergraduate courses in physical education for teachers, healthy active children, and active living across the lifespan. She also teaches graduate courses in research in physical education and research in curriculum studies. Dr. Francis's research focuses on physical education and dance curricular analysis, physical literacy, and movement and embodied learning.

Doug Gleddie, PhD, is an Assistant Professor in Faculty of Education at the University of Alberta. He teaches undergraduate courses in elementary physical education curriculum and instruction. He also teaches graduate courses in physical education curriculum. Dr. Gleddie's research focuses on physical education pedagogy, physical activity motivation, and health promoting schools.

William J. Harvey, PhD, is an Associate Professor in the Faculty of Education at McGill University. He teaches undergraduate courses on inclusive physical activity and physical education pedagogy. He also teaches graduate courses on inclusive physical activity and critical interpretations of physical education pedagogy. Dr. Harvey's research focuses on self-determination and persons with mental health problems, physical activity interventions and children with attention-deficit hyperactivity disorder, and professional development of physical education teachers and clinical kinesiologists.

Clive Hickson, PhD, is an Associate Professor in the Faculty of Education at the University of Alberta. He teaches undergraduate courses in introductory and advanced elementary physical education curriculum and instruction. He also teaches graduate courses in research methodology. Dr. Hickson's research focuses on teacher effectiveness and mentorship.

Brenda Kalyn, PhD, is an Assistant Professor in the Faculty of Education at the University of Saskatchewan. She teaches undergraduate courses in elementary physical education curriculum and instruction. She also teaches graduate courses in curriculum theory and research. Dr. Kalyn's research focuses in the impact of students' and teachers' learning experiences on pedagogy and curriculum specifically related to physical education, holism, culture, and dance.

Jeanne Adèle Kentel, PhD, is a Lecturer in the Faculty of Education at the University of British Columbia. She teaches undergraduate courses in physical education for teachers, healthy active children, and pedagogy. She also teaches graduate courses in research methods, critical pedagogy, and curriculum theory. Dr. Kentel's research focuses on gender, critical pedagogy, and movement understanding.

Ken R. Lodewyk, PhD, is an Associate Professor in the Faculty of Applied Health Sciences at Brock University. He teaches undergraduate courses in motor development, formal games, and pedagogy. Dr. Lodewyk's research focuses on motivation, instruction, and beliefs in sports and physical education.

Rebecca Lloyd, PhD, is an Associate Professor in the Faculty of Education at the University of Ottawa. She teaches undergraduate courses in learning theories and health and physical education. She also teaches graduate courses in research methods, and health and physical education pedagogy. Dr. Lloyd's research focuses on phenomenology, curriculum inquiry, and movement consciousness.

Chunlei Lu, PhD, is an Associate Professor in the Faculty of Education at Brock University. He teaches undergraduate courses in health and physical education. Dr. Lu's research focuses on physical education, health education, and cultural studies.

Nancy Melnychuk, PhD, is a Professor in the Faculty of Education at the University of Alberta. She teaches undergraduate courses in physical education pedagogy and curriculum and instruction. She also teaches graduate courses in physical education teacher education, current research in curriculum and instruction in physical education, research paradigms and methods for thesis and project completion, and curriculum implementation in physical education. Dr. Melnychuk's research focuses on physical education teacher education and bridging the gap between theory and practice.

Barbara Olmsted, EdD, is an Assistant Professor in the Schulich School of Education at Nipissing University. She teaches undergraduate courses in the Bachelor of Physical and Health Education program and physical and health education in the consecutive Bachelor of Education program. Dr. Olmsted's research focuses on pre-service elementary teacher education for physical and health education.

Joanna Sheppard, MA, is a Lecturer in the Faculty of Health Sciences at the University of the Fraser Valley. She teaches undergraduate courses in teaching elementary and secondary physical education, curriculum models, and health education. Ms. Sheppard's research focuses on the importance of life skills teaching, more specifically social and personal responsibility through the use of the Teaching Games for Understanding (TGfU) games model.

Stephen Smith, PhD, is an Associate Professor in the Faculty of Education at Simon Fraser University. He teaches undergraduate courses in instructional activities in physical education, designs for learning in physical education, and introduction to teaching. He also teaches graduate courses in curriculum theory, pedagogical theory, and health education. Dr. Smith's research focuses on phenomenology, pedagogy, and teacher education.

Carolyn Temertzoglou, MA, is a Lecturer in the Ontario Institute for Studies in Education at the University of Toronto. She teaches undergraduate courses in teaching elementary and secondary physical education, curriculum, instruction and assessment with an emphasis in the construction of vision for teaching health and physical education. She also teaches graduate courses in connecting research to practice for teaching quality health and physical education. Mrs. Temertzoglou's research focuses on physical education and teacher education, beginning teachers, and teaching/teacher education practices.

David C. Young, PhD, is an Assistant Professor in the Faculty of Education at St. Francis Xavier University. He teaches undergraduate courses in educational foundations and special education. He also teaches graduate courses in school law, school administration, and inclusive schools. Dr. Young's research focuses on school law and educational policy.

1

Physical Education
Looking Back,
Looking Forward

Physical Education Looking Back, Looking Forward

Nick Forsberg and David Chorney

Overview

The purpose of this chapter is to share the history of physical education (PE) in Canada as well as consider what the future may look like for the field of PE in our country. The chapter examines the roots of PE in Canada, significant events, and Canadian pioneers in the field before contemplating where PE may be headed. The chapter also examines how specific historical events have led to changes in PE.

This chapter allows readers to see how the history of PE in Canada has unfolded and challenges them to think where the PE field is heading as well as what roles there are to play in the continued evolution of PE in Canada.

Introduction

The history of PE in Canada has barely reached the century mark in terms of regular programs existing in schools. To look back and reflect on how PE has evolved over the past century in Canada is truly insightful and encourages one to ponder how much things have changed, yet how some things remain unchanged over the past number of generations.

Physical education in Canada has a storied history. This history is steeped in critical events that often parallel the birth of Canada as a nation. It is rich with individuals and associations, organizations, and departments that played instrumental roles in the development of PE from a simple form of physical training in its early inception to a more complex field of study today. This chapter is intended to provide a historical glimpse of the roots of PE in Canada, examine its evolution through time to where the field resides today, and share some thoughts on what the future might hold for PE in Canada.

Physical Education in the Past

It should not be surprising that the roots of PE in Canada can be traced back to the contributions of Canada's First Nations and immigrants from Western Europe. For example, First Nations games, such as lacrosse and traditional dances, as well as the culturally-rooted games and dances of Western European immigrants might be interpreted as being the initial form of PE at the time. A more structured and organized understanding of PE resulted from the migration of people to larger centres. The establishment of the local YMCAs and YWCAs in these larger centres played a pivotal role in advancing the PE movement in Canada (Gurney, 1982).

Initially, PE "training" had the intent of creating a very able and capable body, a person who would serve and defend his/her country in times of war. The evolution of PE has resulted in a course of study where students become more engaged thinkers, compassionate, supportive, and skilled in a variety of fundamental movement skills. This evolution of PE has been varied and diverse due to the development of unique provincial curricula, as well as provincially developed initiatives such as daily physical activity and comprehensive school health.

The combining of PE with health and wellness education, and outdoor education, has also contributed to the evolution. In addition, the rapid advancement of technology and the integration of new technologies into today's PE classroom are just a few examples of how PE has changed and will continue to change in the future.

The Early Years of Physical Education

One of the first visionaries for PE in Canada was Egerton Ryerson, the first Superintendent of Education for Upper Canada (Cosentino & Howell, 1971; Keyes, 1989; Morrow & Wamsley, 2005). In 1846, he launched an appeal for a PE program in schools: a program that was focused on instilling discipline and moral values in young children (Mandigo, Corlett & Lathrop, 2012). In 1852, he continued this work by publishing a complete course of physical exercises that included military activities such as tactics and marching. In 1865, the federal government began offering a grant of fifty dollars to any school administering "drill and gymnastics." Finally, in 1892, a law made PE and gymnastics compulsory in schools.

Shortly after the turn of the century, the majority of formal public school settings at the secondary level focused on drill and practice, physical training, and sporting games played by the school teams. For the most part these sporting games were also exclusively reserved for the few male athletes within the school. Private schools for boys that were established around this time were not that different as these programs also focused primarily on sports. However, the private schools that were established for girls focused more on activities such as dance and rhythmics, more commonly referred to at that time as "physical culture" (Cosentino & Howell, 1971).

The first Normal School, an institution designed for the training teachers, was established in 1847 and was equipped with a gymnasium so that teachers could be instructed to provide leadership in this area of the curriculum (Innis, 1950). This development demonstrates the growing importance that PE began to receive in teacher training.

In the early 1900s the field of PE continued to flourish. More PE programs began to appear in teacher training institutions. Prior to this the only four institutions that played prominent roles in physical educator training were McGill University and the Macdonald Normal School in Quebec and the University of Toronto and the Margaret Eaton School in Ontario. It should be noted that the Margaret Eaton School, which later joined the University of Toronto, played a major role in the training of women as physical educators (Gurney, 1982). The programs at these schools were heavily influenced by European educators known for their work in movement education. Examples of this influential work include Swedish gymnastics founded by Pehr Henrik Ling, a Czechoslovakian youth sport movement (Sokol) founded by Miroslav Tyrs and Jindrich Fugner, and a Swiss Eurhythmics movement founded by Emile Jaques-Dalcroze (Martens, 1986).

In 1908, the province of Nova Scotia entered into an agreement with the Department of Militia and Defence focusing on the inclusion of PE and military drill in public schools. This included the formation of cadet corps, the teaching of rifle skills, and the training of teachers for certification of competency in teaching for these areas. In return, the Department of Militia and Defence agreed to provide competent instructors to enable teachers to obtain qualifications in physical training and military drill, to pay a bonus to qualified teachers who instructed cadet corps, and to provide supplies and print resources and to conduct examinations and evaluations (Constantino & Howell, 1971).

This plan caught the attention of another Canadian PE pioneer, Lord Strathcona, who was Canada's High Commissioner to Great Britain at that time. Strathcona was so impressed by this plan that on April 17, 1909, he entered into an agreement with the Government of Canada in the establishment of the Strathcona Trust Fund. Within this fund, $500,000 was set aside to be administered by the National Department of Militia. It was intended to provide annual grants to the participating provinces. Recipients of this fund were to incorporate physical training as an integral part of the curriculum in all schools above the primary grades to form cadet corps and to provide physical educator training. The instructors were to be supplied and paid by the Army, provided the provincial department of education would allocate time at the Normal School (a teachers college) for "physical training instruction," and encourage the teachers, once they left the Normal School, to include "physical drill" as part of the school program. Canada had very few professionally trained physical educators, so most provinces availed themselves of the funds established by this trust and entered into an agreement with the federal government. As a result, the work was carried out by army sergeants, and their teaching was supplemented in the Normal Schools by the use of the British syllabus of physical exercises for public elementary schools, printed in 1904, which was based on the Ling system of gymnastics. Years later in 1933, a revised version of the syllabus was released that showcased a very prominent interest in games that were popular among the British.

Physical Education from 1914–1945

During the First World War, PE across Canada did not see any significant growth or substantial evolution. However, during the waning years of the Great Depression when economic crises and unemployment rates throughout the country were prominent, a glimmer of hope emerged for the field of PE and training. The government of Canada passed the *Youth Training Act* on May 19, 1939. The intent of this act was to prepare Canada's young people for gainful employment (Orban, 1965). This *Youth Training Act* led to the first official national fitness program in 1965.

The province of Manitoba is but one example of where great gains were achieved because of this act. However, it should be recognized that in the year prior to the *Youth Training Act* being passed, Manitoba had already established youth training centres on its own initiative under the directorship of Robert Jarman (Manitoba Department of Education, 1909).

The demands of World War II stretched the limits of national funding programs. Additionally, priorities were being diverted away from education (specifically PE), resulting in a decrease in personnel entering the teaching profession and training programs. As a result, school boards began to lower the standards of teacher qualifications. The war effort also affected the ability to manufacture the equipment necessary for PE programming in schools, as the focus of the nation was to ensure the manufacturing of military equipment. The army had priority in regard to equipment, so even in school systems where funds had not been dramatically cut back it was not always possible to purchase the necessary PE teaching supplies and equipment.

During this time, PE programs began to change in philosophy. There was a more concentrated focus on formal calisthenics, where obstacle courses and endurance activities that required minimal or no PE related equipment became the norm. Cadet training was revived, and in most provinces girls as well as boys had compulsory defence training. Physical education also formed the basis of all war service programs for women, with a particular emphasis on health.

In 1943, the *National Fitness Act* in Canada was passed. This was in response to medical examinations carried out prior to and throughout World War II that revealed many men and women to be unfit for military service. The *National Fitness Act* established a $250,000 fund to be provided to provincial governments on a matching basis with a per capita quota for each province. The objective of the act was to promote the physical fitness of the people of Canada through the extension of PE in schools, universities, and other establishments; to help train physical educators in the key principles of PE; to organize activities designed to promote a greater measure of physical fitness; to provide facilities; and to co-operate in an attempt to improve overall well-being through physical exercise. Subsequently, this act encouraged and prompted the majority of the provinces to initiate or expand their PE and recreation programs. In February of 1944, a National Council on Physical Fitness was appointed consisting of a director and nine other individuals, each representing one of the provinces of Canada participating in the National Physical Fitness Plan.

Physical education has undergone many changes in Canada since its inception.

Physical Education from 1946—Present

Following World War II, PE experienced its greatest evolution. A metamorphosis from the more traditional form of training, skill, and practice to a PE model that incorporated a philosophical approach known as movement education began to emerge. This movement originated from the work of Rudolf Laban, an Austrian dance teacher who designed a framework for analyzing movement. Physical educators that immigrated to Canada from England following the war brought this orientation with them to the teaching of PE resulting in movement education finding its way into the teaching of school-based programs (Pangrazi & Gibbons, 2009). This metamorphosis meant that learners were exposed to a variety of movement forms like games, gymnastics, and dance that nurtured the development of the whole child: physical, social, and cognitive (Mandigo et al., 2012).

Not only did the content of PE programs begin to shift, but the methodology of teaching PE also began to change. Movement education promoted a more student-facilitated approach whereby the learners were actively engaged in making decisions about how they would solve movement problems (Hill, 1979). This was in stark contrast to the more traditional forms of PE programming that reflected a gender-specific and teacher-centred approach that was commonplace prior to World War II (Mandigo et al., 2012).

During the 1970s and 1980s, provincial PE curricula began to adopt the movement education foundation. Elementary PE programs were built upon Laban's movement education concepts of body awareness, space awareness, effort, and relationships. Secondary PE programs were also built upon the same foundation but differed with respect to the amount of time devoted to the variety of activity and movement forms.

Canadian Pioneers Who Influenced the Field of Physical Education

Robert Tait McKenzie

Robert Tait McKenzie was born in 1867 and spent his early years in the small town of Almonte in the Ottawa Valley. His childhood was spent actively playing in the outdoors, which was commonplace for children at this time. It would be this love for outdoor play that began to nurture his interest in physical activity and its relationship with the human body. One of McKenzie's childhood friends was James Naismith,

Robert Tait McKenzie

James Naismith

the inventor of basketball. This childhood friendship would continue through their years together at McGill University.

McKenzie received his formal schooling at Almonte and followed this by attending Lisgar Collegiate Institute in Ottawa. In 1885, at the age of eighteen, he entered McGill University eventually earning a degree in medicine (McGill, 1980). As a student at McGill, McKenzie began to acquire an interest in the fields of PE and art. It was also during this time that he took an avid interest and began to participate in gymnastics. This eventually led to becoming Naismith's assistant in teaching gymnastics at the university (Kozar, 1992). Following Naismith's graduation from McGill in 1890, McKenzie assumed the position of instructor in gymnastics, carrying this title and responsibility even beyond his departure from McGill in 1892. Upon graduation he accepted a medical position at Montreal General Hospital but maintained direct involvement at McGill holding several positions (Medical Examiner, Instructor in Physical Culture, Director of Physical Training, and Demonstrator of Anatomy) until his eventual departure to the University of Pennsylvania in Philadelphia as Director of Physical Education and a professor in the faculty of medicine. McKenzie remained in Philadelphia for the rest of his life interrupted only by a brief time spent in service with the British Army during World War I.

McKenzie is recognized worldwide for contributions to the fields of medicine, PE, and the art form of sculpture. His advancements in rehabilitative medicine were highly regarded at the time. His extensive writing and teachings in PE became the foundation for its instruction across the country. This extensive study and practice in medicine and PE provided McKenzie with a unique understanding of both sport and anatomy that led to him becoming one of the world's leading sport sculptors (Kozar, 1992).

Robert Tait McKenzie's contributions to PE are unparalleled. His untiring dedication and commitment to the advancement of PE has been recognized by national associations in both Canada and the United States that have bestowed awards in his honour.

James Naismith

James Naismith was born in 1861 in Bennies Corner, a small community near Almonte, Ontario. It was during his youth growing up near Almonte that he became friends with Robert Tait McKenzie. Naismith attended elementary school in Brownies Corner and high school in Almonte. After graduating in 1883, he attended McGill University earning a BA in physical education. He was regarded as a very talented and versatile athlete participating in

Ethel Mary Cartwright

football, lacrosse, rugby, soccer, and gymnastics. His skill in gymnastics eventually resulted in his becoming the head instructor of gymnastics at McGill. He went on to be an instructor of PE at McGill from 1887–1890 while also pursuing his education in theology at Presbyterian College in Montreal.

Naismith moved to Springfield College in Springfield, Massachusetts, in 1890, assuming a position as an instructor of PE. In 1891 he invented the game of basketball, arguably his greatest contribution to the field of PE. After a brief period in Denver, Naismith become a PE instructor at the University of Kansas in 1898. During his tenure at the University of Kansas, he also assumed responsibilities as basketball coach and university physician. From 1919 until his retirement in 1937, Naismith was also the university's athletic director.

Ethel Mary Cartwright

Ethel Mary Cartwright was born in 1880 in Clapham, England. After completing her education in England, she assumed the position of PE instructor at McGill Royal Victoria College in 1906, eventually transferring to McGill University. While at McGill she was instrumental in instituting mandatory PE for women in each of their four

years of study. Her work and dedication in this field helped lead to the establishment of the McGill Department of Physical Education in 1912 (Cosentino & Howell, 1971). During her tenure at McGill she also worked as a coach and an administrator. In 1928, she left McGill University and accepted a position at the University of Saskatchewan where she remained until her retirement in 1942. While there she organized the women's PE department and also established a women's athletic director. Under her leadership women's sports at the university flourished and gained prominence. The University of Saskatchewan recognizes her tremendous contribution to women's sports and athletics annually by presenting the Ethel Mary Cartwright Trophy to the Huskie female athlete of the year. Her dedication, commitment, and contributions to the fields of PE and sport were also recognized nationally when she received the R. Tait McKenzie Honour Award, the highest award presented by PHE Canada (then known as CAHPER) in 1948.

Arthur Stanley Lamb

Dr. Arthur Stanley Lamb was born in 1886 and raised in Ballarat, Australia. He complete his formal schooling at Ballarat State and Technical School before immigrating to Canada in 1907, and assuming the Physical Education Director position and teaching responsibilities at the YMCA in Vancouver for two years. He graduated from Springfield College with a BPE in 1912. He immediately moved to Montreal and attended McGill University as a medical student while simultaneously working as an instructor of PE. In 1920, he assumed the role and responsibility of Director of Physical Education at McGill. He would also go on to receive MD and CM (Master of Surgery) degrees from McGill and served in various positions at the university until his retirement in 1949.

Dr. Lamb had an avid interest in PE. He was very active as a member, and held executive positions in various health, sport/athletic, and PE associations and organizations. Dr. Lamb worked with such groups as the National Committee for School Health Research, the Canadian Public Health Association, the Amateur Athletic Union of Canada, the Canadian Olympic Association, and the Canadian Intercollegiate Athletic Union Board of Governors. He is generally more widely known and recognized for the leadership he provided to the inception and development of the Quebec Physical Education Association in 1923 and the Canadian Physical Education Association in 1933 (now known as Physical and Health Education Canada). He served as the Association's first president for three terms (six years) until 1939 and held the title of honorary president until his death in 1958.

In various tributes, Dr. Lamb has been referred to as "the father of physical education in Canada," "the father of modern physical education in Canada," and "dean of physical education." For his leadership, dedication, and distinguished service to the fields of PE, health education, and sports and athletics, Dr. Lamb received the R. Tait McKenzie Honour Award in 1948.

Florence Somers

Florence Somers was born in 1889 in Waltham, Massachusetts. She completed all of her formal schooling and post-secondary education in the United States receiving a diploma of PE in 1908 from the Sargent School of Physical Education where she would later become the director. She went on to receive a Bachelor of Science degree in education from Boston University and followed this with a Master of Arts from New York University in 1929. She taught at various elementary and secondary schools in Massachusetts before assuming the position of Director of Health and Physical Education for East Orange Public Schools.

In 1933, she immigrated to Toronto and took the position of assistant director at the Margaret Eaton School before being promoted to the director's position the following year. In 1941, the Margaret Eaton School became affiliated with the University of Toronto and Florence became an assistant professor, responsible for the instruction of professional courses for women. She maintained active involvement in professional associations and organizations, often assuming leadership positions. She was instrumental in furthering the advancements of women in athletics and contributed by being a part of the first advisory board for the Women's Athletics Committee.

Her leadership skills were also evident when she assumed the position of president of the Canadian Physical Education Association in 1939, following Dr. A. S. Lamb and serving as its president for two terms (four years). Perhaps her greatest achievement as president was recognizing the need for the CPEA to gain prominence as a national association. To work toward this end she encouraged and succeeded at having the CPEA hold its 1939 conference in Vancouver which helped to solidify the CPEA as a national association. The dedication, commitment, and contributions of Florence Somers to the fields of PE, outdoor recreation, and athletics did not go unnoticed as she received an honour award from AAHPER in 1940 and the R. Tait McKenzie Honour Award in 1950.

From CPEA to PHEC

The Canadian Physical Education Association (CPEA) was founded in 1933 by Dr. A. S. Lamb of McGill University and is considered to be one of the most important associations that helped advance PE in Canada. From its inception it struggled, particularly in trying to position itself as a national organization. It was through the untiring efforts of individuals such as Dr. A. S. Lamb, Florence Somers, and C. D. "Blackie" Blackstock (who presided as both the *Bulletin* editor from 1937–1950 and the first executive director from 1964–1974), that the association weathered its initial growing pains and began to establish itself as an association that was the voice for PE in Ontario and Quebec. To ensure the fledgling association would continue to thrive, these individuals worked diligently, along with the support of others, to promote the association by expanding its membership and reach beyond the borders of Ontario and Quebec (Gurney, 1982). With the opportunity to host national conferences in Vancouver in 1939 and Winnipeg in 1944, the CPEA began to slowly emerge as a national association. In addition, the advent of the *National Fitness Act* of 1943 resulted in the creation of a National Fitness Council. Several members of the CPEA were also named to this council and some of the first meetings were held jointly with the CPEA executive meetings. This partnership helped strengthen the CPEA and support its growth on the national scene so that by 1945, the CPEA had members from every province except Prince Edward Island. Funding assistance from the National Fitness Council in 1946 also helped the association to be able to publish its conference proceedings for the first time in both official languages. This was followed by the first official bilingual convention in Montreal in 1948 (Gurney, 1982).

Other notable initiatives that elevated the CPEA to be recognized as a national association were the first name change to the Canadian Association for Health, Physical Education and Recreation (CAHPER) in 1947; the continued support for CAHPER branches in the provinces; the production of the first *Journal* in 1957; and the first CAHPER office in 1962. Through the years, the association had recognized the need to continue its evolution through organizational restructuring that reflected the needs of the time. The association continued to position itself as the voice of health education, PE, and recreation, often aligning itself with other national organizations and creating structures within the association responsible for their promotion. This eventually led to another name change in 1994 when the association became the Canadian Association for Health, Physical Education, Recreation and Dance (CAHPERD). This move reflected the critically important work that was being done by passionate advocates of dance across the country and internationally. The name would remain until 2008 when CAHPERD entered its 75th year of service eventually renaming itself again to become Physical and Health Education Canada (PHE Canada) as it is known today.

The association remains strong and vibrant and is unequivocally recognized as a national organization with a mandate that reads: "All children and youth in Canada living healthy, physically active lives." Its membership is far reaching, its representation is in every province and territory, and its reputation continues to grow. This national association has made and continues to make major contributions to the field of PE. It has assumed its rightful place as the voice for PE in Canada.

Physical Education Today

Present day PE is best described through the various curriculum documents developed by the ministries and departments of education in the ten provinces and three territories of Canada. While it cannot be said definitively that curriculum development across Canada is the same, the argument might be made that the procedure follows a very similar process in the various provinces and territories. It should be noted that PE curricula in the Yukon Territory, Northwest Territories, and Nunavut Territory are very often

adopted from the curricula of neighbouring provinces but with a specific mandate that it reflect the ethnic, language, and cultural traditions unique to the residents of the territory.

In most cases, the design, implementation, and evaluation of curricula are completed by a committee consisting of individuals identified as curriculum developers. These committees are very often comprised of government officials identified as PE consultants, physical educators from the field, school-based administrators, and post-secondary education faculty members from faculties or colleges of education or PE.

Curriculum development traditionally centres upon identifying a vision or aim for PE followed by stated goals, and focuses on kindergarten to grade twelve. In some provinces and territories, the development of kindergarten to grade twelve may be further divided by grade levels (see **Table 1.1** on page 15). The goals of a curriculum are achieved through the identification of outcomes and indicators followed by the assessment and evaluation of student learning.

While there are many similarities, the Canadian provinces and territories have different Physical Education curricula.

The process of curriculum development involves a step-by-step procedure and four distinct phases. The initial phase is the creation and design of a theoretical model, foundation, and framework grounded in research and informed by societal realities. This is followed by a pilot phase where the initial creation and design is tested in practice and selected schools. Feedback received from this pilot phase is then reviewed utilizing formative assessment procedures informing the initial design resulting in possible changes to the curriculum document. Once this work has been finalized, an implementation phase is then instituted which allows the curriculum to be put into practice in schools throughout the province or territory. As implementation is in progress the process of assessing and evaluating the curriculum begins. It is often the case that the process of curriculum renewal can be a four- to five-year process.

There are no established guidelines that determine the length of time that a curriculum is used before a review is undertaken and another revised curriculum is created. What is critical to understand is that the process of curriculum renewal results in the creation of a document known as a curriculum guide. As the term implies, this guide provides educators (in this case physical educators) with the foundation and framework for their school-based PE program. Very often the curriculum guide is referred to as "curriculum-as-plan" (Aoki, 1991). The actual teaching of the curriculum in various schools with their unique circumstances, approaches, and philosophical orientations results in what is best described as the "curriculum-as-lived" (Aoki, 1991).

The PE curriculum documents today attempt to help children and youth develop the skills, knowledge, and attitudes to lead healthy, active lives (Mandigo et al., 2012). In the last decade, curriculum revision in some provinces has also recognized the reality that teaching PE crosses boundaries into areas related to health education. As a result, recent provincial curriculum renewal emphasizes and promotes active living and helping children and youth develop skills to make healthy choices through PE (Mandigo et al., 2012). Some provinces have adopted the position of creating curriculum documents that combine the educational fields of PE and health education. In attempts to even further enhance the position of PE in the educational landscape, the term "physical literacy" has emerged. This is in an effort to equate physical literacy in PE with literacy in other subjects such as reading/language arts, mathematics, and science.

For decades, if not since its inception, PE has been marginalized and not viewed as an academic subject. Physical education has constantly battled to be recognized as having a vital role to play in the education of children and youth. There is little doubt that the evolution of PE curricula through time has both influenced and been influenced by the enduring work of those who teach and research the subject, as well as organizations and associations who make it their mandate to promote the field.

Table 1.1 (page 15) provides an overview and links to the various provincial PE curricula in each of the provinces and territories. The provincial/territorial curricula documents referred to in **Table 1.1** provide us with the philosophical and foundational components of what is important in the teaching of PE. The documents also suggest ways in which one can plan, facilitate, assess, and evaluate the instructional learning. However, curriculum documents are not foolproof. Dr. Stu Robbins reminds us that curricula developed with the best intentions are only as effective as the quality programs that implement and teach to the curriculum. His words challenge each of us to decide the role that we will play.

Where is physical and health education?

In many ways physical and health education is like Lewis Carroll's Alice, who came to a fork in the road. She looked at the cat and said, "Which way do I go from here?" The cat replied, "That depends on where you want to go!" I believe that physical and health education is at a crossroads. One path is to continue to occupy children with lots of physical activities. The other is to develop a cohesive and comprehensive program of physical and health education that will educate children to know and understand the benefits of being physically active, that will teach children the physical skills required to use their bodies in a wide variety of situations and will create a love of being physically active for life.

The potential for physical and health education is enormous! Society is beginning to realize that being physically active has great benefits to our health and well being and has the potential to offset the negative effects of a sedentary lifestyle. We seem to be constantly seeking the magic "pill" that will overcome obesity and cardiovascular disease. As Dr. Andrew Pipe has said, "We have that pill in physical activity but refrain from using it!" We have ample evidence to support this claim. We don't need more research evidence. We need to decide to do something before it is too late. We, physical and health education, are at the crossroads. Are we ready to deliver daily, meaningful programs of physical and health education to each and every child? The challenge is ours: we need to decide which way we want to go! [From correspondence with authors].

Physical Education in the Future

Imagine a future 20 years from now where physical education programs are all in a valley of despair. In fact, physical education programs have largely been eliminated from schools, because they failed the test of accountability. Children were not learning in physical education. … Now imagine a future 20 years from now where physical education programs take center stage in the school. Every child has quality instruction provided daily by a specialist and physical activity is centrally important to children, teachers and parents. … Either future is possible. (Sanders & McCrum, 1999, p. 3–4)

The future of PE in Canada can perhaps best be described as not being that different from what might be understood to be the future of PE globally. The research literature in PE identifies both "the decline and fall of physical education" and "the rise and triumph of physical education" (Kirk, 2010).

In his work, Dr. David Kirk describes the contributions of scholars such as Dr. Patt Dodds and Dr. Lawrence Locke, along with Dr. Daryl Siedentop, who were predicting the eventual demise and downfall of PE in the 1980s if there was not a radical shift in the programming away from the dominant model (Locke, 1992). The issue for Siedentop, O'Sullivan, and Tannehill is that PE's resistance to all efforts to reform its failing practices was due to its deep institutionalization in schools (Kirk, 2010). However, Siedentop went even further to include the failure of physical educator preparation programs that provide future educators with the subject-matter knowledge needed to teach PE lessons, but only up to an introductory level (Siedentop, 2002).

Despite the pessimistic view of some of the field's leading scholars, many other notable authors and researchers have imagined a more optimistic future for PE. The work of Don Hellison (1987) accompanied by that of Penny and Chandler (2000) saw that PE could change for the better. This change, however, required that PE concern itself with connecting to, and having an impact on, social issues while also being linked across the curriculum and beyond the school to our society at large (Kirk, 2010). In addition, other scholars such as Jewett, Bain, and Ennis (1995) share a view of optimism for the future of PE that requires a reconceptualization of the teaching of PE to include attention to five value orientations: "discipline mastery, self-actualization, social reconstruction, learning process, and ecological integration" (Kirk, 2010, p. 32). Laker (2003) envisions the future of PE as one of possibilities that contains as Kirk (2010) describes, "some

As physical education continues to evolve, athletes will continue to achieve things previously thought to be impossible.

Physical educators have the opportunity to make an enormous impact on the lives of their students.

genuinely radical and 'progressive' elements, such as the personal and social responsibility, teaching games for understanding (TGfU), sport education, and health-related exercise pedagogical models, a cultural studies approach to popular physical culture, and a theoretical framework provided by the various value orientations" (Kirk, 2010 p. 32).

The following words by Dr. Ellen Singleton on the future of PE provide us with a glimpse of the challenges we still face but also seem optimistic about how far the field has come through time.

Moving past the past—what's the future of PE?

On my more pessimistic days, I find it hard to envision any real change in school Physical Education as we move into the future. Despite our best efforts as PETE educators, many physical educators, particularly at the secondary level, remain focused on reproducing and reinforcing pedagogical practice that is characterized by gymnasium-based activities that are teacher-centered, male dominated, competitively organized, team sport oriented, and evaluated in terms of ability, previous experience, and behaviour in class. Regardless of the campaigns we have waged in the

past, elementary students continue to be taught Physical Education by generalist teachers with (usually) minimal preparation rather than specialists trained in movement, child development and cultural and learning theory as it applies to physical activity.

It is cheering to remember that change, however difficult to discern, is a process that never stops. For Physical Education this has meant the introduction to curriculum documents across Canada of recently rejuvenated definitions of health and Physical Education through the notion of "literacy." Simply introducing these concepts to the members of the field has ignited discussion about the purpose, focus, and pedagogical connections between health education and Physical Education that is long overdue. This discussion is fanned and fuelled with textbooks and journal articles written and edited by Canadian scholars for PETE students, practitioners, and academics that focus on cultural, social, and pedagogical issues facing teachers today and into the future. This knowledge and experience is further disseminated through conferences and local initiatives. For example, programs promoting healthy active schools at elementary, middle/junior, and even secondary schools are highlighting the important connections between nutrition, adequate rest, relief from stress, and many different forms of physical activity. As well as enabling graduate students to connect with mentors anywhere in the world, online classes enable undergraduate and graduate PETE students to discuss their learning experiences and their research, and to develop collegial ties with others across Canada. What is the future of Physical Education? Perhaps we're living it now. [From correspondence with authors]

The United Nations declared 2005 as the International Year of Physical Education and Sport and provided the opportunity for the field of PE to take the leadership required for affecting change in the world and position itself on the international stage. In doing so, the UN was encouraging, but also challenging, the field to recognize the vital role it could play in raising standards of literacy and numeracy, increasing student achievement, improving school attendance and retention, improving personal and social development; raising self-esteem and providing positive alternatives to risk behaviour; and encouraging attitudes of fairness, respect for others, and valuing diversity (Mandigo et al., 2012). It is evident that PE has indeed evolved from its original inception of purely physical training to a field that is now being encouraged and challenged to assume a prominent and critical role in positively influencing the larger issues faced by society and the world today.

It appears that PE finds itself at a significant point in its evolution. The decisions the field makes now will require critical thought and action as it moves forward into the second decade of the twenty-first century. Whatever these decisions are, there is general agreement among many in the field that we would be wise to adhere to two basic tenets. The first is that the future of PE is inextricably linked to an understanding of the past and even more so the present. The second tenet is the essential and important role that the field of higher education plays in the preparation of future physical educators (Kirk, 2010). If there is no shift in the current understanding and the need for change in the preparation of today's physical educators, there is very little chance that change will result in school based PE programming and therefore no change will occur to have a positive impact on the larger issues of society and world.

Conclusion

In closing this chapter, the authors suggest that the future of PE in Canada rests with us all. As educators, it is imperative that we take responsibility and an active role in ensuring a promising future for PE. This future must positively influence the lives of children and youth as well as address the issues faced by society and the world. We believe that individuals who desire to teach PE in schools are the key to this influence. The profession needs aspiring physical educators

Case Studies—Quick Hits

Chapter One, "Physical Education: Looking Back, Looking Forward," provides a comprehensive overview of the history of physical Education in Canada. This rich history highlights many prominent individuals, organizations, and significant events that have helped shape the field today. There is evidence that many cultures have also contributed to the field physical education in Canada.

Questions for Reflection

1 Working with a partner or in small groups, identify a specific culture that has contributed to the field of physical education today and provide specific examples illustrating this contribution.

2 Given the reality that the school you will teach in will most likely reflect a culturally diverse student population, how should your program reflect this diversity?

Dr. Stu Robbins identified that physical education in Canada, "is at a crossroads." These words in part also reflect the thoughts by Sanders and McCrum (page 11) regarding the future of our field. If we believe that we are indeed at a crossroads and that the future of physical education can either be "eliminated from schools" or "take centre stage," the decisions you make as a future teacher of PE will be critically important.

Questions for Reflection

1 Working with a partner or in small groups, describe and detail three specific ways to influence decision makers as to the important role that PE plays in the lives of Canadian children and youth.

2 As a future physical educator, identify and describe three principles that your PE program will be based upon and that you believe are critically important to providing a quality program.

who embody the passion, dedication, and commitment
to want to make change through PE. Are you one of these
aspiring physical educators?

Questions for Reflection

1 From your understanding and perspective of the history
   of PE in Canada what would you identify as the major
   influence that shaped PE in Canada? Why?

2 What contributions has school PE made to society and
   more specifically to the lives of children and youth? What
   do you believe PE can contribute?

3 What messages are being conveyed in the thoughts
   expressed by Dr. Stu Robbins and Dr. Ellen Singleton?

4 What do you think the future holds for PE?

5 As a future physical educator, what are your biggest
   aspirations about teaching PE? What are your biggest
   fears about teaching PE?

Key Terms

- Physical Education
- Normal School
- Movement Education
- PHE Canada
- Curriculum Development

Table 1.1: Physical Education Curricula Across Canada

Physical Education Structure	Physical Education Core Areas	Provincial/Territorial Aims & Goals of Physical Education	Curricular Links
Alberta			
Physical Education K–12	■ Activity ■ Benefits Health ■ Cooperation ■ Do it Daily … for Life!	Aims: ■ Enable individuals to develop knowledge, skills, and attitudes necessary to lead an active, health lifestyle Goals: ■ Focus on three priority wellness outcomes (physical activity, healthy eating, psychosocial well-being). ■ Reduce the number and overlap of learning outcomes. ■ Ensure age-appropriateness of learning outcomes. ■ Recognize and address the dimensions of wellness.	Alberta Ministry of Education: http://education. alberta.ca Alberta Learning Website: www.learning.gov. ab.ca
British Columbia			
Physical Education K–12	■ Active Living ■ Movement ■ Personal and Social Responsibility	Aims: ■ Enable all students to enhance their quality of life through active living. Goals: ■ Students will participate daily in physical activity. ■ Students will develop appropriate knowledge and skills for participating actively, effectively, safely, and responsibly in a wide range of individual and dual activities, games, and rhythmic movement activities. ■ Students will develop the knowledge, skills, and attitudes that enable them to value, attain, and maintain a healthy, active lifestyle.	British Columbia Ministry of Education: www. bced.gov.bc.ca
Manitoba			
Physical Education K–12	■ Movement ■ Fitness Management ■ Safety ■ Personal/Social Management ■ Healthy Lifestyle Practices	■ To provide students with planned and balanced programming ■ To develop knowledge, skills, and attitudes for physically active and healthy lifestyles.	Manitoba Ministry of Education: www.edu.gov.mb.ca
New Brunswick			
Physical Education K–8 Physical Education and Health 9–10 Outdoor Pursuits 110 Health and Physical Education 120	■ Movement Categories ■ Alternative Environment ■ Dance/Gymnastics ■ Games ■ Individual and Dual Activities	Aims: ■ To attain healthy levels of physical activity and fitness for all students ■ To encourage the acquisition of motor skills ■ To develop knowledge and attitudes supportive of continuing active living habits throughout life ■ To develop specific objectives designed to meet the physical growth and developmental needs of all children and youth. Goals: ■ Doing ■ Knowing ■ Valuing	New Brunswick Department of Education: www.gnb.ca

Physical Education Structure	Physical Education Core Areas	Provincial/Territorial Aims & Goals of Physical Education	Curricular Links
Newfoundland and Labrador			
Physical Education K–9 Healthy Living 1200 Physical Education 2100 & 2101	■ Education in Movement (moving and doing) ■ Education about Movement (understanding and applying) ■ Education through Movement (cooperation and responsibility)	Aims: ■ Foster personal and community wellness by empowering students to attain healthy lifelong attitudes and behaviours through physical activity as part of the total educational experience. Goals: ■ Promote the "joy of effort" in activities and provide an element of fun and enjoyment through participation in such activities. ■ Develop a thorough understanding of the principles of movement and foster a greater awareness of and appreciation for the various aspects of human physical activity. ■ Provide differential competitive sports opportunities that consistently challenge the most gifted while motivating and satisfying participation on the part of the least talented. ■ Develop confidence and appreciation of group support by meeting the challenges of survival and of adventure sports (adventure education) in the outdoors. ■ Construct group interaction in a way that reduces sexism, racism, or discrimination of any kind. ■ Create new games and physical recreation activities and discover new possibilities for intercultural communication through dance, sport, and fitness activities	Newfoundland and Labrador Department of Education: www.ed.gov.nl.ca
Northwest Territories			
Physical Education K–12 (using Alberta Curriculum)	■ Basic Skills ■ Functional Fitness ■ Communication ■ Effort	See Alberta's Aims & Goals	Northwest Territories Education, Culture, and Employment: www.ece.gov.nt.ca Alberta Ministry of Education: education.alberta.ca Alberta Learning Website: www.learning.gov. ab.ca
Nova Scotia			
Physical Education K–12	■ Knowing ■ Doing ■ Valuing	Learners experiencing purposeful physical activity and developing knowledge of, skills for, and attitudes toward the health benefits of a physically active lifestyle.	Nova Scotia Department of Education: www.ednet.ns.ca

Physical Education Structure	Physical Education Core Areas	Provincial/Territorial Aims & Goals of Physical Education	Curricular Links
Nunavut Territory			
Physical Education K–6 (using Manitoba Curriculum) Aulajaaqtut 7–12 (various resources)	■ Wellness & Safety ■ Physical, Social, Emotional & Cultural Wellness ■ Goal Setting ■ Volunteerism ■ Survival	See Manitoba's Aims & Goals	Nunavut Department of Education: www.edu.gov.nu.ca Manitoba Ministry of Education: www.edu.gov.mb.ca Alberta Ministry of Education: education.alberta.ca NWT for Health Education and Inuuqatigiit Curriculum: www.ece.gov.nt.ca
Ontario			
Health and Physical Education 1–8 Healthy Active Living Education 9–12 Health for Life 11 Exercise Science 12 Recreation and Fitness Leadership 12	■ Physical Activity ■ Active Living ■ Healthy Living ■ Living Skills	Knowledge and skills acquired in the program will benefit students throughout their lives and help them to thrive in an ever-changing world by enabling them to acquire physical and health literacy and to develop the comprehension, capacity, and commitment needed to lead healthy, active lives and to promote healthy, active living. Goals: ■ Active Living ■ Movement Competence ■ Healthy Living	Ontario Ministry of Education: www.edu.gov.on.ca
Prince Edward Island (under revision)			
Physical Education 1–10 Physical Education—Life Style 10/11 Physical Education – Leadership 11/12	■ Fitness ■ Gymnastics ■ Games ■ Dance ■ Outdoor Pursuits ■ Track and Field	Assist the individual in developing: ■ Efficient and effective motor skills and applying these to a wide variety of activities. ■ And maintaining physical fitness ■ Knowledge and understanding of factors involved in attaining competence in and appreciation of physical activity. ■ And maintaining positive personal attributes and interpersonal relationships including a positive attitude towards continued participation in physical activity	Prince Edward Island Department of Education: www.edu.pe.ca
Quebec			
Physical Education and Health 1–6 Physical Education and Health Cycle 1 & 2	■ Performs motor skills in different physical activity settings ■ Interact with others in different physical activity settings ■ Adopts a healthy, active lifestyle	To help students develop psychosocial skills and acquire the knowledge, strategies, attitudes, and safe and ethical behaviours required to properly manage their health and well-being.	Education, Loisir et Sport Quebec: www.mels.gouv.qc.ca Learn Quebec: www.learnquebec.ca

Physical Education Structure	Physical Education Core Areas	Provincial/Territorial Aims & Goals of Physical Education	Curricular Links
Saskatchewan			
Physical Education K–9 Wellness 10 Physical Education 20 Physical Education 30	■ Active Living ■ Skillful Movement ■ Relationships	Aims: ■ Support students in becoming physically educated individuals who have the understandings and skills to engage in movement activity, and the confidence and disposition to live a healthy, active lifestyle. Goals: ■ Active Living—Enjoy and engage in healthy levels of participation in movement activities to support lifelong active living in the context of self, family, and community. ■ Skillful Movement—Enhance quality of movement by understanding, developing, and transferring movement concepts, skills, tactics, and strategies to a wide variety of movement activities. ■ Relationships—Balance self through safe and respectful personal, social, cultural, and environmental interactions in a wide variety of movement activities.	Saskatchewan Curriculum: www.edonline.sk.ca Saskatchewan Ministry of Education: www.education.gov.sk.ca
Yukon Territory			
Physical Education K–12	See B.C.'s Core Areas	See B.C.'s Aims & Goals	Yukon Department of Education: www.education.gov.yk.ca British Columbia Ministry of Education: www.bced.gov.bc.ca

History of Physical Education in Canada—A Timeline

1846	Egerton Ryerson makes the first official appeal for a physical education program in schools.
November 1847	First normal school is established in Canada. It is built with a gymnasium.
1852	Egerton Ryerson publishes the first short complete course of exercises.
1865	The Government of Canada offers a grant of $50 to any school administering "drill and gymnastics."
1891	Canadian-born James Naismith invents the game of basketball in New England.
1892	Physical Education and Gymnastics is made compulsory in all Canadian schools.
1906	Miss Ethel Mary Cartwright becomes the first physical education director for women in Canada.
1908	A two-year compulsory physical education program is approved in Canada.
1908	The province of Nova Scotia enters into an agreement with the Department of Militia in regard to physical education and military drill in public schools.
April 1909	The Lord Strathcona Trust Fund is established in agreement with the Government of Canada.
1910	The McGill Academic Calendar introduced a large section under "Physical Education" with options for both men and women.
1912	Ethel Mary Cartwright establishes the McGill School of Physical Education.
1933	The Canadian Physical Education Association (CPEA) is funded by Dr. Arthur S. Lamb of McGill University.
May 1939	The *Youth Training Act* is passed on May 19, 1939.
May 1943	The *National Fitness Act* is passed.
1944	A National Council on Physical Fitness is appointed to participate in the National Physical Fitness Plan.
1948	The CPEA is incorporated and changes its name to the Canadian Association for Health, Physical Education and Recreation (CAHPER).
1965	The first official national fitness program is introduced.
1994	CAHPER modifies its name to recognize the value of dance education. It becomes the Canadian Association for Health, Physical Education, Recreation and Dance (CAHPERD).
2008	In its 75th year, CAHPERD changes its name to Physical and Health Education Canada (PHE Canada).

For an enhanced online version of this timeline, please go to www.thompsonbooks.com/tpet

Becoming a Teacher of Physical Education

Tim Fletcher, Carolyn Temertzoglou,
and Nick Forsberg

Overview

The purpose of this chapter is to introduce what we believe to be some of the foundational issues and concepts for students who are becoming teachers of physical education (PE). From the outset, it is important to acknowledge the tremendous complexity and challenges involved in becoming a teacher. For this reason, learning to become a teacher is always represented by uncertainty, ambiguity, and tension—there is no fixed path or set of steps that, if followed, make someone "become a teacher." So while this chapter makes some claims about teaching based on the authors' beliefs and experiences, keep in mind that personal beliefs and experiences will lead to questioning of the issues. Indeed, it is hoped that the issues raised in this chapter are questioned, just as it is hoped students are always encouraged to question what it is they are learning.

Readers of this chapter may be located across Canada, at various points in various university programs, and at different stages of their lives. Some may be in the third year of an undergraduate physical education degree or concurrent degree, some may be in a one- or two-year teacher certification program following the completion of an initial degree. Some will be specializing to teach in elementary and others in secondary schools. Some may be aiming to become specialist teachers of physical education while others may be preparing to become classroom generalist teachers where physical education is taught along with language arts and mathematics, for example. Therefore, to address all readers' needs would be an impossible task; but, regardless of where you are and what your experiences with physical education may be, what is addressed in this chapter is important for teachers' development if they are to have their students' learning as the focus of their teaching. At the same time, it is also important to note that the material in this chapter is not all that one needs to become a teacher.

A core issue focused on throughout the chapter concerns the development of a professional identity. Another topic discussed is the importance of reflecting on your prior experiences of school in general, of physical education, and of other physical activity contexts (such as youth sport), highlighting how these experiences profoundly shape your thoughts and knowledge about students, teachers, teaching, and curriculum. Toward the end of the chapter, we invite you to consider developing a vision for teaching PE, one that will no doubt shift as you progress in your career and as you continue your lifelong journey as a teacher, as a learner, and as a passionate advocate for the teaching of quality school physical education.

Introduction:
Developing a Professional Identity

So what exactly is professional identity, and why is it important? According to sociologist Richard Jenkins (2008), identity is not a thing but a process of being or becoming. Because identity is processual, it is just as apt to think of *identification* as it is to think of identity. How we identify others and ourselves allows us to think about "who's who" and "what's what" and to think about who we are, and how we see ourselves "fitting in" to the human world (Jenkins, 2008). Humans interact with many different people in many different contexts, and so we embody several identities simultaneously. For example, you might identify as a sister, a university student, a dancer, a rugby player, a horseback rider, someone who is bilingual, and a lover of heavy metal music all at the same time. Each of these identities may be equally as important to you depending on where you are in your life. But what also contributes to your identity is how you think other people identify you.

When talking about how we identify in the workplace, it is also important to note that aspects of our personal identities strongly influence our professional identities, and vice versa—the two cannot be disconnected. That is, identifying as a sister, student, dancer, and so on, will influence how you go about your professional activities, which in turn influences your identities outside of work. As such, developing identities is complex and often contradictory.

When thinking about how identities are developed, it is clear that there is an interaction between how we see ourselves (self-image) and our perception of how others see us (public image) (Jenkins, 2008). For example, when in a practice teaching placement you might think about yourself and identify as a university student; however, the students at your host school might identify you as a teacher. This discrepancy in identifying labels might have an impact upon how you teach and how your students react to your teaching. This example also highlights the shifting nature of identity; how you identify will change throughout your life. If we take a moment to consider how your identity has and will continue to shift in school settings, it is not that difficult to see: previously you have identified as an elementary and high school student, you now identify as a university student, and you will likely go on to identify as a teacher. After a few years of teaching you might identify as the head of a department, a school board curriculum consultant, a school administrator, or a university instructor. When these shifts are thought about in conjunction with all the changes and experiences one encounters outside of the professional world, the complexity of how we identify becomes clear. As such, identity is thought to be in a constant state of flux, and should not be viewed as being fixed or stable.

Just as there are multiple ways in which to identify personally, so too can you have multiple identities in your professional life. Many teachers of physical education may have a strong background in physical activities and/or organized sport, and so it is perhaps not uncommon for them to include "athlete" as part of their identity. In turn, physical educators are often attracted to additional roles in a school, such as athletic director, coach, or intramural coordinator, that allow them to be further involved in physical activity (Lawson, 1983)—although there is a high degree of variance between individuals (O'Bryant, O'Sullivan & Raudensky, 2000). The point is that, while these roles are extremely important if students are to be provided with many opportunities to engage in physical activity, they are very different. We believe that the most important role a teacher can play in school is that of a *teacher*. Teachers are generally hired by schools or school boards as *teachers* and it is in this area where you can make the greatest impact upon all students, not just those who are interested in sports participation. As such, when thinking about developing a professional identity, focus your thoughts toward defining and refining your identity as a teacher, not as a coach.

As previously emphasized, identity pervades many parts of our lives—in fact, it is almost impossible to escape thinking about identification (Jenkins, 2008). But in this chapter, the primary focus is the development of a professional identity, which in this case concerns the process of becoming a teacher. Developing a professional identity is particularly important for new teachers because the identities that teachers develop in their early years of teaching "shape their dispositions, where they place their effort, whether and how they seek out professional development opportunities, and what obligations they see as intrinsic to their role" (Hammerness, Darling-Hammond & Bransford, 2005, p. 384). In order to develop a strong and positive professional identity, teachers need to feel that they embody the qualities of good teaching and are worthy of what they believe are appropriate labels for a "good" teacher; they also need to feel that other people (such as colleagues, students, and parents) view them as embodying these qualities (Korthagen, 2004).

It is important to realize that views of what constitute "good teaching" differ substantially. Being a part of a school environment for at least twelve years as a student can lead you to have very strong beliefs about teachers and what might represent "good" teaching. These beliefs will also influence the development of a professional identity. As such, it is fairly easy to see how the concepts of experiences, beliefs, identity, and knowledge are closely related, intertwined, and embedded within one another. So while these concepts are addressed throughout the chapter, focus more on how they influence one another rather than how they differ.

Theory to Practice

Almost anyone who has ever been a student will have strong beliefs about teaching, and these may be difficult to change (Randall, 2012; Tsangaridou, 2006); however, it is extremely important to be open to new ideas and ways of thinking about teaching. Canadian researchers Clare Kosnik and Clive Beck (2009) suggest that university teacher education programs offer opportunities to define and refine beliefs and a professional identity by learning about the possibilities and realities of teaching, and also by thinking deeply about the kind of teacher you want to be. Again, this will be strongly influenced by personal identities, interests, and background.

While there are many opportunities for professional growth during a teacher education program, there are also ways that this growth might be inhibited. For example, your own new and innovative ways of thinking about teaching might be stifled during your teacher education coursework or during the teaching internship as you try to navigate the

Teaching identities can have a big impact on the activities you feel are important for your students to learn.

challenges of staying true to your beliefs while also trying to achieve good grades (just as some of your students might do with you when you are teaching them). During teacher training you might feel that you are being "formed" into a type of teacher that you are not comfortable becoming (such as an authoritarian teacher), and this can be particularly challenging when you are being assessed and evaluated on criteria, practices, and points of view that do not match your views about good teaching. Sirna, Tinning, and Rossi (2008) found this type of conformity to be especially problematic during the teaching internship, as pre-service teachers often felt pressure to go along with the practices, views, and perspectives of departmental colleagues. However, there are ways that pre-service teachers can resist views that stand in contrast to their own even when an evaluation is forthcoming. For example, participating in critical reflection before and during the teaching internship is one method of providing pre-service teachers with strategies and understandings of how physical education sometimes "works" or "plays out" in schools. Additionally, it is important to work with your physical education instructor to communicate the extent to which inappropriate practices or points of view (e.g., sexist, racist, homophobic) are occurring, so that a stronger placement can be organized.

While progressing through a university program (be it an undergraduate physical education degree or an education degree), it is worth considering how learning experiences are influenced by identity *and* how *your* identity influences those experiences. For example, when learning about program planning in PE, you might think about how your identities influence the activities you feel are important for your students to learn, and the time you decide to dedicate to each activity. If you have a strong background in distance running, this might influence your decision to spend longer and go into more depth on a track and field unit than a unit on self-defence for example. It might also influence your thoughts about how to assess student learning in track and field, and how you interact with your students as they participate in tasks. Further still, it might inform or impede the extent to which you are open to learning from students or to trying new approaches or ways of thinking about teaching certain concepts. This point highlights the influential role that your prior experiences play in the processes of learning to teach.

Becoming a Reflective Practitioner

According to the US-based National Research Council (2000), one of the key tenets of how people learn is that "all learning involves transfer from previous experiences" (p. 68). Therefore, as people who are learning to teach, some of the most important ideas that you have about teaching will be based upon your prior experiences of teachers, teaching, and schools. But Korthagen, Loughran, and Russell (2006) point out that it is perhaps inaccurate to assume that learning occurs simply through experience; they contend that learning occurs "through *reflection* on experience and through *interaction* with others" [emphasis added] (p. 1025). Thus, an important process in learning to become a teacher involves revisiting and analyzing prior experiences to recognize how your assumptions about teaching have been shaped, how your knowledge has been constructed, and how your beliefs about teaching and learning have been influenced. Listening to or thinking about the experiences of others is equally as important as reflecting on your own experiences, because their experiences will definitely be different from your own. This process of reflecting on teaching and learning has

a profound influence on your thoughts about becoming a teacher and how you will go about teaching students.

Many people who think and write about teacher education place great emphasis on the importance of becoming a reflective practitioner (Schön, 1983). During a teacher-training program, the term "reflection" will likely be encountered frequently and you may be asked to reflect on your learning. Students often resent these frequent requests to reflect, so why is it important to learn to become a *reflective practitioner*? Tsangaridou and Siedentop (1995) provide one powerful reason, suggesting that "because teacher education programs cannot prepare teachers for every situation they may encounter it is preferable to help them become thoughtful decision makers" (p. 213). Furthermore, being reflective will also help you question the taken-for-granted assumptions you have and display in your teaching, as well as the teaching practices of peers, instructors, or colleagues. In this sense, reflection can lead to an understanding of ways in which you can resist practices and points of view that you perceive as standing in contrast with your own, or alternatively, adopt new practices that better suit the needs of students.

According to Grant and Zeichner (1984), reflective teachers are those who actively reflect upon their teaching and upon the different contexts in which they teach: for example, teaching in an inner city school, a school in a rural community, a high school, or working with students of different abilities. Reflective teachers do not take for granted the assumptions about the problems that they face when teaching; instead, they actively consider how they might best solve teaching problems, taking into account and questioning the social, political, and cultural contexts of their work (Fernandez-Balboa, 1997; Randall, 2012). Later chapters of this book examine how things like gender, sexuality, race, and ethnicity all have strong influences on teaching and learning.

Referring to the work of John Dewey at the beginning of the twentieth century, Grant and Zeichner (1984) outline important attitudinal characteristics for teachers who are to engage in reflective action: open-mindedness, responsibility, and wholeheartedness. In order to embody these characteristics, pre-service teachers should take ownership of their education as they make decisions about the kind of teacher they want to become, and refine their own professional identity. This means critically reflecting on: your prior experiences, what you are learning in your university-based coursework, and what you are learning in your practice teaching placements. Reflecting "critically" does not mean simply criticizing things; it means taking the time to think deeply about situations, and placing yourself in the position of others to decide about appropriate courses of action. Quite often this will mean metaphorically placing yourself in the shoes of your students or, perhaps more literally, being open to learning from your students about what does and does not help their learning.

As you gain more experience, and get to know the students who you are teaching and learn from them, you will likely develop some sense of what types of things work and don't work in certain situations. Understanding what works for you as a teacher and for your learners will allow you to anticipate how teaching situations may play out, and to respond quickly to problems that arise daily. However, experienced teachers can attest to the fact that what works well for one class of students on one day, will not necessarily work for another group of students, or the same group of students, on a different day. This point highlights the uncertainty of teaching and the importance of being open to new ideas and approaches that might emerge from conversations with colleagues or students.

Having established the importance of reflection, many pre-service teachers might wonder exactly how and when to reflect. Like most other aspects of teaching, there is

no clear-cut answer, however, it is important to engage in reflection both during and following a lesson. You might also ask yourself or your students:

- What is it that is helping or hindering the current situation?
- What is it about the activity that students are enjoying or disliking?
- Are the learning experiences that I am facilitating meaningful to my students?
- Are all of my learners engaged in the task?
- How can I change this experience so that it is more beneficial for the students in my class?

Professionals often do things without being able to explain their reasoning—one might think of this as using intuition. Taking a few minutes to pause and reflect on questions like the ones posed above while you are teaching (so during the act of teaching) is what Schön (1983) refers to as *reflection-in-action*. By making explicit the knowledge that you have

Reflecting on your classroom experiences can help you become a better educator.

in any current situation, you can more easily draw from that knowledge in the future. Other ways to reflect on your practice are to write down or audio record your thoughts after each class, and log these in a journal. This is known as *reflection-on-action* (Schön, 1983), or reflecting on things after they have happened. You might also discuss your thoughts and experiences about a class you just taught with a trusted colleague who might help you to think differently or more deeply about your teaching and your students' learning. While it is important to remain aware of potential issues related to using a camera in the classroom (e.g., being respectful of your students' rights), photo journalling may also be a useful way to reflect on your teaching. It might help to use all of these methods or many more to gain the most from your thoughts.

Constructing Knowledge for Teaching Physical Education: Experiences, Content, and Pedagogy

Without getting overly philosophical, knowledge is constructed in different ways and from different sources. Discussions about the nature of knowledge and beliefs about how knowledge is constructed are extremely complex and are represented by many people's (often competing) points of view (Munby, Russell, & Martin, 2001). Some people have viewed teachers' knowledge as consisting of knowledge *for* teaching (which can be learned inside and outside of university coursework) and knowledge *of* teaching (which can only be learned in the context of teaching situations) (Feiman-Nemser, 2008). For the purposes of this chapter, it is not the intention to propose one "best way" to view teachers' professional knowledge. The intention is to provide explanations of how there are different types of knowledge that are important for teaching, and lead to a deeper understand of how these different types of knowledge contribute to professional practice. In the next section the following types of knowledge for teaching are briefly discussed: experiential knowledge (what some may call personal knowledge) and knowledge of content and pedagogy.

Case Study 1: Teaching identity

The words of Matthew, a fourth year pre-service teacher, after finishing his practice teaching placement, serve to capture the importance of the process of reflection and its role in nurturing one's professional identity:

> Throughout my teaching internship experience I had many things that affected how I thought, planned, taught, and even how I felt. I always knew that teaching would be a very busy and hectic job; my teaching internship experience was the busiest I have ever been in my entire life. There were days that I don't remember even going to bed that I had so much to do. I spent so much time planning, prepping, marking, and reflecting for one class, I couldn't imagine how some people do it for four classes!
>
> The biggest thing I struggled with throughout my teaching internship was how to find my own identity as a teacher. Because my co-op [or associate teacher] had such a large presence both in classes and throughout the school, I felt many times that I was trying to follow in his steps. After completing my teaching internship, I believe I have my own identity as a teacher, but I also feel that it will change (probably many times) before I get my first contract, and again once I get established in my first full-time position.

> The greatest thing I learned throughout my teaching internship experience was that a teacher should always be looking to improve on something. If you have the best lesson/unit/strategy and you never evaluate it, I believe you have one lesson/unit/strategy. Since returning to university, my co-op [teacher] has taken things that I have done in the classroom and is applying them in his classes. The fact that a veteran teacher such as my co-op was stealing ideas from me has given me a sense of accomplishment as a teacher. From my experiences and his mentoring I believe I am now ready to contribute to the profession, and could control my own classroom(s), be a part of a staff and a team, be a role model and mentor to students, be a coach and run programs within a school, and be someone who can grow and become an educator.

Questions for Reflection

1 With a partner or in a small group, describe how, like Matthew, the way you see yourself personally and professionally has changed.

2 What specific experiences have led to these changes?

Experiential Knowledge

In the previous section the importance of being a reflective practitioner was discussed. However, the ways that people interpret significant "moments" and use them to develop and inform their professional knowledge will depend largely on beliefs and prior experiences (Borko & Putnam, 1996). Someone who is preparing to become a lawyer, for example, may develop some of their knowledge of the requirements of that profession from their university courses, from participating in a brief internship-type placement, or from books or television shows. Some of this knowledge is developed in formal settings and some in informal settings, and as such, some sources of knowledge are considered more valuable than others (e.g., knowledge about practicing law derived from an introductory university course in contrast to knowledge of law derived from watching *Judge Judy*). As explained previously, what makes teaching so unique compared to other professions is the twelve years already spent in schools observing teachers and teaching. By being immersed in school culture generally, you already have some very strong preconceived notions about what a teacher's role entails, and what teaching should "look like"— before even setting foot in university! Lortie (1975) suggested that experiences of teaching as school students are in some ways "like serving an apprenticeship in teaching" (p. 61), which is why he coined the phrase the *apprenticeship of observation*.

Based on experiences gained during the apprenticeship of observation, many pre-service teachers already have a fair amount of valuable knowledge about teaching. The pioneering work of Hal Lawson (1983) in physical education showed that it is often very difficult to overcome or change the beliefs that pre-service teachers have about teaching from their twelve years in schools. However, learning how to teach requires teaching in ways quite different from your own experiences as a student. This is because most of your experiences of teaching have come "from the other side of the desk" (Lortie, 1975, p. 61). For instance, many aspects of teaching are largely not seen by students, such as what goes into planning lessons or units, managing a classroom, dealing with parents, individualizing instruction, or taking into consideration the many social and cultural factors that influence learning. So, pre-service teachers who cling to views of teaching based on experiences as school students may ultimately lack a deep understanding of the complexities of teaching and have superficial views of what it means to be a teacher (Darling-Hammond & Hammerness, 2005). In effect, pre-service teachers who do cling to these initial views may not be the types of teachers that the diverse student body of today needs (Dowling, 2011; Fernandez-Balboa, 1997). Therefore, it is important to be open to deconstructing and reconstructing the experiences and knowledge of teaching gained from being school students in order to create visions of teaching and learning deemed appropriate for classrooms today.

Different students will respond to material taught in a number of different ways.

The process of deconstructing encourages an individual to be reflective and think more deeply and critically about one's previous experiences in school-based PE programs and question assumptions that one may have about what constitutes quality programs and how learners come to experience these programs. Following this deconstructive process, a foundation for reconstructing or rebuilding an individual's understanding of the knowledge of teaching begins to emerge and take shape. This reconstruction allows an individual to be open to other ways of knowing, to accept ideas, and to share ideas of teaching with the intent to create and sustain their own vision for the teaching of PE.

The symbiotic processes of deconstruction and reconstruction provides an opportunity to engage in a reflective process that results in action. Perhaps the best way to describe this is through the experience of Jane (Case Study 2), a pre-service teacher who, upon reflection of her own experiences as a student of PE, came to a different understanding of what is involved in becoming a teacher of PE.

Regardless of whether your experiences of PE were positive or negative, it is important to reflect on your experiences, beliefs, and attitudes about PE and physical activity throughout your teacher education program in order to identify things that are meaningful and valuable to you. Furthermore, personal life values will also influence how you interact with your job and your students. Ennis (1992) suggests that teachers' professional thoughts and decisions are based on their beliefs or value orientations, which "integrate […] explicit and tacit beliefs about students and context with their knowledge of the physical education subject matter" (p. 318). In turn, these orientations influence teachers' priorities and strongly impact upon their planning decisions. For example, if required to use provincial curriculum documents to guide the planning process, it is important to realize that it is acceptable to not view all of the outcomes equally. If you aim to teach your students at some level of depth, you will need to prioritize which curriculum outcomes you will spend the most, and least, time addressing. As such, the curriculum decisions will be strongly influenced by your personal and professional beliefs about the educational process and the meaning and value of PE.

These points reinforce the notion that personal and professional identities strongly influence day-to-day teaching practices. As Bullock (2011) suggests, "teachers' professional knowledge and values are interwoven and inseparable" (p. 31). Thus, as you reflect on what you value and find meaningful as a teacher and come to acknowledge the influences on your identity, you are in the processes of constructing knowledge about teaching physical education.

Knowledge of Content and Pedagogy

It may seem obvious to suggest that teachers require knowledge of their subject in order to teach well. Simply put, teachers need deep knowledge of both the content (what to teach) and pedagogy (how to teach) of their subjects, whether it is physical education, mathematics, or social studies. Just as importantly, teachers also require knowledge of child and youth development. Grossman and Schoenfeld (2005) suggest that for teachers to become diagnosticians of children's interests and ideas, and to engage pupils in explorations of subject matter that extend the reach of their understanding, "teachers need to understand deeply not only the content they are responsible for teaching but how to represent the content for learners of all kinds" (p. 202). This may mean that, because of the diverse nature of students' backgrounds, teachers should have various ways of teaching the same content to different students. For example, some students may prefer to learn about how to throw a javelin if the teacher uses metaphors or analogies (e.g., imagine throwing a spear for hunting or throwing a model airplane in a flat line versus an arc to achieve distance); others may prefer to watch the teacher or a peer demonstrate javelin throwing technique, while others still may prefer to read instructions that are written down in point form. In another example, some students may prefer to learn how to paddle a canoe if the teacher can relate physics principles from Newton's Laws of Motion, while others may prefer to watch the teacher or a peer demonstrate a specific steering stroke such as the "J" stroke in the stern of a canoe. Some may prefer to learn in small group settings, while some may prefer one-on-one instruction. Juggling the wide range of student needs and learning styles can be a particularly challenging task for teachers, however, it is important to recognize that being a good teacher involves talking and listening to students and finding out their interests and preferences.

When one form of knowledge (i.e., content or pedagogy) is developed in absence of the other, there can be limiting effects for teachers. In taking a point of view that acknowledges both content and pedagogy as essential in subject matter preparation, Shulman (1986) coined the term pedagogical content knowledge (PCK) and argued for its importance in the processes of learning to teach. PCK is described as:

> The most regularly taught topics in one's subject area, the most useful forms of representation of those ideas, the most powerful analogies, illustrations, examples, explanations, and demonstrations—in a word, the ways of representing and formulating the subject that make it comprehensible to others. … Pedagogical content knowledge also includes an

understanding of what makes the learning of specific topics easy or difficult: the conceptions and preconceptions that students of different ages and backgrounds bring with them to the learning of those most frequently taught topics and lessons. (Shulman, 1986, p. 9)

In simple terms, PCK is a blending of pedagogical knowledge and content knowledge, and the concept makes clear that being a good teacher is more than just knowing a lot about a subject. It is for this reason that people who know a lot

about a subject but do not have knowledge of how to teach do not usually make the best types of teachers.

It is also important to recognize that PCK does not only include a deep knowledge of the content and pedagogy of a subject area; it requires teachers to have a similarly deep knowledge of their students, and the communities and contexts in which they work. This insight was supported by McCaughtry (2004) who found that understanding pupils' social and emotional needs was crucial to how physical education teachers understand and navigate:

(i) Curricular decisions

(ii) Instructional decisions

(iii) Student learning

Similarly, Ball (2000) has stated:

Although some teachers have important understandings of the content, they often do not know it in ways that help them

Case Study 2: Reflecting on Physical Education

Jane is a pre-service teacher whose earliest memories of physical activity were clearly defined. She recalled growing up in an area with lots of other children and playing tag games and playing in the park, while her earliest memories of organized sport included going to her first synchronized swimming practice outside of school. She felt that her physical activity experiences, particularly with synchronized swimming, helped shape who she is and allowed her to meet new friends and helped improve her body image.

Jane did not pursue active participation in physical education (PE) courses in high school past grade nine; she disliked the curriculum and the way it was taught. She shared that she dreaded going to class in grade nine because she felt certain students always dominated the activities and no modifications were made so it could be more inclusive of students of all abilities and interests. However, she remained very active in competitive synchronized swimming with memories of winning competitions, travelling, and developing friendships. She is now a fitness instructor. Despite the fact that Jane did not enjoy PE in high school and did not identify herself as an athlete because of limited experience in "traditional" sports (e.g., volleyball, basketball, soccer), she has always liked health and fitness, which motivated her to complete her undergraduate degree in kinesiology.

Jane's experiential knowledge of PE would be very different to someone who participated in and enjoyed PE throughout all of their school years. As a result,

this influenced how she thinks about and experiences coursework and teaching internship experiences. What is important from Jane's story is that her negative experiences did not diminish her passion to pursue teaching PE; if anything, the way that she questioned and analyzed the nature of those experiences provided an increased awareness of her own teaching practice and highlighted some practices she wished to avoid. Jane's beliefs about the purposes of PE and what she might emphasize in her programs include: emphasizing fun and enjoyment through a variety of physical activities, movement experiences, and sports, and fostering a positive, inclusive learning environment that makes meaningful connections between the curriculum and the students' lives. For Jane, reflecting on her experiences prior to and during the university program helped construct her vision and embrace teaching PE with increased confidence and an understanding of herself as a teacher. She also chose to reject many of the teaching practices that she observed as a student, coming to her own understanding of what constituted "good" teaching.

Questions for Reflection:

1 Thinking back to your own experiences of PE as a school student, what teaching practices do you look upon positively, and which do you look upon negatively? What are your reasons?

2 How might you reconstruct your experiences and apply them to future teaching and learning situations?

hear students, select good tasks, or help all their students learn. Not being able to do this undermines and makes hollow the efforts to prepare high quality teachers who can reach all students, teach in multicultural settings, and work in environments that make teaching and learning difficult. Despite frequently heard exhortations to teach all students, many teachers are unable to hear students flexibly, represent ideas in multiple ways, connect content to contexts effectively, and think about things in ways other than their own. (p. 243)

For teachers who specialize in a subject area, it makes sense that they often have personal strengths in that subject. It is to be expected that many preparing to become teachers of PE were active, committed to, and possibly successful in *some* type of physical activity, whether judo, table tennis, hiking, or ultimate. Based on these experiences you may have a certain degree of *physical literacy*, being able to transfer your knowledge and skills from one activity to another without too much difficulty. However, just because "being physically active" comes fairly easy to you does not mean that your students feel the same way. As such, some teachers of PE may struggle to comprehend how and where some students may be having difficulty or face problems understanding concepts and movement. To be able to relate to your students, you need to be able to step out of your shoes and into theirs, and try to develop ways to enhance their learning.

As this section has illustrated, teaching is extremely complex. In order for all your students to be engaged in meaningful learning, you need to have a deep understanding of the contexts in which you are teaching, who you are teaching, what it is you are teaching, in what contexts you

are teaching, and many ways in which material can best be presented to students from a wide variety of ages, abilities, and backgrounds. It is for these reasons that Professor Linda Darling-Hammond of Stanford University recently said in a television interview: "teaching *is* rocket science."

What Is Important to Teach in Physical Education? Forming a Vision for Teaching

Anyone studying in a teacher education program has likely been asked in one course or another to think about developing a teaching philosophy, a description of an approach to teaching, a mission statement, or a vision of teaching—something that outlines your stance and beliefs about teaching, learning, and students. Whatever the preferred terminology of your course instructors, developing a vision for teaching involves much more than simply writing a few paragraphs about PE for a course assignment. Your vision for teaching should reflect the main beliefs, ideas, and principles that you feel are important for you personally and professionally (reaffirming the importance of identity once again), and also the key elements that represent what you value most for your students. According to Hammerness (2006), teachers' visions of classroom practice include what they imagine they could be doing in a classroom with their students: the activities, discussions, projects, and interactions that are going on. It also includes the type of learning environment that students will be living and working in. Kosnik and Beck (2009) suggest that a vision for teaching:

Developing a vision for teaching allows you to articulate why you are teaching what you are teaching.

- Keeps you aware of the wide range of goals and processes of teaching
- Helps you connect the various elements of teaching
- Enables you to explain to your students the purpose of learning activities
- Helps you explain your teaching approach not only to your students but to your students' parents, your colleagues, friends, relatives, and hiring committees (p. 107)

While developing a vision for teaching can be an important and meaningful process in learning to teach, it is necessary

to regularly re-visit your vision throughout your career. As teachers grow, develop, and encounter different students, their vision of teaching also evolves. The influences on your vision will also shift and develop throughout your career. An important reason for doing this—particularly in the first years of teaching—is that new teachers' visions can be quite idealistic. This is not to suggest that you should not have high expectations and strive for ideal visions, but it is important to make sure that your vision reflects goals that are realistic and attainable. If your goals and vision are unattainable, you may be setting yourself up for frustration and disappointment.

One of the core ideas behind developing a vision for teaching is that it allows you to articulate why you are teaching what you are teaching. Teachers need to provide solid reasons behind their professional decisions in a way that goes beyond stating: "Well, it says so in the provincial curriculum." You need to be able to explain to your students why it is important to, for example, participate in ongoing fitness assessment, or to work cohesively in small groups,

Case Study 3: "Mr Fitz"

Loyola FitzPatrick, or "Mr. Fitz" as his students call him, has been an elementary PE teacher in Newfoundland and Labrador for thirty-four years. During that time he has completed two degrees, and has attended and presented at countless local, provincial, and national professional development sessions conferences. Recently, he was a recipient of the PHE Canada Teaching Excellence Award for Newfoundland and Labrador.

While all the accolades and awards are indeed impressive, it is the attitude that Mr. Fitz has as he approaches his role as a teacher that is most impressive to us. You might think that after teaching for thirty-four years, he would think that he knows just about all that there is to know about PE. Well not Mr. Fitz. He arrives at school every day and asks himself one simple but very important question: "What will I learn from my students today?" As Mr. Fitz says, all of his students have different ways of looking at the world, whether it be thinking about multiple ways to jump over a skipping rope, or how to include their classmates in conversations or activities. Not only does this attitude apply to the students from kindergarten to grade seven that he teaches daily, he also adopts it when he works with pre-service PE teachers from Memorial University of Newfoundland. He views the opportunities to work with the pre-service teachers as a chance to learn about teaching PE together. He certainly provides them with excellent advice based on his many

years of experience, but perhaps more importantly, he provides many hours of listening and observation of their teaching practices, as well as opportunities to reflect on why things went the way that they did. Together, they are able to work through the inevitable challenges of teaching and share the joy of their frequent successes and "aha" moments.

Mr. Fitz is a wonderful model of a lifelong learner who has instilled a love of PE to the thousands of students who he has taught in elementary schools. It is perhaps of no surprise that many pre-service PE teachers enrolled at MUN proudly say that Mr. Fitz was their elementary PE teacher, and they would like to be the kind of teacher that he was to them.

Mr. Fitz's story highlights how important it is for teachers to be just as open to learning about new things as we hope our students are. Regardless of his extensive experience working with children and the numerous professional development opportunities he has participated in, Mr. Fitz still views teaching as an incomplete, uncertain, and complex situation. But in his eyes, this is part of what makes teaching so enjoyable; you are very much able to learn something new every day. Equally as important, Mr. Fitz does not rely on his school principal to ask him to engage in professional development: he takes it upon himself to foster his personal and professional growth.

or to respect the feelings and emotions of your peers. Too often students feel that they are participating in tasks simply because the teacher told them to, and consequently, many students do not see any value in participating in a lot of school tasks. If students are able to understand the reasoning behind tasks, they are likely to find more personal meaning in their education, and in turn, enjoy their experiences at school more. Furthermore, this can make *your* professional life as a teacher much more meaningful and enjoyable too.

This Is Just the Beginning: Becoming a Lifelong Learner

As stated at the outset of this chapter, you may be at any one of a number of various points in your university PE program. Furthermore it should be acknowledged that you bring a wide variety of life experiences from PE, physical activity, and sport. All of these experiences play a significant role in how you think of yourself as a teacher of PE. Reflecting on these prior experiences is critically important for the development of beliefs about PE and teaching values. Each of these elements is crucial in shaping a teaching identity that will help foster deep and meaningful student learning. Your vision for teaching PE will no doubt

shift and evolve as you progress in your career and as you continue your lifelong journey as a teacher, as a learner, and as a passionate advocate for children and youth. Over the next several months or years your PE program will challenge you to understand and make sense of many educational theories and practices. What will likely become clear (if it has not already) is that teaching is uncertain and complex, and learning about teaching goes well beyond the several years spent at university. Like many things in life, navigating the complexity of teaching is perhaps more about enjoying the journey than reaching a final destination.

After you have completed your university program(s), you can continue to learn about teaching and being a teacher in many ways. Some of these are formal and some are informal. For example, most schools and school boards provide teachers with many opportunities to engage in formal professional development. This may be in the form of seminars that curriculum consultants might run about general pedagogical practices (such as assessment) or about practices specific to PE. Or it may be in the form of attending a provincial or national conference, such as those run by most provincial PE associations or PHE Canada. These conferences provide many worthwhile opportunities to learn about or stay up-to-date with current ways of thinking about teaching, or keep in touch with your

Professional development can happen in many different ways, including feedback from students themselves.

friends, mentors and colleagues. While such initiatives can re-invigorate teachers or provide them with new ideas, they are often not the most effective form of professional development for teachers. It is equally important to seek out new opportunities, read new books, scan relevant websites for new ideas and/or lesson plans, and reflect on your teaching by asking for student feedback.

Conducting research on PE teachers in the United Kingdom, Armour and Yelling (2004) suggest that most professional development should be based in schools and form part of the daily work of teachers. In this sense, professional development is mostly informal but it is also intentional in that there is some clear purpose in mind. This might involve working collaboratively with departmental colleagues to analyze the strengths and weaknesses of a new approach to teaching gymnastics, for example. An important point to consider here involves weighing the decision to work with colleagues inside and outside of your subject area. There are benefits to doing both. Reflecting, talking, and learning with other teachers of PE can allow for deep insights to be made about the subject's content and pedagogies. Because PE is arguably a unique subject in the school curriculum, having colleagues who understand the challenges of teaching it may make it easier for those involved to develop new and/or common insights to improve their practice. Alternatively, reflecting, talking, and learning from teachers who primarily teach in other subjects allows for new and often unexpected ways of learning to occur—it may just require a little imagination to apply it to a PE setting.

Conclusion

The key point to be made here is that your university PE program is just the beginning of being and becoming a teacher of PE. If you understand that what you learn in your university program can help you begin to make decisions and provide you with tools and strategies to enact your vision of teaching, you will likely graduate with a sense of what is in store for you in schools. However, if you graduate expecting that you have learned all there is to know about teaching, you (and your students) will probably be very disappointed. It is for these reasons that for many teachers, teaching is as much a passion as it is a profession. It can certainly help to improve the lives of some young people but it can also help to improve the lives of those who teach.

Questions for Reflection

1   Describe the type of teacher you want to become. What might your teaching style be? What learning experiences do you hope to provide for your students?

2   Because teachers are very busy and often transition from one class to the next to the next, taking the time to adequately reflect on your teaching can be difficult. What are some strategies that you can use to ensure you will remain committed to reflecting on your practice?

3   If you asked all of your classmates from, say, grade nine, what do you think they would say about their experiences in physical education? How might the experiences of people who were successful in physical education differ from the experiences of people who were not as successful? What led to success?

4   Describe some specific learning experiences in your university program, including the teaching internship (e.g., pedagogical approaches, instructional teaching strategies), that have influenced your understanding of yourself as a prospective teacher of physical education. What made these experiences influential? How have these experiences shaped your knowledge of teaching physical education?

Key Terms

- Professional Identity
- Reflective Practitioner
- Reflection-in-Action
- Reflection-on-Action
- Experiential Knowledge
- Apprenticeship of Observation
- Pedagogical Content Knowledge
- Vision for Teaching

2

Pedagogy of Teaching Physical Education

Curriculum Models

Joanna Sheppard and Doug Gleddie

Overview

"Curriculum work does not produce prescriptions for what teachers and students are to do, but provides provisional strategies." (Jewett, Bain, & Ennis, 1995, p. 123)

The intent of this chapter is to explore a variety of curriculum models for physical education (PE). To set the stage, a brief discussion of the nature of curriculum is included as well as a look at the complex personal and political decisions that need to be made. A number of pre-eminent curricular models are examined including the multi-activity model, teaching games for understanding (TGfU), the personal and social responsibility model, sport education, fitness for life, and an emerging design based on competencies. Readers are encouraged to engage critically with the concepts and processes of curriculum in PE as they examine the purpose, overview, and limitations of each model. Finally, some important contexts are identified that can affect the implementation of PE curricula in schools.

Introduction

Transforming culture—changing what people in the organization value and how they work together to accomplish it—leads to deep, lasting change. (Fullan, 2002, p. 18)

The idea of curriculum itself can be a slippery subject. Historically, PE curriculum has changed and adapted as defined by societal needs and events. From physical training needs in time of war, to a health promotion focus in an increasingly affluent post-war society, the purpose of PE has continued to reflect the perceived and changing needs of society (Kirk, MacDonald, & Tinning, 1997). A common purpose or mission for PE curricula currently across Canada is the concept of lifelong physical activity: students learning the knowledge, skills, and attitudes to be physically active for life.

Put very simply, the curriculum can be "what" is studied or learned, with instruction or pedagogy being the "how." Of course, it is not quite that simple. How does one truly disconnect choices about what to teach from how to teach? How do educational professionals address issues of conflict between formal and personal curricular values? Curriculum, then, can be a bit of a moving target! In Canada, the construction of a formal PE curriculum is the responsibility of each provincial ministry or department of education. Therefore, the required program of study differs from province to province, with territories often choosing to adapt programs from one or more provinces. The concept of curriculum, however, is not limited to the course of study mandated by law. As stated earlier, how you teach the provincial curriculum is also a form of curriculum— you make these choices everyday as you teach. As well, there is the potential for delivery of a hidden or covert curriculum through delivery, expectations, and personal and professional values. For a deeper look at specific curricular and teaching models for PE consider The Curriculum Process in Physical Education (Jewett, Bain, & Ennis, 1995) and Instructional Models for Physical Education (Metzler, 2000).

The Multi-Activity Model

Katie prepares herself for her new school term. As a grade six student she has decided to try out for the girls' school volleyball team. She has really enjoyed learning about the skills needed to play volleyball, basketball, soccer, and gymnastics in her PE class, but wants the chance to play a more formal volleyball game with her teammates for a whole season.

Purpose of the Model

As educators in PE, the main goal of our area of study is to enable our students to become physically active movers throughout their lifetime. By demonstrating and providing examples of many different types of physical activity, students can mold and modify these activities to create a healthy and active lifestyle that meets their needs. The multi-activity curriculum model is one such model that allows for this diversity of physical activities for our students to choose from.

What Is the Multi-Activity Model?

The multi-activity model is historically the most used PE curriculum in North America. Defined as a middle or high school PE curriculum model, the primary focus of this model for the student is on the learning of motor skills while maintaining interest through the exposure to a wide variety of sport and movement (Siedentop et al., 1986; Cothran, 2001). Through many activity units, students are introduced to games, dance, and gymnastic activities with updated inclusions of fitness development. However it should be stated that this model seems to be predominately game/ sport dominated. Unit length can vary between four lessons and ten lessons, therefore introducing the students to the basic skill levels found within each physical activity.

Limitations

Even though this multi-activity model is easy to set-up from an administrative perspective, many programs seem to be lacking organization, which therefore results in student boredom, yearly repetition, and failure to develop past the basic movement skills needed to be a physically active participant (Harrison, Blakemore, & Buck, 2001). Creating a progressive and organized approach to the multi-activity model should be the educator's first priority, not only from month to month but also year to year. Three organizational approaches could be followed when creating the multi-activity model yearly plan.

The Sport Season Approach: Using a unit plan structure that corresponds to the intercollegiate sport schedule is one way of setting up the multi-activity model type of curriculum. Potential positive outcomes of such an approach are increased team and school spirit, leadership opportunities for athletes within your PE program and enhanced interest in those who have not played sport on a competitive level. However using this approach could limit the number of activities taught throughout the multi-activity curriculum year and lead to overdrawn sport units. For that reason, it is important to provide alternative units such as dance, gymnastics, fitness, and outdoor pursuits to provide a well-rounded physical activity curriculum.

Pick a Category Approach: By placing physical activities into different categories, this multi-activity curriculum approach will enable students not only to understand the similarities and differences between games and activities but will also introduce them to new experiences that can be progressively built throughout their school years. Examples of categories may include: cooperative activities (leadership, goal setting), individual sports (archery, darts, golf, etc.), team sports (soccer, basketball, hockey, etc.), recreational games (bowling, billiards, bocce ball), dance (line, ballroom, doing the Dougie), outdoor adventure activities (orienteering, hiking, snowshoeing), and aquatics (swimming, diving, synchronize swimming) (Rink, 2009).

The No-Organization Approach: This approach takes little time to set up and therefore can lead to decreased results and minimal engagement from students. Creating units based on the preference of the educator as well as the equipment or facilities available will limit students' capabilities to advance their knowledge past the basic skills of the physical activities and may lead to boredom.

The Teaching Games for Understanding (TGfU or Sport Model)

Doug walks into PE class and is immediately put into a game of lopsided soccer. He and his classmates are in small groups of eight, divided into two teams of four. Each group has a soccer ball and has been told to play the following game within their designated space. The red team starts with the ball and tries to maintain possession for as long as possible. The green team tries to intercept passes or just touch the ball. The red team can run, the green team can only walk. As soon as the green team touches the ball, the game begins again with green in possession and running and red only able to walk.

Purpose of the TGfU Model

What can Doug and his classmates possibly be learning through this goofy game of keep-away soccer? Much more than you might initially think, according to many researchers and practitioners. Doug is engaged in the first step of the Teaching Games for Understanding (TGfU) model first developed by Rod Thorpe and David Bunker in the 1980s. The impetus for TGfU was derived from dissatisfaction with the ways most games were (and perhaps still are) taught: skill and drill, skill and drill with the hope of a small scrimmage at the end of practice. Bunker and Thorpe (1982) found that children who were taught games through this technical method were largely unsuccessful, had little knowledge of the game itself, learned inflexible technique, had poor decision making, and were dependent performers. In contrast, the "objective in the TGfU model is to offer all

students, regardless of ability or skill level, the opportunity to actively experience, enjoy, and understand games" (Butler & McCahan, 2005, p. 40).

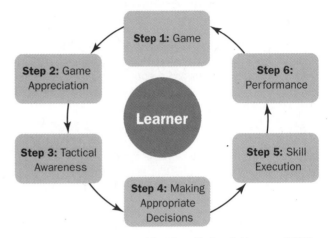

Mandigo, Butler & Hopper, 2007

Figure 3.1: The TGfU Model

What Is the TGfU Model?

Central to TGfU is the concept of "the learner" at the centre of it all, as illustrated in **Figure 3.1**. The needs, motivation, abilities, and developmental level of the student are fundamental to all decisions made by the physical educator. Let's take a closer look at the rest of the model (from Butler & McCahan, 2005; Mandigo, Butler, & Hopper, 2007).

Game: As in the game of lopsided soccer described above, the initial activity should be a modification (rules, numbers, equipment, playing space) of a formal game with a specific objective and allow learners opportunities to experience skills and concepts in context. *In the lopsided soccer example, Doug is able to enjoy a modified game that lets him naturally explore the concept of possession.*

Game appreciation: Through the playing of the initial game, learners will gain an understanding of how the game "works": the interaction of skills, rules, and tactics. *Doug appreciates how passing and receiving interact with mobility, the use of space, and the run/walk rule.*

Tactical awareness: Through playing, learners are able to grasp the existence of offensive and defensive tactics that provide an advantage. *Doug realizes that if he sprints to the open space, he is able to receive a pass before the defence can react.*

Making appropriate decisions: Learners discover through experience how to make quick decisions based on the variety of information provided to them by the evolving game. *Doug recognizes the importance of deciding when to pass immediately and when to dribble clear first.*

Pedagogical Principles of TGfU

- **Sampling**: Many games should be selected in order to show similar and dissimilar aspects to games.

- **Modification-Representation**: Educators can modify the game so that it is playable for the student and is close in structure to the adult game

- **Modification-Exaggeration**: Through small-sided games, educators can exaggerate secondary rules into the game to emphasize tactics and skills into the game play.

- **Tactical Complexity**: By starting out with games with less tactical complexity, such as target games, students can progress throughout more difficult tactics once they have full game understanding.

(Holt, Strean. & Bengoechea, 2002)

Skill Execution: The skills required to play the game have been experienced in context as opposed to isolation. Learners will then realize the importance of proper skill execution and why a particular skill is important. *Doug now recognizes that even though he can make a decision of when to pass for tactical reasons and even what pass to use, he still needs to further develop his actual passing skills with the inside of his left foot.*

Performance: The last step of the cycle is the accumulation of all that has gone before. Game performance (either the original modification or a new modification) should improve with consistent questioning, reinforcement, and feedback from peers and the educator.

Limitations

The Teaching Games for Understanding (TGfU) curriculum model also has some limitations that the educator may need to overcome. For instance, this model was created for game play and therefore should not be used as the only curriculum model throughout the school year. Also, if implemented incorrectly (educator-controlled versus student-controlled), students may not receive the full understanding of when and why they use the game play tactics within the formal game. This model is time consuming to learn but effective for game play growth in students when put into practice. There is, however, a common misconception that TGfU is "just playing games." More education is needed around the true structure and development of this model. Furthermore, there is not a great deal of literature to assist with adapting TGfU for those with movement problems—more work is needed to adapt the model to meet the needs of all students. Physical educators also have to be flexible and prepared for uncertainty when embracing this model as, much like a game, when more control is given to the students, anything can happen!

TGfU Categories:

Games can be grouped into four categories based on essential components such as game intent, congruent concepts and skills, player roles, and similar defensive and offensive strategies. For example, although hockey and basketball are quite different, they share similar intents (invade, score and protect) and concepts (possession, penetration). Therefore, players of one sport may find that some of their skills transfer to another in the same category.

Target	Net/Wall	Striking/Fielding	Invasion/Territory
- Bowling	- Tennis	- Kickball	- Football
- Golf	- Badminton	- Softball	- Basketball
- Curling	- Volleyball	- Lob Ball	- Rugby
- Lawn Bowling	- Handball	- Slo-Pitch	- Lacrosse
- Croquet	- Racquetball	- 3-Pitch	- Ultimate
- Bocce Ball	- Table Tennis	- Cricket	- Ice Hockey
	- Squash	- Baseball	- Field Hockey
	- Paddle Ball		- Floor Hockey
	- Sepak Takraw		

(Playsport www.playsport.net, 2012)

Hellison's Teaching Personal and Social Responsibility (TPSR or Social Model)

Christa walks into her PE class, changes quickly, and prepares herself to be fully engaged in the day's lesson. With little guidance, Christa leads a group of fellow students in a warm-up and small-sided game of soccer. When two players disagree over an infraction, Christa quickly refocuses her peers back into game play by using the rock-paper-scissor method to award possession of the ball. Teaching students such as Christa to assume responsibility over their own behaviour and the behaviour of others is the full intention of Hellison's Personal and Social Development Curriculum Model.

Purpose of the TPSR Model

Teaching life skills and social values within a physically active environment unites a holistic (physical, cognitive, and affective) approach to student's development and personal growth (Gleddie, 2011). Responsibility is just one facet of effective development that plays a role within the PE environment. Responsibility can be defined as "adherence to social rules and role expectation." Relevant to academic achievement are "rules and norms that govern social interaction in the classroom" (Wentzel, 1991, p. 1066). Being accountable for their own well-being and contributing to the well-being of others is a requirement of a student's responsibility that must be taught both inside and outside the gymnasium (Parker & Hellison, 2001).

The opportunity for additional responsibility in a classroom setting should teach students how to be both personally and socially responsible as well as illustrate the importance of self-control, setting personal goals, and caring (Parker & Hellison, 2001). Personal responsibility includes goals such as: self-control, self-motivation and self-effort, independent work, and being a role model. Social responsibility includes goals such as: respecting everyone's right to be included, cooperation, sensitivity and responsiveness to others' needs and interests, and contributing to the well-being of both individuals and the group. It is these precise personal and social characteristics valued within our society that led to the creation of Hellison's TPSR Model.

What Is the TPSR Model?

Acknowledged as a humanistic and social development model for physical education (Siedentop, 1980; Hellison & Templin, 1991), Hellison's Teaching Personal and Social Responsibility (TPSR) model was developed as a teaching tool specifically aimed at adolescent students identified as at risk, underserved, and inner city (Hellison & Walsh, 2002) which led to many research-based interventions (Cummings, 1998; Cutforth, 1997; DeBusk & Hellison,

1989). However, the TPSR model went on to receive a great deal of positive support leading to implementation in a wide range of neighbourhoods as an after-school program and more recently as part of the PE curriculum. The TPSR model was created with the ideology that if students want to be successful individuals within a social environment, they must first learn how to be responsible for themselves and the situations that surround them (Escartí, Gutiérrez, Pascual, & Llopis, 2010).

Hellison's TPSR model consists of five levels of responsibility:

- Respecting the rights and feelings of others
- Participation and effort
- Self-direction
- Helping others and leadership
- Outside the gym

These five levels help both the educator and the student understand what they are responsible for and provide specific targets to strive towards or achieve (Escartí et al., 2010; Hellison, 2003). Moving through each level is at the discretion of both the educator and the student.

Specific steps in planning lessons can be established with the TPSR model and the model can also help with the development of individual lessons (Hellison, 2003). It is important to note that the TPSR model is not a teaching strategy for behaviour management but rather encompasses the attitudes, beliefs, values, and intentions needed to be a responsible student (Hellison, 2003).

Physical activity, including physical education, has been determined as the ideal environment for implementing the TPSR model. This is because physical activity programs offer "unique and social development opportunities" that many other disciplines cannot (Hellison & Walsh, 2002; Hellison, 2003). Physical education enables the use of alternative forms of social organization "in an attempt to constructively redress the social conditions that places some young people's well-being at risk" (Kirk, 1992, p. 4). With this in mind however, Hellison warns that the TPSR model should not be an add-on to the existing physical education program but embedded within the physical education lessons themselves (Hellison, 2003). The embedding or integration of the model within the physical activity lesson will encourage a responsible student environment throughout the entire lesson, not only when prompted by the educator.

The TPSR model also suggests that, by empowering our students within physical activity lessons, the role of the educator will change to one of facilitator, guiding students to make responsible decisions not only for themselves but also when playing with others (Hellison, 2003). This new educator-student relationship can allow the educator to observe their students as individuals rather than part of a whole class (Hellison, 2003), which leads to a deeper understanding of one's students.

Implementing the TPSR Model into a PE class includes a specific six part format beginning with counselling time, awareness talk, the lesson, group meeting, reflection time, and again ending with a counselling time (Hellison, 2003).

Part 1   Counselling Time: Counselling time at the beginning of the formal PE class includes the opportunity for the educator to check in with as many individual students as possible. This quick one-on-one time could include speaking about positive and/or negative behaviour from the previous class and what behaviour the student could work on that day.

Part 2   Awareness Talks: For the beginning of the actual class, the educator brings all the students together to discuss and explain the five goals of personal and social responsibility. As Hellison suggests, this should be done in a gradual and progressive manner so as to not overload the students' affective learning. This awareness talk can also be used as a lesson reminder to the students as to what goal of responsibility they will be focusing on during that class.

Part 3   The Lesson: While students are engaged in the physical or sports-related activities, educators can use this time to integrate the goals of responsibility through the use of suggested teaching strategies, such as awareness strategies, direct instruction, individual decision-making, and large or small group decision-making.

Part 4   Group Meetings: Group meetings should be held close to the end of the class when the educator calls the students in to discuss the day's class. This is a time when students can share with their peers and the educator. They can address issues that occurred during the class and consider possible solutions. This is also a time for students to provide feedback to the educator about what they thought about the class and what they would have changed. Giving the students the ability to give input towards the actual lesson directly connects the lesson to the goals of responsibility.

Part 5   Reflection Time: The purpose of reflection time is to provide the students an opportunity to reflect, and summarize their own behaviour and actions as they relate to the goals of responsibility. This can be used as a self-evaluation tool and documented through the use of journal entries, checklists, the raising of their hands or thumbs, or descriptive sharing of examples about their level of responsibility during the lesson.

Part 6   Counselling Time: The second occurrence of counselling time at the end of the class is used as an additional check in and time for the educator to give feedback on students' behaviour throughout the lesson.

As one of the more researched curriculum models, the TPSR model is a suggested PE curriculum model that requires both the students and the educator a role to play in its success. More importantly, as stated by Hellison, this model is to be used as a basis that is expanded upon by the educator's own values and beliefs as well as the students' needs for personal and social responsibility.

Different educators and different students will respond differently to the variety of curriculum models and how they are implemented.

Consider the specific needs of your students when choosing a curriculum model; what works for one class may not work for another.

Limitations

Limitations to this curriculum model include the amount of time needed for each student as this can make it difficult to provide a quality experience for every student if the class size is large. Also the integration of the affective nature of the goals of responsibility into a physical or sports activity could be daunting to an inexperienced educator. It is also important to note that the TPSR model is most effective when embedded throughout implementation. When the model is simply an "add on," the potential for positive impact is severely reduced.

Goals for Teaching Personal and Social Responsibility:

1 Respect for the rights and feelings of others
   a. Self-control of temper and mouth
   b. Respect everyone's right to be included
   c. Involvement in peaceful and democratic conflict resolution

2 Effort
   a. Self-Motivation
   b. Explore self-effort and try new tasks
   c. On-task persistence

3 Self-Direction
   a. Work independently
   b. Goal-setting progression
   c. Courage to resist peer pressure

4 Helping others and leadership
   a. Caring and compassion
   b. Sensitivity and responsiveness
   c. Inner strength

5 Outside the gym
   a. Trying these ideas outside the physical activity program
   b. Being a role model

(List excerpted from Hellison, 2003)

The Sport Education Model

Sunny is in the middle of her sixth week of curling in physical education class. She has already learned the basic rules and strategies in the sport and is on her way to developing her curling skills in all four positions. This week, Sunny is learning how the Brier is organized by being part of a group of students organizing a bonspiel for their class to occur in the last week of the unit. Her tasks include publicizing the event, organizing the rankings and draw, and booking the facility.

Purpose of the Model

> At the centre of the Sport Education (SE) model are the concepts that sport is a form of play and that play is for all. (Jewett, Bain, & Ennis, 1995, p. 174)

The first assumption is that sport, properly understood, properly conceptualized, and properly implemented is a form of play; that is, sport derives its essential meaning from play and its clear importance in human affairs is attributable to its origins in play. (Keynote Address to the Commonwealth Games Conference, Brisbane, 1982, as cited in Siedentop, 2002)

The goal of the SE model is to develop "competent, literate, and enthusiastic sportspersons" (Siendentop, 2002, p. 3). In this way, students will become knowledgeable players who understand and value sport. They will be able to discern between good and bad sport and will also act in ways that seek to preserve and enhance the culture of sport. Given these constructs, the SE model is a way to help students intensively learn all aspects of a particular sport so they are fully capable of continuing involvement outside of and after school. The SE model differs from the Multi-Activity model in that the focus is on longer seasons of sport (8–12 weeks) and the goal is more in-depth learning rather than exposure to sport. The SE model links well with the LTAD model as it is a form of school-based sport for all students (as opposed to inter-school sport). The SE model also emphasizes the culture of sport and provides multiple opportunities for creativity, leadership, and inclusion.

What is the Sport Education Model?

Sport Education grew out of a typology of play developed by Callois (1961) and grew from Daryll Siedentop's doctoral dissertation on a "play education" curriculum theory (Siedentop, 2002). Siedentop continued to be an important advocate for the model whose purpose is: "to educate students in various sports—to teach them to be players, in the fullest sense of that term" (Siedentop, Mand, & Taggart, 1986, p. 186). The rationale for Sport Education is based on three essential elements: first, that sport is a higher form of play (institutionalized and competitive); second, that sport is

also a part of our collective culture and contributes to health and socialization; and third, if the two previous statements are true, then sport should be part of physical education with an objective for students to become skilled participants and sportspersons.

The SE model includes psychosocial aspects of sport (teamwork, competition, customs), physical aspects (fitness, skilfulness), and cognitive aspects (administration and planning, strategies). Implementation can include modified games, student leadership elements (coaching, officiating, organizing), and often concludes with a culminating event such as a tournament (bonspiel). It should be noted that the goal of the culminating event, and indeed the model itself, is not an elitist type tournament where the less skilled students keep score or run the bracket. SE implementation is intended to allow all students to have the opportunity to play and experience success. The SE model incorporates cooperative learning, peer-teaching opportunities and student-centred learning—all rooted in sport and play. For some students, the "season" experienced at school may be their first or only exposure to sport—the goal is for it to be a positive experience resulting in more opportunities in the future (Jewett, Bain, & Ennis, 1995). In the words of the founder, "Sport Education (is) a way to better serve children and youth with quality sports experiences in the context of physical education" (2002, p. 11).

Limitations

As with other models, the SE model can be misunderstood and incorrectly or poorly implemented. The potential exists for educators to misapply the principles resulting in the implementation of yet another form of elitist sport where the "athletes" play and the "non-athletes" keep score and cheer. Physical educators need to keep the goal of sport for all at the heart of their planning and implementation of this model to ensure appropriate competition and success for all students. The intent of this model is not to "groom" students for inter-school competition. Another limitation of the model is that students will only experience a few sports each year due to the time required to fully explore each season.

The Fitness for Life Model

Jamie is in grade ten and is tired and bored of playing sports all the time in PE class. It's not that he doesn't enjoy it, but rather that he wants to start focusing on his own health. He has starting reading magazines about how to set up a fitness and diet regimen but would like the help of his physical educator to make sure he is choosing the right program for him. He would also like to work out with his friends so he can have a great support system within the comfortable environment of his school.

Purpose of the Model

By the time they are in high school, many students are just like Jamie and would like to focus on their own health within a safe environment. Educators of PE should be promoting this type of ownership over students' own health, and provide the tools necessary for them to succeed. A fitness and wellness curriculum is exactly what is needed in order to do this.

What is Fitness for Life?

Fitness for Life can be defined as "health for everyone with an emphasis on lifetime activity designed to meet their personal needs" (Corbin & Lindsey, 2005). Created by Dr. Charles Corbin, the Fitness for Life model was the response to the need to provide students with a quality physical education program. The model directs its attention to improving a student's fitness levels and developing healthy behaviours. Students (particularly those who are described as passive within regular physical education programs) must actively participate within this type of model by being proactive about their own physical health. Although it is found predominantly within secondary-level PE classes, the Fitness for Life model can be modified to meet the needs of elementary and middle school students as well.

The model uses lectures, lab experiments, and exercise programs that can be progressively used into a student's adulthood. Students learn the importance of measuring heart rate and body fat, calculating calories, and managing weight control while still maintaining their flexibility, endurance, and strength through more recreational and aerobic activities. Within this model, the educator becomes a facilitator and guides students to make positive decisions about their own physical fitness. Students also learn how to assess their physical bodies through the use of different measurements such as the fitness test, as well as learning how to assess their decision-making skills and emotional well-being through journalling and portfolio work (Corbin & Lindsey, 2005).

Limitations

The Fitness for Life curriculum model is a very personal way of teaching PE. In order to use this model effectively, the educator must have full knowledge of all labs, exercise regimes, healthy eating tips, and goal setting tools. Meeting every student's fitness goals is time consuming, however, it will lead to a more independent student and hopefully a more healthy adult in future years.

Competencies—An Emerging Model for PE?

Jo is a recent grade twelve graduate who has moved to a new town in a new province to attend university. After her first term she has noticed significant changes in her personal health. She is not sleeping well, has gained weight, stays alone in her dorm room most nights, and finds her grades suffering as well. After spending Christmas at home visiting and reflecting on her health, Jo decides to make some changes. She starts with keeping a journal that includes how she feels each day, what her activity levels are, and the foods she eats. As a result, she makes a plan to eat according to Canada's Food Guide and take advantage of healthy options in the cafeteria. Jo also researches opportunities at her university and in the community to help her stay active and finds a women's rugby team that needs players—she hasn't played since grade eleven but still loves the sport. Playing rugby and training not only increase her activity levels, but also allow her to meet some very cool, fun people—some of whom happen to be in her Anatomy and Physiology study group. When Jo heads home to her summer job after exams, she feels like she is back in control of her life.

What is Competency?

Jo assessed her situation, recognized areas for improvement, researched and designed a plan for change, and put that plan into action. How was Jo able to make this about-face? She was able to problem solve. She used her knowledge, technical skills, and interpersonal skills to solve her problem of poor health and the negative impact that it had on her life. Problem solving is an example of a broad competency that took Jo time to refine and occurred across her educational experience.

At the time of writing, there is no defined "Competency Model of Physical Education," however, some provinces in Canada have moved, or are in the process of moving, to a model of cross-curricular competencies. These are elements such as critical thinking or creativity (or problem solving) that are addressed in all areas of the curriculum in a manner consistent with subject specific discipline, yet recognizing the essential nature of these competencies to all of education. Often, the terms "competencies" and "skills" are used interchangeably. As a broader concept, however, "competency" is not limited to cognitive elements (involving the use of theory, concepts, or tacit knowledge); it also encompasses functional aspects (involving technical skills) as well as interpersonal skills (e.g., social or organizational skills) and ethical values (Alberta Education, 2011). A "skill" on the other hand "is the ability to perform tasks and solve problems" (Cedefop, 2008) and can be acquired in a matter of months while competencies are acquired over a number of years.

Action competence in health involves young people developing their abilities, their commitment, and their capacity to influence and control their own health, including the factors and determinants that are important to their health (Barenkow et al., 2006). The World Health Organization emphasizes that individual health skills should "enable a young person to apply knowledge and develop attitudes and skills to make positive decisions and take actions to promote and protect one's health and the health of others" (2003). Research conducted by the WHO recommends that health curriculum be written from the position of individual health skills and action competencies. Emphasis should be on the need to move from a topics approach to a holistic approach where students are able to consider issues in the "reality of the social and environmental contexts of their lives" (St. Leger et al., 2010, p. 5). This approach can be further defined as:

> both the formal and informal curriculum and associated activities, where students gain age-related knowledge, understandings, skills, and experiences, which enable them to build competencies in taking action to improve the health and well-being of themselves and others in their community and that enhances their learning outcomes. (St. Leger et al., 2010, p. 4)

As PE is intricately related to health (indeed many provinces have H&PE instead of PE), the competency model is steadily gaining credence as provinces revise PE curricula. Although this is relatively new ground for PE, several provinces have already embedded their PE curricula within this approach. Immense potential exists in this emerging model for cross-curricular learning and links, real-life applicable experiences and assessment, as well as integration and connection with other curricular models such as TGfU or Sport Education.

Case Studies—Quick Hits

Consider the following quote:

> Although people differ in their assessments of the value of school physical education, both while they are students, and later as adults, a significant number report having learned to dislike physically active play, to disrespect physical educators, and to devalue their own capacity to learn movement skills. Given the ostensible purposes of most programs, that constitutes a fair indication that the conventional offering is a failure. Nobody needs to be blamed. We have a programmatic lemon. It is made so by design flaws, the limitations placed on teachers by workplace conditions, changes in youth culture, and the inexorable forces of history. There are no villains. It's just that making lemonade with what we have is beyond most of us, and it probably wouldn't yield the product we really want in any case. (Locke, 1992, p. 363)

Questions for Reflection

1 Although Locke does not directly address curriculum above, given what you've learned in this chapter, what role(s) could curriculum play in the issue described?

2 If you were "in charge" of your provincial curriculum for PE, how would you use curriculum to address the issues that Locke raises?

You have observed that before every physical education fitness class your high school students are drinking energy drinks and potato chips. You are concerned that the importance of nutrition has gone to the wayside even though they are actively involved within your class.

Questions for Reflection

1 How would you teach the importance of healthy eating within your fitness classes?

2 How can you use your assessment tools to help create this behaviour change?

Case Studies—Quick Hits

You have been asked by your administrator to teach about the importance of life skills (responsibility, goal setting, team work, etc.) within your physical education class. More specifically you have been asked to teach about anti-bullying tactics. You have been using the multi-activity curriculum model to organize your physical education classes.

Questions for Reflection

1 How would you address this topic within your multi-activity model PE class?

2 How would you use one or more of the curriculum models explained in this chapter to teach this important life skill?

Limitations

Competencies, by definition, are complex. Provinces that are moving in this direction with curricula are breaking new ground for PE and as such, this process will take time and some trial and error to develop. There is a chance that in-service educators not willing to adapt or change methods and values will simply ignore the model and carry on delivering PE as they usually have (Ha, Wong, Sum, & Chan, 2008). Success will no doubt depend on quality in-servicing, the development of superb resources, and a willingness to embrace this model.

Mixing and Matching of Curriculum Models

Leah is in her fourth year as a physical educator and is preparing for her next year of teaching. She has used a few of the curriculum models throughout her career, however, she has not found one curriculum model that suits all of her teaching values. She has decided to take the best parts of a few models, creating a model that meets the needs for both her and her students.

It is always important as educators to remind ourselves that it is our decision on which curriculum model to use in order to guide our teaching and student learning, and that this decision can involve selecting aspects from more than one curriculum model. This might be the case when a certain model is not working with a certain class of students or when you feel no one model is fully meeting the needs of your teaching values and morals.

Mixing and matching PE curriculum models can be done in a number of ways. One specific example is a combination of the TPSR Model (Hellison & Templin, 1991) and the TGfU Model (Bunker & Thorpe, 1982). While embedding the importance of the five levels of personal and social responsibility, the usual cognitive questioning of the TGfU model can be modified to become a more affective line of questioning. More specifically within stages 3 (Tactical Awareness) and 4 (Making Appropriate Decisions) of the TGfU model, educators can modify the usual cognitive tactical line of educator questioning and exploration (e.g., how did you attack the other team's goal or pins?) to a more affective line of educator questioning and exploration based on Hellison's TPSR levels (e.g., how did you control yourself to make sure that you respected your teammates?). While using both models in combination, the strength of the small-sided approach to games teaching is highlighted from the TGfU model, and complemented by the importance of thinking about one's own personal and social actions within gameplay of the TPSR model. This method provides students the opportunity to work on all three domains (physical, cognitive, and emotional) and allows a deeper sense of what it means to be a responsible game player.

This is only one example of mixing and matching curriculum models in order to enhance student learning. Other combinations have been researched and/or practically utilized within PE classrooms across Canada. It is up to the educator to find out which combination will be the most effective for any given situation.

Contexts for Curriculum Implementation

Regardless of the model(s) you choose to use in your own teaching practice, implementation of curriculum never occurs in a vacuum. What happens in the classroom, field, and gymnasium needs to connect to the larger context of school, community, and/or society. Although the nature of context changes frequently and depends a great deal on factors such as legislation, demographics, and policy, it is worth briefly exploring three important contexts that may impact your choice and delivery of PE curriculum.

Health Promoting Schools Approach

The Health Promoting Schools (HPS) Approach (also called *comprehensive school health* and *coordinated school health*) is a whole-school approach that both encompasses PE and

Table 3.1: Stages of the LTAD Model

	Ages	Description
Active Start	Males and Females 0–6	Learn FUNdamental movements and link them together in play
FUNdamentals	Males 6–9 Females 6–8	Learn all FUNdamental movement skills and build overall motor skills
Learn to Train	Males 9–12 Females 8–11	Learn overall sport skills
Train to Train	Males 12–16 Females 11–15	Build aerobic base, develop speed and strength, further develop and consolidate sport-specific skills
Train to Compete	Males 16–23 +/- Females 15–21 +/-	Optimize fitness preparation and sport-, individual=, and position-specific skills as well as performance
Train to Win	Males 19 +/- Females 18 +/-	Focus on podium performance
Active for Life	Enter at any age	Smooth transition from an athlete's competitive career to a lifelong physical activity and participation in sport

provides a context for healthy behaviours in the school's greater community. HPS was clarified with a set of World Health Organization guidelines (WHO, 1996) and strives to provide a way to link health and education outcomes by including the instruction, supports, and environment of the school setting as part of a foundation that fosters interaction and cohesion among home, school, and community. A growing number of researchers are examining the particularities of HPS and building a solid body of knowledge regarding frameworks, content, implementation and efficacy (Deschenes, Martin, & Hill, 2003; Gleddie, 2011; Inchley, Muldoon & Currie, 2006; Stewart-Brown, 2006).

HPS is increasingly being promoted, followed, and studied across Canada. Linking learning beyond the formal class-room curriculum to the home, school, and community is an important part of current and future PE programming. This coordination can be done through a HPS approach that supports student learning while addressing school health in a planned, integrated, and holistic manner. Such an approach incorporates interrelated components, such as the four pillars of HPS put forth by the Joint Consortium for School Health in the *Framework for Comprehensive School Health*: social and physical environments, partnerships and services, healthy school policy, and teaching and learning (Joint Consortium for School Health, 2010). Physical and Health Education Canada (PHE Canada) also provides HPS framework, supports, and resources to school communi-ties across the country. One of the key elements in the PHE Canada framework is education, which includes not only pro-grams of study and student learning, but also appropriate professional development for educators as well as commu-nity/parent education. HPS promotes a learning experience that is more student-driven and thus holistic:

The classroom health experience is more dynamic and less reliant on information transfer from teachers. Students build skills in advocacy, negotiation and enquiry. Health becomes part of their life, not a set of scientific facts, which are designed to change their behaviours. (St. Leger, 2004)

Long Term Athlete (or Participant) Development Model (LTAD)

The LTAD model encompasses aspects of physical education, such as fundamental movement skills, training, competing, and being active for life. Developed by Canadian Sport for Life, the seven stages follow a developmental approach that acknowledges the interaction of PE with sport and recreation, and promotes physical activity for all. The LTAD model encourages the development of physical literacy (see Chapter 13), especially at the first three stages, and fundamental movement skills through sport participation. It is important for educators to be aware of this philosophy, especially given the groundswell of support for the LTAD program in community, provincial, and national sports organizations. The developmental focus is of particular importance for educators as a variety of excellent resources and tools have been developed to assist with teaching.

Physical Literacy

Over the past decade, the concept of physical literacy has gained incredible momentum in the field of physical education (Mandigo, Francis, Lodewyk, & Lopez, 2009). For example, the Ontario curriculum for H&PE contains explicit reference to the development and need for physical literacy. PHE Canada describes physical literacy with the following:

"Individuals who are physically literate move with competence and confidence in a wide variety of physical activities in multiple environments that benefit the healthy development of the whole person."

For more detail and discussion on this important context, refer to Chapter 13.

Conclusion

As illustrated in this chapter, curriculum models for physical education are diverse and multi-faceted. It is important to remember that although curriculum for PE is developed and mandated by provincial or territorial governments, day-to-day decisions on how to teach are, for the most part, up to the individual educator. These decisions can be based on values, past experiences, identity (see Chapter 2), student and school needs, context, and many more variables. Physical educators can choose to use select models at select times, combine two models, or pick and choose elements from many to create a "poly-curricular collage" that reflects personal identity, experience, and setting. It is important for pre-service physical educators to:

- Know and understand the approaches and models available to them
- Recognize why they may be drawn to teach a certain way
- Understand why others (educator mentors, etc.) use particular approaches
- Be able to draw from multiple sources to create an effective, student-centred, flexible, personal curricular philosophy

We have seen PE curriculum in Canada change over time to meet perceived and changing societal needs. As the purpose of PE continues to evolve from the prevalent "lifelong physical activity focus" to perhaps include more health-focused goals, physical literacy, competencies, and socio-cultural elements, we can certainly expect emerging (and maybe merging) curricular models and approaches to meet the needs of educators and students alike.

Questions for Reflection

1 Discuss how you might go about resolving a conflict with a colleague who teaches PE from a different curricular model than you. How might you find common ground and work together towards a goal of engaging student learning through a high quality PE experience?

2 Given what you have learned about the various models, discuss the strengths and weaknesses of each. How will you combine or integrate the various models to meet your students' needs? Your needs? The curricular requirements of your province?

3 Identify what curriculum model(s) you were taught under. Reflect on your experience and note what you would change and why? Does your recollection and reflection give you the whole picture? Why or why not?

4 Construct a chart or table that outlines critical areas of each model (origin, goal, key characteristics, design components, implementation, student and educator roles, etc.). Using the chart, decide which approaches you may use in your own teaching and why. Discuss your findings with a small group.

Key Terms

- Curriculum Model
- Curriculum
- Multi-Activity Model
- TGfU or Sport Model
- TPSR or Social Model
- Sport Education Model
- Fitness for Life Model
- Competencies Model
- Health Promoting Schools Approach
- Long-Term Athlete Development

Planning for Instruction

Lynn Randall and Daniel B. Robinson

Overview

When many pre-service physical educators think of planning for instruction, they often think of planning the daily lesson. That is, they wonder, "what am I going to do tomorrow?" For those who think a little further in advance, the question they may ask themselves is often, "What sports/dances/gymnastics themes am I going to teach this year?" Planning a quality physical education (PE) program begins well before the beginning of the school year and continues throughout the year. This chapter will give an overview of considerations in the planning process that will help pre-service physical educators plan an instructionally and curriculum aligned, developmentally appropriate, sequential PE program, with a focus on student learning.

Planning is part of what is known as the "instructional process." The instructional process involves three steps. The first step is planning; that is, thinking about, researching, organizing, and developing content for instruction. The second step is actually presenting the content to students; otherwise known as teaching. The planning process is not complete without the third step: assessment. These three steps are repeated continuously. Although the entire instructional process involves three steps, this chapter will focus on the first step only; that is the actual planning process. Teaching and evaluation are the focus of later chapters.

Planning Essentials

Throughout the entire instructional process, and at every level (e.g., yearly, unit, lesson), it is important that physical educators are able to clearly articulate: their intended learning outcomes; their assessment plans and how the assessment plans relate directly to the learning outcomes; how the outcomes will be reached so that students will be prepared for the assessment; and how the needs of individual students will be met. These issues must remain central throughout the entire instructional process (planning, teaching, evaluating). To keep these issues central, there are a series of questions physical educators must repeatedly ask as they proceed through the instructional process. These questions are:

1 **What do I want students to know/be able to do/value?** This question relates to the outcomes/objectives that have been developed for the program/unit/lesson.

2 **How will I know?** This question relates to the indicators of learning or the assessment plan the physical educator has developed to measure the degree to which students have achieved the intended outcomes listed in question 1. Questions 1 and 2 should be directly aligned.

3 **What will I do or how will I get there?** This question relates to teaching the lesson. More specifically, this question addresses the issue of content selection, development, and presentation to students. Similar to the comment made above in question 2, the answer to this question should directly align with the goals and assessments. That is, the physical educator must teach what they intended to teach, and assess what was taught. This is known as instructional alignment and will be addressed later in the chapter.

Recognizing that students' abilities will differ within each unit and lesson, an additional and essential question that must be addressed with respect to Question 3 is: How will I modify the content of the lesson for students with different learning styles? This question relates to knowing how to simplify or extend the content for students who may be struggling or who need more of a challenge.

Beginning to Plan

As stated above, physical educators must be able to clearly articulate their learning outcomes. A learning outcome is a broadly written statement that describes the abilities, knowledge, and attitudes students are expected to be able to demonstrate after having completed a program of study. When deciding where to begin the planning process, the best place to start is by knowing and being able to articulate the end product. For example, after participating in an PE program:

- What are students expected to have learned?
- What are students expected to be able to do?
- What values towards physical activity/movement are students expected to hold?
- How will the physical educator know if students have been successful in meeting the exit expectations?

If the planning process requires the planner to begin at the end, then the physical educator must know and be able to articulate the desired end product of a quality PE program. According to Physical and Health Education Canada (PHE Canada), participation in a quality PE program should lead to students becoming physically literate. Mandigo, Francis, Lodewyk, and Lopez define individuals who are physical literate as those who, "move with competence in a wide variety of physical activities that benefit the development of the whole person" (2009, p. 6). The definition put forth by Mandigo et al., has been adopted by PHE Canada.

The work of PHE Canada influences development of provincial curricula. According to a document released by the organization entitled "What Is the Relationship Between Physical Education and Physical Literacy":

The concept of physical literacy is becoming an important focus in provincial physical education curricula. The recently revised health and physical education curriculum in Ontario identifies **the development of physically literate students as the foundation of student learning from grades one to 12**. In Saskatchewan, physical literacy is considered a critical characteristic of an effective physical education program within its renewed curriculum. In Newfoundland and Labrador, the development of physically literate students is a key outcome in the newly revised Intermediate program. It is only a matter of time until every ministry of education in Canada identifies physical literacy as a foundation of their physical education curriculums. (p. 2, emphasis in original)

Provincial curricula outline the outcomes that students are expected to attain by the end of a program. They often contain the outcomes to be attained on both a program level and yearly basis. For example, on a program level, the outcomes would state what students should be able to do, know, and value at the end of the required course of study, which for most provinces, runs from kindergarten through to at least grade nine. On a yearly basis, the documents outline what students are to be able to do, know, and value at the end of each grade. Thus, the planning process begins with provincial curriculum documents that contain specific or prescribed student learning outcomes for each grade. The British Columbia Physical Education K to 7 Integrated Resource Package 2006 describes specific learning outcomes as:

> the legally required content standards for the provincial education system. They define the required attitudes, skills, and knowledge for each subject. The learning outcomes are statements of what students are expected to know and be able to do by the end of the indicated grade. (p. 7)

Curricular documents in Quebec do not use the term "outcome." Rather, education in Quebec is competency based and defines competency as "a set of behaviours based on the effective mobilization and use of a range of resources" (Government of Quebec, Ministry of Education, 2001, p. 4). There are three interrelated competencies that comprise Quebec's PE program. They are:

- To perform movement skills in different physical activity settings
- To interact with others in different physical activity settings
- To adopt a healthy, active lifestyle (Government of Quebec, Ministry of Education, 2001, p. 273).

Curriculum documents (or guides) do not state specifically what sports, skills, themes, or dances to teach, but rather include more general statements of student outcomes. For example, in relation to the application of basic skills in dance at the grade two level, the Alberta physical education (K–12) curriculum document (2000) states, "students will demonstrate basic dance steps and movement; e.g., creative, folk, line, alone and with others, by using elements of effort, space and relationships" (Outcome A2-8, p. 10). In this regard, physical educators have a lot of autonomy over the content they can select to meet the provincial outcomes.

In summary, curriculum documents outline the general and specific outcomes students are expected to attain at each grade level, but it is the physical educator who selects the specific content that will be used to meet a given outcome. Thus, outcomes provide the physical educator with direction in terms of what students are expected to know, value, and be able to do as a result of instruction, while at the same time allowing a degree of flexibility and autonomy with respect to the content educators can use to reach the outcomes.

Case Study 1: Planning and Balancing

Steven did very well throughout his coursework and teaching internships when he completing his Education degree. The physical educator Steven worked with during his internship continuously stressed two points: 1) the importance of using the curriculum documents as guides when planning a PE program; 2) ensuring that the planned program was balanced. Now that he is starting his first job as a full-time physical educator, Steven is excited to begin planning his own programs, keeping in mind what he learned throughout his teaching internships and university coursework.

Steven is familiar with the curriculum, so throughout the summer he thought about and began to write down some ideas for the units he would like to teach. He also began gathering some new introductory activities and low organized games that could be modified and used with different content, so that he could offer a lot of variety and maintain student interest and enthusiasm.

When he arrives at the school on the first day of planning week, he met his two PE colleagues. During the initial planning meeting, Mike, the department head, draws three school calendars on the white board, one for each teaching space in the school. He then begins filling in the months with content: soccer in September and early October; basketball in late October and November; floor hockey for December; Fitness and Low Organized Games in January to round out the semester. Everyone would be teaching the same content, each in their own teaching space. Once complete, Mike turns to Steven and his colleague and asks, "What do you think?" Steven senses that Mike is open to suggestions.

Questions for Reflection

1 How does Steven's current plan align with your provincial curriculum document? How does Steven's currant plan misalign with your provincial curriculum document?

2 How could the plan, as initially presented by Mike, be better aligned and balanced?

Box 4.1: Education is a provincial responsibility

In 1867 when the provinces united under the name "Canada," the *Constitution Act*, also known as the *British North America Act*, laid out the conditions under which Canada would govern itself. Article 93 of the Act pertains to education. Section 93 begins by stating, "In and for each Province the Legislature may exclusively make Laws in relation to Education ..." (http://laws-lois.justice.gc.ca/eng/Const//page-4. html#docCont). Essentially, the Act granted each province individual responsibility for education. As a result, different curricular documents are developed in each province.

Box 4.2: The Western and Northern Canadian Protocol (WNCP)

In December 1993, the ministers responsible for education in Manitoba, Saskatchewan, Alberta, British Columbia, Yukon Territory, and Northwest Territories signed the Western Canadian Protocol for Collaboration in Basic Education (WCP), Kindergarten to Grade 12. In February 2000, Nunavut also joined WCP. Several cooperative projects have resulted from this alliance, including the development of common curriculum frameworks with learning outcomes in mathematics, language arts, and international languages.

Planning Considerations

With flexibility and autonomy comes responsibility. Physical educators must make responsible choices when it comes to selecting and organizing the content that will be used to meet the outcomes. They must also keep in mind that curriculum documents are often broad in scope, meaning that they are written for an entire province of students. Physical educators need to translate how the curriculum document can be effectively implemented in their particular context, for their specific group of students. To do this effectively there are a number of factors that must be considered before and during the planning process that relate to official documents, the community, the students, and the physical educator. These factors are discussed in the section that follows.

Official Documents

Canada has neither a national education minister nor a national department of education. Rather, education in Canada is the responsibility of provincial and territorial governments **(see Box 4.1)**. As such, each province has independently developed curricular documents while the three territories adapt documents from neighbouring provinces **(see Box 4.2)**.

In addition to the curriculum documents, many provinces have additional policy documents that should be considered when planning. For example, most provinces have an approved safety document that outlines a variety of guidelines and/or procedures that physical educators must follow when teaching PE. The intent of these documents is to minimize the risk of injury and the occurrence of accidents.

Physical educators learn to translate and fully implement the curriculum to meet the specific needs of their students.

Other documents that have been mandated by the province or are specific to a particular school district may also exist. These can cover topics such as the use of athletic facilities away from the school or policies related to securing parent permission for field trips and transporting students to alternative sites. It is an educator's responsibility to be aware of these documents and policies, and follow them accordingly.

The School Culture and Surrounding Community

Within cities, the school and community culture can vary tremendously. Physical educators cannot assume that their school will be similar to one they attended as a student or that the students will have similar interests. The school and community culture will have a big influence on the PE program. Some questions to consider are:

- Does the school and community place a high priority on wellness and athletics? If so, there may be a lot of support for the PE program, but an emphasis on athletics can dominate a PE program.
- Is the school in an economically depressed area? If so, students may not have suitable attire for PE class, parents may care more about courses they feel are more likely to help their child(ren) secure employment. Another consideration in lower-income areas is that many students may have part-time jobs, which can affect participation in a PE program.
- Is the school ethnically diverse? How should this affect the choice of activities?
- Is the school known for its academics? How will this affect support for the PE program?
- Is there a lot of violence in the surrounding neighbourhood? What impact might this have on students' participation in activity outside of school?

Being aware of the culture of the school and surrounding community can help physical educators to make informed decisions during the planning process.

Student Considerations

Interests of the students: When planning the PE program, the end user is obviously the student. Thus, the students' interests must be kept at the centre of the planning process. How can physical educators figure out what students are interested in, what they want to learn, or how they want to spend their leisure time? The easy answer is to ask them! Ask them what they do on the weekends and after school, what activities they would like to become more skilled in, or which activities are popular in the local community. When Ennis (2008) spoke with elementary students, she found students valued content they saw as being connected to their out-of school activities so this type of engagement

with students is valuable. Having students complete a quick survey may be easier than trying to speak to all students individually.

Listening to students is one way to gauge students' interest. Another is to listen to colleagues. How are they talking about their students? Do they feel their students are lazy and disinterested, or engaged and excited about class? In either case, what are they doing to create that environment? Are the activities engaging, relevant, interesting, challenging, and meeting their needs, or is the program basically a repeat of what students did the year before, and the year before that? What elements of the existing program should be kept and which ones should be changed in an attempt to create a positive and engaging movement environment?

Answering these questions can seem intimidating to new educators who have yet to start teaching. One possible solution is to talk with colleagues or peers who have been placed in the school in the past. Another option is to call the school and ask to speak with someone in the PE department. If possible, observing a class may also provide valuable information.

Developmental characteristics/needs of the learners: The developmental characteristics and needs of learners obviously differ from kindergarten to grade twelve. It is important to be fully aware of these differences because they will have an impact on the content that is selected and delivered and could also influence the choice of equipment. For example, being aware that hand-eye coordination is developing in early elementary students could lead physical educators to plan lessons related to improving and strengthening this specific skill. It should be expected that many students struggle with certain skills initially and progress at different rates; knowing this, physical educators may be more likely to plan lessons providing several different practice opportunities over the course of the year.

Knowing the developmental differences and needs of students can also affect school policies or expectations. For example, let's consider departmental policies related to student dress as they relate to the developmental characteristic that young adolescents are often extremely conscience of their appearance. PE departments have important decisions to make in this regard. Students should dress appropriately for class, but what is appropriate? Are shorts allowed and, if so, is there a minimum length? Are sleeves required or are sleeveless or halters allowed? Can shirts or shorts be too baggy? Instead of trying to police student dress, some departments opt for a physical education uniform. If this is the case, who decides what the uniform will be? Will they consider that certain students may find the uniform either physically or emotionally uncomfortable or unflattering? Will choices be available? These are only a few of the questions that may have to be addressed. Being cognizant of the developmental needs and interests of the students will allow for appropriate planning, which is key to delivering quality programs.

Many provincial curriculum documents address the issue of developmental characteristics and include charts or descriptions of the learner characteristics the implications for teaching PE. Three examples are provided in the tables at the end of this chapter: **Table 4.1** is an example from the British Columbia Physical Education K–7 curriculum document (2006) and provides descriptions of learners in grades K to two (typically five to seven-year-olds); **Table 4.2** outlines the characteristics of students in the upper elementary grades (four to six) and is taken from the Ontario curriculum; **Table 4.3** describes the characteristics of middle school students and is from the Nova Scotia Physical Education Curriculum: Grades 7–9 document (1999, pp. 12–13). As you can see, the characteristics, needs, and interests of students change as they grow and mature, and these developmental differences must be taken into account when planning. Keep in mind that the information in these tables is general and that children of the same age and within the same age group can vary in size, maturity, motor ability, and readiness to learn.

Equity issues: Siedentop and Tannehill (2000) pose a series of questions that curriculum designers should ask, but their questions are equally relevant for educators designing and planning a PE program for their particular context. These questions include:

- What groups are best and most served by this curriculum?

  Are males better served than females?

  Are more-skilled students better served than less-skilled students?

- Is the curriculum ethnically sensitive?

  Does it expand the students' capacities to live effectively in an increasingly multicultural world?

  Does it develop students' critical capacities to know when they are being manipulated by powerful economic forces in the health, leisure, and fitness industries?

- Does the curriculum inadvertently work to reproduce the inequities that exist in the worlds of sport, leisure, health and fitness?

  (Siedentop & Tannehill, 2000, p. 143)

Siedentop and Tannehill recognize that there are no easy answers to their questions, but nonetheless, they must continue to be asked and re-asked if relevant programs are to be designed for students.

Physical Educator Considerations

Personal philosophy: As discussed in Chapter 2, all physical educators have a personal vision for teaching. Being able to articulate your vision of teaching and identify where your values lie is important because it is the lens through which the literature is read and interpreted. Some curriculum documents clearly articulate the curriculum orientation, in others they may be implied, and in others they are not mentioned.

Subject matter knowledge and interest of the educator: Many physical educators were successful athletes on school or community teams. For many, this experience results in an expertise or passion for one or two activities in particular. It is natural to want to teach what we know and love. However, never forget that the students are the priority. To fulfill the requirements of the curriculum and meet the needs of the students, a variety of content must be taught. This may include unfamiliar games/sports, dance forms, or other content.

One option for overcoming unfamiliarity is by capitalizing on the strengths of individuals in the PE department. For example, if target games are to be included as content for a middle/high school program and one department member has experience in golf and bowling, he or she could teach the target unit to all classes. In this method, rather than stay with the same class for the entire year, classes are assigned to physical educators based upon the content. Another option is to use a prep period to watch a more experience colleague teach a unit in order to become more familiar with it. Professional conferences also provide great opportunities to acquire skills and knowledge in areas that may be lacking.

Other Considerations

Total available time: The amount of time with students can affect your program greatly. Although both PHE Canada and many PE curriculum documents recommend a minimum of 30 minutes of physical education a day, these recommendations are often not met due to scheduling conflicts or lack of space. As such, meeting all curriculum outcomes can be a challenge. In these situations, important decisions need to be made. For example, is it better to touch on all outcomes briefly and expect a minimal level of achievement, or would it be more beneficial to select those outcomes that are a priority and teach them in depth, expecting students to achieve deeper levels of understanding and ability?

Timetable: In addition to considering the total available time, the weekly timetable presents other time considerations. The first is the length of time allocated to each class. Content selection and delivery will likely vary if the class meets for 20 or 25 minutes as opposed to 50 or 60 minutes. For example, the warm-up and review may be combined in a 20-minute class, but not in a longer one. A second time consideration is the time of day the class meets. For example, some students may be more attentive and energetic during mid-morning lessons as opposed to afternoon lessons. If outdoor spaces are being used, it may be cooler for morning classes and quite hot for afternoon classes. Both scenarios can affect student motivation as well as how much content can be presented in a single class. Another time consideration is class frequency. For example, a class that meets once per week will likely require an extended review. Classes that meet twice a week but on consecutive days are likely to need a thorough review only on the first day.

Available resources: Before beginning the planning process, it is important to know what types of resources are available for instruction. Resources include movement surfaces and spaces, types and amount of equipment in the school, and available community facilities (and access to them). There is little use in planning to include tennis as part of a unit if the school does not have courts or only has four racquets in good condition!

The hidden curriculum: Planning is done for a number of reasons, one of which is to ensure that students learn what educators set out to teach them—what Rink (2009) refers to as "intended" learning. However, students often learn much more than what was intended. The educator's actions, words, and attitudes can convey a host of unintended messages, not all of them positive. For example, if the physical educator tells students about an incident that happened while they were running/working out/playing volleyball, it conveys to the students that the physical educator lives a physically active lifestyle and is serious about the messages they teach during class. On the other hand, if the physical educator arrives late and begins by asking, "what do you want to do today?" what message do you think students pick up about the importance of PE? Also, what messages do the posters (or lack thereof) on the wall convey? Are the people depicted all the same race, gender, or ability? If the students are never evaluated in PE, what message does this convey with respect to the importance of trying, participating, and seeking feedback? This unintended learning that occurs in all subjects is referred to as the null or hidden curriculum (Rink, 2009). Planning is more likely to contribute to more intended learning.

Examining Curricular Documents

As stated previously, the planning process begins with the end. The ultimate outcome of a quality PE program is the development of a physically literate student and the means to achieving this is by meeting the exit outcomes

(or program outcomes) in provincial curricula documents. Exit outcomes are the outcomes students are expected to achieve at the end of a specified period of time and are written on various levels. For example, program level outcomes describe what students are expected to attain after participation in K–12 PE. Most provincial curriculum documents also include key stage outcomes that generally cover the exit outcomes students are expected to attain at the end of elementary, middle, and high school. These key stage outcomes contribute to the overall program or exit outcome(s). Many provincial curriculum documents also contain grade level outcomes that students are expected to attain and which tie in to the key stage outcomes. **Table 4.4** provides examples of the various levels of outcomes that can be found in the Newfoundland and Labrador Physical Education Primary and Elementary Curriculum Guide. The outcomes in Newfoundland and Labrador are divided into three categories: in movement, about movement, and through movement. **Table 4.4** relates specifically to the in movement category.

Thus, to begin to plan for a grade two class, the physical educator would need to have a rough idea of the expected exit outcomes for high school graduation, and a more detailed idea of how the elementary level outcomes contribute to the overall program as well what the grade two

The ultimate goal of quality PE is a physically-literate student.

outcomes specifically are and how they contribute to the overall elementary outcomes. The physical educator can then begin to plan the units and lessons that will help reach the grade level outcomes. Starting with the exit outcomes for high school graduation and working backwards to grade level outcomes is a process known as backward design or designing down (Lund & Tannehill, 2005). A similar process is used when developing yearly plans, unit plans, and lesson plans.

It is imperative that physical educators are cognizant of meeting the curricular outcomes. However, it is unrealistic to pick up a curriculum document and try to teach the outcomes sequentially as they are written. This is not a coherent way to organize or deliver content. As stated previously, various content can be used to reach curricular objectives. Thus, content must be organized in various ways so that when delivered, it is meaningful for students.

There are a variety of ways to organize content. At the elementary level, content can be arranged by using a movement education orientation (Wall & Murray, 1994). With this approach, content that focuses on aspects of body awareness, space awareness, effort qualities, and relationships are explored. The use of skill themes (Graham, Holt-Hale, & Parker, 2007) is another way to organize content. Examples of skill-themes are travelling, jumping and landing, volleying and dribbling, and striking with racquets and paddles. Content can also be arranged by type of skill (Pangrazi & Gibbons, 2003) such as, fundamental motor skills, specialized motor skills, and sport skills.

The content of PE instruction should be organized so that it is meaningful for students.

At the intermediate and high school level, three popular organization methods are by sport or activity (e.g., a unit of team handball, archery, dance, tennis), using categories of movement (e.g., alternative environment activities, dance, games, gymnastics, fitness; see **Table 4.5** on page 65) and by game category (e.g., invasion, net/wall, striking/fielding, and target). In many provinces, curriculum documents outline an organizational structure; in others, physical educators are free to organize content in a manner that best meets the needs of their students.

Developing a Yearly Plan

The next step in the planning process is developing a yearly plan for every grade level.

In addition to the three planning questions mentioned earlier in the chapter, educators must also keep the following in mind when developing a yearly plan: First, the physical educator has some options (Pangrazi & Gibbons, 2003) when deciding how to schedule units of instruction. Units can be scheduled using a "solid block" format where a specific activity is the focus for a specified block of time (e.g., five or ten consecutive days). A modified "solid block" format allows for a day of instruction that deviates from the major unit of instruction (e.g., Fridays may be designated as Fitness Fridays (Pangrazi & Gibbons, 2003) or Dance Day). A "multiple block" format provides the opportunity to teach two or more units concurrently. For example, target games may be the focus on Monday, Wednesday, and Friday, with Tuesday and Thursday begin designated at fitness days.

To develop a yearly plan, develop a table that includes at least three columns. In one column, include every week of the year or semester. In the second column, indicate the content/units that will be taught in each week. The third column can be used to identify the curricular outcomes that each unit will address to ensure that all curricular outcomes will be met. An example is provided in **Table 4.6** on page 66.

When developing the yearly plan, make sure that it has an appropriate scope, sequence, and balance (Pangrazi & Gibbons, 2003). Scope is the content selected to be delivered to students (Lund & Tannehill, 2005; Pangrazi & Gibbons, 2003). Reviewing the scope within the yearly plan can ensure that all necessary content has been covered. For example, a middle level physical educator in New Brunswick would need to ensure their plan includes "at least one unit of Alternative Environment Activities, Dance, Games, Gymnastics and Individual and Dual Activities" (see **Table 4.5**).

Sequence refers to "the order or progression in which learning activities are presented" (Lund & Tannehill, 2005, p. 36). Reviewing the sequence of the yearly plan will ensure that the order in which the material is presented to students is appropriate, and can help make sure students attain any pre-requisite skills required for material to be covered later. For example, it is important to ensure that instruction and practice in basic locomotor skills precede an educational gymnastics unit where students are expected to travel along a variety of apparatus.

Reviewing the yearly plan for balance "ensures that all learning outcomes in the program receive adequate coverage" (Pangrazi & Gibbons, 2003, p. 164), as well as ensuring that they are sequenced in a balanced way. For example, try to avoid a situation where all or part of the yearly plan is dominated by one type of activity (e.g., group games or invasion/territory games). Instead try to re-sequence the content such that a unit that focuses on group interaction/teams is followed with a unit that requires more individual or partner work.

Developing the Unit Plan

With the yearly plan complete, it is time to begin developing individual units of instruction. There are various ways to do this and a variety of items that can be included. Be aware that some districts, schools, or PE departments have a set format or list of items that must be included as part of each unit plan. Some demand much more detail than others. At a minimum, the unit plan should include the objectives of the unit, the assessment tools and evaluation procedures, a block plan that outlines the scope and sequence of the content, and the individual lesson plans. Additional items may be included such as a brief history of the activity, any terms or definitions that may be unfamiliar to students, time, space, and equipment considerations, a brief description of the students whom the unit is being designed for, a management plan, special safety considerations, and lesson modifications for any students with special needs, students who are struggling, or students who have already mastered the content. **Table 4.7** (on page 67) outlines these items and provides a brief description of each item. These considerations need to be addressed early in the unit planning process and are usually included in the front matter.

Establishing Objectives

When developing the yearly plan, provincial curricular outcomes are included with each unit of instruction. The curricular outcomes are relatively broad in scope so physical educators will need to narrow the focus of the outcomes at the unit level and clearly indicate what is to be accomplished in each unit. For example in **Table 4.6**, both week 4 (golf) and week 7 (Tchoukball) have "D4: demonstrate ways to receive, retain, and send an object with increasing accuracy individually and with others" as an objective. Obviously expected

student performance in each activity will vary and be more specific depending on the content taught. More specific outcomes are referred to as objectives **(see Box 4.3)**. Thus, unit planning begins by establishing learning objectives.

Unit objectives answer the question, "what do I want students to learn/be able to do, by the end of this unit?" Therefore, lesson objectives answer the question, "what do I want students to learn/be able to do, by the end of this lesson?" Notice the question asks what the students are expected to do, not what the educator is expected to do. The phrase, "by the end of the unit/lesson" indicates that the important part of the objective is the end result rather than what the student does during class to achieve this end result.

When deciding on objectives, consider what students can do already or what content they have covered in previous years. If the physical educator has taught the students before, he or she should have a good understanding of the students' ability and should plan to extend the content (i.e., introduce more difficult tasks) as opposed to repeating the same material. If the students' ability levels are unknown, consult a colleague or the curriculum document to get a sense of what should have been covered. This will help keep goals and expectations realistic for the students.

Box 4.3: Differentiating Between Outcomes and Objectives

Outcomes are broad in scope. They describe the abilities, knowledge, and attitudes students are expected to be able to demonstrate after having completed a program of study. That is, after participation in a physical education program* what do we expect students to know, value, and be able to do?

Objectives are more specific and detail what students are to learn, generally in shorter periods of time (e.g., a unit or lesson). Outcomes provide direction for objectives. It is through the achievement of a series of objectives that outcomes are met.

*A physical education "program" can refer to: a grade level (e.g., at the end of grade two); a school level (e.g., at the end of elementary school); or an entire educational experience (e.g., at the end of grade twelve).

Since students are the focus, objectives usually begin with, "Students will be able to ..." but some are more specific (and provide more guidance) than others. For

Case Study 2: Stepping Outside Your Comfort Zone

Bridget is excited to begin her position as a physical educator at a local middle school. She was an athlete all through middle school and high school and played for a variety of school and community teams. She continued to play organized sports throughout university through the campus recreation program. During her teaching internship she taught badminton, volleyball, and basketball and she had the opportunity to coach the girl's field hockey and team handball. As a result of many years of playing a variety of sports and recently coaching a couple as well, Bridget is very confident in her abilities to teach a wide variety of sports to her students.

As she reviews the curriculum as the initial step for planning, she becomes increasingly worried. The curriculum document specifically states, "offer a balanced program. A balanced program consists of offering instruction in at least one activity in every movement category. The movement categories are: alternative environments, games, dance, gymnastics, individual and dual activities." "Dance and gymnastics," she quietly says to herself. "I do not know a thing about dance and gymnastics!"

Questions for Reflection:

1 What are some possibilities Bridget could investigate with respect to planning a unit of content with which she has limited experience and confidence?

2 Think of a content area you are unfamiliar with. Where would you begin to plan a unit of instruction for your students (people you would approach, websites you would look into, etc.)?

example, a unit objective that states, "By the end of this unit, students will be able to play a 4 against 4 game of basketball" does not really provide much information about what to expect in terms of student performance or demonstration of certain skills. There is no indication of the content that will be covered in the unit, or the skills students will need to demonstrate in order to successfully meet the objective. A more specific objective such as, "By the end of the unit, students will be able to play a game of 4 against 4 basketball, demonstrating the ability to move the ball by dribbling with control, to pass to an open player, guard opponents, and fake and shoot when the opportunity arises" provides more direction in terms of what must be taught in the unit for the students to reach that objective.

When writing objectives, consider the question: "How can I assess the objective?" What assessment will be used to measure whether students have attained the objective? What type(s) of student performance is expected? Knowing ahead of time what students will be expected to do, know, and value by the end of the instructional period makes writing objectives much easier.

There has been debate in the educational community concerning objective writing and the degree of specificity required for the objective to be meaningful and useful (Rink, 2006). At the unit and lesson level, some comment that the more specific the objective, the more it is able to guide instruction and assessment and that it keeps the focus on content that will help students reach the objective. On the other hand, some educators argue that learning is complex and takes time so expecting a certain level of performance at the end of the lesson is unrealistic especially when one takes into account that students learn at different rates. To these educators, detailed specific objectives tend to narrow the students' learning experiences to only those experiences that can be easily measured. There are many affective objectives (e.g., developing a sense of fair play) and motor skills (e.g., appropriate use of strategies in game play) that are important outcomes for students to learn and experience but are more difficult to measure. In an effort to make objectives both meaningful and useful, Rink (2006) has presented a middle ground suggesting that, "educational objectives should be specified to the degree that they provide direction for the design and evaluation of educational experiences without narrowing those experiences to what is most easily measured" (p. 242).

Types of Objectives: Motor, Cognitive, and Affective

Physical education has the potential to contribute to the physical, cognitive, and affective development of students. This potential is recognized in the definition of a physically literate person and in the exit outcomes of provincial PE curricula. PE exit outcomes are written in three domains: the motor domain, the cognitive domain, and the affective domain. Depending on the province, the domain name may change, but the three are evident in all provincial curriculum documents. The motor domain, also referred to as the psychomotor, the physical, or the doing domain, includes outcomes related to acquiring skills. The affective domain, also referred to as the feeling or valuing domain, includes outcomes related to attitudes. The cognitive domain, also referred to as the knowing or thinking domain, includes outcomes related to acquiring knowledge.

The three learning domains (motor, cognitive, and affective) originated through the work of Benjamin Bloom and a team of educational psychologists. This work resulted in what is known as Bloom's Taxonomy of Educational Objectives (Bloom et al., 1956). The taxonomy was originally developed to assist educators in writing objectives and to encourage them to think about and plan to teach higher order thinking skills. In the development of the original taxonomy, each domain was divided into categories and the categories were ordered from simple to complex and from concrete to abstract (**see Table 4.8** on page 67). Learning at the higher or more complex levels is dependent upon having acquired the knowledge, skills, and attitudes at the lower levels. The cognitive domain of the taxonomy has recently been updated and revised to better reflect learning in the twenty-first century (Anderson et al., 2001). The changes in the revised taxonomy include: replacing the terms "knowledge" and "comprehension" with "remember" and "understand" respectively, switching the order of the top two categories, and changing the names of the categories from noun to verb forms. A comparison of the original and revised cognitive taxonomies is found in **Table 4.9** on page 68.

Case Study 3: Starting from Scratch

Kevin has been an elementary physical educator at Crossroads Elementary School for ten years. During his time at Crossroads, Kevin developed a balanced program based on the provincial curriculum document and incorporated a number of new ideas that he learned at conferences and professional development workshops. Being the only physical educator in the school, Kevin saw the students year after year and was able to ensure that his lessons and units picked up in grade two where the students left off in grade one. The student progress Kevin observed year after year was very rewarding.

However, the student population at Crossroads and another neighbouring school has been declining for years and the district is being forced to close a school. After months of debate and deliberation, the Department of Education decid ed that Crossroads will be shut down. All staff will be transferred to other schools, into positions left vacant by maternity leaves, retirements, and attrition. Kevin was transferred to Three Corners Elementary.

Although sad to be leaving a staff, student body, and community he thoroughly enjoyed working with, Kevin remains positive about the change. He believes that with his experience, the most difficult aspect of teaching at a new school will be learning all the students' names!

September arrives and Kevin begins teaching at Three Corners. It isn't long before Kevin realizes he will have to completely redesign his program. Four years prior to Kevin's arrival, the school, in consultation with District personnel, decided to hire a school literacy mentor in place of the physical educator in an effort to improve the poor results the school was achieving on provincial assessments. Although classroom educators were supposed to be offering regular PE classes to their students, through conversations with the educators and students, Kevin learns that when students were actually brought to the gymnasium, it was mainly as a reward for good classroom behaviour or to play games and blow off steam so they would be better able to concentrate in the classroom. The result was relatively poor skill ability for the majority of the students. With grade five students barely able to demonstrate grade three outcomes, Kevin realizes he is going to have to begin from scratch and redesign his units and lessons.

Questions for Reflection:

1 What steps could Kevin have taken to decrease the surprise (i.e., the students' low ability level) and to decrease the amount of new planning he was going to have to undertake in mid-September?

2 What are some of the considerations Kevin will have to keep in mind as he prepares a new set of units and lessons for the students at Three Corners Elementary?

Objectives are like a road map for learning. They provide direction for planning, teaching, and evaluation. To be useful and measurable, they must be written in a manner that describes behaviour in observable terms. To assist physical educators, in addition to providing categories within each domain, a number of observable behaviours or verbs have been attached to each category. The verbs provide physical educators with suggestions for writing objectives and encourage them to vary the types and levels of objectives they plan for. **Tables 4.10, 4.11, and 4.12** (on pages 68–69) provide examples of the descriptors/verbs within the various domains. **Table 4.10** provides examples for the pyschomotor domain, **Table 4.11** provides examples for the cognitive domain, and **Table 4.12** provides examples for the affective domain.

It is not uncommon for physical educators to focus on motor objectives, mistakenly assuming that the cognitive and affective objectives will be met as a by-product of participating in the lessons. That is, if the rules, strategies, or court boundaries have been explained or outlined as part of the lesson, then students will have learned them (i.e., a cognitive objective of understanding will have been met). Likewise, if students take part in activities where they play with and against each other, then affective outcomes such as teamwork, cooperation, and fair play will be met. If a physical educator has identified cognitive and affective outcomes as part of a unit or lesson, then they must plan to intentionally and explicitly address those outcomes.

Components of an Objective

To provide guidance in writing objectives, it may be useful to consider including three different components in an objective. These three components are: the behaviour students are expected to exhibit (e.g., strike, send an object, dribble); the conditions under which the behaviour is to be demonstrated (e.g., in groups of three spaced two metres apart, from a ball that is served over the net), and the criteria which describes the level of performance the student is expected to achieve. The criteria can be described either quantitatively (e.g., the ball lands in the court at least 80% of the time) or qualitatively, (e.g., with bent knees and a straight back) or both (e.g., contacting the shuttle below the waist on every serve). **Table 4.13** (on page 70) provides examples of objectives written with varying levels of specificity for each of the three learning domains.

Once the unit objectives are written, the next step is to design the assessment procedures for the unit. Doing this immediately after writing the objectives helps ensure that the unit is aligned. Simply stated, instructional alignment helps to ensure that physical educators teach what they intended to teach, and assess what was taught. For example, if a unit objective for a lacrosse unit states that students

will be able to play a 5 against 5 game demonstrating effective scooping, cradling, passing, and catching skills, and the end of unit tests or assessments had students shooting at a stationary target and running through a series of cones while cradling the ball, then your unit would be considered "misaligned" because the assessments do not match the objectives. On the other hand, using the same objective, if the assessment consisted of the use of a specifically developed assessment tool where students were assessed on their ability to pass, catch, scoop, and cradle the ball while playing the game, the unit would be considered aligned as the students would be graded on what the physical educator intended to teach.

Another advantage of completing the assessment immediately after writing the objectives and before planning the individual lessons is that once the assessments have been created or selected, there will be a clear indication of what needs to be taught in order for students to successfully complete the assessments. Using the above lacrosse outcome as an example, the physical educator would not only have to ensure the students could effectively demonstrate the scooping, cradling, passing, and catching, but also have to plan to spend time demonstrating, explaining, and having students practise using those skills in game-like situations. Thus, the inclusion of defenders and how to move and pass around defenders would need to be part of the instruction.

Developing Content

Once the goals/outcomes have been articulated, answer the question, "What must students be able to do to successfully meet this outcome?" Answering this question thoroughly requires a process known as content development (Rink, 2006) or content analysis (Siedentop & Tannehill, 2000) and involves analyzing the content and breaking it down into the various tasks or sequences that are required to reach the desired end goal.

The content development process will also demonstrate the amount of content needed to reach the desired goal. Unit level outcomes may have to be adjusted if there is too much content to cover in the allocated time period. Skill performance takes repeated practice which takes time. There is no use rushing through content for the sake of attempting to meet objectives. In doing so, nothing is gained; student performance does not improve, and it is highly unlikely that the objectives will actually be met. If student learning is truly the goal, a better course of action may be attempting to cover less content and providing more time for students to improve their performance.

Completing the Unit Block Plan

The next step in planning the unit is selecting the content that must be taught to successfully reach the objectives, and the order in which they will be presented. As when completing a block plan for the year, the scope and sequence for the unit needs to be outlined, but on a smaller scale; here, decide what will be covered on each day of the unit. This differs from the yearly plan developed previously in that much more specificity is required than for the yearly plan.

As unit design begins, there are issues to consider. For example, how will the unit be introduced? Will the unit begin with a short motivational video in an effort to get the students excited about the unit? Will a guest speaker be brought in before a unit or would it be more appropriate to bring in guests after the students have had some experience with the content? Maybe students will be allowed free time to explore or play with the equipment. Regardless of how the content is introduced, remember that the introduction is meant to excite the students about the upcoming unit. Also, don't forget the cognitive and affective objectives that have been developed and must be addressed throughout the unit as well.

Once the initial planning considerations have been addressed, the objectives written, assessments developed, and the content development process completed, it's time to complete the unit block plan. Begin by creating a chart that includes one block for each day of the unit. For example, a unit chart for a unit scheduled to last six days will include six blocks. Label each day of the block and then fill in the content that will allow the objectives to be met. The block plan should include enough detail so that an outsider can get a sense of the content that will be covered and see the intended progressions (see **Table 4.14** on page 70 for an example). Remember, the plan is a guide. If students do not progress through the content at the rate expected when the unit was developed, consider revisiting certain content and providing additional instruction, feedback, and practice time so that the unit becomes one where *students learn* (and improve performance) rather than one where the physical educator simply covers content.

Developing the Lesson Plan

Having written unit objectives and completed the unit block plan, the focus shifts to writing individual lesson plans. A variety of formats are available for designing individual lessons and examples can be found in various curriculum documents. A selection of these is provided in the appendix to this chapter (beginning on page 71).

Figure 4.1 is the format suggested by Alberta Education and is an example of a throwing and catching lesson

plan for grades K–three. **Figure 4.2** is an example from Saskatchewan of a fitness-related lesson for grade nine students. **Figures 4.3 and 4.4** are two blank lesson plan outlines from PE curriculum documents supplied by Newfoundland and Labrador and New Brunswick respectively. A number of teacher education programs introduce students to their own formats as a way to focus attention towards specific areas. For example, **Figure 4.5** is the lesson plan outline used at Brock University. The formats vary, but there is similarity in the content. Regardless of the format used, at the very least, your lesson plan should contain lesson objectives, the equipment required, a warm-up, a variety of activities designed to achieve the objectives, a way of measuring if the objectives have been met, and some form of closure.

Figure 4.6 outlines and explains the parts of the lesson plan. The format differs from some of the examples provided in that it will be completed in columns as opposed to para-graphs **(see Figures 4.7–4.9)**. In this manner, the lesson plan is clearer and easier to read and becomes more useful if referred to while teaching the lesson. When completed in columns, it can be read both down and across the columns to check for coherence. For example, by reading down the "organization" column, if the first activity has the students working in pairs, followed by an activity working in groups of three, followed by an activity where students work alone, time is wasted as students moved between the groupings. Seeing this, the physical educator can re-think the organizational formats, and try to reduce the amount of transitioning. Reading across the columns, from left to right, can ensure that the movement activity and the teaching points align. The organizational format will remind the physical educator of how students will be arranged for the activity.

Figures 4.7, 4.8, and 4.9, provide examples of completed lesson plans using the format outlined in **Figure 4.6**. Elementary, middle, and high school examples are provided. **Figure 4.7** is an example of an elementary gymnastics lesson, **Figure 4.8** is an example of a grade seven invasion games lesson, and **Figure 4.9** is an example of a grade nine volleyball lesson.

Notice that the lesson is not scripted. For example, in the first practice task in the grade nine volleyball lesson **(Figure 4.9)**, it does **not** state:

> Bring students in and tell them to form groups of three. Once groups have been formed, use one group to demonstrate how you want students to organize themselves on the court and then begin a demonstration of what you want students to do. Say to the students, "Spread out in a line with the first group member (A) lining up near the baseline facing the net, the second group member (B) will be in the middle of the court facing the sideline, and the third group member (C), will

be near the net, facing player A." Consider taking the place of student B or having a student with good underhand passing skills perform the demonstration for you. Tell students that: A will toss the ball to B who will sideways underhand pass to C. C will catch the ball and toss it back to B who will again, sideways underhand pass the ball to A. Tell students they will switch roles after a few tries in each position. Demonstrate the body position and action for the sideways pass (get under the ball, bend knees, drop shoulder closest to the target, and underhand pass in the direction you want the ball to go).

When lessons are scripted, they become incredibly lengthy and difficult to follow. When lesson plans are created using the methods discussed here, the physical educator's exact words and the finger points of demonstrations and activities will be thought out during the planning process. It is likely that in early planning stages, educators will include more detail than is provided in the examples. However, as experience is gained teaching a variety of content, lesson plans will become less detailed and easier to construct. Remember to include sufficient detail to recall the initial intentions of the activity. The examples provided are simply that—examples. They are each one of several formats available for planning lessons. Even within the formats provided, physical educators should feel free to experiment and make changes.

Conclusion

The ideas presented in this chapter are not meant to be seen as the one and only way to plan. Rather they are intended to provide ideas or possibilities for planning. The planning process can be highly individualized and will become more and more individualized as experience is gained. However, in the early years of a teaching career, it is helpful to have a guide intended to provoke thought about key planning ideas.

Even the best thought out plans can go awry, but if educators think through what it is they want students to learn, how they plan to measure that learning, and how they intend to ensure students attain the objectives, then they're much more likely to teach what was intended and more likely to be able to modify when necessary, and meet the needs of the students.

Readers are encouraged to check out the various documents made available by provincial ministries of education across the country (see **Table 4.16** on page 76).

Questions for Reflection

1 The exit outcome of a quality PE program is that students will be physically literate. A formal definition of "physically literate" has been provided by PHE Canada. Thinking about the program you see yourself planning and delivering to your students, describe the characteristics you would like your students to demonstrate after having participated in your program. How will you know if you are successful (what evidence will demonstrate the degree of your success) in reaching your intended goals?

2 As discussed in the chapter, there are a number of considerations that must be taken into account during the planning process. List the specific factors that you feel are more or less important to consider. On what basis did you make your decision?

3 Examine the curriculum document that you will be expected to use. Is there a clear structure for how content is to be organized and delivered to students? Compare this structure to that of another province or territory. Identify the similarities and differences between the documents. Are some more appealing to you than others?

4 As discussed in the chapter, there are various options for scheduling units of instruction (solid block, modified solid block, and multiple block). What do you see as the potential advantages/disadvantages to each option? Do you think that one option is more appropriate for a specific level (elementary, middle/junior high, or high school)? Do you think one option is better suited to particular content areas?

5 When time is an issue and you cannot possibly meet all the outcomes in the curriculum document, you need to make decisions about what outcomes you will concentrate on. Looking at the outcomes in your particular provincial curriculum document, prioritize the outcomes from most important to least important. On what basis did you make your decisions? Compare your rankings with those of a peer. Are there differences? Can you both defend your rankings?

6 In an attempt to maintain "balance" in terms of content to be included in a program of study (games, dance, gymnastics, for example) and time devoted to outcomes (cognitive/knowing, motor/doing, and affective/valuing), some provincial curricula provide guidelines to this effect. Examine the curriculum document for your particular province/territory to see if such guidelines exist. If guidelines do not exist, how will you balance the time you devote to each learning domain and how much time do you think should be devoted to different movement categories?

Key Terms

- Instructional Process
- Planning
- Teaching
- Assessment
- Assessment Plans
- Learning Outcomes

Table 4.1: Characteristics of Early Elementary Students (Grades K–2) Developmental Level 1 (Approximately ages 5–7, Grades K–2)*

Characteristics and Interests	Program Guidelines
Psychomotor Domain	
Noisy, constantly active, egocentric, exhibitionistic. Imitative and imaginative. Want attention.	Include vigorous games and stunts, games with individual roles (hunting, dramatic activities, story plays), and a few games or relays.
Large muscles more developed; game skills not developed.	Challenge with varied movement. Develop specialized skills of throwing, catching, and bouncing balls
Naturally rhythmic.	Use music and rhythm with skills. Provide creative rhythms, folk dance, and singing movement songs.
May become suddenly tired but soon recover.	Use activities of brief duration. Provide short rest periods or intersperse physically demanding activities with less vigorous ones.
Hand-eye coordination developing.	Give opportunity to handles different objects, such as balls, beanbags, and hoops.
Perceptual abilities maturing.	Give practice in balance—unilateral, bilateral, and cross-lateral movements.
Pelvic tilt can be pronounced.	Give attention to posture problems. Provide abdominal strengthening activities.
Cognitive Domain	
Short attention span.	Change activity often. Give short explanations.
Interested in what the body can do. Curious.	Provide movement experiences. Pay attention to educational movement.
Want to know. Often ask why about movement.	Explain reasons for various activities and the basis of movement.
Express individual views and ideas.	Allow children time to be creative. Expect problems when children are lined up and asked to perform the same task.
Begin to understand the ideas of teamwork.	Plan situations that require group cooperation. Discuss the importance of such.
Sense of humour expands.	Insert some humour in the teaching process.
Highly creative.	Allow students to try new ways of performing activities; sharing ideas with friends encourages creativity.
Affective Domain	
No gender differences in interests.	Set up same activities for boys and girls
Sensitive and individualistic; self-concept very important.	Teach taking turns, sharing, and learning to win, lose, or be caught gracefully.
Accept defeat poorly. Like small-group activity.	Use entire class group sparingly. Break into smaller groups.
Sensitive to feelings of adults. Like to please educator.	Give frequent praise and encouragement.
Can be reckless.	Stress and tumbling
Enjoy rough-and-tumble activity.	Include rolling, dropping to the floor, and so on, in both introductory and program activities. Stress simple stunts and tumbling.
Seek personal attention.	Recognize individuals through both verbal and non-verbal means. See that all have a change to be the centre of attention.
Love to climb and explore play environments.	Provide play materials, games, and apparatus for strengthening large muscles (e.g., climbing towers, climbing ropes, jump ropes, miniature Challenge Courses, and turning bars).

*(taken from Government of British Columbia, Ministry of Education. (2006). *Physical education K to 7: Integrated resource package*. pp. 28–29). Table reproduced from Pangrazi & Gibbons. (2003). *Dynamic Physical Education for Elementary School Children, Canadian Edition*. Pearson Education Canada. Reproduced with permission by Pearson Canada.

Table 4.2: Characteristics of Upper Elementary Students, Grades 4–6

Student Development and Program Implications
Program design and delivery must take into account the physical, cognitive, and emotional development of students. The following descriptions of the developmental characteristics of students in the junior grades are general in nature, and individual student characteristics will vary depending on the child's age, sex, body size, experience, and background.

Physical Domain
Students in the junior grades tend to have significant individual differences, reflecting different growth rates and different life experiences. Some may have begun a major growth spurt. Gender-related differences in development are also evident. As they approach puberty, the average weights and heights of the girls will generally be greater than those of the boys. Some students may begin to develop secondary sex characteristics, and some may feel awkward performing skills as they get used to changes in their bodies. As a result, there is a significant need for differentiated instruction and assessment in these grades. Students in these grades also have more developed locomotor and fine motor skills than students in the primary grades and are developing a greater ability to combine motor skills in sequence. Their bodies are less flexible than those of the younger students, however, unless they work directly on maintaining flexibility.

Programs for these students should provide opportunities to participate in a wide range of activities and should avoid concentrating on only one type of activity, as this can lead to overuse injuries. Providing a wide range of activities also exposes students to new ideas and experiences that may further encourage their commitment to an active and healthy lifestyle. Individual and small-group lead-up activities give all students opportunities to be engaged in their learning. Because of the range of differences in individual development, students will benefit from having a choice of activities or being able to modify activities to suit their varied needs. |

| Taken from: Government of Ontario, Ministry of Education and Training. (2010). *The Ontario curriculum: Grades 1–8: Health and physical education (revised)* (pp. 113–114). Toronto: Ontario Ministry of Education. |

Table 4.3: Characteristics and Needs of Young Adolescent Students (Grades 7–9)

Emotional Characteristics	Physical Educational Implications
Students ■ may be emotional and unpredictable ■ may be extremely sensitive and easily offended ■ may be overly self-critical and hard on themselves ■ have a growing sense of fairness	Students ■ need opportunities to release emotional stress and for discussing their issues and concerns ■ need sensitive adults who are interested in their well-being and development ■ need opportunities for self-exploration and self-definition, and multiple opportunities to experience success ■ need to be treated fairly and consistently
Intellectual Characteristics	**Physical Educational Implications**
Students ■ vary significantly in their intellectual development—some students are learning to think abstractly, many are still in the stage of concrete operations ■ have increasing ability to process and relate information ■ are broadening their interest in the larger world ■ can be disorganized and preoccupied	Students ■ need opportunities to develop their thinking skills ■ need opportunities to question and analyze ■ need exposure to diverse learning opportunities and environments ■ may need help in structuring and organizing activities
Physical Characteristics	**Physical Educational Implications**
Students ■ are experiencing rapid and uneven growth rates ■ may have an abundance of energy and low tolerance for fatigue ■ may be clumsy and awkward in appearance and performance or perceive themselves that way ■ may worry incessantly about appearance ■ are experiencing the onset of puberty and sexual feelings	Students ■ need frequent opportunities for movement, rest, and change ■ respond well to an activity-oriented approach to learning ■ avoid sitting for long periods of time ■ require daily physical activity ■ need information about and opportunities to discuss diet and nutrition, personal hygiene, and physical changes
Social Characteristics	**Physical Educational Implications**
Students ■ are searching for greater autonomy and independence ■ are focusing on friendship and social acceptance by peers ■ are influenced by peer pressure ■ have a growing interest in the larger world ■ are developing a sense of identity ■ are developing personal and social values	Students ■ need choice and increased opportunities for decision making ■ need frequent opportunities to work with peers in small group learning activities ■ need to be exposed to a diversity of cultures ■ need positive role models ■ need to explore ways of dealing with various social situations

Taken from Government of Nova Scotia, Department of Education. (1999). *Physical education curriculum: Grades 7–9* (pp. 12–13). English Language Services, Program Planning.

Table 4.4: An Example of Different Levels of Program Outcomes.

Overall Program Exit Outcome for the "IN MOVEMENT" category:
"Perform efficient, creative, and expressive movement patterns consistent with an active living lifestyle"

Key Stage Level Outcomes (Grades 3, 6, 9, and 12)*

Grade Three	Grade Six	Grade Nine	Grade Twelve
By the end of grade three students will be expected to: 1. Demonstrate a variety of locomotor movements. 2. Demonstrate a variety of non-locomotor movements 3. Demonstrate a variety of manipulative movements. 4. Demonstrate a variety of creative movements. 5. Perform simple movement sequences alone and with other. 6. Explore a variety of individual and group activities. 7. Participate in a variety of warm-up and cool-down activities. 8. Participate in activities in a variety of alternative environments. 9. Demonstrate body and spatial awareness as it relates to movement.	By the end of grade six students will be expected to: 1. Demonstrate a variety of locomotor movements. 2. Demonstrate a variety of non-locomotor movements 3. Demonstrate a variety of manipulative movements. 4. Demonstrate a variety of creative movements. 5. Create and perform a variety of movement sequences. 6. Apply basic motor skills to individual, dual, and group activities. 7. Use appropriate warm-up and cool-down activities. 8. Participate in activities in a variety of alternative environments. 9. Demonstrate body and spatial awareness during activities.	By the end of grade nine students will be expected to: 1. Use appropriate body mechanics in a wide variety of movement activities. 2. Apply principles of body mechanics to improve movement in all activity dimensions. 3. Participate in a variety of activities combining movement and music. 4. Participate in movement activities from a variety of cultures. 5. Participate in a variety of cooperative and competitive group activities. 6. Demonstrate cooperative and competitive strategies in a variety of group activities. 7. Demonstrate appropriate warm-up, work-out, and cool-down activities. 8. Apply movement skills and concepts to a variety of activities in alternative environments. 9. Participate in a variety of personal fitness activities.	By the end of grade twelve students will be expected to: 1. Refine body mechanics in a wide variety of movement activities. 2. Apply principles of body mechanics to improve movement in all activity dimensions. 3. Participate in personally developed activity programs. 4. Participate in student-led activity programs. 5. Participate in a variety of personally developed fitness activities. 6. Use appropriate strategies in game situations. 7. Demonstrate a commitment to personal wellness. 8. Refine movement skills and concepts in a variety of alternative environments.

In addition to the Key-Stage Curriculum Outcomes listed above, there are Specific Curriculum Outcomes for each grade level. These grade level outcomes contribute to the attainment of the Key-Stage Curricular Outcomes. The grade level Specific Curricular Outcomes are organized in themes.

Grade two example:*
From the "IN MOVEMENT" category of the Games—Space, Directions, and Body Awareness theme, the following grade specific outcome is listed:
1. Identify, maintain, and use space adequately.

A number of grade-level Specific Curricular Outcomes are listed for each of the "IN MOVEMENT," "ABOUT MOVEMENT," and "THROUGH MOVEMENT," categories for a variety of themes.

Taken from: Government of Newfoundland and Labrador, Department of Education. (1996). *A curriculum framework for physical education: Adjusting the focus*. Division of Program Development.
* Taken from: Government of Newfoundland and Labrador, Department of Education. (nd). *Physical education, Primary and elementary, Curriculum Guide*. Division of Program Development.

Table 4.5: Content Arranged by Movement Categories

Movement Categories
A physically educated person participates in a balanced physical education program that shall consist of activities selected from all movement categories.

Aquatics	Rhythmics	Simple Games	Educational themes	Athletics (Track & Field)

■ Survival techniques
■ Stroke development
■ Skills application
  -Snorkelling
  -Water games
  -Diving
  -Synchronized swimming
  -Underwater games
  -etc.
 	
Land-based
■ Hiking
■ Backpacking
■ Rock climbing
■ Camping
■ Orienteering
■ Snowshoeing
■ Skiing
■ Snowboarding
■ Skating
■ Horseback riding
■ etc.
 	
Water-based
■ Rowing
■ Canoeing
■ Kayaking
■ Sailing
■ Sailboarding
■ etc.
	■ Singing games
	■ With/without equipment
	■ Aerobic dance
	■ etc.
	
	Creative
	■ Interpretive
	■ Modern
	■ etc.
	
	Cultural
	■ Folk
	■ Square
	■ etc.
	
	Contemporary
	■ Line
	■ Jive
	■ Partner
	■ etc.
	
	Jazz
	■ Traditional
	■ Hip hop
	■ Funk
	■ etc.
	
	Ballroom
	■ Waltz
	■ Fox-trot
	■ Tango
	■ Latin-style
	■ etc.
		■ Schoolyard/backyard
		■ Chasing
		■ Throwing
		■ Kicking
		■ etc.
		
		Innovative
		■ Creative/novel
		■ Initiative tasks
		■ Cooperative challenges
		■ Parachute activities
		■ etc.
		
		Bat and Ball
		■ Softball
		■ Cricket/rounders
		■ T-ball
		■ etc.
		
		Territorial
		■ Soccer
		■ Basketball
		■ Touch football
		■ Hockey (field, floor, ice)
		■ Team handball
		■ Rugby (non-contact)
		■ etc.
		
		Net/Wall
		■ Volleyball
		■ Tennis
		■ Badminton
		■ Pickleball
		■ Table Tennis
		■ Handball
		■ etc.
		
		Target
		■ Archery
		■ Boccie
		■ Bowling
		■ Golf
		■ etc.
			■ Shape
			■ Balance
			■ Weight transfer
			■ Travel
			■ Flight
			■ Take off and land
			■ etc.
			
			Rhythmic
			■ Hoop
			■ Ball
			■ Ribbon
			■ Clubs
			■ Scarf
			■ Rope
			■ etc.
			
			Acrobatic
			■ Tumbling
			■ Pyramids
			■ Artistic
			■ Floor exercises
			■ Uneven bars
			■ Parallel bars
			■ High bar
			■ Vault box
			■ Pommel horse
			■ Rings
			■ Balance beam
			■ etc.
				■ Runs
				■ Jumps
				■ Throws
				■ Combative
				■ Martial Arts
				■ Self-defence
				■ Wrestling
				■ Fencing
				■ etc.
				
				Individual manipulatives
				■ Juggling
				■ Skipping
				■ Hacky sack
				■ etc.
				
				Training programs
				■ Aerobics
				■ Rope jumping
				■ Walking
				■ Jogging
				■ Lap swimming
				■ Cycling
				■ Use of exercise equipment
				■ Weight training
				■ etc.

| Taken from Government of Nova Scotia, Department of Education. (1999). *Physical education curriculum: Grades 7–9* (pp. 12–13). English Language Services, Program Planning. | |

Table 4.6: A Sample Block Plan Including Curriculum Outcomes for the First Term of a Grade 6 Program.

Term 1	Activity	Curricular Outcome (these outcomes are from the NB Middle Level Physical Education Curriculum, grades 6–8)
Week 1	Intro./L.O.G	D1: select, combine, and refine locomotor and non-locomotor skills into movement alone and with others D6: demonstrate sport specific skills through cooperative modified games that involve everyone K4: follow rules, routine, and procedures of safety in a variety of activities and facilities V4: demonstrate a willingness to participate in a variety of activities
Week 2	Indoor Soccer	D7: consistently and confidently demonstrate offensive and defensive positions and strategies K7: identify strategies and concepts related to offensive and defensive positions/ strategies V5: demonstrate fair play and etiquette
Week 3	Indoor Soccer	As above
Week 4	Golf	D5: demonstrate ways to receive, retain, and send an object with increasing accuracy using an implement K5: identify basic concepts in relation to body mechanics and skill analysis V3: demonstrate self-confidence while participating in physical activity
Week 5	Orienteering	D9: demonstrate activity specific motor skills in a variety of alternative environments V3: demonstrate self-confidence while participating in physical activity
Week 6	Fitness	D8: demonstrate ways to achieve a personal functional level of physical fitness through participation in physical activity K1: set and modify goals to develop personal fitness to maintain a healthy lifestyle V1: explain the enjoyment gained from being physically active
Week 7	Tchouchball	D4: demonstrate ways to receive, retain, and send an object with increasing accuracy individually and with others K7: identify strategies and concepts related to offensive and defensive positions/ strategies V2: demonstrate fair plan and etiquette
Week 8	Kin Ball	D4: demonstrate ways to receive, retain, and send an object with increasing accuracy individually and with others K7: identify strategies and concepts related to offensive and defensive positions/ strategies V4: demonstrate a willingness to participate in a variety of activities
Week 9	Badminton	D7: consistently and confidently demonstrate offensive and defensive positions and strategies K6: demonstrate an ability to set goals to improve performance V5: identify and accept responsibility for various roles while participating in physical activity
Week 10	Badminton	As above
Week 11	Fitness	Same as Week 6

Table 4.7: Initial Unit Plan Considerations

Consideration/Item	Description
Outcomes and Objectives	The curriculum outcomes the unit is designed to address and the objectives that are meant to contribute to reaching the outcomes.
History	This is a brief history of important or interesting facts about the activity. The purpose of this piece of information is to provide students with a little bit of background knowledge in order to generate interest in the activity.
Terms or Definitions	This entry in the unit plan would include a list of any new or interesting terms or definitions the educator may want to introduce to the students or has just come across themselves that they may need to remember.
Time	How much time do you have for this unit? This includes both the total number of days the unit will cover and how long each lesson will last.
Space	What facilities do you have? (gymnasium, outdoor field, paved lot)
Students	How many students will be in each class? Are there students with disabilities and if so, what are these disabilities and what accommodations are required? Are the students at a typical developmental stage? What is their previous experience with the content? Are you going to conduct any pre-testing of their abilities and if so, how will this be done and how long will it take?
Equipment	What types of equipment are available, how much equipment is available, and in what condition is the equipment? Can I borrow from a neighbouring school or local club if I need more?
Safety and Management	In addition to the daily class organizational and managerial procedures that you have in place, are there any additional safety or managerial concerns that must be considered for the unit under development? For example, class routines, equipment distribution, or transitions to alternative spaces. Are they any special instructions in the provincial safety documents that must be considered?
Modifications or Adaptations	Think about the various ways content can be modified for students with special needs, students who may struggle with the content, or students who may have already mastered the content. For example, the educator can vary the equipment, the space, the objectives, the game rules, etc.

Table 4.8: Original Taxonomy of Educational Objectives

Domains of Learning		
Motor	**Cognitive**	**Affective**

1. Generic Movement
  1a. Perceiving
  1b. Patterning
	1. Knowledge	1. Receiving phenomenon

2. Ordinative Movement
  2a. Adapting or Accommodating
  2b. Refining
	2. Comprehension	2. Responding

3. Creative Movement
  3a. Varying
  3b. Improvising
  3c. Composing
	3. Application	3. Valuing

	4. Analysis	4. Organization
	5. Synthesis	5. Internalizing values/ Characterization
	6. Evaluation	

Table 4.9: Comparison of the Original and Revised Cognitive Domain

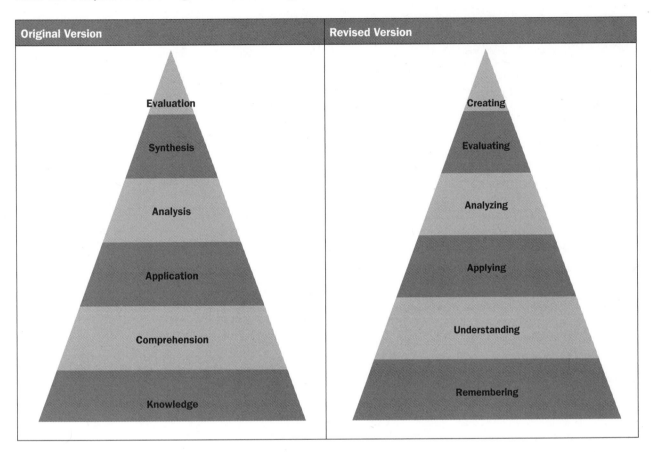

Table 4.10: Examples of Verbs Within Each Level of Behaviour for the Psychomotor Domain

Domains of Learning	
1. Generic Movement	
1a. Perceiving	Identify, recognize, discover, discriminate, imitate, replicate, duplicate, pantomime
1b. Patterning	Perform (shoot), demonstrate (pass), execute (swim), coordinate (jump)
2. Ordinative Movement	
2a. Adapting or Accommodating	Adjust, alter, apply, employ, utilize
2b. Refining	Control, synchronize, improve, synthesize, regulate, perform rhythmically (smoothly, efficiently), integrate, coordinate
3. Creative movement	
3a. Varying	Alter, change, revise, diversify
3b. Improvising	Interpret, extemporize, improvise, anticipate, discover
3c. Composing	Design, compose, symbolize, create, plan

Buck, M. M., Lund, J. L., Harrison, J. M., & Blakemore Cook, C. (2007). *Instructional strategies for secondary school physical education* (6th ed.). New York, NY: McGraw Hill.

Table 4.11: Examples of Verbs Within Each Level of Behaviour for the Cognitive Domain

Levels of Behaviour	Sample of verbs for writing objectives
1. Remembering	Define, match, spell, recite, who, what, where, when, why
2. Understanding	Translate, paraphrase, tell in your own words, summarize, compare or contrast, predict
3. Applying	Solve, apply
4. Analyzing	Analyze, examine, break down, delineate, determine, identify
5. Evaluating	Judge, evaluate, defend
6. Creating	Compose, write, design, invent, hypothesize, plan, create, produce, organize

Taken from: Buck, M. M., Lund, J. L., Harrison, J. M., & Blakemore Cook, C. (2007). *Instructional strategies for secondary school physical education* (6th ed.). New York: McGraw Hill. Changes have been made to the original to reflect the revised taxonomy.

Table 4.12: Examples of Verbs Within Each Level of Behaviour for the Affective Domain

Levels of Behaviour	Sample of verbs for writing objectives
1. Receiving phenomenon	Notice, select, tolerate, be aware or conscious of, listen
2. Responding	Comply, follow, volunteer, enjoy, be satisfied, agree or disagree, react, give opinion, sympathize with, demonstrate appreciation for, attend, read, accept responsibility
3. Valuing	Prefer consistently, support consistently, pursue activities, involve others, debate, argue, value, purchase, improve skills
4. Organization	Discuss codes/standards, formulate systems, weigh alternatives against standards, define criteria, base decisions on values
5. Internalizing values/Characterization	Demonstrate consistent behaviour or methods, integrate total behaviour or values

Taken from: Buck, M. M., Lund, J. L., Harrison, J. M., & Blakemore Cook, C. (2007). *Instructional strategies for secondary school physical education* (6th ed.). New York, NY: McGraw Hill.

Table 4.13: Examples of Objectives Written With Varying Levels of Specificity

	Explicit	Middle Ground	Too broad
Motor	Students will work with a partner to create and refine a movement sequence that includes: two stable balances, each held for five seconds (one balance will demonstrate the concept of counterbalance and the other will demonstrate the concept of counter tension); one balance will be symmetrical, the other will be asymmetrical; use the feet as a base of support in only one of the balances; and the sequence must contain a clear beginning and end.	Students will work with a partner to create a sequence of five movements, two of which include balances that demonstrate both counter tension and counterbalance.	Students will explore counterbalance and counter tension.
Cognitive	Through a pencil and paper test, students will be able to consistently (8/10) identify pictures as examples of counterbalance or counter tension.	Students will be able to verbally describe or physically demonstrate/identify examples of balances that demonstrate the concepts of counterbalance and counter tension.	Students will know and understand the difference between counterbalance and counter tension.
Affective	Students will demonstrate they value educational gymnastics by willingly participating in all activities without prompting, working respectfully with their partner, remaining on task throughout the entire class, and continuously exploring and modifying their movements in an effort to refine their performance.	Students will demonstrate they value educational gymnastics by willfully participating in all class activities.	Students will gain an appreciation of, and value, educational gymnastics.

Table 4.14: Example Grade 2 Educational Gymnastics Block Plan

Unit: Educational Gymnastics—focus on step-like actions, balancing, and rolling		
Day 1 Step-like actions: ■ emphasize use of different body parts, not just the feet ■ explore levels ■ explore directions	Day 2 Using step-like actions to: ■ move onto and off of benches/boxes ■ explore different directions while moving onto and off the small apparatus	Day 3 Rolling: ■ various rolls (logs, shoulder, front, and back) ■ change of direction when rolling ■ begin rolling from various levels (squat, knees, standing)
Day 4 Balances: ■ 4 point, 3 point, 2 point, 1 point ■ at various levels ■ combined with rolling (roll and immediately move into a balance and vise versa)	Day 5 Rolling, balancing, and step-like actions: ■ exploring various combinations of rolling, balancing, and step-like actions ■ step-like actions and balancing with the use of small equipment (benches and boxes)	Day 6 Rolling, balancing, and step-like actions: ■ working in small groups, exploring various combinations of rolling, step-like actions, and balancing both on and off the equipment (small boxes and benches) demonstrating changes in levels and directions

Figure 4.1: Sample Elementary Lesson Plan from Education Alberta

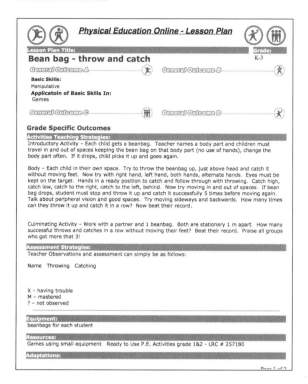

Figure 4.2a: Sample Grade Nine Lesson Plan from Saskatchewan Education—page 1

Sample Grade 9 Physical Education Lesson Plan – Early December

Lesson Focus: Health-related Fitness, Core Strength, Skill-related Fitness, Complex Skills

Opening:
What will students need to know and do? (Outcomes and Indicators):

| Outcome 9.1 (Health-related Fitness) | • Self-identify, and incorporate into action plans, movement activities of personal preference that support increased fitness and enjoyment. |
| Outcome 9.3 (Core Strength) | • Incorporate useful equipment and technology (e.g., stability balls, medicine balls, wobble boards, free weights, professionally led exercises on DVDs) into regular exercise routines that focus on the development of core strength. |

Initiating   Extending   Applying/Challenging

Learning Experience
Students will take responsibility for warm-up activities that students have self-identified previously in their personal improvement plans.

Body:
What will students need to know and do? (Outcomes and Indicators):

| Outcome 9.5 (Complex Skills) | • View and provide meaningful feedback on skill performance, of self and others, that could be a focus for improvement.
• Use feedback from classmates, teacher, and self-assessment strategies (e.g., video, checklists) to determine strengths and weaknesses in performance of self-selected complex skills. |

Initiating   Extending   Applying/Challenging

Learning Experience
Students will be videotaped by classmates (or viewed by classmates) as students perform a skill of choice used in a net/wall game. Each student will self-assess strengths and weaknesses in performance using a pre-created checklist of performance cues (or listen to the feedback from classmates). This feedback will be based on pre-established criteria that include the performance cues for skilful performance. Students will have created this criteria checklist alone or with classmates who want to focus on the same skill. This will provide information to each student from which to build their plan for improvement.

Closure:
What will students need to know and do? (Outcomes and Indicators):

| Outcome 9.4 (Skill-related Fitness) | • Research training techniques that focus on a self-selected skill-related component of fitness. |
| Outcome 9.5 (Complex Skills) | • Apply principles of practice (e.g., whole-part-whole, part-whole) to a self-created or pre-designed plan to improve performance in self-selected complex skills.
• Identify both the health-related components of fitness and the skill-related components of fitness that are the significant influences on the performance of particular complex skills.
• Willingly engage in opportunities for improvement by initiating and taking responsibility for learning how to support own skillful movement. |

Initiating   Extending   Applying/Challenging

Figure 4.2b: Sample Grade Nine Lesson Plan from Saskatchewan Education—page 2

Sample Grade 9 Physical Education Lesson Plan – Early December

Lesson Focus: Health-related Fitness, Core Strength, Skill-related Fitness, Complex Skills

Learning Experience
Through a brainstorming process, students will identify various considerations and sources of information to assist in making a plan to improve the complex skill of choice. The teacher will compile the students' thoughts into a handout that will be the starting point for review and reflection at the beginning of the next class. Students will be expected to bring to the next class, in writing, the title of a written resource or a website address of a source of information that will support them in making their personal plans for improvement (and that could support others).

Assessment and Evaluation (How will I know that students know and can do this part of the process towards achieving the outcome?):
• Each student submits a 'source of information' in writing.
• Students actively engage in working with peers to assess and provide feedback on skill performance.

If students do not know or cannot do this, what will I do?

Figure 4.3: A Sample Lesson Plan Outline Provided by the Department of Education of Newfoundland and Labrador

Sample Physical Education Lesson Plan Template

Class: _____   Lesson/Unit: _____

Date: _____

Specific Outcome (#)	Moving/Doing (YES/NO)	Understanding/ Applying (YES/NO)	Cooperation/ Responsibility (YES/NO)

Introduction/Warm-up (Describe):

Teaching Tips:

Elaborations - Strategies for Learning and Teaching:

Suggested Assessment Strategies:

Closure/Cool Down:

Equipment Required:

Figure 4.4: A Sample Lesson Plan Outline Provided by the New Brunswick Department of Education

APPENDIX C

SUGGESTED LESSON PLAN FORMAT

CLASS: _____   DATE: _____

OBJECTIVE

EQUIPMENT REQUIRED

1. ENTRY ACTIVITY

Having something active to do upon entry into the gym/field or other area encourages students to change quickly and allows immediate activity. This can be a previously learned activity, a warm-up or a review of the previous class.

2. SKILL DEVELOPMENT AND PRACTICE

This would be the core part of the lesson. New learning and practice of newly acquired skills take place during this phase.

3. CULMINATING ACTIVITY

This could be a game, a modified game, a dance or a demonstration of a sequence, for example. It would normally include skills developed in part 2, above, but if the skills are not adequately developed an "old" game, dance, sequence etc. can be used.

4. CLOSURE

Cooling-down, stretching, relaxing and calming activities bring the lesson to an end.

Figure 4.5a: Lesson Plan Template Used by Pre-Service Physical Educators at Brock University—page 1

Figure 4.5: Lesson Plan Template Used by Pre-service Physical Educators at Brock University

Department of Teacher Education
Lesson Plan Template

Subject/Course_____ Lesson _____
Topic_____
Teacher Candidate_____ Lesson Duration _____min
Date_____

1. Curriculum Expectations

Overall:

Specific:

Integrated (if applicable):

2. Lesson Learning Goal(s) Key Question: What do I want students to know and be able to do?

Knowledge and Understanding / Thinking / Communication / Application

3. Assessment Key Question: How will I know each student has learned the concept(s)?

a) Indicator(s) of Lesson Learning Goals:

b) Assessment Strategies and Tools: (Key Question: What will students be doing and what will I use to assess learning?)

4. Differentiated Instruction Key Question: What will I do to assist individual learners or provide enrichment for others?

Accommodation and/or modification:	Extension:

Subject/Course_____ Topic_____
Date_____

Required teacher preparation/materials needed:

Figure 4.5b: Lesson Plan Template Used by Pre-Service Physical Educators at Brock University—page 2

Instructional Plan

Time	Setting the Stage:	Differentiated Instruction	Assessment Opportunities
	Core Learning Activity:		
	Lesson Consolidation/Debriefing with Students:		
Apply new learning: In class / At home			

Post Lesson Reflection

Follow-up/next steps (lesson content/assessment):

Follow-up with particular students (learning and/or behavior):

Opportunities for professional growth:

Figure 4.6a: Sample Lesson Plan Format with Explanations—Page 1

Figure 4.6: Sample Lesson Plan Format with Explanations.

Lesson Plan

Skill Theme: ______________________ *What is being taught?*
Lesson ____ of ___ *Indicate what lesson in the unit this is. It will help keep you on track and remind you where you are in the unit and how much time remains in case adjustments need to be made.*
Grade: ______ *Indicate the grade level the lesson was designed for.*

Note: the material above can also replace the 'Lesson Plan' title above.

Class Length: _________ *How long the lesson is designed for.*
# of students: _________ *Number of students the lesson was designed for.*

Equipment Needed:

In this section, list all the materials required for the lesson. Having this information available up front allows the physical educator to see exactly what needs to be available prior to beginning the lesson so they are not running out of the gymnasium or back to the office because they forgot something. Remember, if you posters or charts for station teaching are being used, don't forget to list 'tape' as part of the required materials. When teaching dance and using an iPod to play the music, don't forget to list the necessary attachment cables required for the sound system or the remote.

Objectives:

This space is used to list the specific lesson objectives that have developed for the lesson. There should be at least one affective and cognitive objective as well as a motor objective.
Some districts/schools also require you to list the curricular objectives as well.

Evaluation:

This can be formal or informal. If formal, include the assessment as an attachment to the lesson plan. If informal, how will you know your objectives have been met? What are you looking for; what level of performance will students be expected to exhibit? Some pre-service physical educators find it easier to list the evaluation techniques for the lesson immediately under the objectives. For some, this helps them ensure these to pedagogical elements are aligned.

Entry Activity:

This is not required, but can be useful. The entry activity is the activity that students do immediately upon entering the gymnasium/field, etc. At the elementary level, many physical educators have their students run, skip, hop, or gallop, in various directions and pathways two or three times around the area. This is a good transition activity from the classroom where students are often sitting to the gymnasium where they are expected to move. Some physical educators have a routine where students enter and immediately proceed into a squad or into their personal space. At the middle and high school level where students are expected to change for class, this often leaves students entering the gymnasium at different rates. Rather than having students stand or sit around, many physical educators make equipment available for students to free play with prior to class beginning. Free play with the equipment sometimes motivates students to get dressed and into the gymnasium quickly.

This is a relatively short activity, generally not lasting more than 3-5 minutes and is often used as a transition from the period before to physical education.

Movement Experience	Organization	Teaching Points

Notice the three headings are spread out across the width of the page. The rest of the lesson plan written in columns with 'movement experience', 'organization' and 'teaching points' as the column headers.
Written in the movement experience column are the actual activities students will participate in or demonstrations/explanations the physical educator will provide. In the organization column, the physical educator draws or explains the organizational format the activity requires, for example, in partners, across the width of the gymnasium; scattered in personal space, groups of 4, etc. The teaching cues or points the physical educator is looking for and has asked the students to focus on during practice, are listed in the teaching points column. If a demonstration and explanation has been provided, the physical educator would have selected two or three points to focus students' attention on. These are the points that the physical educator should be looking for during student practice and should be the points that the physical educator provides feedback on. That is, demonstrate it, look for it, and provide feedback on it.

1. Introductory Activity/Warm Up
This activity, as its title implies, is meant to introduce the lesson and/or provide students with a warm-up to the day's lesson. The warm-up can be lesson specific, for example exploring a variety of step-like actions for an elementary educational gymnastics lesson, or completing a volleyball fitness blast at the beginning a middle/high school volleyball lesson. It is not uncommon to use a variety of low organized games as warm-up activities. Depending on the length and objectives of the

Figure 4.6b: Sample Lesson Plan Format with Explanations—Page 2

2. Review
This part of the lesson is used to review material that was covered the previous class. For those physical educators who want to pre-assess students, this is a good time to conduct that assessment. Depending on the content covered the previous class, the physical educator may want to use the review as the warm-up. For example, if during a dance unit, the previous class ended with a newly learned dance, the physical educator may want to begin the day's class with a review of last classes dance. In this way, the review and the warm-up are the same.
Remember that students' abilities are variable, especially when learning new content, meaning that skills they appeared to grasp the previous lesson may be lacking the following class. If this is the case, then students might need a little longer to return to previous performance levels, thus the review may last a little longer than originally anticipated. Generally, the review lasts 5-10 minutes.

3. Skill Development
This is the part of the lesson where new skills are learned and practice occurs. Thus, this part of the lesson should really encompass the majority of the lesson. During this part of the lesson, aim to provide a variety of experiences under varying conditions. It is important to present material in small chunks, to order your content from simple to complex, and to include extending, refining, and application tasks.

4. Skill Application
This part of the lesson is where students have a chance to 'use' the skills they have been learning and practicing during the skill development portion of the lesson in some form of a game-like or self-testing situation. This part of the lesson allows the teacher and students to see how well they can execute the skills previously practiced. It provides information to the student about their abilities and provides the physical educator with important information regarding what their next lesson should focus on. For example, if the students were practicing faking, dodging, and cutting to move into open spaces to receive a pass, but during a 3 V 3 passing game few passes were made and there were little, if any fakes occurring, the physical educator would realize they needed to spend extra time reviewing this during the next lesson.
Depending on the content being taught, the physical educator can easily integrate various skill application activities throughout the skill development section. In doing so, the skill development/skill application blend together. This would not be uncommon during a folk dance unit for example. During a folk dance unit it would not be appropriate to teach and practice all the steps individually and then expect students to put them all together and dance to the music at the end of the lesson. It is much more realistic that the physical educator would introduce a step or two, dance the steps to the music; introduce another step or two and practice the steps with and without the music, then combine the new steps with the previously learned steps and put these to music and continue until all the steps were mastered. In this way, the skill development and skill application are intertwined throughout the lesson.

5. Closure / Review
This part of the lesson provides the physical educator an opportunity to check for understanding and bring closure to the lesson. If the lessons are progressive and are dependent upon each other, this portion of the lesson allows physical educators to make those connections for students or check to see if students understand the progressions.
This section of the lesson generally only lasts a few minutes.

Differentiated Instruction: *Note: this material can also be included directly in the lesson plan.*	
Accommodations and/or modifications: *List the accommodations and/or modifications that could be implemented to assist students who may have difficulty completing the tasks as outlined.*	**Extensions:** *List the possible ways the content could be made more difficult for those who have already mastered the content and are looking for a challenge.*

Figure 4.7a: Sample Elementary Movement Lesson Plan—Page 1

Figure 4.7: Sample Elementary Movement Lesson Plan

Lesson Plan

Skill Theme: Rising and sinking while traveling (combining non-locomotor with locomotor movements)

Lesson: 2 of 6 **Grade:** 1 **Class Length:** 30 min **# of students:** 22

Equipment Needed:
drum

Objectives:
Students will be able to demonstrate controlled rising and sinking actions while traveling a short distance.

Evaluation:
Teacher observation of students; looking for controlled movements (no 'flopping' or 'shooting stars')

Students will work independently in personal and general space while practicing controlled rising and sinking actions.
Evaluation:
Teacher observation.

Students will be able to demonstrate or explain the difference between sinking and flopping and rising and shooting up.
Evaluation:
Teacher will verbally question at the end of the lesson. Students can demonstrate the difference when asked.

Entry Activity: None for this class.

Movement Experience	Organization	Teaching Points
1. Introductory Activity/Warm Up/Review (Total Time: 5 min)		
Move throughout the space; change the way you are travelling every time you hear 'change' (or the drum beat)	Scattered, moving in personal space throughout the activity area	-possible variations: feet apart, feet together, knees high, walking, running, skipping, galloping-- -use all the space
Emphasize/lead with specific body parts when traveling.	As above	-possibilities: knees leading when skipping, elbows leading when sliding -it should be very clear what body parts are being used to lead the movement.
Combine two different locomotor movements; do each for 8 counts (ex., skipping for 8 counts followed by running for 8 counts). -use drum initially to count beats; remove after a few attempts	As above	-count to yourself -try not to stop when changing one loco-motor pattern to the next... looking for smooth transitions.
After some practice, vary the pathway or direction with each change.	As above	
2. Skill Development		
-Sitting down, print various letters over your head using your hands and elbows. (2 min)	Scattered in personal space	-vary the amount of space used– write big letters, small letters.
■ from sitting position, slowly rise up to a standing stretched position; hold the stretch for 3 seconds, then sink back down to the floor. *after a couple of trials, explain/demonstrate the difference between rising with control and shooting up to standing position; and sinking with control and flopping to the ground ■ repeat several times (4 min)		-use your 'dancing hands' from above to pull you up to standing. -'sink' don't 'flop' – control the movements

Figure 4.7b: Sample Elementary Movement Lesson Plan—Page 2

-rise and sink with a focus on control -repeat above activity to a teacher led count of 4 beats on the drum -repeat several times with drum beat -allow students several opportunities to practice without teacher lead counts (4 min)		-listen carefully to the beat of the drum -smooth movements when you rise up and sink back down
Add travelling: -as you rise, travel a short distance and stop in personal space. Sink in personal space. Repeat several times. (3 min)	Students scattered, traveling through general space.	-rise slowly and with control: do not 'shoot up' and travel but rise while traveling. -clear stop before sinking
Reverse the above -from a standing stretched position, travel a few steps as you sink to a low level; stop and rise to a stretched position. -repeat several times (3 min)		-sink under control: do not 'flop to the ground. -clear stop before rising; rising in personal space.
3. Skill Application		
Travel continuously while rising and sinking -consider using the drum to help with control initially if students need help (4 min)		-try not to stop this time...keep moving -maintain control – rise for a count of 4 and sink to a count of 4 while travelling a short distance.
Can you add a turn during your rise and sink pattern? (3 min)		

4. Closure / Review

Q: What two movements were the focus of our class today?
A: Rising and Sinking
Q: What do I mean when I ask you to 'rise with control?'
A: Rise slowly and be in control of the movement; be able to stop whenever you want; do not 'shoot up' like a rocket!
Q: What do I mean when I ask you to 'sink with control?"
A: Do not flop to the ground; move from high to low level being able to stop whenever you want to.
(2 min)

Differentiated Instruction:	
Accommodations and/or modifications: ■ Teacher can provide slowed and exaggerated demonstrations if necessary. ■ Students needed assistance moving through space can follow a classmate or hold hands with a classmate. ■ Provide visuals of letters for students to copy above head. Or, place visual of letter on floor and have students trace the letters on the floor. ■ Assistance can be provided for students needing help rising and sinking (hold students hands) ■ Students start from a crouched position as opposed to being seated on the floor. ■ Student can focus either on the travelling or the rising and sinking – does not have to focus on two movements at once. Can also eliminate the turn. ■ Focus on control as opposed to moving to a count.	Extensions: ■ Add leading with various parts to rising and sinking and travelling movements. ■ Create individual ways to travel that differ from traditional loco-motor patterns.

Figure 4.8a: Sample Middle Level Lesson Plan—Page 1

Figure 4.8b: Sample Middle Level Lesson Plan—Page 2

Figure 4.8: Sample Middle Level Lesson Plan

Grade 7 Invasion Games Lesson Plan
Lesson: 4 of 10

Skill Theme: creating passing lanes	Equipment Needed:
Class Length: 40 minutes **# of students:** 24	■ soccer balls (minimum of 12) ■ 24 floor hockey sticks (one per person) ■ floor hockey balls (minimum of 12) ■ pinnies

Objectives:
By the end of the lesson, students will be able to create passing lanes by moving into open space to receive a pass, and communicate to the passer when they are open.
Evaluation:
■ Teacher observation: looking for the number of times passes are complete/incomplete; how many passes a team can maintain possession and control of the ball.

By the end of the lesson, students will be able to verbally describe how to get open, and why it is important in invasion games.
Evaluation:
■ Teacher questions throughout the lesson and at the end of the lesson.

Throughout the lesson, students will be work cooperatively with classmates to practice the tasks. During game play, students will actively take part, trying to get open and make quick, accurate passes to their teammates. They will pass when a teammate is open.
Evaluation:
■ Teacher observation of student behaviour and participation during practice tasks and game play.

Entry Activity:
As students enter the gymnasium from the locker rooms, the equipment will be available for free play for students to practice previously learned skills. (4 min)

Movement Experience	Organization	Teaching Points
1. Warm Up Activity		
Mirror Drill: Partners, facing each other. Partner A leads and moves forward, backward, sideways, (about 4 – 5 steps). Partner B mirrors Partner A's movements. Switch after a couple of minutes. (5 min)	Spread out in pairs. A1 A2 B2 B2 C1 C2 D1 D2 E1 E2 F1 F2	■ Be aware of your surroundings ■ Ready position and ready to move ■ Follower: try to stay within one step of the leader
2. Review/Introduction		
What tactic did we practice yesterday? ■ Maintaining possession of the ball/keeping control of the ball. How did we do that? ■ Making good passes. How would you describe a 'good pass'? ■ Accurate (the ball gets to the intended target player), timed well (teammate does not have to wait for the ball or sprint to catch it). Today we are going to continue with passing but focus on a new tactic that involves opening up space by creating passing lanes. (4 min)		

Page 2

3. Skill Development		
Game 1: Soccer: 2 v 1 in half of a badminton court. One of the attackers (A1) is 5 to 10 metres away from the other attacker (A2) and the defender (D1). A1 passes the ball to A2 once A2 has made a move to get open and away from D1. A2 then tries to get to the defender's end line. (5 min)	A1 D1 A2 A1 with ball D1 tries to intercept ball A2 tried to get to D1 end line	-A1 (passer) cannot move -rotate positions after each attempt
What was the objective of the game? ■ Pass to teammate and make it to the opponent's end line. For the initial passer, what did you do to increase the chance of a good pass? ■ Make sure receiver was open For the receiver, what did you do to increase the chance of receiving a successful pass? ■ Get open, make eye contact with the passer, call out when I was open. How did you 'get open' or get away from your opponent? ■ Fake that I was going one way then quickly change directions and move the other way. (4 min)		
Practice Task 1: ■ groups of 3 (2 v 1), on half a badminton court ■ A1 tries to fake and move past D1 to tag A2 ■ A2 must stay at midcourt ■ switch roles after every attempt.	A1 D1 A2	■ use your shoulders, head, feet, to try to deceive your partner to get by your partner and into the open
Game 2: ■ 3 v 1 on half a badminton court ■ using hockey sticks and balls, A1 and A2 try to make 3 successful passes (5 min)	A1 D1 A2	■ use fakes to get away from the defender and create a lane where the passer can make a good pass. ■ eye contact ■ call to passer
4. Skill Application		
■ 3 v 3 on a badminton court ■ choice of floor hockey or soccer ■ 4 complete passes scores 1 point ■ change possession after each point ■ variation: play soccer for first few minutes; change to floor hockey (7 min)	A1 D1 A2 D2 A3 D3	■ both passer and receiver need to get away from the defender; good fakes are necessary ■ get away from defender and create a passing lane to receive the ball ■ show hand, call out to passer, make eye contact
5. Closure / Review		
What game/skill did we work on today? ■ Creating a passing lane to receive a pass For the receiver, what did you do to increase the chance of receiving a successful pass? ■ Get open, make eye contact with the passer, call out when I was open. How did you 'get open' or get away from your opponent? ■ Fake that I was going one way then quickly change directions and move the other way. (3 min)		
Differentiated Instruction: Note: this material can also be included directly in the lesson plan.		
Accommodations and/or modifications: ■ Remove the defender and faking element to work on object control skills. ■ Allow for extra repetitions of the fake if necessary. ■ Practice the fake alone (without the defender). ■ Use 'cold' defender until student is able to fake effectively. ■ Focus on one skill as opposed to both soccer and floor hockey.	Extensions: ■ Work on 2v2 and 3v2 scenarios.	

Table 4.15: Description of Terms

Term	Description
Curriculum	A program of study.
Curriculum Document	The official document developed by provincial departments of education, that identifies and outlines the outcomes students are expected to achieve in each subject, at every level of schooling.
Outcome	A broadly written statement that describe the abilities, knowledge, and attitudes students are expected to be able to demonstrate after having completed a program of study. That is, after participation in a physical education program, what do we expect students to know, value, and be able to do?
Exit Outcome	The overall outcome a program of study is developed to achieve. In Canada, the exit outcome of participating in a quality physical education program, is the development of a physically literate student.
Objective	Statements that detail what students are to learn, generally in shorter periods of time (a unit or lesson for example). Objectives are often more specific than outcomes. It is through the achievement of a series of objectives that outcomes are met.
Instructional Alignment	Matching activities, instruction and assessment to the stated goals/objectives.
Backward Design	Planning that begins with the exit outcome and is intentionally designed toward the exit outcome. For example, beginning the planning process with the grade 12 exit outcome, designing the grade 12 program to meet that outcome and then working backward toward grade 1.
Scope	The content selected to be taught in a particular program.
Sequence	The order or progression in which content is arranged.
Balance	Ensuring that cognitive, affective, and motor outcomes are addressed. Another aspect of balance is to ensure that different types of activities (e.g., individual, dual, team, invasion, net) have been selected and sequenced appropriately.

Figure 4.9a: Sample Secondary Level Lesson Plan—Page 1

Figure 4.9: Sample Secondary Level Lesson Plan

Grade 9 Volleyball Lesson Plan
Lesson: 5 of 14

Skill Theme: (Volleyball) Tactic: Setting up to attack.	**Equipment Needed:**
Skill: Saving miss-hits	■ skipping ropes (8–10)
Class Length: 60 minutes	■ 24 volleyballs (one per student)
# of students: 24	■ 5–10 trainer volleyballs (for those wanting a lighter, softer ball)
	■ 2 courts with nets set up

Objectives:
Using a forehand sideways underhand pass, and reverse/back pass, students will be able to successfully save a ball initially intended for the setter, but that has been accidently volleyed or bumped out of the court.
Evaluation:
■ Teacher observation of the number of times students are getting to the ball, and the accuracy with which students are making passes back to the setter or over the net.

Students will be able to verbalize and demonstrate how to complete a sideways and reverse/back underhand pass; they will be able to verbalize when and why it is important to use these skills.
Evaluation:
■ Students will provide correct answers to teacher questions during and at the end of the lesson.

Students will work cooperatively in groups, providing good tosses during all practice tasks, so that classmates can practice the skills.
Evaluation:
■ Teacher observation

Entry Activity:
Volleyballs will be available for students to engage in free play as they arrive in the gymnasium from the changing rooms.
(4 min)

Movement Experience	Organization	Teaching Points
Introductory Activity/Warm Up		
Three Station Fitness Blast Station 1: Skipping ■ with skipping ropes Station 2: Ball Jumps ■ with ball between knees or ankles (student choice), jump forwards backwards, sideways, and add a turn for a challenge. Station 3: Sprints ■ crossovers 1 length, running backwards 1 length, sprint forward 1 length. Repeat until time is up. Rotate on signal (after 1 ½ minutes). (6 min)	Skipping Ball jumps <---Sprints--->	■ pace yourself so you make it through the minute and a half
Skill and Tactical Development (20-25 min)		

Figure 4.9b: Sample Secondary Level Lesson Plan—Page 2

Setting up to attack: moving to successfully play miss-hit balls -3 v 3 game on ½ court -begin game with underhand lob serve or an underhand lob toss (cannot score on the toss) -score 2 points every time at least two consecutive contacts (on one side) are made – this is the only way you can score points! -alternate serving team after every rally -alternate servers after every serve	NEEDS TO BE RECREATED IN ILLUSTRATOR	-playable serve or toss to begin the rally -two contacts minimum before sending the ball back over the net. -'ready position!'
Post Game Questions:		
What was the purpose of the game? ■ Try to score points by making at two least consecutive hits per side before sending the ball back over What did you need to do in order to make at least 2 contacts on the ball? ■ Make sure we didn't let the ball drop; chase every ball? What if one of the hits went out of bounds...what did you do then? ■ Ran after it! What did you do to try to make it playable again? Use an overhead or side arm pass.		
Practice Task 1: -groups of 3 spread out in a line -B in middle facing sideways to A and C -A tosses to B, B sideways bumps to C. -C tosses to B, B sideways bumps to A. -switch places after 8-10 attempts --teacher will demonstrate and explain, followed by student practice.	NEEDS TO BE RECREATED IN ILLUSTRATOR	■ nice high tosses directly at player B ■ player B: ■ ->line up the ball ■ ->drop shoulder closest to the target ■ ->angle arms towards target ■ ->bend legs for power
Practice Task 2: Repeat above drill, making player B move for the ball	Same set up as above.	■ ready position – ready to move ■ beat the ball – get under it and lined up before it drops too low ■ bend knees to get under the ball ■ ball contact as above
Practice Task 3: Repeat above drill, this time with B facing A. B must reverse pass or back pass to C. B then turns to face A and reverse or back passes to C. -switch roles after 5-10 attempts. Teacher will demonstrate and explain followed by student practice.	Same set up as above.	■ nice high tosses directly at player B ■ player B: ■ ->move quickly to get under the ball ■ ->contact the ball above chin ■ ->arch back and move arms in direction you want the ball to go ■ ->bend legs for power
Practice Task 4: Repeat drill above but make student run for the ball.	Same set up as above.	■ ready position – ready to run ■ need to get under the ball before it drops too low

Figure 4.9c: Sample Secondary Level Lesson Plan—Page 3

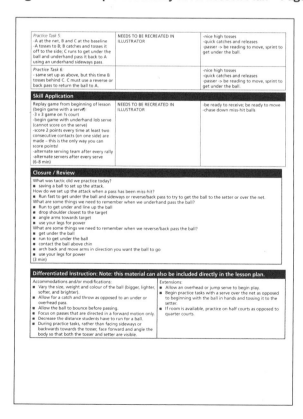

Practice Task 5. -A at the net, B and C at the baseline -A tosses to B; B catches and tosses it off to the side; C runs to get under the ball and underhand pass it back to A using an underhand sideways pass.	NEEDS TO BE RECREATED IN ILLUSTRATOR	-nice high tosses -quick catches and releases -passer - be reading to move, sprint to get under the ball.
Practice Task 6: - same set up as above, but this time B tosses behind C. C must use a reverse or back pass to return the ball to A.		-nice high tosses -quick catches and releases -passer - be reading to move, sprint to get under the ball.
Skill Application		
Replay game from beginning of lesson (begin game with a serve): -3 v 3 game on ½ court -begin game with underhand lob serve (cannot score on the serve) -score 2 points every time at least two consecutive contacts (on one side) are made – this is the only way you can score points! -alternate serving team after every rally -alternate servers after every serve (6-8 min)	NEEDS TO BE RECREATED IN ILLUSTRATOR	-be ready to receive; be ready to move -chase down miss-hit balls
Closure / Review		
What was tactic did we practice today? ■ saving a ball to set up the attack. How do we set up the attack when a pass has been miss-hit? ■ Run fast to get under the ball and sideways or reverse/back pass to try to get the ball to the setter or over the net. What are some things we need to remember when we underhand pass the ball? ■ Run to get under and line up the ball ■ drop shoulder closest to the target ■ angle arms towards target ■ use your legs for power What are some things we need to remember when we reverse/back pass the ball? ■ get under the ball ■ run to get under the ball ■ contact the ball above chin ■ arch back and move arms in direction you want the ball to go ■ use your legs for power (3 min)		
Differentiated Instruction: Note: this material can also be included directly in the lesson plan.		

Accommodations and/or modifications:
■ Vary the size, weight and colour of the ball (bigger, lighter, softer, and brighter).
■ Allow for a catch and throw as opposed to an under or overhead pass.
■ Allow the ball to bounce before passing.
■ Focus on passes that are directed in a forward motion only.
■ Decrease the distance students have to run for a ball.
■ During practice tasks, rather than facing sideways or backwards towards the tosser, face forward and angle the body so that both the tosser and setter are visible.

Extensions:
■ Allow an overhead or jump serve to begin play.
■ Begin practice tasks with a serve over the net as opposed to beginning with the ball in hands and tossing it to the setter.
■ If room is available, practice on half courts as opposed to quarter courts.

Table 4.16: Web Links to Provincial Physical Education Documents

Province	Link
British Columbia	http://www.bced.gov.bc.ca/irp/subject.php?lang=en&subject=Physical_Education
Yukon Territory	Uses the British Columbia program of studies (see: http://www.education.gov.yk.ca/psb/curriculum.html)
Alberta	http://www.education.alberta.ca/teachers/program/pe.aspx
Northwest Territory	Use the Alberta Curriculum Resources which can be accessed through the Alberta Education site (above) or by clicking on 'physical education' from the following link: http://www.ece.gov.nt.ca/
Saskatchewan	Clicking on 'Physical Education' from the link below, will allow the physical educator to select the grade level of their choice. https://www.edonline.sk.ca/webapps/moe-curriculum-BBLEARN/index.jsp?lang=en
Manitoba	http://www.edu.gov.mb.ca/k12/cur/physlhth/index.html
Ontario	Grades 1-8, Health and Physical Education: http://www.edu.gov.on.ca/eng/curriculum/elementary/healthcurr18.pdf Grades 9-10, Health and Physical Education: http://www.edu.gov.on.ca/eng/curriculum/secondary/health910curr.pdf Grades 11 and 12 Health and Physical Education: http://www.edu.gov.on.ca/eng/curriculum/secondary/health910curr.pdf
Quebec	Elementary physical education: http://www.mels.gouv.qc.ca/DGFJ/dp/programme_de_formation/primaire/pdf/educprg2001/educprg2001-091.pdf A list of curricular publications can be found at the following link: http://www.mels.gouv.qc.ca/GR-PUB/menu-curricu-a.htm#elem
Nunavut	A variety of documents and resources are used. For a list of approved resources, educators are encouraged to visit the following link: http://www.edu.gov.nu.ca/apps/UPLOADS/fck/file/K-12/NU%20CUR%20GUIDE%20SEPT%202010.pdf
New Brunswick	Elementary English (K-5) document: http://www.gnb.ca/0000/publications/curric/elementarypysed.pdf Elementary French Immersion Document: http://www.gnb.ca/0000/publications/curric/elemphysedfsl.pdf Middle school (grades 6-8): http://www.gnb.ca/0000/publications/curric/MiddlePhysEd.pdf High School Physical Education and Health Grades 9-10, English: http://www.gnb.ca/0000/publications/curric/PhysicalEducationHealthGrade9-10.pdf High School Physical Education and Health Grades 9-10,French Immersion: http://www.gnb.ca/0000/publications/curric/PhysicalEducationandHealthGrade9-10.pdf Outdoor Pursuits Grade 11: http://www.gnb.ca/0000/publications/curric/Outdoor_Pursuits.pdf Leadership Through Health and Physical Education 120: http://www.gnb.ca/0000/publications/curric/Leadership%20through%20Physical%20Education%20and%20Recreation%20-%20Course%20Outline.pdf
Nova Scotia	To access the actual curriculum documents requires a user name and password, however the outcomes for various grade levels can be found at the following links: Grades Primary to 6: http://www.ednet.ns.ca/pdfdocs/curriculum/LOFsP-6-April20-2012-WEB.pdf Grades 7-9: http://www.ednet.ns.ca/pdfdocs/curriculum/LOFs7-9-April20-2012-WEB.pdf Grades 10-12: http://www.ednet.ns.ca/pdfdocs/curriculum/LOFs10-12-April20-2012-WEB.pdf
Prince Edward Island	Physical Education, Grades K-6: http://www.gov.pe.ca/photos/original/eecd_phyeduK6.pdf Physical Education, Grades 7-9: http://www.gov.pe.ca/photos/original/eecd_physed7-9.pdf
Newfoundland and Labrador	http://www.ed.gov.nl.ca/edu/k12/curriculum/guides/physed/index.html#primary

The Instructional Process

Barb Olmsted and Nancy Melnychuk
(with contributions by Brent Pigott)

Overview

This chapter provides a starting point for pre-service physical educators as they engage in developing relationships with students in their classes. It is not meant to be an exhaustive exploration of the instructional process, but merely an introduction to some key concepts and procedures that contribute to the successful implementation of lessons in an active environment. The instructional process involves a series of interrelated decisions made by both the teacher and the students. The sections found within this chapter will attempt to offer guidance in making decisions with flexibility and commitment to student learning.

Introduction: Why Teach Physical Education?

Physical education (PE) should play an important role in an educational system designed to address the needs of the whole child. Education "through the physical" is another tool to better prepare students for the challenges they may face in the future (Siedentop, 2009). The successful outcomes of a well-planned PE program will contribute to students who are physically and emotionally healthy, and who will be armed with the essential skills needed for making positive decisions about their health and well-being throughout life. Too often, PE has been maligned, marginalized, or ignored due to increased emphasis on other subject areas or school activities deemed to be of higher priority. PE should not be treated as a privilege for good behaviour nor should it be denied to students as a punishment for bad behaviour. Like any other subject area, PE should support and complement all other facets of a healthy learning community within schools.

What Is Teaching Physical Education?

Teaching PE is a very complex endeavour. The physical educator has the responsibility to facilitate instruction so that students are given ample opportunity to acquire the skills, attitudes, and behaviours that may ultimately engage them in physical activity for life. The learning environment must therefore be structured to meet the varying needs of students while respecting learning outcomes prescribed by provincial curricula. As highlighted in the previous chapter, planning is a critical component of successful teaching. The physical educator is challenged to make multiple decisions based on a number of factors, which include:

- Goals of learning (e.g., psychomotor, cognitive, affective)
- Content (as indicated by curriculum, facilities, equipment, scheduling, etc.)
- Skills and abilities of students (pre-assessment)
- Instructional process (the manner in which the learning takes place)
- Class organization (routines, formations, transitions)
- Availability and use of equipment
- Safety of all participants and the teacher (both physical and emotional)
- Time (engagement time)
- Motivating students (gaining and maintaining interest)

However, even the best laid plans may not result in a perfect lesson. The physical educator must continue to make immediate decisions as the lesson proceeds based on these aforementioned factors, which may require some modification of the initial plan. Students are also engaged

in the decision-making process, which allows them to take more responsibility for their own learning (Mosston & Ashworth, 2001). Exemplary physical educators possess this gift: the ability to respond to the changing dynamics of the PE environment by making appropriate decisions to enhance student learning.

Many physical educators enter the profession due to positive experiences in PE in the past or a sense of competence in their ability as athletes, or perhaps both. Many would also attribute their choice of profession to a mentor or role model in the field who created an inclusive, enjoyable environment for learning. Outstanding physical educators implicitly and explicitly address the *affective* learning domain, recognizing that teaching is about developing positive relationships with and among students. By creating a safe emotional environment, physical educators can assist students in developing a positive sense of self-efficacy (perceived competence in a specific situation), a strong predictor of subsequent participation, and therefore the possibility of lifelong engagement in physical activity (Solmon, 2003). The affective learning domain is closely linked to motivation, such that students who have positive, enjoyable experiences in PE are much more willing to engage in subsequent learning opportunities (Rink, 2009). Learning that successfully addresses the affective domain lays the foundation for learning in both the cognitive and psychomotor domains. Provincial curricula also identify affective learning expectations or outcomes as measurable standards by which students' progress is determined.

There is no doubt that the physical educator must play a variety of roles in facilitating students' learning: instructor, mentor, coach, referee, leader, mediator, listener, disciplinarian, observer, and assessor. One of the keys to successful teaching is recognizing when and how each of these roles might be applied, and what situations might demand a particular teaching approach.

Communication Tools

There are various ways to communicate effectively and create a positive atmosphere for learning within a PE environment. Research indicates that a positive learning environment contributes to students developing positive attitudes toward engagement in physical activity during youth and throughout adulthood (Lavay et al., 2006). Most significantly, effective communication helps build and maintain strong relationships between teachers and students that form the foundation for outstanding teaching and learning within a PE lesson. Like many other teaching skills, effectively communicating with students takes practice. The physical educator must be able to send messages clearly, as well as be able to receive and respond to messages from students. It is vital to understand students' perspectives by being an active listener and by incorporating students' points of view. Listening with sensitivity and patience to students is fundamental to creating meaningful relationships with them. Active listening also involves the use of paraphrasing (restating in your own words), supportive body language (e.g., eye contact, body posture/position, gestures), and an awareness of one's own thoughts and feelings. The incoming interpretation of a message from a student might be affected if the teacher is angry or frustrated with that student, and the resulting response may not be as positive if the teacher reacts quickly based on his or her feelings towards the student. As teachers develop their communication skills, they will become aware of personal communication "blockers" that do not have the desired result with students. In fact, they will likely recognize some of these behaviours in their students! Examples of blockers include commanding, judging, delaying the issue, stereotyping, and so on. Ongoing, positive, non-verbal communication such as a smile or thumbs-up gesture by the teacher also reinforces positive attitudes and behaviours inherent in an effective learning environment. Verbal and non-verbal communication skills can be classified in a number of ways depending on the purpose of the message.

What follows is an overview of some of the key communication skills: clarity, demonstrations and visual aids, cues, questioning, observation, and feedback.

Clarity

Being able to transmit clear messages in a short period of time results in greater student understanding of the assigned task(s) and having more time available to complete that task. Physical educators should avoid vague, ambiguous statements or digressing from the original intent of the message, as students may begin to lose interest or the ability to follow instructions when it becomes their turn to respond. Physical educators must use language that is appropriate and relevant to the level of the student. The use of analogy and imagery can also be extremely effective, not only to enhance student understanding, but also to stimulate interest in learning. For example, a statement such as "extend your arms out like an eagle's wings" is much more interesting than "extend your arms out to the side."

Clarity also involves a process whereby the physical educator confirms that the message has been received and understood. Presenting content to students therefore involves several steps to ensure student comprehension and appropriate subsequent physical activity. Communicating content to students does not stop after the initial presentation, it is an ongoing collaborative process throughout each lesson.

Rosenshine and Stevens (1986) emphasize the following characteristics of effective teachers presenting a task to students, which continue to resonate in today's schools. Effective teachers:

- State and reiterate explicit goals for the lesson
- Present material in a logical manner, focusing on one step at a time
- Offer examples or demonstrations with the verbal explanation
- Check for students' understanding

When the goal of the lesson is for students to replicate a specific skill, these teacher characteristics have been particularly successful (Rink, 2009). However, if the goal of the lesson is to elicit problem-solving behaviour or other types of student-centred learning behaviours, the teacher must carefully define the parameters of the task without revealing the appropriate response. In this case, the teacher may offer more than one example of the response, or no example whatsoever to allow the students to develop their own responses. Additionally, the teacher might offer feedback or a series of clues or questions to stimulate cognitive engagement as students progress through the task. Some lessons may involve minimal intervention by the teacher, which may consist only of providing students with the lesson goal and some basic parameters for their participation. The teacher would then carefully observe as the lesson unfolds, and perhaps offer some guidance, reminders, or carefully worded questions to keep students on task. At the end of a lesson, effective teachers review the goal with students, offer general feedback about the achievement of the goal, and ask the students to share or reiterate their learning. Sometimes teachers conduct a *debrief,* particularly in more student-centred or experientially based lessons, where he or she leads or guides a discussion about affective or cognitive learning outcomes.

Regardless of the type of verbal interaction with students, teachers must always consider how they can present the content with clarity, meaning and relevance, and they must use strategies to determine if students understand their message. Additionally, they must be able to judge how much content to present at any given time. Too much content will reduce clarity, and therefore affect the quality of instruction. The content in a grade eight PE class would differ quite significantly from a grade two PE class as dictated by provincial curricula, but teachers are responsible for knowing what their students are capable of learning and doing within one lesson. Teachers must therefore carefully pre-assess their students to determine their abilities and learning needs. Purposeful planning with the learning goals in mind, as discussed in the previous chapter, is critical to presenting lesson content with clarity.

Table 5.1: Characteristics of Effective Demonstrations

Characteristics of Effective Demonstrations	"Do's" with Demonstrations
Developmentally appropriate	Do not apply the "adult" or "expert" model to students who have not yet developed the ability to perform it that way
Mechanically correct	Do demonstrate CORRECTLY—if you cannot demonstrate the skill correctly, ask a student or use another model (e.g., video)
Presented before students try a new skill	Do not allow students to practice a skill the wrong way
Use instructional cues for each phase or movement segment	Do use action words Do use simple language
Slow motion and real time	Do demonstrate at different speeds Do demonstrate parts of the skill
Use imagery and analogy	Do use mental images so students can see and feel the movement in their own minds Do use examples within the experience of the students
Complex skill—whole/part/whole presentation Simple skill—whole	Do break down complex skills into component parts, then slowly work toward combining the parts together
Repeat the demonstration at least three times; reinforce as the lesson proceeds	Do demonstrations from different angles to change the view for observers
Scaffold new skills with existing skills	Do establish a learning progression starting where the students are, gradually adding difficulty or complexity Plan for extension tasks for more advanced students

Demonstrations and Visual Aids

As previously indicated, demonstrations can significantly enhance verbal instructions or explanations. Because of the differing learning styles among students, verbal instructions alone are not likely to transmit the entire message. Research has shown that the combination of presentation modes significantly increases the depth of learning (Townsend & Gurvitch, 2002).

Demonstrations can be used for a variety of purposes, including the presentation of new skills; the demonstration of student movement during a drill, practice, or routine; the concepts or tactics of a game situation; or to present one example of a response to a problem-solving task. In PE, students have an opportunity to immediately apply and practice the demonstrated skill or behaviour in a practical setting. Experiencing the action in this way increases the learning opportunities even further. Teachers must therefore carefully plan how they will demonstrate the skills in a manner that is relevant to their students. Characteristics of effective demonstrations are summarized in **Table 5.1**.

Demonstrations are usually accompanied by clear verbal cues (discussed in the next section) to explain the demonstration in real time. It is also important that teachers explain the context for the demonstration, and the justification for why it is presented in a certain way. It may be the rules of the game that dictate the form of the demonstration (e.g., pivot foot while in possession of the ball in basketball), or it may offer the participant greater advantage if a skill is performed similar to the demonstration (e.g., rotation of the trunk during an overhand throw).

With the ubiquity of technology, many teachers use video clips and images to further emphasize the teaching points and movement and/or mechanical concepts. A separate visual may permit the teacher more freedom to explain the desired outcome rather than being concerned with demonstrating and explaining at the same time. This is also true if the teacher selects a peer model to demonstrate. All these methods can stimulate interest in learning (and support skill learning) in PE. As indicated in **Table 5.1**, teachers must ensure that the visual presented matches the developmental level of the students. For example, a video of a professional basketball player performing a slam dunk is an exciting and motivating thing to watch for many students. It does not, however, offer much in the way of modelling a skill that is within the realm of possibility for elementary students!

Visual aids such as task cards, posters, photographs, or electronic images and videos (e.g., laptop or tablet) may be placed in locations where students may refer to them when they are practicing the skill independently or in groups. They are also a handy reference for teachers. A carefully prepared visual aid is a resource that teachers can use repeatedly so it is worth the time investment.

Table 5.2: Critical Elements and Learning Cues for the Overhead Volley

Critical Elements of the Skill	Teaching Cues
■ Stance is narrowed from ready position ■ Knees bent ■ Elbows out beside the ears ■ Hands form a triangle (thumbs and forefingers) ■ Wrists bent back toward face (wrinkles in wrist) ■ Hands at forehead, waiting for ball (looking through triangle) ■ Contact is made with pads of all fingers and thumbs ■ Arms extend after contact is made ■ Arms fully extend, wrists remain fairly stiff to propel ball up and outward ■ Little involvement of legs (knees may extend)	■ Triangle ■ Pads ■ Extend

Cues for Teaching and Learning

Cues are used by effective teachers to focus students' learning and improve performance, which often means enhancing (motor) skill technique (Pangrazi & Gibbons, 2009). However, teaching/learning cues may also be directed toward improving movement quality (e.g., force production, accuracy, control), knowledge of strategies or tactics in games, or understanding the creation of emotional impact in dance. For example, the teacher may continue to reiterate the phrase, "pass and break into the open" as students play basketball, or he or she may reinforce the feeling of despair with the comment, "stretch outward with head, chest and every limb" as students dance.

The cues should call attention to key points of a performance through brief, precise, action-oriented words. Communication should focus on one aspect of the performance or phase of a skill at a time, yet combining all the cues should present the skill as a whole. For example, a short series of fluid movements may be required in a dance or gymnastics sequence (e.g., jump, roll, balance) or in executing a motor skill for games playing (e.g., step, rotate, throw). For primary students, verbal cues such as "step, chase/hop" may be helpful for learning a locomotor skill like galloping.

Motor skill performance can be characterized by a number of critical elements that describe, in words, how to correctly perform a particular skill. Learning cues, however, should be brief and accurate summary words that imply action are easily remembered (by both teacher and student), and are consistently used in the right order to guide the performer. Demonstrations should always be accompanied by learning cues, and once introduced, the cues can be used for subsequent practice and consolidation of new skills. **Table 5.2** presents an example of one motor skill and its accompanying critical elements and learning cues that may be appropriate for a middle school class.

Questioning

Questioning is a powerful communication tool. Used effectively it can be a diagnostic tool that determines prior learning, a motivational tool that engages students in learning, an assessment tool that determines level of understanding, a modification tool that extends activities, a management tool that maintains lesson focus, or a tool to stimulate creativity and critical thinking. In PE classes, one of the most popular times for questioning is immediately following a demonstration. Termed checking for understanding (CFU), teachers might ask the students a number of questions related to the content contained within the demonstration or the process for meeting the goals of the lesson (Rink, 2003). In this way, teachers can be more confident knowing that their students have comprehended the message and are ready to move on to the next phase of the lesson.

Teachers should determine the purpose for their questions and plan them in advance. Carefully planned questions contain content and vocabulary appropriate for the developmental level of students. Some questions should be straightforward and convergent, while others should be high level and divergent, designed to engage students at multiple cognitive levels. Questions should begin with how, what, where, why, when, or what if rather than who can tell me, is, or can you. A question like, "If the ball touches the net during the serve in volleyball and goes over the net, is the ball still in play?" requires a simple yes or no answer, and involves very little cognitive engagement on the part of students. If the question is rephrased as, "What are three rules regarding the serve in volleyball?" the students are challenged to think beyond just the net serve, and may offer a variety of responses to demonstrate their knowledge of volleyball rules. A question like "Can you show me three types of locomotion?" is a non-specific question that may elicit a simple yes or no response. In most cases, the intent is implicit in the question, and a student responding to the question would offer more than simply yes or no.

Additionally, however, the teacher might use the question as an opportunity to remind students of where they are to move. So, if the question is rephrased to "As you move safely from the red line to the green line, what are three types of locomotion you might use?" the result may be more positive.

Teacher behaviour following a question can be just as important as the question itself. If the teacher does not give students time to process the question and formulate an answer, the question becomes ineffective. Good teachers might count slowly to ten to allow for such processing to occur (a concept called wait time), even if the silence is deafening. If an answer is not forthcoming, the teacher may offer prompts or probes to hint at the solution without giving it away. While waiting, teachers should scan the entire class to engage as many students as possible in considering possible solutions. Body language of students and their willingness to make eye contact will disclose hints about the difficulty of the question. Correct responses should be followed with praise (verbal and/or non-verbal), and comments that build on the response. Incorrect responses should be dealt with in a direct way, rather than indirectly (e.g., "not really" or "almost"). Divergent questions will elicit a variety of creative responses, and teachers must be sensitive to recognize all responses that may be valid in these types of situations.

Encouraging and answering student questions should be done in a thoughtful, direct, and genuine way, and should reflect the positive environment desired for learning. Again, verbal and non-verbal communication should be congruent, something teachers should reflect upon as they conclude each lesson.

Observation

Observational skills play a critical role in PE classes, regardless of the activity (Darst et al., 2012). Teachers must be active observers of the environment at all times to ensure the safety of participants, monitor off task behaviour, assess student learning, and guide students as they learn new skills. An active observer is one who is continually assessing the degree of appropriate engagement of students (both with the content and with one another) and making immediate decisions in response to those assessments. The term *with-it-ness*, originally coined by Kounin (1970), captures the essence of this ability to multitask in a PE context. More commonly referred to as "having eyes in the back of your head," teachers with this ability are aware of what is going on in all areas of the learning space, and they make sure the students are aware of this. PE teachers can enhance this ability by keeping in mind some general principles. These include:

- Maintaining a position in which the teacher can see all participants (even peripherally)
- Circulating around and throughout the space
- Offering feedback to multiple individuals or groups concurrently (often a quick word or two may suffice)

Case Study 1: Lack of Proper Clothing/Habitual Tardiness

At the start of the semester, Miss Jones outlines the importance of the rules regarding being on time in proper clothing for her grade ten PE class. It is explained that students not dressed properly will not be allowed to participate in activity classes and as a result the students' participation marks will be affected.

Two weeks later Betty, one of Miss Jones' students, arrives in class without a change of clothing. Miss Jones has Betty sit in the bleachers for the class away from any other students and asks Betty to remain after class to discuss the situation.

At the end of class, Miss Jones meets with Betty to determine why she does not have the proper clothing. Betty explains that she forgot her gym bag at home. Miss Jones reaffirms the class rules with Betty and the reasons why changing into proper PE attire is important. Since this is the first time, Miss Jones notes the lack of proper clothing on her recording sheet and warns Betty that any further instances will involve detention, possible parental involvement, and, eventually, Vice Principal intervention if the problem persists.

Questions for Reflection

1. How flexible should the teacher's policy be regarding "proper" clothing?

2. Why is it important to have a graduated series of consequences for infractions such as improper uniform and lateness?

3. At what point should the teacher contact a parent/guardian or seek Vice Principal intervention?

Case Study 2: Ensuring Inclusion

Mr. Smith has just finished some basketball skill drills with his PE class of thirty grade nine students and decides to finish the class with games of full court basketball. His class is in a full gym that contains two full courts and ten baskets (four wall baskets and six court baskets). He divides the class into six teams of five players. Three of the teams will play in each half of the gym with one team rotating in every five minutes. Teams will be expected to abide by the basketball rules as established by Mr. Smith and the students, but there will be no referees. Mr. Smith will supervise games to be sure that basic rules are being followed.

As the games progress, Mr. Smith observes that the more skilled players in the game are dominating play. He also observes that some players are not getting involved in the game and try to stay out of the full court running and aggressive play. Clearly, some adjustments will have to be made for the next class.

During the allotted game time of the next class, Mr. Smith divides the class into twelve teams (six teams of three and six teams of two). Two teams will play modified games on each of the six court baskets rotating to play a new team every four minutes.

Questions for Reflection

1 What are the advantages of using smaller teams on smaller courts?

2 What rule modifications need to be made for two teams playing on one basket?

3 How can the modifications used for this game be applied to other sports (volleyball, soccer, baseball, etc.)?

4 Should the teacher be involved in the selection of team members?

- Scanning the class frequently
- Using verbal and non-verbal strategies as reminders to off-task students

As previously indicated, with-it-ness includes the need for immediate intervention if necessary. The nature of the response may simply be a word of encouragement to redirect students, or it may mean stopping a game to make a rule change for safety purposes. Taking immediate action may prevent the situation from straying further from learning goals, and will ensure that students stay safe, have maximum opportunity to participate, experience success, and stay on task.

Regardless of the learning goals, students appreciate regular feedback about their progress. Whether observing for the purposes of providing feedback or making assessments about student learning, ongoing and frequent observation of skills (e.g., error type and frequency, performance accuracy) is essential. Expert teachers have the ability to observe a movement pattern, offer feedback to individual students about accuracy and quality of the movement pattern, and subsequently assess any resulting changes. For example, a student is observed throwing a ball, and the flight of the ball is an upward path lacking distance. The teacher must quickly diagnose the performance error (e.g., ball release is too early), provide prescriptive feedback to the student, and observe subsequent throwing trials (with more feedback). Pre-service physical educators must therefore take every opportunity to hone this observational skill, as the active environment of any PE class will demand their attention in many different directions.

Observation is also an essential skill for assessing and evaluating student learning. Teachers must therefore be able to make quick decisions regarding performance success. With large class sizes, this can become a difficult task. There are two key questions teachers must ask themselves to justify a summative evaluation of any skill or behaviour:

- How many observations must I make for each student to gain a fair evaluation?
- Do I make the observations during a controlled setting, a final performance setting, or an exploratory or practice setting?
- These are questions that will be addressed in Chapter 6, but are worth considering now as observation and assessment are both integral parts of instruction

Feedback

Effectively providing feedback to learners is an essential instructional skill. Feedback communicates important information to students about their behaviour and performance as they progress toward cognitive, affective, and psychomotor goals in PE. Feedback, in both verbal and non-verbal forms, should be delivered immediately following the performance to have the greatest impact. This allows students to apply the feedback during the same lesson in subsequent practice trials. Teachers do not have the luxury of collecting evidence of student performance on paper; they must offer process assessments based on their observations of students in class. Purposefully used, feedback can support learning in meaningful ways: it keeps students focused on assigned tasks, and it can motivate them to maintain their participation. Feedback can be classified in a number of ways based on its intended purpose. It can be summarized in the following manner:

- Positive, negative, or neutral
- General or specific
- Evaluative or prescriptive
- Class, group, or individual
- Verbal or non-verbal

Feedback presented in a positive manner is far more effective than negative or neutral feedback (Rink, 2009). Examples such as "good effort" or "well done," are positive, but do not offer the student information about why their performance was successful, nor do they provide any information about next steps. These types of statements project a feeling, or place a value upon a performance (evaluative feedback). They are also considered general statements because they do not refer specifically to what was good about a performance. A non-verbal alternative might be the "thumbs up" gesture. These vague types of statements are used frequently in PE settings, usually to encourage further effort and participation. If used too often though, they may lose their effectiveness. However, if not used frequently enough, students may not wish to put forth much effort nor will they sense that their participation is important.

Therein lies the challenge for PE teachers: knowing when to use feedback, how frequently to use it, and what type would be most appropriate given the circumstances. A statement such as "Use your shoulder and back muscles as you pull the paddle through the water" is a prescriptive, specific statement that indicates exactly what the performer is being asked to do next. It does not evaluate previous performance (either positively or negatively). Furthermore, it can be used to offer feedback to the entire class, a smaller group, or an individual.

Teachers must be sensitive to the appropriateness of a public statement directed to an individual student, as opposed to speaking with the student privately. For example, a negative comment such as "Michael, don't step before you dribble because you travel every time" delivered from across the gymnasium for the entire class to hear is not likely to enhance Michael's performance. In fact, he may feel ashamed of his inability to perform in front of his peers, which in turn could affect his willingness to continue. Rather, a carefully-worded, positive statement made to Michael in private such as "Michael, be sure to jump stop when you catch the ball" may have a more productive outcome. Teachers can also combine comments for even greater impact. Examples of this include: "Good job, you rotated your body that time" or "Well done, remember to follow through after you release the ball." The first example combines specific, evaluative, positive feedback, and the second example combines specific, prescriptive, positive feedback. In the first instance, the evaluative feedback is a judgment about previous successful performance, whereas the second example includes prescriptive feedback indicating future desired performance.

Non-verbal feedback may include facial and body gestures, but it may also include the physical positioning of the limbs of students so that they can feel the skill or action. Of course teachers must be well aware of cultural practices and/or school policies that might limit touching. There may also be different interpretations of non-verbal gestures in some cultures. Non-verbal feedback may also convey the teacher's displeasure with what he or she observes (e.g., standing with hands on hips, frowning, crossed arms), which

Knowing when and how to use feedback can be a challenge for PE teachers.

may also act to keep students on task without a spoken word from the teacher. Open communication with students about feedback styles is therefore an important part of the instructional process.

Feedback may effectively be used as another tool to engage students in critical thinking and problem solving behaviours. Teachers who ask students to reflect on their own experiences, movement patterns, and performance results are more engaged in learning. If students can explain why they must move in a certain way, describe what factors contribute to successful performance, and evaluate their own movement, they are demonstrating a much deeper understanding of the content (Rink, 2009). Rather than simply telling a student how he or she might improve performance, the teacher should ask the student specific questions about the performance. For example, the teacher might observe a student running or cross country skiing and then ask the student, "When your left foot comes forward, which arm comes with it?" If the student is performing the skill incorrectly, the teacher would continue to ask which

arm should be coming forward and why. This questioning process, though much more time consuming than simply telling the student to alter their movement, demands that the student engage in cognitive processes to more fully understand the purpose of his or her actions. The list below provides a summary of some of the key factors to keep in mind when offering feedback.

Guidelines for Giving Feedback to Students

- Give feedback immediately
- Keep feedback positive
- Focus on the behaviour, not the individual
- Distribute feedback evenly
- Balance evaluative feedback with prescriptive feedback
- Be specific
- Target feedback appropriately (e.g., individual, group, class)

Table 5.3: Motivating Students in Physical Education

Strategy	Examples
Set clear and concise course objectives with students	■ Focus on fun and/or enjoyment through active participation ■ Improve personal fitness and strength ■ Experience as many lifestyle activities as possible
Outline specific methods for achieving course objectives	■ Regular attendance and full participation ■ Give best/complete effort ■ Behave appropriately according to class rules
Explain teacher attitudes in various situations	■ Emphasize skill improvement rather than how one compares with other students ■ Establish clear consequences for non-participation or other inappropriate behaviours
Promote positive attitudes	■ Praise all forms of participation and improvement ■ Praise the last person to finish/complete an activity ■ Do not accept negative comments
Promote equitable and fair participation and sportsmanship	■ Careful selection of teams by/in different ways (modify immediately if necessary) ■ Promote self-monitoring and self-regulating behaviour ■ Have clear and/or automatic rules for unresolved fouls or violations (e.g., offence retains possession)
Inclusion	■ All students involved (even those not properly dressed) ■ Use buddy system with class/peer leaders ■ Subtle adjustment in rules to help less-skilled students ■ Positive reinforcement ■ Maintain smaller groups and teams ■ Offer some choice (type of equipment/apparatus/music, partners/groups, rules, type of task, etc.) ■ Offer levels of participation (varying distance in a cross country run, height of bar in high jump, etc.)
Evaluation Strategies	■ Strong emphasis on participation ■ Stress improvement ■ Pre-warning of test material (e.g., "listen carefully as this will be on the test") ■ Reduce emphasis on comparisons with peers
Success	■ Offer self-competitive tasks or cooperative tasks so everyone can experience success (e.g., personal improvement goals)

Table 5.4: Contrasting Communication Skills Based on the Teaching Approach for a Lesson on Walking on a Low Beam or Bench

	Teacher-Centred Lesson	Student-Centred Lesson
Goal of Lesson	Students will successfully demonstrate the critical elements of forward walking on the beam	Students will successfully demonstrate three ways to travel down the beam on their feet
Clarity	Step-by-step explanation of motor skill	Presentation of lesson goal
Demonstration	Full demonstration by teacher	None
Teaching Cues	Eyes up Arms out Weight on front foot Lift back foot, slide it forward along side of beam Touch beam with toe Transfer weight to front foot	None
Check for Understanding	How do I move my foot along the beam? Where do I look? What do I do with my arms?	How many different ways are we to move down the beam? Can we walk on our hands and knees?
Questioning (e.g., During Lesson)	None	In what ways can you move down the beam? How do you place your feet? What can you do to maintain your balance?
Feedback	"Well done! Next time remember to keep your eyes up."	"Nice job! Show me another way to move down the beam."
Differentiation	None	Based on student's individual ability and choice

- Use non-verbal signals alone, or to support verbal feedback
- Inform students of what they are doing wrong (e.g., "good effort, next time try stepping forward with the other foot")

Motivating Students

Motivating students continues to be one of the biggest challenges for PE teachers. Many theories purport to explain motivational behaviour in students, yet the answer is complex and multifactorial (for a review, please see Erpic, 2011). Though it is not within the scope of this chapter to detail various theories and possible solutions, there are some common strategies that emerge based not only on theory, but also on evidence in the field (Tjeerdsma, 1995). Teachers must therefore be sensitive to each student's level of motivation, and seek a variety of ways to engage all students in their lessons.

Some students will be motivated by a competitive class environment emphasizing team sports and winning, while others would much prefer to challenge themselves in a non-competitive environment emphasizing self-directed goal achievement or cooperative tasks. A balanced approach may therefore contribute to greater student participation over the long term. Students who feel safe and comfortable in a positive environment are more likely to participate in planned activities than those who feel ostracized or different from the rest. Similarly, teachers who have developed positive relationships with their students will have more success in motivating their students. **Table 5.3** (on the previous page) summarizes some of these strategies.

Effective communication skills can make the difference between a lesson that accomplishes its stated goals and one that doesn't. If the teacher is unable to develop a positive relationship with students, then even the best lesson plan can quickly become a disaster. **Table 5.4** contrasts some of the communication strategies between teacher-centred and student-centred approaches to provide the reader with a context for communication.

PE teachers should continually reflect on their communication skills, determine what areas need improvement, and work towards developing their ability to connect with students and their learning. Reflection on each lesson as soon as possible following its conclusion should be a priority for all educators. Determining what went well and what could have been done to improve the lesson contributes to sound professional practice. The next section discusses different types of instructional approaches based on the goals of learning.

Instructional Framework

The instructional framework refers to the methods and strategies teachers use to maximize learning opportunities for students (Rink, 2009). The approach a teacher uses depends largely upon two key factors: the learning goals for the lesson, and the degree of readiness of the students. If the students are to learn a new skill, the teacher may play a more central role in guiding them, whereas if the students are consolidating previously learned skills, they may assume more responsibility for their own learning. Similarly, a lesson focused on problem solving may involve minimal verbal instruction by the teacher, merely some carefully worded questions that guide the students to the appropriate solution(s). Teachers may also combine a number of methods within the same lesson. This has been found to be the case in a traditionally structured lesson that is still frequently in use today. The elements of this type of lesson are:

1. Introductory Phase
2. New Skills Phase
3. Consolidation Phase
4. Application Phase
5. Closure

The introductory phase of the lesson may include an appropriate warm-up, as well as an overview of the learning goals of the lesson. Sometimes referred to as the anticipatory set (Pangrazi & Gibbons, 2009) or pre-impact (Mosston & Ashworth, 2001), the introductory phase prepares students for learning.

The new skills phase involves teacher explanation and demonstration of new skills or concepts.

During the consolidation phase, students will practice the new material in carefully guided, controlled settings (sometimes referred to as "near" contexts). This may involve drills, station learning, and/or partner learning, etc. The teacher monitors this phase closely, offering feedback to as many students as possible while providing multiple opportunities for students to practice their skills. In the application phase, students apply their newly practiced movements or skills in a more formal setting, which may include modified presentations or games; mini games; or full games or presentations depending upon the developmental appropriateness of the situation. For example, application in a dance setting may include combining several movements into a fluid theme-focused sequence with a beginning and ending. Application in a team-oriented sports activity may include games with fewer players or games in a modified space. Often termed "far" contexts, the students have more independence and responsibility for their learning in the application phase, as the teacher may or may not be directly supervising the activity. Mosston and Ashworth (2001) refers to the new skills, consolidation, and application phases together as the "impact" phase of the lesson. It may also be referred to as the instructional phase.

During the closure (or "post-impact") phase, students are gathered for overall feedback regarding their performance, and perhaps some information about upcoming lessons. This is often a time when equipment is stored, and it may involve a cool-down prior to moving to another learning space.

Spectrum of Mosston's Teaching Styles

A teaching "style," as defined by Mosston and Ashworth (2001) is a framework or structure of a lesson independent of personal teaching habits. Based on the interplay among deliberate teaching behaviours, learning behaviours, and the objectives of the lesson, Mosston and Ashworth developed eleven teaching styles. The spectrum of styles is organized along a continuum, each designed to accomplish a particular set of objectives. Differing objectives demand the use of a different style. At one end of the spectrum is the *command style*, a teacher-centred format in which the teacher makes all of the decisions for learning. At the other end of the spectrum is *self-teaching*, a purely student-centred format whereby the student is responsible for teaching him or herself, and communicating that learning to the teacher.

Table 5.5 summarizes the key elements of each style, and the considerations for teachers when selecting an appropriate teaching style (adapted from Mosston & Ashworth, 2001).

Mosston and Ashworth's spectrum of teaching styles has been the subject of much research since it was introduced in 1966. The adoption of all teaching styles has been somewhat limited, as many teachers select teaching styles with which they are comfortable or with which they have had experience. Kulinna and Cothran (2003) found that the most frequently used styles were the command style, the practice style, and the divergent style, even though teachers felt the practice, reciprocal, and inclusion styles would best benefit students. No doubt the teacher's level of comfort and confidence using a range of teaching styles is a key factor in these findings, which speaks to the importance of selecting a variety of styles to best suit the learning needs of students.

Table 5.5: Summary of Mosston's Teaching Styles.

Style	Objectives	Considerations
Command (A)	■ teacher makes all decisions ■ teacher-directed instructions re: location, start time, pace, stop time, demonstration, etc. ■ learner responds to instructions ■ class is set up in an orderly manner ■ teacher feedback is limited ■ examples include yoga, aerobics, golf, javelin, or discus, etc.	■ efficient use of time (time on task is high) ■ learning by recall and repeated performance ■ fixed standard of performance (based on model)
Practice (B)	■ learner performs tasks prescribed by teacher, but learner determines pace, rhythm, start, stop, interval ■ teacher circulates to give individual feedback, ask questions ■ designed for individual practice, class is dispersed ■ examples include kicking a soccer ball, front crawl in swimming, etc. ■ task cards may be used	■ learners held accountable for decisions ■ learners begin to experience independence ■ providing activity for students who finish task early ■ time on task can be affected
Reciprocal (C)	■ class is organized in pairs or threes ■ observer gives feedback, doer performs the skill, feeder, if necessary, feeds object to doer ■ observer makes feedback decisions, rather than teacher ■ use of task cards or criteria sheets designed by teacher ■ teacher communicates only with observers ■ examples include forward skating, wall climbing, etc.	■ greater socialization between students ■ students take more active role in learning process ■ constant presence of teacher not required ■ teacher trusts students to make decisions
Self-Check (D)	■ learners assess themselves in comparison to criteria sheets established by teacher ■ examples include target games, fitness results/weight or resistance training, etc. ■ teacher provides feedback at end of class	■ students monitor themselves ■ self-check is private ■ students learn their own limits, successes, failures ■ more concerned with the results of a movement, not the movement itself ■ learner reflects on own behaviour
Inclusion (E)	■ multiple levels of performance of the same task to allow for success of all learners ■ accommodates individual skill differences ■ student chooses the level of performance based on perceived ability ■ self-assessment ■ teacher provides feedback regarding the decision-making process, not the chosen level ■ examples include gymnastics, basketball shooting (distance from basket), fitness and weight training	■ students can take a step backward to experience success ■ inclusive, invites involvement ■ be aware of the gap between reality and aspiration ■ some students have difficulty choosing a particular level because they are conditioned to being told ■ often a positive style for students who get excluded from other activities

Style	Objectives	Considerations
Inquiry Teaching Styles	**Content is new to the learner** **Higher cognitive engagement**	
Guided Discovery (F)	■ teacher guides students through a series of problems/tasks in which students make decisions to arrive at a predetermined solution ■ each step is based on the response to the previous step ■ teacher must wait for the learner's response and offer frequent feedback or clues (patience) ■ examples include centre of gravity in gymnastics, levers, stability, strength, speed, the need for a variety of passes in basketball	■ lots of preparation on part of teacher ■ teacher must be prepared to experiment with the "unknown" because responses may be unanticipated ■ minimal social contact with other students, but cognitive involvement is high ■ level of physical activity may be low
Convergent Discovery (G)	■ less direct guidance from teacher ■ one possible solution ■ teacher presents the problem, students develop the process to arrive at the solution through exploration ■ students demonstrate their solution to others	■ students must have the requisite skills in order to find a movement solution ■ similar to guided discovery, teacher must be prepared for a variety of responses ■ cognitive engagement is high ■ individual or small group work
Divergent Discovery (H)	■ learner is engaged in discovering a number of solutions to a problem ■ teacher merely encourages responses, does not make judgments ■ teacher may demonstrate one solution, and students discover other solutions ■ examples include rolling the body, getting from one side of the gym to another using limited equipment, combining movements in gymnastics or dance, tactics in sport, game situations, etc.	■ demanding for the teacher, must have expertise in the area ■ creativity of students ■ individual or group problem solving (more social contact)
Learner-Designed Individual Program (I)	■ teacher identifies a broad topic area ■ students design their own learning experiences, including goals and evaluation criteria ■ learner implements, refines program ■ examples include personal fitness plans, improvement plans	■ prior experience in an activity is necessary for learners to engage in this style ■ time consuming—thinking, experimenting, performing, recording ■ teacher provides equipment choices
Learner-Initiated (J)	■ learner makes a request to the teacher to plan an individual learning experience ■ learner makes all of the decisions ■ teacher is involved as a resource and/or at the request of the learner	■ not generally a whole class experience
Self-Teaching (K)	■ outside the realm of physical education classes ■ learner takes on the role of both teacher and student, making all decisions for learning ■ feedback from teacher is provided only upon request	

(Source: Mosston & Ashworth, 2001)

Table 5.6: Understanding the Gradual Release of Responsibility

Component	Description
Modeling ("I do it")	■ Teacher demonstrates, using "I" statements to model thinking ■ Lesson includes instruction about when to use the skill or strategy ■ Lesson includes indicators of success
Guided Practice ("We do it")	■ Students practice in flexible groupings ■ Teacher actively dialogues with students as they practice, keeping them on task and on track with success criteria ■ Teacher uses prompts, cues, redirection as necessary to improve individual practice
Collaborative Learning ("You do it together")	■ Students continue to practice in flexible groupings ■ Tasks are designed so students benefit from group interactions ■ Students are held accountable for individual as well as group learning
Independent Learning ("You do it alone")	■ Independent tasks extend beyond practice to application and extension tasks ■ Teacher works with individuals and small groups as they work on tasks to maintain focus on success criteria

(Quotations from Fisher & Frey, 2008)

Gradual Release of Responsibility

In recent years, there has been an increased emphasis on student-centred methods of instruction that encourage students to become capable thinkers and learners. Research suggests that students who are more engaged in their learning demonstrate greater achievement (Flessa et al., 2010). Engaged learners find extrinsic rewards (e.g., praise, good grades, winning) welcome, but their main motivation arises from their enjoyment and interest in the lesson content. Engaged learners are also more likely to stay on task, persevere to overcome challenges, and commit to developing greater understanding of concepts (Jang et al., 2010). Teachers must therefore consider how they can make learning relevant to students' prior experiences, make links to other subject areas, provide opportunities for students to take responsibility for their own learning, and finally, ask students to articulate their learning.

Students learn in different ways and at different rates based on their particular skills and abilities, so it makes sound pedagogical sense for teachers to plan lessons that present the content with this in mind. Teaching strategies (or instructional strategies) are defined as purposeful actions and behaviours planned and implemented by the teacher to meet lesson goals. They are techniques for engaging learners and delivering the curriculum. Strategies may vary depending on the strengths and personality of the teacher. Some examples of strategies include demonstrations, station activities, peer teaching, and direct instruction. While Mosston's spectrum of styles speaks to the adoption of one particular approach for a lesson or series of lessons, it may also be appropriate to use a variety of strategies within one lesson to present the content in different ways. The gradual release of the responsibility model, originally developed to enhance literacy achievement, has relevance in PE. In fact, the traditional approach to structuring a lesson is strikingly similar. This framework identifies four key components (teaching strategies) that can be used within one lesson or over a series of lessons to support students as they acquire new skills (Fisher & Frey, 2008). It also requires that the teacher shift the responsibility for performing a task to a situation in which the students assume all (or most) of the responsibility for handling tasks in which they have not yet developed skills. The four key components are: modeling, guided practice, collaborative learning, and independent learning. **Table 5.6** summarizes each of the components.

As students assume more responsibility for their learning, they will be better equipped to use their skills in different contexts. The "transferability" of such skills is an important factor in PE settings as well as physical activity settings beyond the school environment. Developing confidence and movement competence (also known as *physical literacy*, see Chapter 13) through this responsibility model may contribute to the adoption of physically active lifestyle habits. This is certainly a major goal for many physical educators.

A variety of curriculum models (see Chapter 3) and curriculum approaches to PE have evolved from community, school, teacher, and/or student beliefs, values, goals, and philosophies. The different models and approaches are adopted and adapted to complement the spectrum of teaching styles providing a foundation for developing interrelationships between content and the instructional process. For example, the TPSR model (Hellison, 2003) would provide a supportive basis and framework for teaching through Mosston's divergent and learner-initiated styles to achieve learning goals.

Differentiated Instruction

Since students differ significantly in their learning styles, abilities, prior experiences, and interests, teaching approaches or strategies should vary accordingly. Successful differentiated instruction caters to all types of learners, and responds according to their changing needs (Ontario Ministry of Education, 2011). Appropriate adjustments can be made with regard to the content (e.g., planning), the process of instruction, and the product (e.g., assessment).

The use of task cards can be helpful in differentiating instruction to accommodate varying developmental levels among students. They can be used effectively in conjunction with several teaching styles (e.g., practice, reciprocal, self-check, divergent), in order to assist individual students in exploring and practising at an appropriate skill level. For example, during a grade nine skating lesson, several skill-focused stations may be set up, each with a task card for either gliding, forward stroking/skating, backward stroking/skating, jumping, or turning. Different levels are indicated by colour or number allowing each student to select entry level and progress as required.

Sample

Gliding (transfer weight using outside and inside edges):

Try increasing your speed before moving onto the next task.

1. Glide through the four pylons (far apart) on two feet forwards.
2. Glide through the four pylons (far apart) on two feet backwards.
3. Glide through six pylons (close together) with one foot forwards.
4. Glide through six pylons (close together) with one foot backwards.

Task cards, in electronic or traditional forms, can also help students experience and observe progress, record results, and compare to personal bests.

The following is a list of other general suggestions to differentiate instruction in a PE class, many of which will be discussed in the next section:

- Use a variety of instructional strategies.
- Use a variety of management strategies.
- Use a variety of learning activities.
- Use a variety of grouping strategies.
- Provide students choice with regard to activities, levels, equipment, etc.

- Monitor and assess student responses and adjust accordingly.
- Provide accommodations and/or modifications that are specified in the individual education plans of students who have special education needs.

The Learning Environment

One of the most important factors related to learning and subsequent achievement in PE is time spent with the subject matter (Rink, 2009). This refers to the active engagement of students in appropriate practice while receiving ongoing feedback and/or task adjustments from the teacher. In this context, "practice" could refer to drills, modified games, full games, or any other activity in which students are given opportunities to respond through physical activity. Similarly, "appropriate practice" refers to the correct performance of a skill or task according to the ability level of the participant. In other words, learning may be limited if students are practicing incorrectly, if the task is too easy or too difficult, or if there are too many tasks presented at one time.

Students' engagement time with motor skill activities is often referred to as Academic Learning Time in Physical Education (ALT-PE). According to Darst et al. (2012, p. 202), ALT-PE is "an activity where students are practicing skills in a setting that enables them to experience success. Learning is related to the amount of time students are involved in productive, on-task activity." Therefore, the allocation of time is one of the priorities for PE teachers. One way to maximize time available for learning is to reduce non-active time. The following section presents a number of strategies to structure the environment to achieve this goal. One must keep in mind that the learning environment includes not just the physical structures, equipment, and activities, but also the relationships between participants.

Rules and Routines—A Behavioural Plan

Sometimes referred to as effective "management" of the learning environment, teachers must establish a number of routines, strategies, and guidelines unrelated to the curriculum to ensure that all students can participate safely as they work towards achieving the goals of the lesson. The development of routines and rules can contribute significantly to the time available for learning. Student involvement in this process may empower students to take greater pride and ownership of rules and routines, thereby enhancing the learning environment. As previously mentioned, teaching and learning involves the building of effective relationships between teacher and student, and between students. Mutual respect for each other, and respect for established rules and routines, will contribute to a positive learning environment.

Routines are repeatable behaviours that contribute to the efficient day-to-day operation of PE classes. These include locker room activities (getting changed, amount of time for getting changed, what to do upon entering the gymnasium, etc.), set up of equipment, gaining the attention of the teacher, lesson closure, attendance, bathroom breaks, and lates/tardiness. Teachers must consider how they wish to conduct their classes, and what routines might be appropriate for their particular teaching approach and grade level of student.

Teachers must make these routines explicit at the beginning of the school year, and continue to reinforce such routines on a regular basis (particularly after vacations). By clearly communicating expectations ahead of time, providing ample opportunity for students to develop the appropriate behaviours, and reinforcing such behaviours, instructional time will increase.

Though teachers should expect students to follow the established routines, in reality this does not always happen. Teachers should therefore have a plan in place to a) reduce opportunities for students to violate the routines, and b) apply consequences consistently and fairly for all students. Students may have a number of excuses for not following routines (including some that may be the result of factors outside the school environment), and in such situations, teachers should reflect carefully on their own teaching practice to determine whether or not this may be the root cause.

Personal qualities such as enthusiasm, approachability, flexibility, and composure are keys to establishing positive relationships with students. Making a personal connection with students will enhance their interest and willingness to arrive at class on time and prepared to be active. Additionally, teachers might reflect on their professional qualities such as starting the class on time, following established rules and routines, being organized for the lesson, and exemplary communication practices. If teachers are not "walking the walk," or demonstrating expected behaviours for their students, then they should not be surprised when students choose not to follow the routines.

The following questions for developing routines might prove to be helpful as a guide for new teachers. Note that there may be additional school-wide routines such as fire drills, power outage/lockdown procedures, or other emergencies that may require specific training on the part of teachers and students.

Case Study 3: Fight in Class

During a floor hockey game in Mr. Brown's grade eleven PE Class, one student body checks another into the dividing wall as they are going down the gym floor toward the net despite the fact that Mr. Brown had emphasized that to prevent injury in class, body checking would not be permitted. Mr. Brown is refereeing the game and blows the whistle to stop play. Tom, the student who was checked, immediately drops his stick and retaliates by pushing John, the offending student, into the wall. This is followed by further pushing and shoving as well as a heated verbal exchange between the two.

Mr. Brown steps between the two students and sends them to opposite ends of the bleachers away from the other students in the class so that they both can cool off. They are told to remain there until the end of class.

Once class is over, both boys are called together to discuss what happened. John admits that the illegal body check provoked the confrontation. Tom admits that the retaliation was not appropriate and that the teacher should have been the one to penalize John's action.

Questions for Reflection

1 What consequences (if any) should each student receive for their actions?

2 Would the consequences be different if punches had been thrown?

3 Is a Vice Principal intervention warranted?

4 Are any further actions by the teacher warranted, (change room supervision once students are dismissed, ensuring conflict is not carried on after students leave class, revisiting rules with the class, etc.)?

Questions to Consider when Establishing Routines:

- Do the students need to get changed? If so, how much time is required?
- How will behaviour in the change room be monitored?
- What will students do as soon as they enter the gymnasium before the formal lesson begins?
- How will I deal with students who do not have the appropriate clothing, or who do not wish to participate (e.g., due to injury or illness)?
- How will I deal with late students?
- How will I deal with attendance?
- How will I deal with requests for bathroom breaks or drink breaks?
- How will I organize the students at the beginning of the lesson?
- How will I gain the attention of the students?
- How do I wish students to gain my attention?
- How will I distribute equipment or set it up?
- How will I signal the beginning (or end) of an activity?
- How will I identify out-of-bounds areas?
- How will I deal with a student who gets injured during class?
- How will I dismiss students?

Rules for social conduct in class may extend to the entire school environment. Examples include respecting others, using equipment appropriately, and cooperating with fellow students. Consequences for breaking the rules must be explicit and strictly enforced in order for standards of behaviour to be maintained. Rules (stated in positive terms) are often posted in a prominent location as a reminder to all. Many teachers engage students in the development of rules so that there is a greater sense of ownership and responsibility for following them.

A positive approach to establishing rules is more effective than a negative approach (Lavay et al., 2006). Rather than waiting for unacceptable behaviour to occur and imposing a sanction, teachers should consider how they might praise acceptable behaviour as a model for others. Valuing positive behaviour will contribute to its perpetuation much more effectively than fear of negative consequences. "Catching" students displaying appropriate behaviours is one strategy to value both the student and the behaviour, and this can be done in such a way that other students will wish to demonstrate those same behaviours. If negative behaviour is evident, immediate intervention should occur to prevent escalation or spreading of that behaviour. By focusing on the specific behaviour (e.g., "you did not complete that task") and not the individual (e.g., "you are unmotivated"), dignity and respect is retained. A follow-up question such as "what can we improve next time?" implies that the teacher still cares about the student and is willing to work together toward a solution.

Clearly, establishing a productive learning environment begins with the relationship that develops between teacher and student. Appropriate behaviours must be explained or demonstrated to students; they do not enter the school or gymnasium knowing what these are, nor will they learn them in one lesson. Teachers who systematically cultivate a positive relationship with their students by being proactive, consistent, fair, and firm will have most success with their behavioural management plan. Most importantly, teachers must model the qualities and behaviours they wish to see in their students.

Establishing routines is an important part of the instructional process in PE.

Case Study 4: Following the Rules

At the start of the school year, Ms. Steiner gathers her grade three class around her in the classroom (on the carpet area), and discusses the rules of the gymnasium with her students. She displays a list of clearly stated rules on one side of the interactive whiteboard, and a class list on the other. She explains each rule and gives examples, and she asks the students for reasons why each rule is important. Ms. Steiner encourages the class to ask questions if they do not understand a rule. After the discussion, Ms. Steiner asks the students, "If you understand the rules, please raise your hand." Next, she asks, "If you promise to give your best effort to follow the rules at all times, please raise your hand." She notices some students were hesitant to raise their hands for the second statement. Ms. Steiner tells them that the rules are also posted on the gymnasium wall as a reminder if they forget the rules. And, before each PE class in September, Ms. Steiner will review the rules before students proceed to the gymnasium. The students appeared much more confident after hearing this, and they raised their hands enthusiastically. Before Ms. Steiner lines up the students to go to the gymnasium, she has each student come up and place a check mark beside his or her name on the whiteboard.

Questions for Reflection

1 How might this series of events assist Ms. Steiner during the school year?

2 Why did Ms. Steiner discuss the rules of the gymnasium in the classroom?

3 Why did Ms. Steiner have the students place a check mark beside their name?

4 What other strategies might be considered for helping primary students learn, understand, and follow the rules in the gymnasium?

5 Make a list of gymnasium rules for a grade three class.

Organizing Students

Depending upon the activities planned for a PE lesson, teachers may select from a variety of organizational formations or physical arrangements of students to increase learning time. Some of these formations may already be embedded into daily routines, such as squad formation at the beginning of class. Some formations may have specific names so that when the teacher calls for that formation, the students know exactly what they are to do without prompting. Other formations might be selected for specific purposes during the lesson. If students are to gather in the centre of the gym as part of an established daily routine, this may save the teacher valuable moments asking the students to gather there and waiting while they comply. Other teachers may allow their students to engage in unstructured, supervised play at the start of class until the signal to stop is given, and then students gather in squad formation. Some teachers may choose to have a "home base" (e.g., squad formation in front of the teacher upon a signal), and will strategically stand in an area of the gymnasium where he or she wishes to begin the next activity, prompting students to automatically gather in that location (upon the signal).

In most cases the teacher would provide instruction to the students while they waited in formation. It is generally more effective to have the students be seated at this point in order to communicate clearly, and see all students' faces. This is particularly important with older students, who, when standing, may tower over the teacher, thus making it difficult to clearly give instructions. Standing students may also be more restless, and sidle up to one another to engage in conversation. Idle students who have equipment in their hands may also become a distraction from the intended message.

Teachers must also consider the importance of their message. There is usually important information to convey at the outset and conclusion of a lesson. If students are asked to gather in the mid-lesson, then any message conveyed should be significant yet concise so that students can quickly get back to the activity. The following questions might be considered when selecting a formation:

- How can the formation maximize active time?
- Which formation will offer the greatest safety in the space provided?
- What formation will maximize the use of equipment?
- What formation will fit best with the planned activity?
- How can the formation contribute to balanced teams, inclusion, and differentiation?

Table 5.7: Common Formations for Organizing Students in Physical Education

Formation	Description	Advantages	Disadvantages
Squads	Students in columns, usually 4–6 squads of 4–6 students, equally spaced	■ Teams/groups already established ■ Leadership roles can be developed within squads if used over long period of time ■ All students facing same direction	■ Same pair each time ■ Uneven numbers may cause problems
Partners	Students self-select Teacher selects Random draw	■ Multiple applications ■ Maximizes contact time with equipment ■ Can easily modify difficulty of task according to individual skill ■ Can increase physical activity levels	■ Role of leader may be uncomfortable for some
Semi-Circle or Line with Leader	4–6 students in a line (or semi-circle) with a leader out in front facing the line	■ Often used for throwing, passing, catching, receiving ■ Rotate role of leader	■ Ability to communicate with all students is compromised if teacher stands in middle ■ Does not simulate game conditions as well as other formats
Circle (close or spread)	Student arranged in a circle, usually with ample space in between	■ Follow the leader activities (e.g., stretching) ■ Everyone faces each other (useful for discussion or debrief)	■ Safety may be a concern if each student has equipment ■ Difficult for teacher to supervise and offer feedback to all
Scattered	Students equally spread throughout space	■ Individual skills ■ Creative movement ■ Teacher can circulate	■ Students waiting to respond unless several pieces of equipment are used
Zig-Zag	Two lines, staggered, facing each other	■ Controlled setting, easier for teacher to monitor ■ Enhances communication among students	■ Students waiting in line
Shuttle	Two lines of students facing each other, spaced apart	■ Can combine throwing/passing/receiving skills with movement	■ Students waiting in line ■ Can become overly competitive (teacher may have difficulty ensuring students follow rules) ■ Quality of performance may be compromised due to competition
Relay	Several columns of students arranged along one side of gym, student movement based on signal or location of other students	■ Can be used as a warm-up ■ Can be used with or without equipment	■ Those with less ability may be singled out
Whole Class Movement	All students arranged along one side of space; mass start	■ Everyone active	■ Difficult for teacher to supervise and offer feedback to all
Staggered Class Movement	Individuals or small groups depart at regular intervals	■ Less comparison between students	

Table 5.7 describes some of the most commonly used formations, along with advantages and disadvantages of each. Teachers must balance skill development with the desire for physically active students when selecting an appropriate formation. New skills may require more static practice, and this will dictate a specific formation. The gradual progression to game-like situations is usually a priority. Therefore, selecting a formation that would offer these possibilities may be preferred. If students are practicing throwing and catching from static positions, the teacher may slowly add more movement to simulate game conditions. For example, once the throw is released, the student might be asked to run to a specific location several steps away, and return to the original location to receive the next pass.

Selecting Partners, Groups, and Teams

Selecting partners and teams can be a challenge for PE educators. If the same strategy is used each time, students will quickly understand that if they stand in a certain position or wear a certain colour they will remain on the same team or in the same group as their friend(s). Therefore, it is important for teachers to use a variety of methods to select groupings of students, so they cannot anticipate the resulting teams. Regardless of the strategy selected for that day, it is important for teachers to purposefully plan for balanced teams, and to select a strategy that can be accomplished in a short period of time. Some strategies to pick teams include:

- Group students by shirt colour, shoe colour, etc.
- Group students by birth month (then combine months to balance teams)
- Group students by gender, then have each group split into two teams, and then combine one gender with another
- Choose the teams ahead of time based on abilities and read/post the list
- Use a random method (e.g., coin toss)

It should be emphasized that allowing students to select their own teams/groups or allowing team captains to select one student at a time can be a demeaning experience for some students. Teachers should be sensitive to this type of alienation, and avoid these situations. If the skill and maturity level of the students is such that they recognize the value of balanced teams and how that contributes to a positive learning environment then self-selected teams may be appropriate.

For many students, selecting a partner can cause anxiety as they may lack the confidence to ask someone to be their partner, or they are afraid that they may not be asked. Teachers should be sensitive to the feelings of those students who may not get a partner, and adjust accordingly. Teachers must also be aware that self-selected partners may result in the same pairings each time and therefore imbalanced opportunities in some activities. One strategy to reduce the anxiety and minimize the opportunities for the same partnerships each time would be to make partnering with someone new of benefit to everyone, or to place value on selecting someone new each time. For example, the teacher may set a goal of selecting different partners for each day of the week, and encourage all students to reach that goal. Alternatively, the teacher may attach the act of selecting partners to elements of the curriculum related to social skills (e.g., interpersonal skills), thereby using it as an assessment tool. And as such, the teacher must explain to students the importance of selecting different partners each time. Students who are asked to pick a new partner frequently, and for short periods of time, will view that behaviour as a more natural process in PE class. This strategy certainly supports the development of positive relationships in a safe, caring environment.

Case Study 5: Building Student Confidence

At the start of the semester Mr. Black asks his grade eight PE class the following questions: "How many of you would like to improve your upper body strength and how many of you would like to improve your level of fitness?" The majority of students respond positively to both questions. Mr. Black decides to start the process by making push-ups and sit-ups (as many as you can do in a set time), as well as a series of continuous running activities, a part of the daily class warm-up. Mr. Black designates Fridays as Max Days. On Max Day all students are asked to do as many push-ups as they can, as many sit-ups as they can do in a minute and then take their thirty second heart rate immediately following the running routine. After each of these tasks, all students are asked to report their scores to Mr. Black individually and a running total is kept of the scores over the semester. Mr. Black modified the tasks for students who could not complete two push-ups or sit-ups until they were able to do so.

Students were asked to try to beat their scores on the push-ups and sit-ups from the previous week as well as observe any changes in heart rate from the previous week. Mr. Black was able to constantly praise students who were showing improvement as they gave their scores, as well as monitor student progress.

Questions for Reflection

1 What are the advantages of having students do as many repetitions of a specific task as they can in a set time rather than a set number of repetitions?

2 Why did Mr. Black have students report scores individually to the teacher as opposed to having them call out their scores in front of the whole class?

3 Why is it important to encourage less skilled students to try modified tasks to help improve skills?

4 How could this type of approach be applied to other activities?

Volunteerism Versus "Voluntoldism"?

In nearly any grade level, the teacher will often require the assistance of one or more students for demonstration purposes. When a teacher asks for a volunteer publicly, it is frequently the confident, strong athletes in the class who readily put up their hand. This may not always be the best person to demonstrate, as he or she may unwittingly place the expectations so high that other students may be discouraged. It may also be an opportunity for the student to show off in front of his or her friends, and the demonstration may not match the explanation of the teacher. Similarly, a student may volunteer in order to demonstrate in an inappropriate way just to get a laugh. Teachers must use their judgment regarding the appropriateness of the volunteer. It may be prudent to ask a specific student (whom the teacher knows would provide a good demonstration) in private prior to the lesson so that the student is not embarrassed if asked at the time.

Transitions

There may be several phases within one PE lesson (e.g., warm-up, new skill learning, individual practice, application, closure). A transition is defined as the time (usually non-active time) required for moving from one phase to the next. Students may use this time to select or set up equipment; get organized into partners, groups, squads, or teams; move from one space to another; or to rotate from one station or game to another. Teachers may need this time to attend to managerial or non-instructional tasks such as distributing equipment, assigning teams, taking attendance, etc. Effective PE teachers minimize the time required for transitions to allow for more learning and activity time. Transitions should be taken into account during the planning phase, and can be built into the normal routines of every class. Students may be slow to respond during these phases since they might interpret non-learning time as an opportunity to socialize with their peers. This can delay the start of the next phase, as the teacher will have to signal and wait for attention before proceeding. Although it seems straightforward and simple, gaining and waiting for the attention of students can delay the start of a class, or reduce the active time available.

Teachers must purposefully plan what signal they wish to use to get students' attention, and they should emphasize to students how to respond appropriately and quickly to that signal. Some teachers may choose to use a single, short whistle blast, which can be effective in a noisy environment. Using multiple whistle signals may create confusion or may be difficult to hear. Once the whistle is blown, students should know exactly what to do (e.g., take a knee and listen, stop, hold the ball, turn and listen, or gather at "home base"

immediately). Alternatively, the teacher may wish to re-direct students to a specific location to begin the next phase of the lesson. In some classes, learning time and/or activity time is severely compromised because students are slow to respond. By reflecting on these situations, teachers may develop effective proactive strategies that work well for their specific students. Avoid penalizing students who do not respond appropriately with physical activity (e.g., "get down and give me ten pushups!"). While this may be effective for certain coaching situations, it will likely not contribute to a positive learning environment. A more positive way to deal with this situation might be to indicate to students the longer it takes to organize, the less time they have for physical activity. Other strategies may include:

- Gather in equipment first, then give instructions
- Include students in the set up and/or take down of equipment; activity does not begin until all equipment is ready
- Bring all participants into a pre-determined location at the beginning or end of a new phase
- Build in automatic rotations or substitutions so there are no stoppages in play
- Establish a method for timing segments within each phase (if appropriate)
- Wait for the attention of all students before beginning instructions for next phase
- Build in motivation for quick transitions

Transitioning from an indoor to an outdoor environment within the same lesson may also present some challenges, including safety concerns. Teachers might consider how they can conduct much of the organizational details of the lesson indoors (e.g., dividing groups, identifying group leaders/partners, organizing equipment, safety) before moving to the outdoor space. Students should know exactly where they are to meet and what they are to do upon arrival, as the arrival of the teacher and/or the rest of the students may be delayed. Equipment should be controlled at this point as well, since outdoor spaces tend to be much larger than indoor spaces, thus giving students an opportunity to spread out (perhaps out of sight or earshot). Purposeful planning for using outdoor spaces can enhance the frequency of their use.

Table 5.8 (on the next page) summarizes a number of strategies related to structuring the learning environment that may be helpful as PE teachers consider non-instructional ways to better engage their students during lessons.

Table 5.8: Strategies to Enhance the Learning Environment

Issue	Strategy	Examples
Physical Safety	Change Physical Environment	■ Use mats/padding ■ Consult safety guidelines for equipment and protective gear use
	Rule Modifications	■ Crease rule (hockey); no body contact; no stick checking; two hands on the stick; cover rule (lacrosse); completed pass rule; contact with ball below the waist ■ Reduce chance of injury by providing "no go zones" ■ Use alternate forms of goals and scoring rather than goalies
	Drill Design	■ Reduce chances of someone being hit by errant flying object; e.g., hit/strike/throw in only one direction ■ Establish method for clearing zone of equipment and participants before next shot or rotation
	Rule Enforcement	■ Strict enforcement by teacher (especially at the outset) ■ Peer engagement (e.g., call own fouls; self regulation as an expectation) ■ Student referees (e.g., use of school team members, or those students with appropriate training)
Opportunity to Participate	Change Physical Environment	■ Add more courts (e.g., half court singles in badminton) or make smaller courts (e.g., three courts of volleyball in half gym) ■ Reduce team size or members per group to maximize contacts ■ Use all physical space and equipment available (e.g., all basketball nets) ■ Use outdoor spaces as much as possible (e.g., local park or green spaces, playgrounds) ■ Use alternative settings if available (e.g., local YMCA, community facilities) ■ Provide individual or partnered activities (e.g., non-competitive focus)
	Rotations	■ Shorter shifts ■ Minimize elimination; re-entry option ■ Timed episodes to equalize play (e.g., four minute games) and minimize wait time
	Well-planned Transitions	■ Use setups to safely maximize numbers participating at one time (e.g., around-the-world, shuttle drill, king-of-the-court) ■ Ball retrieval strategies (e.g., retrieve own ball, central location for ball storage) ■ Routines for equipment/apparatus setup and take down, warm-ups, responding to whistles or other signals, gathering for instructions, etc. ■ Clearly defined method of rotation or movement from one area to the next
	Rule Modifications	■ Establish rules to force all participants to be involved in play on offence and defence, e.g. "cherry-picker's" offside rule
	Balance Teams/ Groups	■ Strategies for selecting partners/teams ■ Teacher-selected teams, groups, squads ■ Hold a draft after period of time
Lack of Success	Equipment Modifications	■ Change size of ball (e.g., smaller, larger) ■ Change type of ball (e.g., elephant skin ball vs. volleyball)
	Change Target	■ Size of target ■ Distance to target
	Reduce Task Complexity	■ Break down the skill into parts ■ Scaffold new learning ■ Suitable time to complete task without compromising technique
Off Task	Increase Clarity of Instructions	■ Use clear and brief expectations; check for understanding; use demonstrations
	Reduce "Talk Time"	■ Plan the instructions; use key words; break up into shorter episodes
	Reduce Wait Time	■ Eliminate lines; add more implements (e.g., balls); add more stations
	Closer Supervision	■ Teacher circulation; frequent and specific feedback
	Optimal Challenge	■ Timed drills rather than finite numbers; provide challenge choices/levels; keep score
	Variety	■ Different drills/activities; change teams; leadership roles

Conclusion

Teaching PE is a complex endeavour, requiring much planning and preparation. But even the most thoroughly prepared lessons do not always proceed as planned. Effective teaching starts with a plan, but changes and flexes according to moment-to-moment events during the lesson. Successful teachers are able to adapt the learning conditions according to these events so that opportunities for student learning are maximized and the goals of the lesson can be met. The three key elements of the instructional process (communication tools, instructional framework, learning environment) presented in this chapter should provide pre-service teachers with a flexible framework within which to adapt their lessons to meet students' needs and learning interests, and to further develop their repertoire of skills and knowledge. Expert teachers continually challenge themselves to broaden their range of abilities, and to courageously try new ways of instructing, organizing, and motivating their students. Successful teaching in physical education is much more than simply delivering the curriculum; it is about developing positive relationships with students so that they will become active young men and women engaged in their learning.

Questions for Further Discussion

1 Select three of the following roles: instructor, mentor, coach, referee, leader, mediator, listener, disciplinarian, observer, and assessor. Describe a specific situation in PE class in which each of those roles might be applied. Reflect on your ability to perform in each role. What skills and abilities do you currently possess, and what might you need to develop in the future?

2 Consider how you might fully involve a student with a physical disability (e.g., visual impairment, locomotor problems, or uses a wheelchair) in your PE class. How would you change your instructional approach? What changes would you have to make to the learning environment for full inclusion?

3 Research your provincial ministry's policies on safe, healthy schools. These may include policies on bullying, daily physical activity, and acceptance. Explore how these policies might inform your teaching, and how you might support these policies school-wide through PE.

4 Students often give their best effort or demonstrate the proper movement pattern when they know the teacher is observing them, yet they may display entirely different behaviour when the teacher is not observing. What steps might you take to ensure students work on the assigned task for the duration of time allotted?

5 How might achievement of learning outcomes in PE support the achievement of learning outcomes in other subject areas? Conversely, how might other subject areas support the achievement of PE learning outcomes? Develop some specific strategies around interdisciplinary teaching and learning.

6 Examine your province's safety guidelines with respect to safe participation in PE. How is this document intended to guide your practice? Use specific examples to demonstrate your knowledge of this document.

7 Why are learner-centred instructional approaches (e.g., independent learning, guided discovery) less prevalent than other approaches? What are the advantages and disadvantages of these approaches?

8 You have planned a soccer lesson for the gymnasium, but the day is warm and sunny, and the field (natural grass) is available for your use. The field is across a busy street from the school. What changes must you make to your management plan? Outline at least three key modifications to your plan.

Key Terms

- Learning Domains (affective, cognitive, psychomotor)
- Communication Skills
- Debrief
- Teacher Demonstrations
- Visual Aids
- Teaching and Learning Cues
- Teacher Questioning
- Teacher Observation
- With-it-ness
- Feedback (verbal and non-verbal)
- Instructional Framework
- Teaching Styles
- Engaged Learners
- Teaching Strategies
- Differentiated Instruction
- Appropriate Practice
- Learning Environment Management
- Organizational Formations
- Lesson Transitions

Assessment and Physical Education

Daniel B. Robinson and Lynn Randall

Overview

This chapter is meant to provide new physical educators with a foundation of knowledge and skills related to appropriate and desirable assessment practices within physical education (PE). New physical educators should have an understanding about assessment and a number of closely related topics and terms (measurement, evaluation, criteria, etc.). Equipped with this foundational understanding, it is possible for physical educators to design assessment tasks with both purpose and potential. Because of assessment's essential and significant role in the planning and teaching process, sound assessment practices contribute to sound planning and teaching practices. While assessment on its own is a complex and multifaceted topic, PE presents some additional unique issues. Consequently, this chapter includes content, assessment samples, illustrative examples, discussion/reflection questions, and case studies directly related to the unique PE context.

Introduction

It is essential for physical educators to have a sound understanding of assessment, measurement, and evaluation. Assessment is generally defined as the process of collecting and organizing information-as-evidence from many sources about students' knowledge, skills, and attitudes. Physical educators (as well as students and their parents/guardians) may then use this information in a number of ways. For example, physical educators are able to make informed educational decisions about their students, provide feedback to their students about their individual learning achievements and needs, and reconsider and/or revisit their own instructional practices (Buck, Lund, Harrison, & Blakemore Cook, 2007).

The collection and organization of students information requires some sort of differentiation. Without such differentiation, identifying varying levels of student learning would be impossible. Measurement is the process by which such differentiation may occur. Measurement might result in some easily quantifiable descriptor (e.g., a student's performance during an immediately measurable task, such as writing a test) or it might result in a qualifiable descriptor (e.g., a student's performance during an observable task, such as presenting a movement sequence).

Assessment and evaluation are terms that are defined in various ways by different physical educators, administrators, and authors. Though sometimes used interchangeably, within this chapter, assessment and evaluation should be viewed as very different constructs. Assessment is the process of collecting and organizing information, while evaluation is the subsequent process of judging students' learning based on that information. To reiterate, the gathering of information about student learning is assessment; making judgments about student learning based on measurements associated with those assessments is evaluation (Davies, 2007).

To further appreciate this difference, consider that while multiple individuals might be given the task of assessing students within PE (e.g., physical educators, students, parents/guardians), only a trained physical educator is capable of making the professional judgments required for evaluation. For example, students might be able to collect and organize information about their peers while they perform a motor skill (such as striking a ball with an implement) in order to provide them with corrective feedback. In this case, they would be assessing one another. However, the physical educator is the best person to determine whether a student's performance when striking a ball is poor, adequate, proficient, or excellent, when compared to the criteria related to the particular outcome or learning objective. Only physical educators may label such learning so that a description and mark may be assigned to it.

Before, After, and During Instruction

Some readily recognize the need for physical educators to assess what students might know, be able to do, or value, *before* instruction. Others recognize the need for them to do so *during* instruction. Historically, most others have readily recognized the need for physical educators to assess what students might know, be able to do, or value, after instruction. Within PE, there is a need for all three of these assessment practices—and generally for clearly different purposes. These assessment practices and purposes are often referred to by terms such as pre-assessment, formative assessment, and summative assessment.

In order to have a clear understanding about assessment practices and purposes, it is important to first have an understanding of the principles of assessment (i.e., that assessment be continuous, collaborative, comprehensive, and criteria-based). Similarly, physical educators should also have an understanding of other important concepts related to assessment such as norm-referenced and criterion-referenced evaluation, validity, and reliability.

Learning Domains

Once they have an understanding of assessment in PE, physical educators are responsible for choosing (and/or designing) appropriate assessment tasks or tools so that they may assess and measure students in all three learning domains (cognitive, psychomotor, and affective; Bloom, 1956) in different movement dimensions (e.g., games, dance, gymnastics). The cognitive domain includes things that students are able to know (knowing or declarative knowledge), the psychomotor domain includes things that students are able to do (doing or procedural knowledge), and the affective domain includes the things that students are able to value (valuing, or affective knowledge).

While these three domains might be conceived as mutually exclusive categories, the current thinking related to physical literacy recognizes an overlapping, and more holistic, notion of these constructs (Francis et al., 2011; Wall, Reid, & Harvey, 2007). For example, psychomotor abilities (e.g., fundamental movement skills and sport specific skills) are interrelated and interconnected with both cognitive abilities (e.g., decision-making and self-regulation) and affective abilities (e.g., social and emotional well-being). Nonetheless, physical educators are responsible for applying assessment tools related to all three of these learning domains, including exit slips, fitness tests, learning logs, and skill tests.

Physical educators are required to make professional judgments based on the collected assessment data. These judgments generally require them to qualify and/or quantify student learning, which often relies upon the utilization of checklists, analytic rating scales, and rubrics. Stated more clearly, while students might be given the task of completing an exit slip or skill test, the physical educator might utilize a related checklist or rubric to measure student learning.

Even educators with a strong understanding of PE assessment will encounter assessment "issues" within schools. Different educational professionals have varying perspectives on some of these issues, which are generally more "grey" than "black and white." With this in mind, the following topics are explored at the end of the chapter: Assessing Student Effort, Participation, and Conduct; Fitness Testing; and Assessing Student Improvement.

Principles of Assessment

Given the three previously mentioned assessment practices and purposes (i.e., pre-assessment, formative assessment, and summative assessment), there are four essential principles that must be constantly respected. Specifically, assessment is an educational practice that must be continuous, collaborative, comprehensive, and criteria-based (Alberta Learning, 2000; Francis et al., 2011). Assessment practices that strive to meet these principles are more likely to enable students to achieve the outcomes of their PE programs **(See Figure 6.1)**.

Figure 6.1: Principles of Assessment

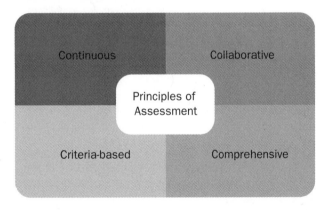

Continuous

Assessment should be an ongoing process so that it may continually enable student learning. It is no longer appropriate to consider assessment as only necessary at the end of a unit or term. Students should be assessed throughout a school year, school term, instructional unit, and in some respects, throughout an individual lesson.

Continuous assessment ensures that physical educators are constantly aware of their students' developing knowledge, skills, and attitudes. Students themselves should be continuously aware of these things as well. Ideally, when assessment is continuous, physical educators are able to receive ongoing feedback about the effectiveness of their

own instruction so that they might, in turn, revisit or re-teach a certain outcome. Equally important, when assessment is continuous, students are made constantly aware of their own progress with respect to their learning of knowledge, skills, and attitudes within their program. With continuous assessment, PE students should be constantly aware of their progress, such that evaluation results and grades provide little-to-no surprise.

Collaborative

The educator should not be the only individual who plays a role in the assessment of students. Both students and their parents/guardians may benefit from involvement in the assessment process. When students are included in this process, they are able to take a much more active role in their own learning. Students with a clear understanding of their own abilities, strengths, and weaknesses are ideally suited to set, monitor, and meet learning goals. Their involvement in the assessment process also enables them to take some responsibility with respect to understanding, and meeting, the outcomes of a PE program.

Including parents and guardians in the assessment process similarly allows them to have a clear understanding and insight about students' abilities, strengths, and weaknesses.

Comprehensive

Comprehensive assessment within PE suggests a need for comprehensive efforts in two regards. First, comprehensive assessment suggests a balance of curricular outcomes ought to be assessed. Such a focus on outcomes necessitates an inclusion of cognitive, psychomotor, and affective outcomes within all of the movement dimensions prescribed within the curriculum. While it may be permissible to privilege certain learning outcomes over others (Wiggins & McTighe, 2007), a balance of outcomes should be assessed.

Second, in addition to comprehensive assessment practices addressing the curriculum, this type of assessment also suggests that a variety of assessment strategies be utilized. For example, while written tests have traditionally been the primary method of assessment in most subject areas, educators with an understanding of the need for more comprehensive assessment practices are increasingly looking to other methods which respect the diversity of learning needs of their students. These might include tasks such as project work. Within PE, physical educators who understand the need for more comprehensive assessment practices are utilizing such things as learning logs, performance tasks, and portfolios rather than relying solely on isolated skill tests.

Criteria-Based

Assessment practices must consider the most critical criteria that describe what students should be able to know, do, or value. Articulating learning outcomes with clearly-defined criteria allows all those involved with assessment to have a clear understanding of the criteria upon which students are to be measured and evaluated. Furthermore, it is essential that these criteria be shared with students (and ideally with their parents/guardians) before and during instruction so that they have a clear understanding of what is expected of them.

Norm-Referenced and Criterion-Referenced Evaluation

Assessment and evaluation require a consideration of students' learning relative to some sort of ideal outcome. These considerations may be made relative to an external ideal defined by the performance of others or they may be made relative to an external ideal defined by criteria.

When a judgment about a student's learning of an outcome is based on how well a student does in relation to others, the evaluation is norm-referenced. Norm-referenced evaluation is often used in conjunction with a pre-determined "normal distribution." This assumes a small number of students will do exceptionally well, a small number will do poorly, and a majority will peak in the middle as average (Rust, 2002). When students are compared to others, the "others" might be based on larger groups such as national norms, school norms, or class norms.

There are some common criticisms of norm-referenced evaluations that have a particular relevance for PE. First, when students are compared to others within an especially small population (e.g., class norms), there is a possibility that the learning results will not follow a normal distribution. This might be influenced by a number of possible factors, some of which should be familiar to any university student who has felt aggrieved by the "bell curve." For example, the students within a class might be especially weak, or strong, or they may have been taught especially poorly, or well. In such instances, norm-referenced evaluations provide little information about students' actual learning. Second, when students are compared to others within an especially large population (i.e., national norms), there is little regard given to the unique teaching and learning context. That is, educators are forced to make judgments about their students relative to others with whom they may have very little in common. Finally, norm-referenced evaluations require some students failing to meet the outcome. For example, in the past, many fitness tests evaluated students in this manner (Rink, 2010).

Case Study 1: Just Getting Started

Matt, a first-year high school physical educator, has replaced the former physical educator who retired after many years at the school. Matt's teaching assignment is strictly PE. In addition to the compulsory course, Physical Education 10, many students at his school have chosen to take Physical Education 11 and Physical Education 12 as electives. In fact, for many years, his school has had many more students enrolling in these electives than other schools in the same school district.

After report cards were sent home at the end of his first term, Matt had many inquiries from his students and their parents/guardians. There were a number of concerns expressed, but the main concern was the grades students received on their report cards. Students and their parents/guardians were genuinely puzzled by the generally lower-than-expected grades. Parents/guardians expressed such sentiments as, "My son's marks were a full ten percent higher last year. What happened?" and "How can my daughter have such a low mark? This is gym."

As a first-year educator, Matt was discouraged. Considering the time and effort he had put into assessing, measuring, and evaluating his students, he could not have anticipated such dissatisfaction. He planned on discussing the situation with a school administrator; before he had a chance to do so, an administrator contacted him. Evidently, some of the same students and parents/guardians had already approached her about the issue. The administrator, speaking first, explained to Matt, "Students take this class to bring their average up. We are used to a class average of around ninety-five percent in gym here..."

Questions for Reflection

1. Discuss what Matt might have done beforehand to avoid this situation. What might he have done in September, and throughout the term?

2. Discuss how Matt might address this situation? What message(s) might he share with the school administrator, students, and parents/guardians?

In contrast, when a judgment about a student's learning of an outcome is based on how well a student does in relation to clearly stated criteria related to that outcome, the evaluation is criterion-referenced. Criterion-referenced evaluations do not assume any particular distribution of grades; there are not necessarily students who will do exceptionally well, or poorly. Student learning is compared only to, and is assessed only according to, the extent to which it meets the criteria established ahead of time. Since PE curricula across Canada are all essentially outcome-based programs, choosing and applying criteria for various outcomes is generally a straightforward task. In fact, many provinces' curriculum support and implementation documents include assessment samples in which student learning may be easily compared to various curricular outcome criteria. While in the past, fitness tests have been norm-referenced (*which* always resulted in some students scoring poorly), more recent fitness tests such as the Fitnessgram® (Cooper Institute, 2007) are criterion-referenced. With these types of fitness tests, it is possible for all students within a PE class to achieve the minimum standards for success. However, it is also possible for no students to achieve the minimum standards for success.

When assessing students, both the validity and reliability of the assessment must be taken into account.

Validity and Reliability

When physical educators collect information about their students for assessment purposes, it is important for them to be certain that the information is valid and reliable. If a measure has validity, its measurements should indicate exactly what is supposed to be measured. If a measure has reliability its measurements should be consistent if repeated. **(See Figure 6.2)**.

To understand these ideas, consider a carpenter who is tasked with measuring and cutting ten 2x4 boards so that they are six feet in length. When measuring and cutting is complete, the carpenter's supervisor notes that all boards are exactly the same length, though they are all a full foot too long. In this case, the carpenter's measuring is reliable (i.e., every time he or she measured and cut the boards, they ended up the same length) but the carpenter's measuring is not valid (i.e., not once did the carpenter measure and cut a six foot board). It is especially important to note here that assessments can be reliable but not valid. However, if an assessment is valid, it is generally reliable (i.e., if all boards had been measured and cut to six feet, both validity and reliability would be achieved).

Validity

Validity is essentially determined by way of physical educators' professional judgment (McMillan, Hellsten, & Klinger, 2011). Assessments are valid when they measure exactly what is intended to be measured. For example, testing a student's ability to set a volleyball as an indicator of that student's ability to play volleyball might not be particularly valid (though it would certainly be a valid assessment of the student's setting ability). Ideally, physical educators are able to select an outcome from their curriculum document and then clearly articulate the most critical and demonstrable qualities of that outcome. Once this is complete, physical educators might then introduce assessment tasks and/or tools to assess student learning.

Physical educators need to ensure three types of validity: content validity, criterion-referenced validity, and construct validity (Fenwick & Parsons, 2009). Content validity refers specifically to how well an assessment measure actually measures a student's learning of what was taught. A physical educator might ensure content validity by choosing assessment tasks that are very clearly aligned with curricular outcomes while also continually being committed to teaching to those outcomes. This point cannot be overemphasized: physical educators should only assess students' learning of the outcomes that have been taught. For example, if a physical educator wishes to assess students' ability to safely use equipment or follow game rules and etiquette, students need to first be taught these concepts.

Figure 6.2: Reliability and Validity

Unreliable and Unvalid   Reliable, not valid   Both reliable and valid

Criterion-referenced validity refers to how well an assessment measure actually aligns with the articulated criteria. A physical educator might ensure criterion-referenced validity by implementing differing assessment tasks while using the same criteria; similar ratings suggest criterion-referenced validity. For example, if a physical educator is to assess students' ability to perform a manipulative task (such as performing an underhand roll), the same criteria might be used to assess students as they play beanbag bocce and bowling. If the ratings on the different tasks (using the same criteria) were similar, criterion-referenced validity would be achieved.

Lastly, construct validity refers to how well an assessment measure actually measures what is supposed to be measured. A physical educator might ensure construct validity by discussing students' intentions with them as they perform a psychomotor task. It is important to note that a performance task may be a poor method (with respect to construct validity) to determine declarative knowledge; interviewing a student would have more construct validity. Consider, for example, the PE student who cannot perform a high jump, but who can very clearly explain the mechanics of doing so. It is in this respect that written (and/or oral) assessments are generally better than performance-oriented assessment tasks at determining students' knowledge. Physical educators should therefore choose assessment tasks and tools that are best aligned with the learning domain (e.g., knowledge, skills, attitudes) being assessed.

Reliability

Similar to validity, reliability is determined by the physical educator. While validity refers to a measure's ability to measure what it is supposed to be measured, reliability refers to a measure's ability to have consistent measurements, each and every time it is used. It is with this logic that a reliable measure may or may not be valid

while an unreliable measure will never be valid (and a valid measure is generally reliable).

Within PE, the same assessment measure should result in similar assessment results every time. The more similar the results, the more reliable the assessment measure. The three types of reliability detailed here are:

1 Test-retest reliability

2 Internal validity

3 Inter-rater reliability

Test-retest reliability refers specifically to how consistent a measure is when implemented on a number of occasions. With all essential elements remaining constant (e.g., no further instruction, similar conditions), students' results should be similar if they are assessed repeatedly using the exact same assessment measure. Of course, there will always be minor variables that can influence a student's performance (mood, diet, sleep, etc.). Though perfect reliability is impossible to achieve (as are completely identical assessment conditions), physical educators should still strive to apply assessment measures capable of consistently revealing similar results.

Internally consistent reliability refers specifically to how well an assessment measure includes components that are equally challenging. For example, if a battery of assessment measures is used to determine a students' ability to play basketball (e.g., dribbling, passing, shooting, guarding), each assessment measure should be similar *if* they are to measure the same thing (i.e., basketball ability) and have internally consistent reliability. Similarly, a multi-item multiple-choice test with forty questions should yield similar results if students' even and odd-numbered responses were to be compared to one another (again, if all questions are intended to measure the same thing and have internally consistent reliability).

Finally, inter-rater reliability refers specifically to how well an assessment measure yields similar results when applied

Figure 6.3: Sample Self Assessment Tool from New Brunswick's Middle Level Physical Education Curriculum Grades 6 to 8

Sample of an individual assessment of interpersonal skills

Physical Education Self-Assessment

Unit: _____

Team Members: _____   _____

_____   _____

_____   _____

_____   _____

Social Development Assessment					
Date:	1	2	3	4	5
Rate yourself in the following categories on a scale of 1–5 (1 being the lowest and 5 the highest).					
1. encouraged other students					
2. played games fairly					
3. helped others improve					
4. shared responsibility in games					
5. resolved conflicts in a positive way					
6. showed respect for rules					
7. showed respect for officials and their decisions					
8. showed respect for opponents					
9. gave everyone an equal chance to participate					
10. maintained self control at all times					

by different people. Clearly, a multiple-choice test with an answer key would have perfect inter-rater reliability. However, assessments of psychomotor and affective outcomes within PE can be more subjective. Ideally, different physical educators using the same assessment measure would arrive at the same, or similar, decisions about students' learning. One way to improve inter-rater reliability is to have physical educators observe and assess the same students and then have them come together to discuss their observations so that they may come to a more clear and common understanding.

Role of Assessment in PE

As previously mentioned, there are many roles of assessment in PE. In order for a physical educator to properly plan instructional activities, it is first important to know what knowledge, skills, and attitudes students already possess.

When teaching lessons or units within PE, physical educators need to be constantly aware of their students' learning. Such awareness allows both the students and their physical educators to have an understanding about what knowledge, skills, and attitudes have been learned, and which require further instruction. Finally, once a lesson or unit of instruction has been taught, physical educators need to have a clear understanding about what students have learned.

It is also advisable for physical educators to ensure that assessment practices be as authentic as possible. Authentic assessment (sometimes also referred to as performance-based assessment) includes tasks that relate to real-life contexts (Ryan, 2005). This often requires assessments to occur in real-life (or contrived) settings (Kovar, Combs, Campbell, Napper-Owen, & Worrell, 2007). For example, assessing students' ability to pass and receive a plastic puck by observing two students passing back and forth would be an artificial setting; invasion games like

Figure 6.4: Sample Peer Assessment Tool from New Brunswick's Middle Level Physical Education Curriculum Grades 6 to 8

Sample of a rubric done with a partner

Directions: Please evaluate your partner and yourself using the following scale:

Scoring	What does it mean?
4	consistently / all of the time
3	usually / most of the time
2	occasionally / some of the time
1	rarely / seldom

Criteria	Self	Partner
Knowledge of steps		
On count with music		
Enthusiastic while learning dance		
Provides "put-ups" to peers		
Does not give up		
Provided input on this checklist		

How did you do?

_____

_____

Are you ready to teach the class?

_____

_____

floor hockey do not generally involve undefended passes. A more authentic task would require physical educators to assess their students' passing and receiving abilities while they were engaged in a floor hockey game, lead-in game, or game-like scenario.

Pre-Assessment

Pre-assessment consists of assessment before instruction. It is also sometimes referred to as diagnostic assessment (Alberta Assessment Consortium, 2005). This may occur at the very beginning of the school year or just prior to instruction in any given unit. While a physical educator may have some general learning outcomes and expectations of students (as defined, largely, by PE curriculum), information gathered through pre-assessments can be used to select and plan for appropriate learning outcomes and expectations, instructional activities, and

subsequent assessments (McMillan et al., 2011). Such initial pre-assessments can provide important individual and collective information to answer the following sorts of questions:

- What pre-existing knowledge, skills, and/or attitudes do students have that are related to the general learning outcomes and expectations?

- What are the differences between students' level of cognitive, psychomotor, and/or affective knowledge with respect to the general learning outcomes and expectations? Are some students behind or ahead?

With pre-assessment information, physical educators are able to individualize instruction by providing appropriate tasks and modifications for their students. For example, students who are found to have an especially strong ability within a particular movement dimension might be given more challenging tasks and activities related to educational outcomes. Similarly, students with a weaker ability might be taught less challenging tasks and activities.

Although pre-assessments allow for such possibilities, their practicality and efficiency have been questioned by those such as McMillan et al. (2011) who suggested that it is doubtful formal pretests given at the beginning of a school year are helpful for planning. It is therefore important for physical educators to choose pre-assessments that are both practical and efficient. Examples of practical and efficient pre-assessments might include a fitness test at the beginning of a term (to be compared to one done at a later date) or an informal observation of students' game play in soccer before planning a soccer unit. Information gathered through pre-assessments should not be evaluated.

Formative Assessment

In recent times, formative assessment has become an increasingly popular concept within education. Indeed, research has indicated that when educators include formative assessment practices in their teaching, student achievement is positively affected (Black & Wiliam, 1998). Despite this evidence of formative assessment's potential, surveys of educator practice suggest that it is yet to become commonplace within many schools (Black, Harrison, Lee, Marshall, & Wiliam, 2003).

Formative assessment generally occurs during a lesson, unit, or program of instruction, and provides ongoing feedback to the student about progress, and to the educator about the effectiveness of instruction (Fenwick & Parsons, 2009; Rink, 2010). The gathered assessment information provides students and educators with information related to curricular outcomes up until that moment in time; which can and should inform future teaching and learning. Formative assessment practices do not need to rely entirely on the physical educators to collect information and provide feedback. For example, with requisite criteria in hand, students can assess their peers (peer assessment—**Figure 6.4)** or themselves (self assessment—**Figure 6.3**).

The benefits of peer assessment include: students improving their ability to observe themselves and others critically and appreciatively, students becoming more aware of their own biases, students being exposed to additional perspectives and observation styles, and students developing the ability to judge according to criteria rather than personal preference or emotional appeal (Fenwick & Parsons, 2009). The benefits of self assessment include: students becoming increasingly engaged in their learning (Bruce, 2001), educators gaining access to information otherwise not available about their students' effort (Rolheiser & Ross, 2000), and students becoming enabled to internalize learning goals so that they may apply them to their future learning (Herbert,

1998). Furthermore, as appropriate and with educator support and direction, students might also engage with their parents/guardians in formative assessment practices.

An example of a formative assessment practice in PE would be when a physical educator has students working in pairs, using a checklist in order to provide feedback to one another as they perform a movement task. Alternatively, students might watch themselves performing a movement task on video and use a checklist to assess their own progress.

Summative Assessment

Summative assessment is much more familiar to new physical educators—it has been the most common assessment practice within schools for many years. Generally occurring at the end of a unit or term (or whenever students need to demonstrate their learned knowledge, skills, or attitudes), summative assessment essentially allows educators to ascertain their students' level of achievement at a particular moment in time. Furthermore, it informs educators, students, and parents/guardians; enables judgments and evaluations about students' learning of outcomes; and its associated information is often submitted into school records (Earl, 2003). Information gathered from summative assessments is generally evaluated. The difference between formative and summative assessment was perhaps made best by Stake (as cited in Scriven, 1991): "When the cook tastes the soup, that's formative. When the guests taste the soup, that's summative" (p. 169).

Evaluation and Grading

Once summative assessment information is collected and measured, students can be evaluated. If marking is defined as the measurement and reporting of learning as indicated on any single assessment of student learning, then grading is the measurement and reporting of that learning at the end of a unit, term, or year (O'Connor, 2009).

Keeping in mind that evaluation requires educators to make judgments about student learning, physical educators should not report grades by determining the average score on a number of measured and marked assessments. A problem arises when educators simply average the scores of all of their students' assessment tasks, since they effectively absolve themselves of the responsibility of making an informed and professional judgment about their students' learning.

Undoubtedly, the task of collecting assessment information for a number of outcomes and reporting that achievement with a single score on a report card is a difficult task. Nonetheless, physical educators, equipped with assessment information gathered throughout a unit, term, or year, are ideally situated to make an overall decision about student learning.

Currently there are many different ways to report students' learning on report cards. These differences may exist between grade levels in the same school, between schools in the same district, between districts within the same province, and between provinces and territories nationwide. These different reporting systems include numerical scores, letter grades (or equivalent qualitative descriptors), pass/fail systems, and analytic rating scales. Numerical scores and letter grades are the most common grading systems in Canadian schools. Increasingly, the use of letter grades is being replaced by the use of qualitative descriptors (e.g., Excellent/Satisfactory/Needs Improvement or meets all outcomes all of the time/most of the time/ some of the time). Pass/fail or credit/no credit systems, by their nature, suggest that educators need only identify the minimum level of achievement necessary to move to the next level. Finally, some report cards now include analytic rating scales for a number of general learning outcomes within each subject area.

Regardless of the system of reporting, most report cards also include educator comments about students' learning; generally these are connected with various curricular outcomes.

Types of Student Assessments

Assessing students' learning of cognitive, psychomotor, and affective outcomes requires physical educators to employ a number of assessment possibilities. These tasks and tools can be employed in both a formative and summative manner; indeed the very same task or tool can be used for both purposes. While assessment tasks such as written tests, fitness tests, and skill tests might be readily recognizable to many, physical educators who value a more comprehensive view of assessment are now employing a number of other assessment strategies. These include, but

are not limited to, exit slips, observations, learning logs, performance tasks, and portfolios.

Exit Slips

Exit slips are written student responses to questions posed by the educator at the end of a class. They are especially practical and efficient as they take minimal time, yet are capable of providing an educator with an indication of students' understanding of lesson outcomes. They may be completed on handouts, index cards, mini white boards, or sticky notes. The educator should pose a question (or questions) for students to respond to. After having ample time to complete their exit slips (no more than five minutes), students simply hand them in to their educator as they leave class. While educators routinely summarize key points of a lesson during closure, students are rarely afforded an opportunity to summarize their learning at the end of a lesson; exit slips give students that opportunity. For an example see **Figure 6.5**.

Fitness Tests

Fitness testing has been a staple of PE programs for over fifty years (Darst & Pangrazi, 2009; Lloyd, Colley, & Tremblay, 2010). Moreover, the advantages and disadvantages associated with fitness tests within PE have been debated for decades (Corbin, Pangrazi, & Welk, 1995; Rowland, 1995). If fitness testing is to be included within a PE program, a number of guidelines should be followed:

- Fitness testing ought to be an integral part of fitness instruction

- Fitness testing results should inform physical educators about their own instruction and their students' learning (when physical activity is taught)

- Physical educators should expect all students to reach the minimum fitness standards for their grade/age level

(Silverman, Keating, & Phillips, 2008)

Figure 6.5: Sample Exit Slip

During physical education class today, we learned some new balances. How are "base of support" and "centre of gravity" related to balance?	Draw a picture showing where your hands and head should be when performing a headstand.

Case Study 2: Docking Marks

Joy had been the sole physical educator at her K–12 school for almost ten years. However, due to declining enrollment, her school recently closed down. Like a number of her colleagues, she has been placed at the nearest school (where all of the displaced students were also sent). Though she has been teaching PE for nearly a decade, her assignment at this new school is the first time she has taught PE as part of a group within a PE department. The other five physical educators have all been at the school for a number of years and seem to be especially close colleagues and friends. There is clearly a bond that has been established within the PE staff room.

Early in September, the PE department head reviewed the department's policies with respect to attendance, changing for class, and late assignments with every-one. Joy learned that if students missed two lessons within any unit, they could not pass the unit. She also learned that students would lose 5% from their term mark for every time they didn't change into appropriate attire, and that late assignments would be docked 5% a day. Joy doesn't really agree with any of these department policies but she feels uncomfortable, as she is the newest physical educator in a department of six.

Questions for Reflection

1 In your opinion, what are the major issues Joy might have with the PE department policies?

2 What message do the department policies give to students?

3 Discuss what Joy might do to share her perspective related to assessment and the school's current PE policies.

Fitness tests most often focus upon health-related fitness components (e.g., muscular strength and endurance), though some physical educators may also focus on skill-related fitness components (e.g., speed and agility). One of the more common fitness tests utilized today is the Fitnessgram® (Cooper Institute, 2007) physical fitness test; it has been found to be relatively valid and reliable. The Fitnessgram® includes a battery of test possibilities so that all health-related fitness components may be assessed. These include the Progressive Aerobic Cardiovascular Endurance Run (PACER) for aerobic capacity, triceps and calf skin folds for body composition, the curl-up test for abdominal strength, the push-up test for upper-body strength, the trunk lift test for trunk extensor strength and flexibility, and the back-saver seat and reach test for flexibility.

Observation

Observation of students is perhaps the most common method of assessing students in PE. Given the nature of PE, physical educators are often able to observe their students' movement throughout lessons. One of the greatest strengths of observation is that it allows students to receive immediate feedback on their performance. Educators' observations and feedback should focus on curricular outcomes. These observations are often closely tied to psychomotor outcomes but they may also relate to affective ones. For example, affective outcomes related to fair play and cooperation lend themselves to observation. Observation might be completed by physical educators or by other students. Observations may be recorded as an anecdotal record with a curriculum-aligned checklist.

Learning Logs

Learning logs provide students with an opportunity to track their own behaviours in class and/or outside of school. Curricula across the country have outcomes related to encouraging students to participate regularly in physical activity, and many have outcomes related to encouraging good nutritional practices. Requiring students to maintain a learning log for these types of behaviours allows two important things to occur. First, physical educators, who obviously cannot monitor these things, are able to effectively gather assessment information by way of their students (and their students' parents/guardians). Second, such a practice allows students (and their parents/guardians) to become more engaged in the assessment process. Students are enabled to become constantly aware of their behaviours, as are their parents/guardians. For an example see **Table 6.1**.

Table 6.1: Sample Learning Log

Style	Time	Considerations	Heart Rate	Description
Sample	30 min.	Swimming	156 bpm	I went to the pool with my family
Sunday				
Monday				
Tuesday				
Wednesday				
Thursday				
Friday				
Saturday				

Table 6.2. Sample Performance Task

Gymnastics Floor Sequence
Hollywood has come to town! A casting agent has spotted you and your friends at the school and has asked you to audition for a new movie. This audition will require you to choreograph a gymnastics sequence as an action scene for a movie. He has given you a list of general dominant movement patterns (DMPs) that you will need choose from and then put together in a gymnastics sequence.
Performance Task
You will be in a group of four students. Each group must have a starting pose, followed by a gymnastics sequence, and ending with an ending pose. Each group member must perform a minimum of three movements from each of the DMPs learned within the unit. These include (1) statics/balances, (2) locomotions, and (3) rotations. Each group member does not have to perform the same movements; the movements students choose should be suitably challenging for themselves. The routine will be a minimum of two minutes, but no more than four minutes, long. Students may include implements/props and/or dialogue and they must include music. Specific assessment criteria will be provided to you.

DMPs	Student 1	Student 2	Student 3	Student 4
Static/Balance	1 2 3	1 2 3	1 2 3	1 2 3
Locomotion	1 2 3	1 2 3	1 2 3	1 2 3
Rotation	1 2 3	1 2 3	1 2 3	1 2 3

Performance Tasks

Performance tasks are often utilized as culminating experiences that allow for a degree of flexibility and variation in students' performances (Rink, 2010) and are usually completed within a class period. Examples of performance tasks include:

- Students performing a gymnastics sequence
- Students performing a dance routine
- Students playing a game or lead-in game
- Students leading an aerobic fitness activity

Performance tasks generally allow for an authentic assessment. They can be assessed as they occur or recorded for assessment at a later time (Rink, 2010). For an example see **Table 6.2**.

Portfolios

Portfolios have long been a common assessment and evaluation method within various professional fields, including art, architecture, photography, and journalism (McMillan et al., 2011). In education, a portfolio is defined as "a purposeful, systematic process of collecting and evaluating student products to document progress towards attained learning expectations or to show evidence that

111

Case Study 3: Dis(abilities) and Assessment

Samantha is an elementary educator who teaches her class all subjects with the exception of music. As a generalist educator, Samantha took only one PE curriculum and instruction course in university. Despite this limited education, she has attended many professional development sessions and has been committed to providing her students with a quality PE program.

She has been focusing on teaching her grade one students a number of fundamental movement skills. She has planned and taught a number of lessons intended to help students improve upon their manipulative skills, particularly throwing and catching. To do so, she has been using some quality teaching resources that focus on these skills. In fact, some of her teaching has included the use of checklists and analytic rating scales.

While she has found these resources' checklists and analytic rating scales to be user-friendly and appropriate for most of her students, they have been less than ideal for some of her students who have differing abilities (i.e., some have some serious intellectual and physical disabilities). For some of these students, their throwing and/or catching abilities are so limited that the assessment checklists and analytic rating scales result in the lowest possible ratings—they have little use.

Questions for Reflection

1 Discuss what Samantha might do to address the needs of her students with disabilities with respect to assessment and evaluation.

2 In your opinion, must all students within the same class be assessed using the same checklist or analytic rating scale (i.e., the same criteria)? Give reasons for your answer.

a learning expectation has been achieved" (McMillan et al., 2011, p. 257). Physical educators and their students, together, should decide upon the contents of a portfolio. Because the portfolio cannot include evidence of all learning, it is especially important that educators and students create a purposeful portfolio with systematically well-organized content materials. Within PE, it is important to include items that address all three learning domains such as written assignments or tests, fitness testing results and goals, photographs of products, journal entries, skill tests results, and student reflections (Darst & Pangrazi, 2009). While portfolios have traditionally included only paper copies of assessment records, recent advances in technology are allowing students to develop multimedia portfolios that can include video of students performing various movement skills. The use of portfolios has several advantages; they are capable of documenting students' growth over a period of time, they involve students directly in their own learning and assessment, they build students' confidence, they provide more holistic measures of learning, and the very act of building them is a learning experience for students (Fenwick & Parsons, 2009). Potential drawbacks include the time-consuming nature of assembling them as well as the difficulty in using them to make judgments for evaluation (Fenwick & Parsons, 2009).

Skill Tests

Educators often design skill tests so that they may assess a student's learning of various movement tasks. For example, a skill test might be employed to assess students' fundamental movement skills (e.g., throwing, catching, hopping) or sport-specific movement skills (e.g., batting, volleying, serving). Skill tests can be administered informally by the students themselves or their peers, or in a more formal manner by the physical educator. The main advantage of skill tests is that they allow physical educators to isolate and focus on particular skills that are clearly included as curricular outcomes. Some of the challenges associated with skill tests include the difficulty of administrating them to everyone in a large group, and the decontextualized (and non-authentic) nature of many of the tests. Physical educators might address the difficulty of administrating large numbers of skill tests by having some students be assessed by the physical educator and others assessed by peers. In cases where skill tests are meant to be summative (and evaluative) assessment practices, physical educators might video record students' skill tests so that they may assess and evaluate at a later time.

The observation that skill tests are sometimes not authentic assessment tasks should be considered. Open skills, in which environmental factors restrict and define possible movement responses, are more appropriately assessed in an authentic assessment scenario (e.g., through game

Table 6.3: Sample Checklist A

Dodge (Locomotor Skill) Criteria	Observation 1				Observation 2			
Student's eyes focused in the direction of travel?	yes	☐	no	☐	yes	☐	no	☐
Student's body lowered during change of direction?	yes	☐	no	☐	yes	☐	no	☐
Student pushes off with outside foot during change of direction?	yes	☐	no	☐	yes	☐	no	☐
Student changes direction with one step?	yes	☐	no	☐	yes	☐	no	☐
Student can change direction in both directions?	yes	☐	no	☐	yes	☐	no	☐

Table 6.4: Sample Checklist B

Fair Play Criteria	Yes	No	Comment
Follows all game rules and demonstrates respect for decisions of the educator/official			
Responds to disagreements with teammates and/or opponents in a fair and considerate manner			
Contributes to the creation of a caring games-play environment by modelling games etiquette			

Table 6.5. Sample Analytic Rating Scale A (Frequency)

Gymnastics (Dominant Movement Patterns) Criteria	Rarely	Occasionally	Frequently	Consistently
Body movements flow smoothly from one to the next				
Body movements occur at low, medium, and high levels				
Performed balances are in control and held for a minimum of three seconds				
Performed rotations are in control and "tight"				
Performed locomotions cover space using multiple pathways and directions				
Notes:				

Table 6.6. Sample Analytic Rating Scale B (Quality)

Overarm Throw Criteria	Limited	Adequate	Proficient	Excellent
Preparation: side facing, throwing arm set back				
Action: transfer of weight forward, hip and body rotation, release point				
Recovery: follow through across body, return to athletic ready position				
Notes:				

play). A skill such as dribbling a basketball can be more authentically assessed by observing a student dribbling a ball around defenders in a game rather than having them perform a skill test in which they dribble a ball around cones. For closed skills, in which a stable and predictable environment has little-to-no effect on possible movement responses (e.g., teeing off a golf ball or serving a tennis ball), skill tests are more appropriate.

Written Tests

Most students should be familiar with written tests in many different subject areas as they are a staple assessment practice within the majority of schools. Written tests are practical assessment methods to assess student knowledge of PE. Trying to infer student knowledge through performance is an almost impossible task—students may have excellent declarative knowledge while having limited procedural knowledge. That is, a student may know what one must do to successfully perform a back roll, but may not have the ability, strength, or flexibility to do so. Written tests allow educators to collect such information from their students.

Within PE, written tests are sometimes misused as physical educators assign written tests that have little-to-no connection with the curriculum. For example, if there are no outcomes about the history of a particular sport, it is not suitable to assess students on that knowledge (and it is certainly not acceptable to include these assessments for evaluative purposes). Written test questions that might be especially suitable for PE might focus on knowledge about performing skills, knowledge about offensive and defensive strategies, and knowledge of safety practices and guidelines.

Measuring Student Learning

Regardless of the type of assessment employed by physical educators, measurement is required to allow educators (and students and their parents/guardians) to make sense of the information. The collection of assessment information requires a consideration against some previously identified criteria. These criteria should be clearly aligned with curricular outcomes and should be easily understandable by educators, students, and parents/guardians. Simply stated, criteria are the standards by which students' knowledge, skills, and/or attitudes may be valued or judged; determining criteria defines "what counts" (Gregory, Cameron, & Davies, 1997). Once criteria are established, student learning may be assessed with a checklist, analytic rating scale, or rubric.

Checklists

Checklists consist of a list of characteristics or behaviours that are generally separated into two discrete and binary categories. For example, categories might include yes or no, present or absent, or achieved or working to achieve (Herman, Aschbacher, & Winters, 1992). Checklists are capable of indicating effective completion of a task related to a particular cognitive, psychomotor, or affective outcome. For examples, see **Tables 6.3** and **6.4**.

Analytic Rating Scales

Analytic rating scales are similar to checklists in that they also include a list of characteristics or behaviours that are separated into discrete categories. However, rather than the two possibilities that checklists characteristically offer, analytic rating scales typically rate students along a continuum of possibilities. These may be quantitative, such as a score between one and four. They may also be qualitative, such as a descriptor from among many on a continuum. Analytic rating scales with qualitative descriptors often differentiate student learning based on either frequency or quality. Descriptors based on frequency might include labels such as rarely, occasionally, frequently, and consistently. Descriptors based on quality might include labels such as limited, adequate, proficient, and excellent. For examples, see **Tables 6.5** and **6.6**.

Rubrics

A rubric is like an analytic rating scale, except with more complete and detailed descriptors. A rubric is essentially a scoring guide that includes clear criteria that allow a physical educator to differentiate between various levels of student learning (McMillan et al., 2011). More than checklists and analytic rating scales, rubrics allow questions, such as the following, to be addressed:

- How should different levels of quality be described and distinguished from one another?
- What does the range in the quality of performance look like?

(Wiggins, 1998)

In order to design and utilize student-friendly rubrics, Gibbons and Robinson (2004) suggest physical educators first determine the number of performance levels they wish to use, write the "minimum standard" level first, and then use simple and specific language. They further suggest physical educators use students' words within rubrics (allowing students to co-create the criteria) as well as catchy terminology (e.g., "ultimate team player" or "on another court") so as to take students' focus away from numerical

Table 6.7: Sample Rubric A

Rubric and Criteria: gymnastics headstand (balance)			
Needs Improvement	**Satisfactory**	**Proficient**	**Excellent**
Can initiate a tripod but is unable to independently balance while inverted	Can independently balance while inverted in a tucked headstand position	Can balance with minimal peer support while inverted in an erect headstand position	Can balance independently with control for at least three seconds while inverted in an erect headstand position

Table 6.8: Sample Rubric B

Rubric and Criteria: demonstrate a healthy cooperative spirit and respect for tennis etiquette			
Needs Improvement	**Satisfactory**	**Proficient**	**Excellent**
Sometimes works with, and is supportive of, their peers; sometimes demonstrates respect and appropriate tennis etiquette (e.g., with respect to shaking hands, recognizing good shots, avoiding others' courts), often with prompting.	Usually works with, and is supportive of, their peers; usually demonstrates respect and appropriate tennis etiquette (e.g., with respect to shaking hands, recognizing good shots, avoiding others' courts) with some exceptions.	Usually eagerly works with, and is supportive of, their peers; usually demonstrates respect and appropriate tennis etiquette (e.g., with respect to shaking hands, recognizing good shots, avoiding others' courts) without prompting.	Always eagerly works with, and is especially supportive of, their peers; always demonstrates respect and appropriate tennis etiquette (e.g., with respect to shaking hands, recognizing good shots, avoiding others' courts) without prompting.

equivalents. While one could have just two categories within a rubric, they generally have three or four.

A good quality rubric should do the following:

- Help students understand what is wanted on an assignment
- Help students understand what a quality performance or product looks like
- Help students understand what they did well and what to do differently next time
- Enable students to self-assess
- Help teachers plan instruction
- Help teachers grade consistently
- Help teachers have sound justification for grades
- Help teachers and student communicate with parents

  (Arter & Chappuis, 2007, p. 31)

For examples, see **Tables 6.7** and **6.8**.

Planning for Assessment

Educators traditionally planned, then taught, then assessed. This linear view of the planning-teaching-assessment process has mostly been replaced by a more up-to-date and educationally sound model in which assessment has a different role. As previously stated, this contemporary view gives assessment more of a primary role in the process, which may seem somewhat backwards to those more familiar with the traditional model. Accordingly, this new model has been labelled "backward design" by Wiggins and McTighe (2007). The backward design model (**Figure 6.6**) requires educators to first decide upon the desired results, determine the acceptable evidence, and then plan for learning experiences and instruction (Wiggins & McTighe, 2007).

Depending on the assessment task, tool, and measure, educators may focus on a single outcome or may assess multiple outcomes. While some assessment samples within this chapter (and within various provincial PE curricula) may seemingly include multiple outcomes within one task/tool/measure, physical educators must always remember to only assess that which has been taught (and that which was an initial selected goal for students to learn).

Given that PE curricular outcomes are generally grouped by domain and that only a few provinces provide guidelines for relative weighting of these domains, physical educators are afforded great freedom and responsibility. This chapter has purposely avoided prescribing these relative weights. Physical educators themselves (or within departments, schools, or school districts) ought to consider their own teaching philosophies and school and community contexts as they make these decisions.

Case Study 4: Assessing Fitness

Ryan is a physical educator who strongly believes that one of the goals of PE should be to help his students become physically fit. It is for this reason that he routinely includes fitness building activities, or "Fitness Blasts," within his PE program. He chooses a number of fitness building activities so that his students may improve upon all of their health-related fitness components (e.g., muscular strength and flexibility). He purposely keeps both his instructions and feedback short and simple in an effort to maximize students' moderate-to-vigorous activity time within PE.

In addition to constantly working to help his students improve their health-related fitness, Ryan regularly has his students engage in fitness testing. He has adopted the Fitnessgram® as his fitness assessment system, appreciating the criterion-based standards for the Healthy Fitness Zone (HFZ). When students engage in fitness testing, he has found that there are basically three types of students. Some participate fully, trying their best to achieve the highest standards possible, always pushing themselves beyond the HFZ to the point of exhaustion/failure. Others participate fully, yet are satisfied to achieve only the minimum standard for the HFZ before stopping. The third group participates minimally (if at all), effectively "going through the motions" with no observable effort or care for the fitness assessment tasks.

Ryan knows that almost all students in his class are more motivated and put forth a greater effort when things "count" for marks. Though he has yet to include fitness assessments in his evaluations, he is wondering if this might get his students to try harder—and to get better assessment results.

Questions for Reflection

1. Considering what you know about fitness and assessment, what reasons are there for not including fitness assessments in evaluations (and marks/grades)?

2. How might Ryan appropriately use assessment to encourage greater engagement and effort on the part of his students?

Common PE Assessment "Issues"

Within PE, there are some assessment issues that seem to be more or less subject-specific. These issues are encountered and addressed by physical educators in a number of ways with different educators seemingly taking up differing perspectives. Nonetheless, new physical educators ought to consider these issues, and be able to enact assessment practices in these areas that are defensible—that is, based on sound PE assessment principles and practices.

Assessing Student Effort, Participation, and Conduct

Many pre-service physical educators might remember their own evaluations in PE including such attributes as effort, participation, and conduct. In fact, it is not unheard of for some physical educators to ascribe a disproportionate percentage of students' grades to such attributes. Such physical educators might proudly declare to their students, "I don't care how well you do at skills as much as I care about how hard you try. Those who try their best will get good grades." Of course, these promises come true as these physical educators might base a full 50% (or more) of their students' grades on their demonstrated level of effort, participation, or conduct.

It is not inappropriate to include attributes such as effort and participation in assessments and evaluations. However, if such behaviours are included, they must be clearly aligned with curricular outcomes. This is generally not too difficult as most PE curricula within Canada include affective outcomes that are clearly aligned to such attributes. For example, an outcome such as "demonstrate respect for others during physical activity" (Ministry of Education, Province of British Columbia, 2006, p. 38) is clearly aligned with conduct and an outcome such as "demonstrate a willingness to participate in a variety of activities and in one new activity that is personally challenging" (Education New Brunswick, 2002, p. 19) is clearly aligned with participation and effort. However, attributing a disproportionate amount of value to these outcomes is suspect. Though there is no prescription for attributing relative value to outcomes in most provinces, a more balanced assessment and evaluation scheme (between the three domains, for example) would be desirable. While the majority of curricula do not detail what relative value ought to be afforded to the three learning domains, some provinces, such as British Columbia and New Brunswick, do provide guidelines.

Figure 6.6: Backward Design (Wiggins & McTighe, 2007)

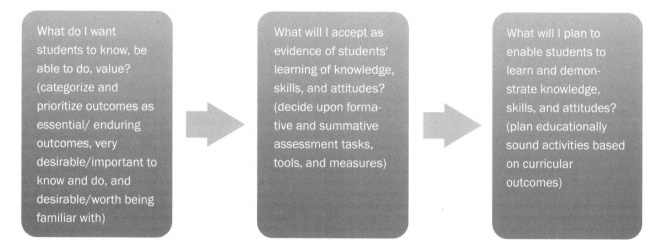

Fitness Testing

The ubiquitous nature of fitness testing within PE needs careful consideration. That is, fitness testing is, by definition alone, a test. If fitness tests were labelled "fitness assessments," perhaps more physical educators might recognize the potential they have as formative assessment tasks, rather than as summative ones. Very often, physical educators who include fitness testing results as though they were summative assessments (measuring, evaluating, and reporting them) do so despite the absence of explicit curriculum outcomes related to attaining a particular fitness standard. Rather, fitness-related outcomes are more often related to the act of aiming to become more fit or healthy (e.g., "apply ways to achieve a personal functional level of fitness," and "design a personal fitness and nutrition plan"; Education New Brunswick, 2002, pp. 17–18). Using fitness test results to determine marks or grades for these sorts of outcomes clearly has limited validity. That is, a fitness test measures students' level of fitness (and, depending on the fitness test and testing conditions, this too might be debatable); it reveals little-to-nothing about fitness training, fitness goal setting, and fitness planning.

This is not to suggest that fitness testing has no place within PE programs. In fact, it can be an important component of a quality program. However, it should be implemented as a formative assessment practice. Fitness testing can make students aware of their health-related fitness status and it can provide educators and parents/guardians with that same information. As students aim to meet curricular outcomes like those previously stated, fitness testing might enable them to set goals and monitor their own progress. Furthermore, as students observe themselves making progress towards their goals through the process of formative assessment, they may become further motivated to participate and be active.

Assessing Student Improvement

Given the range of knowledge, skills, and attitudes of students within PE (and, indeed, within all subject areas), some physical educators opt to assess students' improvement, rather than their learning as compared to outcomes-related criteria. When enacting such assessment practices, physical educators generally have noble intentions. That is, they recognize the differing abilities of all their students and simply wish to have them all improve and meet individual goals. While this rationale might seem sound, there are some potential drawbacks related to such an approach.

First, when assessing student improvement (particularly when students are aware of this assessment process), it is incredibly difficult (and time consuming) to articulate and measure baseline knowledge, skills, and attitudes for every individual student. In fact, it should come as no surprise that students might purposely score poorly on an initial assessment, expecting that they would then be able to exhibit a greater degree of improvement. Second, assessing students' improvement disregards the curricular outcomes for a given grade level. Grade-level curricular outcomes are written so as to indicate what students are to be able to know, do, or value by the end of a period of time. Disregarding these and aiming solely for individual improvement causes educators and their students to lose focus on the provincially mandated learning goals. Third, the highly knowledgeable/skilled student has less room for improvement than the less knowledgeable/skilled student. Consequently, when assigning final grades, it is difficult to definitively know if all students' grades accurately reflect the degree to which each has met the provincially mandated learning goals.

Of course, assessing student improvement has some potential as a formative process. For example, allowing students to set goals with respect to such things as fitness tests, track and field results, or golf scores, would be an ideal practice. Students might know their initial PACER test result, their best shot put result, or their lowest golf score on a mini course. With this initial information, they could compare future results. The degree of improvement could be open to assessment, but not to evaluation.

Conclusion

Assessment is a crucial element of the instructional process within PE. The use of valid and reliable measures, in both formative and summative assessment tasks, is essential for ensuring student learning. Adherence to continuous, collaborative, comprehensive, and criteria-based assessment principles and practices ensures that assessment is meaningful and purposeful. Quality PE programs necessarily include a variety of assessment tasks so that students may have multiple opportunities and methods by which to display their learned knowledge, skills, and attitudes.

Questions for Reflection

1 Reflect upon the assessment practices you remember from your time as a student. How would you describe your former physical educators' assessment practices? How were these assessment practices similar and/or different to the assessment practices in other subject areas?

2 Many educators are frustrated by their schools' policies prohibiting "zeros" and "docking" marks for assignments. What basis might they have for these frustrations? What are some alternatives to assigning zeros and docking marks might you adopt for use in PE?

3 All PE curricula within Canada include outcomes within three domains (cognitive, psychomotor, affective). When physical educators must decide upon a single grade for a term, what relative weight might be given to these three domains? Support your answer.

4 Sometimes during a performance task (e.g., a gymnastics sequence or a dance presentation), students may not perform as well as they are capable of performing. Should students be allowed another opportunity (i.e., a "do-over")? Support your answer.

5 Of the many possibilities for reporting students' grades (e.g., numerical scores, letter grades, pass/fail systems, and analytic rating scales), what would you suggest would be most ideal? Support your answer.

Key Terms

- Assessment
- Norm-Reference Evaluation
- Criterion-Referenced Evaluation
- Validity
- Reliability
- Authentic Assessment
- Formative Assessment
- Summative Assessment
- Evaluation

Appendix 1: Sample Assessment Tool from British Columbia's Physical Education K to 7: Integrated Resource Package 2006

Assessment Instrument
OUTDOOR ACTIVITIES

Name: _____   Date: _____

	Teacher Assessment
My favourite outdoor activity that I've tried is I like this activity because The major muscles involved in this activity are	
One new land-based outdoor activity I'd like to try is I'd like to try this activity because Where I can do this activity in our community	
One new water-based outdoor activity I'd like to try is I'd like to try this activity because Where I can do this activity in our community	

Appendix 2: Sample Assessment Tool from Grade 12 Active Healthy Lifestyles: Manitoba Physical Education/Health Education Curriculum Framework of Outcomes and a Foundation for Implementation

Sample Checklist for Assessment of Final
Complete/Incomplete Designation

Student Name: _____ Class: _____ Date: _____

Use an "x" to indicate that the student has met expectations (complete). Samples have been provided for Module A. To add other assessment tasks, tab and enter content. Fields are limited to approximately 14 characters.

Module A: Physical Activity Practicum	Module B: Fitness Management	Module C: Nutrition	Module D: Personal and Social Development	Module E: Healthy Relationships
GLO 1—Movement GLO 2—Fitness Management GLO 3—Safety	GLO 2—Fitness Management GLO 4—Personal and Social Management	GLO 5—Health Lifestyle Practices	GLO 4—Personal and Social Management	GLO 4—Personal and Social Management GLO 5—Health Lifestyle Practices
☐ Physical Activity Plan	☐ ☐ ☐	☐ ☐ ☐	☐ ☐ ☐	☐ ☐ ☐
☐ Safety and Risk-Management Plan	☐ ☐ ☐	☐ ☐ ☐	☐ ☐ ☐	☐ ☐ ☐
☐ Parent and Student Declaration Forms	☐ ☐ ☐	☐ ☐ ☐	☐ ☐ ☐	☐ ☐ ☐
☐ Physical Activity Log and Reflections	☐ ☐ ☐	☐ ☐ ☐	☐ ☐ ☐	☐ ☐ ☐
☐ Student-Teacher Conferences	☐ ☐ ☐	☐ ☐ ☐	☐ ☐ ☐	☐ ☐ ☐
☐ 55 Hours of Moderate to Vigorous Physical Activity	☐ ☐ ☐	☐ ☐ ☐	☐ ☐ ☐	☐ ☐ ☐
☐ Achieved Student Learning Outcomes	☐ Achieved Student Learning Outcomes	☐ Achieved Student Learning Outcomes	☐ Achieved Student Learning Outcomes	☐ Achieved Student Learning Outcomes

Final Assessment: Complete: ☐   Incomplete: ☐

Appendix 3: Sample Assessment Tool from Alberta's *Physical Education Guide to Implementation (K–12): Assessment, Evaluation, an Communication of Student Learning*

Sample Game Analytic Rating Scale				
Criteria	**Consistently**	**Frequently**	**Occasionally**	**Rarely, if ever**
Demonstrates proper skills				
Uses equipment safely				
Plays fairly, with proper game etiquette				
Encourages and supports others in their participation				
Displays a positive attitude				
Comments:				

Appendix 4: Sample Assessment Tool from Saskatchewan Curriculum: Physical Education 8

An Assessment Rubric for Physical Educator Use

Outcome 8.9—Movement Sequences

Perform, both as a leader and a follower, self-created, collaboratively created, and established sequences of movements with smooth transitions, incorporating skills and combinations of skills from a variety of games (i.e., target games, net/wall games, striking/fielding games, invasion/territorial games, low-organizational and inventive games) and body management activities (e.g., dance, aquatics, educational gymnastics, track and field, Pilates, yoga, wrestling, martial arts, aerobics, alone and with others.

Level 4	Level 3	Level 2	Level 1
Frequently performs sequences of movements with smooth flow and **little to no hesitation**	**Usually** performs sequences of movements with smooth flow and with **some hesitation**	**Usually** performs sequences of movements with **some choppiness** and **much hesitation**	**Frequently** performs complex skills with an **obvious choppiness** and **constant hesitation**
Designs sequences of movements that **always accurately reflect given criteria**	**Designs** sequences of movements that **usually accurately reflect given criteria**	**Designs** sequences of movements that **occasionally accurately reflect given criteria**	**Designs** sequences of movements that **never accurately reflect given criteria**
Frequently uses visual representation to support understanding of movement sequences	**Usually uses visual representation** to support understanding of movement sequences	**Occasionally uses visual representation** to support understanding of movement sequences	**Rarely uses visual representation** to support understanding of movement sequences
Always contributes fair share to the collaborative creation of movement sequences	**Usually contributes fair share** to the collaborative creation of movement sequences	**Occasionally contributes fair share** to the collaborative creation of movement sequences	**Rarely contributes fair share** to the collaborative creation of movement sequences
Easily leads and follows in the performance of movement sequences	**Leads with some hesitation and easily follows** in the performance of movement sequences	**Leads with much hesitation and follows with some hesitation** in the performance of movement sequences	**Rarely leads or follows without much hesitation** in the performance of movement sequences
Frequently, and with no hesitation, verbalizes the appropriate performance cues to support performance of sequences of complex skills	**Usually, and with little hesitation, verbalizes** the appropriate performance cues to support performance of sequences of complex skills	**Occasionally, and with hesitation, verbalizes** the appropriate performance cues to support performance of sequences of complex skills	**Must be prompted to verbalize** appropriate performance cues

Diversities
in Physical Education

Catherine Casey and Jeanne Adèle Kentel
(with contributions by Erin Cameron)

Overview

The lifeworlds of students are forged in history and in a multiplicity of cultures. Matters such as socio-economic status, race, gender, sexuality, and ability influence their daily encounters. Within these daily experiences exists a cultural landscape of oppression whereby students are connected to very real social, cultural, economic, and historical issues that can affect their home and school lives and leave them feeling ignored. In addition, they respond to and are affected by the struggles of their parents, which can further marginalize them. The feeling of oppression is an emotional experience, which afflicts the senses and the spirit. If the oppressive experiences of students are overlooked, physical education (PE) is limited in its transformative potential. Readers of this chapter are invited to consider what is known and understood about individual students and their daily lives.

A lack of diversified curricula has significantly influenced pedagogical practice and knowledge production within the fields of sport and PE in Canada (Douglas & Halas, 2008). As a result the values, practices, and emphases of PE reproduces and maintains a privileged hierarchy that establishes implicit and explicit criteria for exclusive membership and normalizes the prevailing dominant cultural character (white, male, heterosexual, able bodied, able minded, thin, wealthy) common to higher education institutions. In order to engage in a diversified curriculum the meaning and significance of diversity must be understood.

Diversity refers to individual differences and distinctiveness, and encompasses acceptance, respect, and recognition. It is a multi-faceted exploration of differences pursued in an environment that is as safe and welcoming as possible in an educational or societal setting, particularly within a climate of acceptance. The term *acceptance* is purposely used in lieu of terms such as tolerance, which suggest something (or someone) that needs to be endured or allowed. A climate of acceptance implies that one willingly and openly welcomes and receives the diverse identities of others. *Respect* occurs when others are held in esteem, revered, and treated with dignity as part of a shared lived experience. There are no preconditions for respectful treatment; it is unconditional. Recognition refers to the acknowledgement and appreciation of others and their identities in genuine and meaningful ways. It is a deliberate and conscious act carried out in a spirit of gratitude.

In light of the aforementioned understanding of diversity this chapter begins by underscoring the current cultural landscape and context of the PE field. It further delineates some of the systemic influences, concerns, and stereotypes that continue to prevail in the field. In response to the existing dominant culture, this chapter builds upon culturally relevant PE theory (Halas, 2011), a framework to address matters such as equity, social justice, cooperation, and movement understanding. Diversity is examined in the contexts of race, socio-economic status, immigrants/refugees, gender, sexual orientation, religion, dis/abilities, and body mass, shape, and appearance. By drawing on the social justice work of others, a more equitable and just field (Fernandez-Balboa, 1997; Flory & McCaughtry, 2011) is envisioned and a range of ideas for embracing critical pedagogies and culturally responsive practice are presented. To this end, the intent is not only to engage in dialogue about critical pedagogies and practice in PE, but also to inspire action that can potentially transform practice. In closing, this chapter offers an array of tangible ways to address PE's exclusionary culture by attending to diversity concerns.

Introduction

On November 21, 1978, the United Nations Educational, Scientific and Cultural Organization (UNESCO) adopted the International Charter of Physical Education and Sport, a Charter that states that all children have the right to access and participate in sport and physical education (PE). In addition to establishing access to sport and PE as a right, the Charter goes further in articulating how sport and PE programming should meet individual and social needs (Article 3), by paying attention to the "personal characteristics of those practicing them, as well as the institutional, cultural, socio-economic and climatic conditions of each country" (Article 3.1). Thus, this chapter not only ascertains the need

for sport and PE in education more broadly, but also highlights an important quality of such programming—the need to address diversity.

Paulo Freire (1997) reminds educators that, "fighting against discrimination is an ethical imperative...our fight against the different discriminations, against any negation of being, will only lead to victory if we can realize the obvious: *unity within diversity*" (p. 87). While people are from diverse cultures, faiths, classes, abilities, and orientations, according to Freire, all educators are obliged to work towards the common goal of an invitational climate for *all* persons in places of learning. Freire further calls on educators to employ critical pedagogical practices, which are liberatory and democratic. Critical pedagogy disrupts all forms of power and marginalization, and provokes learners to critically appraise the ways representations of dominant orders figure into and do not figure into identities (Kentel 2009; Light & Kentel, 2010; Kentel, 2011).

Many Canadian communities have diverse student populations.

In Canada, a quality PE program is characterized as one that provides children with the opportunity to develop the knowledge, skills, and habits needed to lead physically active lifestyles (Physical and Health Education Canada [PHE Canada], 2010). While development of one's physicality has historically been a common curricular objective, there is growing awareness about the importance of cultural diversity within the PE field. Consequently, some are suggesting the field needs to address its privileged, white, elite, and western cultures (Fernandez-Balboa, 1997; Fitzpatrick, 2011; Lawson, 2005) in order to move towards a more culturally relevant approach that is more in keeping with the experiences of youth in the current time (Halas, McRae & Carpenter, 2012; Halas, 2011; Melnychuk, Robinson, Lu, Chorney, & Randall, 2011; Tinning, 2004).

Halas, McRae, and Carpenter (in press) observe that alongside a growing body of research evidence a number of Canadian researchers are drawing attention to the structural needs of facilitating sport and PE programs that address the macro-level societal issues (i.e., those social forces that shape the cultural landscapes of educators and students), mid-level organizational issues (i.e., the school-based practices that shape educator-student relationships), and micro-level relational issues (i.e., the points of contact between teachers and students). Attending to these matters creates a space where transformation of the learning context can occur—a necessary shift in PE content to accommodate the needs of the learner.

Culturally Relevant Physical Education

Culturally relevant PE as defined by Halas (2011) is "providing programs that are rich in meaningful and relevant activities that affirm the cultural identities of students" (p. 23). Gleaned from Ladson-Billings' (1995) concept of culturally relevant pedagogy, it is not an attempt to insert culture into the PE curriculum; rather, it is a means to "utilize students' culture as a vehicle for learning" (p. 161) and further provoke critical consciousness. It is a student before content approach, which acknowledges that each individual comes with lived experiences that are an intersection of race, ability, gender, sexual orientation, socio-economic status, religion, somatotypes, and cultural and family traditions. It builds on the premise that everyone and everything is interconnected (see **Figure 7.1**).

Culturally relevant PE not only recognizes the diverse cultural identities of students, it aims to affirm them through comprehensive curricular development and responsive pedagogical practices that reach beyond the context of the school.

Figure 7.1: Culturally Relevant Physical Education: A Theory For Engaging All Students In Meaningful Ways (Halas, 2011)

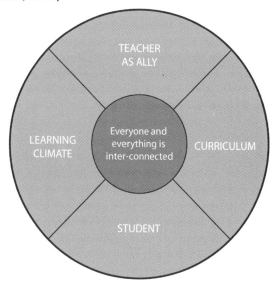

The teacher as ally: In what ways can teachers use their positions of privilege to build equitable, respectful, and supportive relationships with all students?

The student: What is known about students' day-to-day cultural landscape? What are their stories and histories, both personal and collective?

The learning climate: In what ways can a supportive and engaging climate where everyone, regardless of where they are situated in relation to the many axes of difference, feel respected, included, supported, and engaged be created in physical education?

The curriculum: What learning experiences are meaningful and relevant for the students? In what ways can lessons be designed to figure into students' personal and social constructions of themselves? Namely, what is of interest to them?
(Adapted from Halas, 2011)

Contexts for Understanding Diversity

Race

Despite the recognized need for more critical pedagogies and practices that disrupt the current hegemony of whiteness in PE, some Canadian pedagogy experts speak of a lack of expertise and confidence when talking about issues pertaining to race and diversity, and subsequently also fear offending people if they were to do so (Douglas & Halas, 2008). Arguably these fears and reservations are not only limiting the evolution of the field, they are also normalizing the experiences, histories, and world views of the racial majority. Increasingly there is a need for ideas and practices that support students in moving beyond fear and familiarity towards critical pedagogies that recognize Canada's racialized and ethnically diverse population.

Diversity is particularly relevant in the Canadian context where racialized minorities represent the youngest and fastest growing group of the population (Douglas & Halas, 2008). A racial hierarchy is of significant concern since approximately twenty percent of Canadians identify as a racialized minority or Aboriginal, and this number is growing. A pedagogical shift is not only desirable, it is necessary, in order to address the needs of a diverse student demographic and an evolving recognition of multiple identities among Canadian people.

From Theory to Practice

1 **The teacher as ally:** What visible minority groups are marginalized in classrooms or schools? Is there any evidence or examples of racism on sports teams? Are any students being bullied because of their race or the clothing that they wear? Is there any racially motivated gang activity that is of concern? Are there ways teachers can work together with school boards, education ministries, and the community to create spaces where the young can develop positive relationships?

2 **The student:** What activities are students involved in outside of school? Are there games, traditions, or dances they could share with the class? Are there underlying reasons for them not having a change of clothing or being late for class?

3 **The learning climate:** Does the environment tolerate racial slurs, jokes, and references? Is there intervention when racist comments or more subtle alienation occur? Are there ways to talk about race and racism that disrupt the marginalization of minority groups?

4 **The curriculum:** Invite parents, grandparents, and community members to contribute to learning experiences. Invite students to share their ancestries and traditions and contribute to the living curriculum through play, games, music, and dance.

Activity—Green star/no star

■ Read *The Sneetches* by Dr Seuss (1961) or watch the video together (Cat in the Hat Productions, 2010).

■ Discuss the dynamics between the plain belly and the star belly sneetches.

■ Have students make a list of privileges typical in the class (e.g., free time, eating first, free choice, assistance with assignments, computer time)

■ Divide students in groups and have each group experience no privileges for half a day.

■ Have the underprivileged group wear pinnies so they are easily identifiable.

Discuss the experiences of the underprivileged group each day and how being outcast made them feel. Further discuss the experiences of the privileged groups. Invite students to share examples where others are treated differently because of how they look or where they are from.

Socio-Economic Status (SES)

Economic inequality or the gap between the rich and poor is at its widest point ever in Canadian history. While there are increasing concerns for the erosion of the middle class, this ultimate reality was raised nearly a decade ago (Curry-Stevens, 2003). This trend has significant implications for the education of the young. Brownell et al. (2004) found that the poorer a child's neighbourhood the more likely she or he is to have difficulties in school, fail standardized tests, and quit school prematurely. Poverty, therefore, puts many young at risk in reaching their potential.

With the erosion of the middle class and the rising costs of housing, more people are going to be living with inadequate means. Schools are now fundraising to pay for supplies, equipment, and special activities. Teachers are now required to be more aware of economic gaps and how many more children are affected by poverty or financial hardship. Many children from economically disadvantaged homes have to get jobs by the age of fourteen years (or younger) which prevents them from playing on school or community teams. This provides a backdrop for developing a more comprehensive PE program and examining potential school partnerships within the communities where they are located.

From Theory to Practice

1 **The teacher as ally:** Are the students having enough to eat and drink each day? Is a breakfast program needed? What steps can teachers take to ensure those who require a breakfast or lunch program are not singled out? Are teachers aware of the social awkwardness of poverty, what it might look like, and a range of ways to address it? What are the underlying beliefs and assumptions about poor people? Why are people poor? What are teachers' beliefs about economic inequality and the ways this might affect the lives of students?

2 **The student:** What is the cultural landscape of poverty in the class and school? What does the school administration, board, or district do for students who cannot afford sport or activity fees associated with PE? Is consideration given to how embarrassing it is to not have money, a change of clothes, or to not have eaten all day? How can teachers be affirming to these students? What about the intersection of mental illness and poverty? Are there emotional and psychological health issues encountered by the students in addition to the physical and more visible signs of ill health?

3 **The learning climate:** What can teachers do in order to develop an increased awareness of what is happening in their classrooms? Are teachers willing to have conversations about the thorny issues facing students? In what ways can the identities of students who live in poverty or come from poor backgrounds be affirmed? In what ways can teachers collaborate in order to allow all students to participate in various school activities? How can teachers ensure that students feel safe and that there are no barriers to their participation?

4 **The curriculum:** If students do not have the opportunity to participate in outside activities or organized sports due to cost and/or parental availability, provide ways they can have their needs met (such as exposure to a wide variety of activities and initiatives in PE). Widen participation by offering more intramurals and clubs before, during, and after school. Establish community partnerships to create more participatory possibilities.

Activity—The Myth of Meritocracy

- Distribute bags of various coloured Snap Cubes® to all participants in the class. Some students are to get a bag with a few cubes, some with many, and some with no cubes.

- Each person has to try to get four matching cubes (of the same colour).

- Players may only negotiate and trade with the cubes that they have.

This activity reinforces the concept of the myth of meritocracy. Meritocracy suggests that people are disadvantaged because they do not work hard and those who are successful are the ones who deserve it. The fundamental premise that underpins meritocracy is that those who work hard will get ahead in life. This activity reveals that this is not always the case.

Immigrants/Refugees

The challenges encountered by immigrants and refugees in Canada are an intersection of race and socio-economic status. In Canada the intersection of colonization and poverty has produced a racialized lower class (i.e., Aboriginals and immigrants have difficulty finding jobs). Immigrants and refugees face other difficulties because many are qualified professionals but whose credentials are not recognized in Canada. The families need to adjust not only to the economic change but also may need to learn a new language, adapt to new surroundings, and cope with taking jobs for which they are overqualified. Snezana Ratkovic speaks candidly about her experiences of immigratory prejudice and describes how she was a qualified and experienced science teacher in her home country but was relegated to pushing a broom upon emigrating to Canada (Ratkovic & Kentel, 2007).

Case Study 1: Attracting New Canadians

Mr. Patel has been hired to teach at a large suburban high school with a highly diverse student population in Toronto. There is a large population of new Canadians including some students whose families were refugees from the East African nation of Sudan. The teachers at the school are all expected to coach both male and female sports. The Vice Principal asks Mr. Patel what he could do to get the group of immigrant students involved in the extra-curricular program. Mr. Patel proceeds to invite the new students to come after school to his basketball club. While some of the students come, they have never played the game before and the other students become frustrated with the new students when they do things like run with the ball or kick it. Gradually the new students stop coming to the extra-curricular program until they all eventually drop out.

Questions for Reflection

1 Why do you think the new students stopped coming to the extra-curricular program?

2 What do you think about the approach Mr. Patel used with the new students?

3 What are the steps you would take to address the needs of recent immigrants to Canada? What practices would you put in place in order to do this?

Case Study 2: Working in a Challenging Community

Ms. Chang is a teacher in an early-middle years' school in Winnipeg's inner city. The majority of her class is Aboriginal but there are also students from other ethnic backgrounds including some Caucasians.

Ms. Chang spends a lot of time volunteering in the community and getting to know her students and their families. Since many students from her class arrive late in the morning, she started an after-school club where they could learn about topics they were interested in or play games and sports that their parents could not afford the fees for. The club also plans activities that give back to the community by doing things like yard clean ups, helping the elderly, and holding events that enhance community spirit.

After several months of running the club, Ms. Chang experienced burnout and was required to take time off work. Her students missed her and it was difficult for anyone to take over the role that she filled in the school and community.

Questions for Reflection

1　Is there anything Ms. Chang could have done differently to create the learning climate she desired without becoming overwhelmed?

2　What would excite you about teaching at this school?

3　What other challenges might you expect to encounter as a teacher in an inner-city school?

4　Is it possible to do too much for students? If so, in what ways can teachers balance the naturally occurring and extended curriculum they offer?

King (1995) portrays "post-industrial migrants" as the asylum seekers, the refugees, those who emigrated as a result off a "push" factor, or to escape difficult situations. Many children from immigrant or refugee families have witnessed acts of war and horrific treatment of human beings. Thus, as Bagnoli (2007) suggests, experiences of migration can be a source of suffering "and may be the cause of a great deal of pain" (p. 40). Bagnoli further identifies three main factors to assist global nomads in coping with their new surroundings and roles:

1　Understanding of the expectations with which these people emigrated

2　Their ability to form a social network

3　Their mastery of the language

Teachers and schools can assist students by providing additional language supports and creating situations where they can establish friendships.

From Theory to Practice

1　**The teacher as ally:** What opportunities are there for students to use and develop their first language? Are there English language support groups in the school? Are there services in the community that teachers can direct students and families to? Are there sports, play, or dance clubs where students can develop language and friendships while participating in an enjoyable physical activity?

2　**The student:** What adjustments are students who have immigrated making? Have they experienced trauma? What might the visible signs of trauma be? (e.g., not speaking, limited or no eye contact, aggression). Who are the friends of students? What opportunities are there for students to make and build friendships?

3　**The learning climate:** Is there an open dialogue between students and between students and the teacher? Are students comfortable sharing their experiences with a teacher? Are there opportunities for students to open up to a trusted friend? In what ways can teachers become privy to student-to-student dialogue that occurs in changing rooms and playing fields at break times? What examples can teachers provide to students to exemplify respect and dignity in their social interactions?

4　**The curriculum:** Provide cross-curricular learning experiences whereby each student can learn about her/ his place of origin. Explore the landscape, traditions, languages, music, dance, literature, dress, stories, games, and foods. Allow students to make decisions about what they would like to share with others.

Activity—Ethnic Collage

- Invite students to research a special fact about their place of origin. (This could be an event, a famous person, place, or structure, etc.)

- Invite students to write a short vignette or poem about why this is important to them.

- Students may draw or paint pictures or create artifacts to accompany their writing.

- Create a class collage of all the unique characteristics of students' places of origin.

Gender

PE and sport are key areas where masculinities and domination are played out. The very nature of game play is to outdo an opponent and become faster or stronger in the process. Through examining the concept of *libido dominandi*, the desire for domination, Bourdieu (2001) further scrutinizes the human tendency to have power and control and observes:

> It is through the training of the body that the most fundamental dispositions are imposed, those which make a person both inclined and able to enter into the social games most favourable to the development of manliness—politics, business, science, etc. (Early upbringing encourages boys and girls very unequally to enter into these games, and favours more strongly in boys the various forms of the *libido dominandi*.) (p. 56)

Davison (2004) suggests that the development of manliness could be dangerous indicating that the "practices of masculinity which are taken for granted as 'boys will be boys' behaviour is not only harmful to marginalised students but ultimately shapes the learning environment" (p. 145). The development of masculinity can be problematic not only for girls, but for boys, and those who are transgendered as well. While Bourdieu (2001) attempts to disrupt the gender order, he discovers that, "when we try to understand masculine domination we are therefore likely to resort to modes of thought that are the product of domination" (p. 5).

Girls who do not act feminine according to socially-coded rules can encounter a marginalized experience in schools. These experiences can also be encountered by males across the spectrum of hyper-masculinity, masculinity, and effeminacy, yet masculine is not exclusively male and feminine is not solely female. Brown (2006) contends that "masculinity and femininity can 'float free' from men and women" (p. 165) yet in practice this is difficult to accomplish.

According to Duncan (1990) "'masculine' and 'feminine' correspond not to natural, universal differences but to culturally and historically specific constructions of difference" (p. 2). Thus, the theories and ideas that people

Case Study 3: Increasing Participation

Mr. García teaches PE in Pukatawagin, in the north of Manitoba. Throughout the year the lessons are comprised mostly of games.

There is limited equipment and space in the gymnasium so Mr. Garcia divides the class into two teams of boys and two teams of girls. The boys play the boys for five minutes while the girls sit and then the girls play the girls for five minutes while the boys sit. Then one team of girls plays one team of boys and then they switch with the other teams.

During the play there are students who are never passed to and pairs of girls chatting in the corner and off to the side. Students waiting on the sidelines have mixed responses which include yelling and cheering, watching the play, poking each other, pulling on each others' clothing, and playing singing games. This continues until time is up and the students are sent off to change.

As the students return to the changing room they are overheard saying, "Yeah we killed you!" "You guys suck!" "I hate PE" and "Why do we have to play this stupid game?"

Questions for Reflection

1 What are the key elements in the curriculum provided by Mr. Garcia?

2 What is the first element you would change and why?

3 What other components would you change? Why?

hold within society about "reality" and "truth" depend on social attitudes as opposed to biological or physical facts. What is learned to be "true" is based on the contexts of our growing up. While the social construction of gender is complex and troublesome, educators and their students are in a position to transform the current difficulty since schools are essentially social settings.

Sykes (2011) suggests that teachers need to think of gender beyond the binary construct of male and female. Being transgendered is especially difficult in PE because of this construct. According to Sykes (2011) in most PE contexts, "it is still very rare, if not impossible, for students to decide about, develop, and live their transgendered subjectivities" (p. 2).

Disrupting gender stereotypes or attitudes relating to expected roles, behaviours, appearance, and dress of males and females is challenging for most educators. Dislocating stereotypes relating to transgenders and androgynous identities is even more difficult because as Sykes submits there is little understanding of those who identify as the opposite sex of their birth or who do not identify as exclusively female or male. Changing rooms are designated male and female, sports teams and competitions follow suit, and even co-educational classes are often organized into male and female groups.

From Theory to Practice

1 **The teacher as ally:** Are there any personal or pedagogical practices, which may be emphasizing or privileging masculinity? Are there situations that are overlooked when an intervention might support a marginalized student? Are labels such as tomboy and wimp discussed with students in ways that call on them to consider the effects of their use on others?

2 **The student:** Are there girls in the class who would prefer to engage in more aggressive games and activities? Are there boys or girls who are being marginalized in PE for acting feminine? In what ways do the boys respond to feminine activities? In what ways do the girls respond to masculine activities? Are there spaces for transgender students to feel more comfortable when changing their clothes or participating in learning experiences?

3 **The learning climate:** Does the learning climate permit all students to engage in movement and movement understanding equally? Are there ranges of opportunities that are homogenous as well as heterogeneous? Are students engaged in democratic practice so they are equipped to extend an invitational climate beyond the formal learning space to the playing fields and gathering places at break times?

4 **The curriculum:** Develop curricula that allows for equitable engagement among all students. As part of a comprehensive curriculum include learning experiences that comprise the full spectrum of masculinity and femininity. Invite students to critically scrutinize media images and reports related to masculinity and femininity in order to develop an analytical understanding of gender.

Activity—Thought, Word and Deed

■ Distribute a set of three cards to each student labelled, "Thought," "Word," and "Deed."

■ Prepare a list of stereotypical statements and activities related to gendered language and stereotypes (e.g., you throw like a girl, that's women's work, men are pigs, men are better at sports, girls are weak, boys can't dance, girls are smarter, lining up boys and girls separately, playing boys against the girls, etc.). Students can also add their own ideas and experiences to this list.

■ For each statement/action, have the students select the corresponding card if they have thought the statement, spoken the statement, or done the deed.

■ Discuss the ways thoughts, words, and deeds can be harmful to others and brainstorm a list of thoughts, words, and deeds, which are gender sensitive and aware.

Sexual Orientation

Sexuality is one of the most difficult topics in teacher education due in part to the different beliefs, orientations, and values that people bring to the discussion. Heterosexuality is typically more highly valued than homosexuality, which creates tensions in everyday life for marginalized groups.

Homophobia is among the most serious topics in education of the young. Perceived homosexual orientation can provoke bullying (Birkett, Espelage, & Koenig, 2009), which in the most extreme and tragic cases can lead to death by beating or suicide (Gibson, 1994).

Some groups on the religious and political right reject homosexuality and/or bisexuality, which can create increased tensions for educators and can have limiting effects on the curriculum. While religious beliefs are to be respected, they are individual, and therefore, ought not to infringe on the beliefs and values of others.

From Theory to Practice

1 **The teacher as ally:** Have labels such as "dyke," "fruit," and "wuss" or expressions such as "that's so gay" been discussed with students? Is there a process of intervention when these comments occur? What steps are taken in order to promote a climate of acceptance in classrooms? Are there programs in the school and/or the community that support students and teachers in creating safer places for multiple orientations to feel valued?

2 **The student:** Are there any students who are struggling because they are presumed to be or identify as gay or lesbian? Are there any students who identify as gay, lesbian, or bisexual who are being bullied for coming out or taking a stance? Do all students feel welcome to

share their views regardless of orientation? Are situations occurring in the changing rooms where students do not feel comfortable or safe? Is there a place in the school where students can talk about their experiences if they do not feel comfortable or safe to do so in class?

3 **The learning climate:** Are there opportunities in the school to participate in clubs and activities where minority orientations would not feel further marginalized? Are there spaces where students can develop individually as well as in groups? Are there private spaces where students can change their clothes for physical education classes?

4 **The curriculum:** Develop PE lessons and learning experiences that provide a wide range of activities that would interest all sexual orientations. Provide opportunities for individual and dual activities as well as group learning. Work towards a living curriculum that involves students in developing learning experiences that pertain to the difficulties they encounter when confronting matters related to sexual orientation.

Activity—Critical Media Pedagogy

- Invite students to gather specific images and examples from the media that might make some people uncomfortable (e.g., cross-dressing, same-sex affection).

- Invite students to share these images and examples in class.

- Invite students to individually rate their comfort levels with the image or story on a scale of 1 to 10 with 1 being very uncomfortable and 10 being very comfortable.

- Invite students to discuss their rating in pairs or small groups and indicate why they are comfortable or uncomfortable with the media representation.

- Discuss possible ways to retain one's own beliefs and values while respecting the beliefs and values of others.

Religion

In order to present a critical view, it must be recognized that religious groups and persons have historically made and currently make a contribution to society. Zajda et al. (2006) claim that the term "social justice" was coined by a Sicilian priest, Luigi Taparelli D'Azeglio, based upon the work of Saint Thomas Aquinas. While social justice has various meanings in different contexts it would be amiss to overlook the influence of theologians and religious and spiritual philosophers in its development. Religious groups are typically aligned with charitable work and societal efforts to care for those in need.

In contrast, some religious groups become politically engaged in blocking policies that intend to endorse

Religion can present unique challenges to physical educators.

equitable practices among citizens. These efforts are viewed as the religious right and in some instances are both religiously and politically extreme.

Apart from the complexity of religious beliefs and their influence on politics and education, practicing one's faith is a basic human right so long as it does not infringe on another's right to practice his or her religion. This in itself is problematic because some religious groups are privileged over others in particular societies (similar to whiteness and masculinity) and can exert political power that further marginalizes minorities.

Spirituality is not necessarily linked to formal religion yet is an important component of an individual's being that is increasingly absent in schools. Moreover, efforts to eliminate religion from public education have been an insurmountable challenge, partly because it has been historically embedded in schooling but also because ignoring the faith traditions of students can disenfranchise them from their daily lives and experiences.

From Theory to Practice

1 **The teacher as ally:** In what ways might teachers figure into the acceptance of other religious points of view? What process of intervention is enacted when students are ridiculed for wearing religious clothing or jewelry? Is one religion consciously or unconsciously promoted over another in the school, classroom, or community? Is religion favoured over atheism or vice versa? What connections are being made between the school and religious groups in the community?

2 **The student:** What are the religious beliefs and practices of students? What special religious holidays do the students and families in the school observe? How do teachers respond when students indicate they cannot

131

Case Study 4: Health Education and Religion

Mr. Jones teaches at a private religious school in Edmonton. While Mr. Jones has been teaching there for several years he has limited knowledge and understanding about the faith, traditions, and culture of the community. He frequently receives notes from parents indicating that their children are not to participate in dance, sexual health education, or gymnastics due to the traditional dress they wear. While Mr. Jones is frustrated by these notes, he provides another space for those students to work in while he continues with the lessons he has planned. In some instances nearly half of his students are missing class due to some aspect of their religious beliefs. Despite this fact, he continues to follow his pre-planned curriculum as prescribed by the province year after year.

Questions for Reflection

1 Is there anything Mr. Jones could have done differently to include all students in the classes that were taught?

2 What opportunities might be possible to create partnerships and positive relationships between school and community in this setting?

3 What other challenges might you expect to encounter as a teacher in a religious school or as a teacher of religious students?

participate for religious reasons? Is there acceptance of religious dress and customs by students who exercise their faith in these ways?

3 **The learning climate:** Does the school environment reflect respect for an individual's faith and/or religious beliefs without infringing on the views of others? Do teachers permit free expressions of faith among students even if they are in opposition to their personal views? Does the learning climate allow for both religious and non-religious expressions of faith?

4 **The curriculum:** Adapt the curriculum to include students from a range of religious backgrounds. Develop curricula that accommodate faiths that do not observe certain holidays such as Christmas or Halloween, or the singing of national anthems. Develop practices that encourage the participation of students who are required or opt to wear certain types of clothing.

Activity—Faith Statement

- Have students write a faith statement (what they believe in).
- Have students write a definition or statement of social justice.
- Have students compare the two statements and highlight where their beliefs intersect with the meaning and purpose of social justice.
- Discuss ways religion can be in harmony with social justice and religion can be in opposition to social justice.

Dis/abilities

While disabilities (particularly intellectual ones) may present themselves in the mainstream areas of the curriculum, physical, behavioural, and intellectual disabilities can be especially evident in PE.

Fitzgerald (2011) underscores the difficulties with a medicalized view of disabilities and calls for researchers and educators to actively listen to the experiences and stories of children and young people with identified needs. Fitzgerald further highlights the absence of a voice for young people with disabilities in PE and broader educational circles. Unfortunately, inclusive practices are inconsistent and complex.

Efforts towards inclusion have been somewhat fruitless according to Slee and Allan (2001) who state, "we are still citing inclusion as our goal; still waiting to include, yet speaking as if we are already inclusive" (p. 181). Teacher education programs are often not equipped to provide comprehensive inclusive education and for many experienced teachers the practice of inclusion was not part of their initial education. Thus the marginalization of children and youth with special needs may be as much a factor of pedagogical ignorance as it is an intolerant dynamic towards a misunderstood minority group.

From Theory to Practice

1 **The teacher as ally:** Have labels such as "head case," "spastic" (or "spaz") and "moron" and expressions such as "that's retarded" been discussed in the classroom? Have efforts been made to understand the requirements of special needs students? Are there programs and

personnel in the community and school district that can offer expertise and resources?

2 **The student:** Is there an awareness of the special needs in the class? Are any students feeling singled out for any reason? Have resources and equipment been sought out that will allow students to participate and engage more fully in PE?

3 **The learning climate:** Are special needs students sent off to a corner to work with an educational assistant during PE? Does the class environment welcome all levels of ability or does it favour the physically adept? Does the learning climate allow for situations where students of various abilities can interact with and learn from each other?

4 **The curriculum:** Draw on community resources and personnel to develop inclusive programs for students with special needs. Design learning experiences where children of various abilities can fully engage and experience growth and success. Develop a curriculum that allows for students who are troubled by noise or too many objects flying in the air to participate without unnecessary difficulty. Talk to students about how they feel about PE and identify which activities they feel included and enjoy participating in.

Activity—Sensory Empathy

- Have students take turns participating in PE class without the use of their limbs or one of their senses. Use eye coverings, wheelchairs, headsets, mouth coverings, etc., to assist.

- Have these students note the challenges they faced in participating fully in the lessons.

- Have the other students note the ways they need to adapt in order to fully include the learners with special needs.

- Discuss ways both you as the teacher and they as co-learners could be more accommodating for students with special needs in PE.

Bodies and Body Image

We have bodies not just because we are born *into* bodies, but because we *learn* our bodies, that is, we are taught how to think about our bodies and how to experience our bodies (McLaren, 1991, p. 156).

Though perspectives have evolved to some extent over the past several decades, the most accepted body types as portrayed in the media tend to be thin and moderately muscular. As a result younger and younger children are developing eating disorders (Cusumano & Thompson, 2001) and are going on diets to achieve a desirable body (Field et al., 2001).

Case Study 5: Differing Abilities

Miss Saunders teaches PE at a large school in Vancouver. She is a physical education specialist and teaches the same program year after year, delivering the prescribed curriculum to the best of her ability. Students come to her class twice a week and are given lessons in games, gymnastics, dance, and on occasion, alternative activities. Overall, the students are improving in their knowledge and skills so Miss Saunders decides to increase the challenge for students. She arranges the class into pairs and gives one partner the ball. The other partner is to stand with her or his back to the passer until the passer slaps the ball and calls out "right" or "left." The receiver needs to listen to the passer and move in that direction to receive the ball.

After several minutes of this activity Miss Saunders notices that one of the students is not moving to receive the ball. She walks over to the young girl and asks her why she is not moving to receive the ball. The girl's partner intervenes and says "She can't hear you." Miss Sanders was astonished at this revelation. The girl had always been well behaved and fully participated in the class as far as she noticed. She had assumed the girl was just shy when she didn't participate in class discussions and review. Miss Saunders modified the activity to include hand signals instead of call outs and the pair continued with the task.

Questions for Reflection

1 What, if anything, was missing in Miss Saunders' pedagogical approach?

2 Was the task the teacher gave to the students reasonable? Why or why not?

3 Was the modification the teacher provided adequate? Why or why not?

4 In what ways could you incorporate culturally relevant PE into this teaching and learning situation?

Case Study 6: Too Many Problems?

Mr. Carrigan is teaching at a high school in Montreal. In his second week of classes, two students, Cara and Mary, tell him that they are pregnant and cannot participate in PE. The guidance counsellor then informs him that two other students, George and Cecelia, have been diagnosed with serious emotional and behavioural difficulties. Another student, Eddie, has been kicked out of his home by his parents and is "couch surfing" with friends (he has yet to come changed for class). Ben, another student, informs him that he has severe asthma and yet another student, Sharon, tells him she has Type II diabetes. All of these students are in Mr. Carrigan's PE class at the same time.

As the weeks progress Mr. Carrigan becomes more and more frustrated with the needs in his class. He informs Cara and Mary that they have to participate even though they are pregnant. He sends George and Cecelia to the office eight times in ten lessons because they are disrupting the class. He takes marks off of Eddie's grade because he did not dress properly and tells him he would soon fail the class. He tells Ben to sit on the sidelines and Sharon to work harder. Mr. Carrigan feels he just can't get through the curriculum with all of the disruptions that are occurring and is overwhelmed by feelings of failure.

Questions for Reflection

1 Why do you think Mr. Carrigan was feeling overwhelmed in his situation?

2 Do you think there is anything Mr. Carrigan could have done to alleviate his feelings of failure? If so, what?

3 Do you think this class was typical or atypical? Why?

4 What components of culturally relevant PE do you think would be helpful to Mr. Carrigan and his students?

Eating disorders are dangerous and can lead to ill health, hospitalization, and even death. Apart from this, being underweight has been connected to a positive body image among adolescent girls, whereas being overweight and heaviness were related to a lower body image in males and females (Vilhjalmsson, Kristjansdottir, & Ward, 2012).

The obesity epidemic is not only emphasized in the medical field, it is now being taken up by PE researchers and political governing bodies, and subsequently being cascaded to schools to address. Sykes and McPhail (2007) observe that overweight children rarely have positive experiences in PE, and in many cases their experiences are described as "unbearable."

They further describe a culture of "fat phobia" and little tolerance for a spectrum of body types particularly in PE. This is highly problematic due to the considerable role genetics play in body composition and health (Maes, Neale, & Eaves, 1997).

Being sensitive to potential body image issues is especially important when teaching Physical Education.

From Theory to Practice

1 **The teacher as ally:** Are labels such as "fatty," "tubby," "skinny," and "flat" discussed with students? Is there a process of intervention when putdowns are heard? Is more attention paid to students with average body weights? Do teachers disrupt their own beliefs about why children are overweight or underweight?

2 **The student:** Are students eating enough? What sorts of foods are in their lunches? Do students have opportunities to express how they feel about their bodies? Are healthy choices available in the school and the community?

3 **The learning climate:** Does the learning environment allow students to work at their own pace and set reasonable goals for themselves? Does the climate promote a safe space for overweight and underweight students to explore their potential? Are students free to discuss name-calling and body image without encountering further ridicule?

4 **The curriculum:** Develop curricula whereby eating disorders are discussed with and investigated by students. Invite people from the community with eating and weight challenges to speak to the students about ways to overcome an unhealthy body image. Accommodate for different body masses in your lessons and learning experiences. Provide equipment and/or attire that will fit all shapes and sizes of students.

Activity—Body Image Research

- Invite the students to research a topic related to the body (e.g., eating disorders, excessive exercise or training, obesity, fat-phobia, extreme thinness).

- Have students write a story about a hypothetical person based on the research they gathered.

- Invite the students to share their narratives and post them on the wall or in a book.

- The purpose of this activity is to create a space where empathy can be experienced rather than focusing on the grave statistics that underscore the problem.

Actions Toward Culturally Relevant Physical Education

The current underpinning of culturally relevant PE is to focus on the child, the community, and the society at large. While the teacher's role, the learning climate, and the curriculum all intersect with the experiences of the young, the overarching goal of culturally relevant education is to meet the needs of each student.

Cultural relevance comprises all aspects of a young person's life that figure into their daily existence. Is it possible to view issues as neither good nor bad and just a product of one's experiences? The experiences that people live are not right or wrong; rather, experiences shape who we are. It is our responses to another's experiences that shape who we become. Therefore, teachers must work towards disrupting their own preconceptions of who they think their students are and seek to understand who their students *actually* are.

There are many tools that teachers can utilize in order to reach and include each student and become involved at the macro-, mid-, and micro- levels of education. For example, a three-pronged cycle of cultural relevance provokes teachers "(a) to have sophisticated knowledge of community dynamics, (b) to know how community dynamics influence educational processes, and (c) to devise and implement strategies reflecting cultural knowledge of the community" (Flory & McCaughtry, 2011, p. 1). This deepened understanding of cultural relevance can only be realized through involvement in the community and in students' lives that extend beyond the walls of gymnasiums, classrooms, or playing fields.

Questions for Reflection

1 Think back to your school days. Was there one student who stands out in your mind who really had difficulty in school? How did this student perform in PE class versus other classes? What do you think were the underlying factors that might have influenced the student's behaviour in school?

2 Is it harmful or helpful for a student to be categorized as having an emotional or behavioural disorder? Give an example for when it may be helpful and one for when it might be harmful. Are there ways for educators to transform any negative effects?

3 How might the contexts compare for a physical educator in Vancouver, Thunder Bay, or Iqualuit? What different issues and challenges might they encounter? What strategies and resources are available to teachers in these settings?

4 In what ways can PE educators incorporate and support a diversity of voices in authentic, respectful, and constructive ways?

5 In what ways can PE educators act as and partner with cultural allies and border crossers?

6 Do gender stereotypes still exist? To what extent? In all cases? Is there variability dependent upon the context? Do stereotypes change? In what ways can teachers and students act to disrupt stereotypical tendencies?

7 What might it be like for a PE teacher to be part of a cultural and/or linguistic minority? In what ways might this relate to students' experiences? How might teachers and students in diasporic settings navigate and construct knowledge?

8 As a teacher or future teacher, how can you extend your focus beyond individual students to understand the social, cultural, and economic factors in your PE classroom?

9 What information do you need to successfully motivate students to stay actively engaged in your PE classes?

10 How prepared are you to teach PE in a culturally responsive way?

Key Terms

- Lifeworlds
- Diversity
- Acceptance
- Respect
- Recognition
- Culturally Relevant PE
- Learning Climate

Adapted and Inclusive Physical Education

William Harvey
(with contributions by Shawn Wilkinson, Jessica Mackay and Michael Cicchillitti)

The purpose of this chapter is to provide a brief history of disability and an overview of adapted and inclusive physical education (PE) from a North American perspective. The focus will then shift to Canada where these same two issues for people with disabilities will be explored from a national perspective. Our country has enjoyed the benefits of many national organizations, researchers, physical educators, and volunteers who have excelled in the areas of adapted and inclusive PE. The current job responsibilities of physical educators will be explored in the context of inclusion, and a brief questioning of future pathways concludes the chapter.

Introduction

This chapter is made up of three main sections. The first section is called "Where have we been?" It includes definitions of key terms, a discussion of historical perspectives on PE and physical activity in North America, and definitional issues woven throughout the text (e.g., least restrictive environments, individual education plans). It is vital for future physical educators to understand how people with disabilities have been treated in the past in order to more thoroughly understand how they are currently being educated. Furthermore, this historical reconstruction may help to explain why physical educators may experience tremendous difficulties implementing differentiated instruction.

This book chapter is different from many others that address adapted and inclusive PE. The second section, "Where are we now?" is much more practical in nature. It poses questions about how physical educators may perform their job functions in relation to adapted and inclusive PE. The section explores planning for inclusion and concrete steps to take in order to become more inclusive in teaching practice. It does not provide specific activities for including persons with disabilities in PE. Rather, it is meant to stimulate each reader's thinking about their future role in delivering PE to students with disabilities. This categorical approach is not typical in Canadian schools, as each reader will discover in the first section.

The third, and final, section is called "Where are we going?" and addresses future concerns that people with disabilities and physical educators are likely to encounter. Given the history of adapted and inclusive PE, educators have not adapted very well to the needs of people with disabilities. Therefore, a series of pointed questions are posed to drive future teaching practices and research about those with disabilities in PE, and challenge the PE teaching profession to perform much better in the future.

Where Have We been?

One of the major challenges when writing about inclusion and adapted PE is terminology because definitions tend to change over time (Reid, 2003a). Standard definitions of integration, inclusion, physical education, adapted physical education, inclusive physical education, physical activity, and adapted physical activity are provided to guide the understanding of this chapter. There are many acronyms in the text so please refer to **Box 1** in order to distinguish between similar-looking terms. This section will then provide a brief history of people with disabilities that will lead into a historical reconstruction of PE and physical activity for persons with a disability. A story of adapted and inclusive PE in Canada will be told to help situate the reader in this rather short but complicated tale.

Definitions

Integration and inclusion are terms that originated in the 1990s (Reid, 2003a). For the purposes of this chapter, integration will refer to the notion that all people have the right to live in a society that values individual rights and freedoms, and to live a life just like everyone else. This notion implies that each person, in their own respective way, has the right to work, love, and live in the same society and in a similar fashion as their friends, neighbours, and fellow citizens (Reid, 2003a).

Inclusion, for the purpose of this chapter, will be defined in relation to all people and their associated functions in our school systems. Many professionals and lay people may simply think of inclusion as a practice solely within school classes where students with a disability are included (Goodwin, Watkinson, & Fitzpatrick, 2003; Reid, 2003a). However, this chapter aims to convince the reader that inclusion is much more. It is a philosophy, a state of mind, a means and an end to understanding the valuable and integral roles that persons with disabilities can and do play within our school systems. Ultimately, inclusion focuses on self-determination and individual abilities whether the person does or does not have a disability (Block & Obrusnikova, 2007a; Goodwin et al., 2003; Reid, 2003a).

Box 1: List of Acronyms
General Terms

- APA—Adapted Physical Activity
- APE—Adapted Physical Education
- PE—Physical Education
- IPE—Inclusive Physical Education
- IEP—Individual Education Plan
- IDEA—Individuals with Disabilities Education Act
- LRE—Least Restrictive Environment
- MTI—Moving To Inclusion
- PA—Physical Activity
- NCPERID—National Consortium on Physical Education and Recreation for Individuals with Disabilities
- PCK—Pedagogical Content Knowledge
- PL—Public Law
- PETE—Physical Education Teacher Education

Person-Specific References

- ADHD—Attention-Deficit Hyperactivity Disorder
- DCD—Development Coordination Disorder
- MHP—Mental Health Problems
- PDD—Pervasive Developmental Disabilities

The following standard definitions were adopted for this chapter:

"Physical and Health Education (PHE) is a school subject designed to help children and youth develop the skills, knowledge, and attitudes necessary for participating in active, healthy living. As such, Physical Education programs are an integral component of the total school experience for students" (Fishburne & Hickson, n.d.). This term is synonymous with the term physical education (PE), which is more commonly used in Canada and will be used in this chapter.

"Adapted Physical Education (APE) is a subdiscipline of physical education with an emphasis on physical education for students with disabilities. The term adapted physical education generally refers to school-based programs for students ages 3–21" (Block, 2007, p. 12).

"Inclusive Physical Education (IPE) means providing all students with disabilities the opportunity to participate in regular physical education with their peers, with supplementary aides and support services as needed to take full advantage of the goals of motor skill acquisition, fitness, knowledge of movement, and psycho-social well-being, toward the outcome of preparing all students for an active lifestyle appropriate to their abilities and interests" (Goodwin et al., 2003, p. 193).

Physical Activity (PA) is a movement of the body that expends energy; such as participation in sports, dance, and exercise. Physical activity is used in PE programs as a medium for teaching curriculum content. It is the vehicle to become physically educated, just as a book is a vehicle to becoming literate (Fishburne & Hickson, n.d.).

Adapted Physical Activity (APA) can be broadly described as a cross-disciplinary human movement science, concerned about the physical activity needs, skills, and experiences of persons with disabilities over the course of lifespan development (Sherrill, 1998).

History and Persons with a Disability

The Active Living Alliance for Canadians with a Disability has been highly successful in advocating for the use of person-first terminology (e.g., a person with autism) when referring to persons with disabilities. Person-first terminology suggests that the person is of paramount importance and her or his disability is considered important but does not completely define the person. Unfortunately, this type of advocacy and recognition of the individual person was not always the case. The label barrier for people with disabilities has been a significant issue. Rather than using person-first terminology, pejorative terms described people with disabilities. For example, Billy would be described as autistic or as an autistic child and not necessarily referred to by his first name or as a child. The negativity of terms even involved people with intellectual disabilities being referred

to as imbeciles and morons by professionals during the 1950s (Reid, 2003a). Thus, persons with disabilities have not always been treated as people who were capable of governing their own behaviours and actions, and, they were frequently excluded from all walks of life (Reid, 2003a).

Exclusion and Inhumane Treatment

The dictionary definition suggests that the term exclusion refers to a person who may be barred, restricted, or prevented from participating in various life-related activities. Persons with disabilities have historically been excluded from everyday activities.

Stories abound from both ancient and recent times where persons with disabilities were treated inhumanely due to the impairment brought upon by their specific disability. For example, Jansma and French (1994) describe the abandonment or murder of children with disabilities by their fathers as being legally permitted in Ancient Rome. They suggest that society, in general, did not begin to adopt a caring attitude for many people with disabilities until the time period between 1500 and 1900. They also state that those with mental health problems (MHP) were first treated humanely by the famous Louis Pinel at the end of the 1700s. While some may justify this poor treatment of persons with disabilities by saying it happened a long time ago, persons with disabilities, especially persons with MHP, were frequently portrayed as feeble, demonic, villains, or monsters by popular media up until twenty to thirty years ago (Dahl, 1993; Mobily & Ostiguy, 2004). Further, people with disabilities continued to be routinely institutionalized until well into the middle of the twentieth century (Reid, 2003b). In fact, many of those with MHP today remain institutionalized in our current society (Harvey et al., 2010). This point about institutionalization may seem trivial, or even tangential, to the story of PE and people with disabilities. However, the underlying assumption is that this type of segregation may be acceptable at a societal level. The implication is that educators or other people may consider it okay for those with disabilities to be excluded because it is a normal societal action to take or condone. Clearly, this should not be the case from a humanistic or inclusive perspective.

Education, over time, has proven to be one of the better allies of people with disabilities. Reid (2003b) describes the institutionalization and segregation of persons with disabilities that occurred before and during the 1950s. Many were confined to institutions, sometimes for their entire lifetimes. This type of institutionalization often led persons with disabilities to become both segregated and socially isolated. Both Wall (2003) and Reid (2003a) suggest that the social turbulence of the 1960s ushered in many changes for those with disabilities as Wolfensburger's notion of normalization began to seriously influence their treatment by placing an emphasis on allowing them to live "normal" lives.

Reid (2003b) also describes the societal shift that saw people with disabilities removed from institutional exile and being encouraged to live at home and be placed in special classes within "regular" schools. Thus, he also describes the notion of mainstreaming that began in the 1960s, where special education services began to be provided within the regular school system. Children were placed into streams based on educator perceptions and academic achievement and abilities. Students with disabilities were expected to be educated in the regular school setting; however, there were special education classes in regular schools for groups of students with similar disability labels (e.g., the blind class, the behaviour problem class, the autistic class). Students with disabilities could only gain entrance into the regular classroom setting by special recommendation after an educational assessment (Goodwin et al., 2003; Reid, 2003a). For instance, Goodwin et al. (2003) suggest that "in essence, students were asked to 'earn their way' out of special education classrooms to join their peers in regular classrooms" (p. 192).

Persons with disabilities would continue on this brave new path of normalization due mainly to the influence of legislators in the United States. This legislation will be discussed in relation to the provision of PE services but, first, a brief look back at PE and persons with disabilities is necessary for this story to unfold.

Physical Education and Physical Activity for Persons with Disabilities

Both physical education and physical activity for people with disabilities have usually been described through a variety of historical accounts, a series of reconstructionist histories if you will. Many major APA or IPE textbooks contain historical descriptions of various pathways that enabled persons with disabilities to be physically active (Arnheim & Sinclair, 1985; Block, 2007; Jansma & French, 1994; Sherrill, 1998; Winnick, 2000). PE and PA for people with disabilities have been given many labels such as "corrective, orthopedic, therapeutic, remedial, developmental, adapted and special education" (Arnheim & Sinclair, 1985).

Nomenclature can also be associated with different professionals and various points in time. For example, Sherrill and DePauw (1997) coupled the term medical gymnastics with the famous Per Henrik Ling of Sweden who, during the late 1800s, developed rehabilitative exercises for persons with physical disabilities (See Sherrill & DePauw, 1997 for extensive APA history). Thus, it should be noted the medical model, where disability-related challenges were assumed to exist solely within the person (Goodwin, 2003; Reid, 2003b), predominated the PE world for people with disabilities well into the twentieth century.

Hallmark Legislation: Mainstreaming and the Least Restrictive Environment

A major change in the treatment of people with disabilities emerged in the 1970s with major US legislative reforms. Educational legislation played an important historical role in the development of APE and, as a result, IPE. In fact, hallmark legislation in the US is likely the genesis of current APE and APA services and practices for persons with a disability in North America. Most major APA textbooks devote sections to the importance of public law (PL) 94-142 or the *Education for All Handicapped Children Act* of 1975, which entrenched the rights of all Americans to a "free and appropriate education, including physical education, for all eligible children ages 3–21" (Block, 2007, p. 5). American students with disabilities have legal access to PE or some other comparable PA if the school system cannot provide the appropriate services described in the individual education plan. This legislation, currently the *Individuals with Disabilities Education Act* (IDEA), was reauthorized to include early intervention programs (PL 98-189), preschool programs (PL 99-457), transition services to the "regular" community (PL 101-476), and parental participation rights in the planning process (PL 108-446) (Block, 2007).

The legal recognition of PE for persons with disabilities was indeed historically noteworthy, but it has not always brought about smooth transitions for persons with disabilities in PE. Reid (2003a) describes the mainstreaming movement and PE as being misaligned and lists four problems associated with the integration of mainstreaming and PE. First, it was poorly planned. Next, there was a lack of adequately trained personnel. Third, some school boards used mainstreaming as a method to save finances. Finally, the original purpose was to mainstream people with mild intellectual disabilities only. As a result of these four challenges, mainstreaming fell from favour and became a dumping ground that had lost its primary purpose of individualized education (Reid, 2003a).

The notion of the least-restrictive environment (LRE) is also covered by PL 94-142 and the IDEA. The LRE concept was designed to ensure that children were placed in the most normalized educational setting possible (Block, 2007). The LRE has often been defined within a cascade system from the most segregated setting (i.e., twenty-four-hour treatment services, including APE, in a hospital) to the least segregated setting (i.e., instruction in a regular classroom or gymnasium) (Goodwin et al., 2003; Reid, 2003a). This concept reinforces the claim that mainstreaming and inclusion have often been focused on "where" people with disabilities have been placed and taught (Reid, 2003a, 2003b). For example, an American child with pervasive developmental disabilities (PDD) may be taught in a regular educational setting if the school and the individual education plan (IEP) indicate that the necessary supports

Many physical activities can be adapted for those with disabilities.

and services are in place. If not, then the law requires that the child be placed in the next level of the LRE. For instance, a child with PDD could be placed in a specialized school setting where there are more formal supports and the infrastructure needed to provide one-on-one instruction and smaller classroom sizes.

If one believes that the best interests of the child are being identified and met by the multidisciplinary team, then the LRE may seem like a very good idea. Multidisciplinary teams usually consist of many domain-specific professionals (psychologists, general education teachers, resource teachers, physical educators, etc.) who may all contribute individual objectives to assist a student with a disability to meet individual educational objectives. The student and their parents are also part of the team and they are expected to be included in the process so they may provide guidance and feedback. Thus, the LRE may encourage the multidisciplinary team to search out the best solutions for the educational needs of the student. The concept of the LRE should encourage team members to question what the unique teaching objectives and practices are in relation to each and every person.

Ardent proponents of inclusive PE may not agree with these perspectives on the LRE concept. For example, Reid (2003b) suggests the following five difficulties:

1 It may provide a legitimate reason for more segregated environments to exist (e.g., a residential school).

2 It may downplay the services and supports required to adequately include persons with a disability.

3 It is essentially a "readiness" model with few observable process milestones to advance to the next less restricted level.

4 The decision to place someone in any environment is a moral issue that is not best served by professional decision makers.

5 It may be an infringement on human rights.

Please do not be fooled into thinking that this discussion is tangential or unnecessary. Rather, the legislation was used to set the stage for the development of student learning environments and educator working conditions at the time. It still may be used to enhance learning environments and current working conditions!

Thus, legislation to support the inclusion of people with disabilities may be viewed as a double-edged sword. It may be deemed as positive because legislation entrenches the rights of people with disabilities to engage in PE. However, legislation may be considered a hindrance to others. For example, American physical educators are bound to the legal requirements of IDEA (Reid, 2003b) whereas those in Canada are not because formal Canadian legislation does not exist to protect the PE or PA needs of Canadians with disabilities. Although Wall (1990a) valiantly argued that PE and PA opportunities must be provided to persons with disabilities as per section 15 of the *Canadian Charter of Human Rights and Freedoms*, Reid (2003b) clearly stated that no Canadian laws exist for concepts like LRE and inclusion in PE. So what does it matter if there are no legal obligations for PE instruction to be provided for people with disabilities?

The three main issues related to the lack of legislation of PE for Canadians with disabilities are trust, certification of APE specialists, and adequate supports.

1 **Trust:** Canadian physical educators and their respective school boards must be trusted to include people with disabilities in PE classes. We must assume that IPE is happening because of the current inclusion movement in many Canadian schools (Reid, 2003a). For example, Health Canada promoted IPE during the 1990s when they and their national partners distributed copies of the *Moving To Inclusion* (MTI) resource to over 15,000 Canadian schools (Wall, 2003). MTI is currently an online resource that describes ways to make PA inclusive; it is available to university professors and their students for a nominal fee (see www.ala.ca). However, this does not necessarily mean that IPE is alive and well in our schools. There are no firm statistics to suggest that IPE is widely occurring in Canadian schools. It is hard to believe that all physical educators are being inclusive, particularly given the long history of exclusion of people with disabilities.

2 **Certification of APE Specialists:** There is no formal certification to become an adapted physical educator in Canada. Two paths that may lead to a formal APE certification for American PE specialists (as identified by Block, 2007) are the Adapted Physical Education National Standards examination (NCPERID, 2006) or state licensure. There are four prerequisites required to take this exam including a bachelor's degree in PE, 200+ hours of practicum experiences in APE, a three-credit course in APE, and a valid teaching licence (Block, 2007, p. 13). However, school districts are not required to hire these certified specialists and only 30% of US states have developed a specific state licence for APE specialists (Block, 2007). This lack of a professional certification may seem like a minor issue to some PE specialists and an enormous issue for others. Reid (2003b) provides a thorough discussion of the relevance of the term "adapted" when referring to PE or PA for persons with disabilities. Reid (2003b) refers to the existence of a special APA text, which indicates that many of our country's leaders (i.e., the editors and authors of the Canadian APA text; Steadward, Wheeler, & Watkinson, 2003) must have believed that a specialization in APA was justifiable. However, Reid (2003b) also notes that the term APA could lead physical educators to feel unprepared to provide instruction for people with disabilities because it may be viewed as a specialization. Reid suggests that arguments against the term "adapted" may focus on (1) too much specialization, (2) program adaptation when few or no changes may be required, and (3) the potential fostering of segregation through an identification of differences from others rather than identification of similarities and celebration of individual abilities. He further claims that PA for people with disabilities is already a possibility with the current knowledge base and skill sets of physical educators and recreation staff in the community if they possess beliefs in individualization and accommodation. Research in IPE may not support his claims as the attitudes of physical educators towards inclusion have generally been negative (Block & Obrusnikova, 2007b). Furthermore "as adaptations become more extensive, creative, and possibly unique to an individual's disability, it is likely that most physical educators would benefit from the suggestions of adapted physical activity specialists" (Reid, 2003b, p. 22).

The Catch-22 is that there still is no certification in Canada to become an APA specialist. There are Canadian universities that have graduate programs in APA (e.g., McGill University, University of Alberta, Lakehead University), so a physical educator could identify as an APA specialist if she or he were to use their M.A., Ph.D., and job-related experiences as qualifications but the universities currently have no formal certification system in place. Future physical educators could adopt a marketability approach to suggest that an APE or APA specialization would make them more employable because they can include all people in their teaching practice. Specialization could promote quality teaching for all students and put parents and guardians at ease knowing that their children continue to be in the hands of highly qualified professionals. Further, it may also lead to standards, or required professional competencies, to guide practice and hold educators accountable. These types of questions could lead to a very lively debate!

Case Study 1: A Bad Attitude?

Principal Harvey understands that the job of a physical educator is challenging because it encompasses the biological, psychological, and sociological domains of the human experience. Many previous physical educators have told him there is limited time to do their job. Therefore, attempts at inclusion often feel like just another item on a long "To Do" list.

Mrs. Jones made an appointment to speak with Principal Harvey about her son John, who has a mild form of Asperger's syndrome. Her son's physical educator refuses to allow the fourteen-year-old to participate in PE class because, as the educator says, "Johnny just doesn't get how to take part in sports." The mother requests that the physical educator be present at the next IEP meeting, but the educator refuses saying he does not want to waste his time on one kid with a perceived bad attitude when he can be putting his time to good use with his coaching responsibilities.

Questions for Reflection:

1 Why would the educator act this way?

2 What actions would you take if you were Principal Harvey?

3 What actions would you take if you were Mrs. Jones?

4 How do you think that John and his mother feel about their place in the school as a result?

3 **Lack of adequate supports:** The foundations of mainstreaming and APE were built with the recognition that inclusion in education, and by extension PE, should incorporate various types of support to ensure a successful experience (Block, 2007; Reid, 2003a; 2003b, Sherrill, 1998). Block (2007) suggests that physical educators must first determine "who" will provide the support necessary to plan for IPE (i.e., the educator, an APA specialist, occupational therapist, physiotherapist). However, we must question how Canadian physical educators may obtain adequate support for IPE, especially if they are not included on the multidisciplinary teams that formulate the IEP. Many physical educators may feel too busy to attend these meetings and/or they may not be invited to attend (Harvey, 1997).

Thus, it seems that Canadian physical educators will have to count on themselves to identify any type of support for IPE. The four different types of support that may be provided to physical educators are:

1 Resource Support—providing required information about IPE or potential financial and human resources

2 Moral Support—listening empathetically and helping to solve any challenges

3 Technical Support—suggesting assistance about teaching methods, strategies, and potential adaptations to ensure a successful IPE

4 Evaluation Support—providing the physical educator with data collection tools and strategies to collect information that assists with questions surrounding support services

(Block, 2007, pp. 69–70)

The amount of required time for support is also important. These supports can be minimal to pervasive (Block, 2007). For example, a child with a learning disability may periodically require verbal cues to remind them to pay attention while a child with multiple disabilities (e.g., autism spectrum disorder and intellectual disability) may require constant support from a paraeducator to guide and assist them by hand throughout the entire class each day. Please note these supportive actions are quite complicated and they are no small tasks to accomplish. A few concrete strategies are provided to address this topic later in the chapter.

There are some serious questions that need to be asked about the feasibility of IPE in the Canadian context. One should not jump to the conclusion that the lack of legal protections suggests that it would be better to be free of LRE-related issues like alternative placements, costs associated with attending IEP meetings, and developing individual objectives to become part of the overall IEP. If that were the case, IPE would lose the ability to focus on each individual and miss the tremendous opportunity to educate many people with disabilities about adopting active and healthy lifestyles for their lifetimes. Sherrill (1998) suggests the philosophy and products of LRE have enabled the inclusion of most people with disabilities in regular education environments. While Sherrill (1998) and her US colleagues advocate for a variety of PE specific placements options to support the LRE notion, she notes that students with disabilities are usually either placed into a separate APE or regular PE setting. It seems the LRE has helped pave the way to IPE. Perhaps we should heed the words of Reid (2003b) who suggests a redefined and flexible approach to inclusion where individual student needs are better accommodated. For example, physical educators should try to include people with disabilities in class activities as much as possible and, if necessary, run a parallel activity at the same time (and if possible, in the same space). For instance, have all students working on physical fitness tasks, but at their own level, to enhance individual health.

Case Study 2: Certification

Dr. Wilkinson has decided to lead a new certification process for inclusive physical educators in Canada. He has selected the Montreal area and the four local universities as the crucible for his new project. The local school boards would like to support him in this endeavour but want him to construct a solid case for an accreditation process.

He decides to approach universities in the Buffalo, New York, area for support since he grew up there. His American colleagues have difficulty understanding the issues related to inclusion because IDEA legislation has permeated the US culture. Dr. Wilkinson does not really know where to start, but believes firmly in a certification process to protect the right of Canadians with disability to engage in PE and PA.

Questions for Reflection

1 Do you agree that APE specialist certification should be required in Canada? Why or why not?

2 Why should Canadians with a disability have the right to engage in PE or PA?

It stands to reason that legislation should exist to ensure that the PE and PA needs of those with disabilities are being met. Clearly, IDEA has influenced the conceptualization of APE, IPE, and APA in North America. The reader is strongly encouraged to read Wall (2003) for a strong accounting of Canada's PA history for persons with a disability.

Where Are We Now?

The focus of this chapter will now turn to current job responsibilities of physical educators. The relationship between inclusion and planning will be highlighted to ask why, how, and what can be done to include people with disabilities in PE. Concrete steps will be provided for in-service physical educators to follow in order to develop an inclusive program.

Planning for Inclusion

Good quality PE is synonymous with good quality APE (Reid, 2003b; Sherrill, 1998). Quality PE starts with the planning process, particularly when including children with disabilities. However, if a pre- or in-service educator was to read APA texts superficially, then she or he might get the idea that adapted or inclusive PE is primarily outcome-based. For example, "quality physical education encourages individualization through teacher-student interaction, task selection, choice and environmental modifications that encourage different ability levels and needs" (Reid, 2003b, p. 21). However, it is crucial that planning for inclusion is not secondary to the initial planning procedure. Rather, it should be immediately embedded in the planning process and not considered as an afterthought.

Physical educators are, indeed, expected to plan programs from a hierarchy of planning perspective (Rink, 2009). Planning ranges from the highest level possible (i.e., provincial department of education) to the grassroots or classroom level (i.e., year, month, unit, and individual lesson plans). Each educator must first consult their provincial curriculum to identify the priority teaching areas in PE as identified by provincial planners. Educators are required by law to follow these curricula to develop appropriate programs to meet expected provincial and school board outcomes. For instance, in Quebec, each educator is expected to follow the Quebec Education Plan and school board policies to create appropriate program and unit plans as well as accompanying lesson plans to meet legal and local educational demands. It is crucial that pre-service educators adopt an inclusive PE philosophy so that IPE is not conceptualized as a simple bag of tricks or a one-size-fits-all approach.

Each educator is also expected to become a consummate professional who works diligently on the craft and science of teaching. The Quebec Ministry of Education has developed a competency-based curriculum that mandates twelve professional teaching exit competencies for pre-service physical educators. A few of these competencies focus on professional skills and development. For example, the eleventh states that student educators should "demonstrate ethical and responsible professional behaviour in the performance of his or her duties" (Government of Quebec, 2001, p. 145). Thus, the governmental expectation is that educators will continue to improve their proficiency in all professional aspects of teaching. Given this type of expectation, pre- and in-service physical educators must become very well versed in all aspects of PE. It takes countless hours of deliberate practice to become a finely tuned educator who has learned and knows every little intricacy for the teaching of fundamental movement skills, sport-specific skills, specific curriculum models, and lifelong physical activities for all learners. It would probably take a lifetime to just become proficient in a few of these instructional areas. Thus, it is very important that physical educators adopt a lifelong learning approach to their instructional practices. The more current the professional's teaching practices, the better. As will be demonstrated shortly, this wealth of automatized pedagogical content knowledge (PCK) will be vital for those working to include people with disabilities in PE.

Provincial curriculum models usually describe the recommended approach for persons with a disability from the perspective of each respective department of education. However, do not expect major direction from the provincial education legislators and curriculum planners. Usually, there is simply a suggestion to adapt instruction as best as one can to suit the needs of people with disabilities. This type of bare-bones adaptation to PE is about all that persons with disabilities have come to expect. Again, since there are no formal Canadian or provincial laws to ensure PE for people with disabilities (Reid, 2003b), we must trust that Canadian physical educators will do their utmost to include people with disabilities in their classes.

In-service educators must look to the future and try to predict how they may be able to adapt their instruction to better include people with disabilities. Most in-service physical educators in Canada will be required to complete one course in APA for people with disabilities. Despite this, educators often feel unprepared to teach PE to people with disabilities due to a lack of knowledge (Block, 2007; Reid, 2003b; Block & Obrusnikova, 2007b). One suggestion is that physical educators, coaches, and recreation specialists would feel better prepared to provide service to people with disabilities if they were required to take more academic courses in APA (Reid, 2003b). It is not necessarily the case that educators question whether or not to adapt activities for the sake of including people with disabilities, but that many do not know where, what, and how to adapt or include people with disabilities in PE.

Professional Reflections about PE

Pre-service and in-service physical educators should explore their own personal belief systems and philosophical values concerning the role of PE in relation to inclusion. This approach was used by Block (2007) in his text called *A Teacher's Guide to Including Students with Disabilities in General Physical Education*. In the introduction, Block and his colleagues describe and explore:

1   What a physically educated person is,

2   What a physically educated person does, and

3   How PE is devoted to developing people who are active and healthy for their lifetimes.

Of course, this description is consistent with the definition of a physically educated person provided by the National Association for Sport and Physical Education (NASPE), Physical and Health Education-Canada (PHE Canada), and the reading that you have done thus far in this chapter. The third point in the list above is important to note in the context of inclusion. If PE is considered valuable for all people in the process of adopting a physically active and healthy lifestyle for their lifetime, then it should be expected that people with disabilities be included in PE because they are valuable members of society who also require a similar lifelong physically active and healthy lifestyle. It is unacceptable to be included in PE just for the sake of inclusion.

Earlier in the chapter it was suggested that physical educators develop well-automatized PCK. The reason for this suggestion is to demonstrate the need to know the profession very well. For example, the more information that a professional educator really knows well about a content area, the more available thinking space the educator may devote to another facet of their job. For instance, if an educator has developed her or his PE program and knows all of the intricacies of the physical activities and/or sports in the instructional program, then she or he could not only explore issues and identify potential solutions for instructional challenges surrounding inclusion, but also investigate various pedagogical models and brainstorm instructional strategies in relation to program and teaching practices. Thus, it becomes evident that a conceptual approach is necessary to develop a solid foundation for IPE to occur. A conceptual approach focuses on the predominant conceptual framework, or combination of frameworks, that guides service delivery for people with disabilities. For example, empowerment and self-determination are the prevailing constructs for the selection, motivation, and participation in physical activities by persons with disabilities (Reid 2003b; Causgrove Dunn & Goodwin, 2008). Fortunately, a text entitled *Adapted Physical Activity* (edited by Steadward, Wheeler, & Watkinson, 2003) exists to better inform us about the wide depth and breadth of APA philosophies, advocacy efforts, school programs, community practices, policies, and disability sport within Canadian borders and beyond. This text can be an invaluable resource for physical educators as it incorporates a lifespan perspective on PA and describes how PA opportunities have changed tremendously for people with disabilities over the past thirty years. This uniquely Canadian textbook also provides support for the overall objectives of PA and PE that prescribe lifelong physical activity and a healthy lifestyle for everyone.

The question of knowing where, what, and how to adapt activities or include people with disabilities in PE is a complicated one. Goodwin et al. (2003) suggest that consensus seems to have swayed positively so educators are trying to include children with disabilities in the "regular" PE program. Thus, in their opinion, the "where" question has been resolved. The authors further suggest the challenging aspects of IPE, of what to teach (i.e., curriculum) and how to best implement the chosen instructional content, is highly conceptual in nature. Our field should question the depth of individual and group academic disconnectedness by questioning physical educators who work every day in the trenches of education. They must ask the question: How does this information help to include persons with disabilities in my classes? Further, they should need more convincing to believe the "where" question has faded in the PE community.

Physical educators need to search for concrete methods to address the conceptual nature of how to teach IPE as well as any concerns about political correctness that relate to inclusion. The foundation of APA was built on the development of personal and professional experience and expertise. Past efforts to define, categorize, and guide APA were attached to the service delivery needs of persons with disabilities (Reid, 2003b). This "person" element is valuable, as that should remain the focus of professional endeavours (Wall, 1990b). Educators and researchers need to adopt a flexible teaching approach to APE or IPE. There will likely be much trial and error involved when gaining the necessary experience to adapt instruction so that varying levels of inclusion are possible. Apart from the total exclusion or ostracism of persons with disabilities, there are probably fewer mistakes to make than one may imagine. However, planning should be an integral part of the process of adaptation or inclusion in PE. Otherwise, IPE may continue to be conceptualized as simply adapting the instruction that the physical educator is performing.

Seven Concrete Steps to Inclusion

What are the important and concrete steps for the pre-service or in-service educator to be aware of so they can plan to include each person with a disability in PE?

1 Make links between your provincial curriculum and the instructional model (Block, 2007; Metzler, 2011; Rink 2009) that you choose to use for instruction.

2 Understand and select the instructional approach to skill or game development that ties to the instructional model (Goodwin, 2003).

3 Predict and understand the most likely types of abilities and disabilities to be encountered (Jansma & French, 1994; Sherrill, 1998; Winnick, 2000).

4 Identify the types of support needed to encourage inclusive PE (Block, 2007).

5 Identify assessment and evaluation methods that include IEPs (Block, 2007; Rink, 2009).

6 Identify routines, procedures, and other concerns that may utilize a positive approach to behaviour management (Lavay, French, & Henderson, 2006).

7 Speak to the students with disabilities in your class to better individualize PE instruction.

1 Provincial Curriculum and Curriculum Models

The role of models to guide instruction has risen in popularity (Metzler, 2011). Although it seems like just another level of planning, the use of instructional models is important to the informed delivery of instruction. Current instructional models may include direct instruction, indirect instruction, lifetime games and sports, cooperative learning, inquiry teaching, outdoor and adventure education, the TPSR model, and the TGfU model. The latter three models have been quite popular in the past decade (Metzler, 2011; Rink, 2009). For more information on the various curriculum models, see Chapter 3.

2 Instructional Approaches and Instructional Models

Many PE scholars suggest tying a selected instructional model to instructional approaches that underlie the teaching of motor skills. For example, Goodwin (2003) identifies seven instructional approaches that have traditionally been used when teaching motor skills to children with disabilities and explores the theoretical assumptions that underlie each instructional approach. Goodwin's work could be a valuable resource to those attempting to determine which theories are directly or indirectly related to your teaching style. For example, the popular Teaching Games for Understanding

(TGfU) approach groups games and their associated skills into four categories based on the boundaries of the play environment and similarities of movement skills, actions, and strategies used in each category. Educators would do well to know that cognitive and strategic instructional approaches likely underlie the TGfU model. Thus, principles of information processing and metacognition, or conscious thinking strategies, in a problem-solving framework are likely to be a larger part of an educator's understanding when instructing all people at the given moment. These underlying principles will affect how the educator conceptualizes learning and related teaching practices. For example, the educator may assume that all "normal" children will learn games in relation to the environmental boundaries placed on each game category, and that all children will be able to learn how to problem solve and become more proficient at formal games through deliberate practice and experience. This assumption is not likely to hold true for many students with disabilities.

3 Predicting Abilities and Disabilities

Spend some time thinking about the types of disabilities that you may encounter in your PE classes. Perhaps the key to planning for students with disabilities is to understand that educators will likely encounter people with specific types of disabilities. For example, a physical educator is very likely to teach a student with attention-deficit hyperactivity disorder (ADHD) because the prevalence of ADHD is conservatively estimated to be 3–5% of the school-aged population of North America (American Psychiatric Association, 2000; Brault & Lacourse, 2012). Other disabilities to be aware of are autistic spectrum disorder, learning disabilities, physical disabilities, and mental health problems such as anxiety and depression. Many APA texts adopt a categorical approach that advocates understanding the different types of disabilities and associated impairments that may affect people (Jansma & French, 1994; Sherrill, 1998; Winnick, 2000).

This type of approach may be not appreciated by some APE, IPE, or APA professionals because it is based on the prescriptive, medical model where disability-related challenges may be assumed to exist all within the person (Goodwin, 2003; Reid, 2003b). However, more information about specific challenges for students with disabilities may enable educators to be better informed about the impairing effects of various disabilities. In fact, Canadian researchers have been at the forefront of exploring the relationships between PA and persons with physical disabilities (Goodwin, Thurmeier, & Gustafson, 2004), autism spectrum disorder (Reid & Collier, 2002), development coordination disorder (DCD) (Cairney et al., 2005), and ADHD (Harvey & Reid, 2003) as well as other emotional and behavioural difficulties (Halas, 2003). Please note that a person can be affected by more than one disability at one time, a condition referred to as comorbidity.

Pre- and in-service educators should be aware of one of the more common comorbidities, that is, the combination of ADHD and DCD. ADHD is a disorder that is highly prevalent in our schools. The symptoms of inattention, hyperactivity, and impulsivity often lead students to wreak havoc in classrooms and gymnasiums. Most pre-and in-service educators would understand DCD by identifying a student who is physically awkward or clumsy. Yet, 50% of children with ADHD may also experience the effects of DCD (Sergeant, Piek, & Oosterlaan, 2006). This research fact often surprises physical educators who may have previously believed that the majority of children with ADHD were tremendous movers who also learned better through their physical bodies (Anderson & Rumsey, 2002). Furthermore, educators should be aware that there are a substantial amount of children who experience movement skill difficulties in gymnasiums and playgrounds all across our country. In turn, it is recommended that educators avoid a one-size-fits-all teaching approach, and be able to differentiate instructional planning, teaching performance, and student evaluation. (The reader is directed to Harvey and Reid (2003) for more discussion on the important topic of comorbidity). It is highly recommended that educators cater to the abilities of students with disabilities rather than feel hindered by the impairments and challenges related to each specific disability. PE program development should progress as usual, with disability-specific knowledge informing the teaching process.

4 Types of Support

Educators should identify the types of support needed to encourage inclusive PE. Inclusion without appropriate supports is not considered inclusion at all (Block, 2007; Goodwin et al., 2003; Reid 2003a, 2003b).

As mentioned earlier in the section on history and IPE, the educator must be aware of the types of supports available in the school system and beyond. Try to identify the professionals who could be of assistance when including people with disabilities. Make allies with the students and parents, the school psychiatrist or psychologist, resource personnel, paraeducators (sometimes called shadows or community care workers) and involve them in your discussions and planning for inclusion.

For example, paraeducators are sometimes left out of the gymnasium when their assigned children are in PE class. Do not assume that they are taking a break or do not know much about children with disabilities. These people may be one of our best resources as they work every day with the children with disabilities that you will include. A very good resource for involving paraeducators in PE is *Paraeducators in Physical Education: A Training Guide to Roles and Responsibilities* by L. J. Lieberman (2007).

Some disabilities limit participation more than others so communication is key, particularly with young students.

Case Study 3:
"I've seen guys like you come and go"

Mike has just graduated from a PE Teacher Education program in Canada. He has landed a teaching job in PE at the K–6 level and is very excited about this new professional opportunity. The school is an inner city school in a large city. He meets all of the teaching staff, including the other PE specialist, Mr. Smith, on the first day of the job in August.

Excitement is in the air on the first day of school. It isn't hard to sense that the local neighbourhood is a tough one. There are many students with behavioural problems attending the school. Mike can hardly catch his breath because he is so excited. Mr. Smith meets Mike at the gymnasium to wish him good luck on his first day. Mike is surprised when he hears Mr. Smith say, "They don't belong here. They should be in jail with their parents." Mr. Smith then turns and says to Mike "Good luck on your first day because all of these kids will be off their pills and off the walls. Most of them are lazy, crazy, or stupid … Good luck with that." Mike replies by saying "They can't be all that bad. They look like really good kids." Mr. Smith rebukes Mike by saying, "Hmmph, I've seen guys like you come go. I'll be here when you can't take the heat and leave."

Questions for Reflection:

1 What would you be feeling if you were in Mike's shoes?

2 How and why would you reply to Mr. Smith?

3 How could you plan to remain positive to inclusion even in such a challenging environment?

5 Assessment and Evaluation Methods

How do you embed assessment and evaluation in IPE? Assessment should not really change for all people who participate in IPE. For example, differentiated instructional processes include assessment and evaluation methods linked to IEPs. Those seeking more information are strongly encouraged to consult *A Teacher's Guide to Including*

Students with Disabilities in General Physical Education by M. E. Block (2007) for concrete examples of planning, assessment, and evaluation with related forms and checklists. It is also important to know and understand the traditional instructional approaches used in APE and IPE since they are related to assessment, adaptation, and evaluation.

Goodwin (2003) identifies seven instructional approaches that have been used and the assumptions that are linked to each one (i.e., remedial therapy approach, developmental approach, perceptual motor approach, behavioural approach, cognitive approach, ecological systems approach, and strategic approach). For example, many in-service educators will be aware of the developmental approach and developmental task analysis as they will have learned about the relationships between the person, task, and environment variables as well as stage theories in a required motor development course. Developmental task analysis has often been used to analyze environmental factors that may limit motor skill acquisition and help to guide which of the variables may be adapted for successful skill performance (size, weight, speed, trajectory of objects, implements to be manipulated, sizes of equipment, etc.) (Goodwin, 2003). Goodwin presents these instructional approaches in a historical fashion to describe the ever-changing instructional frameworks that exist within APE circles. Thus, the last framework is called the strategic approach and it is linked to metacognition, or higher-ordered conscious thinking processes, where students learn how to analyze and solve problems to promote independent learning. Goodwin further links metacognition to self-regulation and self-determination, which are the prevailing constructs for PA participation by those with disabilities (Reid 2003b; Causgrove Dunn & Goodwin, 2008). Pre-service physical educators are advised to think carefully when deciding to use elements or parts of various instructional approaches. The theoretical assumptions that underlie some approaches may not match or be poorly linked together in actual teaching practice. This is an important point to keep in mind when trying to use assessment and evaluation to make a PE program defensible (Rink, 2009).

6 Routines and Procedures

Sixth, the physical educator needs to explore what systematic approaches, routines, procedures, and other concerns may enable a positive approach to behaviour management. The book *Positive Behaviour Management in Physical Activity Settings* (2nd ed, by Lavay, French, & Henderson, 2006) is a tremendous resource that encourages positive behaviour management for all students. This text is highly recommended reading for all pre-service physical educators. University students in education need to understand that there will always be student behaviours that impede their instruction but not all of the behaviours should automatically be considered "bad behaviour." Instead, new educators must respect their students' varying cultural and religious beliefs and customs while attempting to create a positive learning environment. Lavay et al. suggest this learning environment is mediated by the choice of

1 The systematic approach (i.e., behavioural, humanistic, biophysical approach or combination of them)

2 Positive strategies (i.e., "Catch 'em being good" where the educator praises each child for individual good behaviours rather than focusing solely on punishing each child for poor behaviours), and

3 The design of a proactive management plan to follow.

It would be wise to follow the ten-step approach to design a behaviour management plan as described in the book. While it does represent another layer of planning for all students with and without disabilities, the rationale for this specificity of planning is based on a parallel with sports teams. How much planning does the coach of an elite team do? Preparation and planning are constant, consistent, and deliberate. Why should pre- and in-service physical educators not expect to do the same as future educators? Many educators ask about safety concerns and students with disabilities. While safety is a concern for all children, there is some validity in asking the safety question because most major textbooks do allude to it (e.g., Block, 2007; Sherrill, 1998; Winnick, 2000). Lavay et al. suggest that ADHD, autism, behavioural problems, and traumatic brain injury are the most common disabilities that may affect a person's behaviour negatively (2006). They suggest a variety of effective management strategies like gestures, proximity control, positive reinforcement, behavioural contracts, token economy, the talking bench, and one-to-one or small group instruction. Educators will have a better idea of how to use the behaviour management information provided by these authors if she or he learns all about the specific disability or disabilities that may affect each student. It is highly recommended to be fair, firm, and consistent when incorporating a positive behaviour management approach. Furthermore, it is challenging to be positive when dealing with poor behaviour but educators must resist the temptation to take the asocial behaviour personally (Rink, 2009). The main challenge is not to exclude any child from PE for behavioural problems. The real gem of teaching is learning how to include all children in PA and enjoying the journey along the way!

7 Speak to the Students

Finally, all educators should be encouraged to communicate with any students with disabilities to better individualize

Case Study 4: "An IPE program is expected to start on the first day of school"

Principal Mackay has just returned home from a national educators' conference devoted specifically to inclusion. There were a host of various speakers who relayed their research and practical application ideas about inclusion in subject-specific areas like music, drama, and PE. She was so impressed by one American speaker that she is inspired to make all PE classes at her school fully inclusive. She receives immediate approval from the school board to pilot this approach to PE.

Principle Mackay informs the PE department in early May, ample time in her professional opinion to develop a fully functional and fully inclusive PE program for the beginning of the next school year in September. Although one PE specialist is not supportive of the idea of inclusion, the other advocates for it but is skeptical of whether or not it will be possible to completely overhaul the PE program in such a short period of time. The principal does not agree and makes herself clear, in a meeting with both specialists, that an IPE program is expected to start on the first day of school.

Questions for Reflection:

1 If you were the physical educator on board with inclusion, how would you make a strong case for the extension that you and your colleague require to develop and run a quality IPE program?

2 What important factors can you identify and discuss to make your case?

instruction. This process will likely result in some very positive stories and some very negative stories from the children.

Canadian researchers have led the world in documenting the ambivalent feelings of children with disabilities toward their participation in PE (Goodwin & Watkinson, 2000; Spencer-Cavaliere & Watkinson, 2010) and the ensuing

Case Study Game

You will need one die and a notepad of paper to record each case that you develop during this activity. Roll the die six times (once each for gender, age, disability, impairment(s), support(s), and activity) and record the number and identifier for each category in the game matrix (See **Table 8.1** below).

For example if you were to roll a 3, 5, 6, 1, 6, and a 4, then your case study profile would be a male who is ten years old with ADHD, poor movement skills, and no supports trying to participate in fitness.

Your challenge is to develop an initial plan to provide an APE activity for this person. Furthermore, you will develop a plan of action to include this child in an age-appropriate IPE class of peers without disabilities. Once you are finished one case study, then pick up the die and roll again. To increase the level of complexity of the game, roll the die twice for the disability category and/or the impairment category and you will be able to add a second diagnosis and/or impairment to the case. You will quickly come to understand some of the issues related to comorbidity.

Please refer to Hodge, Murata, Block, and Lieberman (2003) for practice with more case studies.

Table 8.1: Game Matrix						
Number	1	2	3	4	5	6
Gender	Male	Female	Male	Female	Male	Female
Number	1	2	3	4	5	6
Age	6 years	13 years	8 years	16 years	10 years	7 years
Number	1	2	3	4	5	6
Disability	Pervasive Development Disorder-Not Otherwise Specified	Learning Disability	Developmental Coordination Disorder	Physical Disability	Autism Spectrum Disorder	Attention Deficit Hyperactivity Disorder
Number	1	2	3	4	5	6
Impairment(s)	Poor Movement Skill	Letter Reversal	Learned Helplessness	Inability to Use Lower Limbs	No Verbal Communication	Social Isolation
Number	1	2	3	4	5	6
Support(s)	Paraeducator	Moral Only	Resource Teacher	Adapted Physical Activity Specialist	Parents	None
Number	1	2	3	4	5	6
Activity	Throwing and Catching	Badminton	Invasion Games	Fitness	Movement/ Game Skills	Soccer

development of important friendships (Seymour, Reid, & Bloom, 2009; Spencer-Cavaliere & Watkinson, 2010). For example, children with disabilities have spoken about feelings of happiness and acceptance when included in physical activities or feelings of sadness or anger when excluded (Spencer-Cavaliere & Watkinson, 2010).

Where Are We Going?

This final section will address concerns or issues that people with disabilities and physical educators are likely to encounter in the near future. It is hoped that positive changes soon begin to emerge for people with disabilities and physical educators in IPE. Of course, Canadians with disabilities should continue to embark on a brave new path of PE and PA that traces it roots to the influence of US legislation. Yet how do students with disabilities get recognized as students who have equal rights to be educated, with the potential to become active and healthy for their lifetimes? Do we in Canada, as a society, need to lobby the government to have these rights entrenched in the Canadian constitution? Will people with disabilities agree to advocate for this type of legal status? We must explore how people with disabilities can gain a public voice in the IPE discussion. Although Canadian researchers have led this charge for individual expressions about inclusion to emerge, still more needs to be done.

"Where are we going?" is the crucial question as physical educators have not adapted very well to the needs of people with disabilities based on history and evidence-based research. We must ask the following series of questions to people with disabilities and the PE teaching profession.

1   How can we develop the idea that good IPE is good PE?

2   How can we convince all physical educators that our profession is about teaching people and that we meet educational objectives through physical activities?

3   Will there ever be a "perfect fit" for all people in education and/or PE?

4   How can we adopt a more flexible approach to inclusion?

5   Is inclusion something that we do "with" people or "to" people?

6   How can we start a public discourse to include the opinions of all people to define what is "normal"?

7   What would the proponents of full inclusion do or say if people with disabilities chose to be educated outside of the regular classroom?

8   How can we develop the argument that PE requires adequate levels of support to include persons with disabilities?

9   How are we going to deal effectively with some of the more serious mental health issues that seem to be plaguing the youth of our nation (depression, anxiety disorders, etc.)?

Additionally, how can we encourage physical educators to think outside of the box? Pressé, Block, Horton, and Harvey (2011) recommended the use of the Sports Education model which involves having students with and without disabilities participate in a disability sport with abilities adjusted. For example, it may be a welcome change of pace for a class containing a blind or visually-impaired student to play against other students who are either blindfolded or have their vision impaired in some way. Furthermore, how can we increase educator attitudes and perceptions of self-competence for IPE? How can university researchers and PETE programs include more questions, studies, and course offerings to help answer some of the questions posed above? Can new instructional approaches be utilized, such as service learning and situated pedagogy, to create additional experiences for PETE students to learn from people with disabilities in the community (Wilkinson et al., 2012). Finally, people with disabilities need to join forces with educators so IPE may eventually be accepted, conducted, and successful.

Conclusion

This chapter has covered many topics that relate to IPE. The first section started out by briefly exploring the historical exclusion of people with disabilities in society, which in turn had an influence on the gradual inclusion of people with disabilities in schools. The chapter then described the historic US legislation that gave children and youth with disabilities the right to participate in PE. This led to a discussion of mainstreaming and the least restrictive environment so the reader could gain a clearer perspective of how the learning environment has been conceptualized for students with disabilities. Undoubtedly, these pedagogical movements have had an effect on how IPE has been conceptualized and offered in its past and current forms by identifying the supports, or perhaps lack of formal systematic support, needed to ensure the success of IPE.

The second section focused on contemporary issues in IPE, which include the importance of planning for inclusion right from the start rather than relegating IPE to a simple adaptation of physical activities during instruction. It was further suggested that pre-and in-service physical educators engage in active reflection about the purpose of PE to provide a solid rationalization for the inclusion of all students in PE. Seven concrete steps to IPE were provided to guide each pre-service physical educator to develop their own philosophy and differentiated planning and instructional approaches for inclusion.

There is a definite uncertainty about the current state of IPE in Canada, so this chapter ends with more questions than predictions about the future of IPE. Clearly, people with disabilities should have the right to participate in PE. Yet, this belief is grounded by the insight that all Canadians need to band together to gain the winning conditions for the successful implementation of IPE.

Questions for Discussion/Reflection:

1 How can pre-service physical educators change the perceived negative outcomes related to the inclusion of students with disabilities in PE?

2 What strategies would you suggest to include students with disabilities in PE?

3 What are the conceptual differences between adapted and inclusive PE in Canada and the US? How do they matter?

4 Define your conceptual and planning approach for including students with disabilities. How comfortable are you including people with disabilities in PE and how will you strategize to keep motivated and positive about developing and refining instruction for all students?

5 Identify one of the seven instructional approaches (as described by Goodwin, 2003). Discuss how you would go about developing a teaching unit with associated lesson plans and activities based on the selected approach.

6 What information should a physical educator seek when speaking with all children to understand inclusion?

Key Terms

- Integration
- Inclusion
- Adapted Physical Education
- Inclusive Physical Education
- Physical Activity
- Adapted Physical Activity
- Exclusion
- Least-Restrictive Environment
- Individual Education Plan
- Pedagogical Content Knowledge
- Paraeducators

Web Resources for PE and APA

- National Center on Physical Activity and Disability
  www.ncpad.org
- Adapted Physical Education (PE Central)
  www.pecentral.com/adapted/adaptedmenu.html
- Disability Sport Links
  dsusa.org
- International Paralympic Committee
  www.paralympic.org
- Canadian Paralympic Committee
  www.paralympic.ca
- Recreation resources for individuals with disabilities
  www.familyvillage.wisc.edu/recreat.htm
- Active learning and empowerment in APA
  www.adaptip.com
- Project INSPIRE
  www.twu.edu/INSPIRE/
- Active living alliance for Canadians with a disability
  www.ala.ca

Acknowledgements

I thank Mr. Shawn Wilkinson, Ms. Jessica Mackay, and Mr. Michael Cicchillitti for their proofreading, thoughtful reflections, and contributions for this chapter. I am fortunate that these three wonderful graduate students provided me with an opportunity to incorporate their expertise into this text.

Indigenous Knowledge and Physical Education

Brenda Kalyn
(with contributions by Erin Cameron, Yvette Arcand, and Jeff Baker)

This chapter will share perspectives on indigenous knowledge in relation to the teaching of physical education (PE). The knowledge centres around the medicine wheel, visualized through a multi-layered model integrating indigenous teachings with contemporary curriculum (See **Figure 9.2**). The term indigenous knowledge respects and includes First Nations, Métis, and Inuit Canadian cultures that are encompassed by the term "Aboriginal" under Section 35 of the *Canadian Constitution* (Aikenhead & Michell, 2011). The term "indigenous" applies worldwide and further respects other indigenous views.

The goal for teachers studying this chapter is to enter into a journey of learning about indigenous knowledge and further personal understanding regarding how indigenous knowledge can both guide and complement learning in PE. As we learn, we invite students, both indigenous and non-indigenous, to experience indigenous knowledge in their learning. There is no intent that indigenous knowledge is only for indigenous classrooms. Sharing and learning about indigenous perspectives encourages both teachers and students to respect and consider diverse ways of living and learning.

Indigenous peoples hold a unique place within societies and schools. As educators, we must recognize that students come to class from unique and diverse backgrounds, and respond with positive learning invitations for all students. The experiences that students bring to school are part of who they are and what they have come to know through living and being in the world. The potential connections between indigenous knowledge and contemporary western approaches are particularly strong within PE curricula. The holistic philosophy of indigenous peoples embraces the physical, emotional, mental, and spiritual aspects of human nature (Bopp, Bopp, Brown, & Lane, 1985) and is well situated to guide pedagogical practice as we teach PE. The holistic philosophy is about connections and inter-relatedness that transcend beyond isolated subject areas that often occur in schools. In this chapter, PE will be considered inclusive of these holistic teachings and move beyond the singular aspect of the physical.

There should be no assumption that the knowledge or ideas presented here are universal or conclusive. The term "knowledge" respects multiple ways of knowing among indigenous peoples. Although written as knowledge, teachers should be mindful of the plurality of the term. All indigenous peoples have unique ways of knowing and many share similar teachings such as holism. Teachers should consider a broader perspective of knowledge/s while learning about indigenous knowledge. The knowledge, practical ideas, and questions shared in this chapter are a compilation of knowledge/s, thoughts, themes, experiences, and stories gathered from indigenous Elders and teachers, cultural guides, personal teaching experiences, and the literature.

The teaching of holism is widely thematic amongst indigenous peoples (Canadian Council on Learning, 2009). The four aspects of human nature, and the holistic teachings discussed within this chapter, are guided by the Sacred Tree (Bopp et al., 1985). The hope is that you will take the knowledge, grow from it, and begin to see ways to respectfully use it in your teaching.

Introduction

To begin learning about the bridging of indigenous knowledge and contemporary western knowledge in PE, educators must first acknowledge the unique place that indigenous peoples hold within our societies and the knowledge they bring to the world. Since the Royal Commission on Aboriginal Peoples (1996) affirmed the importance of indigenous knowledge, Canadian education curriculum has been challenged to respect indigenous knowledge in schools, and move beyond hegemonic practices that have been a large part of Canadian school culture. Ministries of Learning across Canada (British Columbia, 2006; Saskatchewan,

2010; Manitoba, 2003; Prince Edward Island, 2011;) acknowledge the importance of including indigenous perspectives in PE and move beyond the "insertion or adding-on" of indigenous knowledge through piecemeal activities such as playing a game, making an indigenous craft, listening to music, or watching/participating in the dance without understanding the knowledge and teachings that relate to the activity. Indigenous peoples have reclaimed the right to lead educational initiatives (Battiste, 2002) and these initiatives will lead curricula experiences.

As we teach our subjects, we immerse ourselves in the daily life of curricula, students, teachers, and communities. The term curriculum has over 120 different definitions and one of these definitions states that "curriculum is all the experiences that learners have in the course of living" (Marsh & Willis, 2003, p. 10). Honouring the personal experiences that students bring to school should prompt teachers to ask themselves "can my students see themselves in the curriculum that I teach?" Baskin (2011) affirms that all students should believe that they belong in their classroom and educators must remember that embracing multiple knowledge sources in our teaching acknowledges diverse backgrounds. Learning and applying new knowledge demonstrates a greater awareness and respect for life experiences and cultural knowledge that should be a part of students' learning.

I am a non-indigenous teacher educator who has had the privilege of working and learning alongside indigenous teachers, indigenous students, Elders, cultural advisors, and colleagues for many years. These individuals taught me a great deal about indigenous knowledge from their perspectives. Throughout my journey as a teacher and then a teacher educator, I struggled with the same concerns as many new PE teachers wondering what indigenous knowledge is and how it could be applied to the curriculum in general, and more specifically to PE. Resources were available describing indigenous activities that could be taught in PE; however, there was limited information on the indigenous knowledge that should accompany these activities. This chapter provides insight into the indigenous perspectives that have been shared with me. In every case, the indigenous teachers, Elders, and cultural advisors led the process and provided the knowledge. They all encouraged me to take the knowledge and bridge it with PE curricula to assist teachers in seeing the possibilities for indigenous knowledge to lead contemporary PE curricula. This positive collaboration was the result of building strong relationships with the indigenous people who shared their knowledge with me.

All italicized portions of this chapter are direct quotes from indigenous people regarding their knowledge and experiences in relation to indigenous knowledge and PE. Pseudonyms have been used with the exception of the indigenous pre-service PE teachers. This sharing of knowledge is in the spirit of collaboration and learning, and I hope that the knowledge will inspire your work.

Indigenous knowledge is not something you read or hear once and immediately understand. Learning to listen, reflect, build learning relationships, experience the teachings, and inquire further, are aspects of experiencing indigenous knowledge. It takes time to learn and understand the knowledge and pedagogies of indigenous people. What is important is to open the mind and heart to the teachings. It is through this process that you will learn to build learning relationships with your students, indigenous teachers, Elders, and their communities. Follow them as your guides and respect what they teach you.

Acknowledging Indigenous Knowledge

In addition to being complex and having always existed, Battiste (2002) states that indigenous knowledge is: sustained by indigenous civilizations; often oral and symbolic; transmitted through indigenous language and passed on generationally through modelling, practice, and animation rather than a written context. Knowledge has a sacred purpose, is connected to all of nature, and

teaches people self-responsibility taught through traditions, ceremonies, and daily observations. Indigenous knowledge does not follow Eurocentric ways of knowing so one must be cautioned against transforming indigenous knowledge through a Eurocentric lens. Defining indigenous knowledge is challenging because it transcends cognitive paradigms and the greater challenge is to successfully bridge indigenous knowledge with contemporary education that respects and builds on both knowledge systems.

Eurocentric domination in education historically asserted western and European values, experiences, and ways of knowing on students with the intent of assimilating all students under this structure. The extinction of indigenous knowledge and ways of knowing was a primary goal of Eurocentric education that succeeded in separating families, destroying indigenous languages, and ways of knowing amongst the indigenous peoples. Today, indigenous peoples are re-empowered to affirm and activate their intellectual self-determination, reclaim their knowledge, and situate themselves within the academic and educational places of learning. Indigenous knowledge must be respected through protocol and not misappropriated or claimed in unethical ways. Educators must understand that indigenous knowledge can lead and design learning

Indigenous peoples hold a unique place within Canadian society.

experiences. Battiste (2002) affirms indigenous peoples' desire to balance educational approaches and build learning relationships between knowledge perspectives.

Indigenous communities have particular customs and protocols. Teachers, administrators, and staff should contact their specific community Elders and leaders for guidance and direction on local protocols (Aikenhead & Mitchell, 2011). Educators must move beyond teaching about indigenous knowledge and allow students to engage in learning experiences through indigenous knowledge, which should be done through local indigenous peoples (Battiste, 2002; Alaska Native Knowledge Network, 1998). Following local guidelines is important for validating local knowledge and culture. Ultimately, it is about building trusting educational

relationships between classrooms, schools, and communities. Indigenous people are educational leaders who strive to build learning relationships and work alongside teachers and students within communities. These valued relationships are the cornerstone of good works together (Wilson, 2008).

Fully immersing yourself in a culture is the best way to learn from it and begin to know it. There is cultural copyright on indigenous knowledge and educators must respect that. The space between knowledge is called ethical space where we write relationships between people and knowledge. The protocols are about respect for the boundaries. Just as it would be unreasonable to assume that all western ideas and values are universal, we must allow spaces for differences and commonalities (Baskin, 2011).

Eurocentric understandings of knowledge are often solidified within the written word. Curricula are published documents meant to be activated by teachers to provide enriching learning experiences for students. Teachers are called to bring these documents to life and actively engage students in learning through the enacted curriculum (Marsh & Willis, 2003). Consider the idea that knowledge and curricula are alive, ever growing and changing, and never static.

Case Study 1: Mary's Story

When I was a little girl, my mother and father would take my brothers and sisters fishing every Sunday afternoon in the summer. My dad gave me my own fishing rod, and I found a spot where I thought I might catch a fish. I cast my rod over and over again. Nothing. Suddenly I felt a jerk and started yelling and called my dad to help me. In his quiet way he said, "Kikwaashquepina na?" I was expecting him to come and help, but he continued to fish. I would look at him, but he was not paying attention (I thought). I tried to reel in the fish, but I couldn't: it was too strong for me. My rod kept bending, almost touching the water at times, and I was getting tired. I was scared I would fall in or that the fish would pull me in. My father must have been watching me all this time because out of the blue he said, "Eshcum paki ta piigin." Release it every once in a while. "Taani ayaakosi. Ki kaki kane dan anapi shiwii ko piñata." You will know when it is tired and you can reel it in. I was getting impatient and getting more tired. Finally, I could tell whatever was on my line was getting tired because it was not pulling so much. Slowly I reeled in the line until I could drag the catfish onto the rock formation I was standing on. My father was a hunter, trapper, and fisherman, and he had years and years of experience. The lesson I learned is that by not running over to come and help me, he honoured me by trusting and believing that I could bring that fish in myself. (Kalyn , 2006, pp. 109–110)

Mary's father honoured her ability to bring in that fish. Imagine someone believing in your learning so much that they don't intervene? His wisdom allowed her to experience learning in a holistic manner by acknowledging the multiple ways of knowing that are possible for this one lesson. He gave her the opportunity for self-directed learning by encouraging her to think, experience the physical challenge of catching the fish, feel many emotions and sensations, and ultimately enjoy the satisfaction of completing the lesson learned.

Questions for Reflection

1 Do we honour the knowledge that our students bring to PE or do we think we always have to show our students the techniques for learning to occur?

2 How can teachers follow the teachings in this indigenous story and transfer that to the teaching of motor skills, perseverance, knowledge, relationships, and spiritual aspects?

3 How do perseverance and volition demonstrate self-responsibility in this experience?

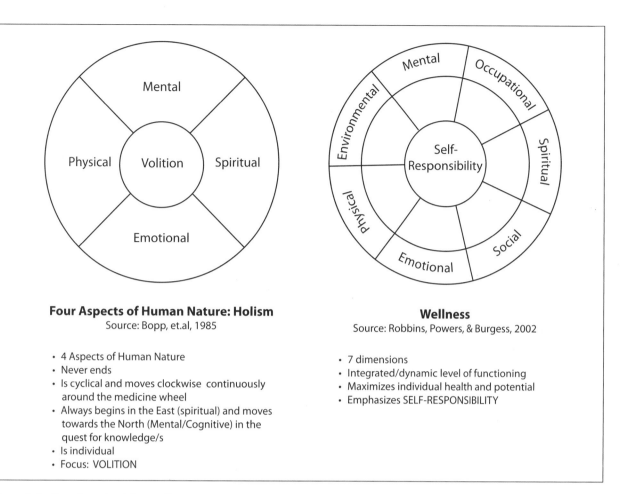

Figure 9.1a: Four Aspects of Human Nature and Figure 9.1b: Wellness

Indigenous people regard knowledge as alive. Carol, a cultural guide explained:

We "borrow" knowledge. It is like asking for permission to invest in this knowledge. This investment is in the self and for others. When we ask a question, hear a story, or inquire about something, we are suggesting that we want to know and learn. As we listen, we take the knowledge and transform it for our personal use and experience to which it should apply in our lives. The knowledge is transformative if it leads to social/personal action. Each person must take the knowledge and learn from it. The knowledge then becomes your own but you don't really own it. It is still out there. We learn to understand each other's knowledge through listening, acting, and through conversation. When we borrow from one way of knowing, we are asking to use the knowledge but it is not like a taking of the knowledge, for you leave it where it is and use what you need. The knowledge is not static. It is alive and growing and becoming, through action, and the lived experience of the individual. Knowledge is built upon. We must ask what purpose the knowledge has. What do we do with the knowledge to keep it viable and not to waste

it? It is like listening to a story. The story is given as a gift. I take it for my use and leave the story whole. I interpret the meaning and value of the story based on what struck me and how the knowledge from the story can be meaningful to me. My grandfather would ask me "what did you learn in school today?" I would tell him and then he would ask me what I was going to do with this knowledge. (Kalyn, 2006, pp. 137–138)

Knowledge is embedded in language and how individuals understand meaning is derived from their language. Translating the term "knowledge" from indigenous languages implies a different message than a Eurocentric ideology of knowing through subject related knowledge, theories, and/or experiences. Indigenous expressions for "knowledge" often translate into "ways of living" or "ways of being" (Aikenhead & Mitchell, 2011). Valuing indigenous knowledge as an action, a way of being in the world brings more life to knowledge and experiences.

Indigenous people are passionate about bridging their sources of knowledge within schools. Part of the process of decolonization is moving away from the Eurocentric lens that interprets the world only in terms of western,

European, or Anglo-American values and experiences. The assumption that all Aboriginal peoples speak their language or understand their cultural knowledge is inaccurate due to their own Eurocentric education and past separation from their cultures (Battiste, 2002).

Indigenous people are re-finding the balance, creating self-spaces, creating stability, and pulling from the best of both worlds to create new knowledge, and influence culturally responsive pedagogy and curricula (Brant Castellano, 2002; Curwen Doige, 2003; Hampton, 1995; Kalyn, 2006). Tizya-Tramm (2012) supported this belief stating that "Although the approaches of First Nations traditional knowledge and western academic knowledge differ, the goal is the same: to be on the edge of knowing" (p. 15).

Holistic Learning and Wellness— A Healthy Journey

The first thing to realize is the tension in referring to PE as "physical education" in reference to indigenous knowledge. The hegemonic compartmentalization of subjects taught and learned from western paradigms is in strong contrast to indigenous beliefs in the holistic nature of learning (Battiste, 2002). The term physical education will be referred to within this text; however, remember that this term, as used within this chapter, includes the physical, mental, spiritual, and emotional aspects of human nature that are reflected in the learner from an indigenous perspective.

Elder David said that we are on this earth to follow a journey and Elder Rose said it must be a healthy journey. They agreed that the spirit is always present from the moment of concep-tion; the child becomes physical upon conception. Elder Rose explained that from the very beginning, when human cells meet and begin to divide, there is motion. The new life is constantly in motion and we are in motion inside our mothers. We cannot escape our physicality (Kalyn, 2006). Our physi-cality does not stand alone. It is dependent on the relation-ship between the physical, mental, emotional, and spiritual aspects of human nature that can be represented through the teachings of the medicine wheel.

The Medicine Wheel

The medicine wheel is an ancient symbol used by indigenous people to show relationships that can be expressed in sets of four and is used to help with teaching and learning (Bopp et al., 1985; Fiddler, Tourangeau, Male, & Marlor, 2000; Graveline, 1998). Indigenous people use symbols to express and represent meaning to derive purpose and understanding. Understanding meaning is important for the health, well-being and wholeness of individuals, their communities, and for living out the beliefs that these symbols represent. The medicine wheel

symbol is relative to local cultures and there are different representations created to reflect the teachings of a particular group and their beliefs.

The medicine wheel is metaphorically referred to as a mirror because it allows an individual to see things not normally visible; it allows an individual to look back on him or herself and better see what is going on within the self (Bopp et al., 1985; Fiddler et al., 2002; Laframboise & Sherbina, 2012). The volition or will (Figure 9.1) is seen as a force centred in the middle of the medicine wheel and it enables an individual to make decisions and act on those decisions by: 1) concentrating; 2) setting goals; 3) initiating an action; 4) persevering; and 5) completing the action. The volition, or will, guides the development of the four aspects of human nature that need constant developing. This volition centres on self-responsibility to live and grow in all four areas and to achieve balance and harmony throughout one's journey in life. When an individual begins extending one's knowledge or physical literacy by learning a new physical skill, game, or dance, it requires concentration, goal setting, action, perseverance, and working towards satisfactory completion of the skill. Throughout this progression and inter-related learning, the individual is focusing on mental capacity to learn the skill, emotional responses to the challenges and successes of the acquired learning, spiritual satisfaction through challenge and success and/or the interaction with the environment (e.g., the outdoors) to learn the skill, and the physical challenges of achieving the goals through the completion of the action. This process requires the individual to be responsible for personal learning and decision making, to focus on the task, and recognize that volition, or free will, guides the actualization of this inter-related learning. Indigenous activities may include participating in a sweat, pow-wow dancing, orienteering in the woods, trapping, hunting, canoeing, roping, and attending a sun-dance to learn the meaning and teachings of the medicine wheel from other participants.

The individual is taught to have a vision of personal poten-tial and to look towards becoming all that he or she can become in life. Most importantly, the teachings stress wholeness and the fact that everything is interrelated and is in a state of constant cyclical change. Change is vital to help the individual grow and become all that he or she can become. Ermine (1995), discussing the sacred tree, stated "The medicine wheel can be used as a mirror by any sincere person" (p. 106) and can reveal the gifts/potential a person has that are yet to be revealed.

Human development never stops and the journey moves cyclically, beginning in the east. Travelling this circular pathway around the four directions teaches the individual new lessons. Each direction represents new teachings and offers new gifts. Upon reaching the north, which is identified as the direction of completion and fulfillment, the individual does not stop learning or moving in the cycle. The north encourages the individual to complete what he or she has begun and no matter how difficult the journey, persevere with the knowledge that the goal can be achieved. As an individual continues throughout life, he or she will begin again in the east with a new teaching or the continuation of a teaching previously learned that takes him or her to a higher state of learning (Bopp et al., 1985).

The First Nations holistic model deals with gradually taking steps to achieving personal goals starting from the East (where life/learning is born) and ending (moving towards the North where one passes on wisdom). It does not end there as you are constantly on the move learning new things. Physical Education is no different, for example, if you are just learning to play baseball, you first start off by throwing/catching a baseball and learning how to handle a bat (east). Gradually, you learn how to play using more advanced skills (south) and in the (west) you begin to understand the rules of baseball and what your role is on a team. Eventually, in the north, you are a pro at playing baseball. If you learn another sport you will begin in the East again with new knowledge about the new sport. (W. Whitstone, ITEP Pre-service physical educator, U of S, personal communication, 2011)

Lamothe (1993) shared a Dene teaching method about becoming a good hunter. To be a successful hunter a person must be able to read animal tracks (mental); read the weather, the land, the seasons, the habits of the moose; and then be able to apply that knowledge to track the moose (physical). Tracking and killing the moose would require knowledge and the development of (physical/emotional) skills such as strength, stamina, lightness of feet, excellent hand-eye coordination, focus, patience, discipline, and timing to execute the actual kill. Young hunters would have learned these skills through careful observation of more experienced hunters. They would be educated through example and, when they were ready, they would hunt their own animal. Giving thanks for the animal (spiritual) helped ensure a successful hunt would follow.

Wellness

Contemporary western wellness philosophies represented through wellness wheels vary, but often include the physical, social, environmental, emotional, spiritual, intellectual, and occupational dimensions of Wellness (**Appendix 1**). Individuals are encouraged to identify personal weaknesses in each area, maintain strengths, and strive for balance. Self-responsibility is at the core of wellness (Robbins, Powers, & Burgess, 2002; Alaska Native Knowledge Network, 1998). Indigenous peoples practiced holistic teachings long before the early 1990s when contemporary practices in this area became a focus in PE. The figures found in the Appendix contrast the two areas.

Physical education is uniquely situated to respond to holistic learning. It is one curricula area that can have a positive influence on the physical, emotional, mental, and spiritual potential of students.

The following three models represent First Nations (**Appendix 1**), Métis (**Appendix 2**), and Inuit (**Appendix 3**) Lifelong Learning Models (Canadian Council on Learning, 2009) and provide further insight into the holistic paradigm and lifelong learning.

The Four Aspects of Human Nature

The following descriptions and examples of the four aspects of human nature are derived from the teachings of the sacred tree (Bopp et al., 1985). The voices of the indigenous pre-service physical educators and indigenous classroom teachers who shared their knowledge and experiences in relation to these teachings have been honoured within this text in a different font. Embedded within these voices are examples of how teachers might consider using the knowledge about the four aspects of human nature and bridging contemporary PE. Each section includes questions to consider and discuss.

My physical, mental, emotional, and spiritual levels are exactly what makes me who I am, what I am, and how I am. These are all intertwined and cannot separate who I am. They are aspects of my body as a whole and to affect one level either positively or negatively, influences my entire body. When people grasp the importance of the mind, body, and spirit relationship and show well-being on all levels, they are more likely to feel at peace with themselves and all other beings. In order to feel this much power, one needs to commit and have personal responsibility. Everything you put into your body or what you do to your body affects all levels. Our bodies were made to serve us well but it is up to us to maintain optimum health. In order for us to maintain that, the first step is to treat our bodies with care and respect. (S. Tootoosis ITEP Pre-service physical educator, U of S, personal communication, 2011)

Spiritual Aspect

Spirituality is a deep connection of the individual with all aspects of life. Spirituality centres on balance in life and is not based on a system of religious beliefs, although it can be, and some individuals combine the two systems. Spirituality focuses on the affective domain and the subjective experiences of the individual. It is a state of mind, centred within the heart, and bears strong connections between morals, values, and education.

According to indigenous tradition, spirituality exists from the moment of conception, is connected to all aspects of the individual, and grows constantly through the experiences an individual encounters in life. We build relationships through our spirit so everything is alive and everything is meaningful. The spirit is something a person can feel, and those around you can feel your spirit. Developing spiritually can be viewed in a variety of physical contexts from fine motor learning, such as beading, to large body movements, or an outdoor learning experience that connects students and nature. One indigenous teacher explained that when she teaches her students beading she also teaches them that their first project must be given away to someone because the giving process will encourage positive spiritual, mental, emotional, and physical aspects in their self. If the student knows who they will be giving the gift to, the recipient should be in the student's positive thoughts as the project is being completed. These activities require a relationship with the self, the object, the environment, and/or others in order to connect the task and the spirit. The whole individual is enhanced through these relationships.

Indigenous Teachers' Knowledge

If I die, people remember who I was because of my spirit. I believe that when we are born we have a spirit where we develop spiritually, emotionally, physically, and mentally as we go along our way. I believe this potential is in us when we are conceived. I have five children and I felt each of their spirits.

If kids get embarrassed or put down in the classroom and teachers are not teaching contrary to this behaviour then a little bit of that person is taken away and that erodes their spirituality.

Teaching sixteen- to eighteen-year-old boys who were quite rough can be tough and putting a lacrosse stick in their hands was a worry. We had a smudging ceremony before beginning to play to teach respect and we prayed for everything to go well in class and that the play would be safe.

Before playing the game of Moose Skin Ball there could be a thanksgiving prayer for the equipment used to play the game. Giving thanks for the hide of the animal, the grass of Mother Earth that went into making the ball to play the game and asking for good relationships during play might be one way of applying the spiritual nature to this game.

It is important to have your spirit connected to your physical movement during dancing. When you are [hoop] dancing and you don't have your spirit connected, you will not do a good job. Try to understand everything [about the dance] before you go out and do it. The more you understand the more meaningful the activity.

I think of my body as a temple and I must treat it with respect. I think of the physical, the spiritual, mental, and emotional and how I am going to strive to be my best.

The body is a gift from the Creator so being physically active combined with spirituality is honouring the Creator and showing respect because you are using your body in a good way.

The spiritual aspect of human nature is often the most problematic for teachers. Teachers should invite all students to apply their personal spirituality to their learning experiences, if the student acknowledges spirituality in his or her life. Teachers do not have to teach spirituality nor consider themselves spiritual persons to create inter-related learning spaces for students.

Lacrosse has been played by Canada's Aboriginal population for almost 1000 years.

Emotional Aspect

To have a healthy heart can also relate to happiness. To have a healthy mind is to be content with one's self. Having a healthy body is to be physically active and fit. These components are important and contribute to how I feel emotionally. (J. Kent, ITEP Pre-service physical educator, U of S, personal communication, 2011)

The emotional side of an individual relates to feelings and how feelings translate into the wider context of his or her social environment and learning. Developing skills of cooperation, understanding, empathy, responsibility, values, confidence, teamwork, perseverance, and goal setting are a part of this aspect in PE.

Athletic students who embrace movement challenges and find success and fulfillment in activity experience satisfaction through physical education; while other students experience kinesthetic challenges. Students who are less athletically inclined; overweight; physically awkward; unable to run, jump, or throw in a skilled manner; excluded from teams or play; or ridiculed by peers are at risk in these situations. These negative emotional situations leave students feeling inadequate and embarrassed and less likely to feel a part of learning in PE. A non-threatening, inclusive environment is imperative in order for students to feel safe and take risks without the fear of ridicule or failure. Encouraging physical activity requires teaching to students' emotional well-being and pedagogies must plan for a healthy, inclusive learning environment. Some generalist teachers who come to PE methods classes with negative past experiences in the subject are afraid to be back in the gymnasium. Professors are challenged to recognize this sensitivity and move towards enhancing these students' self-esteem and emotional well-being before expecting them to succeed personally and envision themselves as teachers of PE. If students lack confidence and emotional strength this could not only affect their physical performance, but negatively affect their personal belief in their ability to achieve physical skills, prohibit them from recognizing their mental capacity to learn the skills, and hamper their spiritual connection to themselves and their learning.

Indigenous Teachers' Knowledge

We have to be careful in physical education and teach to the social/emotional sides of the child. Physical education can be scary because in the classroom if a student lacks a skill he or she may be able to conceal this weakness but in physical education it is more obvious if you lack skill or are left out.

In physical education there is a lot of emphasis on competition. In Aboriginal culture cooperation is more valued than competition. Singling individuals out for praise is not

as effective as praising the whole group. We need to look at developing skills without the presence of competition.

Encountering frustrations in our physical performance can impact success. As a young girl, I recall feeling uncomfortable in physical education when everybody was yelling at me "Come on Karen, you've got legs like a gazelle… run!" I thought "But I can't run! I don't know what's wrong with me. I can run far but I can't run fast." I was ashamed as a young child in physical education. Now, as an adult I go out of my way to make sure that I can prove that I can take a risk and do it [face a physical challenge] but when I was younger I felt uncomfortable.

Physical Aspects

My personal philosophy about holistic health and wellness is that it has to encompass the whole person and not just one aspect of life. To focus on one aspect is an incomplete approach. You must concentrate on incorporating all aspects of life: spiritual, emotional, physical, and mental. The body, mind, and spirit are not independent; rather they are related. What affects one aspect will surely affect the others. (W. Whitstone, ITEP Pre-service physical educator, U of S, personal communication, 2011)

Physicality involves more than using the body to play a game or dance or sing. It encompasses building physical, mental, emotional, spiritual strength, and endurance through personal challenges. Accomplishing physical tasks require perseverance, obedience, and discipline. The over-arching benefits of physical activity impact the other aspects of human nature and teachers suggest that physical activity should be used more often as a way of helping students deal with their emotional problems. The body was meant to move and physical education is a vital component of a student's day in school. Cultural activities should be experienced within curricula so students can see themselves, their experiences, and their cultures reflected inside of the activities and learning experiences.

Indigenous Teachers' Knowledge

The Elder told me to get my students up and do something physical and it will help them feel better and deal with their problems. Last week this happened with one of our kids at school who was working with a counsellor. The student didn't want to talk to anyone. The counsellor suggested that we go for a walk, which we did and the kid opened up.

When we talk of strength there are many different types of strength. When we ask the kids about physical strength, right away they think about being strong but being strong in the physical is just as important as being mentally strong, spiritually, and emotionally strong. If students are edgy I take them outside to get some fresh air or to the gym. If they don't have the physical part of them they are not going to get revived energy like new cells, oxygen going into their body, so we need to do that for them. We need to do that every day. Go for a walk or do some stretching and wake up their physical side.

Instead of sitting students out as a punishment, get them to take a walk around the school and come back in or do some spider push ups to take their minds somewhere else.

Students have emotional problems and sometimes that causes them to feel physically tired and when this happens, I encourage them to go out and sit on Mother Earth, make a connection and try to become revived again. Get out of this stuffy room. I always tell them to say a prayer to connect with the spiritual aspect.

I use the drum in relation to the heartbeat in my class. I gather the children in a circle and sit on the floor. The children find their heartbeat at rest and think of the drum as a heartbeat. They imagine their heart beating the blood through their body that gives them the gift of life. Next, the children engage in cardiovascular dancing to pow-wow music to increase their heart rates. We talk about the blood pumping throughout the body and the lungs filling with oxygen. The children realize the impact of exercise on the heart and learn that the heart is a muscle that needs to be exercised for it to be strong. They learn it is their responsibility to exercise and they can feel pride in taking care of their bodies.

Students have to get some feeling of connectedness with the instructor or the coach and if they can't get that they won't care if it's helping their cardiovascular or whatever, or reduces their risk of diabetes. If nobody at home is showing that physical activity is important then it's just a school thing. It's not a life thing. I ride my bike to school; I ride my bike to work every day. I make my kids ride their bikes, too, so they're seeing it and doing it. You want kids to read, well, they've got to see you sitting there reading. A lot of people are naturally lazy. The teenage mentality is—even if you show them the pictures about illness, there is still the idea that, "It'll never happen to me."

In the past, many people depended on physical activity for survival. Activities such as hunting, fishing, trapping, berry picking, farming, planting, walking, running, and other physical challenges were a part of daily life, which helped strengthen physical capacity. Today, the sedentary lifestyle led by most people has resulted in many diseases, increasingly so amongst children. Physical education programs can promote physical fitness, active living, and skill development, and encourage lifelong physical activity. Teaching

indigenous games in PE classes such as snow snake, moose skin ball, and lacrosse teaches the historical aspects of games, the skills that were involved, the natural equipment used in the past and modified today, and the fun and social purposes achieved through playing games. This is one way of enhancing culturally-responsive pedagogy while teaching the desired concepts, and encouraging physical activity.

Mental Aspects of Human Nature

I attend round dances, feasts, and sweat lodges when I can. Round dances for social and personal enjoyment and it's a good workout on the legs; feasts for social gathering to give thanks and to feed my body to maintain good health; sweat lodges to cleanse my soul of negativity and pray for my ancestors and families as well as myself. I respect my Elders by listening to their stories about their lives and their wisdom, and also shake their hands when I leave their presence. (Kristen Matchee, ITEP Pre-service physical educator, U of S, personal communication, 2011)

There are several components in relation to the mental aspects of the individual to consider in the teaching of PE. Self-responsibility, goal setting, appreciating individuals' strengths and gifts, learning new skills, experiencing perseverance, and applying those skills to improve one's self are important. The mental aspects include allowing students to choose their activities to increase their engagement.

One grade three student was excited about learning to juggle with scarves; however her enthusiasm quickly digressed as the activity became challenging (Kalyn, Paslawski, Wilson, Kikcio, & MacPhedran, 2007). Failing to consecutively sustain one scarf in the air for any length of time she screamed and threw herself onto the floor and said she quit. After allowing time for the student to contain herself, she was encouraged to try again and follow the instructional technique of "tossing and clawing" provided for her. She focused much better during the second practice and as she succeeded she began to smile and demonstrate more confidence in her ability. Progressing to two scarves, she persevered and kept practicing, building skill, patience, and confidence. By the end of the study she was able to successfully juggle three scarves, demonstrated increased confidence in herself, could share verbally the technique involved, and wanted to learn how to juggle small balls. This student demonstrated perseverance, skill development, emotional control, and the mental capacity to connect new knowledge through kinesthetic accomplishments. When this student, through her own self-discipline and volition, made the choice to persevere, she learned obedience to the task and to herself, through her actions and experiences.

Indigenous Teachers' Knowledge

Physically, if you apply visualizations it can help you to move better. It helps you mentally and emotionally. If you listen to the professionals in sport they visualize the movements. They see the home run; all those things they see bring the action into the body from their mind and helps them accomplish that goal. If a child has a problem throwing a ball then help them visualize it. Have them relax and calm themselves. Throwing a ball might be a stressful thing so help them see the goal and relax and they might actually do better.

Choice is a personal decision and there are reasons why we chose to engage in an activity and this choice generally represents our interests and our experiences. We need to recognize the talents that students have in physical education and help them develop physically; then they are also developing emotionally and having success with their self-esteem.

Letting students have a say in the curriculum includes the mental because they need to critically think and decide what they want to learn and how they can learn a certain skill.

Choice in activities provides students with ownership, which directly feeds spirituality because in order to have ownership you have to have some pride in what you are achieving. Older students could have opportunities to teach a dance, for example, to their peers which would give them ownership and responsibility for the activity. This would also provide opportunities for fun, laughter, and recognizing individual strengths. Students would be accountable to complete their tasks and be responsible for their learning.

If we fail to allow students to have a voice in their learning we are actually being disrespectful towards them. We need to respect the fact that kids have knowledge and experiences that they bring to the lesson and these should be acknowledge by allowing them to have a voice.

Teachers are called to plan pedagogically for quality lessons so choice in activity can take on various forms. If you wanted to encourage students to jump to build strength in their legs and think about using their upper body to help them jump then planning should be creative. The task should be motivating and perceived as possible by all students and teach to the four aspects of the student. Asking students to distance jump could be exciting for some; yet difficult, and humiliating for other students. Set up different coloured lines on the floor or markers of some kind. Students would have the choice of jumping to any of these lines and back. The "jackrabbits" could take off and go as far as possible and others could move at their pace and ability. There would always be the possibility to challenge one's self and move to the next level of competency. Imagery could be used in

reference to the lines. The space in-between could be large rivers with rapids to jump over or hunting trails. Students could jump in a circle moving clockwise beginning in the East, in and out of hoops any number of times, use a jump rope, jump in zig-zag or meandering pathways on the floor. Students could make decisions and meet their physical abilities, feel success, think creatively, and enhance their spirit through their achievements and challenges. To avoid students comparing and teasing each other about jumping choices, teach students about respecting each other's choices and decisions before you begin the activity. Teach students emotional outcomes if you want to achieve them.

Students could participate in journal writing regarding their experiences in physical education. Encouraging kids to express themselves in different ways is important and writing is a good way to deal with emotions, questions, or something else that they may not wish to say verbally.

When we teach to the whole child we are able to teach to their potential. We look at them. We see them for who they are at this moment and dream for where they can go.

Perseverance

Perseverance and endurance are concepts closely related to the physical aspects of human nature and involve the whole person. Acquiring motor skills requires patience, practice, endurance, and obedience and is directly related to volition and self-responsibility. It is important not to give up. This cyclical journey builds experience through each progression elevating one to a higher state of knowledge and takes time and patience.

New learning begins in the East (See **Figure 9.2, Layer 4**) in the pre-control stage of motor learning. Movement around the wheel develops skill, patience, and knowledge in all aspects and adding adaptations or progressions to the skill provides further challenges.

Learning to cascade juggle with one scarf, students must apply the learning cues of toss, claw, level, X formation, hand-eye coordination, and timing (Pangrazi & Gibbons, 2009). As students develop skills, they move through the control, utilization, and finally proficiency stages of motor learning while progressing to three scarves (Graham, Holt-Hale, & Parker, 2007). Encouraging students and guiding them toward success is important for developing perseverance and students need to experience possibilities in their learning. The cyclical journey around the wheel advances knowledge and skills, furthering success.

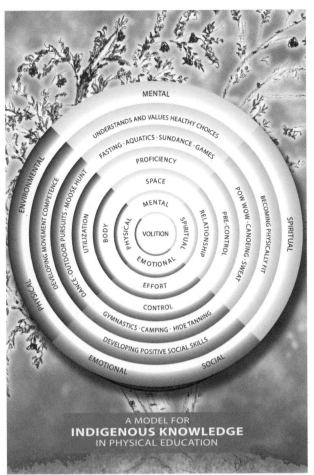

MENTAL
UNDERSTANDS AND VALUES HEALTHY CHOICES
FASTING · AQUATICS · SUNDANCE · GAMES
PROFICIENCY
SPACE
MENTAL
BODY PHYSICAL VOLITION SPIRITUAL RELATIONSHIP PRE-CONTROL
EMOTIONAL
EFFORT
CONTROL
GYMNASTICS · CAMPING · HIDE TANNING
DEVELOPING POSITIVE SOCIAL SKILLS
EMOTIONAL SOCIAL
ENVIRONMENTAL
DEVELOPING MOVEMENT COMPETENCE
DANCE · OUTDOOR PURSUITS · MOOSE HUNT
UTILIZATION
PHYSICAL
POW WOW · CANOEING · SWEAT
BECOMING PHYSICALLY FIT
SPIRITUAL

A MODEL FOR
INDIGENOUS KNOWLEDGE
IN PHYSICAL EDUCATION

Figure 9.2: A Model for Indigenous Knowledge in PE.

Indigenous Teachers' Knowledge

Training the mind to get through challenges requires perseverance. If you go on your journey and try to learn something too fast you may miss something important you should pick up; something you'll need for your journey along the way. We must take our time and this takes perseverance and discipline and it takes time to establish that.

Learning to make a teepee requires strong physical skills and perseverance. Each pole of the teepee represents an indigenous teaching and obedience is one of the most important teachings. Without obedience there is no discipline. Without discipline we don't learn.

To teach obedience I made the kids stand up in silence by their desks for fifteen minutes. It took two or three weeks before everybody could do it. They had to take responsibility for themselves and discipline themselves. This required obedience and perseverance.

I have a student who wants to be a basketball player. I encouraged him and told him that he could achieve what he wants. I guided him back to the centre, the volition/self-responsibility, and told him not to blame anyone else for his failures.

The Elder said you always have to start with you. You have to be proficient for you. In western society we always judge our skills against someone else's skills. We have to consider the skills we bring to the learning situation; the stage we are at in our learning, and assess our own improvement. There is always room to learn more and it is our responsibility to try and improve. It's about choice.

Our belief is that if you didn't learn it [the skill] this time the opportunity to learn will come again. It will come a little bit harder and a little bit stronger the next time. If this continues to happen then there is something that is being said to you that you're not getting and you're not taking the time to understand the learning. If a student can't perform a skill the teacher should address some of the other aspects of the wheel. There might be some other parts of the student that keeps them from meeting their goals. Maybe they are unhappy, someone put them down, or they don't understand what is required to accomplish the skill. The indigenous cultures have a philosophy that would look at the whole person in physical education and not just the physical part.

When we struggle in life we need to ask ourselves what we are supposed to learn from that struggle. When we do struggle we come back stronger for the struggle. If we "don't get it" [the meaning in the lesson] it will keep coming at you until we get it. This is how the wheel keeps moving. Some people are quick learners and others are stubborn. People need to learn that not everything happens the way that we want it to. The lesson challenges us to ask, "what is being said to you, what haven't you learned yet?"

Our lives are like running into the wind. We can keep running and keep pushing. Sometimes it blows us back a bit … but if we let it blow us completely off course, we have allowed that to happen. No matter how tired we are we need to stand and wait for our energy to come back. It goes back to self-responsibility. We need to focus and ask who is in charge here. Even if the wind blows you over we need to get up and walk again. Standing in the wind for a while is always a spiritual connection because the native people believe that they pray to Grandfather wind so if you are just standing in the wind saying a prayer for strength it is answered back through the blowing of the wind.

A Model to Honour Indigenous Knowledge

Figure 9.2 (Kalyn, 2006) demonstrates possibilities for connecting indigenous knowledge and common PE curricula concepts. The model was guided by the teachings of the sacred tree (Bopp et al., 1985); indigenous teachers, Elders, and pre-service teacher educators who contributed to this knowledge and research. When reading through the model discourse (see pages 171–176), the indigenous knowledge has a coloured background, while the curricula content and contemporary ideas do not.

Pedagogical ideas and strategies are provided to assist teachers in understanding how curricula teachings might honour indigenous knowledge. Indigenous knowledge leads this conceptual model and is the foundation for the knowledge framework. The model is described in greater detail in **Appendix 4** (pp. 171–176).

Conclusion

Physical education is a unique curricular area that has the potential to teach the whole student. Responding pedagogically and culturally through indigenous knowledge and the cyclical nature of learning encourages an opportunity for learning in new ways. Students and teachers can experience indigenous teachings and physical activities to enhance and challenge their mental capacities, emotional maturities, physical skills, spiritual connections, endurance, patience, and the development of self-responsibility.

The challenge is to listen more thoughtfully, ask informed questions, and step outside Eurocentric paradigms. Indigenous peoples designed a model of living a healthy life generations ago. We should respectfully borrow this knowledge and develop ways to enhance teaching and learning in PE through this knowledge.

Questions for Reflection

1 Sports teams have engaged in prayer before beginning a game. Can you find parallels between praying, smudging, and feeling a spiritual connection to your physicality while engaged in activity?

2 Can you think of a personal spiritual experience that you would share with your peers to demonstrate how you see spiritual connections and learning in PE?

3 What concerns you the most about incorporating the spiritual aspect of human nature into your PE classes?

4 Can you recall an experience where either you or your peers were emotionally affected in PE class? How do you feel the teacher could have handled the situation differently?

5 How will you affect a positive emotional environment within your PE classes?

6 Consider ways that you have persevered to learn a physical skill. What made you persist instead of quitting? How can you pass these experiences on to your students in PE, especially the reluctant movers?

7 Can you identify with physical movements and an improved feeling of well-being as a result of being active?

8 Have you thought about the mind-body connection in PE? Have you considered the variety of skills and knowledge that is learned through PE?

9 Pre-service physical educators have asked "do we have to write anything down?" while engaging in PE methods classes. Why do you think they would ask such a question? What does that prompt you to consider as a pre-service physical educator?

10 As pre-service physical educators, how will you bridge the four aspects of human nature in your classes?

Suggested Ideas for Teachers

1 Hang visuals such as posters, student-created banners, quotes from indigenous teachers, Elders, and students in your gymnasium, activity spaces, classroom, or hallways that represent indigenous cultures and knowledge. Students should see themselves in your class, their school, and the activities they participate in.

2 Paint a medicine wheel on the floor in the centre of the gymnasium and/or an ice surface and use it as a gathering and teaching place.

3 Have students write their successes with motor skills. Share stories of perseverance. Post these where others can read them.

4 Integrate books, stories, readings, conversations, presentations, and other skills into your language arts class that feature indigenous athletes, hunters, dancers, women, children, and youth in their natural environments involved in physical activities. Bring those experiences into the teaching of motor skills. For example, what type of skills would a dog musher need? How would you develop those skills?

5 Have an indigenous book, audio-visual file in your office. Encourage students to borrow materials.

6 Invite Elders and other members of the indigenous community into your learning spaces to teach physical activities and provide meaning in relation to these activities. Learn the history of the activity, the equipment that was used, what the equipment was made of and why. Discuss the skills and fitness levels required to be successful in these activities. What stage of motor learning are your students performing at as they play these games or participate in the activities?

Always check for protocol with your local school and community regarding the appropriate channels to pursuing knowledge and the individuals to assist you.

Remember to check for safety guidelines in your school and school district with regards to activities. Contemporary issues of safety might affect the ability to implement some activities in some areas. For example, are your students strong enough to try the knuckle hop (Heine, 2006) or could this be a liability and safety issue? Invite indigenous people to provide demonstrations and share knowledge.

7 Use indigenous music in your classes for warm-ups and other activities.

8 Participate in indigenous activities whenever you are invited to do so by your students or community.

9 Be curious about indigenous knowledge and be a respectful listener. You will learn a great deal. Allow your students to teach you.

The following practical ideas are from British Columbia Ministry of Education. (2006). *Shared Learnings*.

1 Arrange a field trip to a gathering, potlatch, pow-wow, or feast where there is likely to be dance performed. Have students think about the following questions in preparation for the field trip: what will we see, hear, smell, taste, and feel? How will we show respect? Debrief with a class discussion about the various movements they may have observed in the dance (e.g., erect stance, starting and stopping with the music, head and hand movements, "heartbeat" movements, footwork, sequence of left-right steps, quick steps, stomping steps, imitating animal movements, changing facial expressions).

2 Ask groups of students to research and learn about a traditional indigenous game or dance to share with the class. Expand this idea to include traditional games and dances from a variety of cultures by asking the students to explore their own cultural experiences.

3 Using local Aboriginal community/school sports organizations as resources, ask students to research the value of games and sports in contemporary Aboriginal communities (e.g., hockey, soccer, baseball). Ask students to research high profile Aboriginal sports events, such as the Prince Rupert Basketball Tournament, the Easter Soccer Tournament in Victoria, canoe races, or other local events.

4 Include in regular classroom displays pictures of and information about Aboriginal athletes. Role models to include are Gino Odjik, Angela Chalmers, Ted Nolan, Grant Fuhr, and Roger Nielson. Ask students to research the life and work of a specific athlete. Examples include Woneek Horn-Miller, Tom Longboat, Jim Thorpe, Fred Sasakamoose, Gaylord Powless, Margo Cane, Maria Tallchief, Gloria Snow, or Rene Highway.

5 In a class discussion, explore reasons for the use of Aboriginal images in sports (e.g., stereotypes of Aboriginal peoples as wild, strong, and/or fast). Provide examples and ask students to discuss whether these images are respectful and appropriate.

6 Ask students to find examples of logos used by various sports teams (e.g., UBC Thunderbirds, Cleveland Indians, Washington Redskins, Chicago Blackhawks, Kansas City Chiefs, Atlanta Braves) and discuss the positive and negative impacts. Ask students to create their own respectful Aboriginal logos for imagined sports teams. Display and have students explain the imagery included in their logo and why it is appropriate to that sport.

Suggested Resources

Bruchac, J. (2004). *Tim Thorpe's bright path*. New York: Lee & Low Books.

CBC Non-Broadcast Sales. (1994). *Inuit throat singers*. [Video]. Retrieved from: www.sources.com/MNN/MeAIndex.htm#I

Cradleboard Teaching Project. Retrieved from: www.cradleboard.org

Erdrich, H. (1993). *Maria Tallchief*. Austin, TX: Raintree Steck-Vaughn.

Garrett, L. (2005). *Tom Longboat: Born to run*. Toronto: Pearson Education Canada.

Heine, M. (2006). *Dene games: An instruction and resource manual*. Yellowknife, NT: Sport North Federation.

Heine, M. (2006). *Arctic sports: A training and resource manual*. Yellowknife, NT: Sport North Federation.

Heine, M. (2006). *Inuit-style wrestling: A training and resource manual*. Yellowknife, NT: Sport North Federation.

Hoyt-Goldsmith, D. (1998). *Lacrosse: The national game of the Iroquois*. New York: Holiday House.

I.C.E. Productions. (2004). *Pow-wow trail: Episode 11 pow-wow fever*. [DVD]. Retrieved from: www.arborrecords.com

Macfarlan, A. & Macfarlan, P. (1985). *Handbook of American Indian Games*. Mineola, NY: Dover.

Marks, D. (2008). *They call me chief: Warriors on ice*. Winnipeg MB: J. Gordon Shillingford.

Miller, C. L., & Peacock, T. (1998). *Collected wisdom: American Indian education*. Boston: Allyn & Bacon.

Muasuzumi, A. (1999). *Caribou hide: Two stories of life on the land*. Yellowknife, NT: Raven Rock.

National Film Board of Canada. (Wapos Bay Productions). (2009). *Going for the gold*. [DVD]. Retrieved from: www.nfb.ca/onf.ca

National Film Board of Canada. (Kent Martin). (2008). *The sacred sundance: The transfer of a ceremony*. [DVD]. Retrieved from: www.nfb.ca

Northwest Territories Education, Culture and Employment. (1996). *Inuuqatigiit curriculum*. Retrieved from: www.ece.gov.nt.ca/curriculum

Northwest Territories Education, Culture and Employment. (1996). *Dene Kede: A Dene perspective*. Retrieved from: www.ece.gov.nt.ca/curriculum

Ontario Ministry of Education. (2010). *Health and Physical Education* (Interim ed. revised). Retrieved from: www.edu.gov.on.ca/eng/curriculum/elementary/health.html

Shilling, V. (2007). *Native athletes in action!* Summertown, TN: 7th Generation.

Acknowledgements

The First Nations, Inuit and Métis Holistic Lifelong Learning Models are reprinted with permission from the Canadian Council on Learning (2009), and were developed by a collaboration of partners. More information can be found at www.ccl-cca.ca/CCL/Reports/RedefiningSuccessInAboriginalLearning/RedefiningSuccessModels.html

The author wishes to gratefully acknowledge:

Academic contributions from Erin Cameron, BA, B.Ed., Dip(Comm), MA(IIComm), Ph.D(c)

Reading of this work by:

Yvette Arcand B.Ed., PGD EAdmin, M.Ed.
Associate Director of Student Affairs
Indian Teacher Education Program
University of Saskatchewan

Jeff Baker B.Ed., M.Ed., Ph.D(c)
Faculty & Staff Coordinator
Aboriginal Programs
University of Saskatchewan

Segments of this work have previously been published by VDM Publishing

Key Terms

- Medicine Wheel
- Indigenous Knowledge
- Wellness
- Four Aspects of Human Nature

Appendix 1

First Nations Holistic Lifelong Learning Model

Living DRAFT
Last Updated: June 6, 2007

First Nations Holistic Lifelong Learning Model

Living DRAFT
Last Updated: June 6, 2007

ABOUT THE FIRST NATIONS HOLISTIC LIFELONG LEARNING MODEL

The *First Nations Holistic Lifelong Learning Model* represents the link between First Nations lifelong learning and community well-being, and can be used as a framework for measuring success in lifelong learning.

For First Nations people, the purpose of learning is to honour and protect the earth and ensure the longterm sustainability of life. To illustrate the organic and self regenerative nature of First Nations learning, the Holistic Lifelong Learning Model uses a stylistic graphic of a living tree. The tree depicts the cycles of learning for an individual and identifies the influences that affect individual learning and collective well-being.

The *First Nations Holistic Lifelong Learning Model* is a result of ongoing discussions among First Nations learning professionals, community practitioners, researchers and analysts. For a complete list of individuals and organizations that have contributed to the development of this learning model, visit www.ccl-cca.ca.

DESCRIBING THE MODEL

The First Nations learner dwells in a world of continual re-formation, where interactive cycles, rather than disconnected events, occur. In this world, nothing is simply a cause or an effect, but the expression of the interconnectedness of life. These relationships are circular, rather than linear, holistic, and cumulative rather than compartmentalized. The mode of learning for First Nations people reflects and honours this understanding.

Lifelong learning for First Nations peoples is grounded in experiences that embrace both indigenous and Western knowledge traditions, as depicted in the tree's root system, "Sources and Domains of Knowledge". Just as the tree draws nourishment through its roots, the First Nations person learns from and through the natural world, language, traditions and ceremonies, and the world of people (self, family, ancestors, clan, community, nation and other nations). Any uneven root growth can de-stabilize the learning system. The root system also depicts the intertwining presence of indigenous and Western knowledge, which forms the tree trunk's core, where learning develops.

A cross-sectional view of the trunk reveals the "Learning Rings of the Individual". At the ring's core are the four dimensions of personal development—spiritual, emotional, physical, and mental—through which learning is experienced holistically. The tree's rings portray how learning is a lifelong process that begins at birth and progresses through childhood, youth and adulthood.

Learning opportunities are available in all stages of First Nations life. They can occur in both informal and formal settings such as in the home, on the land, or in the school. The stages of learning begin with the early childhood phase and progress through elementary, secondary and post-secondary education, to adult skills training and employment. Intergenerational knowledge is transmitted to the individual from the sources within the roots.

The First Nations learner experiences the various relationships within indigenous and Western knowledge traditions through their emotional, mental, spiritual and physical dimensions. The tree's extended branches, which represent the individual's harmony and well-being, depict the development of these experiences. The individual's well-being supports the cultural, social, political and economic "Collective Well-Being", represented by the four clusters of leaves.

Just as leaves provide nourishment to the roots and support the tree's foundation, the community's collective well-being rejuvenates the individual's learning cycle. Learning guides—mentors, counsellors, parents, teachers, and Elders—provide additional support and opportunities for individuals to learn throughout their lifespan.

Appendix 2

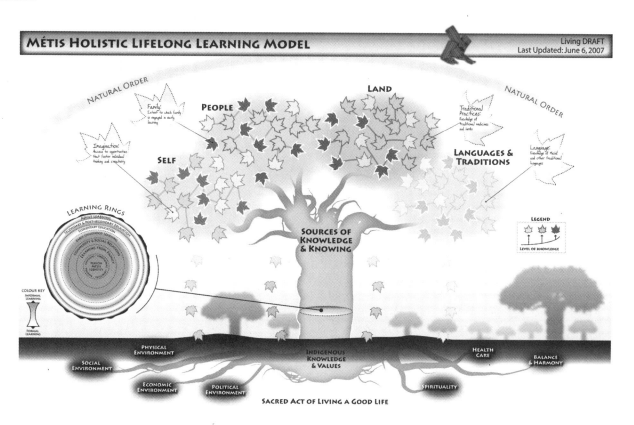

About the Métis Holistic Lifelong Learning Model

The *Métis Holistic Lifelong Learning Model* represents the link between Métis lifelong learning and community well-being, and can be used as a framework for measuring success in lifelong learning.

The Métis understand learning in the context of the "Sacred Act of Living a Good Life," a perspective that incorporates learning experienced in the physical world and acquired by "doing," and a distinct form of knowledge—sacred laws governing relationships within the community and the world at large—that comes from the Creator. To symbolize these forms of knowledge and their dynamic processes, the Métis Holistic Lifelong Learning Model uses a stylistic graphic of a living tree.

The *Métis Holistic Lifelong Learning Model* is a result of ongoing discussions among First Nations learning professionals, community practitioners, researchers and analysts. For a complete list of individuals and organizations that have contributed to the development of this learning model, visit www.ccl-cca.ca.

Describing the Model

The Métis learner, like the tree, is a complex, living entity that needs certain conditions for optimum growth. As conditions change throughout the natural cycle, so will the regenerative capacity of the tree. The health of the tree, or the Métis learner, impacts the future health of the root system and the "forest" of learners.

Métis people view lifelong learning as part of a regenerative, living system—the "Natural Order" that governs the passage of seasons and encompasses a community (or forest) of learners. Within this organic system, relationships are interconnected, and balance and harmony are maintained.

The tree's roots represent the individual's health and well-being (social, physical, economic, spiritual, etc.) and provide the conditions that nurture lifelong learning. The root base of the tree represents the indigenous knowledge and values that provide stability for the Métis learner.

A cross-sectional view of the trunk's "Learning Rings" depicts how learning occurs holistically across the individual's life cycle. At the trunk's core are the spiritual, emotional, physical and mental dimensions of the Métis self and identity. Intergenerational knowledge and values are transmitted through the processes that first influence the individual's development—learning from family, and learning from community and social relations (represented by the two rings surrounding the core). The four outer rings illustrate the stages of lifelong learning, from early childhood through to adulthood; they depict the dynamic interplay of informal and formal learning that occurs at different rates and stages, as represented by the extent of growth across each ring.

Extending from the trunk are the branches—"Sources of Knowledge and Knowing" such as self, people, land and language and traditions. The clusters of leaves on each branch represent the domains of knowledge. The intensity of their colour indicates the extent of individual understanding in any knowledge domain. The leaves of knowledge eventually fall to the ground, signifying how knowledge transmission enriches the foundations of learning and produces more knowledge (more vibrant leaves).

Appendix 3

Figure 4

Inuit Holistic Lifelong Learning Model

The Inuit Holistic Lifelong Learning Model depicts the linkage between Inuit lifelong learning and community well-being, and can be used as a framework for measuring success in lifelong learning.

The Inuit Holistic Lifelong Learning Model is a result of ongoing discussions among Inuit learning professionals, community practitioners, researchers and analysts. For a complete list of individuals and organizations that have contributed to the development of this learning model, visit **www.ccl-cca.ca**.

The Inuit Holistic Lifelong Learning Model uses a stylistic graphic of an Inuit blanket toss (a game often played at Inuit celebrations) and a circular path (the "Journey of Lifelong Learning") to portray the Inuk's learning journey and its connection to community well-being.

Lifelong learning for Inuit is grounded in traditional "Inuit Values and Beliefs," as articulated in Inuit Qaujimajatuqangit (IQ). To illustrate the strength of IQ, the model depicts 38 family and community members, including ancestors, "holding up" a learning blanket, with each figure representing an IQ value and belief. The inclusion of ancestors represents the sacred Inuit tradition of "naming" – a practice which fosters Inuk identity, kinship relations, and the transmission of intergenerational knowledge.

Within the learning blanket are the "Sources and Domains of Knowledge" – culture, people, and sila (life force or essential energy) – as well as their sub-domains (languages, traditions, family, community, Elders, land, and the environment).

The Inuk's lifelong learning journey is ongoing and he/she progresses through each life stage – infant and child, youth, young adult, adult, and elder – and is presented with a range of learning opportunities.

During each learning journey where he or she can experience learning in both informal settings, such as in the home or on the land, or in formal settings, such as in the classroom or in the community. The Inuk is also exposed to both Indigenous and Western knowledge and learning practices, as depicted by the two colours of stitching along the rim of the blanket.

The Inuk emerges from each learning opportunity with a deeper awareness of Inuit culture, people and sila. In turn, the Inuk contributes his or her newly acquired skills and knowledge to the community, thereby contributing to the determinants of "Community Well-being" (identified as physical well-being, economic well-being, social well-being and environmental well-being), and returns to the learning path to continue the lifelong journey.

Appendix 4: A Model for Indigenous Knowledge in PE, Accompanying Text and Descriptions of Layers

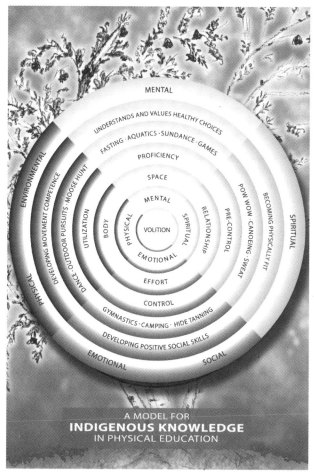

A Healthy Journey

We are all on a life's journey. The journey never ends. To have a healthy journey we need to take care of our spiritual, emotional, physical, and mental aspects. The journey is cyclical and moves clockwise, continuously around the Medicine Wheel. The journey begins in the East (Spiritual) and moves towards the North (Mental) in the quest for knowledge. Experiences build knowledge and the outcomes of my journey depend on me.

A Model for Indigenous Knowledge in Physical Education

This model is supported by the Teachings of the Sacred Tree

- Planted by the Creator where people may gather to find healing, power, wisdom and security
- The roots spread firmly into Mother Earth and the branches reach in prayer to Father Sky
- The fruits of the tree are the gifts given from the Creator (path of love, compassion, generosity, patience, wisdom, justice, courage, respect, humility)
- The life of the tree is the life of the people

The Medicine Wheel

- Is an ancient symbol used by many indigenous people
- Is used to help us see or understand things not normally visible
- Acts as a mirror so an individual can look back on one's self and look within to see where one is going
- Reflects wholeness and interconnectedness
- Demonstrates that everything is in a relationship
- Shows not only what is but what could be possible in our lives
- Demonstrates that the process of human growth in all aspects never stops
- As a cycle moves constantly as the human develops on life's journey
- Involves four directions

Layer 1 : The Centre: Volition

Volition: Centre of the Wheel	Bridging Curricula

■ You are in charge of your healthy journey
■ Involves self-responsibility
■ Helps you realizing potential
■ Requires perseverance
■ Helps you grow in all four aspects of human nature
■ Is a force at the centre of the wheel that helps the individual make and carry out decisions by:
    ■ Concentrating
    ■ Setting goals
    ■ Initiating an action
    ■ Persevering
    ■ Completing the action
	Behavioural changes require self-responsibility, discipline, and action. These are based on five stages of development (Prochaska, Norcross & DiClemente, 1994, p. 54)
	1. Pre-contemplation: The individual resists change and denies that change is needed
	2. Contemplation of change: The individual acknowledges that change is needed
	3. Preparation: The individual intends to take action to change behaviour
	4. Action: The beginning of action and change
	5. Maintenance: The individual stabilizes change and maintaining positive behaviour

Layer 2: Four Aspects of Human Nature

- The Medicine Wheel teaches us that we have four aspects of human nature and each one must be developed to achieve balance in one's life
- These are developed through volition
- Growth in these areas comes through struggle
- Process of developing these qualities is called "True learning"

Special gifts of knowledge are provided from each aspect and one aspect is never left behind while traveling to the next. Each round of the circle creates new knowledge that grows and is obtained through perseverance, patience, and practice. As we stand in one direction we can see the other three directions which assists in balancing one's self...looking back... looking ahead. Standing too long in any one part of the wheel could lead to an imbalance; therefore, we must keep moving in order to grow. The following descriptions provide Indigenous teachings of each aspect on the left column and possible bridging with physical education curricula on the right column.

SPIRITUAL (East) Little Mouse sister does what she does with all of her tiny being	Bridging Curricula

■ First stage in the development of the human will
■ Existed from the moment of conception
■ The direction of childhood, birth, rebirth, new learning
■ All journeys begin in the east
■ A place to learn how to care for others
■ A place to learn to be self-reliant
■ Gift of focus – learning to pay attention
■ The place of innocence – the ability to believe in possibilities
■ Deals with the affective domain
■ Involves the subjective experience
■ Morals and values are taught
■ We can feel each other's spirit
■ Emotions are affected by our spirit
■ We develop relationships with the objects we interact with
■ The self is part of the environment
■ Involves challenge to be the best you can be
■ Involves ceremony
■ Respecting the body
■ Your spirit is connected to your physical movements
■ Setting goals and achieving success
■ Feeling positive about the physical things one does
	■ Teaching morals and values
	    ■ Fair play values
	    ■ Respecting others and self
	    ■ Issues of bullying
	■ The affective domain
	    ■ Appreciating that everyone is important
	    ■ Respecting the abilities of others
	    ■ Helping others to learn
	    ■ Respecting the body as an instrument of movement
	    ■ Appreciating the gift of health
	■ Learning new skills
	    ■ Realizing that each new skill or progression learned is a new challenge
	    ■ Motor learning is never complete
	■ Recognizing athletic ability is a gift
	■ Giving thanks for the life of the animal or plant that has contributed to the game through equipment
	■ Recognize that the player has a relationship with the object of play, the playing space, the opponents/team-mates, and the equipment being used
	■ Recognizing that following these teachings through physical activity can lead to improved self-esteem (emotion), increase in knowledge (mental), (spiritual) growth and (physical) wellness

EMOTION (South)	Bridging Curricula
Cougar teaches concentration ■ Second stage in the development of the human will ■ the place of the heart ■ Learn to make sacrifices and be generous, ■ be sensitive towards others feelings, be loyal ■ Learn about love and be passionate in the world ■ Feelings can be realized and controlled by acts of volition ■ Learn discipline of emotions ■ Develop confidence ■ Is the place of fullness of youth and testing of the physical body ■ The body must be respected ■ Realize that emotional problems can affect your physicality ■ We must make wise choices to keep the body healthy and not let the body control our well-being ■ All of these require exercising of the volition ■ Gifts of the south include grace of movement, appreciation of the arts, power of discrimination ■ If one is working well inside their emotions there will be a strong spiritual connection ■ Pray and connect with Mother Earth	■ Learn to share, be fair, play with everyone ■ Respect others' feelings during play ■ Teach friendly competition and recognize not everyone likes competition ■ Learn about teamwork ■ Demonstrate winning and losing with pride ■ Recognize that exercise releases tension ■ Exercise requires discipline ■ One must exercise the will to maintain an active lifestyle ■ One must choose how they like to move through physical activity ■ Learning stress management to apply pro-active responses to emotion ■ Relaxation techniques and exercise to calm the body ■ One can learn to balance feelings while balancing the body in different ways ■ The centre of gravity can be related to the 'will' where one must find the balance inside and outside of the body in relation to the base of support (Mother Earth/ a balance beam) ■ One must make choices about how they need to live in order to be on a healthy journey
PHYSICAL (West)	**Bridging Curricula**
Black Bear (Strength) Turtle (teaches to go "within" and grants the gift of perseverance) ■ Third stage in the development of the human will ■ Existed from the moment of conception ■ Represents the place of testing and the source of strength which must come from within ■ The place where perseverance can be won through testing ■ Perseverance and testing can be learned through ceremony ■ (sun dance, fasting, hunting, survival, games) ■ Learning to stick to a challenge ■ The direction of power (to heal, protect, defend) ■ Recognize potential ■ A place of sacrifice – nothing should be taken without giving back ■ One must learn to manage power ■ Spend time in prayer to gain insight ■ Learn to love and know the Creator ■ Learn what the Creator would expect of you as a leader ■ Encourage students to set goals for themselves and achieve them ■ Respect the goals that others set for themselves	■ How to make wise decisions (for your healthy journey) ■ Try your best and never give up ■ Challenge yourself and test yourself through your activities to learn more and strive to become more proficient in applying motor skills to your activities ■ Run faster, jump higher, throw farther ■ Control your emotions and recognize the power you have (spiritually, emotionally, physically, mentally) ■ Work on the fitness components of strength, flexibility, cardio-endurance, power, and body composition and use these to test your will and your potential ■ Learn obedience by listening, following instructions, respecting self, others and equipment, playing fair, following the rules ■ Learn to lead with fairness and wisdom when interacting with others

MENTAL (North)	Bridging Curricula
The Great Mountain (symbolic teacher of the North)	■ Relate story-telling to physical activities – create dances, games from stories and legends typically told in the winter
■ The place of winter, white snow is symbolic of the white hair of the Elders	■ Learn to be leaders of others in class, on teams, in partners
■ A place to learn and guide others with wisdom	■ Understand that the mind and the body are connected
■ Dawning of the place of true wisdom	■ Learning motor skills is a relationship between the mind and the body
■ Intellectual gifts are realized in the North	■ Learn to challenge yourself and complete your goals
■ Some of the special gifts of the North: thinking, synthesizing, speculating, predicting, discriminating, problem solving, imagination, interpretation of hidden meanings, organization	■ Set new goals continuously in different aspects of wellness
■ The mind can be trained to become strong	■ Understand the connection between the spiritual, emotional, physical and mental aspects of human wellness
■ Perseverance must be strong to succeed when the task seems too great	■ Understand what it means to become a physically educated person
■ The direction of completion and fulfillment	■ Understand the impact of a healthy lifestyle and value the benefits of health
■ Learning to finish what we have started	■ Teach others in your family and your community the way to wholeness and the relationships between all things
■ Final lesson in the development of the powers of the will- volition	■ Encourage others to become physically active
	■ Value your-self and your will
	■ Recognize that you have been given the gift of choice in life and that these choices impact your healthy journey
	■ Strive to be in balance on the wheel of life

Layer 3: HUMAN MOVEMENT CONCEPTS (Pangrazi & Gibbons, 2009)

These concepts are part of a framework designed for analyzing and extending movement. The concepts help teachers relate the development of movement through the stages of motor learning, and apply creative approaches to movement. The inter-relationship between the concepts is important.

Every movement requires an instrument (the body) to move in space, with effort, in relationship to someone or something.

RELATIONSHIPS	QUALITIES OF MOVEMENT (EFFORT)	BODY	SPATIAL AWARENESS
■ Is the with whom or with what of movement	■ This is the how of movement	■ The body is the instrument of movement ■ Placed in the West (physicality) ■ The body forms many shapes as it engages in movement with people and the environment ■ Focuses on balance, transfer of body weight, flight	■ Is the where of movement ■ Placed in the North (understanding the capacity for movement in space) ■ Where does movement occur in space? ■ General space ■ Personal space ■ In different directions (right (E), left(W), forward, backward, up(N), down(S), clockwise, counter-clockwise) ■ At different levels (high, medium, low) ■ In different pathways (straight(E), meandering(S), zig-zag(W), circular(N)
■ Placed in the east (building relationships) ■ All aspects of movement are related occur with self and/ or others, may occur with an object, and in some relation to space and the environment	■ Placed in the south (represents emotion and feeling) ■ How does the movement look and feel? ■ What force or timing is used in the movement? ■ Is it fast, slow, heavy, light, sneaky?	■ The person in the body strives to achieve the gifts of intuition, senses, emotions, feelings, skills, strength, endurance, perseverance, patience, intellect, spirituality, balance through movement	

Layer 4: MOTOR SKILL ACQUISITION (Graham, Holt/Hale & Parker, 2007)

- Learning a new skill begins in the east, in the infancy stage of the skill, and progress to the north where proficiency is achieved
- All activities require motor skills learned through progressive, developmentally appropriate activities and practice
- There are four stages of motor learning
- The mind, body, Emotion and Spirit are connected in the activity and The learning never stops
- When the body achieves success, the emotion and the spirit are fed and mental capacity increases

1) Pre-control	2) Control	3) Utilization	4) Proficiency
■ Aligned with the East ■ This is the infant stage of motor learning ■ This is the beginning of learning a new skill	■ Aligned with the South - Requires practice and perseverance	■ Aligned with the West ■ PERSEVERE IN PRACTICE ■ Apply motor skills through more advanced progressions ■ Create more advanced opportunities for varied relationships in movement as they relate to the game, dance, or other activity	■ Aligned with the North ■ This is the final stage of motor learning ■ The student is able to use the skills almost "at will" requiring very little concentration.
■ Little control over the object or the body in relation to the object, others, or space ■ Motor learning requires plenty of practice	■ Students gain some control and success with the body, others, and the object ■ Progressions are applied ■ Plenty of practice opportunities required	■ Students enjoy applying the skills to activity due to increased success in motor learning	■ Competent stage of motor learning
■ It can be extending a previously learned skill (where one can find themselves at a pre-control level again)	■ Staying calm and remaining focused are important so the student remains focused or becomes frustrated		■ Can contribute to positive emotional feelings, spiritual wellness, physical strength, and wisdom

Layer 5: ACTIVITY PERSPECTIVES

Physical activity enhances motor learning and skill improves through practice. Teachers need to provide a wide variety of opportunities for students to be physically active. These activities should make connections to students' lives. Cultural knowledge should be respected within activity perspectives. The following examples demonstrate some possibilities.
Canoeing, Tracking, Snow Snake, Archery, Beading, Pow Wow
Aquatics, Dance, Games, Outdoor Pursuits, Gymnastics, Manipulatives, Fitness, Cooperative Activities, Team Building Skills, Roping
Sun Dance, Jigging, Throat Singing, Indigenous Games, Sweat, Moose Hunting, Fasting, Tanning Hides, Mushing, Fishing, Trapping, Berry Picking, Building a Canoe, Round Dance, Camping

Layer 6: BECOMING PHYSICALLY EDUCATED

- The volition connects to the four aspects of human nature
- Movement variables helps students progress through activities and develop motor skills
- Motor skills are learned through and applied to activities
- Knowledge is gained through practice
- Application of knowledge moves students towards the goal of becoming physically educated (National association for sport and physical education, 2004)

Physically Educated Students

■ Are able to make the connections between all aspects of human nature ■ Work towards balance, harmony and interconnectedness on their journey ■ Persevere, set goals, learn patience, enjoy the benefits of a physically active lifestyle that leads to a state of wholeness and wellness ■ Share knowledge with others	■ Develop movement competence (W) ■ Apply movement concepts and skills to activities (W) ■ Strive for physically fitness (E) ■ Understand and value the benefits of being physically active (N) ■ Develop lifetime activity skills (N) ■ Demonstrate positive social skills (S)

Level 7: A HEALTHY JOURNEY

As we strive for a healthy journey we climb many mountains and meet many obstacles. The most important obstacle to deal with is the self—the will—the volition. Bopp et al. (1985, p. 63) stated that the great mountain is one of the symbolic teachers of the North. The higher we climb its slopes, the steeper and more difficult the way becomes. And yet the higher we go, the more we can see and the stronger we can become.

TA Loeffler, Professor of Outdoor Education at Memorial University, Newfoundland has climbed the highest peak on six of the seven continents of the world. She has left to accomplish Mt. Everest. Her journeys highlight the holistic nature of these tasks. Beginning with the challenge, the dream, and tremendous self-doubt; she shared her physical, emotional, spiritual, and mental journey ascending these mountains:

"I knew this mountain was teaching me patience but also perseverance. Hardship. That's life at altitude. Vision. Views from high places. Stark understanding. Rising above. Seeing nothing higher. Seeing in new ways. This is what makes the hardship both bearable and worth it. Seeing, and then coming down having seen. Pushing through. Giving up comfort. Working with my mind. Finding small pockets of fun and absurdity and laughter and connection. Seeing the morning light dance circles. Watching the evening sun drain from the hills. Sinking into a rich rhythm of physical exertion. Learning the lessons that come from days and days of outdoor living, the whispers of the stars, and the drone of the wind. All are my teachers and the mountains exact deep lessons." (Loeffler, 2008, p. 55)

Physical Education, Safety, and the Law

David Young
(with contributions by Antony Card)

Overview

You receive a phone call requesting that you, as a substitute physical educator, deliver some creative game activities to a grade four physical education (PE) class. This is to be your first visit to the school and you are keen to impress them with your talents. That evening you prepare a lesson plan and review your provincial PE safety guidelines to determine best practices for the activities you will be teaching. You arrive to the school to find that the gym is much smaller than expected and a scout group who rented the gym the night before have left equipment scattered around the perimeter of the space. There was also heavy rainfall overnight and it appears that the roof has leaked, leaving a large puddle of water in the middle of the floor. To make matters worse, when the class arrives it is in fact a grade three and four combined class of over forty students. You immediately recognize the dangers of wet floors, loose equipment, and overcrowded spaces for physical activity. Three options come to mind:

- Mark the dangers and warn the students not to go near the obstacles
- Mark and highlight the dangers and have half the class participate at one time
- Cancel the planned activity and take them to an alternate classroom space

The last option is the safest, but you are concerned about how this will be perceived by the school principal, and you do not want the students to miss out on a valuable educational activity. Accidents can and do happen in PE, even when there has been no evidence of negligence by the physical educator. However, if you choose one of the other options have you demonstrated a sufficient duty of care? And furthermore, how could these risks be managed and prevented in the future?

The potential negligence on the part of physical educators is a serious concern. This chapter will provide an overview of the impact of the law on PE. Among the major topics to be discussed are the following: injuries in PE, the law of torts, negligence, legal defences to negligence, and risk management.

Introduction

Liability for school accidents traditionally has depended on the fault-based concept of tort, specifically, negligence. In determining negligence on the part of educators, courts have relied on the 1894 decision by Lord Esher in *Williams v. Eady*, which determined that, in carrying out their duties, educators were expected to use the same degree of care with respect to their students as careful or prudent parents would use with their own children. Recently, several courts have modified this well-established legal principle in cases involving physical educators, holding them to the higher standard of care of a "skilled and competent practitioner"

(Dickinson, 2006, pp. 280–281). This modification has occurred largely as a result of literature that suggests that because a gymnasium, and the nature of the activities undertaken in this venue, is more dangerous than a typical classroom and the activities going on there, physical educators must be held to a higher standard of accountability.

Thus, potential negligence on the part of physical educators is a legitimate concern, because it can result in serious physical harm to students, and emotional, professional, and economic damage to educators who may be sued in tort and sustain liability for significant monetary awards.

Injuries in Physical Education

In terms of student injury, schools are often seen as "oases of safety in a violent world" (Posner, 2000, p. 2). However, in their work *Education Law*, Brown and Zuker (1998) argue that "schools are, by their very nature, fertile grounds for accidents to occur. This is particularly true if pupils are engaged in activities which have an element of heightened or inherent danger, such as sports, technical labs, and science labs" (p. 58). Anyone even vaguely familiar with typical classroom environments recognizes they are fast-paced environments, where the capacity for one educator to completely monitor all students within his or her charge is questionable at best. The demand for "adequate supervision" is further magnified when students are participating in classes with increased risk, such as PE.

Physical Education is essential for students' health and well-being but poses more potential safety risks than other school subjects.

This is an important consideration because experts appear to agree that athletics and PE are the areas of greatest risk for school accidents. However, "there are no precise data on injuries resulting from sports and physical education activities. But we do know that substantial numbers of children are injured during physical education and athletic practice and games" (Posner, 2000, p. 125). In fact, "not only do accidents occur [in physical education and athletics] frequently, but they also tend to be serious enough to evoke lawsuits" (Dickinson, 2006, p. 278). According to Connors (1981), there has been more litigation in the realm of athletics and PE than in all other educational fields combined.

In one study, Kelm, Ahlhelm, Pape, Pitsch, and Engel (2001) found that approximately 5% of all school children are seriously injured during PE classes every year. Yet, "because there is no national system, either private or public, that collects comprehensive data on school injuries" (Posner, 2000, p. 13) we are often left to speculate as to how many children are injured at school each year. In spite of this, Dickinson (2006) points out that the Centers for Disease Control and Prevention (CDC) have concluded that in terms of the United States:

■ Injury is the most common condition treated by school health personnel.

■ Each year, approximately four million individuals sustain injuries at school.

■ The majority of injuries are unintentional. Falls (43%), sports (34%), and assaults (10%) are the most frequent causes of injuries leading to hospitalization.

In addition to the CDC findings, it is also worth noting that the bulk of these injuries are minor. Furthermore, most studies indicate that boys are one and a half times more likely to be injured at school than girls (Posner, 2000).

In thinking about school-related accidents, it seems likely that most people who have taken PE at some point in their lives will have either experienced or witnessed an injury. The author can vividly recall an episode in grade eleven when, while engaged in a game of volleyball, he was struck in the face by a ball spiked by a member of the opposite team. The end result was a red and swollen cheek, coupled with a bruised ego. While the injuries received were slight, the opportunity for greater damage did exist.

The Law of Torts

"Accidents are the business of the law of torts—an area of law largely defined and carried out under the common law, that is, according to judge-made case law" (Dickinson, 2006, p. 279). The term tort is derived from the Latin word *tortus*, which means twisted or crooked. The expression found its way into usage in early English as a general synonym for "wrong" (Linden, 2001, p. 1). "Later the word disappeared from common usage, but retained its hold on the law and ultimately acquired its current technical meaning" (Fleming, 1998, p. 3).

Although there have been many efforts at describing and defining torts, none have been completely successful. In fact, "no definition could possibly depict the richness and variety of the subject matter of tort law" (Linden, 2001, p. 2). Still, a working definition of tort is needed, and the one offered by Prosser (1955) appears to be the most promising. Therefore, in this chapter the term tort refers

to a miscellaneous and more or less unconnected group of civil wrongs, other than breach of contract, for which a court of law will afford a remedy in the form of an action for damages. The law of torts is concerned with the compensation of losses suffered by private individuals in their legally protected interests, through conduct of others which is regarded as socially unreasonable. (p. 1)

Children and teenagers rarely think of the inherent risks in many of their activities.

Thus, torts are civil as opposed to criminal wrongs because what is involved is private rather than public harm. That is, civil liability results from the harmful actions of one person against another. These private wrongs are enforced by the victims, or someone acting on their behalf, in order to recover compensation for the losses sustained (MacKay & Dickinson, 1998). Yet, it should be noted that civil and criminal liability are not mutually exclusive (Dickinson, 2006).

Torts may be either intentional or unintentional in nature. An intentional tort involves an effort by an individual to interfere with or cause harm to another. The four most common types of intentional torts are assault, battery, false imprisonment, and mental anguish (Connors, 1981).

Unintentional torts are usually referred to as negligence. Negligence occurs "when a person ought to have foreseen that his or her actions would cause harm" (MacKay & Dickinson, 1998, p. 3). Whereas very few educators commit intentional torts towards their students, negligence is the most common tort suit in education.

Since the early 1900s, the law of torts has been constantly evolving (MacKay & Sutherland, 2006). It is not an exaggeration to say that when we describe torts, "we are describing the present-day effects of several centuries of creation, elaboration, and explanation" (Fridman, 2003, p. 4). Today,

the law of torts hovers over virtually every activity of modern society. The driver of every automobile on our highways, the pilot of every aeroplane in the sky, and the captain of every ship plying our waters must abide by the standards of tort law. The producers, distributors and repairers of every product, from bread to computers, must conform to tort law's counsel of caution. No professional is beyond its reach: a doctor cannot raise a scalpel, a lawyer cannot advise a client, nor can an architect design a building without being subject to potential tort liability. In the same way, teachers, government officials, police, and even jailers may be required to pay damages if someone is hurt as a result of their conduct. Those who engage in sports, such as golfers, hockey-players, and snowmobilers, may end up as parties to a tort action. The territory of tort law encompasses losses resulting from fires, floods, explosions, electricity, gas, and many other catastrophes that may occur in this increasingly complex world. A person who punches another in the nose may have to answer for it in a tort case as well as in the criminal courts. A person who says nasty things about another may be sued for defamation. Hence, any one of us may become a plaintiff or a defendant in a tort action at any moment. Tort law, therefore, is a subject of abiding concern not only to the judges and lawyers who must administer it, but also to the public at large, whose every move is regulated by it. (Linden, 2001, p. 1)

The above quotation makes it clear that tort law is pervasive. However, to truly understand torts, what is required is an examination of their role. While various rationales have been put forth to account for the creation of tortious liability, deterrence and compensation stand out as the two primary purposes of the law of torts.

Deterring harmful conduct is an important goal of tort law (Cummins, 1999). Legal scholars such as Bentham, Austin, and others argued that the role of tort law was remarkably similar to criminal law—to punish the guilty. Tort law still operates in a similar fashion, with the overarching premise being that by holding defendants liable, future tortious acts will be discouraged. As Linden (2001) puts it,

the threat of tort liability is supposed to deter wrongful conduct and to stimulate caution on the part of those who wish to avoid civil liability for their conduct. In other words, the lesson being taught to society is that tort, like crime, does not pay. In addition to the element of deterrence, tort law serves a compensatory purpose. (p. 4)

Allotting compensatory damages to a tort victim for loss shifts the costs of wrongdoing from the victim to the tortfeasor. "The fault of the tortfeasor provides the legal excuse for the shift of responsibility, making the tortfeasor pay for injuries that are his or her fault" (Cummins, 1999, p. 11). Although the compensatory role of torts may not be perfect, "no one can deny that thousands of injured individuals do collect millions of dollars every year to assist them in getting some comfort and enjoyment from what remains of their shattered lives" (Linden, 2003, p. 460). It is worth pointing out that embedded in the concept of compensating victims is a related principle. Those who are forced to pay damages for their substandard conduct will likely try to avoid a recurrence; the compensatory role thus contributes to the deterrent role played by the law of torts (Linden, 2001).

The Tort of Negligence

In terms of education, negligence is the most significant branch of tort law. It entails the "failure to do something that a reasonable and prudent person would do or the commission of an act that such a person would not commit" (Bezeau, 1995, p. 340). Although no simple definition accurately describes the term, negligence does involve any type of conduct which falls below some pre-defined standard. This position is echoed by Leibee (1965), who defines negligence as:

conduct—either action or inaction—which, it is claimed by the injured person, does not measure up to the standard of behaviour required by the law of all persons in society. Briefly, that standard or measurement may be described as the manner in which a reasonably prudent person would act under the same or similar circumstances as those involved in the case before the court. (p. 8)

A second fundamental principle of negligence is reasonable foreseeability. That is, a prudent person should have the capacity to be able to predict when his or her actions might result in risks that could potentially cause harm to others (MacKay & Flood, 2001). "It is no defence to a claim of negligence to say that you did not foresee the harm if it is true that a reasonable person in the same circumstances would have foreseen it" (MacKay & Dickinson, 1998, p. 3). As MacKay (1984) points out,

> everyone has a duty to conduct himself in such a way so as not to harm others. In order for liability to arise it is necessary that the harm caused and the person injured should have been "reasonably foreseeable." The test often used by the courts is whether a "reasonable person" would have foreseen the accident. If it is foreseeable that someone might be harmed, it is necessary for a person to take whatever steps a reasonable or prudent person would take to avoid injury. (pp. 109–110)

Thus, the courts are charged with holding accountable those parties who have created risks, or have failed to adopt measures which would prevent the possibility of harm to others (MacKay & Sutherland, 2006).

As MacKay and Dickinson (1998) point out, to establish a cause of action for negligence, three elements must be present: (1) a duty of care; (2) a breach of the standard of care; and (3) damage resulting from this breach.

Duty of Care

In determining negligence, courts must first ascertain whether a duty of care was owed to the plaintiff by the defendant either at common law or under statute law. That is, a duty of care must be owed under the law. "Moral or professional duty is not sufficient" (Bezeau, 1995, p. 340). A duty of care can be defined as "the sum total of considerations that would lead an adjudicator to find that a particular plaintiff is entitled to some sort of protection" (Champion, 2004, p. 72). According to Fleming (1998), a duty of care reflects "an obligation, recognised by law, to avoid conduct fraught with unreasonable risk of danger to others" (p. 149).

All these definitions refer, in various terms, to the duty of care as a "responsibility to take reasonable measures to avoid causing harm to others where the injury is reasonably foreseeable" (MacKay & Sutherland, 2006, p. 2). This does not require eliminating the potential for harm, but rather taking steps that would minimize it.

In the 1932 case of *Donoghue v. Stevenson*, Lord Atkin established the "good neighbour principle" of negligence liability. According to this rationale, a duty of care was owed to those deemed to be a neighbour. But, in law, who is a neighbour? For Lord Atkin, neighbours were "persons who are so closely and directly affected by my act that I ought reasonably to have them in contemplation as being so affected when I am directing my mind to the acts or omissions which are called in question" (p. 580). Because of the close proximity of educators and students, the "good neighbour" principle easily applies.

Outdoor activity is crucial for elementary-level children but presents increased supervision challenges.

Building on the special relationship between educator and student, the duty of care established first in schools in the 1894 case of *Williams v. Eady* arises from an application of the *in loco parentis* doctrine (MacKay & Dickinson, 1998). "According to this theory, teachers are given temporary delegation of authority over and responsibility for students and thus, act in place of a parent" (MacKay & Flood, 2001, p. 374). As Winnecke C.J. of the Victoria Supreme Court explained in the case of *Richards v. State of Victoria*, "the reason underlying the imposition of the duty would appear to be the need of a child of immature age for protection against the conduct of others, or indeed of himself, which may cause him injury" (1969, pp. 138–139). This duty of care is a "weighty" responsibility—one which must be taken seriously in order to ensure the safety and well-being of others, and thus avoid potential liability (MacKay & Sutherland, 2006).

Breach of the Standard of Care

A breach is a "failure to conform to the required standard of care" (Fleming, 1998). As Russo (2006) points out, a breach of the standard of care can result from either a failure to act (nonfeasance), or by failing to act properly (misfeasance). Thus, a breach of the standard of care can stem from an omission or an act (Bezeau, 1995).

For example, in the case of *Hussack v. School District No. 33 (Chilliwack, B.C.)*, a grade seven student was injured during a field hockey tournament in a PE class. Devon Hussack had missed the previous in-class instruction on field hockey prior to being allowed to participate in the tournament. The physical educator in this case had divided the class into four teams and reminded the class of basic safety rules related to field hockey. The student was struck in the face, sustaining a concussion, which ultimately resulted in the development of serious psychological issues. The court did not accept the physical educator's assertion that Hussack's prior experience in ice and floor hockey would provide adequate preparation for the game. It was deemed that he should have participated in the progressive "building blocks" prior to participating in the game. Although the standard of care in negligence law varies depending on the situation, generally speaking, courts have applied the "reasonable person" doctrine. In Canadian jurisprudence, the most complete and accurate description of the "reasonable person" is that offered by Mr. Justice Laidlaw in *Arland v. Taylor*.

> [The reasonable person is] a mythical creature of the law whose conduct is the standard by which the courts measure the conduct of all other persons and find it to be proper or improper in particular circumstances as they may exist from time to time. He is not an extraordinary or unusual creature; he is not a superhuman; he is not required to display the highest skill of which anyone is capable; his is not a genius who can perform uncommon feats, nor is he possessed of unusual powers of foresight. He is a person of normal intelligence who makes prudence a guide to his conduct. He does nothing that a prudent man would not do and does not omit to do anything that a prudent man would do. His conduct is guided by considerations which ordinarily regulate the conduct of human affairs. His conduct is the standard "adopted in the community by persons of ordinary intelligence and prudence." (1955, p. 142)

Case Study 1: Adequate Supervision?

John Oakes has been a physical educator at Rosemount High School for five years. During this time he has gained a reputation among the student body as a popular teacher. During one particular PE class in which the students were practicing routine rolls on the mats in the gymnasium, a group of Grade ten boys ask if they can leave the gym and go to an adjacent classroom where they might practice on the parallel bars. While reluctant to grant the request, Mr Oakes eventually gives in and allows the students to practice in the other room. Although he tries to simultaneously supervise both the gymnasium and the classroom, the boys are essentially left to practice on their own. During one particularly difficult dismount, Ethan Boyd loses his balance and comes tumbling to the floor, crying out in pain. After being rushed to the hospital, the student is left with a badly broken arm, and separated shoulder.

Questions for Reflection

1. Was the level of supervision in this case adequate?

2. What, if anything, could the teacher have done differently?

3. What steps would you as a physical educator have taken to minimize the potential for student injury?

The "reasonable person" is a legal fiction, because no person can be completely "reasonable." Nonetheless, the

> test is employed by our courts to evaluate the conduct of the actors that come before them. The exercise is a unique process in which a value judgement based on community standards is reached. In such pursuits it is imperative to control as much as possible the personal biases and whims of the judge and the jury. The reasonable person test is meant to assist in this task. (Linden, 2001, p. 133)

The doctrine is thus important because it is the "measuring rod used in negligence law to judge an actor's conduct" (Linden, p. 130).

In determining negligence on the part of school personnel, courts have typically relied on the case of *Williams v. Eady* in which Lord Esher determined that in carrying out their duties, educators were expected to use the same degree of care with respect to their students as careful or prudent parents would use with their own children. This case involved injury sustained by a student through the explosion of phosphorus. The schoolmaster was held liable for improperly storing the dangerous substance. In his decision, Lord Esher stated that

> the schoolmaster was bound to take care of his boys as a careful father would take care of his boys, and there could be no better definition of the duty of a schoolmaster. Then he was bound to take notice of the ordinary nature of young boys, their tendency to do mischievous acts, their propensity to meddle with anything that came in their way. (p. 42)

This "careful parent" standard "has remained as the quintessential standard of care expected of educators ever since" (Dickinson, 2006, p. 280).

As Dickinson (2006) points out, in applying the "careful parent" standard to cases of negligence in schools, several factors are examined to ascertain whether a breach of the standard of care has occurred, including the following:

- The overall foreseeability of harm
- The nature of the activity
- Student attributes (age, intelligence, experience, strength, coordination)
- Instruction previously received by the student, as well as knowledge of the risks associated with the activity
- Whether there was a history of similar accidents
- Whether approved general practice was employed

If, after an examination of the facts, it is determined that the conduct of school personnel did not meet the standards of the "careful parent" doctrine, liability for negligence may result.

According to Brown and Zuker (1998), the "careful parent" standard is an ideal model to use in school negligence cases. For them,

> it is both fundamentally sensible and sufficiently adaptable. What it amounts to is a reflection of society's expectation that anyone who has responsibility for the safety of a child must take that responsibility very seriously, whether a parent of the child or not. (p. 87)

This support for the "careful parent" standard is shared by Metcalfe (2003), who argues that "the analogy of parental care provides a meaningful understanding of the responsibility of teachers for the physical safety of their students" (p. 276).

However, in spite of these glowing affirmations, within the school context the "careful parent" standard has been heavily criticized. As Hoyano (1984) puts it, "a test devised in 1893 is an anachronism in the context of modern education" (p. 3). Perhaps the "careful parent" standard was appropriate in the days of the one-room schoolhouse with ten or fifteen students. However, in the classrooms of today, where thirty or more students are not uncommon, it does appear outdated as a test for determining the standard of care. Furthermore, the "careful parent" standard is seen as being paternalistic (MacKay & Sutherland, 2006). It has also been described as an "elastic yardstick" which provides the courts with little guidance because the standard is so flexible that it can be bent by judges in any way they desire (MacKay & Dickinson, 1998, p. 11).

Therefore, the standard of care for educators is somewhat of an enigma in that teaching is the only profession in which this standard is an extrapolation of parental behaviour (Bezeau, 1995). Consider the standard of care required of physicians as outlined in the case of *Crits v. Sylvester*.

> Every medical practitioner must bring to his task a reasonable degree of skill and knowledge and must exercise a reasonable degree of care. He is bound to exercise that degree of care and skill which could reasonably be expected of a normal, prudent practitioner of the same experience and standing, and if he holds himself out as a specialist, a higher degree of skill is required of him than of those who do not profess to be so qualified by special training and ability. (1956, p. 143)

Yet, there are "areas where a teacher has a higher duty of care than that of a parent. Parents are not necessarily specialists in gymnastics, in trampoline work [and other physical activities]" (Giles, 1988, pp. 96–97). Because "of the specialized training of the instructors and the complexity of athletic activity, the careful parent standard may no longer be appropriate for physical education instructors" (MacKay & Sutherland, 2006, p. 20). This is consistent with the principle advanced by Fleming (1998) that "those who undertake work calling for special skill must not only exercise reasonable care but measure up to the standard of proficiency that can be expected from persons of such profession" (p. 121).

In this vein, several courts have modified the "careful parent standard" in cases involving physical educators, holding them to the higher standard of a "skilled and competent practitioner." In *McKay v. Board of Govan School Unit No. 29*, which involved a student being injured while performing on the parallel bars, Justice Woods of the Saskatchewan Court of Appeal stated that

> a physical training instructor in directing or supervising an evolution or exercise is bound to exercise the skill and competence of an ordinarily competent instructor in the field. The standard of a careful parent does not fit a responsibility which demands special training and expertise. (1968, p. 523)

In *Thornton v. Board of School Trustees of School District No. 57*, both the trial judge and the British Columbia Court of Appeal held that the standard of care required of a physical educator was that of a "reasonably skilled instructor" with "supra-parental expertise." In this case, which dealt with a student being left a quadriplegic as a result of undertaking a somersault from a springboard, the Court of Appeal found the educator negligent for failing to recognize the inherent danger of the activity. To make matters worse, it was also revealed that the educator was working on school reports at the time of the accident. In its ruling, the Court of Appeal (1976) set down four requirements of the standard of care for physical educators. These four principles, which have been cited in subsequent cases, hold that the standard of care for an activity is satisfied if:

1 The exercise is suitable for a student's age and mental and physical condition.

2 The student is progressively trained and coached to do the exercise properly and avoid danger.

3 The equipment used is adequate and suitably arranged.

4 The performance, having regard to its inherently dangerous nature, is properly supervised.

The standard of the "reasonably competent physical education teacher" invoked by the British Columbia Court of Appeal in *Thornton* was subsequently applied in the 1977 case of *Myers v. Peel (County) Board of Education*. This case focused on an injury suffered by a student while attempting a dismount from suspended rings. Like the Thornton case, the physical educator in question had failed to exercise proper supervision. Interestingly, both the Ontario Court of Appeal (1978) and the Supreme Court of Canada (1981) rejected this standard, preferring to rely instead on the "careful parent" test. However, the Supreme Court did

Case Study 2: How High is Too High?

As part of an exercise routine, physical educator Sherry Clarke has asked her Grade twelve class to jump from a seven foot high beam onto the floor, which was covered with mats. Each of her twenty-nine students has successfully completed the jump, except for Royce Howard. Royce has been diagnosed with a glandular condition, and as a result, he is considered obese. Because of his weight, Royce is reluctant to engage in the activity, but Ms Clarke insists that all of the students in her class complete the activity. Consequently, Royce attempts to jump from the beam, lands awkwardly, and breaks his leg, thus requiring surgery and the insertion of a metal pin.

Questions for Reflection

1 Do you believe Sherry Clarke is liable for the injuries sustained by Royce Howard?

2 What role should the physical fitness of students play when planning an activity?

3 As a physical educator, how would you have handled this situation?

indicate that the "careful parent" rule must be qualified. As Justice McIntyre noted, this standard cannot

> be applied in the same manner and to the same extent in every case. Its application will vary depending upon the number of students being supervised at any given time, the nature of the exercise or activity in progress, the age and degree of skill and training which the students may have received in connection with such activity, the nature and condition of the equipment in use at the time, the competency and capacity of the students involved, and a host of other matters which may be widely varied but which, in a given case, may affect the application of the prudent parent standard to the conduct of the school authority in the circumstances. (1981, p. 279)

By taking into account each of these factors in determining the "careful parent" doctrine, the court has implied that a physical educator may be held to a higher standard of care than a regular classroom educator, due in large measure to the particular level of expertise required as well as the complexity of athletic activities (MacKay & Sutherland, 2006). However, there is still uncertainty as to when and under what circumstances courts will invoke the "careful parent" as opposed to the "competent instructor" standard. "It would make sense that the more the cause of accident [sic] and injury relate to technical aspects of physical education theory and practice, the more one would expect the higher standard of care to be applied" (MacKay & Dickinson, 1998, p. 41).

Damage Resulting from a Breach of the Standard of Care

In addition to a duty of care, and a breach of the standard of care, damage resulting from this breach must also be present for legal liability to be established. As Justice Guy of the Manitoba Court of Appeal stated in the 1968 case of *Long v. Western Propeller Co. Ltd.*, "in negligence actions there is no 'cause to sue' until the third requirement of the A.B.C. rule—i.e., the damage, has occurred" (p. 345).

Although the tendency may be to think of damage solely in terms of actual physical injury, the term also applies to economic losses, emotional distress (see Shariff, 2004), and nervous shock (MacKay & Dickinson, 1998). However, no liability exists unless the damage was caused by the negligent act or omission of the defendant (Fridman, 1990).

> Aside from the judicial requirement of damages, there is a practical economic component. Litigation is an expensive process, and there is no point in pursuing a court action in cases where the recovery would be so minimal that the legal fees would not be covered. Even if litigation succeeds and a court orders the losing party to pay the winning party's costs, the amount the winning party receives rarely compensates him for more than one-third of the actual costs incurred. Thus, the damages claim must be large enough to make the litigation worthwhile. (MacKay & Sutherland, 2006, p. 6)

A practical implication of this for schools is that minor injuries, even if caused by educator negligence, are unlikely to result in litigation (MacKay & Sutherland).

Negligence cases involving school board employees often result in courts finding the respective boards liable according to the doctrine of vicarious liability, which originated in the law of master and servant. "We speak of vicarious liability when the law holds one person responsible for the misconduct of another, although he is himself free from blameworthiness or fault" (Fleming, 1998, p. 409). In the majority of cases, the school board is the primary defendant because it has a responsibility for the acts of its employees committed during the course of their employment and is in the best position to compensate victims financially (MacKay & Flood, 2001).

Insurance purchased by boards of education serve to underwrite liability awards incurred as a result of lawsuits. According to s. 170(1), par. 9 of the Ontario *Education Act*, boards must

> make provision for insuring adequately the buildings and equipment of the board and for insuring the board and its employees and volunteers who are assigned duties by the principal against claims in respect of accidents incurred by pupils while under the jurisdiction or supervision of the board.

Consequently, educators are usually insulated from the financial repercussions that may arise because of their actions. However,

> a teacher, even if not financially responsible for the case, will still be sued as a defendant and thus will be subject to fact-finding processes before and during trial. When an accident has resulted in severe injuries to a child, it is terribly disturbing to be forced to relive the accident under scrutiny of lawyers and judges. (MacKay & Sutherland, 2006, p. 11)

Furthermore, as Shivers (1986) points out, even mere allegations of negligence can cause irreparable damage to the reputation of the defendant educator as well as his or her employer.

Legal Defences to Negligence

In a negligence suit, a defendant's primary defence will be that one or more of the three elements of negligence—duty of care, a breach of the standard of care, and damage resulting from this breach—have not been proven by the plaintiff. If this tactic proves unsuccessful, two main options remain. A claim may be defeated, partially or completely, on the grounds that the plaintiff was contributorily negligent, or that he or she voluntarily assumed the risk of injury. As Russo (2006) points out, these defences recognize that even though a duty of care is owed to students by school employees, they cannot be held accountable for every harm that may occur.

Contributory Negligence

Contributory negligence "rests on the theory that, because there can be numerous parties responsible for causing an injury, including the plaintiff himself or herself, formal and meaningful apportionment of fault should occur" (Dickinson, 2006, p. 288). There are numerous cases where the principle of contributory negligence has been applied. For example, in the *Myers* case, McIntyre J. stated that there was contributory negligence on the part of [the plaintiff] in performing a difficult manoeuvre, fraught with danger, without announcing his move and without the presence of a spotter in a position to break his fall. (1977, p. 14)

If a student is deemed to have been contributorily negligent by failing to act as a reasonable person of like age, intelligence, and experience would have acted, then damages will be reduced in proportion to his or her degree of fault (Dickinson).

As Bezeau (1995) points out, rules for apportioning liability among parties to negligence suits have been enacted by all provinces. In Ontario, according to the *Negligence Act* (1990):

1 In any action for damages that is founded upon the fault or negligence of the defendant if fault or negligence is found on the part of the plaintiff that contributed to the damages, the court shall apportion the damages in proportion to the degree of fault or negligence found against the parties respectively.

2 If it is not practicable to determine the respective degree of fault or negligence as between two parties to an action, such parties shall be deemed to be equally at fault or negligent.

Even though contributory negligence is no longer a complete bar to recovery, it still remains the most common form of defence to a charge of negligence.

Voluntary Assumption of Risk

Voluntary assumption of risk, also called *volenti* as a shortened form of *volenti non fit injuria* (no injury is done to one who consents), is a complete defence to a claim of negligence. The defence of *volenti* "may arise either by an express agreement on the part of the plaintiff to assume the risk or by implication from the conduct of the parties" (MacKay, 1984, p. 153). It is important to note that for this defence to be valid, individuals must understand the risks inherent in the activity (Goodman, 1989). In addition, they must recognize that through their participation in the activity, they are assuming full legal responsibility, and in so doing, agreeing that the educator and school board will not be liable for damages, even if negligence occurs (Dickinson, 2006, p. 286).

The defence of *volenti* is often pleaded in sports injury cases. Students may be deemed to have assumed the normal risks associated with an activity such as floor hockey, but not those that are unusual or abnormal in nature. Therefore, in order for a student to legally consent to a risk, he or she must be fully apprised of the nature of that

Case Study 3: Accidents Happen?

During a warm day in September, physical educator Ram Parma opts to take his Grade six class outside for a game of softball. Ram has provided detailed instructions to his class, and all students are equipped with the necessary equipment. As the children play, Parma serves as umpire, calling balls and strikes. During one at bat, a student fouls off a pitch, and the ball ricochets, striking a female student who is sitting in the dugout. Parma rushes over, and realizes the girl has been struck in the eye, which has resulted in swelling. Parma administers emergency treatment, and in the end, the injury is only minor.

Questions for Reflection

1 Was the level of supervision provided by Ram Parma adequate?

2 What if anything could Mr Parma have done to prevent this injury?

3 What, if any, types of activities in PE require a heightened degree of supervision?

risk. This of course is problematic when young children are involved (MacKay & Dickinson, 1998).

Thus, the defence of *volenti* is difficult to sustain in cases involving children. "It would take a rather exceptional set of facts for a court to agree that a student had accepted the legal risk of injury and effectively released a board from liability" (MacKay & Dickinson, 1998, p. 89).

Risk Management: A Different Kind of Defence

Contributory negligence and voluntary assumption of risk are legally established defences to a claim alleging negligence. Both are essentially reactive measures. The best "defence" however is risk management because it is proactive and aimed at minimizing the likelihood of a mishap. "Rather than simply controlling risk by transferring it to an insurer, boards must accept responsibility for taking active steps to reduce accidents and injuries" (MacKay & Dickinson, 1998, p. 99). Ultimately, this implies that educators should take steps in their classrooms to reduce the potential for risk. While risk cannot be eliminated, it can be controlled (Robertson & Robertson, 1988).

As was pointed out, potential negligence on the part of physical educators can result in serious physical harm to students, and besides this human cost, can lead to lawsuits characterized by significant monetary awards for victims. According to MacKay and Dickinson (1998), accidents are inevitable, and even if not legally required to do so, boards would be well-advised to purchase adequate insurance to defend themselves against lawsuits for negligence. However, they go on to point out that merely compensating victims ignores the moral responsibility that boards have to protect those under their care from potential harm.

In this chapter, risk refers to a situation "when circumstances may (or importantly, may not) turn out in a way we do not wish for" (Steele, 2004, p. 6). Risk thus becomes associated with calculability, whereby decision makers—in this case, physical educators—select activities based on the inherent risks each presents. However, this evaluation should not be some haphazard undertaking, but rather, a conscientious and concerted effort to arrive at a decision that is based on all available facts, and that takes into account the costs and benefits of the activity or activities in question. Theories of risk management therefore come to the fore, and in particular, the theory of risk as a decision-making resource. The ideas grouped under this heading seek to show how

it is possible to take rational action despite lacking certain elements of knowledge. In particular, they suggest that an understanding of uncertainty structured in terms of "risk" allows us to plan our actions despite not knowing how the future will turn out. An approach using ideas of this sort is extensively applied in contemporary management and regulation, for example. But these ideas are also linked to aspects of law and legal theory because they are compatible with ideas of choice and decision-making and thus with issues of individual agency. (Steele, 2004, p. 18)

At the secondary level, team sports can present safety risks.

Academic Value of the Activity

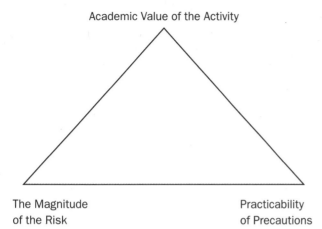

The Magnitude
of the Risk

Practicability
of Precautions

Figure 10.1: A Simplified Risk Management Model

Risk management, in its broadest sense, involves managing both physical and legal risk. "In many respects, the former can be seen as looking after the latter as the proper fulfillment of one's duty to reasonably reduce physical risk should in most instances obviate legal liability" (Dickinson, 2006, p. 288). Therefore, as Dickinson (2006) points out, in terms of PE, risk management is a merger of legal concepts and principles and best practice in the field. Ultimately, the goals are to:

- Prevent injuries
- Prevent potential lawsuits
- Prevent actual lawsuits from being successful
- Minimize the amount of damages in the case of a successful lawsuit
  (Mahoney, Forsyth, Holman, & Moriarity, 2001, p. 19)

To ensure student safety and thus minimize potential for liability, Watson (1996) recommends that the following steps be taken:

1 Risk identification
2 Risk classification
3 Development of risk control measures
4 Implementation of risk control measures
5 Monitoring and modifying of such measures

Risk identification is a physical educator's first step toward ensuring that an activity is safe. This involves careful planning on the part of the physical educator, including actively ascertaining what might potentially go wrong in terms of actual and "constructive notice" risks (Watson, 1996, p. 13). The term "actual risk" refers to those risks that any reasonable person would notice, such as injuries resulting from playing basketball on a gym floor littered with broken glass. Constructive notice is a legal concept which requires that a person recognize those risks that a

Case Study 4: A Preventable Injury?

Brian Gard has taught PE at Clarence High School for twenty-five years. Among the activities he enjoys teaching his Grade eleven boys is rugby. As a passionate advocate of the sport, Mr. Gard encourages his class to "play the game with gusto." As a result, the rugby matches in his class often involve a fair amount of physical contact. During one such match, Anton Volker is tackled head-on, hitting the turf with a thud. The impact of the hit is tremendous, and tragically, Volker is left paralyzed. Bystanders claimed that the game was far too rough; furthermore, Volker's father argued that his son should never have been allowed to participate, because he already had a pre-existing neck condition—a fact known by Mr Gard.

Questions for Reflection

1 Was the level of supervision adequate in this case?
2 How can one create a PE class where all students are included?
3 As a physical educator, what would you have done differently in this case?

professional would identify. An example would be a physical educator who allows an injured student to return to an activity in spite of signs indicating that further medical treatment is required. This dichotomy between actual and constructive notice risks mirrors, to some extent, the legal debate surrounding the "careful parent" and "reasonably skilled practitioner" standards of care.

From the above it would appear that physical educators must first and foremost exhibit a level of "withitness," a term coined by Santrock, Woloshyn, Gallagher, & Marini (2007). This is a management strategy in which educators demonstrate an overall awareness of what is happening in the classroom. By being "with it" educators are in an ideal position to anticipate potential accidents. Foresight is thus an important element of successful risk identification. Again, the linkage to the negligence concept of reasonable foreseeability is apparent.

Once the risks have been identified, a physical educator inevitably will be confronted by the dilemma that there are no activities that are completely safe. As a consequence, in order to decide on what activities will be used, educators must consider factors such as frequency of injury, potential severity of injury, cost of removing the risk, and the overall value of the activity.

In addition to risk identification and classification, steps must be taken to develop and implement risk control measures. Among the possible options are avoidance (not offering the activity); acceptance (offering the activity in spite of the risks, with the provider accepting responsibility); reduction (minimizing risks); and transference (accomplished by purchasing insurance whereby the risk is transferred to the insurance company, and through a voluntary assumption of risk by participants). If an activity is inherently dangerous, and the risks cannot be minimized, it can justifiably be eliminated (Doctor, 2005). However, as Dickinson (2006) points out, in most cases, reasonable steps can be taken to minimize risks by:

- Providing additional personnel
- Seeking the advice of specialists
- Providing adequate training to both educators and students
- Properly maintaining equipment
- Establishing clear rules
- Having contingency plans in place based on foreseeable risks

Although this list is not exhaustive, it is a starting point. As MacKay (1984, p. 107) notes, "children are highly inventive in finding ways to be injured." Therefore, a good rule of thumb in risk management for school boards and educators is to expect the unexpected.

Finally, risk management must involve the monitoring and modifying of procedures and policies, based on existing as well as emerging data (Bird & Zauhar, 1997). Risk management is not static, but rather adapts to emerging realities and demands (Elliott, 2004). This is logical, given that the classrooms of today are in a constant state of flux.

Watson's recommendations are useful for all physical educators to keep in mind. By adhering to the basic steps he recommends, one keeps student safety integral and thus the possibility for legal entanglements is minimized.

Besides the work of Watson, there are numerous other risk management systems in the literature which range from simplistic to extremely advanced. One is the simple model proposed by MacKay and Dickinson (1998, p. 100), reproduced in **Figure 10.1**.

According to this model, three broad questions must be asked before undertaking any activity which involves risk:

1 What are the risks?

2 What can be done to eliminate or reduce the risks?

3 Are the benefits worth the risks?

This schema, while remarkably simple, encapsulates the fundamental issues which physical educators need to consider when planning for and teaching a PE class. Because managing physical as well as legal risk is fundamentally important, physical educators must

take every precaution possible to prevent accidents by providing for the safety of students and other individuals who participate in physical education. If sound risk management precautions are taken, the likelihood of injury is lessened, of a lawsuit is diminished, and of negligence is minimized. (Krotee & Bucher, 2007, p. 439)

While risk management programs look straightforward on paper, implementing them usually proves more difficult (Jefferson & LaBute, 2001). In spite of this, their value is inestimable to all parties involved in education.

Risk Management and Risk Avoidance

An often-voiced objection to the tort system is that because of its attendant fear of litigation, it promotes excessive risk management or risk avoidance (see Young, 2007). Take, for example, the medical field, where "defensive medicine" operates on the basis that physicians act to avoid lawsuits (Klar, 1997). There is evidence to support this notion of excessive risk management also at play in PE. Darst and Pangrazi (2006) point out that many American physical educators and administrators have become extremely cautious and conservative in regards to activities with an element of risk. They go on to claim that some educators refuse to offer new activities for fear of being sued because of student injury.

This risk avoidance behaviour is reflected in the safety guidelines produced by the Ontario Physical and Health Education Association (Ophea). For instance, it is recommended that tackle rugby not be included in the secondary school PE curriculum. Furthermore, tackle football, various outdoor education activities, and some track and field events, specifically the pole vault, are not recommended at the secondary level (2004).

All Canadian provinces have also developed physical education safety guidelines, and it is incumbent upon physical educators to review the guidelines for their respective province. Typically, these documents describe key areas of safety including: facilities (e.g., pre-activity inspections), equipment safety (e.g., avoiding homemade equipment), instruction (modifying activities), supervision (e.g., establishing routines), and clothing and footwear (e.g., removing jewelry). The safety guidelines are helpful in providing need-to-know information related to specific activities, template letters, forms, and checklists. Physical educators should be cognizant that school districts and schools may have their own policies in addition to the guidelines provided by the province.

The Ontario School Boards' Insurance Exchange (OSBIE), whose role is to ensure member school boards against losses and to promote safe school practices, adopts a position similar to Ophea. According to its Risk Management Template, risk avoidance is the first option educators should consider.

As Spada, Simmons, Crawford, and Haynes (2004) have argued, because we live in a litigious society, liability is a major concern for those involved in the teaching of PE. In fact, in some cases, rather than risk student injury that might result from an activity with a heightened degree of danger, educators are simply choosing not to undertake the activity within their classes. This has led some to conclude that "litigation paranoia" may be robbing students of valuable educational experiences (MacKay & Dickinson, 1998).

Data collected from the 1997 British National Unit of Safety Across the Curriculum project is telling. According to this report,

> many [physical education teachers] are resorting to what are considered "negligence avoidance" strategies; simply remove the activity and you remove the risk. Comments like "Far less risky things are undertaken in the gym," "reluctance to try anything very much" and "can lead to withdrawal of some activities therefore children lose out," typify this stance. This clearly has implications for the nature of the curriculum offered to pupils. Responses generally indicated that some schools are terrified of being blamed and sued, and are withdrawing involvement in some activities, thus denying opportunities. (Raymond, 1999, pp. 94–95)

According to Brown (2009), the potential for lawsuits is a very real concern for physical educators and administrators. While fear can be positive in that it forces one to be more preventative, it can also result in educator stress, as well as in limitations to the programs offered in school. Thus, "teachers face the constant challenge of striking a reasonable balance between protecting students and giving enough rein to develop their independence and sense of risk taking" (MacKay & Dickinson, 1998, pp. 16–17).

Conclusion

The value of PE in terms of physical, mental, emotional, and social well-being is evident. The importance of daily physical activity, especially in light of increasing and alarming incidences of childhood obesity, and the health problems accompanying it, elevate the importance of PE in today's schools.

As a physical educator, you should keep in mind that student injury is always a possibility, but you should also remember that it is impossible to insulate children from all potential hazards. Certainly, caution and common sense should assist in dictating your conduct as an educator (Delaney, 2007). As well, remember that a fear of litigation should not cripple you as an educator to the point where you avoid activities that could be educationally valuable to your students. And in thinking about negligence and risk management, try to foresee potential sources of danger and reduce them, thereby preventing your students from being injured. However, if any accident were to occur in your class, always maintain detailed notes of the incident.

As a concluding thought, in the 1980s television police drama *Hill Street Blues*, Sgt. Phil Esterhaus (played by Michael Conrad) always ended roll call with that famous line "let's be careful out there." As a physical educator, remember these words, as they will serve you well in your professional practice.

Questions for Discussion

1 In terms of liability for student injury, do you believe physical educators should be held to the "careful parent" standard or that of the "skilled and competent practitioner" standard?

2 What if any impact does "litigation paranoia" hold for you as a physical educator?

3 As a physical educator, how important is risk management to your practice?

Key Terms

- Torts
- Duty of Care
- Standard of Care
- "Careful Parent" Standard
- Contributory Negligence
- Voluntary Assumption of Risk
- Risk Management
- Risk Avoidance

Critical Approaches to Pedagogy

William Harvey
(with contributions by Shawn Wilkinson
and Michael Cicchillitti)

Hope is alive, but it must be a practical and not a naïve hope. A practical hope doesn't simply celebrate rainbows, unicorns, nutbread, and niceness, but rigorously understands "what is" in relation to "what could be"—a traditional critical notion. No one will let us have our sociopolitical and educational dreams without a protracted struggle. The work is hard, and we will often be vilified for taking part in critical activity. Sometimes we will wonder whether we are the crazy ones as we sit in a crowded room as the only persons making the critical arguments discussed here. (Kincheloe, 2008a, p. x)

Overview

The purpose of this chapter is to introduce critical issues along the entire PE continuum. The term "critical" may be a bit misleading as many people understand the term as logical thinking or logical reasoning where there may an assumed and rather straightforward way of interpreting the world. In this chapter, critical thinking is explored in relation to the professionalization of PE while also providing a primer on quantitative and qualitative research methods. The term "critical" may is also linked to critical theory or pedagogy as examinations of social, cultural, and political issues that may influence our teaching practice. For example, a critical pedagogue would suggest that our pre- and in-service physical educators should be informed consumers of theory/research and practice. A discussion of research methods that outlines the research process and questions the construct of normality from a qualitative perspective, will lead to two suggestions for getting started in critical pedagogy and critical examinations of two contemporary and popular current trends in Canadian PE (i.e., improved cognition through physical activity and discourse surrounding the physical literacy movements).

Physical educators can benefit from cultivating a wide variety of skills.

Introduction

Critical approaches to pedagogy are not for the faint of heart. Advocates of critical pedagogy suggest schools and their associated curricula are highly political in nature. Critical pedagogues study constructs related to social justice, marginalized groups of people, inadequacies of power relationships, and various influences that impact the production of knowledge and teaching practices in schools. The exploration and understanding of relationships between schools and related social, political, cultural, and ethical discourses may enable the development of a strong system of education where our children and youth could thrive (Kincheloe, 2008a). However, forms of critical questioning may leave the impression that no one or nothing is sacrosanct.

Rather than just questioning everything for the sake of questioning (O'Sullivan, Siedentop & Locke, 1992), critical pedagogues challenge the status quo and defend the ideals of democracy and the empowerment of individuals. For example, Kincheloe (2008b) champions the role of critical pedagogy and the democratic right to question the role of governments, including the US government, and their influence on the knowledge produced in, and used for, education. He suggests that ethical, ideological, and pedagogical knowledge construction be explored and changed, where and when necessary, to develop understandings between all people and promote world peace and harmony.

The contexts of pedagogical research and practice are vital to understand as professionals will be expected to hold

their own personal values and experiences that will shape their perceptions and explanations for the functioning of schools and their environments. For example, it is important to understand the personal and professional positioning of the author, who has written this book chapter, because his lived experiences will shape the interpretations of critical pedagogy and how it is viewed and, hopefully, incorporated. Thus, this chapter is being written from the perspective of a university professor who has taught physical education (PE) methods in physical education teacher education (PETE) pedagogy at McGill University for the past seven years. During the past ten years as a researcher, he listened carefully to the people with disabilities and physical educators who participated in his research studies. Further, he was molded by his experiences as a former adapted physical educator who taught PE and devised physical activity programs for children, adolescents, and adults with mental health problems during a twelve-year teaching career at the Douglas Mental Health University Institute (DMHUI) in Montreal, Quebec. Finally, his research and practice have been shaped by his perceptions of growing up, and continuing to live, in the inner city where crime rates and the marginalization of the poor often run rampant. Thus, his professional teaching knowledge and practice has intersected education, health, medical, and social domains.

More physical educators need to make a conscious effort to incorporate critical thinking and critical pedagogy into their professional practice for the future of our profession. Wright (2004) describes how the world has been experiencing profound changes in technology, knowledge, culture, and society. Her descriptions of the influences of these four factors on education and school-based change are insightful because she mentions how technological change enables the transmission of knowledge over all parts of the world and associated cultures. For example, whatever happens at the other end of the earth (e.g., Australia or New Zealand) can become instant news over electronic superhighways. The Internet and computer usage has done much to speed up the transmission of information and news, create huge warehouses of research knowledge, and drive recent social changes through social media campaigns. Wright (2004) further questions how knowledge is constructed and whether it may be fluid rather than crystallized. In other words, knowledge may not be fixed but rather may change over time and across contexts. Finally, she mentions the social diversity that has portrayed our world for many recent years.

Young people in western countries today also live in pluralist societies formed by the increased migration of peoples from a multitude of countries and cultures. Boundaries between cultures both within and across countries are more permeable; the mixing of cultures is not seamless, but produces struggles which are inextricably linked with both structural power and the power of the particular discourses or meanings to define how particular cultural groups might be thought about and acted upon. (Wright, 2004, p. 4)

Our future professional educators, researchers, and everyday citizens need to ask good questions about the research and practice knowledge that is being generated and written. This recommended line of questioning is not meant to be bold, but to legitimately uphold our profession by asking strong questions that challenge the status quo, encourage democratic values, and defend social justice and marginalized groups within schools. For example, Kincheloe (2008a) asks some of the following questions:

What is the sociocultural role of schooling? What is the relation between this role and the dominant power blocs? How does this relationship affect the construction of the curriculum? How does a teacher resist an oppressive curriculum in an age of tight control of teachers? How do we recognize a pedagogy of social control? (p. 108)

This chapter is written from a combined critical thinking and critical pedagogy approach that will challenge the reader's main conceptions about the purpose of PE. It will require personal reflection and analysis of the political, social, and cultural influences that surround PE. This combined critical thinking and critical pedagogy approach may lead to critical engagement as the pre-service physical educator will read and discover through this chapter.

The chapter is made up of four main sections. The first provides a definition of the term critical thinking, a brief discussion of the relationship between the professionalization of PE, PETE programs, and critical thinking as well as a primer on quantitative and qualitative research methods. The constructs of objectivity and normality are also explored. The next section is an introduction to critical pedagogy and provides both a definition and guiding principles. The third section, "Critical Engagement," combines critical thinking and critical pedagogy to provide a pragmatic and relatively moderate approach to social justice issues for undergraduate students. It is an attempt to link theory/research and practice in a critically engaged manner where pre-service physical educators will be encouraged to ask reasonable questions about the critical issues which surround their teaching practices and engage in critical pedagogy. The fourth and final section looks at contemporary and popular trends in Canadian and North American PE, and explores two popular current trends in Canadian and North American PE.

Case Study 1: "You can't wear that dress to the spring dance"

Jeff is in the last days of his final pre-service physical educator teaching experience. He has given every effort that he possibly could to devote his time to the elementary school he was placed at. However, Jeff considered his supervising in-service physical educator as "old school." It was tough, day in and day out, because his supervisor challenged many of Jeff's fundamental beliefs about PE. His supervisor was simply rude, arrogant, and unprofessional.

Jeff has been included in the preparations for a spring dance for all of the children at the school. He stayed late after school to become part of this exciting dance for the children, pleased that it would encourage a healthy and active lifestyle. Both Jeff and his supervisor were sitting in the gym at the end of the day when Susie, a grade two student, posed a few questions to Jeff about the dance. She was concerned about the starting time of the event and also asked if she could wear the new dress she was wearing to the spring dance. Before Jeff had a chance to respond, the supervisor let out a big laugh and exclaimed, "You can't wear that dress to the dance, you're too fat." Suzie ran away with tears running down her face. Jeff was furious and ran after Susie to console her.

Questions for Reflection

1 How should Jeff deal with this situation?

2 Why would an educator demean a student in this way?

3 What should be done to assist this girl after such a denigrating event?

Critical Thinking

Wright suggests that critical thinking may be conceptualized as "logical reasoning where attention is directed to problem-solving, reasoning and higher order thinking skills" (2004, p. 6). She suggests that critical thinking is about knowing when, where, and how to question something. It is a logical process of asking questions to acquire information. However, Wright further suggests that "the emphasis, however, remains on the process, that is the teaching and learning of thinking skills, rather than on what kind of knowledge is questioned" (p. 7).

Yet what kinds of knowledge are applicable in education and PE? Epistemology is the philosophy and nature of knowledge construction where knowledge is considered as being socially constructed (Bredo, 2006; Kincheloe, 2008b). Cognitive psychology has been highly influential with epistemology in education and PE circles (Wall, Reid, & Harvey, 2007). Wright's reference to knowledge would likely be known as declarative knowledge which would be related to the content being taught in a PE unit and class (Wall et al., 2007). For example, content knowledge would be of the activity or game being taught (skills, tactics, rules, etc.).

However, declarative knowledge would not cover how and when to teach content in PE. Procedural knowledge would include how to perform the content being taught (e.g., the actual production of a skill, strategy, or any other physical action). Metacognitive skills, also known as conditional knowledge, would include knowing when and where to apply strategies in activities and games (Wall et al., 2007). This last category is similar to pedagogical content knowledge where educator knowledge is combined for planning and strategic instructional purposes (Griffin, Dodds, & Rovegno, 1996; Schempp, Manross, Tan, & Fincher, 1998; Shulman, 1986). Clearly, there is much more to know about knowledge than one might expect.

A crucial link between critical thinking and knowledge construction lies in the development of physical educator expertise and PE program delivery. Rink (2009) suggests the PE profession is characterized by extensive preparation, a high level of public trust, accountability from within the profession, and freedom from direct supervision. She highlighted the need to create defensible PE programs where student outcomes are emphasized, and assessment guides instructional processes in order to address a perceived historic

As an physical educator, you can create opportunities for your students to work on their critical thinking skills.

lack of accountability in PE programs. The implication is that physical educators are expected to be responsible to students, parents, and school boards where public funding (e.g., taxes) is used to finance the education system and related high stakes assessment and decisions. It seems reasonable that Rink would make the case for a defensible PE program given that the subject is often criticized for lacking clear student outcomes (see Pate, O'Neill, & McIver, 2011). However, can we expect all physical educators to be critical thinkers? Do university or PETE programs teach or encourage pre-service physical educators to be critical thinkers? While Bouffard and Strean state that "critical thinking is about judging using standards" (2003, p. 5), they also suggest that many, if not all, university programs do not teach critical thinking whatsoever.

This chapter is an opportunity to address this point and a perceived lack of teaching about critical thinking may lead to some of the challenges that many physical educators may experience in the field. For example, Rink (2009) clearly identifies planning, assessment, and evaluation as key issues to consider in the delivery of accountable and defensible PE programs. Rink further identifies the three areas as being major challenges for physical educators to perform as they may not necessarily observe the value in performing these main instructional functions. Thus, there are disconnects between theory and practice. A major strength of Rink's text is the research that supports her writing. While academics may realize the importance of this point, would pre- and/or in-service physical educators realize or care about this important research support? If not, why would an educator link theory and teaching practice? This last point is important to understand because, as pre- and in-service physical educators, we may undervalue links between research and practice. For example, new physical educators may perceive many more difficulties in their professional work duties than experienced PE professionals (Macdonald, 1995, 1999). Yet, these initial challenges may be partly explained by pre-service physical educators who suggest they may only incorporate part of what they learn in PETE programs into their teaching practices (Matanin & Collier, 2003). Both pre- and in-service physical educators should be critical thinkers about research if they claim to support their teaching practices or outcomes by mention of any type of research. It is also logical to expect that educators should be well-informed about the art and science of research if they are going to criticize the process and products of research or disregard study results. Thus, a primer on the research process will provide rationale for the importance of research in teaching, and link back to the importance of individual differences in learning and education.

A Research Primer

The scientific method drives how many research studies are conducted. Is teaching a science? Rink (2009) claims that teaching is both building one's profession, or craft, and a science.

There is little doubt that science underlies much of what educators do in PE. For example, there is a fair amount of research literature on many aspects of PE (Kirk et al., 2006), including specific physical educator knowledge, beliefs, and practices (Tsangaridou, 2006a, 2006b), as well as hallmark research data to support the benefits of physical activity for people of all ages (US Department of Health and Human Services, 1996). Thus, it is important both to understand how researchers perform their job and to gain respect for the challenging work that they do. Furthermore, evidence-based teaching practice may allow a teaching program to be defensible and demonstrate the value and credibility of your PE program to parents and school board representatives.

Bee, Boyd, and Johnson (2006) identify the eight interrelated components involved in the research process.

First, researchers **recognize the problem** area(s) that they are interested in. For example, the research program of Harvey (2007, 2009) revolves around self-determination and self-regulation. These constructs are studied by engaging people with attention-deficit hyperactivity disorder (ADHD) because they are often assumed to not self-regulate and more can be learned about self-regulation as a result (see Harvey et al., 2007 & Harvey et al., 2009). Thus, researchers use theories as a framework or lens to view, understand, and attempt to predict outcomes related to their phenomenon of interest.

Second, researchers **define the specific problem** because they develop a general research question about their phenomena of interest. For example, one of Harvey's main research questions is: Why are the movement skills of children with ADHD poor in comparison to their peers without ADHD?

Third, researchers **formulate hypotheses**, which are a specific question(s) purposefully made to help answer the specific problem. For example, Harvey et al. (2007) make the following hypothesis: The fundamental movement skills of children without ADHD will be significantly better than the movement skills of children with ADHD on the Test of Gross Motor Development-2, or TGMD-2 (Ulrich, 2000). The results prove the hypothesis to be true. This finding has enabled a better understanding of the movement skills of children with ADHD and the ability to ask more questions related to the general research question (Harvey et al., 2007).

Case Study 2: "Get out of my class"

You have just met your first professor in PE pedagogy and she has challenged you to write a paper about your views concerning the future of PE. Dr. Black gave her first lecture that seemed to have a very negative tone about it. She wants our profession to give more, to stand up for all students, and to pour all of your energy and caring into being the best educator that you can be. However, she also has noted that the profession seems to be in trouble. We have physical educators who are just going through the paces and rolling out the balls to play.

Dr. Black states that she is sick and tired of physical educators who complain that no one respects them. She wants to change the approach to her PE Teacher Education program. The main purpose of your paper is to identify your social and political views about PE and physical activity. One of your peers stands up in class and demands that the professor retract the assignment, as she does not believe that her social and political views should be the subject of an assignment. Dr. Black ejects her from class and there is a hush that runs over the classroom. The student reports back to the department chair because she feels the assignment and the professor are out of line.

Questions for Reflection

1 Make an argument for and against the identification of your social and political views to your PE pedagogy professor.

2 Pretend that you are Dr. Black and make a case for your assignment. How would you go about defending the assignment and your professional behaviours?

Fourth, researchers **construct a research design** to run their study or series of studies. Essentially, the research design is like the framework of a house where all the key components and plans are laid for a solid construction. Undergraduate motor development or research methods courses usually review the following list of components in research design: cross-sectional, longitudinal, and sequential designs; case study, applied behaviour analysis, true experimental and quasi-experimental designs; independent and dependent variables; participants, experimental, and control groups; and correlation.

Bee et al. (2006) also describe how challenging the fifth component of the research process, **data collection**, may be. It sounds like such a simple thing to do: Go out and collect data for the study. However, it is one of the most challenging and meticulous tasks that a researcher must do very, very well. For example, Bee et al. suggest that researchers must adhere to test administration and research protocols provided in testing manuals. They also point out that data collection usually occurs within set time periods (e.g., days, times) and no matter what the size of the study, it takes much administrative effort and planning to keep all of the information organized and stored safely so others may not access this confidential information. The information gained from data collection is then placed into a standard order for analysis. For instance, Bee et al. describe how researchers input data into computer programs or house visually-based research data into portfolios.

The sixth component of the research process is called **research ethics**, which is a vital part of the researcher's job and civic responsibilities. Bee et al. (2006) clearly stated that ethics approval for research with animals and human participants must pass before and be approved, in writing, by a university Research Ethics Board (REB). Researchers must ensure that study participants are:

- Protected from any harm
- Provided informed consent
- Provided with the right to withdraw from the study at any time and for any reason
- Provided the right to confidentiality
- Provided a written summary of results
- Informed as soon as possible about any deception that may be included as part of the research design

REB approval must be obtained before any research can be conducted and there are serious implications for researchers who break this vital part of the research process. Penalties can be anything from having research funds suspended to being fired from one's academic position.

The seventh component of the research process is **data analysis**, which includes hypothesis testing. Analysis helps to answer the hypotheses and shed more light on the research question. How a researcher analyses her or his data really depends on the analytic approach and the underlying philosophy that accompanies it. Normality and objectivity are two of the fundamental notions of research and one of the main departure points for post-modern scholars who use qualitative analytical approaches in their research process (Sparkes, 2002). A quantitative analytical approach usually suggests that inferential statistics are used. Inferential statistics are usually performed on larger data sets (e.g., those with a sample size of twenty-five or more participants) to allow the analyzed data to be compared across similar populations and provide the ability to make inferences about the phenomenon of interest. For example, the central limit theorem suggests a rule of thumb that scores of twenty-five to thirty or more participants generally distribute equally around a mean with a predictable standard deviation (Glass & Hopkins, 1984; Stevens, 1996). Thus, the larger the sample size, the better and the greater the power to predict and improve the ability to generalize the study results. Most students will understand this concept of normality to be linked to the regular distribution or bell curve. It is a concern that researchers and students alike may understand the term "normal" to mean everyone in society or not to be aberrant. The distribution is normal onto itself because the amounts of numbers are expected

Keeping up-to-date on PE research can help make you a better educator.

to vary this way. Clearly, the notion of normality is not well understood as it usually refers to the sample population being considered and it is not always reflective of the entire population. Sometimes, non-inferential statistics may also be performed on smaller data sets (e.g., sample sizes of six or fewer participants) but the results are usually not generalizeable to other populations besides the same sample used for the study (e.g., single-subject designs, applied behaviour analysis).

There is also the notion of individual differences where a person's test score or performance does not fit the results of a statistical analysis. It may be that some feature or characteristic of the person does not fit the sampling distribution tested and, as a result, this person may not be expected to perform in a similar fashion as others. Large individual differences have often been referred to as outliers in statistical terms and excluded from subsequent analyses (Glass & Hopkins, 1984; Stevens, 1996). However, Bouffard (1993) raised concerns about the phenomenon of individual differences when he suggested that there may be little to no transfer of an average group effect to individual performance. In fact, he claimed the existence of a person by treatment interaction (PTI) because individuals may be expected to react differently than groups of people to the same treatment intervention. Several other authors have also warned against the dangers of generalizing group data to individual performance (Bouffard, 1993; Bouffard & Reid, 2012; Reid, Bouffard, & MacDonald, 2012). This warning is important to understand as there is a continuum of different types of research that are either far-removed from the practical setting (e.g., basic research), or directly situated in the practical setting (Thomas, Nelson, & Silverman, 2010). To complicate matters more, there are studies that may be performed at the population, group, and individual levels (Thomas et al., 2010). Thus, researchers and educators should be aware of the type(s) and level(s) of research studies that are being cited in relation to appropriateness of the generalization(s) that are being inferred. For instance, the generalizeability of qualitative studies has been questioned because study findings provide the ability to make inferences to the research setting only (Creswell, 2007; Thomas et al., 2010). While the results of large, evidence-based studies are often considered the gold standard to make inferences to larger populations (Thomas et al., 2010), the issue of a PTI has not been well understood by many in the scientific community (Bouffard, 1993; Bouffard & Reid, 2012; Reid et al., 2012). Thus, interpretations of large studies that infer results to individual levels must be made with caution. In other words, educators must question if they observe the effects of a recommended intervention with their students rather than just accepting the sweeping and broad inferences often made through the large studies. These points clearly reinforce Tinning's

(2002) suggestion that individual differences are recognized as a basic educational principle. Clearly, one-size-fits-all instruction does not seem to work for all students and educational interventions need to be individualized or placed within small group instruction and tutorials if they are to be effective for all learners (Gredler, 1997; Reid et al., 2012).

Many scholars who claim to be quantitative researchers hold firm to the idea that people are highly subjective and not objective. Thomas, Nelson, and Silverman (2011) wrote a primer on the scientific method, which introduced the reader to the age-old discussion about the ills of subjectivity and varying forms of subjective knowledge. Scientists have traditionally claimed that they are objective because they set up external procedures to ensure the objectivity and reliability of their research (Thomas et al., 2011). The research is deemed credible because other people (e.g., researchers) physically verify the validity and reliability of the research. This objective verification may be referred to as a form of positivism because something must be concrete and tangible in order to exist (Bredo, 2006). For example, if you cannot prove that the phenomenon of interest is concrete, then it does not exist. Emotions are a good example of phenomena that scientists have difficulty measuring and explaining. Further, science tends to reduce complex phenomena into smaller chunks for people to better understand "the truth," and this reductionism may be touted as necessary by most scientists.

On the other hand, many qualitative researchers claim that there are multiple truths and they do not seek to find a single truth (Bredo, 2006). They believe firmly that the individual's voice is vital to understand within a variety of contexts. One could say that they celebrate the subjectivity of human beings and value experience as a central essence to life. These researchers use a variety of qualitative research approaches (e.g., narrative, phenomenological, grounded theory, ethnographic, and case study approaches (Creswell, 2007)) to provide a voice to marginalized groups. Other researchers use mixed-methods research designs to answer their research questions. This approach is relatively new in physical activity research and may not be appreciated by quantitative or qualitative researchers (See Thomas et al., 2011 for a review of all three research approaches).

The eighth and final component of the research process is to **draw conclusions**. Conclusions are always linked back to hypotheses and the general research question about the phenomena of interest. The researcher then makes links back to the appropriate literature to place her or his findings in context. Good research usually produces more questions than answers. Clearly, there is a logical reasoning process that underlies the research process for both quantitative and qualitative researchers. These people are attempting to understand the world better and, if researchers and

educators are open-minded, perhaps we can start to build a mutual conversation to create better teaching and research practices. However, the relationship between research and practice has not always proven to be an easy one to navigate.

Critical Pedagogy

Critical pedagogy is an approach where social, cultural, and political justice issues are examined in relation to teaching practices. It has also been described in the following manner: "Proponents of this approach are primarily interested in assisting students to examine and challenge the status quo, the dominant constructions of reality, and the power relations that produce inequalities, in ways that can lead to advocacy and community action" (Wright, 2004, p. 7). Furthermore, Muros Ruiz and Fernández-Balboa (2005) identify the following five principles of critical pedagogy.

1 People's vocation is to become fully human.

2 Humans are not predetermined, and hence they can change their condition.

3 Hope, freedom, love, and solidarity are necessary conditions for becoming fully human.

4 Humanization requires being with the world (not just in the world) ethically and responsibly. By contrast, domination is found in the "culture of silence," in which people can neither name nor invent the world.

5 Humanization stems from "conscientização"—a constant process of becoming aware of both the conditions that limit people's humanization and the possibilities of transcending these conditions. Conscientização, in turn, emerges from praxis—a perceptual reflective effort to link theory and practice in a cyclical way. (p. 244)

Traditionally, it is doubtful that many PETE programs would highlight the fact that teaching could be considered a political act and related to social justice. Dr. Joe Kincheloe, a leader in the critical pedagogy movement, suggests that all education is inherently political (Kincheloe, 2008a). He clearly states that educators need to be aware of the political, social, and cultural landscapes that surround them and marginalized groups of people in schools. This awareness leads to action to promote social justice and adopt a vision of education that is based on justice and equality (Kincheloe, 2008a). For example, Macdonald (1995) explored the working lives of new physical educators in Australia. The rationale for this study was an exploration of the high drop-out rates of physical educators in the first five years post graduation from university.

Macdonald suggested these educators were being marginalized, deskilled, and disempowered because they were toiling under tremendous workloads, with little opportunity to conceive how their instructional and coaching programs would unfold, or to make higher level program decisions. Macdonald interviewed twenty-two in-service physical educators, eleven women and eleven men with fewer than two years of experience, and found that more than 50% of interviewees were already planning to leave the PE profession. Their lived experiences relayed stories of:

■ Reduced professional status among other teaching professionals

■ PE as a break from the real work of schools

■ Lack of accountability in PE

■ Boredom after teaching similar material over the course of a year

■ Heavy administrative work in carnivals and coaching

■ Disempowerment through the power structures of schools where constant observation of physical educator work performance was perceived to lead to a lack of decision making

■ Disappointment from senior PE colleagues' behaviours that could be considered peer pressure to lower their professional standards or sexual discrimination that was reported but not acted upon by principals.

This study is a classic example of critical pedagogy that should catch the attention of pre-service physical educators because it identifies the challenging personal and professional career choice that they are about to embark on. Perhaps being forewarned allows them to be forearmed for the challenges and prepared to deal with adversity in the workplace. While this study focused on physical educators, usually there are more traditional at-risk groups of people who are identified as being marginalized. For example, these groups may include, but are not limited to, people with disabilities, students from economically disadvantaged areas, First Nations and Aboriginal communities, and people who have cultural, sexual, and gender differences in comparison to people from traditional white, middle to upper class backgrounds and communities.

Muros Ruiz and Fernández-Balboa (2005) suggest that critical pedagogy is quite a challenging endeavour for university professors to teach as well as for university students to understand and adopt into their repertoire of skills. They caution that pre-service physical educators should be provided with more than just simple exposure to critical pedagogy without being provided the means to defend themselves in the rough and tumble real world of education. Two concrete steps are provided to assist the pre-service physical educator with an initial understanding of critical pedagogy. First, pre- and in-service physical educators

Case Study 3: "Just let them bring their damned running shoes to school!"

It is your first day of student teaching and you are excited to see so many young and excited children running around the school yard. Your student teaching partner, Mr. Phelps, has also been observing the students attentively. However, for some reason, he does not seem to share your perceptions of the children in this lower socioeconomic area. He doesn't seem to be smiling and is not as excited as you are to get the day started.

You enjoy a full day of student teaching and meet afterwards with Mr. Phelps to reflect and discuss your experiences. Your morning assessment of him was correct. His every word and sentence about the children are negative. You are amazed when he goes off on a rant. He suggests that he could predict poor social skills and sedentary behaviours of the students because their parents sent them to school in second-rate clothes. You defend the students and their parents by saying that these poor working folks are trying their best to provide everything that they can for their children and, really, there were not many behaviour problems in the class. You had heard that the average Canadian works, on average, ten more hours per week than they did thirty years ago. You exclaim, "Can't we just treat people like people and encourage them to be active and healthy?" You are floored by your partner's response: "Just let them bring their damned running shoes to school."

Questions for Reflection

1 Why do you think your teaching partner acted like he did?

2 How will you approach your teaching partner in the future and why?

3 How will this discussion and your knowledge of the children's poor family income levels influence your teaching strategies?

should identify their own personal and professional positioning because their unique values and experiences will also shape their perceptions and explanations for the functioning of schools and associated environments.

The following questions will help the reader to perform this vital positioning exercise:

- How would you describe your cultural background?
- How does your culture value education? Social rights?
- How does religion affect your cultural beliefs and daily actions?
- What expectations do you have about the community that you live in?
- How do you believe that people are socialized within their cities?
- How do children form friendships?
- Where do they play and with whom?
- What are your political beliefs?
- Are you a conservative, liberal, or libertarian thinker?
- What political parties and leaders do you vote for and why?
- What types of financial, social, and community implications may your political choices lead to for yourself and others?
- How do your political beliefs influence your teaching practices and treatment of students, parents, and colleagues?

Next, visit and explore the case studies in this chapter after completing the exercise of personal and professional positioning. The case studies represent a concrete introduction to critical pedagogy. Ask the following questions when starting each case study.

- Which group may be marginalized? Why?
- What person or group may stand to benefit from the perceived social injustice?
- What are the political, social, and/or cultural issues that need to be identified and addressed?
- What does the associated research indicate and how well does it match or not match the current issues being explored?
- How could the issue be solved? How is my own unique positioning affecting my perceptions of the particular case studies?

Critical Engagement

Tinning (2002) questions how pre-service educators are taught critical pedagogy and suggests that universities are not really preparing these young professionals for an uncertain world. He speaks about creating a "modest pedagogy" where educators develop more modest forms of pedagogy that utilize a critical approach but are open to various solutions.

Perhaps this task can be accomplished by combining critical thinking and critical pedagogy so our physical educators are critically engaged. Wright describes critical engagement as the "capacity to speak up, to negotiate, and to be able to critically engage with the conditions of their working lives" (New London Group, 1996 as cited by Wright, 2004). Tinning further notes that many physical educators of the 1970s and '80s were not taught about the ideas linked to critical pedagogy (e.g., self-determination, ideology, emancipation). A critically engaged approach will enable our young professionals to become more aware of the critical issues in PE. The key will be to ask reasonable and respectful questions about critical issues to both educators and researchers alike. Yet we also must be more skeptical and less utopian as Tinning suggests.

Why would physical educators be required to problem solve if they believed that no problems or issues exist in their teaching? If this reasoning is extended, perhaps PE is in a seemingly constant state of disarray because few physical educators seem to use higher order thinking, or metacognition, and critical pedagogy in their teaching practices. PE continues to be questioned from the perspectives of physical activity and health outcomes (Pate, O'Neill & McIver, 2011). Fortunately, while questioning the outcomes of PE, forward-minded thinkers have included PE as part of the physical activity policy agenda (Woods & Mutrie, 2012). Clearly, physical educators and PETE programs need to step up their teaching and research game to maintain the benefits gained by students and the survival of the PE profession.

Our professional discourse needs to advance from being marginalized in the school curriculum and being blamed for not addressing the increasing epidemic of physical inactivity despite having a reduced role in the lives of children as service providers (Woods & Mutrie, 2012), to becoming the best teaching and research professionals that our country has to offer. Our profession should be asking pointed questions to many provincial, national, and international stakeholders who claim to know the purpose of our profession.

Critical Reflections

A critical perspective is needed so we may become better educators and researchers as well as make better links between teaching and research for the benefit of our major stakeholders—our children and youth! What are the areas of PE that require a critical questioning? Traditionally, critical pedagogy has focused on social justice and marginalized groups. Major discussions usually centre around issues related to sexuality, gender, religious considerations, cultural studies, etc. (Kincheloe, 2008a).

Since some of these discussions have occurred in other parts of the text, two other subjects have been chosen here for critical reflection because they have been in the PE spotlight for the past few years.

Cognition and Physical Activity—Critical Reflections

Dr. Stephen Norris was the keynote speaker at the National Conference for PHE Canada in May 2012 (Norris, 2012). His speech emphasized that physical educators need to drive change because physiologists have failed to cry out to politicians and the public about the benefits of PE and physical activity for the health, welfare, and education of our children. He suggested that children are being marginalized, and that they will benefit from PE and physical activity programs, especially in health, brain functioning, and academic achievement. Longitudinal research has long demonstrated that participation in PE will lead to improved, non-significant trends in test scores, and no deleterious effects on other subject area test scores (Shephard, Lavallée, Volle, LaBarre, & Beaucage, 1994). Dr. Norris stated in his keynote address that the debate in Canadian PE should start with the book, *SPARK: The Revolutionary New Science of Exercise and the Brain* (Ratey, 2008).

Physical educators and physical activity professionals, among others (including Aristotle and Plato), have long known that physical activity is vital to the functioning of the human body and mind. These professionals relied on their intuition about the beneficial effects of physical activity programs, which include physical exercise programs, until the release of the US Surgeon General's report on physical activity and health (US Department of Health and Human Services, 1996).

SPARK (Ratey, 2008) should be applauded for informing the general public about the beneficial effects of exercise on brain functioning (e.g., increased brain-derived neurotropic factor, increased volume of hippocampus, etc.). Further, a recent meta-analysis suggests that there are small and significant effects of acute exercise on cognition (Chang, Labban, Gapin & Etnier, 2012).

However, improved brain functioning through physical activity does not automatically guarantee improved cognition, nor does it recognize the valuable contributions of a great educator on the learning outcomes of students. Hence, the debate in Canadian PE should start with the effects of physical activity on the global health and welfare of our children and youth as has been clearly known for the past twenty years. Serious consideration must be given to the recommendations of McKenzie (2007) who suggests that physical educators need to have a public health policy edge to their educator training, where PE may be revised to play a significant role in disease prevention, health promotion, and physical activity service delivery.

Pre- and in-service physical educators need to know how to read and evaluate texts that offer reductionist answers to complex problems. For example, while it is, wholeheartedly, agreed that children with ADHD should exercise daily, physical activity research worldwide would seem not to support at least three major claims made in the SPARK chapter devoted to ADHD.

First, the author claims that children with ADHD end up playing sports and doing well (Ratey, 2008, p. 146). According to available research knowledge on physical activity and children with ADHD, this claim is unfounded as there are currently few to no research studies to support the statement. In fact, approximately 30–50% of children with ADHD may also have developmental coordination disorder (DCD) (Sergeant, Piek, & Oosterlaan, 2006). In other words, a large percentage of children with ADHD are physically awkward and experience tremendous difficulties when performing human movements. A critical perspective would suggest that these children would be set up for public failure because they would be expected to perform well on the basis of a stereotype. Public failure in PE and physical activity must be understood as potentially debilitating for any person to experience.

Second, many children with ADHD will experience failure when performing the types of recommended activities. While there is disconnectedness with the physical activity research literature, mothers were also marginalized with the following passage that implied they may not like their children to engage in high-risk activities: "Less traditional sports, such as rock climbing, mountain biking, whitewater paddling, and sorry to tell you, Mom—skateboarding are also effective in the sense that they require complex movements in the midst of heavy exertion" (p. 148).

Complex movements are problematic for people with DCD so it is doubtful that the technical movements involved in the identified sports would, indeed, activate a vast array of brain areas. If children with ADHD have problems doing the movements, then the hypothesis is likely incorrect because they would not perform the movements at all or sparingly. Brossard-Racine et al. (2011) performed a literature review which suggested that cortical activation dysregulation, cerebellar dysfunction, or delayed white matter maturation were hypothesized neurobiological mechanisms for the poor movement skills of children with ADHD. They cautioned that motor skill assessments and neuroimaging techniques should be better linked together before confirmation of any specific neural claims are made.

Third there was a claim that children with ADHD have less body fat (Ratey, 2008). There was discordance in the literature about the relationship between ADHD and obesity by the year 2007. Some articles suggest that children with ADHD were also obese (e.g., Holtkamp et al., 2004; Hubel et al., 2006; Tantillo et al., 2002) while others stated the opposite (e.g., Curtin et al., 2005; Wigal et al., 2003). This disagreement still exists in the research literature today.

Another related example where the research evidence may not full support the conclusions is a text called *Perceptual-Motor Activities for Children: An Evidence-Based Guide to Building Physical and Cognitive Skills* (Johnstone & Ramon, 2011). No research studies were cited in the bibliography of Johnston and Ramon's text which claims to build cognition through physical activities.

The point is that these texts, like many others, offer important insights on why physical activity should be promoted more in schools. They are very important works, but a critical perspective is always required. All that is written need not be taken as absolute truth. All works need to be read with a critical eye.

Lately, the words of Kincheloe have been ringing loud and clear: "As I tell all my students, whenever individuals tell me they are providing me with the objective truth I guard my wallet" (2008a, p. 5).

The Physical Literacy Movement—Critical Reflections

Our second example of critical reflection focuses on the physical literacy movement. Physical educators will be aware of the discourse that surrounds the physical literacy movement. But is there a hidden agenda here? For example, one university professor first became aware of the term in 2007 when teaching third year students in an undergraduate PE pedagogy class. There was a group assignment to research a major issue related to PE (e.g., academic achievement, gender, metacognition, student beliefs, educator beliefs, educator knowledge). Each group was expected to:

1 Identify and discuss the major issues related to each topic in general education.

2 Identify and discuss the major issues related to each topic in PE.

3 Describe the research methods used and discuss the findings of two PE studies on the topic area. They were also expected to discuss the strengths and weaknesses of each research study.

4 Identify and discuss the implications of this research on their teaching practice.

5 Perform a twenty-five-minute group presentation on their topic.

Case Study 4: "I'm willing to listen!"

Mr. Singh is a physical educator at your local elementary school. He is very upset by the C grade that PE received in the *Active, Healthy Kids Canada Report Card* (Active Healthy Kids Canada, 2012). Based on this information, Mr. Singh approaches the school principal and demands that more schedule time be provided immediately so PE can be delivered on a daily basis.

The principal, Ms. Appleby, listens attentively to Mr. Singh's demands. She informs Mr. Singh that there is nothing that she can currently do to change the situation. However, she is willing to listen and receive recommendations and an action list to support schedule changes over time. Mr. Singh leaves the principal's office dejected and unmotivated to work.

Questions for Reflection

1 Do you think both professionals acted in an appropriate fashion?

2 How could Mr. Singh and Ms. Appleby become partners to solve his perceived problem?

3 What types of critical questions would you pose if you were in the shoes of Mr. Singh? Ms. Appleby?

4 What potential solutions would you propose to them?

6 Write a seven to ten page paper that discusses the implications of the research on teaching in PE.

Physical literacy was included as a topic for this assignment and two pre-service physical educators took up the challenge. The results of literature searches were surprising.

Despite the existence of major physical literacy movements in the United Kingdom and Canada, there was found to be very few research studies had been performed. In fact, the two undergraduate physical educators (to their credit) emailed Dr. Margaret Whitehead, the creator of the physical literacy model (Whitehead, 2001), to ask her how many research studies had been done in physical literacy. Her reply was incredible because she deemed that only one study had been performed to date. How could two to three national advocacy movements be created when there appeared to be such limited data to support the notion of physical literacy?

This prompts the question: What is the definition of physical literacy? This is the question that a critically-engaged pedagogue and researcher should ask.

Many provincial and national organizations are promoting this concept. Definitions and frameworks are being advanced by national organizations. For example, Higgs (2010) suggests the term could be utilized for a variety of reasons, such as the obesity crisis that is facing not only our nation but many nations worldwide. He further alludes to the political nature of the term:

> Governments understand the concepts of literacy. One needs to learn to read as a child in order to become a fully functioning member of society; through the use of the term physical literacy, many stakeholders have come to understand that children and youth need a repertoire of physical skills, or "physical literacy"—that will enable them to become physically active, and therefore healthier, adults. (2010, p. 7).

We must ask the following critical questions:

- What is the concept or construct of physical literacy?
- If the definitions keep changing with the winds of the politicians, then is physical literacy really a concept?
- Do governments really understand what is meant by literacy?
- How can a marginalized group of people who are physically illiterate be identified?
- Physical eduators, kinesiologists, coaches, and recreation professionals also need to ask how they are expected to achieve physical literacy when its definition and measurement change rapidly over time?
- Will this lack of clarity further reduce the professional status of physical educators when they cannot clearly

Case Study 5: "Tell me my child will grow up to attend university"

Mr. Fit is a physical educator with five years' of teaching experience at the elementary school level and he loves to do his job each and every day. He is reading popular books that have confirmed what he knew all along. Exercise will fundamentally change the brain, improve thinking, and increase test scores for all of his students. Mr. Fit has even convinced the school principal to buy treadmills and exercise bikes to place in the grade five class that has many children with behaviour problems, including children with ADHD. The school starts a ten-week physical activity program to improve test scores for this class. Mr. Fit guarantees academic success to all of the children's parents since he suggests that strong research backs up his claim.

The project has gone well by the December holiday break and about 60% of the students seem to be benefitting from the aerobic exercise program. However, there are some noticeable academic failures in class and Mr. Fit is quite concerned about parent-educator interviews. How will he explain these failures to the parents of the students? He does his homework and finds out that 5% of the failing children have been skipping school periodically. A few of the parents of the failing students, who do not skip school, show up and start to ask questions. How and why did this failure happen with their child? Mr. Fit suggests that there may be many reasons why improvements did not occur for their children but he and the students will redouble their efforts. One father is early for his interview with Mr. Fit and he confronts him, brushing his tears to one side, and says, "Tell me my child will grow up to attend university."

Questions for Reflection

1 What types of information would you prepare for parent-educator interviews?

2 Do you believe the parents of the failing students are entitled to an explanation?

3 How would you respond to this concerned parent?

measure and account for physical literacy to government and social policy makers?

- Will the term encourage a discussion to link sport and PE?
- What are the funding implications for these organizations, communities, schools, students, and their families?

Much of the information about physical literacy (developmental stage theories, motor patterns, traditional sports, etc.) has been taught during undergraduate PETE degrees for more than twenty years. Thus, is physical literacy really repackaging old ideas to seem like they are new ones? Is physical literacy just another attempt at getting more Canadians to the podium at the Olympics so that politicians and like-minded citizens can feel good about their competitive country? How do the majority of Canadians get supported for their lifelong physical activity opportunities? Is physical literacy being used as a medium for some of the sports and PE communities to teach traditional, hedgemonic, sporting values to children and youth? Fortunately, the Long-Term Athlete Development (LTAD) model does include people with disabilities and recreational participants (please refer to www.canadiansportforlife.ca/learn-about-canadian-sport-life/ltad-stages for more information on the LTAD model).

These and other questions can be raised in the context of a supportive but critical reflection on modern trends in physical education research and practice. For further background, readers are encouraged to examine Phillips and Roper (2006) for a good discussion about the history of PE that includes the historical struggle for political power between PE and sport.

Conclusion

This chapter introduced the concepts of critical thinking and critical pedagogy to encourage pre-service physical educators to become critically engaged. Personal and professional positioning and critically-informed viewpoints

The foundations of physical literacy can begin to be taught at a young age.

on education, health, and well-being issues will be required for all new and experienced physical educators in the field.

It is solid and critical, professional practice to question and reflect on your own instructional practices as well as those of other educators, school administrators, and researchers. All educators have a tough job but an educator's job is crucial to serving the needs of all children by providing a safe, secure, and humanizing learning environment that all human beings have the right to live in. This chapter started with a quote from the late Joe Kincheloe and it will end with a quote from him. He was a colleague and friend who exemplified the struggle and empowerment of critical pedagogy.

Nothing is impossible when we work in solidarity with love, respect, and justice as guiding lights. Indeed the great Brazilian critical educator Paulo Freire always maintained that education had as much to do with the teachable heart as it did with the mind. Love is the basis of an education that seeks justice, equality, and genius. If critical pedagogy is not injected with a healthy dose of what Freire called "radical love," then it will operate only as a shadow of what could be. Such love is compassionate, erotic, creative, sensual, and informed. Critical pedagogy uses it to increase our capacity to love, to bring the power of love to our everyday lives and social institutions, and to rethink reason in a humane and interconnected manner. (Kincheloe, 2008a, p. 3)

Questions for Discussion/Reflection

1   Why are you choosing to become a physical educator? How may your cultural, social, and political beliefs affect how you teach children?

2   Which groups of people would a critically engaged educator identify as marginalized in Canada? Why?

3   Why should a physical educator adopt a critical perspective to education?

4   Write a definition for the term hegemony and explain what this term means in everyday teaching situations.

5   Research all of the different definitions of physical literacy. What are the similarities and differences between the definitions? How do the definitions differ between countries and our own provincial and national organizations?

6   How many Canadian children and their families would not be able to pay the funds to qualify for the child sports tax credit? Why does this matter in the sense of critical pedagogy?

Key Terms

- Critical Thinking
- Critical Pedagogy
- Critical Engagement

Whole Class Assignment—A Critically Engaged Inquiry

Dr. Smith has decided to have your class explore the findings of the *Active, Healthy Kids Canada Report Card* because it just produced its seventh straight failing grade on the physical activity levels of Canadian youth for meeting recommended Canadian Guidelines for Physical Activity (Active Healthy Kids Canada, 2012). While there are a variety of sources used to create this report card, the information is usually based on surveillance at the population levels. In other words, much of the data analysis, resultant grades, and inferences are derived from epidemiological or population level studies.

She would like you to investigate why the report card suggests that there have been few improvements in activity levels or very poor grades if, as the authors claim, the findings of the report have raised awareness about sedentary living. Dr. Smith has assigned different parts of the report card to small working groups in your class. She clearly states in the project explanation that you will be required to read and learn about epidemiology, test construction, and the development of report cards (e.g., measurement and reporting). What are the similarities and differences between epidemiological and group/individual approaches to measurement and report cards? How are report cards designed? How many of this type of report card exist? Which countries also employ a report card? How are comparisons made with other countries if Canada is provided failing grades? Poor grades or continued failures are not always the fault of the individual. They may indicate a cellar, or floor, effect (Glass & Hopkins, 1984) where the continuing low scores may be due to the physical activity evaluation criteria (e.g., guidelines) being too strict. Will Canadian youth and society benefit from the messaging being relayed by the report card?

The primary purpose of the assignment is to perform a critically engaged analysis. Each group will be expected to:

1 Identify the specific criteria used to make the grading decision for the assigned area of the report card.

2 Review the specific recommendations for improvement in each section of the report card.

3 Develop a list of critically engaged questions to ask about their assigned section.

4 Present their material in a health poster board presentation to the entire cohort of pre-service physical eduators in their university.

Dr. Smith firmly believes that good questions form the basis of exemplary teaching and research so she wishes to create a new critical pedagogy and engagement process in your department.

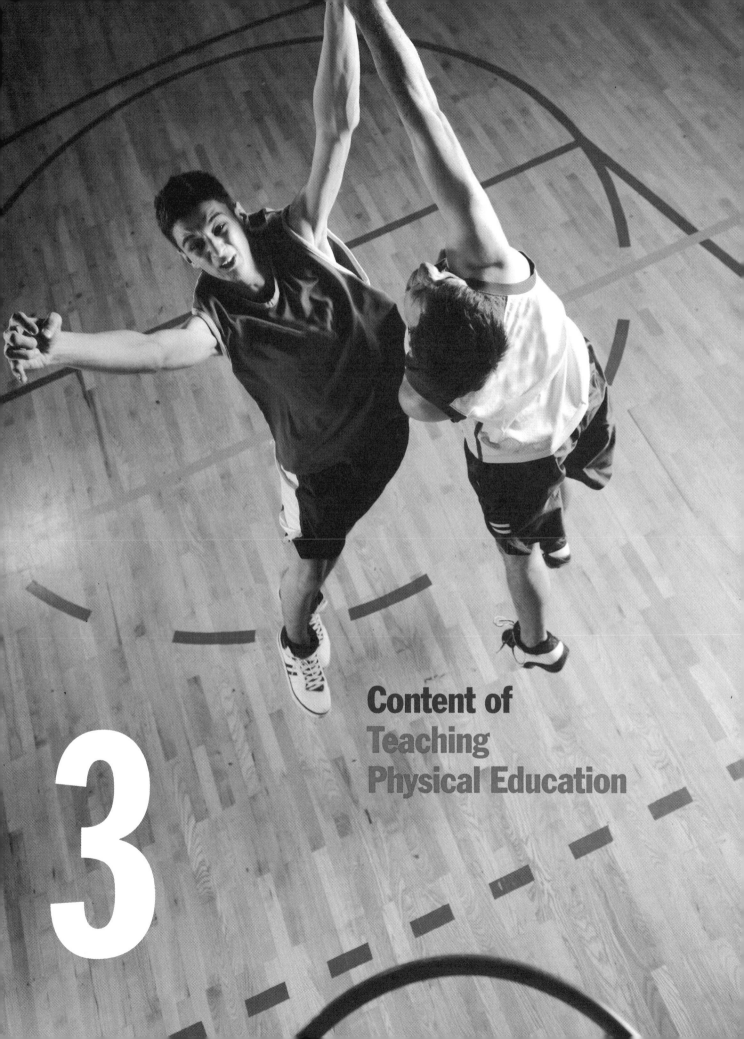

3

**Content of
Teaching
Physical Education**

Movement Domains

Chunlei Lu, Nancy Francis, and Ken Lodewyk

Overview

The purpose of the chapter is to introduce the movement domains that describe five major categories of physical activity for physical education (PE). Each movement domain has unique characteristics and provides students with an array of experiences intended to empower them physically, intellectually, socially, and emotionally through their developing skills, abilities, and experiences. These movement domains offer variety in PE programs and their sound implementation can help promote students' physical literacy and positive attitudes (e.g., joy of movement) towards lifelong active living.

The five movement domains are DAIGG:

- Dance
- Alternative environment physical activities
- Individual physical activities
- Games
- Gymnastics

Instruction using these movement activities should be developmentally appropriate, engage the affective and socio-emotional realms, and foster movement competence, healthy living, and enhanced fitness. For example, students can learn respect for self, others, and their environment, and increase their appreciation for the role of activity in health and well-being. Students will also learn about movement through concepts, skills, tactics, and patterns found in the array of movement domains. Laban's movement framework provides the fundamental concepts related to the body, the space in which someone moves, the effort quality of that movement, and the relationships to others and objects. By integrating the movement domain, movement concepts, and fundamental movement skills like locomotion (travelling), stability (non-manipulation), and manipulation, the three foundational building blocks of PE lessons are established.

Introduction

The goal of PE is to assist children and youth to develop the knowledge, skills, and attitudes necessary for a healthy, active lifestyle. To do so, a variety of physical activities must be introduced to all students, regardless of their diverse needs. A comprehensive framework of physical activities (DAIGG) is provided (see **Table 12.1**) to help physical educators to understand the broad spectrum of physical activities and to facilitate their planning in PE curricular design, implementation, and evaluation (Lu & De Lisio, 2009). These five movement domains are generally reflective of curricula from across Canada. Each of the five categories is unique and cannot be replaced by another. It should be noted that some activities fit in more than one domain (e.g., aerobic dance).

Although the framework does not include an exhaustive list of physical activities in school, all five categories and major sub-categories of physical activity should be introduced to students. In elementary school, movement skill competency is typically achieved through a balanced program of games, gymnastics, and dance, blending fitness into each.

Physical activity is a crucial part of a healthy lifestyle.

As students move into high school, the emphasis towards individual physical activities and alternative environment activities increases; however, physical educators should develop their program in consultation with students based on instructional goals and objectives, student needs and preferences, the physical educators' expertise, the availability of resources (e.g., facilities, equipment, assistants, transportation) and time, administrative and parental approval, and school tradition and culture. It is critical that the selection of physical activities should align with the current philosophies and goals of PE. For example, priorities may be given to those that may foster lifelong, health-oriented, recreational, enjoyable, learner-based, cooperative (i.e., less competitive), and community-related physical activities.

Each activity must be regarded as the raw movement material that should be modified or adjusted to be developmentally appropriate for the learner's needs and abilities and to nurture their positive experiences. Schools should develop a variety of programs and structural organizations to promote sustainable physical activity for all students such as clubs (e.g., dance, walking, skating) and themed school days (e.g., skipping day, multicultural games day). These programs and structural organizations may be developed under the frameworks of comprehensive school physical activity (e.g., PE class, intramural and after-school activities) and comprehensive school health (i.e., health-promoting schools).

Movement Concepts

Teaching PE through movement concepts forms the basis of a lesson's movement theme and facilitates students becoming educated in and through movement as they learn about movement (Wall & Murray, 1994). Laban and Lawrence's (1947) descriptive analysis of human movement allows us to describe any human activity. The four broad movement concepts answer the following questions:

1   What is the body doing? (body concepts: body shape, body parts, locomotion, balance, body functions)

2   Where is the movement going? (spatial concepts: directions, levels, pathways)

3   What is the dynamic content or quality of movement? (effort quality concepts: time, weight, space, flow)

4   With whom or to what is the mover relating? (relationship concepts: to people and objects)

Figure 12.1

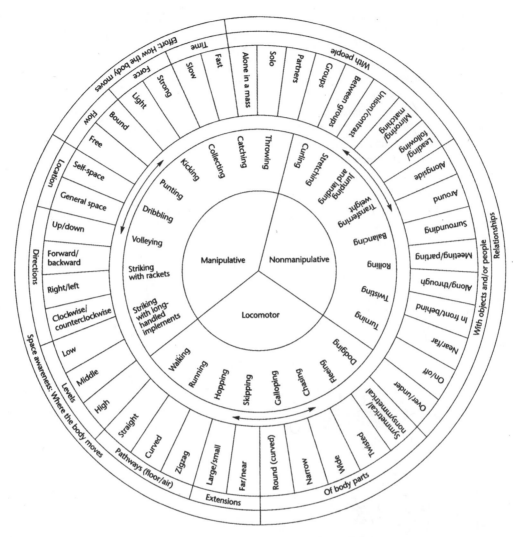

(Graham, Holt/Hale, & Parker, 2007, p. 284)

Besides being able to describe any movement, we can also teach a new skill, and develop and refine existing skills through observation, discussion, and analysis by using the movement concepts to modify and alter the learner's movement patterns.

The concepts enable us to:

1 Structure learning tasks and ask strategic questions

2 Observe and analyze movement

3 Communicate with others by using common terminology

4 Evaluate students movement and the content of the program

Fundamental Movement Skills

Fundamental movement skills (FMS) are the most basic movement skills found in any complex skill. They provide individuals with the requisite understanding and ability to be able to advance to more complex skills. Fundamental movement skills are not acquired naturally; they must be taught. For example, dribbling a soccer ball requires the skills of running, dodging, turning, and changing speed (PHE Canada, 2011b). Fundamental movement skills contribute to an individual's physical literacy and include skills such as running, stopping, turning, rolling, balancing, jumping, skipping, galloping, hopping, leaping, kicking, throwing, and catching. **Figure 12.1** illustrates the interrelationship amongst Laban and Lawrence's movement analysis, fundamental movement skills, and some specific skills from the movement domains (stability is commonly used to describe non-manipulative skills).

Table 12.1: Movement Domains (DAIGG)

Movement Concepts				
Fundamental Movement Skills				
Dance	**Alternative environment activities**	**Individual physical activities**	**Gymnastics**	**Games**
Rhythmic ■ Singing and clapping ■ Step dancing Educational ■ Creative ■ Modern Folk ■ Aboriginal ■ Hip-hop Ballroom and Social ■ Jive ■ Latin	Land-based ■ Hiking ■ Orienteering Ice/snow-based ■ Curling ■ Ice skating Water-based ■ Swimming ■ Canoeing	Exercise without equipment ■ Walking ■ Running Exercise with equipment ■ Cycling ■ Inline skating Fitness ■ Personal fitness ■ Weight training Mindfulness exercise ■ Yoga ■ Eastern martial arts	Educational gymnastics ■ Alone or in small groups ■ With small or large equipment Rhythmic gymnastics ■ Ribbons ■ Hoops	Low organizational games ■ Chasing ■ Catching Target ■ Golf ■ Bocce Net/Wall ■ Volleyball ■ Badminton Territory/Invasion ■ Basketball ■ Soccer Batting/Fielding ■ Baseball ■ Softball
Note: This is not a complete list of physical activities within each category.				

Movement Domains

There are numerous benefits to categorizing physical activities in PE: facilitating the understanding and conceptualization of physical activities, helping physical educators to provide a variety of physical activities for students in curricular planning in physical education, and designing other programs (e.g., intramurals, after school) to ensure that student movement preferences are offered. **Table 12.1** outlines the five movement domains and forms each may take.

Another aspect to consider is the variety found in each with respect to rules, use of equipment (e.g., balls, gymnastic boxes, skis), social expectations (e.g., collaboration, co-operation, competition), the environment (e.g., playing field, dance studio), and the ultimate purpose of the activity; that is, whether it is functional (e.g., games), expressive (e.g., dance), or pursued for the pleasure of engagement in the environment (e.g., snowshoeing).

Dance

Dance has received much attention in the media in recent years, perhaps because of its demanding physicality and skill, evocative emotion, and the tremendous variety within the art form. But dance is not new, as "every age has had its dance; … dance is consistent with life" (H'Doubler, 1940, p. 3). Over the centuries, dance has existed in some form in every culture and society as it fulfills social, recreational, competitive, religious, therapeutic, and artistic functions (Oliver, 2009). Dance is so interwoven into human behavioural patterns that, although the forms may change according to the practices and values of the particular society, involvement is a hallmark of being human (Hill, 1982).

Overview

Dance lessons provide an opportunity for students of all ages to express, and be, themselves. Dance education is valued because it offers the student a different way of knowing, a means for thinking, and a form for expression and understanding of self and others, issues, and events

(Dewey, 1934; Eisner, 1998; Shapiro, 1998). The inclusion of dance depends upon whether the physical educator considers it important for students to become skillful in and knowledgeable of expressive movement. Many physical educators assume that they cannot teach dance if they do not know dance. When physical educators begin with what they know and are comfortable with, and engage their skills of observation, and movement analysis towards students' skill refinement, effective lessons can ensue.

Sometimes the question is asked if dance is part of the PE program, part of the arts education program, or a stand-alone subject. On reflection, it may not matter where dance is located in the curriculum. What is important is that children have learning experiences in the expressive form of movement.

The Material of Dance

When we dance, we either "replicate pre-set movements or we create our own movements" (Rutledge, 2006, p. 87). We may learn dances that have been established for a long time, such as folk and social dances; we may learn new dances from DVDs and the Internet. However, it is important that students create their own dances to invoke their creativity and critical thinking to extend their movement understanding.

Regardless, dance lessons should be enjoyable for both physical educators and students. These lessons are times for exploring movement; sharing, selecting, and rejecting ideas; participating in the creativity of others; observing dances being developed; and evaluating so physical educators and students refine and clarify the product. Adshead (1981) advocates for students learning to effectively create, perform, and observe dance. This implies that students should have the opportunity to develop and dance their own dances, perform dances that others have choreographed, and observe one another as well as professional dancers.

Dance is a physical activity based upon fundamental movement skills. It is also an art form with a specific language and a social forum through which students' life skills can be developed. Defined as such, educational theorists such as Eisner (1998), Gardner, (1983), and Vygotsky (1934) would likely endorse the educative value of dance. Once the movement material is identified, one or two relevant movement themes chosen by the physical educator will guide the lesson idea and focus the students' skills. For example, in most Latin dances the movement of the hips is paramount, as is the rhythm. Therefore, the physical educator should focus the initial lesson on body parts (hips) and time. When students are more proficient in the step patterns, the physical educator may focus on the steps in

relation to a partner (theme of partner relationships) or add the complexity of changing directions (directions theme).

Anthoney's writing (1979) is helpful because it alerts us to the unique role of the physical educator in dance as opposed to other movement forms. In dance, the physical educator and students transform everyday movement into an artistic experience. This, according to Anthoney, occurs at three levels, which provide us with a focus when we plan learning experiences for students.

Level 1: Movement for movement's sake, to develop an awareness of enjoyment in moving. Dance beginners of any age need this particular kind of focus in their lessons.

Level 2: The concern here is with having an aesthetic experience. Our everyday movements are transformed into a form with new meaning. A quality dance program should give the students this level of dance experience.

Level 3: This completes the transition from everyday to artistic movement. The intention is "to give form … to create a structured dance … to show someone the dance" (Dewar, 1980, p. 28). An arts program, rather than a PE program, would aim to reach this level of experience with all of the students.

Each of the three levels is a legitimate dance experience, and more or less emphasis will be placed on each of them at different stages of learning, according to the focus of the learning experience.

Dance Forms

Because Canada is so tremendously diverse in its culture, the number of dance forms that a physical educator can include is almost endless. We have pockets of step-dancing, Ukrainian dancing, Aboriginal dancing, urban or hip-hop dancing, line dancing, square dancing, French-Canadian, Latin, Filipino, and Indian (just to name a few), as well as educational forms of dance such as creative and modern dance. Some students may have had private dance studio training and be skilled in the dance forms of ballet, jazz, lyrical, musical theatre, acro (acrobatic), or tap in which case they may wish to share their skills and knowledge in socially sensitive and developmentally appropriate ways.

The physical educator's choice of dance forms should be based on the students' backgrounds, interests, needs, and capabilities at that particular time. As well, dance content may overlap with other subject areas and provide relevant and enriching educational material. For example, the physical educator may decide that the students need help in working cooperatively with others and so select a particular cultural dance that includes this. The physical educator may wish to prepare students for an upcoming graduation dance and teach the jive, waltz, or a particular dance that reflects the students' culture. The students may be dealing with bullying and asked to create a dance about friendship and respect for others through the physical educator's guidance in creative or modern dance.

Folk and Social Dance

Most of us have images of established folk dances and social dances such as the waltz and jive. However, most dance forms actually began as folk dances as they originated from the folk of the time. Even hip-hop, urban dance, and jazz were originally considered folk dances. Folk and social dance is really borrowed from the adult world as they were the social dances of the people. When schooling became compulsory and some form of physical activity was considered essential for the children, adult movement activities were scaled down

and included in the curriculum. Physical educators knew the dances, and they were considered easy to teach.

Over the years, folk and social dance has become firmly established in many school programs, and it is probably one of the most common dance forms taught. Students of all ages can have very positive learning experiences when established dances are taught by sensitive and confident physical educators who are able to select and adapt predetermined dances to meet the developmental needs of their particular students, ensuring that all students are included.

Because there are a plethora of resources available for physical educators who wish to teach pre-set dances, the steps involved will not be presented here. Rather, readers are encouraged to seek out the many printed and electronic resources available from sites such as www.humankinetics.com/dance.

Case Study 1: Top-down or Bottom-up?

Two grade seven educators vary in their approach to teaching an eight-lesson unit on the concepts of formal net games such as badminton.

Educator One applies a top-down approach in which the lessons are designed with badminton in mind. The unit begins with a teaching of the rules and then progresses through the main skills, tactics, and affective qualities needed to succeed at badminton. Drills and lead-up games are used so students become increasingly proficient in their badminton playing performance; and most lessons end with game play. The educator designs, models, implements, and teaches all of the content and gives all students plenty of feedback and questions to answer to maximize their learning. The final two lessons include a class badminton tournament using the official rules and time for the educator's assessment of students' skills.

Educator Two utilizes a bottom-up approach designed to meet the learning objectives relative to formal net games. Since net games such as badminton and volleyball share similar fundamental rules, skills, and tactical problems, Educator Two implements a unit of instruction that

focuses on the relationships to people and levels (of the birdie and ball). In other words, the chief aim becomes meeting the net-game themes rather than performing a particular formal net-game. Sample net-game themes could be finding or covering space with optimal footwork and communication, using the appropriate type and force of shot according to the game situation, and being aware of how each of these vary when using a racquet, hand, or foot. Lessons use movement tasks that are increasingly complex by having both the educator and students involved in altering the conditions of play (e.g., changing the rules, equipment, number of players), conducting assessments, and providing further information and feedback. Lessons often begin and end with a modified game so that students experience a motivating context upon which to construct their learning.

Questions for Reflection

1 To which of the described approaches to teaching games have you been most exposed?

2 List and then discuss the main advantages and disadvantages of each.

Creative and Modern Dance

Creative and modern dance offer students a diverse dance experience, and requires a carefully designed lesson to promote skill development and sequential movement. Students may dance alone, with a few chosen friends, or individually within the whole class. The movement material or skills of these educational dance forms may be simple rhythmic step patterns or descriptive verbs (and actions), which emanate from ideas or concepts. These verbs may be chosen by the physical educator, may be found in poetry or stories, or may be created by the students themselves under the guidance of the physical educator.

Effective dance lessons incorporate movement material that relates to the specific interests of the students. Stimuli for dance lessons can be found in a favourite character from a movie or television show, a song ("If I Had $1,000,000"), social issues (bullying, the environment), or a news event. Ideas can be explored by discussing, analyzing, improvising with or without any accompaniment, synthesizing, and transforming the ideas into concrete, repeatable movement patterns or motifs.

The Dance Process

It is imperative that physical educators know what dance skills or actions will serve as the focus of the lesson so that student movement may improve and become more refined. These may include any of the following, depending upon the dance form taught.

Locomotor actions: walk, run, skip, gallop, jump, leap, hop, turn

Expressive actions: stretch, curl, shrink, explode, creep, pause, wring, slash

Folk or social dance steps: step-hop, two step, box step, jazz-square, grapevine, polka step, pony, slide, pop-lock

A Dance Teaching Progression

The following progression is a suggestion for physical educators to use in creative or modern dance.

1 Students brainstorm with the physical educator about the concept to be developed in the dance sequence (e.g., friendship, family, sports) and the physical educator records the relevant words.

2 The physical educator then translates those words into verbs or action words with the students.

3 The physical educator assists the class in selecting between three and five different words or actions that can be develop with the students with or without music.

4 The physical educator then works with students through each word—one at a time—in a fairly direct way by asking questions, to find specific qualities for each word.

5 The students (alone, in pairs, or small groups) choose three actions that they will develop into a dance.

6 If students demonstrate the ability to organize themselves in groups of four, they will decide who will move when, where, and how in response to the physical educator's parameters set (e.g., thirty-two counts for this; sixteen counts of that).

Simple Dance Ideas

1 The physical educator plays popular music and reviews all verbs as stated below, reminding students that there is no right or wrong way. Students get into groups of 4 and pick an action from the envelope that the physical educator has prepared. Each person creates a movement to teach others so there is a sequence of 4 actions of 8 counts each.

Walk	Jump	Turn	Step-Kick	Hands Wave
Turn	Pivot	Clap/Stamp	Shake	Push

2 Telephone choreography- Each movement gets a number; the physical educator reviews all movements with the students physically so that movement is of quality. Each student creates a sequence using his/her phone number.

1: Turn slowly	2: Hop	3: Jump/leap
4: Balance	5: Grapevine step	6: Reach
7: Pony/polka step	8: Stretch	9: Skip

Gymnastics

Most students delight in running, jumping, rolling, and climbing, so the gymnastic experience is generally a positive one for all age groups (Wall & Murray, 1994). These basic skills involved are fundamental movement skills and are used in many sports, including gymnastics. Gymnastic movement is worthy of emphasis within the PE program due to the physical demands it requires. Muscles of the arms, legs, and trunk are taxed as students balance, spring, climb, and hang. Body control is the major objective of gymnastics; efficient movement is necessary in a variety of situations, both on the floor and when using an apparatus. Experience with large apparatus provides excitement and challenge, and demands conceptual understanding. Students learn skills such as collaboration, planning, critical thinking and predicting as they solve movement problems alone, with a partner, or with a group.

Forms of Gymnastics

Gymnastics is an aesthetic sport (like diving or figure skating) that is concerned with movement itself, the focus being how and where the body moves in relation to the floor or an obstacle. What the action is and how it is performed is the essence of gymnastics, not the result of the action, nor the effect of the action (as it is in games). At all times we are trying to prove that we can defy gravity in a variety of specially constructed situations. Through the centuries, variations in gymnastic forms have evolved; however, the two most appropriate forms for school PE are rhythmic gymnastics and educational gymnastics.

Rhythmic Gymnastics

Modern rhythmic gymnastics is a dance-like movement form, which incorporates elements from dance and games to create a sequence in which a ball, rope, hoop, ribbon, or club is manipulated in time to music. Children and adolescents can enjoy the rhythmic elements of movement, and when they can catch, bounce, and throw objects with proficiency, they will react positively to the challenge of performing these skills to music. They will also enjoy the challenge of composing a simple gymnastic sequence to popular music.

Educational Gymnastics

Educational gymnastics is aptly termed because its main goal is education. This implies that the student is most important, as opposed to the activity or movement skill. This is a form we believe should be included in school PE programs as well as in recreational programs.

In educational gymnastics, students work at their own level on tasks structured to develop understanding and skill in applying selected movement themes (see **Table 12.2**). While each student responds to the same task, the theoretical framework allows for skill progression appropriate for each individual child. The physical educator's role is to observe and analyze students' responses, and provide encouragement through increasingly detailed feedback, either individually or to the entire class, which promotes the solving of movement problems through gymnastic activity.

Body awareness is heightened through a focus on the body's shape in jumping, landing, rolling, balancing, hanging, swinging, and climbing. Students learn to control body parts and use them effectively to receive and support their weight as they perform various activities. They will discover that sudden, forceful movement is necessary at times, while energy must be harnessed to create an effective movement at other times. They will learn the importance of timing and rhythm, so movements may progress smoothly through a

Case Study 2: "Can I Golf With You?"

A physical educator arranges for his grade ten PE class to play four holes of golf at a local golf course. One student named Terry plays a par four hole in the following way:

Terry drives his ball off the tee first because he arrived to the tee area first. He hits his ball deep into the woods (out of bounds) and swears loudly as he does so. Terry stands a safe distance directly behind the next person to tee off and begins to verbally tease his friend about his lofty score on the last hole. He stops this once all the players in their group of five have taken their first shot.

Upon arriving at the point of entry into the woods of his first shot, Terry climbs over a fence to access the out-of-bounds area where his ball landed. He looks for seven minutes and gives up only when players waiting to tee off behind him ask him to hurry up. He tosses a new ball into the middle of the fairway and strikes his next shot with all of the others in his group waiting for him on the green. His shot careens off a tree and into a sand trap near the green. In an angry response, he throws his golf club up and forward halfway to the green.

He takes a few practice swings in the sand trap carving out a divot in the sand on each one. Upon chipping the ball, it rolls close to the cup for which his group congratulates him. Another player farther from the cup is waiting to putt but Terry walks over the projected line of that player's shot and putts. He misses the cup so he putts the ball again before it stops rolling and finally enters the cup. He announces that he has earned a score of four and walks off to the next tee before the others have finished putting.

Questions for Reflection

1 List all of the violations of golf etiquette in the description above.

2 Why is it useful for physical educators to teach the etiquette rules of various games?

Table 12.2: Gymnastic Themes

Body concepts	Space concepts	Effort concepts	Relationship concepts
■ Body parts ■ Body shape ■ Body functions ■ Locomotion ■ Flight	■ Directions ■ Levels ■ Pathways	■ Time ■ Flow	■ Partner work: copy, contrast, mirror, match, balance ■ To the apparatus (or partner): over, under, around, through

sequence of activities. Spatial dimensions will be explored so that height and distance are judged accurately in relation to both the body and objects.

Educational Gymnastic Content

The concepts of what the body is doing, where the body is moving, and how the body is moving in relation to the floor or apparatus are constantly being explored. Small apparatus, such as mats and hoops, as well as large apparatus such as benches and boxes provide additional stimuli. When students work together, challenge is also increased. A partner may contribute to the movement sequence as an obstacle, a leader, or follower; one who matches the movements, provides contrast, or one who assists a partner's movements.

Fundamental Gymnastic Skills

Fundamental gymnastic skills can be categorized into six dominant movement patterns. These categories are helpful in assuring that the array of gymnastic movement is covered as students work alone or as part of a group; without apparatus and with small or large apparatus. The six dominant movement patterns include: locomotion, statics (balances), rotations (turning around an axis), springs, landings, and swings. The categories are not mutually exclusive, meaning that an action may be a combination of two or more categories. These gymnastic skills may be developed through lessons that focus on various movement themes.

1 **Locomotion:** Locomotion implies travelling to a new place. Common types of locomotion used in gymnastic activities focus upon the feet (e.g., running and jumping), feet and hands (e.g., cartwheeling), rolling, and various types of weight transference.

  ■ *Weight Transference:* Weight transference implies a change in base of support, either on the spot or through moving the body to a new place. Weight transference can be accomplished in various ways. The body may stay on the spot and merely change position as new body parts take the weight as in the headstand, handstand, or shoulder stand. Weight may also be transferred from one body part to the same body part through flight. Stepping

actions, rolling actions, or jumping actions can initiate momentum for transference of weight. When apparatus is used, there is an even greater potential for weight transference because a range of body parts may support weight in balancing, hanging, and swinging actions.

  ■ *Stepping Actions:* Stepping actions are a form of locomotion involving only the feet or hands, or both feet and hands to travel. Walking on hands or travelling along a bar while hanging, cartwheeling, and scampering with feet and hands, all involve stepping.

2 **Statics:** Statics denote balances, which are static or stationary shapes and are held for a period of time. Static balance involves balancing on a specific body part or parts. Common static balances include headstand, handstand, frog stand (where the head provides the base of support and the body is in a curled shape, with knees resting on elbows), and back arch. Statics may also include holding a shape while hanging from bars, rings, or a rope.

There are four specific types of balances:

  ■ *Overbalance:* Overbalance involves balancing and then slightly shifting the weight (centre of gravity) outside of the base of support in order for transference of weight to occur. A common example of overbalance is a handstand or headstand into a forward roll.

  ■ *Counter-resistance:* Counter-resistance involves two (or more) people pushing against one another in order to achieve stability. A typical example of this is two people leaning into each other, shoulders contacting to create an inverted V.

  ■ *Counter-tension:* Counter-tension involves pulling away from a partner (or partners) to achieve balance. A typical example of this is two people clasping hands while face to face and then leaning backward, creating the shape of a V.

  ■ *Suspension:* Balancing on an apparatus can take the form of either supports or hangs. In supports, the head is above the base of support (e.g., gripping on horizontal bar, hips resting on the bar). In hangs, the head is below the base of support (e.g., hanging inverted by the knees on a horizontal bar).

3 **Rotations:** Rotations occur around any of the three axes (horizontal, vertical, and anteroposterior) and include rolling, cartwheeling, and spinning. Rolling partially provides for the individual's safety upon landing while forming the basis for rotation in gymnastic movement. When a program involves climbing, travelling in unconventional ways, springing off apparatus into the air, or travelling backward, the physical educator must provide additional safety mechanisms to prevent injury. The ability to tuck the body in a curled shape and continue moving until the momentum is dissipated limits the risk of injury. Rolling has tremendous value for the child, not only as a safety precaution but also because it necessitates focus on the use of body parts, body shape, weight bearing, and transference of weight. As a result, the sequence of *run, jump, land, and roll* must be learned early in a gymnastic program. The cartwheeling action involves the transference of weight towards the side from a stretched shape. Less skilled students are challenged to retain the stretched shape in transition when weight is on the hands. Spinning is an enjoyable challenge as it can occur with weight on the feet, stomach, bottom, or shoulders and requires significant core strength in order to maintain one's body shape.

4 **Springs:** Springs involve any part of the body producing flight, which is when the body is without support and totally off the ground. Jumping is a form of spring in which there can be a transfer of weight from two feet to two feet, one foot to two feet, two feet to one foot, one foot to the other (leap), or one foot to the same foot (hop). Jumping demands strong and sudden curling and stretching of the legs and trunk and is first experienced when a toddler steps down from a height. From there it progresses to jumping on the spot and later, running and jumping. Finally, jumping onto a raised surface may be mastered. For this reason, the progression of jumping down, then up, over, and later onto apparatus should be employed. Other types of springing actions can occur using various body parts such as the legs and or arms to propel the body from one part to another, such as springing from the hands onto the feet, or from the shoulders and hands behind the head onto the feet.

5 **Landings:** Landings occur when the body becomes stable after flight, even if only for a short period. Most typically we land on our feet when jumping from a height or distance or onto a piece of apparatus. However, we may also land on our hands, which makes it more difficult to achieve stability. Critical in landing is the ability to absorb force through the entire body and all its parts, including ankles, knees, hips, trunk, shoulders, and arms. Because safe landings are so critical in

Case Study 3: Teaching for Difference

Two grade five educators vary in their approach to teaching a selected skill in gymnastics.

Educator One is of the opinion that all students should learn how to perform a cartwheel and informs the students that is their learning goal for the day. Once students have warmed-up by running around the gym, he demonstrates the cartwheel numerous times so they can copy his action. For the students who couldn't already perform a cartwheel, the outcome is that some gain varying degrees of skill and some repeatedly fail and give up.

Educator Two is of the opinion that all students can learn various ways in which to transfer their weight through stepping actions. The warm-up consists of travelling on the feet in various ways followed by taking weight on the hands when reaching a mat. At mats, the educator encouraged the students to find two different, non-adjacent, body parts (e.g., one shoulder, one foot) to take your weight on, alternating between them in order to travel. Students explored various body parts on their own, then observed half the class and discussed which methods worked better than others. The educator then suggested that everyone take a small hoop and work on a feet-hands-feet action, placing hands only inside the hoop (feet always outside) making suggestions to each student for refinement. Students had tremendous variety in their final skills and were delighted with their progress.

Questions for Reflection

1 What specific teaching strategies did each educator use to promote individualized skill development?

2 In what way is Educator Two using constructivist teaching principles?

gymnastics, it is important that students learn how to jump, land, and roll early in their skill development.

6 **Swings:** Swings provide delightful free-flowing movement opportunities when apparatus is available. Swings are usually accomplished by hanging by hands or knees from bars, ropes, and rings.

Summary

Gymnastics plays a vital role in a student's development of physical literacy. The focus is on the body and how and where it moves in relation to the floor, others, or apparatus. The movement concepts of the body, effort, space, and relationships are applied to particular gymnastic skills for variety in the lesson focus.

The games category encompasses both indoor and outdoor activities.

Games

The purpose of this section is to describe the basic nature, structure, purpose, skills, tactics, activities, pedagogical strategies, and helpful resources associated with teaching games in PE. Games tend to be the largest component of the PE curriculum for most schools (Hardman & Marshall, 2000). They provide a generally engaging means of enhancing functional movement skills, knowledge, and behaviours.

What are games and how do they relate to sports? A game "has explicit rules, specified or understood goals, the element of opposition or contest, and a sequence of rules and actions which is essentially repeatable every time the game is played" (Estes & Mechikoff, 1999, p. 14). In contrast to games, sports represent a broader cultural institution particularly through their poignant influence on human lifestyle through the attitudes and values they model through physical performances, politics, and the media. Educationally, games are more like play than institutionalized sport through their heightened focus on being inclusive, developmentally appropriate, optimally challenging, and aim of meeting holistic learning objectives. The fundamental aim of sport is more competitive (to win), specialized (e.g., sport-specific training), quantified (precise records of performances), and more closely follows the standardized formal rules that are bureaucratically governed and managed both internationally and locally.

Many PE programs teach games as sport—at the expense of many students' full participation—in order to strengthen their school sports program or to succumb to a prevailing socio-political agenda or image of sport reflected in the media and culture. While such trends are troubling, the culture of sport does have an important role in fulfilling particular educational objectives of PE (see Pope, 2011 for a review) especially if students are taught the role of sport culture and "sport as one exemplar of a culturally relevant physical activity" and if it is taught to them "by demonstrating ways in which sport can contribute to leading a full and valuable life" (Almond, 1997, p. 15).

Table 12.3: Game Definitions

Term	Definition			
Developmental (Low-Organization) Game	Bears little resemblance to formal games. Consists of simple elements found in many games (running, dodging, guarding), makes little demand on the players in terms of roles, strategy, and rules, and no game form is specified (e.g., tag, "Red Light, Green Light") (Wall & Murray, 1994).			
Lead-Up Game	More complex and bears greater resemblance to formal games as it consists of a combination of elements (manipulative and non-manipulative skills, positional play, and tactics) found in a selected formal games form (e.g., Danish Rounders for striking-fielding) (Wall & Murray, 1994).			
Formal Game	Institutionalized game/sport that provides competitive opportunities between players or teams and that are governed by rules which allow equal opportunity for success (Adapted from Ellis, 1983).			
	Target	**Striking-Fielding**	**Net-Wall**	**Territorial**
	Golf, curling...	Baseball, cricket...	Badminton, squash...	Soccer, ultimate disc...

Games Theory

In educational movement settings, games are often differentiated by their formality; that is their relative structure, purpose, and complexity. As illustrated in **Table 12.3**, developmental games tend to emphasize more basic lead-up features (e.g., skills, tactics, and understandings) of more formalized (or institutionalized) games such as tennis and rugby. All games are either individual or partner focused (e.g., running, jumping, and throwing activities associated with track and field) or more team-oriented (e.g., ultimate disc) and emphasize one or more environments such as performing on the ground, with ice/snow, or in the water or air (e.g., diving).

Games within each of these categories share similar fundamental rules, skills, and tactical problems that reflect movement strategies common within a formal game category (see **Table 12.4** for tactical examples). This can help physical educators to transfer the movement learning of their students thematically across games in the same or another game category. For example, a low organizational game involving underhand throwing or rolling an object around obstacles towards a target shares movement themes with formal target games such as curling, ultimate, golf, or bocce. Low-organizational games can teach students more about how body parts can be used to deliver the object, the pathway (and level as in golf) of the object, the amount of weight required for a successful delivery, and the relationship between the objects(s) and the target. These target game concepts are also relevant in the other game categories of striking-fielding (e.g., softball), net-wall (e.g., handball), and territorial (e.g., rugby). Further, the tactic of covering space is very similar across striking-fielding games whereas creating space is shared in most territorial games. Such an integration of movement skills, concepts, tactical awareness, and socio-emotional qualities is a staple of the Teaching Games for Understanding (TGfU) pedagogical approach which is one reason it has been emphasized in the H&PE curricula of provinces such as Ontario.

Games Literacy

The development of games literacy is a key aim of games instruction in PE. Mandigo and Holt (2004) report that

> students are games literate if they (a) have knowledge and understanding that enables them to anticipate patterns of play, (b) possess technical and tactical skills to deploy appropriate and imaginative responses, and (c) are able to experience positive motivational states while helping to facilitate motivation among others involved in the game.

Table 12.4: Game Tactics

Game Category	Relevant Movement Themes	Generic Offensive Tactics	Generic Defensive Tactics
Target Games	■ Body parts ■ Body shape ■ Pathways ■ Weight ■ Relationship to objects	■ Accuracy ■ Raise	■ Setting up guards ■ Take-outs
Striking-Fielding Games	■ Body parts ■ Locomotion ■ Levels ■ Pathways ■ Weight ■ Relationships to others	■ Strike to an open space ■ Knowing when to run ■ Helping another runner to advance ■ Protecting the strike zone	■ Positioning to covering (limit) space ■ Making the ball (spin) difficult to strike ■ Communicating with and backing up teammates
Net-Wall Games	■ Body parts ■ Body shape ■ Weight ■ Timing ■ Levels (of self and object) ■ Pathways (of self and object) ■ Relationships to others	■ Striking to open space ■ Variation of shot type and placement ■ Adding spins and fakes ■ Strategic attacks (e.g., smashes/spikes)	■ Footwork, positioning, and anticipation ■ Returning to a neutral position and posture ■ Blocking and digging
Territorial Games	■ Body parts ■ Body shape ■ Weight ■ Timing ■ Levels (of self and object) ■ Pathways (of self and object) ■ Relationships to others	■ Creating (finding) open space (width, depth, and support) ■ Short, quick, and accurate passes ■ Give and go ■ Special plays (e.g., free kicks, throw ins)	■ Diagonal teammate support ■ Marking the opponent (and variations in degree) ■ Zone or person-to-person systems ■ Clearing the implement ■ Tackling and rebounding

Case Study 4: "Let's Go for a Fun Run"

The educator, an avid runner, was keen to take her PE class for a jog around the perimeter of the school block to enjoy the glorious spring weather. She told the students to line up at the gym door wearing their outdoor clothing and carrying their water bottles. When everyone was ready, the line of students ran through the playground, splashing through the pools of muddy water towards the street. The jog began well; however, as time progressed, the distance between the faster students and slower students grew. One student's winter boot fell off as he was running, which made everyone laugh because he continued to run in socks. Students, who were feeling hot, threw off their winter coats and slowed to a walk. Some students ran across a busy street to catch up with the others. The students at the end of the line complained that they brought water bottles but were still thirsty. As the students entered the schoolyard, the faster students jeered the slower ones with cries of "Slow poke; slow poke!" The educator was furious. The run was a disaster.

Questions for Reflection

1. Select a specific age group for this scenario and write a list of things that the educator should have done.

2. What are some principles for ensuring student safety that may be generalized to an array of situations?

Rather than being literate in a single game, children with games literacy will be able to engage with poise, confidence, and enthusiasm in a wide range of games. (p. 4)

Knowing the primary characteristics about game rules, skills, and tactics (such as body and space awareness, effort qualities, and relational concepts) for a variety of games along with how they relate to those of other games is important for game performance. Knowledge consists of declarative (the "what" about a concept or skill), procedural ("how" to perform it), and conditional-strategic knowledge (knowing about "when" and "where" to apply it tactically). For example, in the game of badminton a student should not only be familiar with the knowledge of what constitutes a drop shot and the rules pertaining to its use (declarative), but also how (procedural) and when/where (conditional/strategic) it is best used (i.e., when the opponent is in their backcourt). Those with more movement skill tend to rely increasingly on procedural rather than declarative knowledge to more automatically control their movements. In addition to the role of knowledge, researchers such as McPherson and Kernodle (2003) have noted links between game expertise and better working memory, recollection of game-specific information, and superior cognitive processing speed and accuracy in recognizing patterns of play, all of which enable more strategic decisions.

Games literate participants also need to be able to perform a variety of physical skills—both technical (e.g., passing, dribbling, shooting) and tactical (e.g., guarding, deciding, moving when not in possession of the ball)—for effective games performance in a variety of contexts. One's movement competency that can be improved through games consists of the physical proficiencies (e.g., strength, endurance, coordination, agility), sensory and perceptual-motor abilities (e.g., visual perception, rhythmic, timing), and the fundamental motor abilities of stability (e.g., bend, twist, balance), locomotion (e.g., run, jump), and manipulation (e.g., catch, throw, kick, punt, strike) necessary for performance in games. Competence in fundamental movement skills allows one to apply them in diverse game settings that require advanced elaborations, combinations, and specializations of movements. For example, if one is able to run, field, jump, and throw with power and accuracy, this combination of skills can be applied in specialized game settings such as softball, basketball, and other recreational activities—all of which can contribute to a more active lifestyle.

Socio-affective factors such as positive relationships, intrinsic motivation, and feelings of competence, enjoyment, safety, and support are being increasingly recognized as critical for games literacy. For example, Biddle et al. (2004) report that levels of enjoyment, feeling included, positive mood, positive body image, sense of well-being, perceptions of competence, and peer relationships are associated with degrees of engagement in game settings. They add that positive experiences in games also have demonstrated links to improved life skills such as empathy, critical thinking, respect, and self-control.

Games Curricula and Pedagogy

There appear to be two primary curricular approaches to teaching games. A top-down approach formulates an instructional unit around the content (e.g., skills, tactics, rules) of a particular formal game or sport with lessons designed to meet the learning objectives relative to that sport. Francis (2009) reports that such an approach was historically more technical or skill-focused in order to enable playing the game at the adult level. In this approach, the physical educator was the authority, expert model, and source of information, direction, and feedback. Alternatively, a bottom-up approach is more common in elementary PE curricula and reflects units of instruction and sequential lessons that highlight the key movement strategies (e.g., skills, tactics, rules) related to the themes within particular game forms/categories (target, striking-fielding, net-wall, territorial). As a result, mastering the game's themes becomes the chief aim rather than mastering the formal game or sport. Sample transferable skills in this approach could be catching and passing wisely and quickly, finding open space, using the most efficient footwork, and using strategic positions to maximize effectiveness.

Games pedagogy tends to fit somewhere between the two extremes of direct educator-centred (or behaviourist) and indirect (or constructivist) learning theory (Rink, 2010). There is ample evidence that when done well, direct instruction can facilitate the learning of motor skills, particularly skills with several required technical elements such as the golf swing or the tennis serve. Meanwhile, teaching indirectly has been linked to improved affective and cognitive outcomes (e.g., cooperation and tactical awareness in games). When using this method in the form of instructional models such as TGfU, peer teaching, cooperative learning, or sport education, students are empowered to construct their own learning while working collaboratively with others (hence the term constructivist). Games instructors using this method might, for example, structure the lesson to include:

- Cooperative problem-solving about the equipment
- Rule modifications needed to enhance their learning or experience tactical and skill challenges and solutions
- Having students function in certain team roles (e.g., coach, manager) to help meet mutual team and lesson goals

In TGfU, for example, playing a sample of games from the four main game categories (which cover most sports) serves as a vehicle for shared learning and engagement in PE. Games are structured and regularly modified by the physical educator or learner to be developmentally appropriate (e.g., optimally complex) and inclusive (see PHE Canada, 2011c, Volume III for more). Storey and Butler (2010) highlight the potential role of TGfU in teaching games as "inherently complex learning systems" (p. 142). They state that

> If educators accept that games are sites of communal learning and adaptation for learners, then the purpose of games for society and the individual, from a values perspective, is an important consideration. If, on the other hand, we seek social efficiency (in which the purpose of our games is to foster competition and individualism in order to survive in our constructed economic and public spheres), then we do not need to rethink zero-sum children's games and common notions of winners and losers. If, on the other hand, we seek social reconstruction and want our teaching to create alternatives to the status quo, then alternative understandings of competition and cooperation (such as ecological understanding) provide insights into potentially different outcomes of the communal adaptation that can occur during games. (p. 142)

Activities for Teaching Games

For enhanced experiences in games it is important to include lead-up activities that are inclusive, relatively novel, creative, tailored to learning objectives, developmentally appropriate, optimally challenging, as "game-like" as possible (versus educator-centred drills), and that reduce public comparisons (as in activities with long wait times where idle students watch one another). As an aid, Rink (2010) posits the following four stages for games based on their complexity:

1 Developing control of the object

2 Complex control and combinations of skills

3 Beginning offensive and defensive strategies

4 Complex game play

Rink emphasizes that the two middle stages tend to be the most neglected in PE and that "skill development out of context for a long time followed by game playing for a long time is an inappropriate approach to teaching games and sports" (p. 301).

Another way to enhance game activities is to modify activities to either simplify or extend them (i.e., make them more complex). For example, the size and shape of the playing area, basic rules, equipment (e.g., ball type, goal size), number of participants, and other game conditions can easily be altered to engage more learners in the activity. It can also be helpful if the physical educator or peers provide short, memorable, helpful, and timely skill and tactical refinements (learning cues and feedback) to participants.

Individual Physical Activities

Individual physical activities are activities that are performed alone but may be enjoyed socially as well. They are enormously important because of our lifetime need for physical activity as an integral part of our lifestyle.

Overview

Individual physical activities are easily implemented in our daily routines with minimal cost and scheduling flexibility, and are not dependent upon others for engagement. The most popular physical activities performed by Canadians are individual ones such as walking, swimming, and bicycling (Canadian Fitness & Lifestyle Research Institute, 1998). Nonetheless, there are not many resources or programs available to support individual physical activities in schools or communities. This may be due to the fact that individual physical activities are not commonly conceptualized as a category of physical activities. Many individual activities are related to activities of alternative environments (which will be discussed in the forthcoming section on alternative environment activities) and many, such as fitness classes, swimming, and jogging, can be conducted in groups. The popular and simple individual activities include walking, jogging, running, personal fitness, mindfulness exercise such as yoga, martial arts, and Pilates as well as outdoor activities such as cycling, inline skating, skate boarding, and horseback riding (Canadian Fitness & Lifestyle Research Institute, 1998). Individual physical activities are generally convenient, self-regulated, and simple to be integrated into an individual's daily life.

Basic Knowledge and Skills

Walking is probably the most popular physical activity because it is an easy and convenient exercise to do for almost everyone. Walking is different from jogging or running; when walking, one foot is always in contact with the ground which is not the case with jogging or running. There are three types of walking: simple walking, power-walking (speed-walking), and race-walking. In school settings, programs should be developed to promote walking, for example, walking to school, walking clubs (e.g., intramural, after school), and a school-wide walking day. Ideally urban planning should assist safe commuting on foot by designing or re-designing pedestrian friendly roads to support maximal walkability for school, shopping, and recreation. Considerations in safe walking activities include prohibiting earphones for safety reasons, whether to walk individually or in groups, and walking as a form of stress relief (see details on mindfulness exercise later in this section). Pedometers may be used to count steps and monitor students' progress.

Running is to move steadily using springing steps in order to have both feet leave the ground (in the air) at once. Jogging is running at a slow and gentle pace while sprinting is running at very fast pace usually for a short distance. Running is likely as old as human existence and has been involved in sports for survival, hunting, and recreation (e.g., ancient Greek sports). Types of modern running include track, road, cross-country, trail, and mountain (hill) running for both recreation and competition. In an educational context, enthusiastic students may be assisted by online programs, which instruct and assist beginners to develop regular running, through scheduling. Safety considerations for jogging and running include having medical clearance, proper attire (e.g., running shoes, socks, suitable clothing), finding an appropriate route, appropriate warm-up and cool-down, and plentiful water.

Physical fitness is the ability to function efficiently and effectively in regular daily life, work, and leisure activities. It is also a physical state of well-being influenced by genetic inheritance, diet, and exercise (Pangrazi & Gibbons, 2009). Physical fitness is different from weight training (which emphasizes muscular strength) or weight related sports such as competitive weightlifting and bodybuilding. The two types of physical fitness are health related and skill related (also known respectively as functional fitness and performance fitness—see **Table 12.5**) (Pangrazi & Gibbons, 2009).

Individual activities can be either structured or more recreational.

Table 12.5: Health-Related and Skill-Related Physical Fitness

Health-related fitness	Skill-related fitness
Cardiovascular endurance	Agility and coordination
Muscular strength and endurance	Balance
Flexibility	Speed
Body composition	Power

Health-related fitness must be emphasized and should be integrated into students' daily lives. The FITT principle provides a framework; FITT stands for: frequency of exercise, intensity (measured by heart rate levels), time (e.g., workout duration), and type of exercise. A personal exercise (or fitness) plan (PEP) may include: a goal and specific measurable objectives, time frame for completion, current health-related fitness level (e.g., fitness test results), weekly planned activities (using FITT principle), weekly or monthly tracking records (e.g., when, what, how), desired fitness level (e.g., aims or goals for fitness test results) at the end of the plan, and reflection and considerations for the next PEP. Fitness tests must be used with sensitivity to educate students about their own fitness levels, inform them of their progress, and motivate them to improve (process vs. product). Test results must be confidential, and should be used for comparison with one's own progress, not for comparison with other individuals or for awards. It is preferable to have simple, short, and routine fitness activities in PE classes, school daily physical activity (DPA), intramural activities, and at home. The goal of teaching fitness is to help students integrate fitness into their daily life both individually and with family members.

Mindfulness exercise as a term used here is not intended to suggest that other physical activities do not engage the mind. Rather, mindfulness is used to address the importance of integrating the body, mind, and spirit for the whole self, as opposed to engaging in activity and being lost in thought about something totally unrelated to what one is doing (PHE Canada, 2011a). In fact, any exercise can become mindfulness exercise if it directly addresses the state of being fully engaged in the present moment, here and now. The most popular mindfulness exercises currently include East-Asian martial arts, yoga, qigong, and Pilates (PHE Canada, 2011a). Aiming for holistic health, these activities are executed with an inward-directed focus on a body-mind connection, breathing, controlled and deliberate movements, flow, centre, balance, and repetitious movement. Critical knowledge and techniques include:

- **Breathing:** Be aware of breathing all the time, and breathe naturally or follow movements (inhaling when opening body and exhaling when closing body). Try to use deep abdominal breathing.

- **Avoid multi-tasking:** Do not have music or the television on when doing exercise. Let your mind go along with your movement.

- **Focus on the process:** Perform every single movement well and do not rush.

- **Appreciate the surroundings:** Impartially feel inanimate surroundings (e.g., equipment, gym, playing fields) and the animate environment (flowers, trees, a creek, others playing games).

- **Accept self and others:** Appreciate one's self and others regardless of body size, movement ability, race, ethnicity, etc., without much judgment trapped by artificial categories.

- **Connect body-mind:** Do not conceptualize the exercise only for the physical aspects (e.g., heart, muscle) or mental aspects (e.g., stress, calmness).

Resources

- www.canadianfitness.net/
- www.mindfullivingprograms.com/
- www.runnersworld.com/
- www.thewalkingsite.com/
- http://ojs.acadiau.ca/index.php/phenex/article/viewFile/30/21

Alternative Environment Activities

Alternative environment activities are those not normally performed in the gym or on the school playing field. They are usually conducted outdoors and are either land-based (e.g., hiking, orienteering), ice- or snow-based (e.g., curling, snow skiing), or water-based (e.g., swimming, canoeing). In addition to the health and fitness benefits, learning these types of physical activities is crucial to students developing active lifestyles through their adulthood. Furthermore, engaging in these activities is a unique way to appreciate nature and integrate other subjects such as geography, social studies, or biology.

Safety must be a top priority when engaging in these physical activities as they are not normally carried out in highly-controlled settings. The policies and guidelines of the school, school board, and province regarding these activities must be followed. In cases when certification is required, properly trained instructors can be invited to teach (preferably on a volunteer basis). Parents may be involved to increase the adult to student ratio for safety. Local facilities (e.g., parks, trails, swimming pools) should be considered first when planning such activities. This will emphasize the link between the activities to the community and reduce the need for transportation. Two sample activities within each of the three categories are introduced.

Basic Knowledge and Skills

Land-oriented physical activities are recreational and usually non-competitive physical activities. As the name suggests, they are conducted on land and include activities such as hiking, orienteering, navigation, backpacking, camping, horseback riding, caving, and rock or mountain climbing.

- **Hiking** involves walking in natural outdoor environments (e.g., wilderness, grasslands, parkland), usually on a marked trail, for recreational and health purposes. The equipment needed includes proper footwear (e.g., hard sole, closed-toe shoes or boots), clothing that is appropriate for both the weather and the environment, and other protective products such as insect repellent and sunscreen. For longer trips, additional equipment needed includes drinking water, food, a first-aid kit, mobile phone, map, compass, whistle, and flashlight.

- **Orienteering** is a sport that involves navigational skills primarily using a map and compass to navigate from point/location to point in a defined, unfamiliar terrain (e.g., school yards, local parks, forests, lakes). It can be recreational or competitive, done individually or in groups, and on foot or using equipment such as canoes or bicycles. Competitive orienteering requires participants to locate a series of designated control points in the shortest time possible. Equipment in orienteering includes maps, compasses, proper clothing, footwear, drinking water, and a whistle.

Ice/snow-based physical activities are conducted on ice or snow and include curling, snow skiing, ice-skating, snowshoeing, and sledding.

- Curling is a target game played on ice that involves players sliding curling rocks towards a target. It is in the same family of games such as bowling and shuffleboard. Curling is one of the most popular winter sports in Canada and an official sport in the Winter Olympic Games (Pangrazi & Gibbons, 2009). Many communities in Canada have curling facilities and clubs. Equipment needed for curling includes junior curling rocks for young players, brooms, and proper footwear (two "gripper" shoes for novices). Alternative curling games can be played in the gym using a taped sheet course and hockey pucks or beanbags as stones.

- Skiing and snowboarding are snow-based recreational or competitive activities that involve travelling on snow. The different types of skiing are cross-county, telemark, backcountry, and alpine. These activities can be performed on a hill, flat terrain, trails or open snow. Snow skiing has great benefits for fitness, especially muscular strength and endurance, cardiovascular endurance, coordination, and balance. The equipment includes suitable skis, poles, boots, proper attire with layers, hats or helmets, gloves/mitts, and goggles. The more risky types of skiing (e.g., backcountry, freestyle, ski jumping) should not be practised in an educational setting.

Canada's climate presents many winter activity options.

Water-based physical activities are recreational or competitive physical activities conducted on the water (e.g., boating, rowing, canoeing, kayaking, dragon boat race, surfing), in the water (e.g., swimming, aquafit, water polo), or under the water (e.g., scuba diving, snorkelling).

- **Swimming** is one of the oldest and most popular water-based physical activities. It is also a physical activity that all individuals should learn, as 1.2 million people around the world die by drowning each year (more than two people per minute according to the International Life Saving Federation, 2012). Unlike many animals that instinctively know how to swim, humans must learn how to swim and survive in the water. It is among the most valuable lifelong fitness activities and a type of exercise that is accessible regardless of age, sex, ability, or cultural background. Equipment for learning to swim may include pool noodles, kickboards, pull buoys, float belts, personal flotation devices (PFD), instructional floatation devices (IFD), swim fins, and, of course, proper swimming attire. Learning sequences may include water orientation, holding positions (e.g., entry), basic swim skills (e.g., float, glide), basic survival skills (e.g., survival floating, treading water, elementary backstroke), strokes (e.g., front crawl, back crawl, breaststroke), and diving (e.g., slide in, sitting, standing).

- **Canoeing** is a water-based physical activity that can be conducted individually or in groups on most types of bodies of water. The equipment needed includes canoes (available in various shapes and sizes), oars or paddles, and approved personal floatation devices (PFDs). A progressive learning sequence may include selecting a canoe, a paddle, and a PFD; carrying a canoe; boarding a canoe; basic paddling skills; self and buddy rescue skills; and strokes (e.g., forward, sweep, draw, pry, J-stroke) in still shallow water. It is also helpful to learn how to paddle in the bow (while looking for obstacles and hazards) as well as paddling in the stern and steer. In addition, it is important to learn how to right a capsized canoe.

Resources

www.olympiasportscamp.com/outdoor-education/index.php

www.redcross.ca/article.asp?id=000881&tid=024

Conclusion

This chapter addresses fundamental movement skills, movement concepts, and the five movement domains. Physical educators should introduce the whole spectrum of physical activities in order to educate students, promote movement competence in a wide variety of activities, enhance movement knowledge and understanding, promote physical fitness, and foster life skills.

Review Questions

1 Does the comprehensive framework (chart) of physical activities address the whole spectrum of physical activities that should be taught in school?

2 How would you select physical activities in your future PE, intramural, and after-school PA programs to foster healthy active lifestyles? Why?

3 What is the difference between sports and games? What is the difference between developmental, lead-up, and formal games?

4 List the characteristics of games literacy. Why is it important to demonstrate tactics, skills, and knowledge that are transferable within and between game categories?

5 Discuss five values inherent in dance education.

6 Describe and discuss the roles of movement skill and movement theme for either gymnastics or dance education.

Key Terms

- Movement Domains
- Movement Concepts
- Fundamental Movement Skills
- Dance
- Gymnastics
- Games
- Individual Physical Activities
- Alternative Environment Activities

Physical Literacy

Rebecca Lloyd and Stephen Smith

Overview

The purpose of this chapter is to address the teaching of physical education (PE) through the lens of physical literacy. The PE focus is programmatic in that there is an emphasis on questioning ways in which the physical activities that comprise the curricula of PE are best described, categorized, sequenced, and connected. The lens of physical literacy allows one to look closely at the so-called "building blocks" of physical skill acquisition and movement competency to discern an expanded activity basis for the claim of physical literacy development and the contributions of PE to the wider realm of literacy development.

The chapter begins by exploring the historical roots of physical literacy, its links to movement education, and its antecedents. Often mistakenly thought of as a new concept, physical literacy has significant historical meaning and appreciable relevance for contemporary PE, sport, and recreation programming. Such an exploration points toward a conception of physical literacy requiring the development of a repertoire of locomotions, manipulations, and body management actions that can be channelled into the skill progressions of various games and sports, gymnastic disciplines, and dance forms. Yet, in addition to having a basis in fundamental movement skills and a mastery of activity-specific skills, the physically literate person also develops the requisite physiological capacities and motor abilities (function), the contextualized capabilities (form), expressive possibilities (feeling), and energetic consciousness (flow) necessary to engage in a wide range of activities that give meaning to the daily pursuit of a healthy and active lifestyle. Such an expanded conception of physical literacy both aligns with and expands Physical and Health Education Canada's recommendation that a physical educator attend to the development of the whole child which includes dimensions of fitness and skill development, cognition, and affect (Francis, Johnson, Lloyd, Robinson, & Sheehan, 2011).

This broadened conception of physical literacy takes us into the second section of the chapter where consideration is given to the wider contexts of literacy and literacy education. Physical literacy is presented as one of the multiliteracies currently concerning educators and as representing a distinctive modality of teaching and learning. In fact, the function, form, feeling, and flow dimensions of physical literacy which are introduced in the first section of the chapter characterize a modality of teaching and learning that is attuned to a social vision of diversity and inclusion.

Such a vision is illustrated in the third part of the chapter where an exemplar is provided to make sense of connecting physical literacy to multiliteracy theory and cross-curricular contexts. Student interviews reveal perceptions of becoming physically literate within an alternative activity, specifically climbing, across the subjects of PE, science, language arts, and drama. Various multimodal forms of expression, as in the use of journals, movies, books, drama, private wikis, and private social networking, illustrate an expanded set of possibilities for acquiring physical literacy. As students learn to climb and express their senses of climbing, they come to a deeper understanding of function, form, feeling, and flow as it is both physically experienced and expressed across literacies.

The overarching intention in this chapter is thus to expand the dominant Canadian rendition of physical literacy as "fundamental movement and sport skills" in keeping with the vision of Physical and Health Education Canada (PHE Canada) which, in their 2009 position paper (Mandigo, Francis, Lodewyk, & Lopez, 2009), acknowledged that physical literacy within education settings must differ from other sport contexts such as Canadian Sport for Life (CS4L). This chapter extends the acknowledgement of physical literacy as involving more than the requisite skills of games, sports, dance, gymnastics, and alternative environment activities, along with the health knowledge and cultivated dispositions of healthy, active living. The perception and conception of physical literacy is expanded in this chapter in order to align it with the potential inherent in multiliteracies theory, namely, the development of a social future of interactive and proactive inclusivity.

The chapter concludes by presenting some challenges and curricular responses to a more fully realized and expanded literacy ambition for physical educators. Such challenges pertain to:

- The confinement of PE to just the teaching of "fundamental movement and sport skills"
- The reduction of these skills to decontextualized sport techniques
- The compartmentalization of activity domains that become teaching and learning ends in themselves

These challenges prompt educators to consider how physical literacy can be realized as a way of reading and responding to others in a variety of environments that include the contexts of games, sports, gymnastics, and dance, yet also extend into less bounded, openly public spaces and natural environments.

The Concept of Physical Literacy: Its History and Contemporary Relevance

Physical Literacy Defined

Physical literacy, a concept put forward by a British physical education and phenomenological scholar Margaret Whitehead (2010; 2007; 2005; 2004; 2001), is at the heart of PE curriculum revision in Canada (Ontario Ministry of Education, 2010; PHE Canada, 2010; Higgs, 2010) and elsewhere (Whitehead, 2010). Based on her doctoral research exploring meaningful existence and embodiment in physical education, Whitehead sought to disrupt the predominance of Cartesian dualism, which is a way of thinking and acting in which the body is regarded as a mere mechanistic entity (e.g., a thing to be worked out, drilled through repetitive practice, or molded into shape) and the mind is understood as will, cognitions, and emotions that can be addressed separately from the body (1990). As such, Whitehead explains physical literacy through the following overarching characteristics:

> a physically literate individual … moves with poise, economy, and confidence in a wide variety of physically challenging situations. Furthermore the individual is perceptive in "reading" all aspects of the physical environment, anticipating movement needs or possibilities, and responding appropriately to these, with intelligence and imagination. (2001, p. 3)

A foundation of physical literacy is crucial in all sports and activities.

Whitehead thus defines the concept of physical literacy through an embodied perspective that is informed by her doctoral readings of existential philosophers such as Merleau-Ponty and Sartre and casts it as a "monist view of the human condition" (2005, p. 3) in which there is no mind-from-body separation. By introducing the concept of physical literacy in this way, Whitehead hopes that students might acquire a "literacy of the motile aspects of the human embodied dimension" (2004, p. 4), a capacity with which we are all endowed, and one that has the potential to make a significant contribution to one's quality of life.

As a new physical educator you might be wondering what significance physical literacy and its philosophic underpinnings has on your emergent practice. Perhaps you are planning to include "mind-body exercise" (Gavin & McBrearty, 2006), such as yoga, in your PE program and are quite looking forward to also including segments on fitness and dance as well as games and sports. Perhaps you are also thinking about gymnastics, circus arts, flow arts, martial arts, and a range of alternative environment activities such as kayaking, climbing, skiing, swimming, diving, and slacklining. This broadened curricular scope of PE would certainly be a step in the direction of increased physical literacy. Yet Whitehead suggests something more is involved. The adoption of the term means that we do not simply focus on the type of content that is taught in PE but broaden attention to consider the holistic physical, mental, and emotional development of the physically active child. She explains that "as appropriate to each individual's endowment, physical literacy can be described as the motivation, confidence, physical competence, knowledge and understanding to maintain physical activity throughout the lifecourse" (Whitehead, 2010, p. 5).

Curriculum learning outcomes aligned with the concept of physical literacy have thus shifted away from what has previously been associated with what it means to become physically educated, which typically entails the mastery of a prescribed set of sport, dance, and gymnastic skills (Whitehead, 2004, p. 5), to that of becoming "physically literate" in terms of the comprehension, critical mindedness, confidence, and competence to be physically healthy and active. In PE curricular terms, to teach towards the intended outcome of becoming physically literate one cannot simply expect to base PE classes on mindless drills, activities, and games to keep students active. Rather, physical educators need to approach the teaching of physical activity with the goal of developing:

a   Knowledge and understanding

b   Critical and creative thinking

c   Communication through various modes

d   The ability to apply knowledge and skills from one context to the next

(Mandigo, Francis, Lodewyk, & Lopez, 2009)

Curricular goals of becoming physically literate have the potential to shift the subject of PE away from "a prescribed activity-centred performance model to a person-centred participation model" (Whitehead, 2004, p. 5) where students develop the knowledge, skills, and attitudes to become active and healthy throughout their lifespan. **Figure 13.1** depicts such a desired curriculum outcome for Canadian physical educators. Note the particular emphasis on the cognitive, movement, and affective dimensions of physical literacy as well as the desired outcome to help students become active for life.

The Historical Emergence of Physical Literacy: The Origin of Movement Education

Although the present-day understanding and prominence of the term "physical literacy" can be attributed to Margaret Whitehead, the concept can be traced back to Francois Delsarte in the mid to late 1800s. Delsarte's life work was dedicated to the systematic reading of bodily postures, positions, and gestures that carry emotional meaning (Shawn, 1965, p. 16). His approach to analyzing movement was a precursor to the notation and field of movement education articulated by Rudolf Laban (1948) many years later. Note that "gesture," in the Delsartian sense, extends beyond what might be categorized as non-verbal communication in acts such as pointing, beckoning, shushing, or waving. In the Delsartain sense "gesture" is more broadly defined as any form of physical expression from any part of one's body, such as the subtle meaning one might gather in reading facial expressions to the obvious gesticulations of arms and hands. Imagine for example, how one might discern the differences between an exploding smile generated from the surprise visit of a loved one and a strained smile put on if the visitor is someone not overly liked.

Discerning such physical expressions of movement is not restricted to reading the emotions of another person. Movement educator and phenomenologist, Maxine Sheets-Johnstone (1999), details how one might turn attention to reading the timing, amplitude, and tensions visible in any movement from the lifting of one's hand to a walk down the street. While it might seem strange to consider the importance of reading such subtle details of nuanced physical expression, particularly as a new physical educator who is keen to get children active and moving, consider what might be communicated in terms of sensing and responding to a student's postures, positions, gestures, and expressions of emotional well-being. An energetic hand, shooting skyward, waving back and forth sends a different message than the child who pauses and holds a hand halfway up when a question is posed. Similarly, a child walking across the gym to an activity station with broad, open shoulders and a bounce in her stride sends a very different message than a child walking at a snail's pace with eyes downcast.

Physical Literacy for Life

A Model for Physical Education

Individuals who are physically literate move with competence and confidence in a wide variety of physical activities in multiple environments that benefit the healthy development of the whole person (Physical & Health Education Canada, 2010).

This model is intended for educators and emphasizes life-long development of physical literacy with active for life as the central aim. Physical Literacy stems from three dimensions of a physically literate person: cognitive, motor (movement), and affect (social, emotional, spiritual) while also linking to health and nature (the environment). Movement takes the central position and has enjoyable play as a central theme. It is bordered by the cognitive and affective dimensions all of which integrate continuously throughout the life-span. The wide variation in maturation and development by age and the lack of credible cut-off age-points for various characteristics of such warrants the use of developmental clusters (early, intermediate, and mature) rather than age or grade levels. The circular arrows between the phases and dimensions reflect the ongoing recursive and spiraling nature of the interactions between each.

Figure 13.1: Physical Literacy for Life: A Model for Physical Education (This figure has been developed by Physical & Health Education Canada and reprinted with permission. For more information, visit www.phecanada.ca).

Case Study 1: Timid Toby

Toby is a grade seven boy who has never liked PE class. He is not a sports person in the traditional sense and does not like the way he feels in most activities his physical educator chooses to instruct such as volleyball. When everyone stops to look at him serve, he freezes and worries about how his serve will affect his team's score. It is not that he lacks the coordination, since he taught himself to juggle some years ago and has now become quite adept with clubs, hoops, and even knives. His juggling has led to an interest in bo sticks, buugeng, and fire poi. Jason seems like a loner at school, yet he has set up a blog about juggling and tweets with a wide net of flow artists around the world.

Questions for Reflection

1. What are the implications for students like Toby of the curriculum goal of becoming physically literate?

2. In what ways might Toby become physically literate with a volleyball beyond the traditionally constructed constraints of a volleyball game?

3. Can PE programs connect with students whose activity interests lie outside the present curricula of games and sports, artistic gymnastics, and social dance?

4. How would physical literacy apply to students like Toby whose activity interests are represented and communicated via digital media?

More than a reading of whether a child is ready and receptive to engage in physical activity, acquiring such a keen sense of the timing, amplitude, and tension in movement also plays into the way one might approach the refinement of movement quality. For example, imagine students engaged in a passing activity. While there might be some motor skill criteria and performance outcomes that you would like your students to consider, (e.g., ways of holding the ball, body position, wind-up, point of release, and target measures), there is also the possibility of reading the many individual physical expressions that emerge along the way (as discussed in Lloyd & Smith, 2010; Lloyd, 2011a) as well as how the students themselves may be encouraged to become literate in reading such expressions. Adaptations may thus be made in regards to the way one passes a ball to a peer, in terms of softening, quickening, or amplifying the motions of the wind-up and ball release so that there is an awareness of the partner's receptivity and a greater chance of a catch being made.

While such an approach to teaching PE may seem new, reading and responding to movement expression in this way ties in with the Laban-informed movement concepts that are at the heart of PE curricula (e.g., Manitoba Education, 2000, p. 27; Government of Saskatchewan, 2010, p. 27). In the province of Ontario, movement competence is contextualized in terms of fundamental movement skills (e.g., stability, locomotion, manipulation), movement concepts (e.g., body awareness, effort, spatial awareness, and relationships), and strategies (e.g., tactics). Movement competence, thus contextualized, is one of the three inter-related strands that form the PE curriculum. In fact, the development of movement competence might be considered to be the foundation of the curriculum as it provides a means and a pathway to approach active, healthy living. Accordingly, it is no surprise that the curriculum states that the "development of fundamental movement skills in association with the application of movement concepts and principles provides the basic foundation for physical literacy" (Ontario Ministry of Education, 2010, p. 23). Perhaps after reviewing some of the relevant history that has to do with the emergence of physical literacy, you may better understand the connection between reading physical postures, positions, gestures, and expressions in the nuanced, lived process of acquiring fundamental movement skills and situating that reading within the development of PE curriculum and pedagogy. (For further reading about the philosophical history of physical literacy, see Lloyd, 2011b.)

Fundamental Movement Skills: Metaphorical Building Blocks

Teaching children fundamental movement skills based on principles of stability, locomotion, and manipulation has become the central focus of developing physical literacy within and beyond the realm of PE. Both PHE Canada (a non-profit organization that advocates for quality, daily H&PE) and Canadian Sport for Life or CS4L (a governing body that aims to improve the quality of sport and recreation in Canada), have developed books, programs, and resources that align the acquisition of fundamental movement skills with physical literacy to the extent that the terms are interchangeable (e.g., Francis et al, 2011; Canadian Sport for Life, 2011). According to CS4L, "fundamental movement and sport skills are the basic building blocks of physical literacy." (p. 3)

The building block metaphor, also common within the curricular uptake of physical literacy (e.g., Ontario Ministry of Education, 2010; PHE Canada, 2010, 2008; Higgs, 2010), is based on the premise that if you learn the fundamentals of movement you are then prepared to participate in a wide variety of activities, just as one who learns to read is then prepared to read a variety of books in various genres. The process of becoming physically literate has thus been described as the acquisition of foundational skills such as "walking, running, jumping, climbing, skipping, catching, and throwing … [which] provide a sound basis upon which all refined sport skills are based" (Francis et al., 2011, p.14). The premise is that if you can run, you have the building block required to take part in games that are based on running such as soccer, baseball, volleyball, track and field, squash, badminton, rugby, and tennis. If you can throw, you have the foundational skill to take part in activities that involve throwing such as baseball, softball, cricket, bowling, darts, and shot put.

Children can begin learning fundamental movement skills from a very young age.

Whitehead (2010) reframes the building block, fundamental movement skill metaphor as a "bank of movement competencies" (p. 53). Accordingly, the more one has in the bank, the more one will respond to a wide variety of situations in a way that is automatic to the individual. A physically literate individual who kicks a ball within a game, for example, no longer has to stop and think to perform the movement. Rather, the motile act of kicking exists within a repertoire of movement possibilities. Whitehead (2010) refers to such movement patterns as one's vocabulary and relates the process of becoming fluent in such action to the Piagetian notion of assimilation and accommodation.

The link between teaching fundamental movement skills in isolation and the skillful use of such movements within the complexity of game play is not necessarily a particularly strong one. In fact, the transposition of a rehearsed, repetitive drill of passing a ball may be quite problematic, as advocates of the Teaching Games for Understanding (TGfU) approach assert. Passes within a game (or the execution of other such fundamental movement skills) may depart from what is depicted in mechanistic breakdowns of the ideal

Physical literacy is important in both formal and casual game settings.

form. The use of fundamental movement skill curricular supporting technologies such as Dartfish (2011), a software program that illustrates mechanistic breakdowns of fundamental movements and skills as well as other visual charts that depict the ideal phases of movement in various sport contexts through the visual representation of movement (i.e., Canadian Sport for Life, 2011), may therefore be viewed with critical awareness and understanding. One such caution is the likely tendency to focus on the externalization of movement rather than the expressive, dare we say "mindful," qualities of movement on which the philosophy of physical literacy is based. Just as the historical perspective of physical literacy drew attention to the reading of the timing, amplitude, and tension that give recognizable quality to particular movements, one might also consider a game reading ability (Mandigo & Holt, 2004) that can be acquired as players come to understand not just the tactics but also the characteristics and unique patterns of play that constitute the flow of games and sports (Lloyd & Smith, 2010).

Becoming Physically Literate

The proposition that fundamental movement and sport skills are the prerequisites of physical literacy may be likened, in reading and writing, to the phonetics and phonemics of word awareness that are connected to the grammatical and syntactical awareness of phrases and sentences and, indeed, to the semiotics of paragraphs, passages, and full texts. To not just "read" a game, but also to be able to move such that one is able to "write" and "author" the passages of play requires requisite movement and sport skills "vocabulary"; yet this level of proficiency also requires a knowledge of, and feel for, the game or sport and its constitutive features that come as a result of a broader PE than one focused just on the skills and tactics of games and sports.

A closer look into the definition of physical literacy that is guiding present initiatives in PE is thus warranted. "Individuals who are physical literate move with competence in a wide variety of physical activities that benefit the development of the whole person" (Francis et al., 2011, p. 2).

Notice within the sport context, physical literacy is also equated to long-term sport performance and participation.

> Physical literacy is the mastering of fundamental movement skills and fundamental sport skills that permit a child to read their environment and make appropriate decisions, allowing them [sic] to move confidently and with control in a wide range of physical activity situations. It supports long-term participation and performance to the best of one's ability. (Canadian Sport for Life, 2011)

It is worth mentioning that the term "sport literacy" is used elsewhere to describe PE programs that are based exclusively on the "physical, cultural, personal, social, and cognitive experience" of games and sports (Drummond & Pill, 2011, p. 173). But this "sport literacy," while better acknowledging the dominant activity focus of PE, sidesteps the extent to which a focus on fundamental movement skills and fundamental sport skills fosters long-term athlete development as well as the more generalized abilities, capabilities, and capacities involved in living a fully healthy, physically active life.

These twin aspirations for the physically literate person, namely sporting excellence and active, healthy living, seem to require a more generalized terminology than the "knowledge, skills, and attitudes" or what PHE Canada categorizes as "cognition, movement, affect" related to particular games and sports. After all, a fully healthy, physically active life is not necessarily a product of games and sports, nor is it necessarily expressed in these forms of healthy, physical activity over a person's lifespan. What is needed is a broader conceptualization of the requisite features of physical literacy that is inclusive of fundamental movement skills and fundamental sport skills but not confined to them. Accordingly, four key indicators of physical literacy can be described as:

1 Functional capacities

2 Contextualized capabilities

3 Expressive possibilities

4 Flow consciousness

These categories differ from PHE Canada's conceptual pillars of cognition, movement, and affect as depicted in **Figure 13.1**. Such categories have been introduced as they are more congruent with the language and philosophy of physical literacy as put forward by Whitehead. They are not at complete odds however. A conceptual mapping between the two categorizations reveal essences of connectedness. The functional capacities category (which will soon be explained) aligns most strongly with what PHE Canada categorizes as movement. Contextualized capabilities map onto both categories of cognition and movement as addressing thoughtful movement formed from a responsive relationship to the environment. The expressive possibilities category aligns most strongly with PHE Canada's affect category and flow consciousness can be conceptualized as an equal merging between all three cognition, movement, and affect categories. To facilitate the naming and remembrance of these categories, they may be thought of as aspects of movement function, form, feeling, and flow that are constitutive of the "Function to Flow" or F2F model (Lloyd, 2011c; Lloyd & Smith, 2009).

Functional capacities (function) provide more fundamental building blocks of physical literacy than just the foundational movement skills of walking, running, jumping, throwing, kicking, striking, catching, and trapping. They indicate the physiological and kinesiological prerequisites of moving in certain ways with particular body parts and "must surely include capacities such as balance, coordination, flexibility, agility, control, precision, strength, power, endurance, and the ability to move at different speeds—that is explosively, right though to sustaining movement over a long period of time" (Whitehead, 2001). Some of these capacities and abilities are addressed in the "ABCs—agility, balance, coordination and speed" of physical literacy (Canadian Sport for Life, 2011). Yet it seems that a more extensive alphabet of movement needs to be considered as required for, say, throwing and catching objects of varying weights, textures, sizes, and forms. The capacity for physical literacy rests on health-related fitness parameters of body mass, cardiovascular endurance, muscle strength, and flexibility coupled with the skill-related capacities of agility, balance, coordination, and speed.

The contextualized capabilities (form) category refers to the wide range of motions and movement sequences that can be performed on the basis of the functional capacities listed above. Such capabilities may be initially thought of as the fundamental movement skills (locomotion, stability, and manipulation). These skills can be reduced to techniques of, say, jumping for distance and landing to preserve that distance, balancing in a handstand and then rolling forwards, or throwing a basketball with a chest pass. Yet a skillful action rests essentially on the capability of executing a motion or movement sequence in a particular activity context. It is, after all, the particular configuration and composition of the long jump pit that determines the nature of the leap and landing. The mat's resilience invites the handstand and cushions the roll. The movements of players on the basketball court suggest the expediency of the chest pass. Yet, whereas the contextual references for movement capabilities have traditionally involved just the constructed environments of gymnasia, studios, indoor and outdoor courts, and playing fields, the contextualized capabilities of physical literacy include a much wider range of activity settings.

As Whitehead points out: Children need to learn how to engage with the "phenomena of the natural world" such as "gravity, gradient, fixed and moving objects, and water" (2001, n.p.). The motions of such engagement need to also be applied to the activities that take place in constructed environments, and increasingly so, those environments in which the activities are technologically mediated, from the use of simple tools and equipment to digital media. This array of contexts then suggests not simply the application of fundamental movement skills to particular games and sports, gymnastics, dance, and alternative environment pursuits, but also an exploration of movement capabilities that may well be constitutive of newly created activity forms. The incorporation of meditative and martial arts (see Ragoonaden, Cherkowski, & Berg, 2012) along with circus arts and flow arts (see Price, 2012) in PE programs is indicative of the range of contextualized capabilities that can be developed. (Further exemplification of this point will be provided late in the chapter in the section addressing the PE innovation of "JungleSport.")

The expressive possibilities (feeling) category refers to what are often called communication skills. We communicate verbally with the explicitness of words and the nuance of voice intonation, visual imagery, and sound mixture. However, we also communicate with our bodies, through facial expressions, hand gestures, and body positions. In specific activity contexts we communicate very physically through the effort qualities of the movements enacted, the spatial arrangements and relationships created in the passages of play, and in the body shapes taken to convey specific intention. According to Whitehead:

a physically literate individual should be able to deploy his/her embodied dimension to achieve intentions that focus on self expression. We are manifest in the world in bodily form and through our embodiment we demonstrate/display/communicate many aspects of our personality. This aspect of physical literacy could relate to situations in which self-presentation and non-verbal communication are central. These situations could also extend to those related to art forms such as dance and drama. (2001, n.p.)

Physical education curricula tend to interpret such self expression in conceptual and cognitive terms, suggesting that it is based on an explicit awareness of what the body does, where it moves, how it moves, and with whom (e.g., Ontario Ministry of Education, 2010, p. 24). However, one might consider that this communicative competence involves a more primary, visceral sense of the body and its expressive possibilities based on the movement exploration of breathing, balancing, timing, and touch. By exploring the qualities of kinesthetic sensibility through breathing activities such as running, swimming, yoga, balancing activities in gymnastics, circus arts and climbing, timing activities in dance, juggling and hooping, and touch activities in martial arts, contact sports, and horse riding, one learns to physically "read" the overt intentions of others and to communicate one's own.

Physical literacy can be obtained both in a school setting and in the home.

Flow consciousness (flow) refers to the state of mindfulness, or thoughtful action, to which we can aspire. It is not just an action state of mind as Csikszentmihalyi (2000) affirms, but also an interactive facility that is responsive, from one moment to the next, to changing environmental conditions and the dynamics of engaging with and against others (Lloyd & Smith, 2006; Lloyd, 2011a; Lloyd, 2011b). At times it is going with the flow; at other times it is going against it. Flow consciousness entails being receptive to the ebbs and flows, the bursts, rushes, and explosions of energy as well as the wanings, crashes, and softenings of energetic personal, group, and team expression (Lloyd & Smith, 2010).

Here we again agree with Whitehead's characterization of the physically literate person as "a mover with a rich bank of established movement responses acquired through interacting with a wide range of challenging environments" (2001, p. 7). The person has acquired a rich repertoire of functional capacities, contextualized capabilities, and expressive possibilities that allow "intelligent movement interaction with the world through perceptive reading of the environment, astute application of existing responses, effected alongside newly created responses where needed" (Whitehead, 2001, p. 8). This kind of reading, comprehension, and composition is premised on the high maintenance of physiological and biomechanical functions, the wide exploration of activity forms, and the deepening of kinesthetic sensibility. Flow consciousness is the sense of being in the moment, in the zone, fully alive and awake to respond with movement fluency.

This characterization of physical literacy suggests an unlimited capacity for movement receptivity and creativity. There is no point in time that one can claim to be fully physically literate. In other words, becoming physically literate, in this manifold sense, is an aspiration rather than ever being a fully-fledged achievement. In the following chapter section, further clarification is given to how becoming rather then being physically literate makes sense by looking through some wider lenses of literacy development.

Lenses of Literacy

> Traditionally, sport and physical education has focused upon the "physical" development of individuals. Although this is critical and central to professional practices, the "physical" is only one half of the term. To truly understand the term "physical literacy," a clear understanding of literacy is needed. (Mandigo, Francis, & Lodewyk, 2007, p. 5)

Mandigo et al. provide a number of literacy definitions worth considering and outline the components of literacy as involving "knowledge and understanding" of content, "critical and creative thinking skills," "communication in

Case Study 2: Helen the Hockey Star

Helen plays hockey most days of the week. Her goal is to make it to the Canadian Women's Hockey League (CWHL) and to her credit she is gaining the attention of some scouts. PE is her favourite subject. It makes her feel good and in some ways she exudes a persona that she "rules the roost." After receiving a mark of a B in physical literacy on her interim report card, she is not only puzzled, but also angry. She is by far the most talented student from a fundamental movement skill perspective, in fact, she is the best in the class.

Questions for Reflection

1 Why might Helen have received a low mark?

2 What components of physical literacy will you assess in your lessons, units plans, and cumulative marks? (Clue: consider the dimensions of physical literacy.)

3 What would you say to Helen's parents if they approach you with concerns about her mark in physical literacy?

various forms," and the "application of knowledge and skills to make connections within and between various contexts" (p. 5). These components appear in the *Ontario Curriculum for Health and Physical Education: Grades 1–8* as "providing a solid foundation of language, communication, and thinking skills on which children and youth can develop the skills, knowledge, and attitudes that they need to make healthy decisions with competence and confidence" (Ontario Ministry of Education, 2010, pp. 36–40).

What is now added to the literate understanding of physical literacy draws upon recent consideration of multiliteracies, multimodalities, and social futures that have been articulated by literacy theorists. The intention behind such an expansion is not to venture too far from physical literacy, but rather to provide some literacy-inspired lenses through which to sharpen a focus on what it means to become physically literate.

The Lens of Multiliteracy

In the mid-nineties a group of international scholars came together to consider what was happening in literacy education. Known as the New London Group, these scholars developed a particular sociocultural pedagogical stance, which they have continued to articulate (Cope & Kalantzis, 2000). "Multiliteracies" is the term they use to describe the attentiveness to the multiple ways in which meaning is communicated.

> The New London Group see many types of expression and communication as literacies, whether formal or informal; spoken, gestured, written, or graphic; official or unofficial; correct or "incorrect"; and so on. Among school subjects, they view science, mathematics, history, art, music, etc. as literacies. To a degree, this broad concept of literacy has been around for some time. Terms such as computer literacy and mathematical literacy are now common. However, the New London Group have broadened the definition of literacy much further and provided systematic justification for doing so. (Rowsell, Kosnik & Beck, 2008, p. 112)

This plurality of literacies provides evidence of the manifold ways in which one makes sense of one's life. There is recognition of the "lifeworlds" each of us inhabits, from classrooms to playgrounds, music studios, art rooms, computer labs, work offices, and public places. What we need to make meaning of these various "lifeworlds" is not just the textual literacy of print material, but also a media literacy that allows one to discern, critique, and deconstruct the influx of advertising and marketing messages. There is a need of health literacy as the discriminatory knowledge required to make responsible decisions about personal and population well-being. There is also a need of science literacy, as the education necessary to be informed about the natural laws and principles that govern our lives. There is even the requirement of becoming literately numerate, having a grasp of the mathematics necessary in the workplace and/or daily life. Now physical literacy is added to this list of the realms of meaning making that enable one to live with increasing awareness of life's complexities.

Yet the recognition of multiliteracies is not just a matter of naming the domains of life to which meaning making, and the means used to do so, refer. Multiliteracies bring to light the "metalanguage" of semiotic structures that undergird the various lifeworld literacies. This metalanguage contains various terms such as genre, discourse, voice, and style. "More informally, we might ask 'What's the game,' and 'What's the angle'? … Here our starting point is the social context, the institutional location, the social relations of texts and social practices in which they are imbedded" (Cope & Kalanzis, 2000, pp. 24, 25). It is no accident, however, that mention is made of "games" in this metalanguage consideration. Literally speaking,

soccer and basketball are both games of territory, yet in terms of genre, discourse, voice, and style, by which we mean their histories, cultural contexts, particular rules and conduct of play, and styles of movement production, they are remarkably different, with variations even between regions and countries that compete together. What they share, at a metalanguage level, is the fact that they are played competitively, expressing an agonistic impulse and being understandable within cultural valuations of scoring, winning, and triumphing over one's competitors. They exist primarily as forms of sport, sharing the discourse of skill acquisition, tactical awareness, game sense, and the relevant cultural knowledges of the place and public value of soccer and basketball.

The metalanguage of multiliteracies allows us to step back from sheer immersion in particular lifeworlds, including the various sport worlds and play worlds, to better grasp the meanings of the multiple and manifold practices of living, playing, and competing. Here we have the argument for attending not only to the motor skills, movement concepts, principles, and strategies needed to play a game or sport, but also to the skills of personal and social responsibility and, in fact, to the critical thinking skills that enable us to understand the wider significance of the time and effort invested. This metalanguage also allows us to better appreciate the "increasing complexity and interrelationship of different modes of meaning" (Cope & Kalanzis, 2000, p. 25), particularly where these modalities show the interconnection of physical and other literacies.

The Lens of Multimodality

> Now becoming increasingly important are modes of meaning other than Linguistic modes, including Visual Meanings (images, page layouts, screen formats); Audio Meanings (music sound effects); Gestural Meanings (body language, sensuality); Spatial Meanings (the meanings of environmental spaces, architectural spaces); and Multimodal Meanings. Of the modes of meaning, the Multimodal is the most significant, as it relates the other modes in quite remarkable dynamic relationships. (Cope & Kalanzis, 2000, p. 28)

Physical literacy expresses a feature of multimodality in referring to the "gestural meanings" that accompany other meanings; it also refers to the movement grounding of all meaning-making, whether the movements be those fine motor skills of digital interfacing or the larger, gross motor skills of dance and sports. There is something significantly multimodal to physical literacy insofar as movement provides the grammar and syntax of all meaning-making to a greater of lesser extent.

The grammar of movement relates to movement education's vocabulary, movement phrases, and the gerunds, prepositions, and creations of movement sentences. Yet the grammar of movement is not just the ability to parse meaning within any one context of action; it also pertains to the metalanguage terms of posture, position, gestural and expressive action, interaction, object of reference, order, style, and facility that allow for shifting between different codes of movement, different forms, disciplines, and cultures of physical activity. Games and sports are then literally different from dance forms, gymnastics, martial arts, and circus and flow arts, not just in the most obviously visible ways, but also in terms of the distinctive ways they utilize the metalanguage of movement proficiency. It is, furthermore, the facility of play with, and interplay between, various styles of pursuing movement competency that produces invention, whether in the form of new games, new dance forms, circus arts and flow arts creations, and in the hybridizations of movement and digital technologies.

This potential of physical literacy requires that one look a little critically at current definitions and see where the potential multimodality of becoming fully physically literate has been underappreciated. One need look no further than the literacy worlds of the children and youth we teach as their worlds are highly technologically-mediated. They are characterized by sophisticated visual imagery mixed with gestural communication. The media with which these children and youth are proficient, from gaming consoles to smartphones, provide clear evidence of a multimodality that appears to be missing when activities are compartmentalized in PE programs. Conversely, what multimodal physical awareness might be tapped into if foot juggling, hacky sack, Tae Kwon Do, and kickboxing movements along with the regular motions of soccer were included? What multimodal spatial, visual, audio, and gestural awareness might be developed if physical literacy were the result of playing across the conventional bounds of games, sports, gymnastics, dance, and the alternative environment and arts-referenced movement disciplines? Such a line of inquiry provides further insight and possibility for what it might mean to move "in a wide variety of physical activities in multiple environments," which is a central component of PHE Canada's definition of physical literacy (PHE Canada, n.d.).

Physical literacy is an important component in an ongoing healthy active lifestyle.

The Lens of Inclusion

This third literacy lens brings us to a social vision that has great significance for PE along with each of the other subjects taught in schools. As Cope and Kalanzis point out: "an authentically democratic new vision of schools must include a vision of meaningful success for all" (2000, pp. 12, 13).

The basis of this vision lies in the recognition of the multiplying and hybridizing ways of making, communicating, and receiving meaning. What is learned is no longer confined to particular regions, taught as particularly preferred activities, in standardized ways.

> Local diversity and global connectedness mean not only that there can be no standard; they also mean that the most important skill students need to learn is to negotiate regional, ethnic, or class-based dialects; variations in register that occur according to social context; hybrid cross-cultural discourses; the code switching often to be found within a text among different languages, dialects or registers; different, visual and iconic meanings; and variations in the gestural relationships among people, language and material objects. (Cope & Kalanzis, 2000, p. 14)

The multiplication of lifeworlds and their overlapping edges now require "an epistemology of pluralism that provides access without people having to erase or leave behind different subjectivities" (Cope & Kalanzis, 2000, p. 18). This "pluralized notion of literacy" (Jewitt, 2008, p. 255) "sets out to redesign the social futures of young people across boundaries of difference" (p. 245). In schools this means giving due attention to the different literacies, not privileging written and oral forms over the visual, tactile, and kinesthetic forms, and provoking a critical literacy "focusing on issues related to fairness, equity and social justice" (Ontario Ministry of Education, 2010, p. 62).

Critical literacy is an essential part of the lens of inclusion in PE. What activity selections advantage some children over others in terms of prior learning, family and community support for participation, and reflection in dominant cultural images? What kinds of instruction and criteria of assessment practices benefit some children over others? What functional capacities, contextualized capabilities, expressive possibilities, and even modes of flow consciousness are privileged in PE? These are some of the questions we need to consider when delivering PE programs.

One can thus come to appreciate the multiliterate, multimodal, and inclusive ambitions of physical literacy. From the physical side there is great potential to explore more widely and deeply the development of movement competency.

Yet this competency is not an end in itself; rather, it is the means of better understanding one's place in the world and one's connection to others who may be quite different in their activity preferences, their capacities, capabilities, expressions, and engagements with us. From the literacy side, then, we see the intrinsic connection of PE practices with the wider practices of literacy in a multicultural, multilingual world comprised of diverse and interconnected lifeworlds.

Content Exemplar

David Kirk (2010) describes the dominant "physical education-as-sport-technique" paradigm, where PE lessons are based and assessed on the teaching of isolated fundamental movement skills. A departure from this and a turn towards the multicultural, multilingual world is paramount if the curricular goal of becoming physically literate is to be adopted. Considering the concept of physical literacy in terms of its history, holistic philosophy, and place within a larger multiliteracy framework, beginning and seasoned educators alike can no longer justify the reproduction solely of the sport education model (Gurvitch & Metzler, 2010) and feel they are teaching students to become fully and fluidly physically literate.

Expanding the Programming of PE to Include Alternative Activities

What stands in the way of physical literacy curricular reform is the ingrained nature of assessment in PE, that is, assessment that is paired with the acquisition of techniques associated with familiar or traditional sports. This is not to say PE programs are not expanding in terms of activities to which students are exposed beyond games and sports (Metzler, 2005). However, what is missing is a conceptual framework for physical educators and students alike to make sense of how they may become physically literate in what might be considered alternative physical activity contexts such as hiking, climbing, or even hula-hooping.

To highlight such a way of thinking, excerpts from interviews with five seasoned physical educators who participated in a climbing-based, JungleSport phenomenological study (as detailed in Lloyd, 2012) reveal that alternative movement forms such as climbing are becoming part of PE programming, yet an understanding of the learning process within such an alternative pursuit is lacking. While the following excerpts are specific to a research project situated within a JungleSport program, the lessons they offer can be applied to a broadened understanding of what physical literacy means within and beyond a curriculum that includes traditional sports.

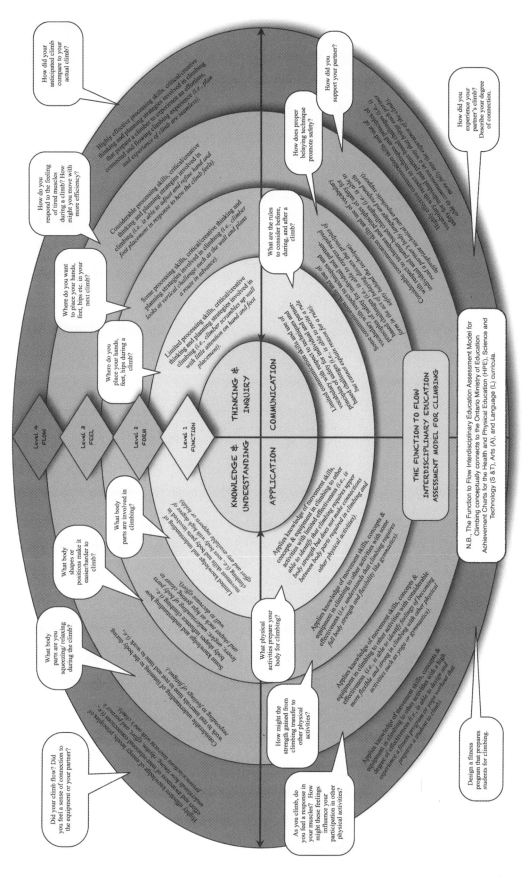

Figure 13.2: Visual Assessment Chart

Here, a grade nine physical educator explains why he includes climbing in his programming:

> I think that JungleSport gets some of them out of their shells and gives the less athletic students a chance to succeed … it's a real kind of leveling of the playing field … that can help if you're using different muscles and using different things. Basically, you want to expose students to as many different things as possible.

The notion of wanting to add variety in PE programming with the intention of exposing students to activities they may continue outside the PE context (and with the long-term intention that it becomes an activity they might pursue as they approach adult life) is also shared by a grade five PE specialist. He explains:

Case Study 3: Sarine Has the Soccer Moves

Sarine arrived in Canada with her family as refugees. She is placed in grade eight, but doesn't speak English well and works daily with Marina, a language support teacher. Marina observes that the PE class is the one place where Sarine seems to understand quite well what is going on. This week her class has started soccer, with drills of dribbling, passing, and shooting, and a mini-game at the end of the period. Sarine stands out, displaying soccer skills that are far superior to those of her classmates.

Questions for Reflection

1 How might Sarine's soccer abilities provide a basis for learning activities with which she is not familiar?

2 What might Marina do to bring Sarine's skills and knowledge of soccer into the classroom lessons?

What I'm interested in is exposing the students to as many activities as possible, hoping that something sticks long term. At least if they find one thing that sticks with them for life, I feel like I've done my job. We do curling, fencing, and many different things. We throw activities at the students and try to get them to try new things.

A grade one educator also speaks positively about the need for introducing variety in her programming:

> What we mostly do is on the ground kind of stuff, if you will, bouncing balls, running, that kind of stuff … . There are some students you may say are more athletic in terms of body strength and that really makes a difference … having that body strength or taking that risk. So, I think that for them, being able to say that "hey, I'm the one who went the highest," or "I was able to do that," or "I was confident enough," it's just such a bonus for them as far as them doing it. Because a lot of them have upper body strength that you don't get to use in a lot of sports.

The consensus after speaking with five educators from five different schools covering grades one, five, seven, eight, and nine, however, was that no matter how much they perceived that the climbing program evened the playing field in terms of offering an opportunity for "non athletic" students to shine and build confidence, not one of them assessed their students beyond basic levels of participation. When asked during the first year of the three-year, SSHRC-funded study, the educators expressed an interest in assisting with the process of developing and testing out an assessment tool that would connect climbing to the four quadrants of physical literacy as detailed in the Ontario Health and Physical Education Achievement Chart (Ontario Ministry of Education, 2010).

The visual assessment chart (**Figure 13.2**) provided educators with interactive prompts was thus created after in-depth phenomenological observation and focus group interviews of students experiencing the JungleSport program in five schools. (Lloyd, 2012). The visual chart was then provided to educators in the second year of the JungleSport study for feedback and suggestions for improvement.

This assessment tool helped the seasoned educators conceptualize learning beyond the dominant sport education model and the "physical education-as-sport-technique" (Kirk, 2010) paradigm. A grade nine educators commented:

> A lot of teachers use JungleSport as a participation activity. And this chart kind of brings the thinking and all of the different skills they bring to it to the forefront. So, until you came last year, it was just a fun activity the kids did. I didn't really think of it any other way then. They had fun, they were active. Whereas now, this tool is putting a different spin on it.

Student Perceptions of Experiencing an Interdisciplinary and Multimodal Approach to Becoming Physically Literate

In addition to the creation of an assessment chart, which features the various dimensions of becoming physically literate as depicted in **Figure 13.2**, an interdisciplinary education approach to becoming physically literate was also introduced in the second year of the JungleSport study.

Prior to visiting each school, the primary researcher was able to coordinate meetings between educators of science, language arts, drama, and PE, in three different intermediate schools in the Ottawa-Gatineau region. What emerged from these meetings were a series of several interdisciplinary and multiliteracy learning activities that pertained to the process of becoming physically literate through climbing. Namely: the watching of climbing documentaries, reading, and acting out excerpts from stories about climbing expeditions, Prusik knot tying, creative writing and social networking through a private Wiki (referred to in their interviews as blogging), and participating in the experience of climbing itself.

Comments from focus group interviews gathered from students in three different grade seven and eight classes from three different schools reveal their experiences and perceptions of being involved in these interdisciplinary and multiliteracy activities:

> the rock climbing was really cool and neat … for science it really helped us to see the real world and how real rock climbers feel when they climb the rocks. For the phys ed part, it was really fun because we get to challenge ourselves, we get to stay fit and we get to work our lower and upper body. For the English it was really fun because we got to share our opinions on the blogs and we got to learn how to use a blog and stuff.

> I thought that doing the blogs really helped the climbing because you can share your experiences with other people and they can relate to you and you can also use links from the other world to relate to like pictures and stuff. Pictures of mountains and rocks and you can really relate to that. And you can comment on other peoples' blogs so that can really help too.

> When I was writing my blog I did a text to world thing … I put a picture of a monkey on vines for the gorilla challenge … . We got to climb on a rope and swing around to get to the other side and like monkeys do that all the time, so it was kind of cool to relate to that. And some people were saying how exciting it was and I was replying "yeah, I can't wait for the next day."

> I thought that the blog was a good idea because you got to write how you felt about climbing and other people could relate and comment on what they thought. And, yeah, I gave

some people comments, like advice and stuff. And I got some comments saying "good job for making it to the top" and "oh, you must have a good partner who kept encouraging you," and stuff like that.

> I think it helps because some people were a little afraid to say what is on their minds and it's easier to say it on their blog. And other people could help them out with advice.

Insights shared by these students speak positively to the emergence of interdisciplinary, multiliterate understandings. Mention of improvements in fitness, connections to others and the natural world as well as overall boosts of self-esteem are but some of the positive results that emerged from the various ways students were encouraged to express themselves and articulate their experiences. Graphics such as the F2F Interdisciplinary Model shown in **Figure 13.2**, which contextualizes the dimensions of physical literacy as defined through the Ontario H&PE Curriculum, within the climbing context provide physical educators and students alike with a way of conceptualizing the learning process beyond Kirk's defined paradigm of "physical education-as-sport-techniques" (2010).

In sharing both the graphic and interview excerpts, it is hoped that broadened conceptions of assessing physical literacy may emerge within other alternative as well as traditional sports.

Conclusion

Almost fifty years ago, Ted Shawn, the renowned dance choreographer and performer, made an appeal for a physical literacy focus in PE. He wrote:

> I hope the day comes when all children, from their first start in the primary grades, learn to use human movement as a language equally and along with their learning to communicate by speech and by writing. We would then have in a few generations a physically "literate" adult population; for today, in spite of "physical education" (which confines itself largely to teaching athletic sports) we have mostly physical illiteracy—only one in a million can communicate and read communications through gesture." (1965, pp. 89–90)

Many years later Margaret Whitehead pressed the case for physical literacy by pointing out that

> the overarching characteristics of a physically literate individual are that the person moves with poise, economy and confidence in a wide variety of physically challenging situations. Furthermore the individual is perceptive in "reading" all aspects of the physical environment, anticipating movement needs or possibilities and responding appropriately to these, with intelligence and imagination. (2001, p. 3)

241

We now see widespread adoption in Canada and elsewhere of the term "physical literacy." Yet, it remains questionable to what extent the term is consistent with what is understood about literacy in general, multiliteracies, and indeed about the functions, forms, feelings, and flows of physicality that comprise the domain of activities and practices in PE.

The JungleSport study provides evidence of an emergent sense of physical literacy that includes not only reading the environment, but also creating meaning for oneself, and communicating that meaning within the specific activity context and more broadly in the context of other literacies. In this way we can begin to see physical literacy as being a process of becoming versed in movement, in and across the boundaries of activities that comprise the PE curriculum, and a process of becoming versed through movement in and across the boundaries of other literacies.

Questions for Discussion and Reflection

1 How can physical literacy be addressed within (and beyond) the prevailing "physical education-as-sport-technique" (Kirk, 2010) paradigm (i.e., lessons based on the teaching of fundamental movements skills in isolation)?

2 What issues of curriculum planning and provision (timetabling, staffing, coordinating cross-curricular multimodal literacy projects, etc.) need to be addressed in order to fulfill the physical literacy promise?

3 What are the benefits and limitations of conceptualizing physical literacy as a fundamental movement skill building block?

4 How would you assess physical literacy in a PE lesson?

5 How would you assess physical literacy beyond the PE context?

6 What are your perceptions of curriculum revision based on the concept of physical literacy? What will stay the same? What will change?

7 What have you learned about the concept of physical literacy that will change the way you plan, teach and/or assess your lessons?

Key Terms

- Physical Literacy
- Movement Education
- Fundamental Movement Skills
- Physical Literacy Indicators
- Multiliteracy Lens
- Multimodality Lens
- Inclusion Lens

Health Literacy

Stephen Berg, Clive Hickson, and Antony Card

Overview

Across Canada, there are many effective physical education (PE) programs being conducted from kindergarten to grade twelve. However, there are concerns throughout the nation that many social health issues are not being properly addressed within the school setting. For children and youth to acquire the knowledge, skills, and attitudes necessary to become health literate, opportunities need to be provided for young people to critically assess various health-related topics, and the school environment is a ideal setting. But how can educators, administrators, and other school officials plan for quality health programming? The purpose of this chapter is to address this question.

First, the chapter presents an overview of what health literacy is and what issues we are currently facing in terms of Canadian children's health. Next, information on the dimensions of health, and the need for health and wellness programming in the schools is presented. Finally, an overview of comprehensive school health programming will be given, along with sample case studies so readers can critically think how, as future physical educators, they can help children and youth become truly health literate.

Introduction to Health Literacy

In 2007, the Canadian Council on Learning suggested that 60% of adults in Canada lack the capacity to gather, understand, and take action on information and services to make appropriate health decisions. This statistic is a concern from many perspectives as it illustrates that health issues will continue to be a concern for many adults regardless of the information and services available to them in their communities. However, from another perspective that can easily be overlooked, this statistic may also be equally problematic for children and youth in Canada. This is due to the fact that some of these adults, perhaps even the majority, may also be parents or caregivers to children and youth. As children and youth are often reliant on the knowledge of the adults in their lives, their health has the potential to be negatively affected.

It is important that children and youth in Canada are provided with opportunities to gain knowledge and skills for themselves to support their own health and well-being. They need to be given opportunities to develop their own understanding of health issues in order to make life choices that will benefit their health and well-being. They need to become health literate!

What Is Health Literacy?

Traditionally in education, the term literacy has been used primarily in the context of language arts programs (Zimmer, Dorsch, Hoeber, & LeDrew, 2011). However, in recent years, the use of this term has been expanded, used more broadly, and applied to many other areas. For example, the term physical literacy is used to describe how well a person is able to move efficiently and effectively in the physical activity domain and this term is now frequently found in PE and coaching literature. Similarly, the term health literacy emerged in the area of PE and has become increasingly featured in health and wellness literature.

In the late 1980s a number of reports were published in Canada and the United States that established clear connections between education and health outcomes. For example:

- Better educated people experience lower mortality rates.
- An increase in education reduces the risk of illnesses such as heart disease as well as the probability of reporting ill health and lost work days.
- Increased levels of education often are associated with better access to health care.
- Increased levels of education normally result in increased employment. Employed people experience better health and lower mortality rates than unemployed people.

- Overall differences in health are particularly noticeable when years of education are increased beyond high school graduation.

The findings from these reports garnered considerable interest in Canada and were a catalyst for the creation of the National Literacy and Health Program in 1994 by the Canadian Public Health Association in an attempt to establish health literacy as an area of inquiry. As a result of actions such as this, the concept of health literacy has been built on a strong foundation of research with over 1,000 published articles on the topic (Canadian Council on Learning, 2007).

Many provinces have expanded their PE curricula to include the study of health and to promote health literacy.

Definitions of health literacy are purposefully broad in nature. This is due to the wide range of skills and actions required from an individual. According to the Canadian Public Health Association (2010) health literacy involves "the ability to assess, understand and act on information for health" Similarly, the Canadian Council on Learning (2007) suggests that health literacy refers to the degree that individuals can access and use health information for healthy decision-making and to maintain their basic health. In agreement, Berg, Hickson, and Fishburne (2010) also suggest that when a person has developed a sound foundation of health literacy he or she will have the skills to gather, understand, and act upon information and knowledge to improve their health and well-being.

These definitions, and similar ones from other health organizations, educators, and researchers, have considerable commonality. In particular, they all focus upon the requirement for individuals to access, understand, and act upon information in order to generate change for the betterment of their health.

Why Is Health Literacy Important?

It is well known that one's quality of life and health status are a combination of actions, genetics, and what's known as the social determinants of health (Green & Kreuter, 2005). According to the World Health Organization (2008), there has been increasing awareness over the past three decades that both the majority of the global burden of disease and the major causes of health inequities found around the world arise from the conditions in which people are born, grow, age, live, and work in. Mikkonen and Raphael (2010) note that despite the assumption that most "Canadians have personal control over these factors, in most cases the living conditions are—for better or worse—imposed upon us by the quality of the communities, housing situations, our work settings, health and social service agencies, and educational institutions with which we interact" (p. 7). And yet, although the health status for children and youth in Canada varies across the country, children and youth generally enjoy a good standard of health (Statistics Canada, 2002).

Even though there has been a virtual elimination of many diseases, other challenges have begun to emerge that are of great concern. For example, many children and youth in Canada engage in sedentary lifestyles, have poor nutritional habits, and participate in high-risk behaviours. Consequently, health issues such as type 2 diabetes, heart disease, and obesity are now at levels that have not been seen previously in past generations (Berg et al., 2010). As Zimmer et al. (2011) succinctly state, children and youth deserve more than a lifetime of health problems.

Figure 14.1: Examples of Everyday Health Literacy Issues

- Teasing and "put downs"
- Rumours
- Bullying
- Cyber-bullying
- Media and body image
- Healthy and unhealthy food choices
- Food labels and Nutrition Facts tables
- Adhering to Canada's Food Guide
- Active lifestyle choices
- Inactivity issues and TV/computer use
- Protective gear usage in sports/work activities
- Safety warnings on packaging and signs
- Proper use of medication
- Proper use of sunscreen
- Drinking water daily rather than carbonated sugar drinks
- Headphones versus earbuds
- Cell phone use (particularly while driving)
- Playground cliques
- Being a bystander to unhealthy behaviours and not intervening
- High-risk behaviours (e.g., smoking, drug/alcohol abuse)
- Benefits of high self-esteem and dangers of low self-esteem

It is commonly accepted that health behaviours are learned and, as such, can be influenced and potentially changed. The acceptance of this concept is important, as the adoption of such a view recognizes that it is possible to create a strong foundation of knowledge and skills that can be utilized by children and youth in order to promote health and also minimize those attitudes and behaviours that are detrimental to health and well-being. **Figure 14.1** lists some examples of potential health literacy issues that children and youth face on a daily basis.

it is critically important that children and youth are equipped to gather relevant information on health and well-being, understand and appreciate the value of this information, and have the commitment to act appropriately upon the information that they have encountered. This is recognized in documents such as the Health and Physical Education Curriculum from the Ontario Ministry of Education (2010). This document introduces educators to the importance of fostering health literacy. It attempts to move physical educators away from a curriculum devoted to playing sports and receiving didactic style instruction in health to a program that will serve students throughout their lives and develop the capacity, comprehension, and commitment to choose healthy, active lifestyles (Ophea, 2010).

Given the current spiraling costs of health care in Canada, developing an effective approach for the delivery of health programming that develops effective health literacy in children and health should be a high priority for Canada (LeDrew, 2008). Therefore, the need to promote health and wellness in children and youth is at a critical point in Canada. It is essential that opportunities be provided to children and youth to develop the knowledge, skills, and attitude to develop healthy lifestyles (Berg et al., 2010).

What Are the Benefits of Health Literacy?

The knowledge and skills gained through the development of health literacy can benefit children and youth throughout their lives. It can help them thrive and navigate their pathway in a world that seems to constantly present new challenges. Importantly, it can also lead them to not only adopt healthy active lifestyles for themselves but also to promote the advantages of healthy living to their peers and all those around them (Ophea, 2010).

The effective implementation of programming that develops health literacy assists in exposing children and youth to not only the immediate effects of healthy choice making, but also the potential of a lifetime of increased well-being. One might further contend that the development of health literacy can actually empower children and youth and provide them with the skills needed to take to control of their well-being. As the children and youth of today become the adult backbone of our communities of tomorrow, health literacy can help to create healthy communities in the future.

Another important benefit of health literacy is the impact it can have on the overall education of children and youth. Studies have consistently demonstrated a strong link between literacy, level of education, and level of health. At all ages, there is evidence that health and learning are closely intertwined. Research has clearly illustrated that the higher a person's attained level of education, the better that person's health (Canadian Council on Learning, 2007; Rootman & Gordon-El-Bihbety, 2008).

Another benefit that has the potential to be realized through the development of health literacy is the elimination of health disparity between different population groups. In their review of health literacy in Canada, Rootman and Gordon-El-Bihbety (2008) state that health literacy varies significantly across the country, with Yukon, Saskatchewan, and Alberta experiencing the best average levels.

Health literacy is part of a healthy active lifestyle.

However, they also point out that the average scores in each province and territory are low, meaning that large portions of the population have a low health literacy level—with immigrants, persons with disabilities, and those with low levels of formal education experiencing the lowest levels. Recognizing that educational programming has the power to reach students from all backgrounds and circumstances is critical, especially if health literacy is to be achieved by all children and youth in Canada.

The Canadian Council on Learning (2007) suggests that researchers and policy-makers in the health and education fields regard health literacy as a critical tool in addressing health disparities between different population groups as well as a sound predictor of overall population health.

Canada is not the only nation recognizing the potential benefits that health literacy can bring to a society. In the late 1990s the American Medical Association recognized and reported that poor health literacy is a strong predictor of poor levels health and is linked to higher rates of hospitalization and high societal economic costs (American Medical Association, 1999). Further, the Centers for Disease Control and Prevention (2012) state that it should be a national educational aim that all children in American schools graduate with health literacy skills that can help them to live healthier lives as children and as future adults.

Barriers to Health Literacy in Canada

It is difficult for individuals to become health literate on their own; society must also support an individual's efforts. It is a joint responsibility; therefore, it is critically important to understand and recognize the barriers that can impede the acquisition of health literacy by children and youth. Individual barriers include issues such as cultural beliefs, a low level of education, or a lack of understanding of health issues. These personal features can cause difficulty for those trying to achieve health literacy.

Systemic barriers can be equally problematic (Rootman & Gordon-El-Bihbety, 2008). For example, a lack of coordination among provincial, regional, and/or national systems can serve to increase any detrimental effects. Rootman and Gordon-El-Bihbety (2008) suggest that schools, communities, and the health care system can all be systemic barriers to health literacy. For example, although schools can be excellent providers of health knowledge and skills, they can be negatively affected by issues such as depleted budgets or a lack of educator expertise.

Addressing these barriers is essential if health literacy is to be achieved by children and youth in Canada. To eradicate these barriers, attention needs to be paid to such issues as: the creation of comprehensive school health programming; the provision of culturally-appropriate health services; and the development of public campaigns to raise awareness of health issues (Rootman & Gordon-El-Bihbety, 2008).

What Is the Relevance of Health Literacy to Children and Youth?

Health issues offer opportunities to discuss, debate, and interpret topical issues of current interest. Creating connections between academic concepts and real-life situations enables children and youth the opportunity to explore the world around them and develop insight for future behaviours and actions (Anderson, 2004). Therefore, for children and youth to appreciate the true relevance of health literacy, it

is critical that educational opportunities are connected and linked to authentic life situations. For example, discussing the media portrayal of body shape and size or role-playing the effects of playground cliques can add authenticity to the classroom. Such experiences can enable children and youth to better face the challenges that they are likely to meet in their day-to-day lives and also some of the decisions that they may be confronted with as adults (Ophea, 2010).

The Importance of Educator Health Literacy

Peterson, Cooper, and Laird (2001) suggest that educators must have the knowledge, skills, and attributes to address the variety of complex health-related issues that children and youth can bring to the school environment. Consequently, pre-professional and staff development programming should provide opportunities for prospective and practising educators to enhance their understanding of critical issues and teaching strategies in child and youth health. Peterson et al. (2001) further suggest that educator health literacy is critically important, as developing health-literate students can only be achieved by high quality teacher education programming that enhances educator health literacy (see **Figure 14.2** for strategies of how educators can support health literacy).

Health literacy can provide keys to future success for children and youth. When provided with effective learning strategies, children and youth can understand the links between what they learn and what they experience in their lives. They can then begin to positively change their actions and follow a healthy, active lifestyle.

What Is Health? What Is Wellness?

Health topics are everywhere. Canadians are constantly bombarded with health-related information through the news, on the radio, on the Internet, in advertising, and various other media. The latest "trends" in exercise prescription, mental health, and nutritional programming are multi-billion dollar industries and it is increasingly difficult for Canadians to discern accurate health facts from fallacies. But what exactly is health, and what does it mean for a person to be healthy?

The World Health Organization (WHO) defines health as a state of complete physical, spiritual, cultural, mental, and social well-being and not merely the absence of disease or infirmity (WHO, 2010) and Pruitt, Allegrante, & Prothrow-Stith (2007), suggest that in the past, if you did not have an illness or disease, you were considered healthy. However, today the term health no longer just means the absence of illness, and the notion of good health has evolved in recent years. Our definition of health has changed as we have come to understand more about the various lifestyle factors

Figure 14.2: Examples of How Educators Can Support Health Literacy

1. **Create and develop cooperative learning environments**

   Cooperative tasks promote understanding and respect for self and others

   Participation encourages responsibility and recognition of choices and actions

2. **Create discussion circles**

   Provides a forum for expressing and exploring ideas and thoughts

   Allows for discussion in a controlled setting

3. **Foster independent learning**

   Allows for the exploration of topical issues of interest

   Takes learning from the classroom to the home and beyond

4. **Encourage journal writing**

   Allows for the expression of thoughts, opinions, and reflections in a private manner

   Allows educators to guide thinking or present ideas for thought

5. **Incorporate role-playing**

   Provides opportunities to practice and act out new skills in a safe environment

   Enables students to recognize potential solutions to issues

6. **Utilize peer educators**

   At times, peers are more effective in the delivery of material than adults

   Provides leadership opportunities for the peer educators

7. **Promote the use of technology**

   Allows students to gather information from a variety of sources

   Students can have experiences that may not be readily available otherwise

8. **Student presentations**

   Students can gather and demonstrate their understanding on a wide variety of topics

   Personal interest or chosen topics can be pursued

9. **Access expertise**

   Invite qualified community resource people to present to students

   Can supplement school-based programming

10. **Field trips**

    Brings relevancy to school-based learning

    Connects school and community

Adapted from Berg et al. (2010)

that bring about illness and affect a person's health (Hoeger & Hoeger, 2011). In contrast to previous thinking, present understanding requires a focus on the factors that precede illnesses rather than being concerned with disease once it strikes.

Although there tends to be no single agreed upon definition of wellness, common themes can be identified in definitions developed by a variety of governments, agencies, and organizations. Wellness has been identified as an all-inclusive umbrella covering a variety of related factors. A state of wellness requires the implementation of positive programs to change behaviour and thereby improve health and quality of life, prolong life, and achieve total well-being (Hoeger and Hoeger, 2011).

Anspaugh & Ezell (2010) state that wellness can be viewed as a balanced state of well-being. It comprises physical, social, spiritual, environmental, intellectual, and emotional components and assumes an individual must take personal responsibility for his or her own well-being and balance of these dimensions. In agreement, Hoeger et al. (2007) also suggest optimum wellness requires the consideration of an occupational component.

Regardless of the lack of a universal definition of health and wellness, our present understanding refers to an individual's overall response to the variety of challenges of living. However, it is critical to remember that within these definitions is the acknowledgement that health and wellness is not something that just happens overnight. It requires a conscious and active commitment from a person to work to improve on all aspects of his or her life.

Dimensions of Health

Health is a balanced state that enables individuals to achieve their full potential in life. Personal wellness occurs when a commitment to lifestyle choices is based on healthy attitudes and actions. Optimum health balances seven dimensions: emotional, environmental, mental/intellectual, occupational, physical, social, and spiritual (Berg et al., 2010).

The following are descriptions of each of the seven components of health.

1 **Emotional:** A person's ability to acknowledge, understand, manage, and express thoughts and feelings through self-control and self-acceptance in a constructive manner.

2 **Environmental:** This component relates to human environment and relationships including family, friends, home, schools, workplaces, culture, community, and country. It also extends to preserving, protecting, and improving one's external environment.

3 **Mental/Intellectual:** This component enhances a person's curiosity and ongoing learning. It implies the effective use of information, the application of learning, the creation of opportunities to extend learning, and the engagement with the world around you. It is also the ability to interpret and analyze, think critically and creatively in order to meet challenges in order for a person to reach his or her full potential.

4 **Occupational:** This occurs when a person broadens and gains new skills. This enables one to have some sense of control concerning their daily actions. It also refers to a person's ability to collaborate with others, commit to tasks, and develop a sense of satisfaction in performance.

5 **Physical:** A person's healthy growth, development, and overall care of the body including proper diet, medical and dental care, and sufficient exercise and sleep.

6 **Social:** This component involves enabling a person to create and maintain satisfying and respectful interpersonal relationships and develop a positive connection with the environment.

7 **Spiritual:** A person's ability to understand his or her own values and beliefs leading to a sense of meaning or purpose. The ethics, values, and morals of spiritual health and wellness can guide a person to create meaning and direction in life and understand the world and his or her role within it.

Physical educators can help facilitate health literacy among their students, and beyond them to their friends and families.

The Need for Health in Schools

Health education is a lifelong process. School-based health education programming can play an important role in the primary prevention of a variety of health issues and should be a fundamental contribution to the development and well-being of youth. A well-planned and well-implemented health and wellness education program can be effective in helping youth reduce their risk of numerous health-related diseases and injuries and in some cases even prevent them. When these components of a health and wellness program are in place, children and youth will have a greater opportunity to become health literate. As children and youth develop awareness of the varying components of health and wellness, and begin to incorporate them into their daily lives, they will begin to assume responsibility for, and actively participate in, their own healthy decision-making.

Issues in Canada

Over the past century, once-common diseases that led to disability or early death have been virtually eliminated. However, despite advances in the treatment of childhood disease, there are new threats despite the fact that we live in a society filled with medical breakthroughs. The number of overweight and obese children in Canada has reached epidemic levels. Further evidence indicates that significant numbers of young people are experiencing mental health issues. Evidence also suggests that, if left unchecked, the prevalence of diseases such as type 2 diabetes, cancer, and heart disease will reach levels previously unheard of.

The following is a lists of risk factors faced by Canadian children and youth.

Physical Inactivity

- The rate of obesity in Canadian youth has tripled in the last twenty-five years (Tjepkema & Shield, 2005).
- Only 9% of boys and 4% of girls are meeting the recommended amount of sixty minutes of moderate-to-vigorous physical activity per day (Active Healthy Kids Canada, 2010).

Case Study 1: The House Party

Grade six students Marie and Heather are walking to the bus stop after school when they are approached by a group of older teenagers. Marie recognizes some of the members of the group as they used to attend Marie and Heather's school a year or so previously. Heather, being a new student to the school, does not know any of the group. One of the group, which consists of boys and girls, invites the girls to go to an empty house a few blocks away to "enjoy themselves." The rest of the group start to gather around Marie and Heather and encourage the two girls to say yes.

Marie is a little wary of the situation as she had heard that a couple of the girls in the group were involved with alcohol and drugs when they attended Marie's school. Heather, eager to make new friends in the community, whispers in Marie's ear, "Should we go? You know them don't you?" Marie knows that she probably shouldn't go and thinks that Heather shouldn't go either but doesn't want to say anything in front of the group.

A boy places his arm around Heather and remarks, "I don't know you but come on, this will be a lot of fun. We have some drinks and we can buy stuff at the store along the way." Heather, now a little nervous, is still unsure and looks to Marie for advice. Marie at that moment takes a deep breath and states in strong voice, "No, we can't go. We are on our way to dance lessons. Come on Heather, we are going to be late!"

With the announcement still ringing in the air, Marie takes Heather's arm and pulls her away from the group toward the bus stop where there are some other students and several adults from the community waiting for the next bus. Heather is a little confused, but understands that something is wrong, and does not object to being pulled away. As they walk to the bus stop Marie's legs feel a little shaky as she explains to Heather what she knows about some of the group members and what some of the dangers might have been if they had gone with them.

Questions for Reflection

1 How is Marie displaying her health literacy?

2 Discuss the types of lessons or activities that could be provided to students so that they too can acquire the skills to handle such a situation.

Comprehensive school health can help contribute to health literacy.

- Less than 50% of Canadian children are active enough each day to meet the Health Canada guidelines for healthy growth and development (Health Council of Canada, 2006).

- 73% of parents indicate their children aged five to seventeen years watch TV, play computer/video games, or read in the after-school period (Canadian Fitness and Lifestyle Research Institute, 2010).

- Less than 20% of children meet the Canadian Pediatric Society's recommendation of less than two hours of screen time daily. More than 50% watch two to four hours of TV daily and approximately 33% spend two or more hours in front of a computer (Government of Alberta, 2007).

Nutrition

- Over half of Canadian children and youth consume less than the recommended minimum four to eight servings of fruits and vegetables per day (Statistics Canada, 2003).

- Approximately a third of Canadian children aged four to nine do not meet the recommended two servings of milk products a day (Heart and Stroke Foundation, 2004).

- Approximately a third of children living in North America visit a fast food restaurant on any given day (Canadian Council of Food and Nutrition, 2006).

Mental Health

- Although emotional health is similar for boys and girls in grade six, by grade ten girls experience poorer emotional health than boys. The critical period for girls appears to be between grades six and seven when their emotional health becomes markedly poorer (Freeman, 2008).

- Youth aged fifteen to twenty-four are more likely to report mental illness and/or substance use problems than other age groups (Statistics Canada, 2003).

Substance Abuse

- Approximately one third of Canadian grade nine and ten students indicate that they have smoked (Saab & King, 2008).

- Over 50% of grade nine and ten students report that they have tried alcohol (Saab & King, 2008).

- Although a substantial number of drugs show a decline in use over time for grade nine and ten students, the use of medical drugs to "get high" has increased (Saab & King, 2008).

Sexual Activity

- 22% of grade nine and ten students report that they have had sexual intercourse (Saab & King, 2008).

- In 2003, approximately one third of youth reported they had not used a condom the last time they had sex (Statistics Canada, 2005).

- 92% of parents agree that sexual health education should be provided in the schools (SIECCAN, 2010).

Bullying

- 36% of Canadian students in grades six to ten report being a victim of bullying (Craig & McCuaig Edge, 2008).

- 51% of teenagers have had negative experiences with social networking (Ipsos Reid, 2011).

- 2002 data shows Canada ranked 26th out of 35 countries in terms of the proportion of young people reporting involvement in bullying and victimization (Craig & Harel, 2004).

- In 2006, 21% of girls and 14% of boys in grades six to ten reported that they had experienced cyber bullying (Craig & McCuaig Edge, 2008).

- In one Canadian study, 41% of students from grades four to seven reported that they were victims of bullying and/or bullied others on a monthly basis. Further, girls reported that they were more likely than boys to bully socially and to be victims of this form of bullying (Totten, Quigley, & Morgan, 2004).

Case Study 2: Helping a Friend in Need

Michael is a grade eight student. His best friend Brian likes many of the same things as him. The two get along great and hang out together all the time. Recently, Michael has noticed that Brian has become a little withdrawn and quiet. Michael has also noticed that despite the warm spring weather, Brian has been wearing long sleeve shirts and sweaters. After the last PE class, he noticed that Brian changed in a toilet stall rather than in the changing room with everyone else. When he thought about it a little more, Michael realized that Brian had been doing so for the last couple of weeks.

After they left the locker room, Michael jokingly asked, "So what are you afraid of?" Brian angrily replied, "It's none of your business!" and stalked off to the science lab for his next class. Michael, a little stunned, shrugged his shoulders and walked off to his math class. At the next break, Michael saw Brian at his locker and went over to patch things up. "Look I didn't mean anything by that. Are you okay?" At the same time, Michael grabbed Brian's arm and Brian recoiled in pain. Michael noticed blood seeping through Brian's sleeve. "What's that from?" Michael asked. Brian, sheepishly replied, "Nothing, I will see you at lunch."

At lunch, Michael confronted Brian and asked him to explain what was going on. Not taking no for an answer, Michael pressed Brian and stated, "You can tell me or I can go and tell someone else that something is wrong." After a few moments of awkward silence, Brian showed Michael a series of recent cuts and scars on his arms and admitted that he had started cutting himself and didn't know how to stop. Michael listened intently and when Brian stopped talking he said, "I think you need some help. I'm always here to help you but you need someone else besides me. Let's work out who we can go and talk to."

Questions for Reflection:

1 Where could Michael take Brian to get the support and help he needs?

2 What message does Michael send Brian with his response to the issue?

3 How are physical educators uniquely situated to assist in situations such as this?

Benefits of Health Education

One of the main benefits of health education is that it allows children and youth to learn different methods and habits that will enable them to feel better in all dimensions of health. Health behaviours can be learned but they can also be changed. There is no better time to begin the development of knowledge, skills, and attitudes than in the school years when children and youth are at an age where they may be more willing to accept positive health behaviours.

It is also important to acknowledge that children and youth spend a considerable amount of their formative years in school environments, therefore it is only logical to attempt to utilize these years to support the development of health behaviours. Such development can allow children and youth to lead fulfilling lives while equipping them with information to make decisions that will continue to promote good health. In addition, an early approach to health education can help children and youth to avoid health issues that result from, for example, poor nutrition, lack of exercise, abuse of drugs and alcohol, and other unsafe behaviours.

The responsibility of schools, educators, and parents to provide a coordinated, comprehensive framework for health education has never been greater. In fact, a comprehensive approach to health education has shown tremendous promise in schools (Murray, Low, Hollis, Cross, & Davis, 2007).

What Is Comprehensive School Health?

Comprehensive school health (CSH) is an overarching approach that applies a health-promoting perspective to all activities in the school environment. The Canadian Association for School Health (CASH) describes it as, "a broad spectrum of activities and services which take place in schools and their surrounding communities in order to enable children and youth to enhance their health, to develop to their fullest potential and to establish productive and satisfying relationships in their present and future lives" (CASH, 2006).

In Canada, comprehensive school health is generally the accepted term although it is also referred to as "health promoting schools," particularly in Europe and Australia. In the US, it is known as "coordinated school health." The approach has been endorsed by the WHO, the International Union for Health Promotion and Education (IUHPE), and the International School Health Network. The development of the CSH model by various governments and organizations was predicated on the WHO's Ottawa Charter (1986). According to the Ottawa Charter:

Case Study 3: Health Versus Profit

The student and parent advisory councils at Alderpoint Junior High School have joined forces to try to raise money for important projects that students have identified as a high priority for student morale. High on that list was a new digital scoreboard for the gymnasium. All the other local schools had acquired such boards in recent years, often through soft drink machine sales or the selling of chocolate bars. Desperately wanting to outfit the gymnasium for their athletic teams and raise school and student morale, the two groups of council members hold a series of meetings to discuss the options. The school staff and administration, although appreciative of the work being done and the ideas being generated, were really hoping that a decision could be made from a health perspective, especially since they had just recently agreed to declare Alderpoint School a "health-promoting school" at the start of the upcoming school term.

After much discussion and investigation into the various options, the three groups realized they have some very difficult choices ahead of them. Chocolate sales and soft drink machines gained a good profit line but all agreed that the health of students is also relevant to student morale. Wrapping paper and fruit sales were the new agreed upon ideas. It would likely take a little longer but it was a better direction for everyone!

Questions for Reflection:

1 Health promotion can face many challenges. Consider and discuss the different viewpoints of this scenario.

2 Discuss how the rest of the parents could also be brought on-side with this decision.

Health is, therefore, seen as a resource for everyday life, not the objective of living. Health is a positive concept emphasizing social and personal resources, as well as physical capacities. Therefore, health promotion is not just the responsibility of the health sector, but goes beyond healthy life-styles to well-being. (WHO, 1986)

The Ottawa Charter recognized the need for a paradigm shift in government thinking, from a focus on primary care to a focus on health promotion. This shift also opened up the possibility of increased funds and support for health promotion work in schools.

Although the model of comprehensive school health goes by different titles, and some of the components of the model have been given different labels, the tenets of the model are essentially the same. Some organizations have contracted or expanded the components of the model to make it more easily understood by various audiences. For instance, IUHPE

(2009) describes the essential components of a health promoting school as:

1   Healthy school policies

2   The school's physical environment

3   The school's social environment

4   Individual health skills and action competencies

5   Community links and health services

The CDC in the United States lists eight components of a coordinated school health program. In an attempt to create a better fit for Canadian schools, Lewallen & Vamos (2006) expanded the model to the following eleven components:

1   School health program (district coordination, policy, and support)

Figure 14.3: Pillars of Comprehensive School Health

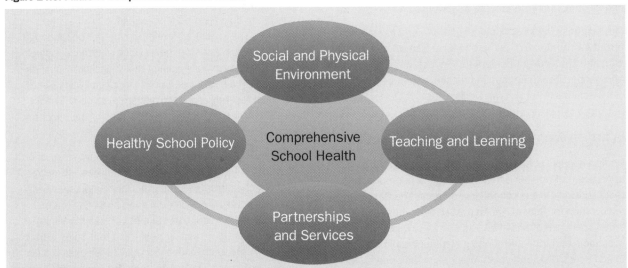

Social and Physical Environment includes the quality of the relationships among and between staff and students in the school, the emotional well-being of students and the influence of relationships with families and the wider community. The physical environment includes the buildings, grounds, play space, and equipment in and surrounding the school and basic amenities such as sanitation and air cleanliness.

Teaching and Learning refers to the resources, activities, and provincial/territorial curriculum where students gain age-appropriate knowledge and experiences and helping build the skills to improve their health and well-being.

Healthy School Policy addresses the management practices, decision-making processes, rules, procedures and policies at all levels that promote health and wellbeing, and shape a respectful, welcoming and caring school environment.

Partnerships and Services are considered to be the connections between the school and students' families and the supportive working relationships within schools (staff and students), between schools, and between schools and other community organizations and representative groups. The importance of health, education, and other sectors working together to advance school health is recognized along with community and school-based services that support and promote student and staff health and well-being (JCSH, 2008).

2   Coordination of school health program (school facilitation of program)

3   Healthy emotional and social environment

4   Family and community involvement

5   Healthy physical environment

6   Health education

7   Physical education and physical activity

8   Nutrition services

9   School health services (prevention and control of diseases)

10 Counselling, psychological, and social work services

11 School health promotion for staff

(Adapted from Lewallen and Vamos, 2006, p.25).

The Joint Consortium for School Health (JCSH) represents the interest of health and education provincial ministries across Canada and, in describing comprehensive school health, has categorized the components into the "pillars" of: social and physical environment, teaching and learning, healthy school policy and partnerships and services **(see Figure 14.3)**.

Many school boards, health authorities, and other organizations across Canada have developed their own versions and graphical representations of the comprehensive school health framework. Examples include Action Schools! B.C., Alberta Project Promoting active Living and Healthy Eating (APPLE) Schools, Living Schools (Ontario), and Healthy Students Healthy Schools (Newfoundland and Labrador). These organizations typically provide resources and tools to assist in the implementation and evaluation of comprehensive school health. One example is the work of Ever Active Schools in Alberta and Physical and Health Education Canada (PHE Canada) who categorize the comprehensive school health model as the "4 Es":

■ **Education:** Supporting a culture of learning for all school community members including wellness-related programs for students and health promotion learning opportunities for educators, staff, and parents.

■ **Everyone:** Collaborating in a meaningful way with the people involved in the everyday life of the school and equal and inclusive opportunities for everyone to make healthy choices.

■ **Environment:** Fostering safe social and physical environments in the school, home, and community; implementing policies that enable healthy active lifestyles; and cultivating a place where everyone knows they belong.

■ **Evidence:** Collaboratively identifying goals, planning for action and gathering information to indicate the effectiveness of actions to support healthy active lifestyles throughout the school community. (PHE Canada, 2012)

The 4 Es remind us that the approach is intended to be "whole school" inclusive, holistic, and about creating the right environment. The need for evidence in planning, supporting action, evaluating, and further planning is also emphasized.

Why Comprehensive School Health?

Schools have an important strategic role to play in addressing the health and social needs of young people because virtually all children and their families can be reached through schools (Sallis & Owen, 1999). In Canada, the comprehensive school health framework or model is recognized as the optimal approach to promoting the health and wellness of students, staff, parents, and others in the wider school community. Schools can have a substantial impact on health and are the most ideal public setting to reach young people. Schools teach knowledge, understanding, and values, but they are also settings where young people socialize, eat meals, are kept safe, enjoy recreation, are treated, screened, vaccinated, teased, bullied, engage with others, are sometimes alienated, and so forth (Rootman, 2004). Further, parents can be targeted with health messages through their children in schools. The CSH approach provides an opportunity to empower students through engagement with the community, to collaborate with outside groups and individuals, and to recognize that the health and wellness of staff is also important.

The health of children and their educational attainment are inextricably linked. Allensworth and Kolbe (1987) argue that a student who is not healthy will not learn well and an individual who does not form healthy attitudes and beliefs will be more likely to suffer from ill health.

The question of how schools can capitalize on their strategic positions to develop the health and social needs of young people has garnered much international attention. The comprehensive approach to school health (World Health Organization, 1986) is widely acknowledged as the optimal approach and has been adopted by many countries around the world (Allensworth & Kolbe, 1987; Kolbe, 2005; Lewallen & Vamos, 2006; McCall & Roberts, 2006; Stewart-Brown, 2006). Evidence suggests that the approach can have positive impacts on health behaviours such as physical activity levels, nutrition, mental health, substance abuse, and bullying. Unfortunately, no reported interventions have considered all of the components in their entirety (Stewart-

Brown, 2006). However, it is worth noting that "there is a substantial overlap between the successful components of a health promoting school and effective schools" (St. Leger, 2001, p. 197).

The positive influence of CSH on health behaviours was demonstrated in the Annapolis Valley Health Promoting Schools (AVHPS) project in Nova Scotia and this became widely accepted as a "best practices" model (Fung et al., 2012). Subsequently, the Alberta Project Promoting active Living and Healthy Eating (APPLE) Schools has shown that students who attend APPLE schools ate more fruits and vegetables, consumed fewer calories, were more physically active, and less likely to be obese in comparison to students attending control schools. It is important to note that APPLE schools has provided a comprehensive school health model that can be transferred to other school settings and has highlighted the importance of having facilitators in schools to act as change agents.

How Is Comprehensive School Health Implemented?

The comprehensive school health model is a call to action for everyone connected with school settings; it requires us to view all activities that are undertaken in schools through a health-promoting lens. For instance, if a school is planning an event or a fundraising activity, thought needs to be given to the opportunities for being physically active, the promotion of positive social behaviours, and the provision of healthy snacks.

The starting point for every school is going to be different given that schools differ by "their objectives, leadership, enrolment criteria, curricular demands due to language or religious instruction, socio-economic factors, physical structure and community support. A standard protocol for the implementation of CSH is therefore not feasible" (Veugelers & Schwartz, 2010, p. 6). School administration and the school health committee play a role in identifying school health priorities. MacDougall (2004) cites numerous examples where forming a school health committee to guide and plan healthy initiatives within a school has been found to be effective. New school health committees are formed or existing committees assume this responsibility. Typical membership of the committee would include a school administrator, educator(s), a public health or school board representative, other community representatives, and students. A mechanism for linking to the public health authority and/or school board provides the opportunity to garner external funds and supports.

The need to have champions who could bring the resources of health and education authorities in schools was identified as far back as 1943 when Wilkey talked about the need for wholehearted cooperation between school educators and

Children of all ages can learn to be health literate.

medical officers to eradicate tuberculosis from Canadian schools. While the attention that the school health agenda has received over time has varied, the need for coordination between the health and education sectors has remained constant (Allensworth et al., 1997). Comprehensive approaches that are facilitated by a coordinator have been recognized as effective (Card & Doyle, 2008).

A systems approach to comprehensive school health recognizes that having champions and coordination at all levels and across sectors is important. The CSH model also requires a coordination of effort at the government level, school board and health authority level, and at the school level. Bassett-Gunter, Yessis, Manske, and Stockton (2012) suggest that policy makers, practitioners and researchers, and national organizations such as the JCSH and PHE Canada, have shaped comprehensive school health in Canada. However, the practices of individual provinces, school boards, health authorities, and schools themselves have had a significant impact on determining the efficacy of comprehensive school health in schools. Allensworth and Kolbe (1987) argue that "sympathetic cooperation" is required between different agencies, particularly those with a health or education focus. For instance, in addressing mental health issues in schools, Noblé (2009) argues educators should not take on more work themselves, but rather focus their efforts on acquiring integrated support from external professional agencies.

According to Bond, Glover, Godfrey, Butler, and Patton (2001), the reason for the failure of some interventions aimed at health promotion in schools has been because the interventions were "piecemeal, short-term packages." Bassett-Gunter et al. (2012) caution that implementing a strategy focused in one area without a broader consideration for the other components of CSH will not be effective or sustainable. The complexities and interactions between the components become clear as schools progress towards becoming health-promoting schools.

The difference between a CSH school and a non-CSH school is that a CSH school has assessed, monitored, and developed a plan of action that takes account of all the components. Further, a CSH school attempts to implement its action plan in a coordinated fashion. Non-CSH schools, therefore, lack an action plan and the coordination of efforts. While it is useful to make the distinction between the two types of schools, labelling a school as CSH or non-CSH may not be helpful as all schools attempt to address the components of the model to some extent.

In summary, the "whole" school approach to comprehensive school health requires all those connected with schools to adopt a health lens and to value a systems approach to evidence-informed action and evaluation. There is a need to identify and support champions, leaders, and school health committees in their work with multiple, coordinated strategies that focus on the social and physical environment, teaching and learning, policy, and partnerships and services.

Questions for Discussion

1   What do you consider to be some of the challenges for providing and promoting health education in schools today?

2   When planning, what could you do in terms of classroom environment, teaching strategies, use of technology, and other methods to give students the chance to become truly health-literate individuals?

3   Are there other barriers that you can come up in regards to health literacy?

4   Do you think these issues are the same in other countries?

5   What do you believe are some of the challenges a physical educator faces when it comes to health education?

6   How can you, as a physical educator, involve parents in comprehensive school health programming?

7   What would be some differences between elementary, middle, and high school when planning for comprehensive school health?

8   What personnel would be needed to develop an action plan for comprehensive school health? Why?

Key Terms

- Health Literacy
- Social Determinants of Health
- Wellness
- Dimensions of Health
- Comprehensive School Health

Online Health Resources

Active Healthy Kids Canada
www.activehealthykids.ca

Be Free from Bullying
www.b-free.ca/home.html

Bicycle Helmet Safety Institute
www.bhsi.org

Bullying in Canada
www.bullyingcanada.ca

Canada's Food Guide to Healthy Eating
www.hc-sc.gc.ca/hpfb-dgpsa/onpp-bppn/food_guide_
rainbow_e.html

Canada's Physical Activity Guide to Healthy, Active Living
www.paguide.com

Canadian Association for School Health
www.schoolfile.com/CASH.htm

Canadian Dental Association
www.cda-adc.ca

Canadian Fitness and Lifestyle Research Institute
www.cflri.ca

Canadian Health Network
www.canadian-health-network.ca

Canadian Institute of Child Health
www.cihi.ca

Canadian Institutes for Health Information
www.secure.cihi.ca/cihiweb/splash.html

Canadian Mental Health Association
www.cmha.ca

Centre for Disease Control Health Information A–Z
www.cdc.gov/az.do

Child and Family Canada
www.cfc-efc.ca

Coalition of Active Living
www.activeliving.ca/

Cyber Bullying
www.cyberbullying.ca

Drug Abuse Resistance Education (DARE)
www.dare.com

Ever Active Schools
www.everactive.org

Family Service Canada Anti-Bullying
www.talk-helps.com

Go for Green—Active Living and the Environment
www.goforgreen.ca

Health Canada
www.hc-sc.gc.ca

Joint Consortium for School Health
www.eng.jcsh-cces.ca

Kids Health
www.kidshealth.org

KIDSAFE
http://www.cha.ab.ca/healthsite/pk4075sh.asp

Leisure Information Network
www.lin.ca

Lifesaving Society
www.lifesaving.ca

Physical and Health Education Canada (PHECanada)
www.phecanada.ca

Pink Shirt Day for Bully Awareness
www.pinkshirtday.ca

Prevent Alcohol and Risk-Related Trauma in Youth
www.partyprogram.com

Road Sense for Kids
www.icbc.com/Youth/road sense_kids.asp

Safe Kids Canada
www.safekidscanada.ca

SAFE KIDS Worldwide
www.safekids.org

Stay Alert and Stay Safe
www.sass.ca

Talking with Kids about Tough Issues
www.talkingwithkids.org

Virtual Resource Centre for Sport in Canada (SIRC)
www.canadiansport.com

World Health Organization
www.who.org

YMCA of Canada
www.ymca.ca

YWCA of Canada
www.ywcacanada.ca

Technology in Physical Education

David Chorney

Overview

The purpose of this chapter is to share ideas and propose options on how technology may be appropriately integrated into a well-thought-out and pedagogically sound school physical education (PE) program. A variety of topics related to technology will be discussed, and practical ideas will be presented on how to include various devices and online tools into the planning and teaching of PE. Ideas on how to incorporate tablet computers, heart rate monitors, and exergaming devices into a quality program, as well as identifying appropriate applications and websites are just some of the topics that will be discussed and examined.

By the end of this chapter, readers will see how the integration of technology into the physical education classroom is possible. Other information pertaining to digital literacy, the history of the Internet, and key Internet terms will also be shared.

Introduction

When considering integrating technology into curriculum, PE is not often the first subject area that comes to mind. However, it is a discipline that lends itself very easily to incorporating a vast array of technological devices, including gaming consoles, audio and visual hardware, a plethora of web-based tools, and an ever-increasing number of applications.

It is possible to integrate technology into the PE curriculum but many people still think that the only goal of PE programs is to get and keep students active. Along this narrow line of thinking are those that believe integrating technology into PE only includes using computers, stereos, and PowerPoint presentations.

Today's physical educators must be open to new ideas while also being receptive to possibilities that may stray from the traditional methods of teaching PE. A few ways to increase physical activity yet not lose focus of what is to be learned within PE lessons can include the implementation of exergames, geocaching, and sports simulation equipment. We must remember that while PE incorporates movement, it has never been solely about movement. We must be cognizant of the whole body and create learning experiences for students that attend to the thinking, feeling, and doing aspects of learning as well.

Technology is here to stay and will only continue to grow and evolve at dizzying speeds. We must also remember that the term "technology" can be defined in many ways and we must not let personal bias, or fear of trying something new, limit our planning and teaching for the benefit of our students. It is important to remember that what works well for one class may not work for another, so it's vital to get to know our students' technological capabilities and make them feel as though they are an integral part of the teaching/learning process.

It's better to try and fail than to never try at all. This chapter is intended to provide a variety of practical ideas to support all physical educators who consider themselves somewhere between a novice and an expert when it comes to technological knowledge and experience associated with technological integration in teaching.

Understanding the Internet and Terminology

Internet History

While the complete history of the Internet could easily fill a few books, the following timeline touches briefly on a few key milestones and events related to the growth and evolution of the Internet between 1969 and the present day. To view an enhanced online version of the timeline, go to www.thompsonbooks.com/tpet

1969: Computers at Stanford and UCLA are connected for the first time on October 29 (Chapman, 2009). In effect, they were the first hosts on what would one day become the Internet.

1971: Ray Tomlinson first develops email as we know it today (Zakon, 2011). Tomlinson made the decision to use the "@" symbol to separate the user name from the computer name (which later on became the domain name).

1973: The first trans-Atlantic connection of email occurs between the US and England.

1975: As emailing becomes more popular, the first modern email program is developed by John Vittal, a programmer at the University of Southern California (Zakon, 2011).

1978: The first unsolicited commercial email message (later known as spam), was sent out by Gary Thuerk to 600 California users (Zakon, 2011).

1989: A proposal for the World Wide Web is written by Tim Berners-Lee (Chapman, 2009) in an attempt to persuade CERN (European Organization for Nuclear Research) that a global hypertext system is in CERN's best interest. Originally called "Mesh," the term "World Wide Web" is coined while Berners-Lee is writing the code in 1990 (Chapman, 2009).

1990: The World, the first commercial dial-up Internet provider, is launched.

1993: The first widely downloaded Internet browser, Mosaic, is released (Chapman, 2009). While Mosaic wasn't the first web browser, it is considered the first browser to make the Internet easily accessible to non-techies.

1994: Mosaic's first big competitor, Netscape Navigator, is released.

1995: Considered by many to be the first year the web became commercialized.

1996: HoTMaiL (the capitalized letters are an homage to HTML), the first webmail service, is launched (Zakon, 2011).

1997: Although they had been around for a few years in one form or another, 1997 was the first year the term "weblog" was used.

1998: Google goes live, revolutionizing the way in which people find information online. Napster also launches, opening up the gates to mainstream audio file sharing over the Internet.

2003: Skype is released to the public, giving a user-friendly interface to Voice over (Internet Protocol) IP calling. Also in 2003, MySpace becomes the most popular online social network.

2004: The Facebook, a social networking site for college students, is launched. The site would later change its name to simply Facebook and go on to become the most popular social networking site (which, as of early 2013 it still is).

2005: YouTube launches and brings free online video hosting and sharing to the masses.

2006: Originally to be called twittr (inspired by Flickr) the social networking site Twitter launches. The first Twitter message ever sent was "just setting up my twttr."

More recent innovations include the invention of smart phones (e.g., Apple's iPhone, Samsung Galaxy phones) and tablet computers (e.g. Apple's iPad, Amazon's Kindle Fire, RIM's Playbook). Smart phones (specifically the iPhone) are almost wholly responsible for renewed interest in mobile web applications and design. The next few years will surely include countless more digital innovations.

Digital Literacy—Use, Understand, Create

Internationally, there is considerable discussion about what it means to be digitally literate. Other countries have created digital literacy working groups to define their own standards, so perhaps Canadian politicians and educators alike need to determine the skills required by today's young people to fully contribute to, participate in, and benefit from a digital society.

Just as traditional literacy goes beyond comprehension to include the more complex skills of composition and analysis, digital literacy includes, but goes beyond, simple technology skills to a deeper understanding of, and ultimately the ability to create a wide range of content with various digital tools. Established and internationally accepted definitions of digital literacy are generally built on three principles: (a) the skills and knowledge to use a variety of digital media software applications and hardware devices, such as a computer, a mobile phone, and Internet technology; (b) the ability to critically understand digital media content and applications; and (c) the knowledge and capacity to create with digital technology.

Technology can only enhance learning if students are taught to think critically about online content and evaluate their own behaviour against a set of shared social values. Digital literacy is not about technical proficiency, but about developing the critical thinking skills that are central to lifelong learning and citizenship. To meet the challenge, schools must focus on pedagogy, and provide training and support to help educators incorporate technologies into all elements of the curriculum in ways that facilitate individualized learning, and teach students how to collaborate with learners both within and outside the school community.

Use, understand, and create are the three verbs that characterize the active competencies of a digitally literate individual (Prensky, 2001). The term "use" represents the technical fluency needed to engage with computers and the Internet. This skill set forms the basis for deeper digital literacy development. Essential technical skills include the ability to use computer programs such as word processors, web browsers, email clients, and other communication tools. In order to develop these skills, students must have access to, and be comfortable utilizing, equipment and knowledge resources such as broadband services, computers, software tools, Internet search engines, and online databases.

The term "understand" denotes the ability to comprehend, contextualize, and critically evaluate digital media. A critical understanding of digital media enables students to reap the benefits, and mitigate the risks, of full participation in the digital society. This skill set also includes the development of information management skills and an appreciation of one's rights and responsibilities in regards to intellectual property. In a knowledge economy, today's youth need to know how to find, evaluate, and effectively use information to communicate, collaborate, and problem solve in their personal lives and future careers.

When discussing digital literacy, the term "create" can be defined as the ability to develop content and effectively communicate using a variety of digital media tools. Creation with digital media means more than the ability to use a word processor or send an email: it includes the ability to adapt communication to various contexts and audiences; to create and communicate using rich media such as images, video, and sound; and to effectively and responsibly engage with Web 2.0 user-generated content such as blogs and discussion forums, video and photo sharing sites, social gaming, and other forms of social media. The ability to create with digital media ensures that students are not just passive consumers but active contributors to the digital society.

Infrastructure and physical access to the tools are the foundation for digital literacy. To maximize participation, however, investments in infrastructure must be accompanied by investments in training current and future educators on how to use these tools. In turn, these practical skills support the development of the higher-level digital literacy skills that move students beyond participation into the transformative areas of innovation, constructive social action, and critical and creative thinking.

Digital Copyright Resources for Educators

Digital copyright is a relatively new field of law that is constantly evolving. The Copyright Board of Canada regularly makes decisions that impact the day-to-day practices of educators, even though most educators are unaware of them. While Canadian educators can look forward to updated copyright laws in the coming years, these resources provide a good overview of the current state of basic digital copyright laws and policies.

- **Copyright Board of Canada:** The Board is an economic regulatory body empowered to establish, either mandatorily or at the request of an interested party, the royalties to be paid for the use of copyrighted works, when the administration of such copyright is entrusted to a collective-administration society. The Board also has the right to supervise agreements between users and licensing bodies and issues licences when the copyright owner cannot be located.

- **Copyright Matters:** Copyright Matters is a comprehensive guide of practical copyright guidelines for educators. The document was commissioned by the Council of Ministers of Education, Canada; the Canadian School Boards Association; and the Canadian Teachers' Federation and was most recently revised in 2012. It is a thorough overview of what educators can and cannot do in the classroom in terms of copyright. Digital copies can be obtained from the CMEC website (www.cmec.ca) and hard copies can be obtained by contacting the CMEC directly.

- **Copyright and Teaching:** What You Need to Know: This site provides an archive of educational resources and materials for educators, relating to copyright in the classroom. (www.2learn.ca/ydp/copyrightabout.aspx)

- **Common Sense Media:** Copyright Resources: A set of resources and lesson plans to teach students about copyright issues. The lessons are generic enough that they do not focus specifically on the laws of one country, but instead focus on broader copyright issues that apply to students everywhere. (www.commonsensemedia.org/search/copyright)

From a digital literacy perspective, the basic skills learned through formal education at the primary and secondary levels, and informally through self-study and social interaction, is the foundation of the skills subsequently developed through high school and post-secondary education (Prensky, 2001). A recent survey of 4,374 students across 13 institutions in the US revealed that the vast majority of them (93.4%) own computers and use them most often for word processing (99.5%), email (99.5%), and web browsing (99.5%). But, the researchers found that only a minority of the students (21%) were engaged in creating their own multimedia content (Bennett, Maton, & Kervin, 2008). This evidence suggests that assumptions about this generation of "digital natives" may be misguided, and that we may be giving more credit to today's technology consumers than they deserve.

As a final and possibly most important point, as physical educators we need to remember that just because our students may know how to use a software program or an electronic communications device, it does not mean they fully understand the context within which it operates, or the content it may be capable of producing. The pedagogy behind digital literacy and the curriculum links to broader learning are what we need to stress and plan for if we intend to effectively implement technology into our teaching, and create spaces in our education for technology and digital literacy to be present. For more information about digital and media literacy, visit the Media Smarts website at www.mediasmarts.ca.

Technology is a huge factor in every subject now, including PE.

Social Networking and Physical Education

Social media and social networking are firmly entrenched in today's society and in our schools today. The use of Twitter, Facebook, YouTube, and many other social networking sites has become the norm for today's youth. It is easy to see how students enrolled in PE classes today may engage in the learning of the subject unlike ever before.

The following section will provide some examples of how and why certain social networking sites can be integrated into any PE program. When using social networking sites, particularly those that involve students being photographed or videotaped, make sure to be aware of any relevant board policies that exist and ensure that signed media release forms are obtained if necessary.

Twitter

The basic idea behind this popular platform is the sharing of information in a maximum of 140 characters. With the simple creation of a Twitter account any physical educator or student can connect with like-minded people from all over the world. The instant ability to have questions answered, or to have files, pictures, or lessons shared can be phenomenal for knowledge acquisition as well as being a big time-saver. In the PE classroom.

Twitter can be used to help explore current world issues or current events. Imagine grade eight students making real world connections and gaining followers from the other side of the world. Physical educators interested in doing this can start by setting up a class Twitter account and giving students access to this via a school computer or a school-owned mobile device (such as a tablet or media player).

YouTube

One of the largest social networking communities in the world is YouTube with nearly 500 million registered users. So what is the value for today's physical educators in using YouTube?

1 **Demonstrations:** With a plethora of videos being added every minute, YouTube has become an amazing source of content for people in all fields, including PE. Many are using it to access sports instruction videos or skill sequences and showing these to students via mobile devices, essentially creating a second educator in the classroom.

2 **Film Crew:** If video-recording devices are available for use in the classroom, students can take up the role of "film crew" with the task of capturing special moments that make up a practical lesson. This might include anything from skill training to game play and tactical instruction. They could then be involved in the editing and distribution of the class video via YouTube. With a little guidance from the physical educator, the film crew would essentially be completing a modernized peer assessment. Once the content has been uploaded and is online, students could easily comment and review their own and others' technique, creating what would essentially be an online portfolio demonstrating the learning of new skills.

3 **Video Coaching:** With the same video-recording devices mentioned above, students can teach a game or skill to another person or people anywhere in the world via video. Using this method, coaching and learning can be done by anyone, from anywhere, and at any time. Great physical educators from around the world have paired up with schools and PE professionals to share lesson content and cultural activities.

Edmodo

Edmodo is the education equivalent of Facebook, allowing physical educators to instantly create a personalized social network for them and their students. Once registered, students can enter a unique class access code given to them by their educator, which enables them to easily share resources with each other. Edmodo can handle all types of media, including images, documents, videos, and URLs which makes it a fantastic place to develop rich discussions around PE and other related topics.

Wikispaces

By setting up a free Wiki website, any physical educator can easily post recorded lectures, handouts, and other digital content for students to access whenever they desire. Content placed in a Wiki website can be easily edited and added to, which makes it easy to store useful content while keeping students up-to-date and interested. This approach can reclaim PE learning time by allowing students to access lessons and assignments outside of school hours, and to always have access to the content throughout the course. Additionally, students today are heavily engaged in mobile technologies, making it possible for them to complete the tutorial side of the class in what was once wasted time, such as travelling or waiting for the school bus. This method also allows students to not only develop a deeper understanding of the curriculum but also to reclaim their active engagement time within their class.

Internet Safety

Educators should not assume that students know what it takes to keep themselves safe online. For actions related to teaching it is an educator's responsibility to safeguard his/her students in the classroom, in the gym, on the field, and online. The following resources may help physical educators to proactively address some of the online safety issues that their students may encounter on the Internet.

Common Sense Media

www.commonsensemedia.org

This site offers a large archive of student handouts and activities that relate to online safety and digital literacy. Most lessons contain printable handouts for both students and educators, as well as lesson plans. The site also features a number of professional development resources for educators.

Define the Line

www.definetheline.ca/

A practical guide written by academics at McGill University, Define the Line provides resources for students, parents, educators, and policy-makers about what actually works when educating students about cyber-bullying and socially responsible digital citizenship.

What's the Deal? Internet Safety

deal.org/the-knowzone/internet-safety/

A website developed by the RCMP that provides practical advice for students about Internet safety issues such as cyber-bullying, interacting or chatting online safely, and protecting online profiles.

Be Web Aware

www.bewebaware.ca/

Be Web Aware is a bilingual education program developed by the Media Awareness Network, Bell, and Microsoft Canada. The program is aimed mainly at parents and focuses on how they can help ensure their child's online safety. It is a good resource for educators to share with parents.

NetSmartz Teens

www.nsteens.org/

This site, run by the US Center for Missing and Exploited Children, contains games, videos, presentations, and educator resources relating to appropriate online behaviour. The site contains an archive of videos about students who have experienced the consequences of risky online behaviour. It also offers a presentation kit for teens who want to do presentations for younger students and/or peers about appropriate online behaviour.

Educators should follow these three key rules when using the Internet with their students in any teaching/learning context:

1 When using the Internet in presentations to students, the educator should always preview any site being used.

2 When students are working at computer stations on an activity designed by the educator, the educator should preview and save the sites to be used by the student whenever possible.

3 When students are required to search the Internet, the educator must emphasize that students should only visit sites that are appropriate to the goal. Students should be monitored throughout the activity.

There are many resources available to help students with online safety.

Multimedia—Hardware/Software

This section describes various types of multimedia equipment and software. A digital camera, video camera, or flip cam can be a huge asset to a physical educator. These devices can be used within all lessons where student activity is present (again, be sure to check school board policies and be aware of media release forms). Most cell phones are equipped with video and still photography capabilities and some feature video editing software.

Webcams

A webcam is a camera that connects to a computer. It records video that can be broadcast over the Internet. The software within the webcam captures frames (still images) from the camera at preset intervals, for example, once every ten seconds. Frame rate is the number of images the software can capture in one second (Layton, 2000). High frame rate is what enables streaming video, which is video viewed in real-time.

Webcams can be used to send video emails, and for video chatting or videoconferencing. The recipient of a video email does not need special software to view the message, but in order to video chat, both users must each have a webcam. Video quality is not usually very high, but the resolution can be adjusted in a webcam's software settings. However, higher quality settings can lead to choppier video frame rates (Saltzman, 2008).

In a teaching context, webcams, flip cams, tablets, cell phones, and other handheld media devices can all be used in purposeful ways to capture students' learning, movement, and construction of knowledge.

Video analysis has long been a powerful tool for exploring movement but it used to come with an expensive price tag that made it hard for schools to afford. Now, there are different options such as TimeWarp 4 software (www.siliconcoach.com/products/timewarp#introduction).

This software, which can be purchased by educators at a discount, allows physical educators to capture student movement to be immediately reviewed after the movement has been performed. When a digital camera is connected to a computer running the software it has the capacity for powerful replay functions. Students should be encouraged to use a checklist to assess their competencies over a variety of skills. After they have completed an action, this software allows them view themselves via replay.

Video recording can be used to provide augmented feedback, which means using an external stimulus to increase learning and motivation (Schmidt & Wrisbert, 2004 as cited in Banville & Polifko, 2009).

Case Study 1: Fighting Tradition

Donna is a new high school physical educator who has just graduated from teachers' college. Donna is very comfortable using technology and is interested in implementing it in her PE classes. Donna is one of five educators in the school PE department. She realizes very soon that technology has not been implemented in any way within the PE courses being offered at the school.

Although she is very enthusiastic to try some new things and implement creative technological ideas in the PE classes she has been assigned, she finds resistance among her colleagues and little support to try anything new.

Questions for Reflection

1 How might Donna convince her colleagues that technology is not scary and can add real value to the learning/teaching process?

2 What are some basic ideas she may have in mind to begin implementing technology into her teaching of PE?

If available, a flip cam can be a useful tool for physical educators.

Video cameras can be used in a PE class as a method of providing feedback to students (Mitchell, 2001 as cited in Banville & Polifko, 2009). Students can view their recorded performance and review strengths and weaknesses with guidance from their physical educator. With the help of video software, the recorded performance can be played in slow motion so that both the student and the physical educator can analyze all movements in greater detail.

Dartfish

www.dartfish.com

Founded in Switzerland in December 1998, Dartfish is a company that develops video applications that allow users to edit and analyze videos in detail. The basic software packages allow you to "draw" on videos, measure angles/ distances, or capture still images from video. The advanced software packages offer more sophisticated functions.

There is a smartphone app available called Dartfish EasyTag. It is an add-on to Dartfish software and is used for capturing and recording information during a game or activity and can allow users to conveniently take notes on a mobile device.

Video analysis software can be an effective way for physical educators to engage students and make them a part of the learning and assessment process. Use of this software can help improve communication with students thanks to objective visual support. The software allows students to see themselves perform by providing them with automatic, instant, or delayed visual feedback. As a physical educator, you can break down activities, compare video clips, and highlight technique development. One of the other benefits of this software is the ease with which physical educators or students can publish the video analyses of exercises or movements into clear and easy to use interactive documents. All video content can be shared with other users.

Tablets

The first widely-used tablet computer (the iPad by Apple), was introduced to the US market in April 2010. In just over four months, the iPad reached 51 billion dollars in sales—the fastest ever for a consumer device. Various tablet computers are now available to consumers and many have a built in microphone and a camera capable of still photography and video recording. When using a tablet to record video in a PE environment, a tripod is strongly recommended.

Tablet computers are becoming more and more popular, particularly amongst young people.

Cell Phones

Most students have cell phones or smart phones and are often more than willing to use them in purposeful ways if given the opportunity. In PE classes today, cell phones can be viewed as tools that have a useful function. Most of today's mobile phones have many features that can make learning in PE very enjoyable and more meaningful than ever before. Remember, even if not all students in your class own a cell phone or have access to a cell phone, you can plan activities where students are paired or work in groups.

Here are some practical ideas for using cell phones in PE classes:

1 **Photo and Video Camera Analysis:** In a dance or gymnastics learning context, where students are required to compose routines and build off of required skill sets, students can use their phones to record some or all of their routine which can then be shared with other students in class. This method could be used to allow students to design parts of a routine and share videos in order to build an overall routine.

2 **MP3 Players:** Most mobile phones have the ability to play MP3 files and record sound files. This can allow physical educators to record podcasts as homework or simply as information for students on different topics and then ask that these podcasts be loaded onto students' mobile devices. In addition, the students can create their own podcasts as a means of sharing and interacting virtually.

3 **Stop Watches:** A mobile phone with a built-in stopwatch can be a very useful tool to engage the students in their learning. There are many options for utilizing the stopwatch feature, but some examples include timing one another on fitness-related activities (e.g., fitness blasts, interval training), or keeping track of total time on an activity.

4 **QR Codes:** A QR code is similar to a bar code, but can contain much more information. Cell phone cameras equipped with the correct reader software can scan the image of the QR code which causes the phone's web browser to launch and redirect to the programmed website. They are an excellent link between the physical world and the digital world, and an innovative way to create real time learning in an outdoor environment. Some mobile phones come with QR code reader software pre-loaded, others will need to have the software installed. There are several websites available to generate QR codes.

Multimedia Apps and Websites

The following is a list of quality applications specifically designed to support and assist physical educators when recording student movement and using video for assessment and learning purposes.

Coach's Eye: This program allows physical educators to record students performing a skill then play it backwards, in slow-motion, or frame by frame. It also offers the option to draw on screen or record a playback with verbal comments. Overall, a really great app for skill assessment allowing instant feedback for students. (www.coachseye.com)

Video Coach: Video Coach is a useful training tool for coaches as it allows for real-time analysis of sport mechanics. The program is both a video recorder and a player and also features HD video capture, single-frame video playback with graphic overlay, video organization, and wireless file transfer. Available through iTunes.

TimeMotion: TimeMotion is a program designed for recording video of athletes engaging in sporting activities that also allows for analysis of existing videos. For example, if taping a soccer game, the program will allow users to track possession of the ball or the frequency of possessions for either a whole team or individual players. The data generated by the program can be easily shared with others. Available through iTunes.

Excelade: With Excelade, any coach, amateur, or athlete can record, analyze in slow motion, and improve and track technique. Available from the iTunes App Store.

Here are a few great websites that will also assist you in using video as part of your teaching of PE:

YouTube and Vimeo: These sites can allow physical educators to put students in charge of their own learning situations. Physical educators can have students teach a movement skill or concept and film it for uploading to YouTube. Physical educators can then consider how the uploaded video can be assessed or critiqued by classmates or others from around the world or across the street.

TubeChop: This site allows physical educators to select a certain section from the abundance of videos on YouTube and share only that section. It is a great tool for filtering much of the nonsensical content showcased on YouTube.

Skype: Used properly in a PE setting, this free site allows users to connect via video or phone connection with other Skype users around the world. Students can be connected with other PE students from different parts of the province, country, or world to debate PE related topics. Students and physical educators can also connect with the authors of various literature, or interview sports figures or influential members of society or the local community. All that's needed is a Skype account, an Internet connection, and a webcam-equiped computer or mobile device.

Posterous: This site can be an asset if anyone wanting to create an online digital portfolio. Simply upload any sporting performance, routine, or combination of skills to be reviewed and analyzed over time. Recorded video file can be sent within an email to post@posterous.com. This will turn a user's email into its own unique website where the video can be watched online. To include a new video or document, simply send another email.

Energy Expenditure Devices

Measuring performance in physical activity is a practice that has evolved over many years and despite much progress with physical activity assessment, the limitations concerning the accurate measurement of physical activity are often amplified in young people due to the cognitive and physiological changes that occur during natural growth. The following section briefly outlines some specific devices that can be used in a PE setting as well as some practical ideas for using these devices with students.

Pedometers

A pedometer is a practical and accurate tool for measurement and motivation in physical activity. It is an inexpensive piece of technology, which, when attached to a waistband, records the number of steps taken in a given time period. Although pedometers do not assess the intensity of the activity, they can provide physical educators with valuable information as well as insight into improvements that can be made for students to become more active. Today there are even smart phone applications available that act as pedometers. A key point to remember is that it is step count goals for students be personalized considering baseline values, specific health goals, and sustainability of the goal in everyday living. Know why you want to use pedometers with students and know what you hope will be achieved.

Accelerometers

An accelerometer is a tool for measuring the intensity of physical activity that can be especially useful for students in PE classes or on sports teams. Accelerometers record body acceleration minute to minute, providing detailed information about the frequency, duration, intensity, and patterns of movement. Counts from accelerometers are used to estimate energy expenditure. This information can be very useful for physical educators as they are able to monitor and assess the intensity that students are giving during engagement in physical activities. The information can also serve as useful to the student when he or she is training or working

on fundamental movements skills as planned by the physical educator. The relatively high cost of accelerometers ($200–$300 per unit, compared to $10–$30 per unit for pedometers) limits their use in large-scale physical activity settings but some free smart phone apps are currently available.

Heart Rate Monitors

Heart rate monitors monitor the user's heart rate, which can be used to measure exercise intensity, as heart rate is related to oxygen uptake. Estimates of energy expenditure from heart rate can be affected by factors such as temperature, humidity, hydration, and emotional stress. However, for the most part, they are as applicable to PE students as they are to highly trained, competitive athletes.

Here is one example of how these devices can be used in a PE setting: Allow a class of students to wear the heart rate monitors prior to beginning a game such as soccer or netball. Instruct the students sitting on the sideline to monitor the heart rates of the players at different intervals, and make the data available after the game. Use this data to encourage a discussion about how player positions may affect the results, or whether or not a player spent much time handling the ball and if so, did that increase or decrease his/her heart rate during the activity?

Indoor and outdoor activities can be enhanced with technology.

The World of Application Software "Apps"

Application software, applications, or more commonly "apps," is computer software designed to help users perform specific tasks. Examples include accounting software, graphics software, and media players. Many application programs deal principally with documents. Apps may be bundled with the computer and its system software, or may be published separately.

The following section highlights some examples of applications that can be used by physical educators. The categories below are intended to offer practical suggestions of apps for specific areas of PE.

Organization and Management Apps

Teacher's Assistant: Physical educators can use this program to keep track of student actions, behaviour, infractions, and achievements in the classroom. This documentation can allow you to communicate quickly and easily with parents and administrators.

Teacher's Roll Call: Teacher's Roll Call is an app designed to help physical educators keep track of student attendance. It makes data entry and management both quick and efficient allowing physical educators to focus more on teaching.

Easy Assessment: Easy Assessment is an app designed for capturing and evaluating student performance in a number of different classroom scenarios.

Numbers: Numbers is a spreadsheet app designed to make spreadsheet creation easy. You can add tables, charts, photos, or other graphics without even using a keyboard.

Team Shake: Team Shake lets your technology choose teams for you. No need to worry about scraps of paper, just enter the names into a compatible mobile device and then give it a shake. The app will then create a random set of colour-coded teams that can be immediately used in a game or saved via email.

Bracketmaker: This app allows users to bring the excitement of the tournament structure of March Madness or Wimbledon to the classroom by creating your own tournament bracket. The program can customize team names for up to thirty-two teams.

MusicWorkout—Interval Timer for Fitness and Exercise: MusicWorkout is an interval timer program that incorporates a user's personal music collection to let you know when it is a rest period or when you should increase your intensity. Users select the duration of the work and rest periods along with the number of sets and the program does the rest.

Teaching Tool Apps

Giant Scoreboard: This app can be used for any activity that requires a scoreboard. It displays an editable timer/countdown and editable team names.

Educreations Interactive Whiteboard: Educreations turns your tablet into a recordable whiteboard. Diagram a sports play through voice recording, realistic digital ink, photo imports, and simple sharing through email, Facebook, or Twitter.

Pocket Body (Musculoskeletal): This app features a fully searchable interactive atlas of the human body.

FitnessHD: This app provides tools for physical educators and students to improve their health by tracking their progress with a calorie counter and body tracker as well as view diagrams and videos of exercises and workouts.

Pocket Heart by Pocket Anatomy: This is an interactive educational app that shows how the human heart works in 3D. It's a great learning tool for cardiac anatomy and physiology.

Whiteboard HD: This app works as a real-time collaborative teaching tool. Connect with any compatible Apple product over Wi-Fi to draw pictures and customize a demonstration. The app also allows you to import your own pictures to display.

Pocket First Aid & CPR from the American Heart Association: Pocket First Aid & CPR from the American Heart Association is always being updated to reflect the heart association guidelines on CPR and emergency cardiovascular care. The app includes stored videos and high resolution illustrations.

Beep Test: This app allows you to administer the beep test (also known as the pacer test and shuttle run test), a standard fitness test used by professionals to test cardiovascular fitness.

StopWatch: This stopwatch app shows time on a digital display as well as on an analog clock face. The analog clock face is easy to collect information from during timing of a physical activity task or test. After the timing has finished, it is most convenient to read the precise time from the digital display.

Student Centred Apps

Nutrition Tips: This app gives you hundreds of interesting and useful nutrition tips and nutritional health facts that are concisely written for quick and easy review.

Fotobabble: Fotobabble is a real-time photo-sharing app that allows you to share images using email, Facebook, or Twitter.

Snapguide: Snapguide is a simple way to share and view step-by-step how-to guides. Students can show skill progression or demonstrate the rules of a game by creating their own guides and sharing them through email, Twitter, Facebook, and more.

Cardiograph: Cardiograph is a heart rate monitor app that allows users to save their results in order to track their progress and fitness level. The program can keep track of multiple people with individual profiles.

Case Study 2: Internet Safety

Aziz has been teaching PE for fifteen years and has just recently become interested in using cell phones as part of his teaching. One of his ideas is to allow students to use their own cell phones to record videos of their gymnastics routines that he has asked them to create as part of their grade ten PE class. Additionally, he is asking the groups to upload their routines onto the Internet so that all classmates may see the completed routines and offer feedback and possibly partake in some peer assessment.

Questions for Reflection

1 What are some key things Aziz should always tell his students about using their cell phones as part of his PE class?

2 Should parents and administration be made aware that he is doing this in his PE class? Why or why not?

3 What are some of the key issues Aziz cannot forget to mention to his students as part of this experience?

Pedometer: Pedometer will work as you walk, run, or jog, even on the treadmill. The special algorithm—the same as used in hardware pedometers—is implemented in the application.

Exergaming

Computer games and video gaming devices are extremely popular among children and adolescents today (Nippold et al., 2005). Although excessive video game play has been noted in the literature as a contributor to childhood obesity, newer gaming technology, sometimes referred to as exergaming, has been designed to capitalize on the reinforcing effects of video games to increase physical activity (Sanders & Hansen, 2008).

Exergaming combines video games and physical activity into a video sports game that is based on actual sports, and is used to encourage participation in physical activity by introducing students to sports in a non-threatening environment (Scott, 2012). Exergaming technology is interactive. Video games or various auditory or visual stimuli are paired with different types of exercise equipment and activity, and the individual must engage in physical activity to play the game or produce the auditory or visual stimulation (Sanders & Hansen, 2008). Exergaming uses various innovative exertion and motion interfaces such as electronic dance pads, motion platforms, bicycle ergometers, haptic devices, mobile phones, and motion-tracking cameras.

One proposed reason for the increased interest in exergaming is the concern over the high levels of obesity in Western society (Sinclair et al., 2007). According to Gorgu et al. (2009) the reasons for obesity include high calorie diets and a serious lack of physical activity in children's daily lives. It has been argued that video games are one of the main causes for physical inactivity (Vandewater et al., 2004; Luepker, 1999; Parizkova & Chin, 2003; Riviere, 2004; Sothern, 2004), because the games that children like to play are not physically engaging in their nature. The emerging exergames genre tries to change this by encouraging players to perform physical movements during game play. The hope is that the enjoyment that traditional video games produce can be harnessed to encourage children to embrace more general physical activity.

Although exergames have become a popular form of entertainment for today's youth it must be stressed that exergaming should not be central to teaching PE. Exergames may increase the physical activity levels of some disengaged students but fundamental movement skills, fitness level and overall game play are likely not significantly increased or improved.

History of Exergaming

In 1982, Atari developed an exercise bike that connected to a game console called the Atari Puffer project (Sinclair, Hingston, & Masek, 2007). In the mid 1980s, HighCycle was developed by Autodesk, which allowed users to pedal an exercise bike across a virtual landscape (Rizzo, 2007 as cited in Sinclair, Hingston, & Masek, 2007). In 1983, Amiga released a foot-operated pad that allowed users to control a game by standing on a board (Sinclair, Hingston, & Masek, 2007). Essentially, the user and foot-operated pad acted as a joystick. Nintendo released the Power Pad in 1987 (Sinclair, Hingston, & Masek, 2007).

After foot-operated pads, motions sensors became the new trend. Nintendo released the Power Glove in 1989, in which a motion sensor was built into a glove worn by players (Sinclair, Hingston, & Masek, 2007). In 2006 Nintendo released the Nintendo Wii, which included controllers with built-in motion sensors (Sinclair, Hingston, & Masek, 2007). Wii Sports is a software package that is compatible with the Nintendo Wii, and includes games such as tennis, bowling, golf, boxing, and baseball.

Some progressive thinking physical educators have already seen the potential benefits of using these games with all students in their classes but especially those students with issues around motivation and participation as well as students with physical and cognitive challenges.

Effectiveness and Potential Use of Exergaming

Exergaming holds promise as a teaching tool that is easy to implement with an entire class and requires little effort from the physical educator. Physical activity levels during PE may increase because children start to engage in physical activity right away. In addition, implementing an exergaming lab in the school may lead to an increase in opportunities for physical activity because these labs could also be available to students before and after school, providing them with a safe location to engage in physical activity.

Some examples of the most popular exergaming devices on the market include Microsoft's Xbox, Xbox 360, Xbox kinect, Sony's Playstation 3, and the Nintendo Wii. All of these devices can have a place in a PE program, however the physical educator must know why she/he is going to use the device and which curricular outcomes will be focused on.

Exergames are a way of engaging students who have lost interest in traditional forms of physical activity (Sheehan & Katz, 2010). This form of interactive fitness is a good motivational tool because students want to play in order to advance to higher and more difficult levels. There is also a level of competition in these games, which motivates children to keep playing in order to win.

A game like Konami's Dance Dance Revolution is a fun way for students to learn about rhythm, tempo, dancing, and choreography (Hicks & Higgins, 2010). Active video games have been found to significantly increase heart rate and step counts (Maddison et al., 2007 as cited in Mears & Hansen,

The video game market continues to expand and incorporate other interests. Exergaming is an example of this growth.

2009). Energy expenditure for children playing interactive games was comparable to brisk walking, jogging, or climbing stairs (Nye, 2011). Games that involve both upper and lower body movement have been found to elicit the greatest heart rate increase and energy expenditure (Graves, Ridgers, & Stratton, 2008 as cited in Nye, 2011). Although exergames are fun and engaging for students, they are not as beneficial as actually playing the real game (Biddiss & Irwin, 2010 as cited in Nye, 2011).

From a practical perspective, if using exergames in a PE setting it is often best to have more than one device in play at the same time in order to maximize the number of students involved. As well, think about using a portable data projector to display the exergame content on a gymnasium wall for added interest and greater ease of viewing.

The following section lists a sampling of exergames and how they may be utilized in a typical PE class. Remember, you will need to plan how many students can actually partake in the activity and think about the curricular outcomes that are part of the reason why you chose the specific exergame in the first place.

- **Konami's Dance Dance Revolution (DDR):** This game consists of a dance pad on which a player moves his or her feet to a set pattern that matches the general rhythm or beat of a song shown in front of the player on the screen.

- **Gamercize with Sony Play Station Batman and Robin:** This is a form of gamercize in which a stair stepper machine interfaces with a video game console, and motion from the stepper provides a signal to the interface module. The interface allows interaction between the game controller and game console only when the signal is present.

- **Three Rivers Game Cycle with Sony Play Station Monster 4 × 4:** This exergame is a game cycle in which an upper body ergometer bike requires children to control on-screen actions by pedalling and steering the bike with their arms instead of their legs.

- **Electronic Sports Dog Fighter Simulator:** Dog Fighter is a form of a virtual bike that resembles a traditional bike and allows children to control all on-screen actions, including steering, speed, turns, firing mechanisms, and other strategies. The faster the player pedals, the faster the objects on the screen move.

- **Cateye Virtual Bike with Sony Play Station:** Dirt Biking is another form of a virtual bike that functions like the Dog Fighter.

- **Nintendo Wii Sports:** This exergame allows users to participate in virtual sports like baseball, tennis, boxing, or bowling. The game can provide replays; however, the player may choose to skip this option.

- **iTech Fitness XrBoard:** This game uses a balance board simulator that allows children to snowboard down a mountain or practice complicated skateboarding tricks.

- **Fit Interactive 3 Kick:** This exergame is a martial arts simulator designed with resilient foam pads in three locations that that are punched or kicked in response to visual and auditory signals.

Case Study 3: Online Privacy

Mr. Gregson teaches grade eight PE at a Canadian middle school. He assigns his students the task of working in pairs to create a two-minute exercise video to be posted on YouTube. Within his assignment guidelines, he asks students to modify certain settings for the videos they post online, including making the video "unlisted" so that only people who have the link can see it, and removing the ability to post comments on the videos. After they are finished, the students are to submit the link for their video and share it with their classmates on the class Moodle site.

A few days after the assignment is submitted, Mr. Gregson receives an angry email from a parent. His daughter has given him the link to her group's exercise video and when he look at it, he noticed that comments were still enabled and that there were a number of defamatory comments posted on the video, including comments about the girls' weight and lack of physical ability. He is very upset and demands that Mr. Smith remedy the situation immediately.

Questions for Reflection

1 What should Mr. Gregson do in response to this parent's complaint? What actions should he take and whom should he notify?

2 If the parent were to press charges, do you think Mr. Gregson could be held liable for the content posted in the YouTube video comments? Why or why not?

3 What could Mr. Gregson have done differently to prevent this situation from occurring? How might he modify this assignment so that it can be used again next year?

Geocaching

Geocaching (which is pronounced "geo-cashing") is a world-wide game of hiding and seeking treasure. A geocacher can place a geocache anywhere in the world, pinpoint its location using GPS technology and then share the geocache's existence and location online. Anyone with a GPS unit can then try to locate the geocache. A typical cache is a small waterproof vessel containing a logbook. Geocaches are currently placed in over 110 countries worldwide and on all seven continents. After ten years of activity, there are over 1.1 million active geocaches published on various websites devoted to the activity.

As a physical educator, geocaching provides a great way to be outdoors with your students and enjoy the benefits of learning and moving in natural environments. You can simply log on to www.geocaching.com, search for a cache within your area, and begin your hunt with the GPS. The hidden cache may require more smarts than meets the eye and reward you with a special prize; it really depends on the cache.

How to Use Geocaching in a Physical Education Program?

1 Have your class race to find a series of geocaches located around their community that require them to work as a team to solve puzzles in order to receive the next geocache coordinate.

2 Have your students make a virtual tour of their own town or community and establish various caches to be found and enjoyed by others.

3 Use geocaching as a way to explore interesting natural environments in the local area. Simply set up geocaches at points of interest and include a series of questions or discussion prompts for the location. This will hopefully make their learning and enjoyment richer.

For a quick tutorial on how geocaching is done, there are several good video tutorials on YouTube.

Conclusion

The world of technology is continually evolving and changing. Today's physical educators have begun to embrace technological tools and implement technology in their teaching. This chapter is intended to provide concrete ideas, to stimulate thinking and perhaps decrease the fears of how technology can and should be integrated into today's planning and teaching of PE.

Technology will only continue to evolve and become more prominent in the lives and teaching of both physical educators and students alike. It is therefore incredibly important for today's physical educators to familiarize themselves with current technologies and remain up to date for their own knowledge acquisition and also to share this knowledge and provide current and meaningful learning opportunities for today's children and youth.

Questions for Reflection

1 With the continued evolution of technology and technological devices, is it realistic to imagine a school offering a PE class that is taught entirely online? What are the advantages and disadvantages for the students and for physical educators?

2 What are the concerns we need to be aware of in terms of using cell phones in our PE classes? What are the protocols that we should follow prior to using cell phones and uploading content to the Internet?

3 Should physical educators receive extra funding for technology equipment or should traditional equipment and technological tools be classified similarly? Explain your rationale.

4 What are some of the ways assessment in PE can be improved with the use of technology? Please give examples.

5 As physical educators and potential users of technology in teaching, how can we ensure all students will be able to properly use any and all of the technological devices we introduce to them? What are some of the assumptions we might make about students and their use and competence with varied technologies?

Key Terms

- Digital Literacy
- Smart Phone
- Tablet
- Social Networking
- Multimedia
- Applications ("Apps")
- Energy Expenditure Devices
- Pedometer
- Accelerometer
- Heart Rate Monitor
- Exergaming
- Geocaching

Beyond Physical Education: School-Based Physical Activity Programming

Joe Barrett

Overview

Canadian public schools play an important role in developing healthy children and offer the government lengthy and consistent opportunities to promote lifelong health and physical activity (PA) practices (Harris, Kuramoto, Schulzer, & Retallack, 2009; Public Health Agency of Canada, 2011). This chapter examines Canadian approaches to providing school-based PA programs. It first looks beyond the physical education (PE) classroom to examine Canadian efforts to integrate student PA across subject disciplines, including three provincial Daily Physical Activity (DPA) mandates. Additionally, it examines intramural and interscholastic PA programming and provides practical considerations related to these two more traditional school-based PA programs.

Introduction

Today children and youth are facing the prospect of living shorter lives than their parents because they are not active enough (Daniels, 2006). Who and what can be blamed for child and youth inactivity? Despite a barrage of research citing a number of well-documented benefits associated with PA among children and youth, including improvements in health, fitness, academic performance, focus, attention, and self-confidence, Canadian families are still struggling to identify and address factors influencing the PA behaviours of their children (Active Healthy Kids Canada, 2009, 2010, 2011; Lu, Barrett, & Steele, 2013; Ploughman, 2008; Tomporowski, Davis, Miller, & Naglieri, 2008). Rink, Hall, and Williams (2010) suggested that the problem of inactivity is much more complex than identifying and addressing a single factor; rather, it is associated with many factors, including changes in (Canadian) lifestyles, school policies, and the communities in which we live.

The declines in spontaneous and self-directed active play by children and youth have consequentially put pressure on Canadian schools to maintain and/or improve child and youth inactivity as parents and families struggle with the increasing challenges and demands associated with living in modern Canadian society (Active Healthy Kids Canada, 2012). What can be safely articulated is that most children in Canada are not physically active enough for healthy purposes (Active Healthy Kids Canada, 2009, 2010, 2011; Canadian Fitness and Lifestyle Research Institute, 2008; Centers for Disease Control and Prevention, 1997; WHO, 1998).

Physical Activity Guidelines in Canada for School-Aged Children and Youth

In 1995, the Canadian Society for Exercise Physiology (CSEP) and the Public Health Agency of Canada (PHAC) together developed guidelines for childhood PA, known as the Canadian Physical Activity Guidelines. These established PA recommendations for four distinct populations: (a) children aged 4–11, (b) youth aged 12–17, (c) adults aged 18–64, and (d) older adults 65 years of age and older. Over the years, the recommended guidelines have changed, reflecting new knowledge and research examining the relationship between PA participation and health benefits for Canadian populations. Each new iteration of the guidelines has resulted from increased cooperation between health-promoting stakeholders and a more rigorous scientific process.

The most recently published guidelines issued by CSEP and PHAC call for children (5–11 years) and youth (12–17 years), regardless of gender, race, ethnicity, or socio-economic status, to participate in at least sixty minutes of moderate-to-vigorous PA each day (Canadian Society for Exercise Physiology, 2011). The guidelines also emphasize the

importance of each population participating in safe, enjoyable, and developmentally appropriate physical activities. A summary of the recent 2011 revisions to the Canadian Physical Activity Guidelines can be found in **Figure 16.1**.

School-Based Physical Activity

The physical environment in which an individual lives is increasingly being recognized as a predictor of physical activity levels in both children and adults (Duncan, Duncan, Strycker, & Chaumeton, 2002; Fein, Plotnikoff, Wild, & Spence, 2004; Spence & Lee, 2004). Thus, the public school system becomes a key environment in which to target children and youth with interventions promoting health (Bates, 2006).

Schools make an appealing venue for population health initiatives, given that they serve the majority of constituent children (Kahn et al., 2002). Since school-aged children and youth between the ages of four and seventeen spend much of their time in school settings in Canada, this structured and consistent time provides schools and teachers a tremendous opportunity to influence student participation in physical activities through school-based curricular, intramural, and interscholastic programs.

Children spend a lot of time at school which makes it the perfect place to promote physical activity.

Are Children Getting Enough Physical Activity in School?

Despite provincial/territorial mandates and calls for quality daily PE, most Canadian children do not receive it. Physical & Health Education Canada (PHE Canada), a national organization concerned primarily with promoting the healthy development of children and youth by advocating for quality, school-based PE, has pointed to a serious decline in the quantity and quality of school PE programs owing to numerous issues. Among these are reductions in school PE budgets and increased pressure for other core curricula (CAHPERD, 2006). Still, despite these challenges, Canadian schools have offered alternatives for students to be physically active through organized cross-curricular, intramural, and interscholastic PA programs.

Over the last decade, at both the elementary and secondary school levels, provinces and territories have evolved to allow for the provision of a wider variety of school-based PA programming. Certain jurisdictions have introduced new health policies designed to ensure that student populations participate daily in physical activity. Other provincial jurisdictions have allowed for the introduction of school-based specialized sport programming delivered, in some combination, through flexible curricular, intramural, and interscholastic offerings.

Are schools providing sufficient opportunities for Canadian students to participate in school PA programs? According to Active Healthy Kids Canada (2011), the answer is yes. Active Healthy Kids is a national organization whose primary goal is to improve the PA levels of Canadian children and youth through the dissemination of relevant scientific research and advocacy work with stakeholders.

In its most recent annual report, the organization gave Canadian schools a B grade for their efforts to provide sport and PA programs in schools. Their report cited recent data collected from a 2010 Physical Activity Monitors (PAM) survey, which asked Canadian parents to report on (a) the availability of school-based PA and sports programs, (b) child participation rates, and (c) whether the school programs met the needs of their child. Findings revealed that 77% of parents believed that schools were providing PA programming beyond PE, while 52% indicated that their child participated in school programs (Canadian Fitness and Lifestyle Research Institute, 2010).

The PAM results, and subsequent positive grade from Active Healthy Kids Canada, are promising, yet greater clarity related to PA program offerings, participation rates, and school PA program fidelity is still to be realized through further research examining school-based PA programs in Canada.

Figure 16.1: Canadian Physical Activity Guidelines for Children (5–11 years) and Youth (12–17 years)

For health benefits, children aged five to eleven years and youth aged twelve to seventeen years should accumulate at least sixty minutes of moderate- to vigorous-intensity physical activity daily.

This should include:

- Vigorous-intensity activities at least three days per week.
- Activities that strengthen muscle and bone at least three days per week.
- More daily physical activity provides greater health benefits.

Let's Talk Intensity!

Moderate-intensity physical activities will cause children and teens to sweat a little and to breathe harder. Activities like:

- Skating
- Bike riding
- Playground activities

Vigorous-intensity physical activities will cause children and teens to sweat and be "out of breath." Activities like:

- Running
- In-line skating
- Swimming

Being active for at least sixty minutes daily can help children and teens:

- Improve their health
- Do better in school
- Improve their fitness
- Grow stronger
- Have fun playing with friends
- Feel happier
- Maintain a healthy body weight
- Improve their self-confidence
- Learn new skills

Reproduced with permission from the Canadian Society for Exercise Physiology.

www.csep.ca/guidelines

Factors Influencing the Provision of School-Based Physical Activity

What influences the provision of PA programming in schools? Some factors are the school setting, the administration, and the teachers.

Schools in many instances are the great equalizer beyond the influence of teachers and programs. Specifically, the school setting offers unique universal access to facilities, equipment, and instruction that support many different opportunities for PA for all children, regardless of race, ethnicity, gender, or socio-economic status. The school and its carefully crafted culture in which PA programs are presented may influence student interest or willingness to participate. Gone are the days of the one-size-fits-all PA program. Canadian schools, reflecting changes in the nation's cultural and social diversity, need to work to cultivate varied

and developmentally appropriate program options to meet the needs and desires of today's students (Mandigo & Thompson, 1998).

To reengage students in PA after decades of behavioural changes, schools and school policies should consider ease of access for all students, safe and convenient spaces for participation, well-maintained equipment and resources, programs targeting student interest (e.g., specialized sport programming, wellness programming), and the challenge of creating a school culture and context that embraces PA (Higgins et al., 2003; Humbert et al., 2006).

The role of the administrator in implementing PA programs has also consistently been cited as a key barrier or success factor (Alberta Education, 2008; Barrett, 2011; Beets et al., 2008). Teachers need to see that administrators believe in the value and importance of school-based PA programming. Often in communicating with parents and the community, administrators will celebrate and champion PA program options as a key aspect of curricular, intramural, or interscholastic options offered in their schools. But beyond communicating the program options available, administrators could also recognize the time, commitment, and value of their teachers' efforts in providing rich and varied PA programming. For a school to succeed in achieving desired PA program goals, administration support is necessary for

Case Study 1: Do As I Say?

In preparation for a pre-service physical educators' teaching internship, one Canadian Faculty of Education requires its students to complete a series of observation days. These scheduled days provide pre-service physical educators with opportunities to build rapport with their associate teacher and teaching internship class students. Additionally, they allow the pre-service physical educators an opportunity to learn more about school day structures, culture, and norms. On some of these days, associate teachers may ask the visiting pre-service physical educators to lead certain instructional activities. The professor for the PE Methods course requires her students to keep a journal detailing how practising teachers deliver curricular PA opportunities to students. What follows are entries from two students:

"She stressed to me the importance of participating in DPA and how it influences student behaviours and activity levels in a positive way. My teaching internship class has a hard time following instructions, so my associate finds it difficult to get through the regular curriculum material without trying to find extra time for DPA. She said teaching DPA helped the students who were restless focus."

Another female pre-service physical educator shared an anecdote regarding how her associate teacher encouraged her to offer DPA:

"We often spoke about what activities we could do on days when we had DPA time scheduled. On my observation days, she always encouraged me to teach DPA, and I appreciated her allowing me to teach activities that I was comfortable with. We both felt it was crucial that the students move before shifting to a new subject to allow them to focus on the next subject lesson."

Questions for Reflection

1   Comment on the journal entries.

2   Do you consider PA an essential component of the instructional day? Why or why not?

3   What should you do if your associate teacher indicates that he or she does not want you to offer cross-curricular physical activities? What can you do?

providing time in the school schedule, championing the program, role modelling the program's ideals, supporting and celebrating the efforts of teachers, and encouraging and reinforcing PA programming (Lu, Barrett, & Steele, 2013; Beets et al., 2008).

Finally, studies continue to provide compelling evidence of teachers' overwhelming belief in the value of school-based PA and the important role it plays in the lives of Canadian children (Alberta Education, 2008; Barrett, 2011). In addition, teachers support the belief that PA benefits the social, emotional, and cognitive domains (Morgan & Hansen, 2008). But in Canada, fewer and fewer elementary schools have specialist elementary PE teachers, making it increasingly difficult to provide PE due to the loss of experts in the field (Robinson & Melnychuk, 2008). With this loss, one could surmise that Canadian elementary teachers also feel they lack the skills and knowledge necessary to institute a PA program designed to improve health and wellness and help prevent obesity.

Yet despite this loss of expertise, Canadian elementary and secondary teachers across the country continue to play important roles in providing and delivering curricular, intramural, and interscholastic PA opportunities for Canadian students. Teachers are the central figures in PA program delivery, acting as facilitators, volunteers, coaches, or instructional leaders. All these duties are penultimate to their responsibility to support and encourage children and youth engagement in PA programming.

In Canada, thirteen jurisdictions—ten provinces and three territories and their respective departments, or ministries of education—are responsible for organizing, delivering, and assessing education at the elementary and secondary levels (Council of Ministers of Education, n.d.). Beyond provincially mandated PE programming at these levels, provinces and territories have varied somewhat in how they provide school-based PA. Here we will examine three common components of Canadian school-based PA programs:

(a) curricular PA programming, focusing on the Daily Physical Activity (DPA) initiative offered in three provinces

(b) intramural programming

(c) interscholastic programming

Intramural and interscholastic programming are two program options offered in all jurisdictions that provide students opportunities to explore and experience a variety of PA options outside the classroom.

We will also look at practical considerations, such as sample program delivery models, the role of the teacher, health and safety considerations, and resource supports available to the classroom teacher.

Figure 16.2: Teachers can . . .

Reinforce student participation

- Ask students about their participation in PA at home and in the community
- Offer praise and attention during student participation
- Incorporate cross-curricular PA
- Help students generate fun and engaging ideas for PA participation

Support the provision of PE

- Show an interest in learning in PE
- Connect learning in physical education to learning in other subject disciplines
- Show respect for the provision of PE

Make PA a positive experience for children and youth

- Choose activities that are inclusive and that focus on student success

- Focus on the joy and benefits associated with PA participation

Never use the elimination of PA as punishment

Choose not to take away opportunities to be physically active

Use physical activity to manage and improve student learning and behaviour

Involve parents and the community

- Help promote student involvement in community PA
- Encourage students to get outside and play
- Offer suggestions to parents to support efforts to increase PA participation
- Increase student awareness of the availability of community activities

Adapted from Rink, Hall, & Williams. (2010). *Schoolwide Physical Activity: A Comprehensive Guide to Designing and Conducting Programs.* Champaign, IL: Human Kinetics.

Curricular Health and Safety Quick Facts

When can students begin participating in curricular programming?

First they must do the following (start of year/start of course):

1 Retrieve a board/authority approved medical form from their teacher.

2 Retrieve a board/authority approved parent/guardian permission/acknowledgement of risk form.

3 Bring back both forms completed and signed by the parent(s)/guardian(s). Students cannot participate in curricular programming until both these forms are submitted to the teacher.

4 Have appropriate clothing and shoes for participation.

5 Be briefed on rules, routines, and acceptable behaviours.

Curricular Physical Activity

Curricular physical activities are designed to provide opportunities for students during instructional time. These activities are taught or supervised by teachers in Canadian schools and include both mandated and optional PE programs, DPA, and cross-curricular PA programs approved by departments or ministries of education. In addition to providing students regular and consistent opportunities to be physically active, the primary function of curricular PA programming is to develop student physical literacy (Mandigo, Francis, Lodewyk, & Lopez, 2009). It is hoped that by giving students such opportunities, they will (a) develop competence across a broad spectrum of physical activities; (b) demonstrate a personal commitment to, and understanding of, their own health and wellness through daily participation; and (c) develop the capacity, or the ability to understand, communicate, apply, and analyze different forms of movement in their lives.

Curricular PA forms one foundation of the comprehensive school health model, and curricular programs play a central role in the development of physically active lifestyles by make PA programming accessible to all children and youth (Centers for Disease Control and Prevention, 2010; Lu, Barrett, & Steele, 2013; Public Health Agency of Canada, 2011; WHO, 2010b).

Case Study 2: Tick Tock, Tick Tock

Ms. Layne has been hired as the new grade four teacher at an elementary school. In the first few months, she noticed that her class occasionally acts out. In recent weeks, despite her best efforts to pull the class back on task, she is finding her efforts less than successful in managing the increasingly disruptive behaviour. At lunch hour one day, Ms. Layne shares her concerns with the grade six teacher, Mr. Abuja. He listens attentively to Ms. Layne's challenges and offers her the following advice: "When things begin to get a little out of hand in my class, I have a tried and true method to pull my students back in line. I walk over to the clock, point at the clock, and begin to count the seconds and minutes that it takes for my students to catch on and quiet down. I tell my students that for every second and minute that they are disruptive in class, that is how much time I will take off of their DPA and recess time. The kids take care of themselves, I don't have to say another word."

Questions for Reflection

1 What lessons are Mr. Abuja's students being taught?

2 Describe Mr. Abuja's classroom management philosophy?

3 Brainstorm five ways in which integrated PA could be used to help remedy the off-task behaviours in Ms. Layne's class.

4 Referencing your own personal experiences as students, discuss the relationships between PA and academic performance, focus, and stress management. Discuss how your established personal beliefs influence your own teaching beliefs and philosophy.

A Mandate for Daily Physical Activity

In 2005, Alberta Education and the Ontario Ministry of Education each introduced provincial mandates for the inclusion and provision of DPA in public schools. In 2008, British Columbia's Ministry of Education followed suit, introducing its own comprehensive DPA mandate. Each mandate is unique in its structure and proposed method of delivery, and each targets slightly different student populations in K–12 education. Despite these differences, the programs have much in common.

All three provinces have positioned their mandate around the need to target inactive lifestyles and the growing concern that Canadian children and youth are not active enough for healthy purposes (Canadian Fitness and Lifestyle Research Institute, 2009; Public Health Agency of Canada, 2007; WHO, 2004). All three provincial governments, in introducing their mandates, have positioned DPA and the need for regular and consistent opportunities for student PA around evidence-based research, offering promising links between DPA and improved academic performance, readiness to learn, and student behaviour. Each program aims to change student behaviours and attitudes toward PA participation, increase PA opportunities for students in schools, and maintain or improve the overall health and wellness of its constituent student populations. **Tables 16.1**, **16.2**, and **16.3** provide an overview of the provincial DPA mandates.

In addition to these examples of provincially mandated DPA, all member provinces and territories have policies in place that prominently highlight the importance of and need for regular and consistent school-based PA.

For example, Saskatchewan's In Motion initiative has introduced measures designed to increase PA opportunities for children and youth at home, at school, and in the community (Saskatchewan Ministry of Education, 2010). As a partner, and in support of the movement, the Saskatchewan Ministry of Education (2010) has introduced DPA recommendations for school districts/authorities and schools designed to support their efforts to make schools healthier places to learn and grow.

Sample DPA Delivery Models

Whole school DPA: Schools may choose to meet the DPA requirement using a discrete and consistent block of time in the school day. In this model of delivery, all or a portion of the student body may participate in developmentally appropriate activities at the same time. The benefit of this model of delivery lies in its consistency and its place in the school schedule. Research has shown that providing DPA using this model of delivery alone or in combination with other models results in a high degree of DPA program fidelity and participation (Barrett, 2011). In this model, a committee, and/or a PE specialist, and/or individual classroom teachers may be involved in the design, planning, and ongoing monitoring of the DPA program.

Table 16.1: Alberta Education Daily Physical Activity (DPA) Mandate

Program Facet	Expectation
Duration	DPA must consist of at least 30 minutes of physical activity daily
Scheduling	DPA can take place during instructional time. Participation in PE classes can be to meet the DPA requirement. Otherwise, teachers are encouraged to incorporate physical activity into other subject instruction. Alternatively, DPA requirements can be met during non-instructional time (during lunch or recess). Schools can provide students with opportunities to sign out equipment and allow use of indoor space (e.g., gyms) during lunch and recess.
Location/Space	Alberta Education has used school space as way to categorize physical activities that schools may use to meet provincial DPA requirements. These categories include classroom or small spaces, gym or open space, outdoors, and whole school or large group.
Grade Level	DPA must be provided for all students in grades 1–9.
Activities	DPA should vary in form and intensity, take into account individual student abilities, consider resources available within the school and larger community, and allow for student choice.
Provision	DPA should be offered in as large a time block as possible, but can be offered in time segments that allow students to meet the minimum 30 minutes per day (e.g., two blocks of 15 minutes, three blocks of 10 minutes).
Accountability	School authorities and school administrators are responsible for monitoring and reporting on implementing DPA. Adjustments to school implementation plans and reporting on school planning and progress are specific responsibilities held by individual school administrators.

(Source: Alberta Education. (2006). Daily Physical Activity: A Handbook for Grades 1–9 Schools.)

Table 16.2: British Columbia Education Daily Physical Activity (DPA) Mandate

Program Facet	Expectation
Duration	Students in kindergarten through grade 7 are to receive at least 30 minutes of DPA each day. Students in grades 8 and 9 must receive either 30 minutes daily or 150 minutes weekly. As a graduation requirement, students in grades 10 through 12 must document a minimum of 150 minutes of weekly physical activity
Scheduling	Schools have the autonomy to use school time as they see fit to implement DPA for kindergarten to grade 7. Schools may choose to deliver DPA as a discrete, dedicated part of the timetable or an integrated aspect in other curricular disciplines, or may use a combination of these two approaches. Of note, students can meet their DPA requirement in activities scheduled during both instructional and non-instructional portions of the school day.
Location/Space	Teachers are encouraged to use a variety of school locations to deliver DPA.
Grade Level	DPA is mandated for all students in kindergarten through grade 12. What varies within the BC program is how students in certain grade levels can meet the mandated requirements.
Activities	Students participate in activities that develop strength (e.g., ball games, push-ups) and cardiovascular and muscular endurance (e.g., brisk walking, swimming, soccer, dancing), and activities that develop flexibility (e.g., stretches, yoga). The importance of participating in moderate-to-vigorous physical activities is emphasized.
Provision	Kindergarten to grade 7 students should participate in blocks of at least 10 minutes, totalling a minimum of 30 minutes of DPA. Students in half-day kindergarten are expected to participate in at least 15 minutes of DPA per school day. In Grades 8–12, participation involves either 30 minutes of DPA or a minimum of 150 minutes of physical activity each week. Individual schools can choose how they wish to structure their DPA programs.
Accountability	Student achievement of the prescribed learning outcomes of DPA are recorded on term and final reports. School boards or authorities are responsible for developing policies and procedures to track DPA. Individual schools can use locally or provincially developed tracking tools to monitor student progress.

Source: British Columbia Ministry of Education. (2011). Daily Physical Activity: Kindergarten to Grade 12, Program Guide.

Table 16.3: Ontario Education Daily Physical Activity (DPA) Mandate

Program Facet	Expectation
Duration	DPA must consist of at least 20 minutes of sustained moderate-to-vigorous physical activity daily.
Scheduling	DPA must take place during instructional time (not during lunch, recess, or nutrition/activity breaks). DPA is considered an enhancement to a quality H&PE program and is not meant to replace mandated H&PE programming. Participation in 20 minutes of moderate-to-vigorous physical activity fulfills the daily requirement for DPA.
Location/Space	Teachers are encouraged to use a variety of school locations to deliver DPA.
Grade Level	DPA must be provided for all students in grades 1–8; kindergarten teachers are also encouraged to provide their students with DPA.
Activities	All activities must include a warm-up and cool down, be developmentally appropriate, and adapted to ensure that all students can participate. Adaptations must be consistent with the accommodations or modifications found in a student's Individual Education Plan. On days when health and H&PE are not scheduled, integrating physical activity into other curricular areas is encouraged.
Provision	Since individual classes may be at different stages of implementation, DPA may initially occur in several short sessions (minimum of 10 minutes each) over the course of the school day.
Accountability	Elementary school principals will make their best effort to ensure that students are receiving at least 20 minutes of sustained moderate-to-vigorous DPA during instructional time.

Source: Ontario Ministry of Education. (2005). Policy/Program Memorandum No. 138: Daily Physical Activity in School, Grades 1 to 3; Grades 4 to 6, Grades 7 to 8

Teacher-driven DPA: This model of delivery designates the classroom teacher as the one responsible for planning and providing DPA. The teacher designs the activities and is responsible for scheduling DPA into the instructional or non-instructional class schedule. Research has shown that schools where this is the predominant model of delivery show wide-ranging levels of commitment and program fidelity to the program mandate (Barrett, 2011). In this delivery model, once again, a committee or physical education specialist or grade level/division teams may be involved in supporting the individual classroom teacher's efforts to design, plan, and deliver DPA programming.

Student-facilitated DPA: This model of delivery not only facilitates provision of the DPA mandate, but also serves a greater purpose in Canadian schools, since it puts students at the centre of program design, planning, and delivery. With the aid of a committee or teacher facilitators, student leaders are designated to support the school's efforts to meet its mandate. Senior students might lead activities at a prescribed time in the school day or in individual classes. Students might organize activities at lunch, recess, or nutrition/activity breaks under teacher supervision. Student leaders can serve a variety of functions, and the more senior the student, the greater the responsibility he or she can share in meeting the mandate. Responsibility

for training these students falls to supervising teachers or committees responsible for DPA. This type of program has the potential to lead to greater student leadership capacity in schools, which in turn could produce more successful program outcomes and student participation.

In your observations and teaching internship placements, you may see schools using one or a combination of these models to meet provincial DPA requirements. Additionally, you may see other innovative practices, since schools, administrators, and teachers have proven their ingenuity and resourcefulness in striving to improve student learning and the student experience in school time and again.

Role of the Teacher

We teach students, not subjects. Historically, it would not have been unusual to hear teachers identify themselves as, for example, "the science teacher" or "the grade three teacher." A shift towards identifying oneself as a teacher of students reflects the importance of putting the student at the centre of learning. In planning DPA, we must first consider the needs of our students to ensure that our design and planning are inclusive in nature and reflect the participatory needs of our students.

DPA initiatives are one method of boosting school-based physical activity.

Planning: Planning the provincially mandated content used to teach our students involves various levels, including long-range, unit, and daily-lesson planning (Rink, Hall, & Williams, 2010). Those responsible for designing and planning a DPA program should consider all three aspects equally. They must also determine if DPA will be delivered discretely, embedded across other subject disciplines, in non-instructional settings, or though a combination of delivery methods.

Having decided how DPA will be structured, teachers can consider developing the scope and sequence of DPA instruction over the course of an entire school year. Discrete themes or units of instruction can be developed (Rink et al., 2010), or alternatively DPA can be embedded within subject units (e.g., music, science, mathematics). Individual lessons can then be planned to help students meet provincially developed learning goals or expectations associated with the DPA mandate. See Chapter 4 for a more detailed approach to planning curricular programming.

"Walking the talk" — role modelling and support: Student learning is social in nature. Students observe and imitate other student actions and behaviours, even those considered less desirable. Significant social learning also takes place through observing and imitating teacher behaviours. We, as teachers, are role models and what we say and do in our schools is closely watched by a captive audience who often emulates our behaviours and dispositions. The act of leading and teaching students thus provides significant and consistent opportunities to shape student values, beliefs, and especially their actions. The simple act of participating alongside our students in DPA activities can therefore be powerful. Our participation not only promotes our own health but may also influence student participation in, and perceptions of, DPA. Our ability to influence students should thus be carefully considered and positively leveraged to get the most out of them while stoking an interest and passion for PA. Demonstrating passion and enthusiasm for PA through our own physically active behaviours with students, as well as our encouragement and support of student interest and participation, may promote their participation in such activities, as well as their enjoyment (Humbert et al., 2006; Rink et al., 2010).

Curricular Health and Safety Considerations

The safety of our students should be the first priority. It is the responsibility of school districts/authorities, schools, and teachers to mitigate potential risks and provide safe spaces for students to learn and grow. As teachers, we may be guided by common sense, but that alone is not enough. Fortunately, in all provinces and territories, support has been provided in the form of guidelines to help teachers determine what is safe and what is not. As part of the

Case Study 3: Marching at the Gates

Mr. Taren has recently been hired as a new teacher at an elementary school. In his interview, when asked about getting involved in the life of the school, he indicates that he is very interested in coaching the coeducational intermediate volleyball team. Since this is a new school, this would be its first such team. The school draws students from three recently closed elementary schools, all of which had well-developed intramural programs, with volleyball featured prominently in both intramural and interschool program offerings. The principal indicates that he believes interest around the school would be very high. A week prior to Mr. Taren's tryouts for the school team, he posts a series of flyers around the school; he also prepares two announcements that are read each morning leading up to the day of the tryout. On tryout day, Mr. Taren packs away his school materials and changes his clothes for the activity. He strolls out of the teachers' change room to find roughly seventy-five students waiting patiently to attend the tryout.

Questions for Reflection

1. What are the challenges Mr. Taren faces?

2. On your own or as a class, brainstorm ten things Mr. Taren could have done differently leading up to the tryout?

3. Suppose the principal indicates that Mr. Taren can take only ten students. How should he handle this situation? What can he do? Why might the principal make this decision?

4. On your own or as a class, develop a clear and well-defined set of selection criteria.

5. What are the implications associated with cutting sixty-five students who wish to participate?

6. Develop ten well-thought-out arguments against cutting students in elementary interschool athletics.

7. What might be done to service those sixty-five students cut from the school team?

comprehensive design and planning for DPA, teachers must become familiar with these board, school, and provincial safety guidelines, and should consult them prior to providing any DPA activity.

Supervision: Teachers have a responsibility to teach students about safe participation practices and the importance of assuming responsibility for both their own safety and that of their fellow students. This process begins with developing safe school and classroom routines and behaviours. Teachers also need to continue to reinforce expectations, behaviours, and rules related to safe participation throughout the school year.

Space: There are many school spaces (e.g., classrooms, the gym, multipurpose rooms, hallways, outdoor play spaces, and fields) available that teachers can use to meet mandated DPA requirements. Teachers should become familiar with these various spaces, ensure appropriate supervision, and check that safety concerns have been identified and addressed prior to student participation.

Equipment: Students need to be taught how to use equipment safely. Teachers also need to ensure that equipment used in DPA activities is safe and in good condition (e.g., seeing that balls are properly inflated, hazards are removed, and equipment is developmentally appropriate).

Students of varying abilities can get involved in intramural activities.

Intramural Physical Activity

Intramural physical activities are designed to provide opportunities for students of wide-ranging interests and abilities to participate in a variety of activities in a fun and inclusive environment (Lu, Barrett, & Steele, 2013).

The Ontario Physical Education Safety Guidelines (2011) classifies intramural activities into four categories: sport imitations, low organization activities, special events, and clubs. The difference between intramural physical activities and curricular and interscholastic activities involves their structure and purpose. Intramural activities are held within a school with teams and participants composed solely of students from the school, and their primary purpose is participation (National Association for Sport and Physical Education, 2008; Physical & Health Education Canada, n.d; Rink et al., 2010). They also deemphasize instruction, skill proficiency, or performance, instead stressing diverse program options and inclusivity with enjoyment through participation. Depending on availability of resources, facilities, supervision, and organization, intramural activities can be structured before, during (lunch or recess), or after school.

Sample Intramural Delivery Models

Traditional model: Students are typically organized into teams and compete in leagues following predefined schedules. Common activities include sport imitations (e.g., floor hockey, badminton) or low organization games (e.g., relays, dodgeball). Students may or may not have input into selecting the league activities. Activities may run for a defined period, followed by the introduction of a new league and new activity. When a new league activity is introduced, the team composition may remain unchanged, or new teams may be created through assignment or student sign-up procedures.

Pick-up model: In this model, students arrive on specified days at a set time and place to play either predetermined activities or activities based on student consensus that day. Students are assigned to teams or make their own teams and compete in games and activities. It is common to see students participating in both formal and informal games and activities on these days. Rules and game play are more likely to be modified based on the varying levels of skill and competitive interest.

Free play model: This model encourages students to use a set space for PA purposes. Formal activities and games are typically unstructured. The role of the teacher in this model is primarily as supervisor of student free play. The supervisor makes equipment available to the students, who are then free to play with their peers or on their own for a set time. This model may provide a less intimidating environment for those less comfortable in more-structured PA settings. Students can choose to participate based on their own level of comfort.

Whole school model: In this model, students have the opportunity to participate in a variety of activities in a set amount of time. Whole school activities may be structured around special events, themes, or school-centric initiatives, and over the course of an entire school day, one or more lunch periods, or during after-school hours. Activities and competitions are organized by class, grade level, team, or house. This delivery model places greater emphasis on mass participation, positive social development, and school community building. Activities may also require significant investment in both instructional and non-instructional time, planning, and supervision.

Leadership model: This model presents tremendous opportunities to build ongoing student leadership within schools. Students here play a central role in developing, organizing, delivering, promoting, and celebrating the intramural program. Teachers guide student committees and working groups through developing and executing the program. Schools using this model are more likely to see the intramural program become a traditional part of school culture. As students graduate and move on, new students move into leadership positions and train in the various roles defined by the student committees and supervising teachers. After the initial training and the establishment of roles, responsibilities, and routines, fewer day-to-day responsibilities are placed on the teachers. In this model, except for the lead teachers on intramural committees, activity supervision is the primary responsibility of teachers.

Figure 16.3: Managing Risk—DPA
The teacher must consider the following elements of risk:

■ The teacher must make sure the DPA activity is developmentally appropriate.

■ The teacher must consult the provincial/board/authority safety guidelines and determine that he/she has the knowledge and ability to teach/supervise the activity safely.

■ When considering an activity not addressed in provincial DPA handbooks or provincial/board/authority safety guidelines, the educational value versus the entertainment value of the activity must be determined (e.g., is dodgeball an appropriate choice for a DPA activity?). If you are unsure about an activity, use common sense and seek the counsel of your principal for advice on evaluating the activity.

After the activity has been approved by a board/authority official as having educational value, the teacher must identify and minimize inherent risks.

Adapted with permission from the Ontario Physical and Health Education Association. (2009). The Ontario Physical Education Safety Guidelines-Elementary Curricular Guidelines.

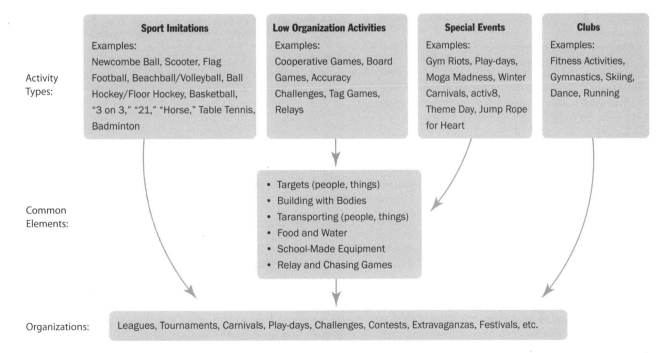

Source: Reproduced with permission from the Ontario Physical and Heath Education Association. Ontario Physical Education Safety Guidelines-Intramural Activities (2011).

Figure 16.4: Categories and Common Elements of Intramural Activities

Role of the Teacher

The foundation of any well-developed intramural program begins with a belief that students should be provided opportunities to participate in enjoyable physical activities. In addition to the benefits of regular activity, schools and teachers may use intramural programs to promote and reinforce positive social behaviours, build student leadership capacity, and instill a sense of community and inclusion. Often these programs are a source of school pride and can involve the participation of a significant portion of the school population. In most instances, the coordination of a school's intramural program is a voluntary task taken on by a teacher or group of teachers at the school.

The nature of this commitment can vary from school to school, but these programs can only be run with the voluntary contributions of teachers. In Canadian schools, teachers may take on one or more of the following roles:

Coordinator/lead teacher: Teachers may be responsible for the development, promotion, execution, and ongoing monitoring of the intramural program. They may also build student leadership capacity through intramural committees and training opportunities for students.

Official: Teachers may be responsible for officiating at certain intramural activities taking place during the school year. Additionally, they may also be in charge of training volunteer student officials.

Teacher volunteer: Some teachers may choose to volunteer to support all aspects of the intramural program, while others may simply decide to play a specific and finite role, such as serving as an intramural supervisor. Either way, the program benefits from the contributions of these individuals.

Chief celebrator of all things intramural: This is likely the most important role teachers can play in an intramural program. It is important to recognize the efforts of volunteers. As often as possible, celebrate the successes and efforts of the volunteers. People choose to get involved and support student experiences for different reasons, but regardless of whether these are altruistic, self-serving, or some combination thereof, it is important to show appreciation of their efforts. A teacher should also endeavour to celebrate and recognize the participation of all students in intramural programming. Throughout the year, find moments to celebrate student participation, achievement of program goals, and the program's contributions to the school community.

Intramural Health and Safety Considerations

Supervision: Students participating in school intramural programs must be supervised by a school official. This may be an administrator, school staff member, an approved volunteer (e.g., pre-service physical educator, parent, or occasional teacher), but in most instances this responsibility falls to a teacher willing to volunteer. This individual is responsible for ensuring safe spaces, safe behaviours, and safe play. Prior to students participating in an intramural activity, supervisors must consult intramural provincial safety guidelines for that activity to ascertain the category of supervision required. As risk factors increase (e.g., number of participants, complexity of task or activity, skill level required to participate), so, too, should the level of supervision and number of supervisors.

Equipment: Many intramural games and activities that students participate in involve modifications to rules, spaces, number of participants, and in some cases use of equipment. These modifications can make intramural play more enjoyable and inclusive. Consideration must be given to ensure that use of equipment is both safe and developmentally appropriate for students. Inadequate, developmentally inappropriate, or limited equipment can make such activities less safe and enjoyable.

Facilities: Teachers should consult provincial intramural safety guidelines to review facility requirements for specific activities. It is the responsibility of the supervisor, not the students, to ensure that the facility or space is free of debris or hazards. The supervisor must identify all foreseeable risks and take appropriate action to mitigate risks to students. Student use of equipment and facilities is prohibited unless supervised by a school official.

Figure 16.5: Categories of Supervision

- "Constant visual" supervision means that the teacher/intramural supervisor is physically present, watching the activity in question. Only one activity requiring constant visual supervision may take place while other activities are going on.

- "On-site" supervision entails teacher/intramural supervisor presence, but not necessarily constant viewing of one specific activity. Momentary presence in adjoining rooms to the gymnasium is considered part of the on-site supervision.

- "In-the-area" supervision means that the teacher/intramural supervisor could be in the gymnasium while another activity is taking place nearby. The teacher/intramural supervisor must be readily accessible, and at least one of the following must be in place:
  1 The teacher/intramural supervisor is circulating.
  2 The teacher/intramural supervisor is visible.
  3 The exact location of the teacher/intramural supervisor is known and the location is nearby.

Adapted with permission from the Ontario Physical and Health Education Association. (2009). Elementary/Secondary Intramural Safety Guidelines.

Figure 16.6: Key Benefits of Regular Physical Activity

The key benefits of regular physical include:

- Better health
- Improved fitness
- Better posture and balance
- Higher self-esteem
- Weight control
- Stronger muscles and bones
- Feeling more energetic
- Relaxation and reduced stress
- Continued independent living in later life

Public Health Agency of Canada

Interscholastic Physical Activity

Interscholastic physical activity programs are endorsed by schools, districts, and provincial and territorial athletic associations. Interscholastic programs typically consist of a combination of structured individual and team competition in local, regional, and provincial settings.

Participation in interscholastic programming is in most cases voluntary, and often these activities serve only a small portion of either an elementary or secondary school population. In many cases, the ability to participate is determined through a formal evaluation process, such as tryouts, conducted by a coach. Success in these tryouts is achieved based on predetermined criteria usually focusing in part on skill proficiency and competitive behaviours. Teams may be organized by people who may or may not be employed by schools or school districts, and activities are normally conducted outside the instructional day. Interscholastic programs place greater emphasis on competition and winning and have little relationship to provincial or territorial curricular objectives. In Canada, such programs are an important part of the culture and provide PA opportunities to the more athletic students (Lu, Barrett, & Steele, 2013).

Sample Interscholastic Athletic Delivery Models

Elementary model: In most Canadian provinces, elementary students in grades four through eight are provided with unique and wide-ranging interscholastic programming opportunities. Canadian schools often feature interscholastic programming as a key aspect of the school culture and experience. It is also often the primary school-based PA option available to elementary students during after-school hours.

Case Study 4: Where There's a Will, There's a Way

During lunch hour, you and a few of your teacher colleagues run a daily intramural program. With the help of a well-organized student intramural council, almost 80% of the students in your school are participating in the lunch-hour program. Each day, teachers supervising and coordinating the program eat their lunch in the first twenty minutes of the lunch hour, then supervise the daily activities in the final forty minutes, on a rotating basis. Today, on your way to the lunchroom, you pass by the gymnasium, where you notice that the door is slightly ajar, and so you open it and walk in. There you find Mia, Aria, Simona, Lucas, Bronwyn, Mateo, and Griffin, all members of your intramural athletic council, alone in the gymnasium, two of them playing basketball, while the rest are lying on the gymnastic mats beside the bleachers. You ask the students how they were able to get in there and access the equipment . . . SILENCE. One student yells out, "We're just eating our lunch before the games today." Another student, taking a jump shot, shouts out, "We just wanted to shoot some hoops ... what's wrong with that?"

Questions for Reflection

1. How would you handle this situation? Consider appropriate consequences, if any?

2. Discuss potential risks for the students.

3. Discuss potential risks for you as the lead teacher?

4. If someone were injured, what would be the potential implications? Who would be responsible?

5. What do the intramural provincial safety guidelines say about supervision?

In this delivery model, activities are generally predetermined, focused on sports, and offered seasonally; schools will also generally offer a limited number of PA opportunities to students over the course of a school year. Across Canada, elementary interscholastic sport offerings may include, but are not limited to, activities such as basketball, badminton, volleyball, track and field, and cross country running. Student participation in most instances is voluntary, and in some cases students wishing to participate are required to go through a selection process or tryout. Because this can lead to the perception that participating on elementary school teams is a privilege as opposed to a right of all students, an emerging emphasis is being placed on winning and outcomes as opposed to participation and social development. Elementary district or authority athletic associations often cite a variety of benefits of taking part in interscholastic programs (e.g., development of skills, school pride, responsible behaviours, morals, and character). Depending on school size, an administrator may be responsible for coordinating the elementary interscholastic program; in other instances,

the role of coordinator might fall to a lead teacher or group of teachers responsible for managing the program.

Secondary model: The secondary model is likely the one that most Canadians can identify with, since secondary interscholastic programming has been part of Canadian school culture for almost a century. Most Canadian secondary schools, if not all, offer some form of interscholastic athletic program. Similar to the elementary model, secondary programming tends to be the primary option available for PA participation outside of school hours. But students are also offered broader and more diverse teams and individual program options than in the elementary model. Also, depending on age, students are eligible to participate in three levels of interscholastic school programming, namely, freshmen/midget, junior/junior varsity, and senior/senior varsity. Individuals and teams may compete in sanctioned sports against other secondary schools in highly structured and organized leagues at local, regional, provincial, and national levels. In most instances, participation in league or tournament competition is demanding, predicated on winning, and may culminate with a playoff structure and championship. Participating in these activities is entirely voluntary, and in almost all instances, students are required to take part in a selection process or tryout. Selection tends to be based on skill and competitive behaviours. Despite more diverse program options and broader opportunities, secondary interscholastic programming also tends to be more exclusive, serving a small percentage of a school's population. In almost all instances, an

Case Study 5: What Did I Get Myself Into?

Part A

Mr. Sharma is the new teacher hired at a middle school and has volunteered to coach the soccer team since the previous soccer coach has retired. At a parents' night one month prior to tryouts, a parent of a student Mr. Sharma does not teach makes a point of visiting with him. A minute or two into the conversation, the parent begins to complain about the previous coach. The parent claims that the old coach mismanaged the soccer season from the first tryout to the conclusion of the last game. The parent then spends fifteen minutes heatedly asserting how the selection of the school team should occur. Mr. Sharma leaves the conversation concerned.

What does Mr. Sharma need to know and do before his first tryout? Divide the class in half or by partners. Each half or partner takes either "know" or "do" and lists all possibilities. Next, classify the responses under each category under common themes. Discuss as a class.

In this case, the parent reaction is a symptom caused by an underlying issue. Discuss possible issues that may have affected this parent, leading to the heated conversation.

Part B

As tryouts are concluding, Mr. Sharma realizes that the child of the parent who spoke to him will not make the team under his selection criteria. He has decided to run the team with twenty members, and thirty came out for the tryouts. After the team selection is made, the parent calls the school asking to speak with Mr. Sharma about it. The secretary mentions to Mr. Sharma that the parent sounded upset.

Questions for Reflection

1 Discuss how Mr. Sharma should go about notifying successful and unsuccessful students?

2 Discuss how he should prepare for the parent conversation?

3 In small groups, role play this scenario.

athletic director or PE department head assumes responsibility for coordinating the interscholastic program.

Role of the Teacher

Athletic director: Either the athletic director or a group of teachers may be responsible for overseeing a portion of or the entire interscholastic program. Responsibilities may include, but are not limited to, the following: upholding a coaching code of conduct in line with school and district values, resolving conflicts (coach–student, coach–parent), ensuring coaches are adhering to interschool athletic policies, sourcing and supporting qualified volunteer community coaches when necessary, scheduling practices and games, organizing transportation for school teams, managing an athletic budget, purchasing uniforms and developmentally appropriate equipment, and ensuring that all reasonable steps have been taken to ensure that students are protected and safe.

Teacher coach: Canadian teachers are often expected to take on athletic coaching or PA roles in schools. Although the duties associated with these roles are not contractually required, the underlying assumption is that teachers will, in some capacity, participate in the school's interscholastic program. The role of teacher-coach can add richness and joy to the professional teaching experience. Teacher-coaches may choose to get involved for different reasons, including: a passion for school sport, an interest in providing students with experiences they had as students, or an opportunity to work with students in a different capacity outside the classroom.

The teacher-coach may be responsible for developing student athletes through safe, quality, and progressive sport instruction. He or she is also responsible for supervising and role modelling positive sport behaviours in both competition and practice, and ensuring that all reasonable steps have been taken to ensure that students are protected and safe. Finally, a key responsibility is to ensure open and consistent communication with parents or guardians.

Teacher sponsor: In recent years, schools across Canada have at one time or another been faced with a scenario where students are interested in participating in a PA program but no qualified teacher-coaches are willing to take it on. This may happen for a number of reasons including changes in duties and responsibilities in the classroom, at school, or at home. Taking on an interschool team requires a great deal of time and comes with tremendous responsibility. Some teachers may wish to be part of the interschool program serving as teacher sponsors of a sanctioned school sport or activity. Teacher sponsors are primarily responsible for assisting the volunteer community coach who has agreed to coach an interschool team. A volunteer community coach can be defined as someone who is coaching at a school but is not employed by the school or school board. In the role of

teacher sponsor, responsibilities may include supervising students, handling administrative duties (transportation, maintenance of accurate team records, adherence to school and association guidelines), ensuring that all reasonable steps have been taken to ensure that students are protected and safe, and acting as a liaison between students, parents, and the volunteer community coach.

Interscholastic Health and Safety Considerations

Supervision: Similar to both curricular and intramural PA safety in Canada, district/authority and provincial safety guidelines govern the safe participation of students in interschool sports. In addition to the well-established rules and routines inherent in specific sports, coaches should have access to interschool safety guidelines and must be familiar with the specific requirements outlined for their sport before their team or students participate in a single tryout or practice. Some interschool programming offered in Canada presents greater risk to students and is therefore governed by specific and detailed guidelines for participation. These guidelines have been established to minimize risks, ensure safe participation, and help protect coaches.

Interscholastic activities are more common at the secondary level but also take place at the elementary level.

289

Figure 16.7: Recommendations for the Responsible Teacher-Coach

1. Develop a personal coaching philosophy in line with the school district/authority and school mission and values. The coaching philosophy provides insight into behaviours, decisions, and choices made in the role of teacher-coach.

2. Schedule team/sport information meetings for prospective student participants.

3. Use announcements and various promotional areas in the school to invite student interest.

4. At the information meeting, consider the following:

   - Outlining the commitment associated with participation
   - Providing a tryout/practice/season schedule
   - Sharing coaching and teaching philosophy with the students
   - Outlining expectations for student participation
   - Handing out required parent/guardian participation consent forms, medical forms, and a parent information letter. Students are not to participate in any tryout, practice, or competition until both the parent/guardian consent forms and medical forms are returned to the teacher coach/teacher sponsor.
   - Providing an opportunity for students to ask questions

5. In the parent letter, share your expectations and philosophy of coaching.

6. Review and have available, at all times, a copy of the provincial safety guidelines for the interschool sport. These guidelines must be adhered to for all interschool athletics.

7. If students will be put through a formal selection and tryout process, lay out the specific criteria and schedule that will be used to make judgments. Students should be keenly aware of what the teacher-coach is looking for in making his or her determinations. NOTE: At the elementary level, efforts should be made to encourage all students to participate. Those who are willing and able to commit to an interscholastic team should be allowed to participate. Cutting students at the elementary level is not an acceptable practice and is strongly discouraged.

8. If a decision is made to cut students, develop a notification process that is respectful of the students' dignity and feelings. All students in some capacity struggle with team selection, and teachers have the responsibility to be very careful with students' hopes and dreams. They are encouraged to notify students in a private manner. The notification should offer the following:

   - Reasons they were not successful
   - Developmental strategies for improvement
   - A mechanism for feedback

9. After forming the team, consider scheduling a parents' meeting. At the meeting, consider sharing the following information:

   - Coaching philosophy
   - Roles and responsibilities (e.g., teacher-coach, parents, student participants)
   - Team rules and expectations for students
   - Team schedule
   - Outline school district/school transportation policies and procedures with parents. Ensure that all parents/guardians have completed a transportation permission form.
   - Outline of any costs associated with participation
   - Solicitation of help for fundraising initiatives
   - Q&A session

10. Become familiar with accident reporting procedures and emergency action plans for your school. Make copies for reference and use.

11. Set realistic goals and help students achieve those goals.

12. For practices, consider the following:

    - Take attendance at every practice
    - Develop thorough practice plans
    - Teach developmentally appropriate skills and strategies progressively
    - Ensure the safety of students (supervision, facilities, equipment)

13. For games, consider the following:

    - Be consistent with all student athletes
    - Role model positive sport behaviours
    - Teach students lessons associated with both winning and losing
    - Be fair and consistent and expect fair play

Figure 16.7 continued

- Be keenly aware of and adhere to school district/school transportation policies and procedures for school athletics

14. Participate in sport-specific professional development opportunities provided through the school board/authority or by sport organizations and sport governing bodies.

15. Have fun. We need to remind ourselves and our students of the joy associated with participating in physical activity.

16. All successes are significant. Winning is but one reason to celebrate. Celebrate student improvement, social developments, and opportunities to learn and growth through interschool physical activity participation.

Figure 16.8: Categories of Supervision: Interschool

During track and field practice, some students are involved in the high jump, some in relay, and others in distance running.

- Constant visual supervision: High jump (initial instruction): coach is at the event and observing activity.
- On-site supervision: Relay: students are participating on the track/field and can be seen by the coach.
- In-the-area supervision: Distance running: students are running a prescribed route through the school neighbourhood.

Reproduced with permission from the New Brunswick Department of Education. (2002). New Brunswick Physical Education Safety Guidelines, Module 6: High School Interschool Athletics Guidelines.

Equipment: Each interschool sport has its own distinct equipment requirements for safe participation and play. Coaches and student-athletes need to ensure that the equipment used in interschool practices or games is safe and meets the appropriate sport-specific guidelines for the activity. Often schools differentiate between equipment that can be used in curricular and intramural PA from that which can be used in interschool sport programs. In certain instances, students may wish to utilize personal equipment (e.g., hockey helmets, lacrosse sticks). This is often acceptable provided that such equipment meets the standards set out in the provincial safety guidelines and is in good condition. Schools, school athletic associations, and teams may also raise funds to purchase equipment that is unique and is required for interschool participation (e.g., rowing shells and oars, specialized volleyball systems). This too is acceptable, provided the equipment meets provincial standards and guidelines produced by sport-governing bodies.

Facilities: Coaches should consult board/authority or provincial safety guidelines to review facility requirements for specific interschool activities. Coaches need to actively mitigate potential risks and eliminate all hazards prior to practices or competitions. This rule of thumb applies in both home and away situations. Regardless of where the practice or competition takes place, coaches and supervisors are responsible for ensuring that student athletes can participate safely in the facility or space provided. In many cases, spectators are an important part of the interschool experience but should not put participating students at risk. Within reason, spectators should also be kept from situations where their own health or safety may be at risk.

Conclusion

Despite clearly defined and widely accepted physical activity guidelines for Canadian children, evidence continues to suggest that our children are not active enough for healthy purposes. Consistent and regular school-based PA programming can and should be a part of the solution to improve and increase childhood physical activity behaviours. Schools, administrators, and most importantly, teachers, offer our Canadian children unique, universal access to facilities, equipment, and programming that support many different PA opportunities for all children regardless of race, ethnicity, gender, or socio-economic status. Beyond PE, Canadian schools can and will continue to offer alternative PA programs (e.g., Daily Physical Activity, specialized sport programming) often through a combination of curricular, intramural, and interscholastic options that support student wellness and physical literacy development.

To our future teachers, you, too, can demonstrate a passion and enthusiasm for school-based PA programming by participating, interacting with students, and through the provision of encouragement and support for student interest and participation in school-based PA programming.

There is a need for schools and teachers to affect great change in students' PA behaviours and attitudes towards PA participation. Together, we can offer fun, engaging PA programming that helps our students

(a) develop competence across a broad range of activities,

(b) demonstrate personal commitment to, and understanding of, their own health and wellness through regular participation, and

(c) develop capacity, or the ability to understand, communicate, apply, and analyze different forms of movement in their lives.

Questions for Reflection

1　How can teachers best ensure that children and youth have opportunities to be active during instructional time? Identify potential barriers and propose solutions to address them.

2　Describe the physical, social, and cognitive benefits of (a) curricular, (b) intramural, and (c) interscholastic PA programs.

3　Share both a negative and a positive experience you remember from your own school-based PA experiences.

4　Brainstorm reasons why teachers might or might not want to volunteer their time in a school-based PA program.

5　Discuss how PA programs have failed students at both the elementary and secondary level, and why? Discuss where they have succeeded, and why?

6　As an extension to this chapter, explore examples of school-based specialized sport programs in your own province. Discuss the merits of such program options versus the more traditional broad-based PA program options.

Key Terms

- Physical Activity Guidelines
- Curricular Physical Activity
- Intramural Physical Activity
- Interscholastic Physical Activity
- Daily Physical Activity
- Whole School DPA
- Teacher-Driven DPA
- Student-Facilitated DPA
- Categories of Supervision

References

Preface

Active Healthy Kids Canada (2011). Don't let this be the most physical activity our kids get after school. *The Active Healthy Kids Canada 2011 report card on physical activity for children and youth*. Toronto: Active Healthy Kids Canada.

Ludwig, D. S. (2007). Childhood obesity: The shape of things to come. *New England Journal of Medicine, 357*, 2325–2327.

Waddell, C., McEwan, K., Shepherd, C. A, Offord, D.R., Hua, J. M. (2005). A public health strategy to improve the mental health of Canadian children. *Canadian Journal of Psychiatry, 50*(4), 226–233.

Chapter 1

Aoki, T. (1991). *Inspiriting curriculum and pedagogy: Talks to teachers*. Occasional Paper on Curriculum Praxis, Department of Secondary Education, University of Alberta.

Cosentino, F. & Howell, M. (1971). *A history of physical education in Canada*. Toronto: General Publishing Company.

Gurney, H. (1982). *The CAHPER story 1933–1983: Fifty years of progress*. Ottawa: T.H. Best Printing Company Ltd.

Hellison, D. (1987). Dreaming the possible dream: The rise and triumph of physical education. In J.A. Massengale (Ed.), *Trends toward the future in physical education* (pp. 137–52). Champaign, IL: Human Kinetics.

Hill, R. (1979). "Movement education: What's in a name?" *CAPER Journal, 46*(1), 18–25.

Innis, M. (1950). *A history of the YMCA in Canada*. Toronto: McClelland and Stewart .

Jewett, A., Bain, L.L. & Ennis, C.D. (1995). *The curriculum process in physical education* (2nd ed.). Dubuque: Brown.

Keyes, M. (1989). Sport and physical education in schools and universities. In D. Morrow, W. Simpson, F. Consentino & R. Lappage (Eds.), *A Concise History of Sport in Canada*, (pp. 69–87). Toronto: Oxford University Press.

Kirk, D. (2010). *Physical education futures*. New York: Routledge.

Kozar, A. (1992) *The sport sculpture of R. Tait McKenzie*. Windsor, ON: Human Kinetics

Laker, A. (Ed.). (2003). *The future of physical education: Building a new pedagogy*. London: Routledge.

Locke, L.F. (1992). Changing secondary school physical education. *Quest, 44*, 361–72.

Mandigo, J., Corlett, J., & Lathrop, A. (2012). Physical Education in the twenty-first century: To infinity and beyond? In E. Singleton & A. Varpalotai (Eds.), *Pedagogy in motion: A community of inquiry for human movement studies*, (pp. 15–44). London, ON: The Althouse Press.

Manitoba Department of Education. (1909). *Program of studies*. Winnipeg: Department of Education.

Martens, F. (1986). *Basic concepts of physical education*. Champaign, IL: Stipes Publishing Company.

McGill, J. (1980). *The joy of effort: A biography of R. Tait McKenzie*. Oshawa, ON: The Alger Press Ltd.

Morrow, D. & Wamsley, K. B. (2005). *Sport in Canada: A history*. Oxford: Oxford University Press.

Orban, W. (1965). The fitness movement. In M. L. Van Vliet (Ed.), *Physical education in Canada*. Toronto: Prentice Hall.

Pangrazi, R. & Gibbons, S. (2009). *Dynamic physical education for elementary school children*. Toronto: Pearson Education Canada.

Penny, D. & Chandler, T. (2002). Physical education: What future(s)? *Sport, Education and Society, 5*, 71–87.

Sanders, S. & McCrum, D. (1999). "Peaks of excellence, valleys of despair": What is the future of physical education? *Teaching Elementary Physical Education, January*, 3–4.

Siedentop, D. (2002). Content knowledge for physical education. *Journal of Teaching in Physical Education, 21*, 368–77.

Chapter 2

Armour, K. M. & Yelling, M. (2004). Continuing professional development for experienced health and physical education teachers: Towards effective provision. *Sport, Education & Society, 9*(1), 95–114.

Ball, D. L. (2000). Bridging practices: Intertwining content and pedagogy in teaching and learning to teach. *Journal of Teacher Education, 51*(3), 241–247.

Borko, H. & Putnam, R. T. (1996). Learning to teach. In D. C. Berliner & R. C. Calfee (Eds.), *The handbook of educational psychology* (pp. 673–708). New York: Macmillan.

Bullock, S. M. (2011). *Inside teacher education : Challenging prior views of teaching and learning*. Rotterdam, The Netherlands: Sense.

Darling-Hammond, L. & Hammerness, K. (2005). The design of teacher education programs. In L. Darling-Hammond & J. Bransford (Eds.), *Preparing teachers for a changing world: What teachers should learn and be able to do*. (pp. 390–441). San Francisco: Jossey-Bass.

Dowling, F. (2011). "Are PE teachers' identities fit for postmodern schools or are they clinging to modernist notions of professionalism?" A case study of Norwegian teacher students' emerging professional identities. *Sport, Education & Society, 16*(2), 201–222.

Ennis, C. D. (1992). The influence of value orientations in curriculum decision making. *Quest, 44*(3), 317–329.

Feiman-Nemser, S. (2008). Teacher learning: How do teachers learn to teach? In M. Cochran-Smith, S. Feiman-Nemser, D. J. McIntyre & K. E. Demers (Eds.), *Handbook of research on teacher education*. (3rd ed.). (pp. 697–705). New York, NY: Routledge/Association of Teacher Educators.

Fernandez-Balboa, J.-M. (1997). Physical education teacher preparation in the postmoderne era: Toward a critical pedagogy. In J.-M. Fernandez-Balboa (Ed.), *Critical postmodernism in human movement, physical education, and sport* (pp. 121–138). Albany, NY : SUNY Press.

Grant. C. A. & Zeichner, K. M. (1984). On becoming a reflective teacher. In C. A. Grant (Ed.), *Preparing for reflective teaching* (pp. 103–14). Boston: Allyn & Bacon.

Grossman, P. & Schoenfeld, A. (2005). Teaching subject matter. In L. Darling-Hammond & J. Bransford (Eds.) *Preparing teachers for a changing world: What teachers should learn and be able to do* (pp. 201–31). San Francisco: Jossey-Bass.

Hammerness, K. (2006). *Seeing through teachers' eyes: Professional ideals and classroom practice*. New York: Teachers College Press.

Hammerness, K., Darling-Hammond, L. & Bransford, J. (2005). How teachers learn and develop. In L. Darling-Hammond & J. Bransford (Eds.), *Preparing teachers for a changing world: What teachers should learn and be able to do*. (pp. 358–89). San Francisco: Jossey-Bass.

Jenkins, R. (2008). *Social identity* (3rd ed.). London: Routledge.

Korthagen, F. A. J. (2004). In search of the essence of a good teacher: Towards a more holistic approach to teacher education. *Teaching & teacher education, 20*(1), 77–97.

Korthagen, F. A. J., Loughran, J. J. & Russell, T. (2006). Developing fundamental principles for teacher education programs and practices. *Teaching & teacher education, 22*(8), 1020–41.

Kosnik, C. & Beck, C. (2009). *Priorities in teacher education: The 7 key elements of pre-service preparation*. New York: Routledge.

Lawson, H. A. (1983). Toward a model of teacher socialization in physical education: The subjective warrant, recruitment, and teacher education. *Journal of teaching in physical education, 2*(3), 3–16.

Lortie, D. C. (1975). *Schoolteacher: A sociological study*. Chicago: University of Chicago Press.

McCaughtry, N. (2004). The emotional dimensions of a teacher's pedagogical content knowledge: Influences on content, curriculum, and pedagogy. *Journal of teaching in health and physical education, 23*(1), 30–47.

Munby, H., Russell, T., & Martin, A. K. (2001). Teachers' knowledge and how it develops. In V. Richardson (Ed.), *Handbook of research on teaching* (4th ed.). (pp. 877–904). Washington, DC: American Educational Research Association.

National Research Council (2000). *How people learn: Brain, mind, experience, and school*. Washington, DC: National Academy Press.

O'Bryant, C. P., O'Sullivan, M. & Raudensky, J. (2000). Socialization of prospective physical education teachers: The story of new blood. *Sport, education & society, 5*(2), 177–93.

Randall, L. (2012). Teacher resistance. In E. Singleton & A. Varpalotai (Eds.) *Pedagogy in motion: A community of inquiry for human movement studies*. (pp. 123–46). London, ON: The Althouse Press.

Schön, D. A. (1983). *The reflective practitioner: How professionals think in action*. New York: Basic Books.

Shulman, L. S. (1986). Those who understand: Knowledge growth in teaching. *Educational Researcher, 15*(4), 4–14.

Siedentop, D. (2002). Content knowledge for health and physical education. *Journal of teaching in health and physical education, 21*(4), 368–77.

Sirna, K., Tinning, R., & Rossi, T. (2008). The social task of learning to become a physical education teacher: Considering the HPE subject department culture. *Sport, Education & Society, 13*(3), 285–300.

Tsangaridou, N. (2006). Teachers' beliefs. In D. Kirk, D. Macdonald & M. O'Sullivan (Eds), *The handbook of health and physical education*. (pp. 486–501). London: Sage.

Tsangaridou, N. & Siedentop, D. (1995). Reflective teaching: A literature review. *Quest, 47*(2), 212–37.

Chapter 3

Alberta Education. (2011) Curriculum redesign project. Retrieved from: http://education.alberta.ca/department/ipr/curriculum.aspx

Barnekow, V. et al. *Health-promoting Schools: A Resource for Developing Indicators*. Woerden, The Netherlands: European Network of Health Promoting Schools (now Schools for Health in Europe), 2006. Retrieved from: www.euro.who.int/Document/E89735.pdf

Bunker, D. & Thorpe, R. (1982). A model for the teaching of games in the secondary school. *Bulletin of Physical Education, 18*(1), 5–8.

Burrows, L. (2005). Proposed Key Competencies and Health and Physical Education in the New Zealand Curriculum. Retrieved from: www.tki.org.nz/r/nzcurriculum/references_e.php

Butler, J. & McCahan, B. (2005). Teaching games for understanding as a curriculum model. In L. Griffin & J. Butler (Eds.), *Teaching games for understanding: Theory,* research, and practice (pp. 33–54). Windsor: Human Kinetics.

Canadian Sport for Life: Long Term Athlete Development Plan. Retrieved from: www.canadiansportforlife.ca/

Callois, R. (1961) *Man, play and games*. New York: Free Press.

Cedefop: European Centre for the Development of Vocational Training (2008), *Terminology of European education and training policy: A selection of 100 key terms*. Luxembourg: Office of Official Publications of the European Communities.

Corbin, C. & Lindsey, R. (2005). *Fitness for Life,* (5th ed.). Champaign, IL: Human Kinetics.

Cothran, D. (2001). Curriculum change in physical education: Success stories from the front line. *Sport education and society 6*(1), 67–79.

Cutforth, N. J. (1997). What's worth doing: Reflections on an after-school program in a Denver elementary school. *Quest, 49*(1), 130–39.

Cummings, T. (1998). *Testing the effectiveness of Hellison's personal and social responsibility model: A dropout, repeated grade, and absentee rate comparison.* Unpublished master's thesis, California State University, Chico.

DeBusk, M. & Hellison, D. (1989). Implementing a physical education self-responsibility model for delinquency-prone youth. *Journal of Teaching and Physical Education. 8*, 104–12 .

Deschesnes, M., Martin, C., & Hill, A. J. (2003). Comprehensive approaches to school health promotion: How to achieve broader implementation? *Health promotion international, 18*(4), 387–96.

Ennis, C., & Chen, A. (1993). Domain specifications and content representativeness of the revised value orientation inventory. *Research quarterly for exercise and sport, (64)*, 436–46.

Escartí, A.; Gutiérrez, M.; Pascual, C.; Llopis, R. (2010). Implementation of the personal and social responsibility. *International Journal of Psychology and Psychological Therapy. 10*(3), 387–402.

Fullan, M. (2002). The change leader. *Educational Leadership*, May, 16–20.

Gleddie, D. L. (2011). A journey into school health promotion: district implementation of the health promoting schools approach. *Health promotion international*. Advance online publication. doi: 10.1093/heapro/dar053

Griffin, L. & Butler, J. (2005) Teaching games for understanding: Theory, research and practice. Champaign, IL: Human Kinetics.

Gutierrez, P. & Llopis, 2010: Application of Hellison's teaching personal and social responsibility model. *The Spanish Journal of Psychology, 13*(2), 667–76

Ha, A. S., Wong, A. C., Sum, R. K., & Chan, D. W. (2008). Understanding teachers' will and capacity to accomplish physical education curriculum reform: The implications for teacher development. *Sport, education and society, 13*(1), 77–95.

Harrison, J. M., Blakemore, L., & Buck, M. M. (2001). *Instructional strategies for secondary school physical education*, (5th ed.). Boston: McGraw-Hill.

Hellison, D. (2003). Teaching personal and social responsibility in physical education. In S. J. Silverman & C. D. Ennis. *Students learning in physical education: Applying research to enhance instruction*. Champaign, IL: Human Kinetics.

Hellison, D. & Templin, T. (1991). *A reflective approach to teaching physical education*. Champaign, IL: Human Kinetics.

Hellison, D. & Walsh, D. (2002). Responsibility-based youth programs evaluation: Investigating the investigations. *Quest, 54*(4), 292–307.

Holt, N., Strean, W., & Garcia Bengoechea, E. (2002). Expanding the teaching games for understanding model: New avenues for future research and practice. *Journal of teaching in physical education, 21*, 162–76.

Inchley, J., Muldoon, J. and Currie, C. (2006). Becoming a health promoting school: Evaluating the process of effective implementation in Scotland. *Health promotion international, 22*(1), 65–71.

Jewett, A., Bain, L., & Ennis, C. (1995). *The curriculum process in physical education* (2nd ed). Madison, WI: Brown & Benchmark.

Joint Consortium for School Health. (2010). *What is comprehensive school health?* Retrieved from: http://eng. jHPS-cces.ca/.php?option=com_content&view=article&id= 40&Itemid=62

Kirk, D. (1992) *Defining physical education: The social construction of a school subject in postwar britain*. London: Falmer.

Kirk, D., MacDonald, D., & Tinning, R. (1997). The social construction of pedagogic discourse in physical education teacher education in Australia. *The Curriculum Journal, 8*(2), 271–98.

Locke, (1992). Changing secondary school physical education. *Quest, 44*, 361–72.

Mandigo, J., Butler, J, & Hopper, T. (2007). What is teaching games for understanding: A Canadian Perspective. *Physical and Health Education. 73*(2), 14–20 .

Mandigo, J., Francis, N., Lodewyk, K., & Lopez, R. (2009) *Position Paper: Physical Literacy for Educators.* Ottawa: Physical and Health Education Canada.

Metzler, M. W. (2000) *Instructional models for physical education.* Boston: Allyn & Bacon.

Parker, M. & Hellison, D. (2001). Teaching responsibility in physical education: Standards, outcomes and beyond. *Journal of physical education, recreation and dance, 72*(9).

Rink, J. (2009). *Teaching physical education for learning.* (6th edition). Boston: McGraw-Hill.

Siedentop, D, (1980) *Physical education: introductory analysis.* Dubuque: Wm. C. Brown.

Siedentop, D. (2001). What is sport education and how does it work? *The journal of physical education, recreation & dance, 69*(4).

Siedentop, D. (2002). Sport education: A retrospective. *Journal of Teaching in Physical Education*, 2, 409-18 .

Siedentop, D., Mand, C., and Taggart, A. (1986). *Physical education: Teaching and curriculum strategies for grades 5–12.* Palo Alto: Mayfield.

Stewart-Brown, S. (2006). What is the evidence on school health promotion in improving health or preventing disease and, specifically, what is the effectiveness of the health promoting schools approach? *Health evidence network report.* Copenhagen: WHO Regional Office for Europe.

St. Leger, L. (1999). The opportunities and effectiveness of the health promoting primary school in improving child health: A review of the claims and evidence. *Health education research, 14*(1), 51–69.

St. Leger, L. (2004). What's the place of schools in promoting health? Are we too optimistic? *Health promotion international, 19*(4), 405–08.

St. Leger, L. et al. (2010). *Promoting health in schools: From evidence to action.* Saint Denis, France: International Union for Health Promotion and Education.

Wentzel, K. (1991). Relations between social competence and academic achievement in early adolescence. *Child development, 62*(5), 1066–78.

World Health Organization. (1996). *Regional guidelines: Development of health promoting schools: A framework for action* (Health promoting schools, series 5). Manila: WHO Regional Office for the Western Pacific.

World Health Organization. (2003). "Skills for Health." *Information Series on School Health, Document 9.* Retrieved from: www.who.int/school_youth_health/media/en/sch_skills4health_03.pdf.

Chapter 4

Anderson, L. & Krathwohl, D. (Eds.), (2001). *A taxonomy for learning, teaching, and assessing: A revision of Bloom's taxonomy of educational objectives.* New York: Longman.

British Columbia Ministry of Education (2006). *Physical education K–7 integrated resource package.* Victoria, BC: Author.

Bloom, B. (Ed.), Engelhat, M., Furst, E., Hill, W., & Krathwohl, D. (1956). *Taxonomy of educational objectives: The classification of educational goals. Handbook 1: Cognitive domain.* New York: David McKay.

Buck, M. M., Lund, J. L., Harrison, J. M., & Blakemore Cook, C. (2007). *Instructional strategies for secondary school physical education* (6th ed.). New York: McGraw Hill.

Constitution Acts, 1867–1982. Government of Canada, Department of Justice. Retrieved from: http://laws-lois.justice.gc.ca/eng/Const/

Ennis, C. D. (2008). Examining curricular coherence in an exemplary elementary school program. *Research quarterly for exercise and sport, 79*(1), 71–84.

Government of Alberta, Department of Education. (2000). *Physical education (K–12).* Edmonton, AB: Alberta Learning.

Government of British Columbia, Ministry of Education. (2006). *Physical education K to 7:* Integrated resource package.

Government of New Brunswick, Department of Education and Early Childhood Development. (2002). *Middle level physical education curriculum, grades 6-8.* Educational Programs & Services Branch, Curriculum Development Unit.

Government of New Brunswick, Department of Education and Early Childhood Development. (2000). *Elementary physical education curriculum, kindergarten-grade 5.* Educational Programs & Services Branch, Curriculum Development Unit.

Government of Newfoundland and Labrador, Department of Education. (1996). *A curriculum framework for physical education: Adjusting the focus.* Division of Program Development.

Government of Newfoundland and Labrador, Department of Education. (nd). *Physical education, Primary and elementary, Curriculum Guide.* Division of Program Development.

Government of Nova Scotia, Department of Education. (1999). *Physical education curriculum: Grades 7-9.* English Language Services, Program Planning.

Government of Ontario, Ministry of Education and Training. (2010). *The Ontario curriculum. Grades 1-8. Health and physical Education (revised).* Toronto, Ontario: Author

Government of Quebec, Ministry of Education. (2001). *New directions for success. Preschool education. Elementary education.* Quebec Education Program.

Government of Saskatchewan, Ministry of Education. (2009) Physical education and training (Middle school) Curriculum and E-Learning. Humanities Unit.

Graham, G., Holt/Hale, S. A., & Parker, M. (2007). *Children moving: A reflective approach to teaching physical education* (7th ed.). New York: McGraw Hill Higher Education.

Lund, J. & Tannehill, D. (2005). *Standards-based physical education curriculum development.* Mississauga, ON: Jones and Bartlette.

Mitchell, S., Oslin, J., & Griffin, L. (2006). *Teaching sport concepts and skills. A tactical games approach.* Champaign, IL: Human Kinetics.

Mandigo, J., Francis, N., Lodewyk, K., & Lopez, R. (2009). *Position paper: Physical literacy for educators.* Ottawa: Physical and Health Education Canada. Retrieved from: www.physical-literacy.ca.

Pangrazi, R. & Gibbons, S. (2003). *Dynamic physical education for elementary school children. Canadian edition.* Toronto: Pearson Education Canada.

Physical & Health Education Canada. (nd). *What is the relationship between physical education and physical literacy?* Retrieved from: www.phecanada.ca/advocacy/advocacy-tools/what-relationship-between-physical-education-and-physical-literacy

Rink , J. (2006). *Teaching physical education for learning.* New York: McGraw-Hill.

Rink, J. (2009). *Designing the physical education curriculum. Promoting active lifestyles.* New York: McGraw-Hill.

Rose, M. (2000). *Step lively two.* Vancouver: Community Dance Project.

Siedentop, D. (1994). *Sport education.* Champaign, IL: Human Kinetics.

Siedentop, D., Hastie, P., & van der Mars, H. (2004). *Complete guide to sport education.* Champaign, IL: Human Kinetics.

Siedentop, D. & Tannehill, D. (2000). *Developing teaching skills in physical education,* (4th ed.). Toronto: Mayfield Publishing Company.

Wall, J. & Murray, N. (1994). Children & movement. *Physical education in the elementary school.* Dubuque, IA: Wm. C. Brown Communications, Inc.

Chapter 5

Darst, P., Pangrazi, R., Sariscany, M., & Brusseau Jr., T. (2012). Dynamic physical education for secondary school students (7th ed.). San Francisco: Pearson.

Erpic, S. C. (2011). Motivation for physical education: A review of the recent literature from an achievement goal and self-determination perspective. *International Journal of Physical Education, 48*(2), 2–14.

Fisher, D. & Frey, N. (2008). *Better learning through structured teaching: A framework for the gradual release of responsibility.* Alexandria, VA: Association for Supervision and Curriculum Development (ASCD).

Flessa, J., Gallagher-Mackay, K., & Ciuffetelli-Parker, D. (2010). "Good, steady progress": Success stories from Ontario elementary schools in challenging circumstances. *Canadian Journal of Educational Administration and Policy, 101,* 632–703.

Hellison, D. (2003). *Teaching responsibility through physical activity* (2nd ed.). Champaign, IL: Human Kinetics.

Jang, H. Reeve, J., & Deci, E. L. (2010). Engaging students in learning activities: It is not autonomy support or structure but autonomy support and structure. *Journal of Educational Psychology, 10*(3), 588–600.

Kounin, J. (1970). *Discipline and group management in classrooms.* New York: Holt, Rinehart, and Winston.

Kulinna, P. A. & Cothran, D. J. (2003). Physical education teachers' self-reported use and perceptions of various teaching styles. *Learning and Instruction, 13,* 597–609.

Lavay, B. W., French, R., & Henderson, H. L. (2006). Positive behavior management in physical activity settings. (2nd ed). Champaign, IL: Human Kinetics.

Mosston, M. & Ashworth, S. (2001). *Teaching physical education.* (5th ed). Boston: Benjamin Cummings.

Ontario Ministry of Education. (2011). *Learning for all: A guide to effective assessment and instruction for all students, kindergarten to grade 12 (draft).* Toronto: Ontario Ministry of Education.

Pangrazi, R. P. & Gibbons, S. L. (2009). *Dynamic physical education for elementary school children* (2nd Canadian ed). Toronto: Pearson.

Rink, J. (2003). Effective instruction in physical education. In: Silverman, S. J. & Ennis, C. D. (Eds.). *Student learning in physical education: Applying research to enhance instruction* (pp. 171–98). Champaign, IL: Human Kinetics.

Rink, J. (2009). *Teaching physical education for learning* (6th ed). Boston: McGraw-Hill. Rosenshine, B. & Stevens, R. (1986). Teaching functions. In M. Wittrock (Ed.). *Handbook of research on teaching* (3rd ed) (376–91). New York: Macmillan.

Rosenshine, B. & Stevens, R. (1986). Teaching functions. In M. Wittrock (Ed.). *Handbook of research on teaching* (3rd ed) (376–91). New York: Macmillan.

Siedentop, D. (2009). *Introduction to physical education, fitness, and sport* (7th ed). New York: McGraw-Hill.

Siedentop, D. & Tannehill, D. (1999). *Developing teaching skills in physical education* (4th ed.). Mountain View: Mayfield Publishing Company.

Silverman, S. J. & Ennis, C. D. (Eds.). (2003). *Student learning in physical education: Applying research to enhance instruction*. Champaign IL: Human Kinetics.

Solmon, M. A. (2003). Student issues in physical education classes: Attitudes, cognition, and motivation. In Silverman, S. J. & Ennis, C. D. (Eds.). *Student learning in physical education: Applying research to enhance instruction* (pp. 147–164). Champaign IL: Human Kinetics.

Thomas, K. T., Lee, A. M., & Thomas, J. R. (2008). *Physical education methods for elementary teachers* (3rd ed). Champaign, IL: Human Kinetics.

Tjeerdsma, B. L. (1995). How to motivate students … without standing on your head! *Journal of Physical Education, Recreation & Dance, 66*(5), 36–39.

Townsend, J. S., & Gurvitch, R. (2002). Integrating technology into physical education: Enhancing multiple intelligences. *Teaching Elementary Physical Education, 13*(2), 35–39.

Chapter 6

Alberta Assessment Consortium. (2005). *A framework for student assessment* (2nd ed.). Edmonton, AB: Alberta Assessment Consortium.

Alberta Learning. (2000). *Physical education guide to implementation (K–12): Assessment, evaluation and communication of student learning*. Edmonton, AB: Alberta Learning.

Arter, J., & Chappuis, J., (2007). *Creating & recognizing quality rubrics*. Upper Saddle River, NJ: Pearson Education.

Black, P., Harrison, C., Lee, C., Marshall, B., & Wiliam, D. (2003). *Assessment for learning: Putting it into practice*. New York: Open University Press.

Black, P., & Wiliam, D. (1998). Assessment and classroom learning. *Assessment in Education, 5*(1), 103–10.

Bloom, B. (1956). *Taxonomy of educational objectives, handbook I: The cognitive domain*. New York: David McKay.

British Columbia Ministry of Education. (2006). *Physical education K to 7: Integrated resource package 2006*. Vancouver: British Columbia Ministry of Education.

Bruce, L . B. (2001). Student self-assessment: Encouraging active engagement in learning. *Dissertation Abstracts International*, Vol. 62-04A, 1309.

Buck, M. M., Lund, J. L., Harrison, J. M., & Blakemore Cook, C. (2007). *Instructional strategies for secondary physical education* (6th ed.). Boston: McGraw Hill.

Cooper Institute. (2007). *Fitnessgram/Activitygram test administration manual* (4th ed.). Champaign, IL: Human Kinetics.

Corbin, C. B., Pangrazi, R. P. & Welk, G. J. (1995). A response to "The horse is dead: let's dismount." *Pediatric Exercise Science, 7*, 347–51.

Darst, P. W., & Pangrazi, R. P. (2009). *Dynamic physical education for secondary school students* (6th ed.). San Francisco: Pearson Education.

Davies, A. (2007). *Making classroom assessment work* (2nd ed.). Courtenay, BC: Connections.

Earl, L. M. (2003). *Assessment as learning: Using classroom assessment to maximize student learning*. Thousand Oaks, CA: Sage.

Education New Brunswick. (2002). *Middle level physical education curriculum grades 6 to 8*. Fredericton, NB: Educational Programs & Services Branch.

Fenwick, T. J., & Parsons, J. (2009). *The art of evaluation: A resource for educators and trainers* (2nd ed.). Toronto: Thompson Educational Publishing.

Francis, N., Johnson, A., Lloyd, M., Robinson, D. B., & Sheehan, D. (2011). *Fundamental movement skills: The building blocks for the development of physical literacy. An educator's guide to teaching fundamental movement skills*. Ottawa: PHE Canada.

Gibbons, S. L., & Robinson, B. A. (2004). Student-friendly rubrics for personal and social learning in physical education. *Physical and Health Education Journal, 70*(4), 4–9.

Gregory, K., Cameron, C., & Davies, A. (1997). *Setting and using criteria: For use in middle and secondary school classrooms*. Merville: Connections.

Herbert, E. (1998). Lessons learned about student portfolios. *Phi Delta Kappan, 79*(8), 583–85.

Herman, J. L., Aschbacher, P. R., & Winters, L. (1992). *A practical guide to alternative assessment*. Alexandria, VA: Association for Supervision and Curriculum Development.

Kovar, S. K., Combs, C. A., Campbell, K., Napper-Owen, G., & Worrell, V. J. (2007). *Elementary classroom teachers as movement educators* (2nd ed.). New York: McGraw Hill.

Lloyd, M., Colley, R. C., & Tremblay, M. S. (2010). Advancing the debate on "fitness testing" for children: Perhaps we're riding the wrong animal. *Pediatric Exercise Science, 22*(2), 176–82.

Manitoba Education, Citizenship and Youth. (2009). *Grade 12 active healthy lifestyles: Manitoba physical education/ health education curriculum framework of outcomes and a foundation for implementation*. Winnipeg, MB: Manitoba Education, Citizenship and Youth.

McMillan, J. H., Hellsten, L. M., & Klinger, D. A. (2011). *Classroom assessment: Principles and practice for effective standards-based instruction*. Toronto: Pearson.

Ministry of Education, Province of British Columbia. (2006). *Physical education grade 2: Integrated resource package 2006*. Vancouver : British Columbia Ministry of Education.

O'Connor, K. (2009). *How to grade for learning: K-12* (3rd ed.). Thousand Oaks, CA: Corwin.

Rink, J. (2010). *Teaching physical education for learning* (6th ed.). Boston: McGraw Hill.

Rolheiser, C., & Ross, J. A. (2000). Student self-evaluation – What do we know? *Orbit, 30*(4), 33–6.

Rowland, T. (1995). The horse is dead: let's dismount. *Pediatric Exercise Science, 7*, 117–20.

Rust, C. (2002). Purposes and principles of assessment. *Oxford Centre for Staff and Learning Development: Learning and Teaching Briefing Papers Series*. Oxford: Oxford Brookes University.

Ryan, T. H., (2005). *The reflective physical educator*. Calgary, AB: Detselig Enterprises.

Saskatchewan Ministry of Education. (2009). *2009 Saskatchewan curriculum: Physical education 8*. Regina, SK: Saskatchewan Ministry of Education.

Scriven, M. (1991). *Evaluation thesaurus* (4th ed.). London: Sage.

Silverman, S., Keating, X. D., & Phillips, S. R. (2008). A lasting impression: A pedagogical perspective on youth fitness testing. *Measurement in Physical Education and Exercise Science, 12*, 146–66.

Wall, A. E., Reid, G., & Harvey, W. J. (2007). Interface of the knowledge-based and ecological task analysis approaches. In W. E. Davis & D. Broadhead (Eds.), *Ecological approach to analyzing movement* (pp. 259–77). Champaign, IL: Human Kinetics.

Wiggins, G. P. (1998). *Educative assessment: Designing assessments to inform and improve student performance*. San Francisco: Jossey-Bass.

Wiggins, G. P., & McTighe, J. (2007). *Understanding by design* (2nd ed.). Alexandria, VA: Association for Supervision and Curriculum Development.

Chapter 7

Bagnoli, A. (2007). Between outcast and outsider: Constructing the identity of the foreigner. *European Societies, 9*(1), 23–44.

Birkett, M., Espelage, D. & Koenig, B. (2009). LGB and questioning students in schools: The moderating effects of homophobic bullying and school climate on negative outcomes. *Journal of Youth and Adolescence, 38*(7), 989–1000.

Bourdieu, P. (2001). *Masculine domination*. Stanford: Stanford University Press.

Brown, D. (2006). Pierre Bourdieu's "masculine domination" thesis and the gendered body in sport and physical culture. *Sociology of Sport Journal, 23*, 162–188.

Brownell, M., Roos, N. P., Fransoo, R., Guevremont, A., MacWilliam, L., Derksen, S., Dik, N., Bogdanovic, B., Sirski, M. (2004). How do educational outcomes vary with socioeconomic status? Key findings from the Manitoba child health atlas. *Manitoba Centre for Health Policy*. Retrieved from: http://mchp-appserv.cpe.umanitoba.ca/reference/ch.atlas.pdf

Cat in the Hat Productions. (2010). *The sneetches*. Retrieved from: http://www.youtube.com/watch?v=2kz3yZkOiKc

Curry-Stevens, A. (2003). Arrogant capitalism: Changing futures, changing lives. *Canadian Review of Social Policy/Revue Canadienne de politique sociale, 51*, 137–45.

Cusumano, D. L. & Thompson, J. K. (2001). Media influence and body image in 8–11-year-old boys and girls: A preliminary report on the multidimensional media influence scale. *International Journal of Eating Disorders, 29*(1) 37–44.

Davison, K. G. (2004). Texting gender and body as a distant/ced memory: An autobiographical account of bodies, masculinities, and schooling. *Journal of Curriculum Theorizing, 20*(3), 129–49.

Douglas, D., & Halas, J. (2008). Resistance? What resistance? Identifying racial inequities in faculties of physical education: Challenging the colour of domination. Paper presented at *"To remember is to resist:" 40 Years of Sport and Social Change, 1968–2008 Conference*, Toronto, ON.

Duncan, M. C. (1990). Sports photographs and sexual difference: Images of women and men in the 1984 and 1988 Olympic Games. *Sociology of Sport Journal, 7*, 22–43.

Fernandez-Balboa, J. (1997). *Postmodernism in human movement, physical education, and sport*. Albany, NY: State University of New York Press.

Field, A. E., Camargo, C. A., Taylor, C. B., Berkey, C. S., Roberts, S. B, & Colditz, G. A. (2001). Peer, parent, and media influences on the development of weight concerns and frequent dieting among preadolescent and adolescent girls and boys. *Pediatrics, 107*(1), 54–60.

Fitzgerald, H. (2011). Knowing disability: "I'm the alien from outer space". In J. Kentel (Ed.). *Educating the young: The ethics of care*. London: Peter Lang Publishers.

Fitzpatrick, K. (2011). Brown bodies, racialization and physical education. *Sport, Education and Society,* iFirst, 1–19.

Flory, S. B. & McCaughtry, N. (2011). Culturally relevant physical education in urban schools: Reflecting cultural knowledge. *Research Quarterly for Exercise and Sport, 82*(1), 1–12.

Freire, P. (1997). Pedagogy of the heart. D. Macedo & A. Oliveira (trans.) New York: Continuum.

Gibson, P. (1994). Gay male and lesbian youth suicide. In G. Remafedi (Ed.). *Death by denial: Studies of suicide in gay and lesbian teenagers,* (pp. 15–68). Boston: Alyson.

Halas, J. M. (2011) Aboriginal youth and their experiences in physical education: "This is what you've taught me." *PHEnex Journal, 3*(2), 1–22.

Halas, J., McRae, H., & Carpenter, A. (2012) The quality and cultural relevance of physical education for aboriginal youth. In J. Forsyth & A. Giles (Eds.). *Red and white: Aboriginal people and Canadian sport.* Vancouver: UBC Press.

Kentel, J. A. (2009). Pretty boys and butch girls: Examining the development of masculinities in physical education. Paper presented at the *Council of University Professors and Researchers (CUPR)* Annual Meeting, April–May 2009, Banff, Alberta, Canada.

Kentel, J. A. (2011). The stronger side of feminine: Conflicting perceptions of gender in physical education. Paper presented at the *AERA Annual Meeting*, April 8-12, 2011, New Orleans, Louisiana.

King, R. (1995). Migrations, globalisation and place. In D. Massey & P. Jess (Eds.). A place in the world? *Places, culture and globalization,* Volume 4 (pp. 5–44). Oxford: Open University Press.

Ladson-Billings, G. (1995). But that's just good teaching! The case for culturally relevant pedagogy. *Theory Into Practice, 34*(3), 159–65.

Lawson, H. (2005). Empowering people, facilitating community development, and contributing to sustainable development: The social work of sport, exercise, and physical education programs. *Sport, Education and Society, 10*(1), 135–60.

Light, R. & Kentel, J. A. (2010). Soft pedagogy for a hard sport(?) Disrupting hegemonic masculinity in high school rugby through feminist-informed pedagogy. In M. Kehlen, & M. Atkinson (Eds.). *Boys' bodies* (pp. 133–52). Oxford: Peter Lang Publishers.

Maes, H. H. M., Neale, M. C. & Eaves, L. J. (1997). Genetic and environmental factors in relative body weight and human adiposity. *Behavior Genetics, 27*(4), 325–51.

McLaren, P. (1991). Schooling the postmodern body: Critical pedagogy and the politics of enfleshment. In

H. Giroux (Ed.). *Postmodernism, feminism, and cultural politics: Redrawing educational boundaries* (pp. 144–73). Albany, NY: State University of New York Press.

Melnychuk, N., Robinson, D., Lu, C., Chorney, D., & Randall, L. (2011). Physical education teacher education (PETE) in Canada. *Canadian Journal of Education. 34*(2), 148–68.

Physical and Health Education Canada (2010). About quality daily physical education. Retrieved from: www.capherd.ca/eng/physicaleducation/about_qdpe.cfm

Ratkovic, S. & Kentel, J. A. (2007). Immigration, oppression, and professional identity: Death of a science teacher. A paper presented at the *ISATT* Conference, July 5–9, 2007, St. Catharines, Ontario.

Seuss, Dr. (1961). *The sneetches and other stories.* Toronto, ON: Random House.

Slee, R. & Allan, J. (2001). Excluding the included: A recognition of inclusive education. *International Studies in Sociology of Education, 11*(2), 173–91.

Sykes, H. (2011). *Queer Bodies: Sexualities, genders and fatness in physical education.* New York: Peter Lang Publishing Inc.

Sykes, H. & McPhail, D. (2007). Unbearable lessons: Contesting fat phobia in physical education. *Sociology of Sport Journal, 25,* 66–96.

Tinning, R. (2004). Rethinking the preparation of H&PE teachers: Ruminations on knowledge, identity and ways of thinking. *Asian-Pacific Journal of Teacher Education, 32*(3), 241–253.

UNESCO. (1978). International charter of physical education and sport. Retrieved from: www.unesco.org/pv_obj_cache/pv_obj_id_0A0B499EE53437D0D87BCF53A52CD0991D580000/filename/SPORT_E.PDF

Vilhjalmsson, R., Kristjansdottir, G. & Ward, D. S. (2012). Bodily deviations and body image in adolescence. *Youth Society, 44*(3), 366–84.

Zajda, J., Majhanovich, S., Rust, V. (2006). Education and social justice: Issues of liberty and equality in the global culture. In J. Zajda, S. Majhanovich & V. Rust (Eds.). *Education and social justice* (pp. 1–12). Dordrecht, The Netherlands: Springer.

Chapter 8

American Psychiatric Association (2000). *Diagnostic and statistical manual of mental disorders,* (4th ed.). *Text Revision.* Washington, DC: Author.

Anderson, A., & Rumsey, R. (2002). Channeling energy using bodily-kinesthetic intelligence: Helping children with ADHD. *Physical and Health Education Journal, 68*(3), 20–26. Gloucester, ON: CAH&PERD.

Arnheim, D. D., & Sinclair, W. A. (1985). *Physical Education For Special Populations*. Englewood Cliffs, NJ: Prentice-Hall Inc.

Berliner, D. (1994). Expertise the wonder of exemplary performances. In J. Mangieri and C. Collins Block (Eds.). *Creating powerful thinking in teachers and students diverse perspectives*. (pp. 1–42). Fort Worth, TX: Harcourt Brace College Publishers.

Block, M.E. (2007). *A teacher's guide to including students with disabilities in general physical education*. (3rd ed.). Baltimore: Paul H. Brookes Publishing Co.

Block, M. E., Elliott, S., & Stewart Stanec, A. D. (2007). What is physical education? In M. E. Block (Ed.), *A teacher's guide to including students with disabilities in general physical education*. (3rd Ed.) (pp. 1–14). Baltimore: Paul H. Brookes Publishing Co.

Block, M. E., & Obrusnikova, I. (2007a). What is inclusion? In M. E. Block (Ed.), *A teacher's guide to including students with disabilities in general physical education*. (3rd ed.). (pp. 15–28). Baltimore: Paul H. Brookes Publishing Co.

Block, M. E., & Obrusnikova, I. (2007b). Inclusion in physical education: A review of the literature from 1995–2005. *Adapted Physical Activity Quarterly, 24*, 103–24.

Brault, M. C., & Lacourse, E. (2012). Prevalence of prescribed attention-deficit hyperactivity disorder medications and diagnosis among Canadian preschoolers and school-age children: 1994–2007. *Canadian Journal of Psychiatry, 57*, 93–101.

Cairney, J., Hay, J., Faught, B., Mandigo, J., & Flouris, A. (2005). Developmental coordination disorder, self-efficacy toward physical activity, and play: Does gender matter? *Adapted Physical Activity Quarterly, 22*, 67–82.

Causgrove Dunn, J., & Goodwin, D. L. (2008). Youth with movement difficulties. In A. L. Smith and S. J. H. Biddle (Eds.), *Youth physical activity and sedentary behavior*. (pp. 239–259). Champaign, IL: Human Kinetics.

Dahl, M. (1993). Role of the media in promoting images of disability—Disability as metaphor: The evil crip, *Canadian Journal of Communication, 18*, 1–6.

Fishburne, G. J., & Hickson, C. (n.d). What is the relationship between physical education and physical activity. Ottawa: PHE Canada. Retrieved from: www.phecanada.ca/sites/default/files/advocacy_tools/PE_PA.pdf.

Goodwin, D. L. (2003). Instructional approaches to the teaching of motor skills. In R. D. Steadward, G. D. Wheeler, & E. J. Watkinson (Eds.), *Adapted Physical Activity* (pp. 255–84). Edmonton, AB: The University of Alberta Press and The Steadward Centre.

Goodwin, D. L., Thurmeier, R., & Gustafson, P. (2004). Reactions to the metaphors of disability: The mediating effects of physical activity. *Adapted Physical Activity Quarterly, 21*, 379–98.

Goodwin, D. L., & Watkinson, E. J. (2000). Inclusive physical education from the perspective of students with a physical disability. *Adapted Physical Activity Quarterly, 17*, 144–60.

Goodwin, D. L., Watkinson, E. J., & Fitzpatrick, D.A. (2003). Inclusive physical education: A conceptual framework. In R. D. Steadward, G. D. Wheeler, & E. J. Watkinson (Eds.), *Adapted Physical Activity*. (pp. 189–212). Edmonton, AB: The University of Alberta Press and The Steadward Centre.

Government of Quebec (2001). Teacher training. Orientations and professional competencies. Quebec City: Ministry of Education.

Halas, J. M. (2003). Culturally relevant physical education for students who experience emotional and behavioral difficulties. In R. D. Steadward, G. D. Wheeler, & E. J. Watkinson (Eds.), *Adapted Physical Activity*.(pp. 285–304). Edmonton, AB: The University of Alberta Press and The Steadward Centre.

Harvey, W. J. (1997). Editorial: Some thoughts on persons with disabilities and physical activity. *The Canadian Association for Health, Physical Education, Recreation, and Dance Journal, 63*(3), 35–36.

Harvey, W. J., Delamere, F. M., Prupas, A., & Wilkinson, S. (2010). Physical activity, leisure, and health for persons with mental illness. *PALAESTRA, 25*(2), 36–53.

Harvey, W. J., & Reid, G. (2003). A review of fundamental movement skill performance and physical fitness of children with ADHD. *Adapted Physical Activity Quarterly, 20*, 1–25.

Hodge, S. R., Murata, N. M., Block, M. E., & Lieberman, L. J. (2003). *Case studies in adapted physical education*. Scottsdale, AZ: Holcomb Hathaway, Publishers.

Jansma, P. & French, R. (1994). *Special physical education: Physical activities, sports and recreation*. Englewood Cliffs, NJ: Prentice-Hall, Inc.

Lavay, B. W., French, R., & Henderson, H. L. (2006). *Positive Behavior Management in Physical Activity Settings* (2nd ed.). Champaign, IL: Human Kinetics.

Lieberman, L. J. (ed.) (2007). *Paraeducators in physical education: A training guide to roles and responsibilities*. Champaign, IL: Human Kinetics.

Metzler, M. (2011). *Instructional models for physical education*. (3rd ed.). Scottsdale, AZ: Holcomb Hathaway.

Mobily, K. E. & Ostiguy, L. J. (2004). *Introduction to therapeutic recreation: US and Canadian perspectives*. State College, PA: Venture Publishing, Inc.

National Consortium on Physical Education and Recreation for Individuals with Disabilities (NCPERID). (2006). *Adapted *physical education national standards* (2nd ed.). Champaign, IL: Human Kinetics.

Pressé, C., Block, M. E., Horton, M., & Harvey, W. J. (2011). Adapting the Sports Education Model for Children with Disabilities. *JOPERD, 82*(3), 32–39.

Reid, G. (2003a). Moving toward inclusion. In R. D. Steadward, G. D. Wheeler, & E. J. Watkinson (Eds.), *Adapted Physical Activity.* (pp. 131–47). Edmonton, AB: The University of Alberta Press and The Steadward Centre.

Reid, G. (2003b). Defining adapted physical activity. In R. D. Steadward, G. D. Wheeler, & E. J. Watkinson (Eds.), *Adapted Physical Activity.* (pp. 11–25). Edmonton, AB: The University of Alberta Press and The Steadward Centre.

Reid, G., & Collier, D. (2002). Motor behavior and the autism spectrum disorders – Introduction. *PALAESTRA, 25*(2), 20–27, 44.

Rink, J. E. (2009). *Teaching physical education for learning* (6th ed.). Toronto: McGraw-Hill.

Sergeant, J. A., Piek, J. P., & Oosterlaan, J. (2006). ADHD and DCD: A relationship in need of research. *Human Movement Science, 25*, 76–89.

Seymour, H., Reid, G., & Bloom, G. A. (2009). Friendship in inclusive physical education. *Adapted Physical Activity Quarterly, 26*, 201–19.

Sherrill, C. (1998). *Adapted physical activity, recreation and sport: Crossdisciplinary and lifespan* (5th ed.). Dubuque, IA: WCB McGraw-Hill.

Sherill, C., & DePauw, K. P. (1997). Adapted physical activity and education. In J. D. Massengale and R. A. Swanson (Eds.), *The history of exercise and sport science* (pp. 39–108). Champaign, IL: Human Kinetics.

Spencer-Cavaliere, N., & Watkinson, E. J. (2010). Inclusion understood from the perspectives of children with disability. *Adapted Physical Activity Quarterly, 27*, 275–93.

Steadward, R. D., Wheeler, G. D., & Watkinson, E. J. (2003). *Adapted Physical Activity.* Edmonton, AB: The University of Alberta Press and The Steadward Centre.

Wall, A. E. (1990a). Fostering physical activity among Canadians with disabilities. *Canadian Association for Health, Physical Education, Recreation, and Dance Journal, 53*(5), 13–20.

Wall, A. E. (1990b). Skill acquisition research with persons with developmental disabilities: Research design considerations. In G. Reid (Ed.), *Problems in Movement Control* (pp. 31–63). North Holland: Elsevier Science Publishers B.V.

Wall, A. E. (2003). The history of adapted physical activity. In R.D. Steadward, G.D. Wheeler, & E.J. Watkinson (Eds.), *Adapted Physical Activity.* (pp. 27–47). Edmonton, AB: The University of Alberta Press and The Steadward Centre.

Wilkinson, S., Harvey, W. J., Bloom, G. A., Joober, R., & Grizenko, N. (2012). Student teacher experiences in a service-learning project for children with attention-deficit hyperactivity disorder. *Physical Education and Sport Pedagogy.* DOI:10.1080/17408989.2012.690385

Winnick, J. P. (2000). *Adapted physical education and sport.* (3rd ed.). Champaign, IL: Human Kinetics

Chapter 9

Aikenhead, G. & Michell, H. (2011). *Bridging cultures: Scientific and indigenous ways of knowing nature.* Toronto: Pearson Education Canada.

Alaska Native Knowledge Network. (1998). *Alaska standards for culturally-responsive schools.* Fairbanks, AK: Alaska Native Knowledge Network.

Baskin, C. (2011). *Strong helpers' teachings: The value of indigenous knowledges in the helping professions.* Toronto: Canadian Scholars Press.

Battiste, M. (2002*). Indigenous knowledge and pedagogy in First Nations education: A literature review with recommendations.* Retrieved from: www.afn.ca/uploads/files/education/24._2002_oct_marie_battiste_indigenousknowledgeandpedagogy_lit_review_for_min_working_group.pdf

Brant Castellano, M. (2002). Updating Aboriginal traditions of knowledge. In G. J. Sefa Dei, B. L. Hall, & D. G. Rosenberg (Eds.). *Indigenous knowledges in global contexts: Multiple Readings of our worlds.* (pp. 21–36). Toronto: University of Toronto Press.

Bopp, J., Bopp, M., Brown, L., & Lane, P., Jr. (1985). *The sacred tree.* (2nd ed.). Lethbridge, AB: Four Worlds International Institute for Human and Community Development.

British Columbia Ministry of Education. (2006). *Shared learnings.* Retrieved from: www.bced.gov.bc.ca/abed/shared.pdf

Canadian Council on Learning. (2009). *Holistic lifelong learning models.* Retrieved from: www.ccl-cca.ca/ccl/Reports/RedefiningSuccessInAboriginalLearning/RedefiningSuccessModels.html

Curwen Doige, L. (2003). A missing link: Between traditional Aboriginal education and the western system of education. *Canadian Journal of Native Education, 27*(2), 144–60.

Ermine, W. (1995). Aboriginal epistemology. In M. Battiste & J. Barman (Eds.), *First Nations education in Canada: The circle unfolds* (pp. 101–12). Vancouver: UBC Press.

Fiddler, T., Tourangeau, N., Male, J., & Marlor, E. (2000). *The Elders: Keeping the circle strong.* Saskatoon, SK: Stewart Resource Centre.

Graham, G., Holt/Hale, S. A., & Parker, M. (2007). *Children moving: A reflective approach to teaching physical education* (7th ed.). New York: McGraw-Hill.

Graveline, F. G. (1998). *Circle works: Transforming Eurocentric consciousness.* Halifax, NS: Fernwood.

Hampton, E. (1995). Towards a redefinition of Indian education. In M. Battiste & J. Barman (Eds.). *First Nations education in Canada: The circle unfolds* (pp. 5–46). Vancouver: UBC Press.

Heine, M. (2006). *Arctic sports: A training and resource manual.* Yellowknife, NT: Sport North Federation.

Kalyn, B. (2006). *A healthy journey: Indigenous teachings that direct culturally responsive curricula in physical education.* (Unpublished doctoral dissertation). Edmonton: University of Alberta.

Kalyn, B., Paslawski, T., Wilson, C., Kikcio, T., & MacPhedran, D. (2007). *The effect of small space physical activity on school performance.* Project # 165. Saskatoon, SK: Dr. Sterling McDowell Foundation for Research into Teaching.

Laframboise, S. & Sherbina, K. (2012). *The medicine wheel.* Retrieved from: www.dancingtoeaglespiritsociety.org/medwheel.php

Lamothe, R. (1993). *Dene teaching methods.* Yellowknife, NT: The Dene Cultural Institute and The Native Women's Association of the NWT for The Royal Commission on Aboriginal Peoples.

Loeffler, TA. (2008). *More than a mountain: One woman's Everest.* St. John's, NL: Creative Publishers.

Marsh, C. & Willis, G. (2003). *Curriculum: Alternative approaches, ongoing issues.* (3rd ed.). Upper Saddle River, NJ: Pearson Education.

Manitoba Education. (2003). *Integrating Aboriginal perspectives into curricula: A resource for curriculum developers, teachers, and administrators.* Retrieved from: www.edu.gov.mb.ca/k12/docs/policy/abpersp/index.html

National Association for Sport and Physical Education. (2004). *Moving into the future: National standards for physical education.* (2nd ed.). Reston, VA: Author.

Pangrazi, R. P. & Gibbons, S. L. (2009). *Dynamic physical education for elementary school children.* (2nd Canadian ed.). Needham Heights, MA: Allyn and Bacon.

Prince Edward Island Department of Education. (2011). *Prince Edward Island Physical Education Curriculum K–6.* Retrieved from: www.gov.pe.ca/photos/original/eecd_phyeduK6.pdf.

Prochaska, J., Norcross, J. C., & DiClemente, C. C. (1994). *Changing for good.* New York: William Morrow.

Robbins, G., Powers, D., & Burgess, S. (2002). *A wellness way of life.* (5th ed.). New York: McGraw-Hill.

Royal Commission on Aboriginal Peoples (RCAP). (1996). *Report of the royal commission on Aboriginal peoples* (Vol. 3). Ottawa, ON: Author.

Saskatchewan Ministry of Learning. (2010). *A time for significant leadership: A strategy for implementing First Nations & Metis Educational Goals.* Retrieved from: www.education.gov.sk.ca/ATFSL-pdf

Tisya-Tramm, E. (2012). Vuntut Gwitchin put the "edge" in traditional knowledge. *Yukon: North of Ordinary, 6*(2), 15.

Wilson, S. (2008). Research is ceremony: Indigenous research methods. Black Point, NS: Fernwood Publishing.

Young, M. (2003). Anishinabemowin: A way of seeing the world: Reclaiming my identity. *Canadian Journal of Education, 27*(1), 101–07.

Chapter 10

Statutes

Education Act (Ontario), R.S.O. 1990, c. E.2.

Negligence Act (Ontario), R.S.O. 1990, c. N.1.

Cases

Arland v. Taylor, [1955] O.R. 131 (C.A.).

Crits v. Sylvester, [1956] O.R. 132 (C.A.).

Donoghue v. Stevenson, [1932] A.C. 562 (A.C.).

Hussack v. School District No. 33 (Chilliwack), 2009 BCSC 852.

Long v. Western Propeller Co. Ltd (1968), 67 D.L.R. (2d) 345 (Man. C.A.).

McKay v. Board of Govan School Unit No. 29 (1968), 68 D.L.R. (2d) 519 (S.C.C.).

Myers v. Peel (County) Board of Education (1977), 2 C.C.L.T. 269 (Ont. H.C.J.).

Myers v. Peel (County) Board of Education (1978), 5 C.C.L.T. 271 (Ont. C.A.).

Myers v. Peel (County) Board of Education (1981), 17 C.C.L.T. 269 (S.C.C.).

Richards v State of Victoria, [1969] V.R. 136 (V.S.C.).

Thornton, Tanner et al. v. Board of School Trustees of School District No. 57, [1975] 3 W.W.R. 622, 57 D.L.R. (3d) 438 (B.C.S.C.).

Thornton et al. v. Board of School Trustees of School District No. 57 (Prince George) (1976), 73 D.L.R. (3d) 35 (B.C.C.A.).

Thornton v. Board of School Trustees of School District No. 57 (Prince George) (1978), 83 D.L.R. (3d) 480 (S.C.C.).

Williams v. Eady (1894), 10 T.L.R. 41 (C.A.).

Secondary Literature

Bezeau, L. M. (1995). *Educational administration for Canadian teachers* (2nd ed.). Toronto: Copp Clark.

Bird, S. & Zauhar, J. (1997). *Recreation and the law* (2nd ed.). Toronto: Carswell.

Block, M. E. (1994). *A teacher's guide to including students with disabilities in regular physical education.* Baltimore: Paul H. Brookes.

Brown, A.F. (2009). *Legal handbook for educators* (6th ed.). Toronto: Thomson.

Brown, A.F., & Zuker, M.A. (1998). *Education law* (2nd ed.). Toronto: Carswell.

Champion, W.T., Jr. (2004). *Fundamentals of sports law.* St. Paul, MN: West Group.

Connors. E.T. (1981). *Educational tort liability and malpractice.* Bloomington, IN: Phi Delta Kappa.

Cummins, R.R. (1999). *Tort law.* Upper Saddle River, NJ: Prentice Hall.

Darst, P.W., & Pangrazi, R.P. (2006). *Dynamic physical education for secondary school students* (5th ed.). San Francisco: Pearson.

Dickinson, G.M. (2006). Teaching within the law: Liability for physical harm and the need for proper risk management. In E. Singleton & A. Varpalotai (Eds.), *Stones in the sneaker: Active theory for secondary school physical and health educators* (pp. 277–302). London, ON: The Althouse Press.

Doctor, E. (2005). Avalanche disaster: Lessons to be learned. In R. Flynn (Ed.), *Law and education: The practice of accountability.* Proceedings of the Fifteenth Annual Conference of the Canadian Association for the Practical Study of Law in Education, 97–111.

Elliott, D. (2004). Risk management in sport. In J. Beech & S. Chadwick (Eds.), *The business of sport management* (pp. 414–430). Harlow, UK: Pearson.

Fleming, J. G. (1998). *The law of torts* (9th ed.). Sydney: LBC Information Services.

Fridman, G. H. L. (2003). *Introduction to the Canadian law of torts* (2nd ed.). Markham: LexisNexis Butterworths.

Fridman, G. H. L. (1990). *Torts.* London: Waterlow.

Gensemer, R. E. (1985). *Physical education: Perspectives, inquiry, applications.* New York: Saunders College Publishing.

Giles, W. H. (1988). *Schools and students: Legal aspects of administration.* Toronto: Carswell.

Goodman, S. F. (1989). *A study of liability, negligence, and risk management in boards of education/municipal recreation departments in Ontario and physical education and recreation programs in Canada.* Unpublished doctoral dissertation, University of Toronto.

Hoyano, L. C. H. (1984). The "prudent parent": The elusive standard of care. *University of British Columbia Law Review, 18*(1), 1–34.

Janzen, H. (1995). The status of physical education in Canadian public schools. *Canadian Association for Health, Physical Education, Recreation and Dance Journal, 61*(3), 5–9.

Jefferson, G. M. & LaBute, D. L. (2001). Insurance for sport and fitness organizations. In M. Holman, D. Moriarity, & J. Forsyth (Eds.), *Sports, fitness and the law: North American perspectives* (2nd ed.) (pp. 199–221). Toronto: Canadian Scholars' Press.

Kelm, J., Ahlhelm, F., Pape, D., Pitsch, W., & Engel, C. (2001). School sports accidents: Analysis of causes, modes, and frequencies. *Journal of Pediatric Orthopaedics, 21*(2), 165–168

Klar, L. N. (1997). Tort and no-fault. *Health Law Review, 5*(3), 2–8.

Krotee, M. L. & Bucher, C. A. (2007). *Management of physical education and sport* (13th ed.). New York: McGraw-Hill.

Leibee, H. C. (1965). *Tort liability for injuries to pupils.* Ann Arbor, MI: Campus Publishers.

Linden, A. M. (2001). *Canadian tort law* (7th ed.). Markham, ON: Butterworths.

Linden, A. M. (2003). The joy of torts. In S. Beaulac, S.G.A. Pitel, & J.L. Schulz (Eds.), *The joy of torts* (pp. 459-474). Markham, ON: LexisNexis.

Luke, M. D. (2000). Physical and health education curriculum: Cross-Canada perspectives. *Canadian Association for Health, Physical Education, Recreation and Dance Journal, 66*(2), 4–12.

Lumpkin, A. (1994). *Physical education and sport: A contemporary introduction* (3rd ed.). St. Louis: Mosby.

MacKay, A. W. (1984). *Education law in Canada.* Toronto: Emond-Montgomery.

MacKay, A. W. & Dickinson, G. M. (1998). *Beyond the careful parent: Tort liability in education.* Toronto: Emond Montgomery.

MacKay, A. W. & Flood, T. L. (2001). Negligence principles in the school context: New challenges for the "careful parent." *Education & Law Journal, 10*(3), 371–392.

MacKay, A. W., & Sutherland, L. (2006). *Teachers and the law* (2nd ed.). Toronto: Emond Montgomery.

Mahoney, M., Forsyth, J., Holman, M., & Moriarity, D. (2001). A practical look at risk management. In M. Holman, D. Moriarity, & J. Forsyth (Eds.), *Sports, fitness and the law:*

North American perspectives (2nd ed.) (pp. 19–31). Toronto: Canadian Scholars' Press.

Metcalfe, J. L. (2003). "[T]here could not be a better definition": A defence of the careful or prudent parent standard. *Education & Law Journal, 13*(2), 257–276.

Ontario Ministry of Education. (2000). *The Ontario curriculum, grades 11 and 12: Health and physical education.* Toronto: Queen's Printer for Ontario.

Ontario Physical and Health Education Association. (2004). *Ontario safety guidelines for physical education.* Toronto, ON: Author.

Ontario School Boards' Insurance Exchange. (2003). *Risk management at a glance.* Guelph, ON: Author.

Posner, M. (2000). *Preventing school injuries: A comprehensive guide for school administrators, teachers, and staff.* New Brunswick, NJ: Rutgers University Press.

Prosser, W. L. (1955). *Handbook of the law of torts* (2nd ed.). St. Paul, MN: West Publishing.

Raymond, C. (1999). Physical education. In C. Raymond, (Ed.), *Safety across the curriculum* (pp. 93–110). London: Falmer.

Robertson, B. W. & Robertson, B. J. (1988). *Sport & recreation liability and you!: For parents, coaches & sport organizers.* Vancouver: Self-Counsel Press.

Russo, C. (2006). Negligence. In C. Russo (Ed.), *Key legal issues for schools: The ultimate resource for school business officials* (pp. 83–97). Lanham, MD: Rowman & Littlefield.

Santrock, J. W., Woloshyn, V. E., Gallagher, T. L., & Marini, Z. A. (2007). *Educational psychology* (2nd Canadian ed.). Toronto: McGraw-Hill Ryerson.

Shariff, S. (2004). Keeping schools out of court: Reasonable tort standards for schools to address psychological harm. In R. Flynn (Ed.), *Law in education: Help or hindrance?* Proceedings of the Fourteenth Annual Conference of the Canadian Association for the Practical Study of Law in Education, 655–79.

Shivers, J. S. (1986). *Recreational safety.* Toronto: Associated University Press.

Spada, S., Simmons, J., Crawford, S. A. G. M., & Haynes, R. (2004). Is liability a growing concern for the HPERD professions, and, if so, what can be done about it? *Journal of Physical Education, Recreation & Dance, 75*(5), 10–12.

Steele, J. (2004). *Risks and legal theory.* Portland: Hart.

Watson, R. (1996). Risk management: A plan for safer activities. *Canadian Association for Health, Physical Education, Recreation and Dance Journal, 62*(1), 13–17.

Young, D. C. (2007). Physical education, tort law and risk avoidance. *Education & Law Journal, 17*(2), 223–43.

Young, J. C. (1996). Current trends and issues in physical education. In B. F. Hennesy (Ed.), *Physical education sourcebook* (pp. 3–11). Champaign, IL: Human Kinetics.

Chapter 11

Active Healthy Kids Canada (2012). *Is Active Play Extinct? The Active Healthy Kids Canada 2012 Report Card on Physical Activity for Children and Youth.* Toronto: Active Healthy Kids Canada.

Bee, H., Boyd, D., & Johnson, P. (2006). *Lifespan development* (2nd ed). Toronto: Pearson Canada.

Bouffard, M. (1993). The perils of averaging data in adapted physical activity research. *Adapted Physical Activity Quarterly, 10*, 371–91.

Bouffard, M., & Reid, G. (2012). The Good, the Bbad, and the Uugly of evidence-based practice, *Adapted Physical Activity Quarterly, 29*, 1-–24.

Bouffard, M. B., & Strean, W. B. (2003). Critical thinking and professional preparation. In R. D. Steadward, G. D. Wheeler, & E. J. Watkinson (Eds.), *Adapted Physical Activity* (pp. 1–10). Edmonton: The University of Alberta Press and The Steadward Centre.

Bredo, E. (2006). Philosophies of educational research. In J. Green, G. Camilli, & P. Elmore (Eds.). *Complementary methods in education research* (pp. 3–31). Washington, DC: American Educational Research Association.

Brossard-Racine, M., Majnemer, A. & Shevell, M.I. (2011). Exploring the neural mechanisms that underlie motor difficulties in children with attention-deficit hyperactivity disorder. *Developmental Neurorehabilitation, 14*, 101–11.

Chang, Y. K., Labban, J. D., Gapin, J. I., & Etnier, J. L. (2012). The effects of acute exercise on cognitive performance: A meta-analysis. *Brain Research, 1453*, 87–101.

Creswell, J. W. (2007). *Qualitative inquiry & research design: Choosing among five approaches.* (2nd ed). Thousand Oaks, CA: SAGE.

Curtin, C., Bandini, L. G., Perrin, E. C., Tybor, D. J., & Must, A. (2005). Prevalence of overweight in children and adolescents with attention deficit hyperactivity disorder and autism spectrum disorders: A chart review. *BMC Pediatrics, 5*, 48–55.

Glass, G. V., & Hopkins, K. D. (1984). *Statistical methods in education and psychology* (2nd ed.). London: Allyn and Bacon.

Gredler, M. E. (1997). *Learning and instruction: Theory into practice.* (3rd ed.). Upper Saddle River, NJ: Prentice-Hall Inc.

Griffin, L., Dodds, P., & Rovegno, I. (1996). Pedagogical content knowledge for teachers. *Journal of Physical Education, Recreation & Dance, 67*(9), 58–61.

Harvey, W. J., Reid, G., Bloom, G., Staples, K., Grizenko, N., Mbekou, V., Ter-Stepanian, M., & Joober, R. (2009). Physical activity experiences of boys with ADHD. *Adapted Physical Activity* Quarterly, 26, 131–150.

Harvey, W. J., Reid, G., Grizenko, N., Mbekou, V., Ter-Stepanian, M., & Joober, R.(2007). Fundamental movement skills and children with ADHD: Peer comparisons and stimulant effects. *Journal of Abnormal Child Psychology, 35*, 871–82.

Higgs, C. (2010). Physical literacy—Two approaches, one concept. *Physical & Health Education Journal, 76*(1), 6–7.

Holtkamp, K., Konrad, K., Muller, B., Heussen, N., Herpertz, S., Herpertz-Dahlmann, B., et al. (2004). Overweight and obesity in children with attention-deficit/hyperactivity disorder. *International Journal of Obesity, 28,* 685–89.

Hubel, R., Jass, J., Marcus, A., & Laessle, R. G. (2006). Overweight and basal metabolic rate in boys with attention-deficit/hyperactivity disorder. *Eating and Weight Disorders, 11,* 139–46.

Johnstone, J. A., & Ramon, M. (2011). *Perceptual-motor activities for children: An evidence-based guide to building physical and cognitive skills.* Champaign, IL: Human Kinetics.

Kincheloe, J. L. (2008a). *Critical pedagogy primer* (2nd ed.). New York: Peter Lang Publishing, Inc.

Kincheloe, J. L. (2008b).Critical pedagogy and the knowledge wars of the twenty-first century. *The International Journal of Critical Pedagogy.* Retrieved from: http://freire. education.mcgill.ca/ojs/public/journals/Galleys/IJCP011.pdf

Kirk, D. Macdonald, D., & O'Sullivan, M. (2006). The handbook of physical education. London: Sage Publications.

Macdonald, D. (1995). The role of proletarianization in physical education teacher attrition. *Research Quarterly for Exercise and Sport, 66*, 129–41.

Macdonald, D. (1999). The "professional" work of experienced physical education teachers. *Research Quarterly for Exercise and Sport, 70*, 41–54.

Matanin, M., & Collier, C. (2003). Longitudinal analysis of preservice teachers' beliefs about teaching physical education. *Journal of Teaching in Physical Education, 22*, 153–68.

McKenzie, T. L. (2007). The preparation of physical educators: A public health perspective, *QUEST, 59*, 346–57.

Muros Ruiz, B., & Fernández-Balboa, J. M. (2005). Physical education teacher educators' personal perspectives regarding their practice of critical pedagogy. *Journal of Teaching in Physical Education, 24*, 243–64.

O'Sullivan, M., Siedentop, D., & Locke, L. F. (1992). Toward collegiality: Competing viewpoints among teacher education. QUEST, *44*, 266–80.

Norris, S. (2012). Keynote address. Presentation at the PHE-Canada-TAPHE 2012. A harbor of hope: Health and physical literacy. Dalhousie University, Halifax, Nova Scotia.

Pate, R. R., O'Neill, J. R., & McIver, K. L. (2011). Physical activity and health: Does physical education matter? *QUEST, 63*, 19–35.

Phillips, M. G., & Roper, A. P. (2006). History of physical education. In D. Kirk, D. Macdonald & M. O'Sullivan (Eds.), *The handbook of physical education.* (pp. 121–40). London: Sage Publications.

Ratey, J. J. (2008) *SPARK: The revolutionary new science of exercise and the brain.* New York: Little, Brown and Company.

Reid, G., Bouffard, M., & MacDonald, C. (2012). Creating evidence-based research in adapted physical activity. *Adapted Physical Activity Quarterly, 29,* 115–31.

Rink, J. E. (2009). *Teaching physical education for learning* (6th ed.). Toronto: McGraw-Hill.

Schempp, P. G., Manross, D., Tan, S. K. S., & Fincher, M. D. (1998). Subject expertise and teachers' knowledge. *Journal of Teaching in Physical Education, 17*, 342–56.

Sergeant, J. A., Piek, J. P., & Oosterlaan, J. (2006). ADHD and DCD: A relationship in need of research. *Human Movement Science, 25*(1), 76–89.

Shephard, R. J., Lavallée, H., Volle, M., LaBarre, R., & Beaucage, C. (1994). Academic skills and required physical education: The Trois Rivières experience. *CAH&PER/ACSEPL 1994 Research Supplement, 1*, 1–12.

Shulman, L. S. (1986). Those who understand: Knowledge growth in teaching. *Educational Researcher, 2,* 4–14.

Sparkes, A. (2002). *Telling tales in sport and physical activity: A qualitative journey.* Champaign, IL: Human Kinetics.

Stevens, J. (1996). *Applied multivariate statistics for the social sciences* (3rd ed.). Mahwah, NJ: Lawrence Erlbaum Associates, Publishers.

Tantillo, M., Kesick, C. M., Hynd, G. W., & Dishman, R. K. (2002). The effects of exercise on children with attention-deficit hyperactivity disorder. *Medicine and Science in Sports and Exercise, 34,* 203–12.

Thomas, J. R., Nelson, J. K., & Silverman, S. J. (2011). *Research methods in physical activity* (3rd ed.). Champaign, IL: Human Kinetics.

Tinning, R. (2002). Toward a "Modest Pedagogy": Reflections on the problematic of critical pedagogy. *QUEST, 54*, 224–40.

Tsangaridou, N. (2006a). Teachers' beliefs. In D. Kirk, D. Macdonald, & M. O'Sullivan (Eds.). *The handbook of physical education* (pp. 486–501). London: Sage Publications.

Tsangaridou, N. (2006b). Teachers' knowledge. In D. Kirk, D. Macdonald, & M. O'Sullivan (Eds.). *The handbook of physical education* (pp. 502–15). London: Sage Publications.

Ulrich, D. A. (2000). *Test of Gross Motor Development* (2nd ed.). Austin, TX: PRO-ED, Inc.

US Department of Health and Human Services (1996). *Physical activity and health: A report of the Surgeon General*. Atlanta, GA: US Department of Health and Human Services, Centers for Disease Control and Prevention, National Center for Chronic Disease Prevention and Health Promotion.

Wall, A. E., Reid, G., & Harvey, W. J. (2007). Interface of the knowledge-based and ecological task analysis approaches. In W. E. Davis and D. Broadhead (Eds.). *Ecological approach to analyzing movement* (pp. 259–77). Champaign, IL: Human Kinetics.

Whitehead, M. (2001). The concept of physical literacy. *European Journal of Physical Education, 6*, 127–38.

Wigal, S. B., Nemet, D., Swanson, J. M., Regino, R., Trampush, J., Ziegler, M. G., & Cooper, D. M. (2003). Catecholamine response to exercise in children with attention deficit hyperactivity disorder. *Pediatric Research, 53*, 756–61.

Woods, C. B., & Mutrie, N. (2012). Putting physical activity on the policy agenda. *QUEST, 64*, 92–104.

Wright, J. (2004). Critical inquiry and problem-solving in physical education. In J. Wright, D. Macdonald & L. Burrows (Eds.), *Critical inquiry and problem-solving in physical education.* (pp. 3–15). London: Routledge.

Chapter 12

Adshead, J. (1981). *The study of dance*. London: Dance Books Ltd.

Almond, L. (1997). *Physical education in schools*. London: Kogan-Page.

Anthoney, M. (1979). An introduction and position statement. In J. Emmel, D. Molnyeux, & N. Wardrop (Eds.), *Values into action* (pp. 171–175). Australian Council for HPER.

Baumgarten, S., & Pagnano-Richardson, K. (2010). Educational gymnastics enhancing children's physical literacy: Harnessing the natural actions of children offers a great way of developing body management. *The Journal of Physical Education, Recreation & Dance, 81*(4), 18–25.

Bergmann Drewe, S. (1996). *Creative dance: Enriching understanding*. Calgary: Detselig Enterprises Ltd.

Biddle, S. J. H., Gorely, T., & Stensel, D. J. (2004). Health-enhancing physical activity and sedentary behaviour in children and adolescents. *Journal of Sport Sciences, 22*, 679–701.

Brehm, M. A. & McNett, L. (2008). *Creative dance for learning: The kinesthetic link*. New York: McGraw Higher Education.

Canadian Fitness and Lifestyle Research Institute. (1998). Popular physical activities. *Progress in Prevention, 32*, 1–4. Retrieved from: www.cflri.ca/media/node/177/files/pip32.pdf

Carline, S. (2011). *Lesson plans for creative dance: Connecting with literature, arts and music*. Windsor, ON: Human Kinetics.

Coelho, J. (2010). Gymnastics and movement instruction: Fighting the decline in motor fitness. *The Journal of Physical Education, Recreation & Dance, 81*(1), 14–18.

Dewar, P. (1980). Teaching creative/modern dance in the schools. *CAHPER Journal, 46*(4), 27–29.

Dewey, J. (1934) *Art as experience*. New York: Perigree Publishing Co.

Ellis, M. (1983). *Similarities and differences in games: A system for classification.* Paper presented at the AIESEP Conference, Rome, Italy.

Eisner, E. (1998). *The enlightened eye: Qualitative inquire and the enhancement of educational practice*. New York: Macmillan.

Estes, S. G., & Mechikoff, R. A. (1999). *Knowing human movement*. Toronto: Allyn and Bacon.

Francis, N. (2009). What's new within the U? Historical development of games education and current curricular relevancy of TGfU in Canada. In T. Hopper, J. Butler, & B. Storey (Eds,), *TGfU… Simply good pedagogy: Understanding a complex challenge* (pp. 35–47). Ottawa: PHE Canada.

Gardner, H. (1983). *Frames of mind*. New York: Basic Books.

Graham, G., Holt/Hale, S.A., & Parker, M. (2007). *Children moving: A reflective approach to teaching physical education* (6th ed.). Toronto: McGraw-Hill.

Graham, G., Holt-Hale, S. A., & Parker, M. (2010). *Children moving: A reflective approach to teaching physical education* (8th ed.). New York: McGraw-Hill.

Griffin, L., Mitchell, S., & Oslin, J. (2005). *Teaching sport concepts and skills – A tactical games approach. (2nd Ed.)*. Windsor, ON: Human Kinetics.

Hardman, K. & Marshall, J. (2000). The state and status of physical education in schools in international context. *European Physical Education Review, 6*(3), 203–29.

H'Doubler, M. (1940). *Dance: A creative art experience.* Madison: The University of Wisconsin Press.

Hill, R. (1982). Let's teach sport and dance. *CAHPER Journal 48*(4), 13–16.

Hoeger, W. & Hoeger, S. (2012). *Lifetime physical fitness and wellness: A personalized program* (12th ed.). Belmont, CA: Wadsworth.

International Life Saving Federation (2012). *Drowning facts and figures.* Retrieved from: http://ilsf.org/drowning/facts

Laban R. & Lawrence, F. (1947). *Effort.* London: Macdonald & Evans.

Lu, C. & De Lisio, A. (2009). Specifics for generalists: Teaching elementary physical education. *International Electronic Journal of Elementary Education, 1*(3), 170–87.

Mandigo, J. L., & Holt, N. L. (2004). Reading the game. Introducing the notion of games literacy. *Physical and Health Education Journal, 70*(3), 4–10.

McPherson, S. L., & Kernodle, M. W. (2003). Tactics, the neglected attribute of expertise. In J. L. Starkes & K. A. Ericsson (Eds.), *Expert performance in sports: Advances in research on sport expertise* (pp. 137–67). Champaign, IL: Human Kinetics.

Oliver, W. (2009). *Dance and culture: An introductory reader.* Reston VA: National Dance Association.

Pangrazi, R., & Gibbons, S. (2009). *Dynamic physical education for elementary school children* (2nd Canadian ed.). Toronto: Pearson.

PHE Canada. (2011a). *Fundamental movement skills: Alternative activities and pursuits.* Ottawa: PHE Canada.

PHE Canada. (2011b). *Fundamental movement skills: The building blocks for the development of physical literacy.* Ottawa: PHE Canada.

PHE Canada. (2011c). *Fundamental movement skills (Volumes I - IV).* Ottawa: PHE Canada.

Pope, C. C. (2011). The physical education and sport interface: Models, maxims and maelstrom. *European Physical Education Review, 17*(3), 273–85.

Rink, J. E. (2010). *Teaching physical education* (6th ed.). New York: McGraw Hill.

Rodgers, B., & Douglas, S. (1998). *The complete idiot's guide to jogging and running.* New York: Alpha Books.

Rutledge, M. (2006). Dancing is for sissies! In E. Singleton & A. Varpalotai (Eds.), *Stones in the sneaker: Active theory for secondary school physical and health educators* (pp. 87–100). London, ON: The Althouse Press.

Schmottlach, N., & McManama, J. (2009). *The physical education activity handbook* (12th ed.). San Francisco: Pearson Education.

Schrader, C. A. (2005). *A sense of dance: Exploring your movement potential* (2nd ed.). Champaign, IL: Human Kinetics.

Shapiro, S. (1998). *Dance, power and difference: Critical and feminist perspectives in dance education.* Windsor: Human Kinetics.

Stanton, J. (2009). *Walking: A complete guide to walking for fitness, health, and weight loss.* Toronto: Penguin Canada.

Storey, B., & Butler, J. I. (2010). Ecological thinking and TGfU: Understanding games as complex adaptive systems. In J. I. Butler & L. L. Griffin (Eds.), *More teaching games for understanding: Moving globally* (pp. 139–54). Champaign, IL: Human Kinetics.

Vygotsky, L. (1934/1986). *Thought and language.* Cambridge: MIT Press.

Wall, J., & Murray, N. (1994). *Children and movement: Physical education in the elementary school.* Dubuque, IA: William C. Brown.

Chapter 13

Butler, J. & McCahan, B. J. (2005). Teaching games for understanding as a curriculum model. In L. Griffin & J. Butler (Eds.). *Teaching games for understanding: Theory, research, and practice.* Champaign, IL: Human Kinetics.

Canadian Sport for Life (2011). Physical Literacy. Retrieved from: www.canadiansportforlife.ca/learn-about-canadian-sport-life/physical-literacy

Cope, B. & Kalantzis, M. (Eds.) (2000). *Multiliteracies: Literacy learning and the design of social futures.* New York: Routledge.

Csikszentmihalyi, M. (2000). *Beyond boredom and anxiety: Experiencing flow in work and play.* San Francisco: Jossey-Bass.

Dartfish (2011). Education Software- physical education. Retrieved from: www.dartfish.com/en/education_software/physical-education.htm

Drummond, M. & Pill, S. (2011). The role of physical education in promoting sport participation in school and beyond. In Steve Georgakis and Kate Russell (Eds.) *Youth sport in Australia* (pp. 165–78). Sydney: Sydney University Press.

Francis, N., Johnson, A., Lloyd, M., Robinson, D., & Sheehan, D. (2011). *An educator's guide to teaching fundamental movement skills.* Ottawa: Physical and Health Education Canada.

Gavin, J. and McBrearty, M. (2006). Exploring mind-body exercise modalities. *IDEA, Health and Fitness Association.* Retrieved from: www.ideafit.com/fitness-library/exploring-mind-body-exercise-modalities

Government of Saskatchewan (2010). *Physical education 1 Curriculum*. Retrieved from: www.education.gov.sk.ca/pe-curricula.

Gurvitch, R. & Metzler, M. (2010). Keeping the purpose in mind: The implementation of instructional models in physical education Settings. *Strategies, 23*(3), 32–35.

Higgs, C. (2010). Physical literacy: Two approaches, one concept. *Physical & Health Education Canada Journal, Spring*, 6-7.

Jewitt, C. (2008). Multimodality and literacy in school classrooms. *Review of Research in Education*, 32, 241–67.

Killingbeck, M., Bowler, B., Golding, D. and Sammon, P. (2007). Physical education and physical literacy. *Physical Education Matters. 2*(2), 21–23.

Kirk, D. (2010). *Physical education Futures*. London: Routledge.

Laban, R. (1948). *Modern educational dance*. London: Macdonald and Evans.

Lloyd, R. J., & Smith, S. J. (2006). Interactive flow in exercise pedagogy. *Quest, 58,* 222–41.

Lloyd, R. J. (2011a). Teaching Games with Inner Sense: Exploring Movement Consciousness in Women's Volleyball. *PHEnex journal*/revue phénEPS 3(2), 1–17.

Lloyd, R. (2011b). Awakening Movement Consciousness in the Physical Landscapes of Literacy: Leaving, Reading and Being Moved by One's Trace. *Phenomenology & Practice, 5*(2), 70–92.

Lloyd, R. J. (2011c). Running with and like my dog: An animate curriculum for living life beyond the track. *Journal of Curriculum Theorizing, 27*(3), 117–33.

Lloyd, R. J. (2012). Moving to learn and learning to move: A phenomenological exploration of children's climbing with an interdisciplinary movement consciousness. *The Humanistic Psychologist, 40*(1), 23–37.

Lloyd, R. J. & Smith, S. J. (2009). Enlivening the curriculum of health-related fitness. *Educational Insights, 13*(4).

Lloyd, R. J., & Smith, S. J. (2010). Feeling 'flow motion' in games and sports. In J. Butler & L. Griffin (Eds.), *Teaching games for understanding* (pp. 89–103). Champaign, IL: Human Kinetics.

Mandigo, J. L., & Holt, N. L. (2004). Reading the game: Introducing the notion of games literacy. *Physical and Health Education Journal, 70*(3), 4–10.

Mandigo, J., Francis, N. & Lodewyk, K. (2007). Physical Literacy Concept Paper. *Canadian Sport for Life (CS4L)*. Retrieved from: http://www.canadiansportforlife.ca/resources/physical-literacy-concept-paper.

Mandigo, J., Francis, N., Lodewyk, K. & Lopez, R. (2009). *Position Paper*

PHE Canada (2008). FMS Tools for Schools. Retrieved from: www.canadiansportforlife.ca/upload/.../FMS%20Tools%20for%20Schools.pdf.

Physical Literacy for Educators. Retrieved from: www.phecanada.ca/programs/physical-literacy/what-physical-literacy.

Manitoba Education (2000). K-12 (K-S4) Physical Education/Health Education Manitoba Curriculum Framework of Outcomes for Active Healthy Lifestyles. Retrieved from: www.edu.gov.mb.ca/k12/cur/physhlth/framework/index.html

Metzler, M. (2005). *Instructional models for health and physical education* (2nd ed.). Scottsdale, AZ: Holcomb Hathaway, Inc.

Ontario Ministry of Education (2010). The Ontario curriculum, Grades 1-8: Health and Physical Education, Interim Edition. Retrieved from: www.edu.gov.on.ca/eng/curriculum/elementary/health.html

PHE Canada (2010). Physical literacy in Canada. Retrieved from: www.phecanada.ca/developingphysicalliteracy/e/

PHE Canada (n.d.) What is physical literacy? Retrieved from www.phecanada.ca/programs/physical-literacy/what-physical-literacy

Price, C. (2012). Circus for schools: Bringing a circo arts dimension to physical education, *PHEnex Journal, 4*(1).
Ragoonaden, K., Cherkowski, S., and Berg, S. (2012). New directions in daily physical activity: Integral education, yoga and physical literacy, *PHEnex Journal, 4*(1).

Rowsell, J., Kosnik, C., and Beck, C. (2008). Fostering multiliteracies pedagogy through preservice teacher education, *Teaching Education 19*(2), 109–22.

Shawn, T. (1965). *Every little movement: A book about François Delsarte: The man and his philosophy, his science and applied aesthetics, the application of this science to the art of the dance, the influence of Delsarte on American dance*. Brooklyn, NY: Dance Horizons.

Sheets-Johnstone, M. (1999). *The primacy of movement*. Philadelphia: John Benjamins Publishing.

Tremblay, M. & Lloyd, M. (2010). *Physical literacy measurement: The missing piece. Physical and Health Education Journal, 76*(1), 26–30.

Whitehead, M.E. (1990) Meaningful existence, embodiment and physical education. *Journal of Philosophy of Education. 24*(1), 3–13.

Whitehead, M. E. (2001). The concept of physical literacy. *British Journal of Teaching Physical Education*. Retrieved from: www.physical-literacy.org.uk/jpe-1990.php.

Whitehead, M. E. (2004). Physical literacy – A debate – Pre-Olympic Congress Thessaloniki. Retrieved from: www.physical-literacy.org.uk/greece2004-abstract.php

Whitehead, M. E. (2005). Physical literacy – A developing concept. *British Journal Teaching of Physical Education*. Retrieved from: www.physical-literacy.org.uk/durham2005-abstract.php

Whitehead, M. E. (2007). Physical Literacy: Philosophical considerations in relation to the development of self, universality and propositional knowledge. *Sport Ethics and Philosophy 1*(3), 1–27.

Whitehead, M. (2010). *Physical literacy: Throughout the lifecourse*. New York: Routledge.

Chapter 14

Active Healthy Kids Canada. (2010). *Healthy habits start earlier than you think. The active healthy kids Canada report card on physical activity for children and youth*. Toronto: Public Health Agency of Canada.

Allensworth, D. & Kolbe, L. (1987). The comprehensive school health program: Exploring an expanded concept. *Journal of School Health, 57*(10), 409–13.

Allensworth, D. Lawson, E. & Nicholson, L. (Eds.). (1997). *Schools and health: Our nation's investment*. Committee on CSH Programs in Grades K–12. Divisions of Health Sciences Policy. Institute of Medicine. Washington, D.C.: National Academic Press.

American Medical Association. (1999). *Health literacy*. Retrieved from: http://jama.ama-assn.org/content/281/6/552.full.pdf+html

Anderson, A. (2004). Health promoting schools: A community effort. *Physical & Health Education Journal. 70*(40), 4–8.

Anspaugh, D. & Ezell, G. (2010). *Teaching Today's Health* (9th ed.). Upper Saddle River: Pearson Education.

Bassett-Gunter, R. Yessis, J., Manske, S., & Stockton, L. (2012). *Healthy school communities concept paper*. Waterloo, Ontario: Propel Centre for Population Health Impact, University of Waterloo.

Berg, S., Hickson, C., & Fishburne, G. J. (2010). *Teaching children about health and wellness*. Edmonton, AB: Ripon Publishing.

Bond, L., Glover, S., Godfrey, C., Butler, H., & Patton, G. (2001). Building capacity for system-level change in schools: Lessons from the gatehouse project. *Health Education and Behaviour, 28*(3), 368–83.

Canadian Association for School Health. (2006). Homepage. Retrieved from http://www.cash-aces.ca/

Canadian Council of Food and Nutrition. (2006). *Tracking nutrition trends*. Retrieved from: www.cfdr.ca/Downloads/CCFN-docs/TNTVI---_TNS-C1062_-2006.aspx

Canadian Council on Learning (2007). *Health literacy in Canada: Initial results from the international adult literacy and skills survey*. Retrieved from: www.ccl.cca.ca/ccl/reports/HealthLiteracy/HealthLiteracy2007.html

Canadian Fitness and Lifestyle Research Institute. (2010). *The 2010 physical activity monitor*. Ottawa: Canadian Fitness and lifestyle research institute.

Canadian Public Health Association. (2010). Health literacy portal. Retrieved from: www.cpha.ca/en/portals/h-1.aspx

Card, A. & Doyle, E. (2008). School health coordinators as change agents, *Health and Learning, 7*, 3–11.

Centers for Disease Control and Prevention. (2012). Goal 3: Incorporate accurate, standards-based, and developmentally appropriate health and science information and curricula in child care and education through the university level. *Health Literacy*. Retrieved from: www.cdc.gov//healthliteracy/PlanAct/Goals/goal3.html

Craig, W. M. & Harel, Y. (2004). Bullying, physical fighting, and victimization. In C. Currie, C. Roberts, A. Morgan, R. Smith, W. Settertobulte, O. Samdal, & V. Barnekow Rasmussen (Eds.). Young people's health in context: International report from the HSBC 2001/2002 survey. *WHO Policy Series: Health Policy for Children and Adolescents, 4*, 133–44.

Craig, W. M. & McCuaig Edge, H. (2008). Bullying and fighting. In W. F. Boyce, M. A. King & J. Roche (Eds). *Healthy Settings for Young People in Canada* (pp. 91–104). Ottawa: Public Health Agency of Canada.

Freeman, J. (2008). Emotional health and well-being. In W. F. Boyce, M. A. King & J. Roche (Eds). *Healthy Settings for Young People in Canada* (pp. 119–36). Ottawa: Public Health Agency of Canada.

Fung, C., Kuhle, S., Lu, C. Purcell, M., Schwartz, S., Storey, K. & Veugelers, P.J. (2012). From "best practice" to "next practice": The effectiveness of school-based health promotion in improving healthy eating and physical activity and preventing childhood obesity. *International Journal of Behavioral Nutrition and Physical Activity. 9*, 27. doi:10.1186/14795–8689–-27

Government of Alberta. (2007). *Healthy kids Alberta! A wellness framework for Alberta's children and youth*.

Green, L. W. & Kreuter, M. W. (2005). *Health program planning: An educational and ecological approach*. (4th ed.) New York: McGraw-Hill.

Greenberg, J.S., (2004). *Health education and health promotion*. (5th ed.). New York: McGraw-Hill.

Health Canada and Statistics Canada. (2004). *Canadian community health survey: Cycle 2.2, nutrition focus*. Ottawa: Health Canada and Statistics Canada

Health Council of Canada. (2006). *Their future is now: Healthy choices for Canada's children and youth*. Retrieved from: http://www.healthcouncilcanada.ca/tree/2.25-HCC_ChildHealth_EN.pdf

Heart and Stroke Foundation. (2004) *Report card-2004: Fat is the new tobacco.* Retrieved from: www.heartandstroke.com/site/apps/nlnet/content2.aspx?c=iklQLcMWJtE&b=4955951&ct=4512817

Hoeger, W. W. K. & Hoeger, S. A. (2011). *Fitness and wellness.* Belmont, CA: Thomson Wadsworth.

Hoeger, W. W. K., Turner, L. W., & Hafen, B. Q. (2007). *Wellness: Guidelines for a healthy lifestyle.* (4th ed.). Belmont, CA: Thomson Wadsworth.

International Union for Health Promotion and Education (IUHPE) *Achieving health promoting schools: Guidelines for promoting.* Retrieved from: www.iuhpe.org/uploaded/Publications/Books_Reports/HPS_GuidelinesII_2009_English.pdf

Ipsos Reid Poll. (2011). *The Internet a new schoolyard for bullies?* Retrieved from: www.ipsos-na.com/news-polls/pressrelease.aspx?id=5556

Joint Consortium for School Health (JCSH). (2008). *What is comprehensive school health?* Retrieved from: http://eng.jcsh-cces.ca/upload/JCSH%20CSH%20Framework%20FINAL%20Nov%2008.pdf

Kaltiala-Heino, R., Rimpela, M., Marttunen, ,Rimpela, ,& Rantanen, P. (1999). Bullying, depression, and suicidal ideation in Finnish adolescent: School survey. *British Medical Journal, 319*(7206), 348–351. doi: http://dx.doi.org/10.1136/bmj.319.7206.348

Kolbe, L. (2005). A framework for school health programs in the 21st century. *Journal of School Health, 75*(6), 226–28.

LeDrew, J. (2008). Thoughts from my pensive: Linking literacy, health literacy and children's health in the primary classroom. *Health and Learning Magazine, 2008*(7), 23–27.

Lewallen, T. & Vamos, S. (2006). A tool to support healthy school communities the healthy school report card. *Health & Learning,* 2006(1), 23–28.

MacDougall, C. (2004). School health committee: Making "healthy schools" happen. *Physical and Health Education Journal, 70*(1), 27–29.

McCall, D. & Roberts, G. (2006). Comprehensive school health. *Health & Learning,* 2006(1), 3–5.

Mikkonen, J. & Raphael, D. (2010). *Social determinants of health: The Canadian facts.* Toronto: York University School of Health Policy and Management.

Murray, N. D., Low, B. J., Hollis, C., Cross, A., & Davis, S. (2007). Coordinated school health programs and academic achievement: A systematic review of the literature. *Journal of School Health, 77*(9), 589–99.

Noble, E. (2009). Mental health, safe & caring schools and teachers, *Health & Learning Magazine 2009*(8), 2.

Ontario Ministry of Education. (2010). *The Ontario curriculum grades 1–8: Health and physical education.* Toronto: Ontario Ministry of Education. Retrieved from: www.edu.gov.on.ca/eng/curriculum/elementary/healthcurr18.pdf

Ophea. (2010). Building health & physical literacy for schools & communities across Ontario. *Physical & Health Education Journal, 76*(2), 28–31.

Peterson, F. L., Cooper, R. J., & Laird, J. M. (2001). Enhancing teacher health literacy in school health promotion: A vision for the new millennium. *Journal of School Health. 71*(4), 138–44.

Physical and Health Education Canada (PHE Canada) (2012). Health promoting schools. Retrieved from: www.phecanada.ca/programs/health-promoting-schools

Pruitt, B. E., Allegrante, J. P., & Prothrow-Stith, D. (2007). *Prentice Hall Health.* Boston: Pearson Prentice Hall.

Rootman, I. (2004). *What we know and don't know about school health.* School Health Workshop, Vancouver, February 13–14.

Rootman, I. & Gordon-El-Bihbety, D. (2008). *A vision for a health literate Canada: Report of the expert panel on health literacy.* Retrieved from: www.cpha.ca/uploads/portals/h-l/report_e.pdf

Saab, H. & King, M. (2008). Health risk behaviours. In *Healthy Settings for Young People in Canada,* (pp. 57–89). Ottawa: Public Health Agency of Canada.

Sallis, J. F. & Owen, N. (1999). *Physical activity and behavioural medicine.* Thousand Oaks, CA: Sage.

Sex Information and Education Council of Canada (2010). *Sexual health education in the schools: Questions and answers.* (3rd ed). Ottawa: SIECCAN.

St. Leger, L. (2001). Schools, health literacy and public health: Possibilities and challenges. *Health Promotion International, 13*(3), 223–35.

Statistics Canada. (2002). *Health reports: How healthy are Canadians?* Retrieved from: www.statcan.gc.ca/pub/820–03-s/2002001/pdf/4195132-eng.pdf

Statistics Canada. (2003). *Canadian community health survey: Mental health and well-being.* Ottawa: Statistics Canada.

Statistics Canada. (2005). Early sexual intercourse, condom use and sexually transmitted diseases. *The Daily.* Retrieved from: www.statcan.gc.ca/daily-quotidien/050503/dq050503-eng.pdf

Stewart-Brown, S. (2006). *What is the evidence on school health promotion in improving health or preventing disease* and, specifically, what is the effectiveness of the health promoting schools approach? Copenhagen: WHO.

Tjepkema, M. & Shield, M. (2005). Measured obesity: Overweight Canadian children and adolescents. *Nutrition: Findings from the Canadian Community Health Survey. Statistics Canada, 1.*

Totten, M., Quigley, P. & Morgan, M. (2004). *CPHA safe school survey for students in grades 47–.* Ottawa: Canadian Public Health Association and Department of Justice Canada. Retrieved from: www.cpha.ca/uploads/progs/_/safeschools/47–_student_survey_e.pdf

Veugelers, P. J. & Schwartz, M. E. (2010). Comprehensive school health in Canada. *Canadian Journal of Public Health, 101,* S5-S8.

World Health Organization. (1986). *Ottawa charter for health promotion: First International Conference on Health Promotion, Ottawa, 21 November 1986.* Retrieved from: www.who.int/healthpromotion/conferences/previous/ottawa/en/

World Health Organization. (2008). *Closing the gap in a generation: health equity through action on the social determinants of health.* Commission on Social Determinants of Health final report. Retrieved from: www.who.int/social_determinants/thecommission/finalreport/en/

World Health Organization. (2010). *Health action in crisis.* Retrieved from: www.who.int/hac/about/definitions/en/

Zimmer, J. A., Dorsch, K. D., Hoeber, L. N., & LeDrew, J. E. (2011). Health literacy: A multi-disciplinary approach to physical activity promotion in elementary schools. *Physical & Health Education Journal. 76*(4), 22–27.

Chapter 15

Banville, D. & Polifko, M. F. (2009). Using digital video recorders in physical education. *Journal of Physical Education, Recreation & Dance, 80*(1), 17–21.

Bennett, S. Maton, K. & Kervin, L. (2008). The 'digital natives' debate: A critical review of the evidence. *British Journal of Educational Technology, 39*(5), 775–86. doi:10.1111/j.1467-8535.2007.00793.x

Chapman, C. (2009). The history of the Internet in a nutshell. Retrieved from: http://sixrevisions.com/resources/the-history-of-the-internet-in-a-nutshell/

Gorgu, L. et al., 2009. *Towards Mobile Collaborative Exergaming.* 2nd International Conference on Advances in Human-oriented and Personalized Mechanisms, Technologies, and Services, Porto, Portugal, 61–64.

Hicks, L., & Higgins, J. (2010). Exergaming: Syncing physical activity and learning. *Strategies: A Journal for Physical and Sport Educators, 24*(1) 18–21.

Layton, J. (April 1, 2000). How webcams work. Retrieved from: www.howstuffworks.com/webcam.htm

Luepker, R., 1999. How physically active are American children and what can we do about it? *International Journal of Obesity, 23* (Supplement 2), 12–17.

Mears, D. & Hansen, L. (2009). Active gaming: Definitions, options and implementation. *Strategies: a Journal for Physical and Sports Educators, 23*(2), 26–29.

Nippold, M. et al. (2005). Literacy as a leisure activity: Free-time preferences of older children and young adolescents. *Language, Speech and Hearing Services in Schools, 36*(2), 93–102.

Nye, S. (2011). Exergaming and physical education: Do these game consoles get kids active? *Virginia Journal, 32*(1), 7–8.

Parizkova, J. and Chin, M., 2003. Obesity prevention and health promoting during early periods of growth and development. *Journal of Exercise Science and Fitness, 1*(1), 1–14.

Prensky, M. (2001). Digital Natives, Digital Immigrants. *On the Horizon, 9*(5), 1–6.

Riviere, D. (2004). Metabolic functions and sport. *Bulletin de l'Académie Nationale de Medicine, 188*(6), 913–22.

Saltzman, M. (2008). Webcam basics: How do they work? *Microsoft Home Magazine.* Retrieved from: www.microsoft.com/canada/home/communications-and-mobility/articles/webcam-basics-how-do-they-work.aspx

Sanders S. & Hansen L. (2008). Exergaming: New directions for fitness education in physical education [Policy Brief]. Tampa: University of South Florida, College of Education, David C. Anchin Center.

Scott, F. (2012). Video games and education [PowerPoint slides]. Retrieved from: https://eclass.srv.ualberta.ca/mod/folder/view.php?id=135115

Sheehan, D. & Katz, L. (2010). Using interactive fitness and exergames to develop physical literacy. *Physical & Health Education Journal, 76*(1), 12-19.

Sinclair, J., Hingston, P., & Masek, M. (2007). Considerations for the design of exergames. *Computer Graphics & Interactive Techniques in Australasia & South East Asia,* 289–95.

Sothern, M. (2004). Obesity prevention in children: Physical activity and nutrition. *Nutrition, 20*(7-8), 704–08.

Statistics Canada. (2010). Canadian Internet use survey, 2009. *The Daily.* May 10, 2010. Retrieved from: www.statcan.gc.ca/daily-quotidien/100510/dq100510-eng.pdf

Vanderwater, E. A. et al. (2004). Linking obesity and activity level with children's television and video game use. *Adolescence, 27*(1), 71–85.

Zakon, R. (2011). Hobbes' Internet Timeline 10.2. Retrieved from: www.zakon.org/robert/internet/timeline/

Chapter 16

Active Healthy Kids Canada. (2009). *Report card on physical activity for children and youth.* Retrieved from: http://dvqdas9jty7g6.cloudfront.net/reportcard2009/ahkc-longform_web_final.pdf

Active Healthy Kids Canada. (2010). *Report card on physical activity for children and youth.* Retrieved from: http://dvqdas9jty7g6.cloudfront.net/reportcard2010/2010ActiveHealthyKidsCanadaReportCard-longform.pdf

Active Healthy Kids Canada. (2011). *Report card on physical activity for children and youth.* Retrieved from: http://dvqdas9jty7g6.cloudfront.net/reportcard2011/ahkcreportcard20110429final.pdf

Active Healthy Kids Canada (2012). *Report card on physical activity for children and youth.* Retrieved from: http://dvqdas9jty7g6.cloudfront.net/reportcards2012/AHKC%202012%20-%20Report%20Card%20Long%20Form%20-%20FINAL.pdf

Alberta Education. (2006). *Daily physical activity: A handbook for grades 1–9 schools.* Retrieved from: http://education.alberta.ca/media/318500/handbook.pdf

Alberta Education. (2008). *Daily physical activity survey report, 2008.* Retrieved from: http://education.alberta.ca/media/756341/dpasurveyreport.pdf

Barrett, J. M. (2011). *Teacher candidates' perceptions of the daily physical activity initiative and their emerging self-efficacy as daily physical activity instructors.* (Doctoral dissertation). Available from ProQuest Dissertations and Theses database. (UMI No. 3459116)

Bates, H. (2006). *Daily physical activity for children and youth: A review and synthesis of the literature.* Edmonton, AB: Alberta Education.

Beets, M., Flay, B., Vuchinich, S., Acock, A., Kin-Kit, L., & Allred, C. (2008). School climate and teachers' beliefs and attitudes associated with implementation of the positive action program: A diffusion of innovations model. *Preventive Science, 9,* 264–75.

British Columbia Ministry of Education. (2011). *Daily physical activity: K–12 program guide.* Retrieved from: www.bced.gov.bc.ca/irp/pdfs/daily_physical_activity/program_guide.pdf

Canadian Association for Health, Physical Education, Recreation, and Dance (CAHPERD). (2006). *The need for quality daily physical education programs in Canadian schools.* Retrieved from: www.nationalchildrensalliance.com/nca/pubs/2006/Quality%20Physical%20Education%20Programs%20Policy%20Brief.pdf

Canadian Fitness and Lifestyle Research Institute. (2008). Kids can play! Encouraging children to be active at home, at school, and in their communities. *Bulletin, 1,* 1–5.

Canadian Fitness and Lifestyle Research Institute. (2009). *The research file.* Ottawa: ParticipACTION.

Canadian Fitness and Lifestyle Research Institute. (2010). *The 2010 physical activity monitor.* Ottawa: Canadian Fitness and Lifestyle Research Institute.

Canadian Society for Exercise Physiology. (2011). *Canadian physical activity guidelines.* Retrieved from: www.csep.ca/english/view.asp?x=804

Centers for Disease Control and Prevention. (1997). Guidelines for school and community programs to promote lifelong physical activity among young people. *The Journal of School Health, 67,* 202–19.

Centers for Disease Control and Prevention. (2010). *Coordinated school health program.* Retrieved from: www.cdc.gov/HealthyYouth/CSHP/

Council of Ministers of Education-Canada (n.d.). *Canada-wide information.* Retrieved from: www.cmec.ca/en/

Daniels, S.R. (2006). The consequences of childhood overweight and obesity. *The Future of Children, 16,* 47–67.

Duncan, S., Duncan, T., Strycker, L., & Chaumeton, N. (2002). Neighbourhood physical activity opportunity: A multilevel contextual model. *Research Quarterly for Exercise and Sport, 73,* 457–63.

Fein, A., Plotnikoff, R., Wild, T., & Spence, J. (2004). Perceived environment and physical activity in youth. *International Journal of Behavioural Medicine, 11,* 135–42.

Harris, K. C., Kuramoto, L. K., Schulzer, M., & Retallack, J. E. (2009). Effects of school-based physical activity interventions on body mass index in children: A meta-analysis. *Canadian Medical Association Journal, 180,* 719–726.

Higgins, J., Gaul, C., Gibbons, S., & Van Gyn, G. (2003). Factors influencing physical activity levels among Canadian youth. *Canadian Journal of Public Health, 94,* 45–51.

Humbert, L. M., Chad, K. E., Spink, K. S., Muhajarine, N., Anderson, K. D., Bruner, M. W., ... Gryba, C. R. (2006). Factors that influence physical activity participation among high- and low-SES youth. *Qualitative Health Research, 16,* 467–83.

Kahn, E., Ramsay, L., Brownson, R., Heath, G., Howze, E., Powell, K., . . . Corso, P. (2002). The effectiveness of interventions to increase physical activity. A systematic review. *American Journal of Preventive Medicine, 22*(4 Suppl), 73–107.

Lu, C., & Barrett, J. M., Steele, K. (2013). *Active living: Toward the development of a comprehensive* school physical activity program (CSPAP). Manuscript in preparation.

Mandigo, J., Francis, N., Lodewyk, K., & Lopez, R. (2009). Physical literacy for educators. *PHE Canada Journal, 75*, 27–30.

Mandigo, J. L., & Thompson, L. P. (1998). Go with the flow: Using flow theory to help practitioners intrinsically motivate children to be physically active. *The Physical Educator, 55*, 145–59.

Ministry of Education, Ontario. (2005). *Policy/program memorandum no. 138*. Retrieved from www.edu.gov.on.ca

Morgan, P., & Hansen, V. (2008). Physical education in primary schools: Classroom teachers' perceptions of benefits and outcomes. *Health Education Journal, 67*, 196–207.

National Association for Sport and Physical Education (2008). *Comprehensive school physical activity programs: A position statement from the National Association for Sport and Physical Education.* Retrieved from: www.aahperd.org/naspe/standards/upload/Comprehensive-School-Physical-Activity-Programs2-2008.pdf

New Brunswick Department of Education and Early Childhood Development. (2002). *New Brunswick physical education safety guidelines: High school curricular, intramural, and interschool guidelines.* Retrieved from: www.gnb.ca/0000/publications/curric/hssg.pdf

Source: Ontario Ministry of Education. (2005). Policy/Program Memorandum No. 138: Daily Physical Activity in School, Grades 1 to 3; Grades 4 to 6, Grades 7 to 8

Ontario Physical and Health Education Association. (2009). *The Ontario physical education safety guidelines: Elementary intramurals/club guidelines.* Toronto: Ophea.

Physical & Health Education Canada. (n.d.). *Quality school intramural recreation.* Retrieved from: www.phecanada.ca/programs/intramurals-leadership

Ploughman, M. (2008). Exercise is brain food: The effects of physical activity on cognitive function. *Developmental Neurorehabilitation, 11,* 236–40.

Public Health Agency of Canada. (2007). *Family guide to physical activity for children.* Ottawa: Public Health Agency of Canada.

Public Health Agency of Canada (2011). *Obesity in Canada: A joint report from the Public Health Agency of Canada and the Canadian Institute for Health Information.* Retrieved from: www.phac-aspc.gc.ca/hp-ps/hl-mvs/oic-oac/assets/pdf/oic-oac-eng.pdf

Rink, J. E., Hall, T. J., & Williams, L. H. (2010). *Schoolwide physical activity: A comprehensive guide to designing and conducting programs.* Champaign, IL: Human Kinetics.

Robinson, D., & Melnychuk, N. (2008). Discourse, teacher identity, and the implementation of daily physical activity. *Alberta Journal of Educational Research, 54*, 245–57.

Saskatchewan Ministry of Education. (2010). *Inspiring movement.* Retrieved from: www.education.gov.sk.ca/physicalactivity

Spence, J., & Lee, R. (2004). Towards a comprehensive model of physical activity. *Psychology of Sport and Exercise, 4*, 7–24.

Tomporowski, P., Davis, C., Miller, P., & Naglieri, J. (2008). Exercise and children's intelligence, cognition, and academic achievement. *Educational Psychology Review, 20,* 111–31.

World Health Organization. (1998). *Promoting active living in and through schools: Policy statement and guidelines for action.* Geneva: WHO Department of Noncommunicable Disease Prevention and Health Promotion.

World Health Organization. (2004). *Global health strategy on diet, physical activity and health.* Geneva: World Health Organization.

World Health Organization. (2010a). *Physical activity and young people.* Retrieved from: www.who.int/dietphysicalactivity/factsheet_young_people/en/index.html

World Health Organization. (2010b). *What is a health promoting school?* Retrieved from: www.who.int/school_youth_health/gshi/hps/en/index.html

Glossary

Accelerometer – An accelerometer is an energy expenditure device that records body acceleration minute to minute, providing detailed information about the frequency, duration, intensity, and patterns of movement. Counts from accelerometers are used to estimate energy expenditure.

Acceptance – In this context, the term acceptance is purposely used in lieu of terms such as tolerance, which suggest something (or someone) that needs to be endured or allowed. A climate of acceptance implies that one willingly and openly welcomes and receives the diverse identities of others.

Adapted Physical Activity – Adapted physical activity (or APA) can be broadly described as a crossdisciplinary human movement science, concerned about the physical activity needs, skills, and experiences of persons with disabilities over the course of lifespan development (Sherrill, 1998).

Adapted Physical Education – As defined by Block, adapted physical education (or APE) is "a subdiscipline of physical education with an emphasis on physical education for students with disabilities. The term adapted physical education generally refers to school-based programs for students ages 3–21" (2007, p. 12).

Affective Learning Domain – The affective learning domain is the part of educating that addresses a student's feelings or emotional state. It involves developing positive relationships with and among students. This domain is closely linked with motivation.

Alternative Environment Activities – In the context of this book, alternative environment activities is one of the five movement domains that describe the categories of physical activity. Alternative environment activities are those not normally performed in the gym or on the school playing field. They are usually conducted outdoors and are either land-based, ice- or snow-based, or water-based.

Applications ("Apps") – Applications are the software that causes any computer or computerized device to perform useful tasks beyond the running of the computer (or device) itself. A specific instance of such software is called a software application, application or app. Today the term most commonly refers to apps available for smart phones.

Apprenticeship of Observation – A phrase coined by Lortie (1975), in an education context, "apprenticeship of observation" refers to the fact that by being immersed in school culture generally, you already have some very strong preconceived notions about what a teacher's role entails, and what teaching should look like.

Appropriate Practice – Appropriate practice refers to the correct performance of a skill or task according to the ability level of the participant. In other words, learning may be limited if students are practicing incorrectly, if the task is too easy or too difficult, or if there are too many tasks presented at one time.

Assessment – Assessment in this context is the third step in the instructional process. Assessment involves evaluating and measuring students in order to ascertain whether they have achieved certain curriculum objectives.

Assessment Plans – A method used by educators to prepare for evaluating students.

Authentic Assessment – Authentic assessment (sometimes also referred to as performance-based assessment) includes tasks that relate to real-life contexts (Ryan, 2005). This often requires assessments to occur in real-life (or contrived) settings (Kovar, Combs, Campbell, Napper-Owen, & Worrell, 2007).

"Careful Parent" Standard – The careful parent standard is a legal term that relates to negligence in schools. In determining negligence on the part of school personnel, courts have typically relied on the case of Williams v. Eady in which it was determined that in carrying out their duties, educators were expected to use the same degree of care with respect to their students as careful or prudent parents would use with their own children. The "careful parent" standard "has remained as the quintessential standard of care expected of teachers ever since" (Dickinson, 2006, p. 280).

Categories of Supervision – There are three categories of supervision as defined by Ophea's *Elementary/Secondary Intramural Safety Guidelines*. The three categories are constant visual supervision, on-site supervision, and in-the-area supervision.

Cognitive Learning Domain – The cognitive learning domain is the part of educating that addresses a student's mental skills or knowledge.

Communication Skills – In the context of this book, communication skills are one of a number of skills that are crucial to being a successful teacher. Someone with good communication skills is better equipped to clearly transfer knowledge to students, enabling them to help meet curriculum objectives.

Competencies Model – The competencies model is an emerging curriculum model in PE. The model involves cross-curricular competencies, which are elements such as critical thinking or creativity (or problem solving) that are addressed in all areas of the curriculum in a manner consistent with subject specific discipline. The model recognizes the essential nature of these competencies to all of education.

Comprehensive School Health – Comprehensive school health (CSH) is an overarching approach that applies a health-promoting perspective to all activities in the school environment.

Contributory Negligence – Contributory negligence is a legal term. The concept of contributory negligence "rests on the theory that, because there can be numerous parties responsible for causing an injury, including the plaintiff himself or herself, formal and meaningful apportionment of fault should occur" (Dickinson, 2006, p. 288). In an educational context, if a student is deemed to have been contributorily negligent by failing to act as a reasonable person of like age, intelligence, and experience would have acted, then damages will be reduced in proportion to his or her degree of fault (Dickinson, 2006).

Criterion-Referenced Evaluation – A criterion-referenced evaluation is when a judgment about a student's learning of an outcome is based on how well a student does in relation to clearly stated criteria related to that outcome. Using this type of evaluation, student learning is compared only to, and is assessed only according to, the extent to which it meets the criteria established ahead of time.

Critical Engagement – In the context of this book, critical engagement is a combination of critical thinking and critical pedagogy. It is further described by Wright as the "capacity to speak up, to negotiate, and to be able to critically engage with the conditions of their working lives" (New London Group, 1996 as cited by Wright, 2004).

Critical Pedagogy – In the context of this book, critical pedagogy is an approach where social, cultural, and political justice issues are examined in relation to teaching practices.

Critical Thinking – In the context of this book, critical thinking is best defined by Wright who suggests that critical thinking may be conceptualized as "logical reasoning where attention is directed to problem-solving, reasoning and higher order thinking skills" (2004, p. 6). She also suggests that critical thinking is about knowing when, where, and how to question something.

Culturally Relevant PE – Culturally relevant PE is a student before content approach, which acknowledges that each individual comes with lived experiences that are an intersection of race, ability, gender, sexual orientation, socio-economic status, religion, somatotypes, and cultural and family traditions.

Curricular Physical Activity – Curricular physical activity is designed to provide opportunities for students during instructional time. These activities are taught or supervised by teachers in Canadian schools and include both mandated and optional PE programs, DPA, and cross-curricular PA programs approved by departments or ministries of education.

Curriculum – In the simplest terms, the curriculum defines what should be instructed or studied in a given subject area in an education system.

Curriculum Development - Curriculum development traditionally centres upon identifying a vision or aim for physical education followed by stated goals, and focuses on kindergarten to grade twelve. In some provinces and territories, the development of kindergarten to grade twelve may be further divided by grade levels.

Curriculum Model – A curriculum model is a method of approaching a curriculum in a given subject area for your specific province or territory. For PE, curriculum models include the multi-activity model, the TGfU model, and the TPSR model among others.

Daily Physical Activity – In the context of this book, daily physical activity (or DPA) refers to education initiatives whose aim it is to ensure that children

Dance – In the context of this book, dance is one of the five movement domains that describe the categories of physical activity. In its most basic definition, dance is an expressive form of movement.

Debrief – In the context of this book, a debrief is a tool that can be used by teachers to reflect on a lesson with students. Typically used after more student-centred or experientially based lessons, the teacher would guide a discussion about affective or cognitive learning outcomes.

Differentiated Instruction – The term differentiated instruction refers to using a variety of teaching approaches or strategies in order to cater to the differing learning styles and abilities of your students. Adjustments can be made with regard to content, the process of instruction, and the product.

Digital Literacy – Just as traditional literacy goes beyond comprehension to include the more complex skills of composition and analysis, digital literacy includes, but goes beyond, simple technology skills to a deeper understanding of, and ultimately the ability to create a wide range of content with various digital tools.

Dimensions of Health – Optimum health balances seven dimensions: emotional, environmental, mental/intellectual, occupational, physical, social, and spiritual (Berg et al., 2010).

Diversity – Diversity refers to individual differences and distinctiveness, and encompasses acceptance, respect, and recognition. It is a multi-faceted exploration of differences pursued in an environment that is as safe and welcoming as possible in an educational or societal setting, particularly, within a climate of acceptance.

Duty of Care – Duty of care is a legal term that relates to the legal concept of "negligence." In determining negligence, courts must first ascertain whether a duty of care was owed to the plaintiff by the defendant. That is, a duty of care must be owed under the law.

Energy Expenditure Devices – A device that measures performance during physical activity such as a pedometer, a heart rate monitor, or an accelerometer.

Engaged Learners – Engaged learners welcome extrinsic rewards , but their main motivation arises from their enjoyment and interest in the lesson content. Engaged learners are also more likely to stay on task, persevere to overcome challenges, and commit to developing greater understanding of concepts (Jang et al., 2010).

Evaluation – In the context of education, evaluation requires educators to make judgments about student learning, generally in order to determine the grade a student will receive.

Exclusion – In the context of this book, exclusion refers to persons with disabilities being excluded from everyday activities.

Exergaming – Exergaming combines video games and physical activity into interactive video games that are based on actual sports. Video games or various auditory or visual stimuli are paired with different types of exercise equipment and activity, and the individual must engage in physical activity to play the game or produce the auditory or visual stimulation (Sanders & Hansen, 2008).

Experiential Knowledge – Experiential knowledge refers to the ways that people interpret personal beliefs, prior experiences and significant moments and use them to develop their professional knowledge. In the context of education, experiential knowledge includes time you yourself spend as a student in the school system.

Feedback (verbal and non-verbal) – Effectively providing feedback to learners is an essential instructional skill. Feedback communicates important information to students about their behaviour and performance as they progress toward cognitive, affective, and psychomotor goals in PE.

Fitness for Life Model – The fitness for life model is a curriculum model for PE. It was created by Dr. Charles Corbin and directs its attention to improving a student's fitness levels and developing healthy behaviours. Students (particularly those who are described as passive within regular PE programs) must actively participate within this type of model by being proactive about their own physical health. It is predominantly used at the secondary level but can be modified for elementary and middle school students.

Formative Assessment – Formative assessment generally occurs during a lesson, unit, or program of instruction, and provides ongoing feedback to the student about progress, and to the educator about the effectiveness of instruction (Fenwick & Parsons, 2009; Rink, 2010).

Four Aspects of Human Nature – The four aspects of human nature as described by Bopp et al. (1985) are physical, mental, emotional, and spiritual.

Fundamental Movement Skills – Fundamental movement skills (FMS) are the most basic movement skills found in any complex skill. They provide individuals with the requisite understanding and ability to be able to advance to more complex skills. Fundamental movement skills are not acquired naturally; they must be taught. They include skills such as running, stopping, turning, rolling, balancing, jumping, skipping, kicking, throwing, and catching.

Games – In the context of this book, games is one of the five movement domains that describe the categories of physical activity. In its most basic definition, a game "has explicit rules, specified or understood goals, the element of opposition or contest, and a sequence of rules and actions which is essentially repeatable every time the game is played" (Estes & Mechikoff, 1999, p. 14). Educationally, games are more like play than institutionalized sport through their heightened focus on being inclusive, developmentally appropriate, optimally challenging, and aim of meeting holistic learning objectives.

Geocaching – Geocaching is a worldwide game of hiding and seeking treasure. A geocacher can place a geocache in the world, pinpoint its location using GPS technology and then share the geocache's existence and location online. Anyone with a GPS unit can then try to locate the geocache. A typical cache is a small waterproof vessel containing a logbook.

Gymnastics – In the context of this book, gymnastics is one of the five movement domains that describe the categories of physical activity. In its most basic definition, gymnastics is a form of activity that incorporates running, jumping, rolling, and climbing.

Health Literacy – According to the Canadian Public Health Association (2010) health literacy involves "the ability to assess, understand and act on information for health"

Health Promoting Schools Approach – The Health Promoting Schools (HPS) Approach (also known as comprehensive school health or coordinated school health) is a whole-school approach that both encompasses PE and provides a context for healthy behaviours in the school's greater community. HPS strives to provide a way to link health and education outcomes by including the instruction, supports, and environment of the school setting as part of a foundation that fosters interaction and cohesion among home, school, and community.

Heart Rate Monitor – A heart rate monitor is an energy expenditure device that tracks a user's heart rate, which can be used to measure exercise intensity, as heart rate is related to oxygen uptake. Some heart rate monitors will also keep track of other variables such as activity time.

Inclusion – In the context of this book, the term inclusion goes beyond the practice of making sure students with a disability are included in school practices and activities. It is a philosophy, a state of mind, a means and an end to understanding the valuable and integral roles that persons with disabilities can and do play within our school systems.

Inclusion Lens – In the context of this book, the inclusion lens is one of three literacy lenses. The basis of this approach lies in the recognition of the multiplying and hybridizing ways of making, communicating, and receiving meaning. What is learned is no longer confined to particular regions, taught as particularly preferred activities, in standardized ways.

Inclusive Physical Education – As described by Goodwin et al., inclusive physical education (or IPE) is defined as "providing all students with disabilities the opportunity to participate in regular physical education with their peers, with supplementary aides and support services as needed to take full advantage of the goals of motor skill acquisition, fitness, knowledge of movement, and psycho-social well-being, toward the outcome of preparing all students for an active lifestyle appropriate to their abilities and interests" (2003, p. 193).

Indigenous Knowledge – The term indigenous knowledge respects and includes knowledge of those who identify as First Nations, Métis, or Inuit Canadian, cultures that are encompassed by the term "Aboriginal" under Section 35 of the Canadian Constitution (Aikenhead & Michell, 2011). The term "indigenous" also applies worldwide and further respects other indigenous views.

Individual Education Plan – An individual education plan (or IEP) is a written plan describing the special education program and/or services required by a particular student. It identifies learning expectations that are modified from,

or alternative to, the expectations given in the curriculum policy document for the appropriate grade and subject or course, and/or any accommodations and special education services needed to assist the student in achieving his or her learning expectations.

Individual Physical Activities – In the context of this book, individual physical activities is one of the five movement domains that describe the categories of physical activity. Individual physical activities are activities that are performed alone but may be enjoyed socially as well.

Instructional Framework – The instructional framework refers to the methods and strategies teachers use to maximize learning opportunities for students (Rink, 2009). The approach a teacher uses depends largely upon two key factors: the learning goals for the lesson, and the degree of readiness of the students.

Instructional Process – The instructional process involves three steps: planning, teaching, and assessment. These three steps are repeated continuously.

Integration – In the context of this book, integration refers to the notion that all people have the right to live in a society that values individual rights and freedoms, and to live a life just like everyone else. This notion implies that each person, in their own respective way, has the right to work, love, and live in the same society and in a similar fashion as their friends, neighbours, and fellow citizens (Reid, 2003a)

Interscholastic Physical Activity – Interscholastic physical activity programs typically consist of a combination of structured individual and team competition in local, regional, and provincial settings. Participation in most cases is voluntary, and often these activities serve only a small portion of a school's population. Interscholastic programs place greater emphasis on competition and winning and have little relationship to provincial or territorial curricular objectives.

Intramural Physical Activity – Intramural physical activity is designed to provide opportunities for students of wide-ranging interests and abilities to participate in a variety of activities in a fun and inclusive environment (Lu, Barrett, & Steele, 2013). The Ontario Physical Education Safety Guidelines (2011) classifies intramural activities into four categories: sport imitations, low organizational activities, special events, and clubs. These activities deemphasize instruction, skill proficiency, or performance, instead stressing diverse program options and inclusivity with enjoyment through participation.

Learning Climate – The learning climate is a term that refers to a supportive and engaging climate where everyone, regardless of where they are situated in relation to the many axes of difference, can feel respected, included, supported, and engaged.

Learning Environment Management – For effective learning environment management, teachers must establish a number of routines, strategies, and guidelines unrelated to the curriculum to ensure that all students can participate safely as they work towards achieving the goals of the lesson. The development of routines and rules can contribute significantly to the time available for learning.

Learning Outcome – A learning outcome is a broadly written statement that describes the abilities, knowledge, and attitudes students are expected to be able to demonstrate after having completed a program of study.

Least-Restrictive Environment – The concept of the least-restrictive environment (or LRE) was designed to ensure that children were placed in the most normalized educational setting possible (Block, 2007). The concept of the LRE should encourage educational team members to question what the unique teaching objectives and practices are in relation to each and every person.

Lesson Transitions – In PE, lesson transition is defined as the time (usually non-active time) required for moving from one phase of a class or activity to the next. Students may use this time to select or set up equipment; get organized into partners, groups, squads, or teams; move from one space to another; or to rotate from one station or game to another. Teachers may need this time to attend to managerial or non-instructional tasks.

Lifeworlds – Lifeworlds is a term used in relation to the diversity found between students. The lifeworlds of students are forged in history and in a multiplicity of cultures. Matters such as socio-economic status, race, gender, sexuality, and ability influence their daily encounters. Within these daily experiences exists a cultural landscape of oppression whereby students are connected to very real social, cultural, economic, and historical issues that can affect their home and school lives and leave them feeling ignored.

Long-Term Athlete Development – The LTAD model encompasses aspects of physical education, such as fundamental movement skills, training, competing, and being active for life. Developed by Canadian Sport for Life, the seven stages follow a developmental approach that acknowledges the interaction of PE with sport and recreation, and promotes physical activity for all.

Medicine Wheel – The medicine wheel is an ancient symbol used by indigenous people to show relationships that can be expressed in sets of four and is used to help with teaching and learning (Bopp et al., 1985; Fiddler,

Tourangeau, Male, & Marlor, 2000; Graveline, 1998). The medicine wheel symbol is relative to local cultures and there are different representations created to reflect the teachings of a particular group and their beliefs.

Movement Concepts – The four broad movement concepts answer the following questions:

1 What is the body doing?
2 Where is the movement going?
3 What is the dynamic content or quality of movement?
4 With whom or to what is the mover relating?

Movement Domains – Movement domains are a method of describing five major categories of physical activity for PE. Each domain has unique characteristics and provides students with an array of experiences intended to empower them. The five movement domains are: dance, alternative environment physical activities, individual physical activities, games, and gymnastics.

Movement Education – An approach to physical education that emerged in the period after World War II. It involved a metamorphosis from the more traditional form of training, skill, and practice to a PE model that incorporated a more philosophical approach. Movement education originated from the work of Rudolf Laban, an Austrian dance teacher who designed a framework for analyzing movement. Movement education exposes students to a wider variety of movement and nurtures the development of the whole child.

Multi-Activity Model – The multi-activity model is curriculum model for PE. The primary focus of this model for the student is on the learning of motor skills while maintaining interest through the exposure to a wide variety of sport and movement (Siedentop et al., 1986; Cothran, 2001).

Multiliteracy Lens – In the context of this book, the multiliteracy lens is one of three literacy lenses. Multiliteracies is a term coined by a group of international scholars known as the New London Group. The group came together in the mid-nineties to consider what was happening in literacy education. They developed a particular sociocultural pedagogical stance, which they have continued to articulate (Cope & Kalantzis, 2000). Multiliteracies is the term they use to describe the attentiveness to the multiple ways in which meaning is communicated.

Multimedia – Multimedia is media and content that uses a combination of different content forms. This contrasts with media that use only rudimentary computer displays such as text-only or traditional forms of printed or hand-produced material. Multimedia includes a combination of text, audio, still images, animation, video, or interactive content forms.

Multimodality Lens – In the context of this book, the multimodality lens is one of three literacy lenses. Multimodality is an educational approach that incorporates different modes of meaning besides linguistic modes, including visual meanings, audio meanings, gestural meanings, spatial meanings, and multimodal meanings.

Norm-Referenced Evaluation – A norm-referenced evaluation is when a judgment about a student's learning of an outcome is based on how well a student does in relation to others. Norm-referenced evaluation is often used in conjunction with a pre-determined "normal distribution." This assumes a small number of students will do exceptionally well, a small number will do poorly, and a majority will peak in the middle as average (Rust, 2002).

Normal School – Normal Schools were institutions designed for the training of teachers. They are now more commonly referred to as teachers' colleges. The first Normal School in Canada was established in 1847.

Organizational Formations – Organizational formations are physical arrangements of students that educators can use in order to maximize learning time. Some examples of organizational formations are squad (or column), semi-circle, partner, scattered, and circle.

Paraeducators – Paraeducators (also known as shadows or community care workers) are school employees who work under the supervision of teachers or other professional practitioners. Their jobs are instructional in nature and they provide other direct services to children and youth and their families.

Pedagogical Content Knowledge – In simple terms, PCK is a blending of pedagogical knowledge and content knowledge, and the concept makes clear that being a good teacher is more than just knowing a lot about a subject. It is important to recognize that PCK does not only include a deep knowledge of the content and pedagogy of a subject area, it requires teachers to have a similarly deep knowledge of their students, and the communities and contexts in which they work.

Pedometer – A pedometer is an energy expenditure device whose primary function is to count the total number of steps taken by the person wearing the pedometer in a given time period.

PHE Canada – Physical and Health Education Canada is Canada's premier professional organization for physical and health educators. First established in 1933 as Canadian Physical Education Association (CPEA), the organization has undergone several name changes in its continued evolution. PHE Canada members are predominantly educators working in the school system, administrators who support them,

and the university professors engaged in pre-service teacher training or H&PE research.

Physical Activity – Physical activity (or PA) is a movement of the body that expends energy; such as participation in sports, dance, and exercise. Physical activity is used in PE programs as a medium for teaching curriculum content. It is the vehicle to become physically educated, just as a book is a vehicle to becoming literate (Fishburne & Hickson, n.d.).

Physical Activity Guidelines – The Canadian Physical Activity Guidelines were developed by the Canadian Society for Exercise Physiology (CSEP) and the Public Health Agency of Canada (PHAC) in 1995. They established physical activity recommendations for four distinct populations: (a) children aged 4–11, (b) youth aged 12–17, (c) adults aged 18–64, and (d) older adults 65 years of age and older. Over the years, the recommended guidelines have changed, reflecting new knowledge and research.

Physical Education – The instruction of games, sports, activities, and health living within the school system. Physical education is often taught in conjunction with health, wellness, and outdoor education.

Physical Literacy – Physical literacy as a concept was developed by Margaret Whitehead. The concept has been at the heart of PE curriculum revision in Canada and around the world. Based on her doctoral research exploring meaningful existence and embodiment in physical education, Whitehead sought to disrupt the predominance of Cartesian dualism, which is a way of thinking and acting in which the body is regarded as a mere mechanistic entity and the mind is understood as will, cognitions, and emotions that can be addressed separately from the body (Whitehead, 1990).

Physical Literacy Indicators – The four key indicators of physical literacy are functional capacities, contextualized capabilities, expressive possibilities, and flow consciousness

Planning – Planning in this context is the first step in the instructional process. Planning involves thinking about, researching, organizing, and developing content for instruction.

Professional Identity – In the context of this book, professional identity concerns the process of becoming a teacher (or more specifically, a physical education teacher. In order to develop a strong and positive professional identity, teachers need to feel that they embody the qualities of good teaching.

Psychomotor Learning Domain – The psychomotor learning domain is the part of educating that addresses a student's manual or physical skills. This is the learning domain most commonly associated with PE but the affective and cognitive domains are also integral to the subject.

Recognition – Recognition refers to the acknowledgement and appreciation of others and their identities in genuine and meaningful ways. It is a deliberate and conscious act carried out in a spirit of gratitude.

Reflection-in-Action – As an educator, taking a few minutes to pause and reflect on questions about a current situation (e.g., regarding how it's going or how it could be going better) is referred to by Schön (1983) as reflection-in-action.

Reflection-on-Action – As an educator, taking time to look back over a teaching experience after it's happened and reflecting on it (e.g., writing down or recording your thoughts after a class or discussing a class with a colleague) is known as reflection-on-action.

Reflective Practitioner – Being a reflective practitioner means being a thoughtful decision maker. It is important to be a reflective practitioner as educator training can only prepare you so much. Being reflective will also help you question the taken-for-granted assumptions you have and display in your teaching, as well as the teaching practices of peers, instructors, or colleagues.

Reliability – In the context of PE, validity refers to a measure's ability to measure what it is supposed to be measured. It is with this logic that a reliable measure may or may not be valid while an unreliable measure will never be valid (and a valid measure is generally reliable).

Respect – Respect occurs when others are held in esteem, revered, and treated with dignity as part of a shared lived experience. There are no preconditions for respectful treatment; it is unconditional.

Risk Avoidance – The term risk avoidance refers to how many educators (particularly PE educators) have become overly cautious or conservative in regards to activities with an element of risk. Some educators refuse to even offer some activities for fear of being sued over a student injury.

Risk Management – Risk management, in its broadest sense, involves managing both physical and legal risk. "In many respects, the former can be seen as looking after the latter as the proper fulfillment of one's duty to reasonably reduce physical risk should in most instances obviate legal liability" (Dickinson, 2006, p. 288). Ultimately, the goals are to: prevent injuries; prevent potential lawsuits; prevent actual lawsuits from being successful; and minimize the amount of damages in the case of a successful lawsuit (Mahoney, Forsyth, Holman, & Moriarity, 2001).

Smart Phone – A smart phone is a type of mobile phone built on a mobile operating system with advanced computing capabilities and connectivity. Smart phones often feature portable media players, digital cameras, GPS navigation, and/or touch screens

Social (TPSR) Model – The social or TPSR model is a curriculum model for PE that was developed as a teaching tool specifically aimed at adolescents identified as at risk, underserved, and inner city (Hellison & Walsh, 2002). It has been expanded beyond such students with the ideology that if students want to be successful, they must first learn how to be responsible for themselves and the situations they find themselves in (Escartí, Gutiérrez, Pascual, & Llopis, 2010). The model consists of five different levels of responsibility.

Social Determinants of Health – According to the World Health Organization, the social determinants of health are the economic and social conditions (and their distribution among the population) that influence individual and group differences in health status. They are risk factors found in one's living and working conditions, rather than individual factors that influence the risk for a disease, or vulnerability to disease or injury.

Social Networking – A social networking service is a platform to build social networks or social relations among people who share, for example, interests, activities, backgrounds, or real-life connections. A social network service consists of a representation of each user (often a profile), his/her social links, and a variety of additional services. Most social network services are web-based.

Sport Education Model – The sport education model is a curriculum model for PE whose purpose is "to educate students in various sports—to teach them to be players, in the fullest sense of that term" (Siedentop, Mand, & Taggart, 1986, p. 186). The rationale for Sport Education is based on three essential elements: first, that sport is a higher form of play (institutionalized and competitive); second, that sport is also a part of our collective culture and contributes to health and socialization; and third, if the two previous statements are true, then sport should be part of PE with an objective for students to become skilled participants.

Sport Model (TGfU) – The Sport or TGfU model is a curriculum model for PE, the objective of which is to offer all students an opportunity to experience, enjoy, and understand games, regardless of their respective ability or skill levels (Butler & McCahan, 2005). The model involves six steps and groups activities into four different categories in order to make them easier to teach.

Standard of Care – In tort law, the standard of care is the degree of prudence and caution required of an individual who is under a duty of care.

Student-Facilitated DPA – Student-facilitated DPA is one of the DPA delivery models. This model not only facilitates provision of the DPA mandate, but also serves a greater purpose in Canadian schools, since it puts students at the centre of program design, planning, and delivery.

Summative Assessment – Summative assessment has been the most common assessment practice within schools in recent years. Generally occurring at the end of a unit or term (or whenever students need to demonstrate their learned knowledge, skills, or attitudes), summative assessment essentially allows educators to ascertain their students' level of achievement at a particular moment in time. Information gathered from summative assessments is generally evaluated.

Tablet – A tablet (or tablet computer) is a one piece mobile computer. Devices typically have a touchscreen, with finger or stylus gestures replacing the conventional computer mouse.

Teacher Demonstrations – In the context of this textbook, teacher demonstrations are one of the communication skills that teachers should strive to develop. Demonstrating for students can significantly enhance verbal instructions or explanations. They can be used for a variety of purposes, including the presentation of new skills; the demonstration of student movement during a drill, practice, or routine; the concepts or tactics of a game situation; or to present one example of a response to a problem-solving task.

Teacher Observation – Teacher observation is a crucial skill for educators. Teachers must be active observers of the environment at all times to ensure the safety of participants, monitor off task behaviour, assess student learning, and guide students as they learn new skills.

Teacher Questioning – Teacher questioning can be a powerful communication tool for educators. Used effectively it can be a diagnostic tool that determines prior learning, a motivational tool that engages students in learning, an assessment tool that determines level of understanding, a modification tool that extends activities, a management tool that maintains lesson focus, or a tool to stimulate creativity and critical thinking.

Teacher-Driven DPA – Teacher-driven DPA is one of the DPA delivery models. This model designates the classroom teacher as the one responsible for planning and providing DPA. The teacher designs the activities and is responsible for scheduling DPA into the instructional or non-instructional class schedule.

Teaching – Teaching in this context is the second step in the instructional process. Teaching involves presenting content to students.

Teaching and Learning Cues – Teaching and learning cues are used by effective teachers to focus students' learning and improve performance, which often means enhancing (motor) skill technique (Pangrazi & Gibbons, 2009). Teaching and learning cues may also be directed toward improving movement quality, knowledge of strategies or tactics in games, or understanding the creation of emotional impact in dance.

Teaching Strategies – Teaching strategies (or instructional strategies) are defined as purposeful actions and behaviours planned and implemented by the teacher to meet lesson goals. They are techniques for engaging learners and delivering the curriculum. Strategies may vary depending on the strengths and personality of the teacher. Some examples of strategies include demonstrations, station activities, peer teaching, and direct instruction.

Teaching Styles – A teaching "style," as defined by Mosston and Ashworth (2002) is a framework or structure of a lesson independent of personal teaching habits. Based on the interplay among deliberate teaching behaviours, learning behaviours, and the objectives of the lesson, Mosston and Ashworth developed eleven teaching styles organized along a continuum, each designed to accomplish a particular set of objectives.

Torts – A tort refers "to a miscellaneous and more or less unconnected group of civil wrongs, other than breach of contract, for which a court of law will afford a remedy in the form of an action for damages." (Prosser, 1955, p. 1).

Validity – In the context of PE, validity refers to assessment. Assessments are valid when they measure exactly what they were intending to measure.

Vision for Teaching – A vision for teaching is something that outlines your stance and beliefs about teaching, learning, and students. Your vision for teaching should reflect the main beliefs, ideas, and principles that you feel are important for you personally and professionally, and also the key elements that represent what you value most for your students.

Visual Aids – Visual aids can be an effective communication tool for students. Visual aids such as task cards, posters, or photographs may be placed on the wall in a prominent location where students may refer to them when they are practicing the skill independently or in groups. They are also a handy reference for teachers.

Voluntary Assumption of Risk – Voluntary assumption of risk, also called volenti as a shortened form of volenti non fit injuria (no injury is done to one who consents), is a complete defence to a claim of negligence in a legal setting. For this defence to be valid, individuals must understand the risks inherent in the activity. In an educational setting, they must recognize that through their participation, they are assuming full legal responsibility, and in so doing, agreeing that the teacher and school board will not be liable for damages, even if negligence occurs (Dickinson, 2006, p. 286).

Wellness – Wellness has been identified as an all-inclusive umbrella covering a variety of related factors. A state of wellness requires the implementation of positive programs to change behaviour and thereby improve health and quality of life, prolong life, and achieve total well-being. It comprises physical, social, spiritual, environmental, intellectual, and emotional components and assumes an individual must take personal responsibility for his or her own well-being and balance of these dimensions.

Whole School DPA – Whole school DPA is one of the DPA delivery models. Schools may choose to meet the DPA requirement using a discrete and consistent block of time in the school day. In this model of delivery, all or a portion of the student body may participate in developmentally appropriate activities at the same time.

With-it-ness – The term with-it-ness, originally coined by Kounin (1970), captures the essence of the ability to multi-task in a PE context. More commonly referred to as "having eyes in the back of your head," teachers with this ability are aware of what is going on in all areas of the learning space, and they make sure the students are aware of this.

Photo Credits

Index